Off the Motorway

About the Author

Christopher Pick, who was educated at the Universities of Kent and East Anglia, worked in publishing before becoming a full-time writer specializing largely in travel, heritage and history. Author of *Children's Guide to London* and *The Railway Route Book* among many other works, he is an enthusiastic explorer of out-of-the-way places in both town and countryside. He lives in south-east London with his wife and daughter.

Off the Motorway

CHRISTOPHER PICK

SECOND EDITION

CADOGAN BOOKS
LONDON

Cadogan Books Ltd
16 Lower Marsh, London SE1.

First published 1984.

Second edition published 1987.

ISBN 0–946313 11 3

Phototypeset in Sabon on a Linotron 202
Printed and bound in Great Britain by Redwood Burn Limited,
Trowbridge, Wiltshire.

For Jenny once more, with love

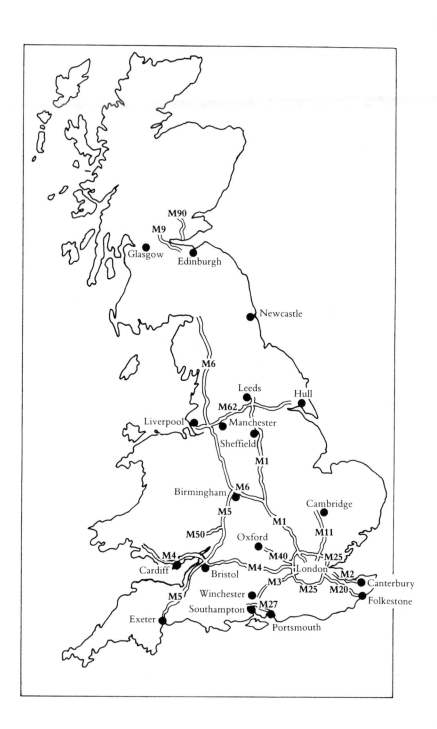

Contents

Preface to First Edition

This book had its origins in a regular series of trips I made 200 miles up and down the M1 for half a year or so. I got bored – extremely bored indeed on occasions. Unlike on main A roads (the A1, for instance, which was my alternative route) there was nothing to catch my interest. No places, since the motorway bypasses them all; no tempting country lanes with the prospect of a pleasant picnic spot; no signposts or advertisements even to tell me about a nice-sounding pub, or an interesting museum, or a fun-filled safari park just 2 or 3 miles away. As a result, not knowing where to get off the motorway, I stayed on it; drank my coffee and ate my buns at the service stations; and continued to be bored.

This book – *Off the Motorway* – is the one I wish I had had on those long journeys. My aim is simple: to describe as many places of interest as possible not too far from exits on all Britain's major long-distance motorways.

I have been as generous as possible in the sort of sights and attractions described. There are picnic spots, views, walks and nature trails; country parks and town ones too; great cathedrals and abbeys, tiny parish churches; zoos, safari parks and wildlife reserves; grand country houses; museums and art galleries of every description; and plenty of historic remains, from ancient Britain, from the Roman occupation and from the Industrial Revolution; and much more besides. The great thing about researching this book – and I visited every exit, driving some 5000 miles in all – was the astonishing variety of places I found. It made me realize what a fantastic place this country is, and how lucky we are that so much of its historic heritage has managed to survive. (Not that that should make us complacent about its continued survival, however....)

Quite deliberately, this book isn't simply a listing of tourist attractions, with dates and times of opening and admission prices. I wanted to share the fun I had exploring the byways as well as the highways, and I have chosen to describe the places I visited. I haven't hesitated to state my impressions and reactions – and criticisms where appropriate. In the end, a book like this can only represent one person's selection. I freely confess that my tastes and preferences are for remoter places, for good walks (the lonelier, the better) and, in the museum world, for working and industrial museums that recall the life of ordinary people, rather than that of the grandees. I also like cityscapes as well as country landscapes. Not everyone shares these preferences, of course, and so, while retaining the personal element (in any case, I like guide-books I can disagree with – they help to stimulate my feelings about a place), I have tried to be reasonably comprehensive. Equally, I have tried to find something of interest near every exit – although in some cases that hasn't been possible.

As far as pubs, restaurants and cafés are concerned, I have been much more selective. I have listed those that look good, particularly when I or reliable friends have tried them. I have also tended to mention them in rural areas where refreshments may be difficult to find. But this is no more than a small selection, and I haven't even attempted to be comprehensive. There are plenty of guides for gourmets and real-ale drinkers already!

How far off the motorway is 'off' the motorway? Inevitably, this varies a good deal. My rule of thumb was not farther than 6 miles. If there is a mass of interesting and recommendable attractions nearby, I haven't mentioned the places farther off, at least not in any detail. Where there is something really good a few miles distant, I have included it, especially if the junction is otherwise unpromising. On the whole, I have deliberately missed out large towns and cities, except to say that they are there. City-centre traffic can't be most people's idea of a break from motorway driving.

Times of opening are given: both the actual hours during which an attraction is open, and the days and/or months it is closed. This information usually refers to the 1983 season, which is all that was available when the research was done in autumn 1983. On the whole, 1984 will be much the same as 1983. But do check in advance, especially if you are planning a special detour to see something. Assume too that most attractions are closed on Christmas Day and Boxing Day. Unless otherwise stated, a phrase such as 'between May and September' means from 1 May to 30 September.

I have given reasonably detailed directions for getting to the various attractions from the nearest motorway exit. But my prose isn't a substitute for some quick work with a map. I apologize too to all those who find themselves reading my book backwards, simply because they happen to start their journey at the 'wrong' end of the motorway. It seemed most sensible and practical to follow the standard junction numbers. Whenever, as is often the case, you can leave the motorway at one junction, take your break, and return to the next junction, I have tried to give clear directions. A few longer excursions are also given.

A book like this could never have been written without the help and cooperation of many people: the staff of regional tourist boards, local tourist information centres, reference libraries and local council offices, and at the individual attractions themselves. Almost everyone put themselves out to help me, passing on information and answering questions by letter and telephone and when I visited. Collectively, they gave the lie to current assertions about the inefficiency of the public sector. Thanks are also due to officials of various national organizations, including the Countryside Commission, the Forestry Commission, the National Trust, the Nature Conservancy Council and the Royal Society for the Protection of Birds, who were likewise very helpful. Then there are the many friends and relations – all conveniently living just off one motorway or the other – who put me up, and fed and watered me, as I drove round the country doing my research. Thanks go to Sue Beales and John Broderick; Audrey and Dick Bishop; Alison and David Brittle, Tom and Mary; Gill and Allan Davies, and Donna; Carole and Tom Pitcairn, Jamie and Ian; Colin and Joyce Try; and Jane Try. Last but not least, I owe a great deal to my wife Jenny and my daughter Alison. They put up with my absences from home; came with me on one long research trip, which made it much more fun; tolerated my spending many hours in front of the typewriter; and were, in a very real and special sense, the start of it all.

Christopher Pick
London SE21
9 *February 1984*

Preface to Second Edition

The completion of the M25 in autumn 1986 has provided a direct link from the shorter southern motorways to the long-distance routes already described in the first edition of this book. For this second edition, as well as the M25 I have added the M2, M20, M27, M3 and M40, working on the same basic principles outlined in the preface to the first edition. On the whole, I have confined my comments to places within 2 or 3 miles of junctions, since these motorways all run through densely populated and busy parts of the country; any longer excursions off the motorway would probably take too much time.

For this second edition, the original text has been substantially revised to take account of the numerous new attractions opened during the last three years and the even greater number of improvements made to the places of interest already described. Opening times and other details have all been checked with the relevant authorities, and every effort has been taken to make the text as up-to-date as possible.

Once again, I have many people to thank: the numerous people in tourist information offices, local authorities, statutory bodies and tourist boards and at each individual attraction who answered my queries; and family and friends for hospitality, especially Stephen and Jan Tregidgo, David, Simon and Alan. As in the first edition, I give a special thank you to Jenny and Alison for putting up with a writer as husband and father.

Christopher Pick
London SE27
12 January 1987

Places of Outstanding Interest

This is a checklist, for quick and easy reference, of what are in my opinion the highlights of each motorway.

The M1

JUNCTION 15: PAGE 19
>**Stoke Bruerne:**
>the Waterways Museum; Rural Life Museum; canal basin; towpath walks.

JUNCTION 24: PAGE 26
>**The Donington Collection:**
>museum of racing cars.
>**Shardlow:**
>inland canal port; village trail; Clock Warehouse with exhibition.
>**Elvaston Castle Country Park:**
>walks in lovely gardens; working estate museum.

JUNCTION 26: PAGE 31
>**Eastwood:**
>D. H. Lawrence's birthplace; Birthplace Museum; town walk.

JUNCTION 42: PAGE 43
>**Temple Newsam House:**
>16th- and 18th-century house; walks in grounds; Home Farm exhibition (described under junction 30 of M62, page 275).

The M11

JUNCTION 8: PAGE 48
>**Hatfield Forest:**
>walks and picnics in former medieval forest.

Chatham Historic Dockyard:
museum of dockyard history in fine 18th-century dockyard buildings.
Fort Amherst:
late 18th-century fortification with exciting tour through tunnels.

The M20

The M27

Mary Rose:
Tudor warship raised from the bed of the
Solent more than 400 years after she sank;
fascinating museum with artefacts from on
board.

The M3

The M4

The M40

The M5 and M50

The M6

Leighton Hall:
fine Adam mansion.
Drive through lovely country to –
Levens Hall, with fine topiary garden and
grounds, and **Sizergh Castle**, both originally
medieval fortified houses, substantially
remodelled later.

JUNCTION 39: PAGE 251
Shap Abbey:
late 12th-century ruined abbey in lovely
country.

The M62

JUNCTION 6: PAGE 258
Knowsley Safari Park:
fine collection of wild animals.
Prescot Museum of Clock and Watch Making:
interesting museum on local industry.
Pilkington Glass Museum, St Helens:
described under junction 23 of M6 (page 238).

JUNCTION 21: PAGE 263
Hollingworth Lake Country Park:
lakeside and country walks in Pennine
landscape.

JUNCTION 23: PAGE 269
Scammonden Water:
Pennine views and walks.
Colne Valley Museum, Golcar:
fascinating Museum in old weavers' cottages.

JUNCTION 24: PAGE 271
Halifax:
Piece Hall and Pre-Industrial Museum;
Calderdale Industrial Museum; fine Victorian
town centre and Town Hall; town trail.

JUNCTION 30: PAGE 275
Temple Newsam House:
lovely Tudor mansion with 18th-century
interior; walks in grounds; Home Farm
exhibition.

The M9

The M90

The M1

Brent Cross to Leeds

INTRODUCTION

The M1 is the grand-daddy of the British motorway system. The southern section celebrated its silver jubilee in November 1984. The drive today is a far cry from those early days when, as I recall them, there were great lengths of pristine carriageway, dotted with just the occasional car. Nowadays it is a hectic mass of traffic, with large numbers of determined commuters and equally determined trucks, and, particularly for the first 30 miles or so, you need all your attention and more on the road. Not that this matters too much. St Albans notwithstanding, the off-motorway sights at the southern end of the route are not all that special. Only when you reach Bedfordshire, and the pace relaxes slightly, is it worth considering turning off. From then on there is a good variety of things to do. The countryside isn't spectacular, but it is almost always pleasant and enjoyable: typical English shire country, with rolling hills, good walks and views, interesting churches and country houses. The southern half of the M1 follows a traditional route north from the capital. The A5, which is based on the Roman Watling Street, is quite close; so too are the Grand Union Canal, and the railway to Birmingham and the north-west, which was the first line built north out of London. On one stretch in Northamptonshire, motorway, canal and railway are all within a few hundred yards of each other. Further north, there is an interesting mixture of rural and urban, with handsome market towns like Chesterfield, interesting industrial sites (Shardlow and Worsbrough Mill, for instance) and pleasant country in the eastern foothills of the Pennines.

The M1 starts in a scrappy and uninteresting part of north London, at a major junction with the North Circular Road (the A406) and the A5, some 8 miles north-west of Charing Cross and about 1 mile west of Brent Cross, where there is a large, purpose-built shopping centre with department stores and supermarkets. In my experience, the best route from the West End (i.e. Victoria, Hyde Park Corner, Marble Arch and so on) is north on the A41, through St John's

1

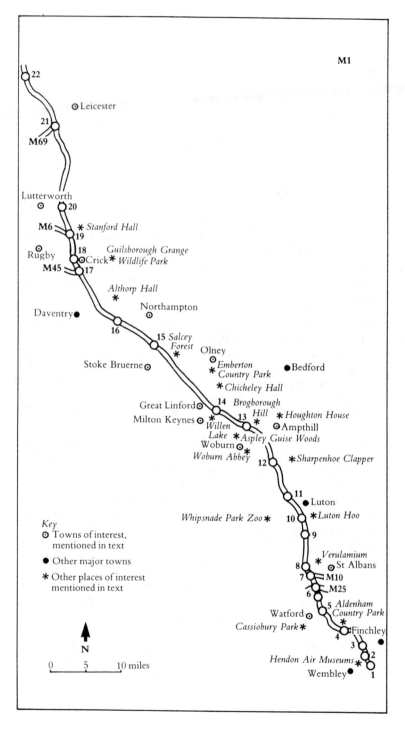

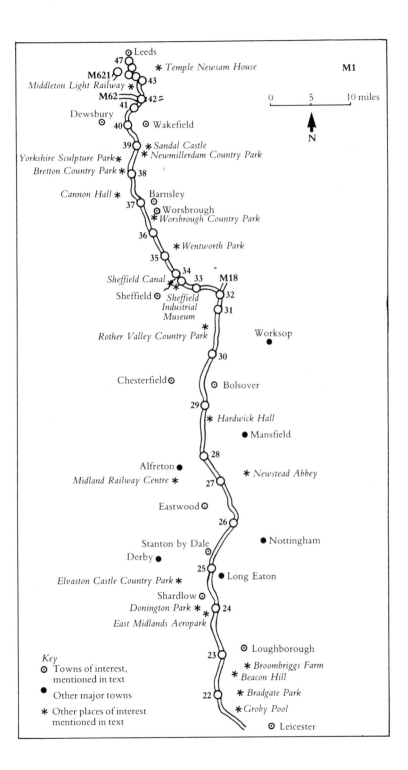

Leeds
47
M621
Middleton Light Railway *
43
M62
41
42
Dewsbury
40
⊙ Wakefield
39 * Sandal Castle
* Newmillerdam Country Park
Yorkshire Sculpture Park *
Bretton Country Park * 38
Cannon Hall *
37 Barnsley
⊙ Worsbrough
* Worsbrough Country Park
36
35 * Wentworth Park
34
Sheffield Canal ** 33
Sheffield ⊙ Sheffield M18 32
Industrial 31
Museum
Rother Valley Country Park * Worksop ●
30
Chesterfield ⊙ ⊙ Bolsover
29
* Hardwick Hall
Mansfield ●
28
Alfreton ● * Newstead Abbey
Midland Railway Centre * 27
Eastwood ⊙
26
Stanton by Dale Nottingham ●
Derby ●
25
Elvaston Castle Country Park * ⊙ Long Eaton
Shardlow ⊙
Donington Park * 24
East Midlands Aeropark
⊙ Loughborough
23
* Broombriggs Farm
* Beacon Hill
22 * Bradgate Park
* Groby Pool
⊙ Leicester

* Temple Newsam House

M1

0   5   10 miles

N

Key
⊙ Towns of interest,
  mentioned in text
● Other major towns
* Other places of interest
  mentioned in text

Wood and Swiss Cottage towards Finchley. (From Swiss Cottage the road is known as the Finchley Road.) Turn left at the junction with the North Circular Road, on to that road going west, keep in the left-hand lane and then filter left. Turn right at the roundabout under the flyover to reach junction 1. There is not much to see or do in the area, and in any case most people will want to get on with their journey. **Hampstead Heath** is a large and extremely pleasant area of open ground easily reached if you are travelling north out of London on the A41. Bear right at the start of the Finchley Road in Swiss Cottage and continue straight on through Hampstead village, and you will reach the top of the Heath by the pond.

JUNCTION 1 HENDON AIR MUSEUMS

Aircraft buffs and nostalgia addicts for the last war will want to make a diversion to the **Hendon Air Museums**, a large complex of aircraft museums housed on the former airfield at Hendon. The first to be opened was the **Royal Aircraft Museum** in 1972, followed in 1978 by the **Battle of Britain Museum** and in 1983 by the **Bomber Command Museum**. All three are housed in some striking modern buildings (not much to my taste, as it happens), with huge halls big enough to accommodate large numbers of aircraft. For it is these that are the centrepiece of each exhibition. In the RAF Museum there are all the famous names: the Sopwith Camel, the Supermarine Spitfire, Bristol Beaufighter, Gloster Meteor, English Electric Canberra, Hawker Hunter and many more; only 40 or so of the total collection of 150 are on display. An interesting recent addition is the MiG–15, the first Warsaw Pact aircraft to be put on permanent display in Britain. In the Battle of Britain Museum, the Spitfire and Hurricane steal the show, of course, but there are plenty more, including the Gladiator, Blenheim IV and many Luftwaffe machines as well (the Heinkel 111, Ju88, Me110, Me109 and Ju87G). The great days of Bomber Command are recalled by the Sopwith Tabloid, the Avro Vulcan, the Vickers Wellington, the Handley Page Halifax and many others.

But it would be misleading to suggest that these Museums are all machinery and nothing else. The men who flew the aircraft are remembered too, and well-designed galleries in each Museum bring the personal, social and technological context to life. In the RAF Museum there are aero-engines, propellers, navigational aids, uniforms and decorations, and reconstructions of a Royal Flying Corps workshop (the RFC was the RAF's predecessor), Women's Royal Air Force huts from both world wars, and a First World War armaments lecture. The chief feature of the Battle of Britain Museum – and a fascinating one it is too – is a replica of the No. 11 Group

Operations Room at RAF Uxbridge. It was from here that fighter squadrons defending the south-east and the approaches to London were controlled. Of their pilots – colloquially known as 'the few' – Winston Churchill said that 'never in the field of human conflict was so much owed by so many to so few'. The reconstruction portrays the operations room exactly as it was at 11.30 on 15 September 1940, a day subsequently named 'Battle of Britain Day', when the contest between the British and German air forces – the fight in fact for Britain's survival – was at its peak. Churchill visited Uxbridge on that day. Asking about Fighter Command's reserves, he received the celebrated answer that there were none. The first-floor gallery is a graphic display area, including exhibits associated with Group-Captain Sir Douglas Bader and Flight-Lieutenant Nicholson, the only RAF fighter pilot to be awarded the VC, an information unit depicting a typical day in the Battle of Britain and a mock London underground station, a touching reminder of the human suffering and spirit shown during the Blitz. In the Bomber Command Museum there is a full-size reconstruction of Sir Barnes Wallis's office. It was Wallis who invented and designed the famous 'bouncing bomb', used by No. 617 Squadron – the 'Dambusters' – to such good effect in breaching the Möhne and Eder dams in Germany. Quite properly, a good part of this Museum is devoted to the US Army Air Force, whose bombing offensives in Europe were of great significance, and a B25 Mitchell and a Flying Fortress are on display. The Museums are all open from 10.00 to 6.00 on Mondays to Saturdays and from 2.00 to 6.00 on Sundays. There is a well-stocked museum shop, and a cafeteria too.

To reach the Museums from junction 1 take the North Circular Road east and turn left on to the A41 going north. Continue through Hendon on the same road. Going down the hill, get into the nearside lane of the dual carriageway. Look out for a signpost to the Museums, turn left at the traffic lights, and follow signposts to the Museums. If you are coming out of central London on the Finchley Road, simply carry straight on along the A41 at Brent Cross. If you are coming into London from the north, or intend driving north after visiting the Museums, use junction 4 (see below).

Junction 2, at Mill Hill, has restricted access. You can join the north-bound carriageway and leave the southbound one. This is the junction to take if you are making for the City along the A1.

Junction 3 does not exist.

JUNCTION 4 ALDENHAM COUNTRY PARK
Junction 4 also has restricted access, and drivers can join the north-

bound carriageway and leave the southbound one. Close by, the **Aldenham Country Park** is worth escaping to if you want a quick breath of fresh air and a reasonably attractive place for a brief picnic; but don't expect too much of this 175-acre stretch of Green Belt. The focal point of the Park is Aldenham Reservoir, on which there is sailing; it was built in 1796 to maintain water levels in rivers affected by the newly constructed Grand Union Canal, and more recently has been used as a reserve public water supply. There is also riding and walking, plus an adventure playground and a picnic area. To reach the Park, take the A41 north from the junction for about 1 mile, turn right and the Park entrance is on the right after less than ½ mile. Opening hours are from 9.00 to dusk daily.

The Hendon Air Museums, described under junction 1 (see page 4), can also be reached from junction 4. Take the A41 south and continue along the dual carriageway towards Mill Hill. Then follow the clear signposts through Mill Hill Broadway to the Museums.

JUNCTION 5 WATFORD

Junction 5 is the exit for Watford, which I can't recommend for a brief off-motorway diversion, even though I was born there! The main attraction is **Cassiobury Park**, which leads down to the **Grand Union Canal**, where there are pleasant towpath walks. But between the Park and the motorway there lies a busy town centre, and in any case much more interesting stretches of the canal are met further north, especially at Stoke Bruerne (see junction 15, page 19). The **Watford Museum** in the High Street has displays on local history and on printing, paper-making and the manufacture of printing ink, all of which are important local industries. The Museum building was once part of a brewery, so exhibits on brewing are also included. The picture gallery has changing exhibitions of works by artists who lived or painted in the area, as well as contemporary material. Opening times are from 10.00 to 5.00 Mondays to Saturdays.

Junctions 6 and 8 and junction 1 of the M10 are all turn-offs for St Albans. Junction 6 leads to junctions 21 and 21a of the M25 (see page 69). Junction 8 also serves Hemel Hempstead, but there is nothing to justify a diversion there.

JUNCTIONS 6 & 8: ST ALBANS

The two main attractions in **St Albans** are the cathedral and, in the valley below, a fascinating complex of Roman buildings, the remains of the great city of **Verulamium**, once the third largest centre in Roman Britain. The modern city is also worth some time.

There are car parks in the centre of town, but the streets are narrow and busy, and my advice is to use the large car park next to the museum and then walk across pleasant water-meadows – over the Roman city, in fact, which lies beneath the turf – and uphill to the cathedral and the shops. Probably the best place to start is at the well-laid-out **museum**, which tells the whole story of Verulamium and displays many of its most interesting finds. There was a pre-Roman settlement here – quite a large one, it seems – but not much has been discovered of it. The first Roman presence was a fort, erected rapidly after the area was taken and succeeded within a very few years by a *municipium* – a self-governing township – with streets and timber-framed shops along them. That was overwhelmed in AD60 or 61 by Boudicca and her forces, and it was only late in the next decade that rebuilding began in a big way. There was another setback in 155, when fire swept through the city, destroying the private dwellings, which were built of timber. In its heyday – from the reconstruction after the fire until some time after 400 (coins stopped being minted in about 430) – Verulamium was a magnificent and prosperous place. There was a fine theatre, built in 155 and reconstructed and enlarged several times, with seating for as many as 5000 or 6000 people: reconstruction drawings suggest a large, impressive building. There was a forum, the meeting-place, and a basilica, the main administrative building, plus several temples. The private houses were impressive, many of them furnished with mosaic floors, painted wall plaster and red tesserae on the corridor floors. And it is the mosaics that are the most interesting of all the museum exhibits. Their lyrical beauty can hardly be described on paper, and is best appreciated by standing and looking for a while. One expert, Roger Wilson, writes that 'the earliest and most unusual is the scallop shell mosaic, laid between AD130 and 150, brilliantly designed and executed with subtle and pleasing use of colour'. To each side are a mosaic with a geometric design and one with a sea-god sprouting claws from his head; he was perhaps intended to look ferocious but has turned out rather benign instead. There are also some panels of reconstructed wall- and ceiling-plaster.

After the museum, the most convenient tour starts with the **theatre**, a few yards down a minor road on the opposite side of the main A414 from the museum. (The museum and the theatre are open on weekdays from 10.00 and Sundays from 2.00, closing at 5.30 between April and October and at 4.00 during the rest of the year.) Then make your way back past the museum again and through the car park to the large public park and the well-signposted **hypocaust** (open at the same time as the museum but closed on winter Mondays to Fridays). Entering through a modern bungalow, you find part of the bath-wing of a 2nd-century town house. Taking a bath in Roman times was a complicated affair. Servants stoked a fire in a small furnace-room, and the heat passed along channels beneath the different rooms in the bath-suite – an early form of underfloor heating, in fact – and up hollow box tiles into the walls. You began in the *tepidarium*, the moderately hot bath; this is the room on show here, with some attractive geometric mosaics. Then you proceeded to the *caldarium*, or hot room, where, after sweating it out for a while, your body was scraped down with a strigil, a blunt knife-like instrument, and then massaged. Hot and cold plunge-baths then followed.

The other principal Roman site to be visited, on the way from the hypocaust to the cathedral, is a long stretch of the **city wall**. At 8 to 10 feet, it is half its original height, so the experts believe. The wall dates from the 3rd century; artillery machines were placed on the projecting bastion. Nearby, the plan of the south-east, or London, gate has been marked out; this was one of the main gates into the city, built in the late 2nd or early 3rd century.

The stroll up to the **abbey** is a pleasant one, past a lake and over the river Ver near the Fighting Cocks pub. (There are also two good-looking pubs in St Michael's village, the Six Bells and the Rose and Crown, just down the road from the museum.) St Albans has been a place of Christian worship for a very long time – certainly since the end of the 4th century AD, for Alban was the first British martyr, executed in about 303 for converting to Christianity and helping a persecuted priest to flee. The present abbey – reached from Verulamium through the lovely Great Gateway, all that remains since the dissolution of the monastery's outer buildings – dates from the late 11th century, although improvements and additions have been made in almost every century since then, including the present one. The nave was built in two distinct styles, Early English and Decorated, a century or more apart. Other highlights include the choir ceiling, decorated in about 1400 with royal shields and sacred monograms, and the exquisite high altar screen, completed in 1484 and one of only two of its kind in England (the other is in Winchester Cathedral). The many statues – of the Twelve Apostles, many other saints and assorted worthies such as the Venerable Bede, King Offa, Edward the Confessor and Pope Adrian IV – were removed at the Dissolution, and new figures were only provided at the end of the 19th century. The chapter house now includes a shop and a refectory with excellent food – a new trend this, here and in many other cathedrals, and a most welcome one too.

There is good shopping in the town, with antique and clothes shops prominent. The lovely early 15th-century **clock tower** in the Market Place can be climbed, and there are good views from the top. (Opening hours are from 10.30 to 5.30 at weekends and Bank Holidays from Easter to mid-September.) The **City Museum** on the Hatfield road has material on local history and geology and also an excellent collection of craftsmen's tools, the Salaman Collection, some of which are displayed in reconstructed workshops. Opening times here are from 10.00 to 5.00 on Mondays to Saturdays. Of rather more specialist appeal, and certainly less accessible by virtue of its opening times (from 2.15 to 4.30 on Sundays), is the **Organ Museum** in Camp Road, where there is a collection of automatically operated organs and other musical instruments.

There are two other attractions, both near the Verulamium museum. The **Kingsbury Watermill Museum** (open daily from 10.00 to 6.00), on the Ver in St Michael's village is a 16th-century cornmill with a working waterwheel and a display of old farm implements. Then, finally, there is **Gorhambury House**, further down the road past the Roman theatre, and home of the Grimston family since 1652. The present Palladian mansion was completed in 1784, supplanting the previous Tudor residence, which had been the home of Francis Bacon, Lord Chancellor of England; the ruins of the Tudor structure can still be seen in the grounds. Outside, the present House looks much as it did 200 years ago. Inside, the tour takes in the five principal rooms and a fascinating collection of family books, portraits (almost every family member from the 15th to the 20th century is depicted) and treasures. The House is open from 2.00 to 5.00 on Thursdays between May and September.

If you are coming from the south, leave the motorway at junction 6, take the A405 north-east, and continue straight on at the first roundabout on the B4630. After you have crossed the M10, turn left along King Harry Lane by the church in St Stephen's and then right on to the A414 if you are making for the Verulamium museum and car park (about 4 miles). The entrance is on the right after a few hundred yards. For the town centre and the cathedral, carry straight on along the B4630. The **Gardens of the Rose**, the headquarters of the Royal National Rose Society, 1 mile away in **Chiswell Green**, contain over 1000 different types of rose. Opening times are 9.00 to 5.00 Mondays to Saturdays and 10.00 to 6.00 Sundays between mid-June and September. If you are travelling from the north, leave the motorway at junction 8 for Verulamium and at junction 1 of the M10 for the town centre. From junction 8 take the A4147 west, and then turn left on to the A414; Verulamium is on the right after about

4 miles. From junction 1 of the M10 (the conclusion of that motorway), turn left and follow the signposts to the town centre (about 1 mile).

Junction 7 is the junction with the M10 and there is no access on to ordinary roads. You can join the M10 from the southbound carriageway of the M1, and can get on to the M1 from the northbound side of the M10.

JUNCTION 9 WHIPSNADE PARK ZOO

Junction 9 is near Markyate in a not especially attractive part of the Chilterns. Use this junction if you are travelling to **Whipsnade Park Zoo** from the south. Take the A5 north and then turn left on to the B4540 at the Packhorse pub. The road climbs slowly to Whipsnade village and then to the Zoo itself (about 5½ miles from the motorway), which is situated on a lovely stretch of the Chilterns with splendid views. In these days of safari parks and wildlife reserves, the concept of keeping animals in large outdoor paddocks, with plenty of room to move about and some attempt made to provide a natural habitat, is hardly startling. In 1931, when the Zoological Society of London opened its doors here, the idea was quite novel. The original purpose of the Park was to display in English surroundings animals from the tropics, but that was quickly overtaken by breeding programmes – over 80 per cent of the mammals to be seen here were born in the Park – and by conservation work with endangered species. It was all part of the slow trend away from regarding animals as man's creatures, to be hunted or put on show, and towards accepting them as independent species with a right to existence: an idea still by no means universally accepted. Whipsnade is really worth a whole day out, and if you do come here for an off-motorway break you would do well to keep to one part of the 500-acre Park. There are some 2000 animals from 200 different species, and everyone will have their own favourites. Mine, well remembered from childhood, are the hippos and the collared peccaries. (Whipsnade once complained that in the adopt-an-animal scheme there were no takers for these marvellously grubby and muddy creatures; within a few days the offers flooded in.) On a rather more serious note, the white rhinos are a remarkable success story. Whipsnade is the first white rhino conservation area outside Africa, and from a herd of 20 that arrived in 1970 numerous calves have been produced. There have been similar successes with Przewalski's horses and Père David's deer, and many other rare animals too. The Whipsnade Railway takes visitors round the part of the Park devoted to animals from Asia. The railway runs daily from 12.00 until an hour before the Zoo closes between Easter and September and in winter at weekends and during school holidays. The Park itself is open daily from 10.00, closing at 7.00 on Sundays and Bank Holidays and at 6.00 or dusk, whichever is earlier, on other days. Early afternoon might be a good time to come. The sea-lions are fed at 2.30 in summer, the lions at 3.30, the tigers at 3.45 and the penguins at 4.15. (Winter times are 2.00, 2.30, 2.45 and 3.15.) There is a zoo shop, plus a cafeteria and refreshment kiosks, and a bar in summer as well. **Whipsnade** village, just outside the Park gates, has the Hunter's Inn restaurant and the Chequers pub, and if you are coming from junction 9 you could turn off the A5 ¼ mile or so north of the motorway to the Spotted Dog and the Three Blackbirds pubs; the latter also has a restaurant.

If you are travelling north, the quickest route back to the motorway is to make for junction 11. Leave the Zoo on the B4540 east through the village, and turn left almost immediately on to the B4541, which runs along the edge of Dunstable Downs, where there are fine views and good walks. Turn right on to the B489 and carry straight on at the junction with the A5 at the centre of Dunstable, along the A505 which leads direct to the motorway (about 5½ miles).

JUNCTION 10 LUTON HOO
Junction 10 is the junction with a tiny spur motorway, only about ½ mile long, which ends at junction 10a, on the southern edge of Luton. The only reason for coming here – Luton itself being a remarkably unattractive place – is to visit **Luton Hoo**. Turn left at the end of the motorway, then almost immediately right following the signposts, and then right again to the park entrance (3 miles). This is an astonishing place: not so much because of the house itself, a fine Robert Adam mansion, nor because of the 1500-acre park landscaped by Capability Brown, magnificent though they both are, but because of the contents. The estate was bought by Sir Julius Wernher in 1903. He had made his fortune as a diamond magnate in South Africa, a fortune substantial enough to enable him to refurbish the interior of the house in the most opulent Edwardian style and to build up a quite fabulous collection. There are paintings, Rembrandts and Titians amongst them, tapestries, furniture, medieval ivories, bronzes, jewels and porcelain – some of the finest work of the most skilled craftsmen of centuries. There is also a fascinating Russian collection of portraits and personal mementoes of the Russian czars (the late Lady Zia Wernher, Sir Julius's daughter-in-law, was the daughter of the Grand Duke Michael and grand-daughter of Czar Nicholas I) and a quite stunning collection of jewelled objects

by Fabergé. This is said to be the only collection of Fabergé pieces on public view in this country. The house and gardens are open daily except Monday (but including Bank Holiday Mondays) from 2.00 to 5.45 between mid-April and mid-October.

Junction 11 lies between Luton, to the south-east, and Dunstable, to the west. If you are travelling south, this is the exit to take for Whipsnade Park Zoo. (The Zoo and the route to it are described under junction 9, see page 10.) I don't advise a trip into the centre of **Luton**, along the A505. All that could possibly draw you there is the Luton **Museum and Art Gallery** in Wardown Park, about 1 mile north of the town centre, where there are displays on the history and manufacture of straw hats and lace, both products for which Luton in traditionally famous. Take the A505 towards Luton, turn left on to Stockingstone Road, continue straight on at the junction with the A6 (the New Bedford Road) and then turn right on to the Old Bedford Road. The Museum entrance is on the right. Opening times are weekdays 10.30 to 5.00, Sundays 1.30 to 6.00, although Sunday closing is at 5.00 from October to March.

JUNCTION 12 SHARPENHOE CLAPPER

There is a pleasant diversion from junction 12 to National Trust land at **Sharpenhoe Clapper**, 2½ miles off. This is a majestic north-facing spur of the Chilterns, an ideal spot, one might think approaching it from the valley below, for a fortified stronghold. The steep Chilterns form three sides, and only the fourth needs to be fortified: a classic promontory fort, in fact. And this is indeed what seems to have happened. Trial excavations have revealed an early medieval rampart, and below it a trench for a middle Iron Age timber palisade. There may be an external ditch as well. There are good walks along the hillside, and the wooded hilltop makes a good picnic spot. From the motorway take the A5120 north, and then take the second right. Keep straight on through modern estates at the edge of Harlington village and then turn left, following the road round until it reaches the not very exciting looking Lynmore pub in Sharpenhoe. The Streatley road runs along the edge of the Clapper.

JUNCTION 12 AMPTHILL

Another worthwhile diversion here is north along the A5120 to **Ampthill**. This is a lovely 18th-century town with some fine 19th-century buildings as well, the sort of town England does so well: it has a few distinguished individual houses, but the main attraction is the ensemble, the meshing together of buildings to create a pleasant, mature environment. For once, modern developments are relatively few and do not obtrude too much; and the volume of traffic has decreased because of the newly opened bypass to the south and west of the town. It is worth taking a little time to stroll through the town. The **White Hart Hotel** is a handsome building in Dunstable Street and there are some attractive houses in Church Street and Woburn Street. The highlight, for me at least, is **St Andrew's Church**, set in the middle of a tiny, elegant square, with the **Feoffee Almshouses**, established in 1690, along one side. Ampthill's history goes back well beyond the 18th century. Henry VIII was very fond of the town and Catherine of Aragon stayed here after she had been thrown over by the King, a cross was erected in her memory in 1773.

Ampthill Park on the north-west edge of the town has some fine walks; the entrance is on the right off the Woburn Road. A short drive north on the B530 to the top of Ampthill Hill brings you to the ruins of **Houghton House**, built, it is believed, by Inigo Jones in about 1613. The House is Bunyan's House Beautiful in *Pilgrim's Progress*, and the Hill on which it stands is the Hill of Difficulty.

Ampthill is roughly equidistant from junctions 12 and 13, so make for the latter if you are travelling north. Take the A507 west from the town and then turn right along a well-signposted road in Ridgmont. Woburn Abbey, described under junction 13 below, can also be reached from junction 14; the route is given on page 16.

JUNCTION 13 WOBURN ABBEY

Junction 13 brings you to one of the most celebrated of all the stately homes of England – perhaps the most famous of all: **Woburn Abbey**. Once, about 20 years ago, Woburn was viewed with a good deal of cynicism, as a slightly vulgar piece of popularization. On the whole, the reality is quite different, and the Abbey's recent history is something of a success story. When the twelfth Duke of Bedford died in 1953, £5 million in death duties became due; the whole of the east wing and parts of the north and south wings plus the indoor riding school and tennis court had recently been demolished because they were irreparably infested with dry rot; and many of the surviving rooms were a disorganized mess of paintings and furniture. It was the achievement of the thirteenth Duke to bring the Abbey to its present immaculate state, work that is maintained by his son, the Marquess of Tavistock, who now lives at the Abbey with his family. The first buildings here were monastic – hence the term 'abbey' – erected for the Cistercian community founded in 1145. Under Henry VII, the abbey escaped dissolution, but it was confiscated and eventually granted to Sir John Russell, who later became the first Earl of Bedford. (The elevation to dukedom came in the fifth Earl's day, in the 17th century.) There were improvements in the mid-17th century, but major reconstruction came only in the mid-18th century, when the present Palladian style was imposed. The interior is a cornucopia of treasures: far too many to describe here without turning this book into a catalogue of all that is most exquisite and sumptuous. Let us mention just three rooms: the Chinese Room, the Canaletto Room and the Long Gallery. The first of these is an almost perfect example of the 18th-century delight in chinoiserie. The porcelain and wallpaper were brought from China in the middle of the century, probably on an East Indiaman built by the Bedfords. There is a flowing lyrical beauty to the wallpaper – all greens and blues in a river scene that runs right round the room, with clearly identifiable animals and birds. The Canaletto Room has a collection of 21 views by the Venetian master, all commissioned by the fourth Duke. The paintings have hung in this room since 1800; today it is used as a family dining room – a magnificent dinner service is laid – although it has served as both a drawing room and a library. The Long Gallery is an 18th-century creation, replacing the earlier gallery that seems to have been little more than a corridor. It is a good example of the care lavished on the house's fabric and contents; the entire gallery was repainted in the winter of 1980/81, the paintings cleaned and re-hung and the furniture restored.

The Abbey at Woburn is just the start of a series of things to do and see. But, so long as you have time enough to enjoy its splendours, it is undoubtedly the most interesting and worthwhile. Outside, the deer park, landscaped by Humphry Repton at the start of the 19th century, is full of wildlife. There are no fewer than nine species of deer here, including one of the largest breeding herds of the rare Père David deer. Woburn's conservation work saved the species from almost certain extinction; in 1985, 22 Père David deer were given to the People's Republic of China in an attempt to re-establish the herd in its native land. You can also walk in the gardens and pleasure grounds and visit the pottery and garden centre and camping exhibition. The antiques centre has 40 shops, each of whose fronts has been rescued from demolition. There is a pleasant coffee shop.

Woburn's 'Wild Animal Kingdom' is yet another successful venture of the Bedfords, among the first and still among the best safari parks in the country. The drive takes you past rhinoceroses, elephants, lions and tigers, giraffes, bears and camels, and through a 'forest of the monkeys', ending at a large and attractive picnic area. Attached to the Wild Animal Kingdom is a leisure park with attractions such as sea-lion shows, Rainbow Ride, Ghost Train, Carousel and Tiger Bouncer, and a restaurant.

Between April and October the Abbey is open from 11.00 to 5.00

on weekdays, to 5.30 on Sundays. In January, February and March the Abbey is open on Saturdays and Sundays from 11.00 to 4.00. In summer months the park's opening times are from 10.00 to 4.45 on weekdays, and to 5.45 on Sundays; in January, February and March the park is open from 10.30 to 3.45. Both park and Abbey are closed throughout November and December. However, the antiques centre and the pottery are open throughout the year. The safari park is open from 10.00 to dusk between mid-March and the end of October. From the motorway at junction 13, take the A4012 through Husborne Crawley. Turn left in the centre of Woburn village through the gates to the Abbey grounds. Alternative routes to the safari park only are well signposted. Access from junction 12 is also easy. Take the A5120 west into Toddington, turn right on the side road of Milton Bryan and then right again on to the A4012 for Woburn. If you are travelling south, an alternative route from the motorway is to leave at junction 14 and take the A5130 south through Woburn Sands to Woburn village.

If all this seems a bit much, you may want to content yourself with taking a brief look at Woburn village and then a drive through the park, quite free and quite permissible on the public road. **Woburn** village is mainly the creation of the fourth Duke, who rebuilt it after a serious fire in 1724. St Mary's, the parish church, went up in the 1860s. It's a pleasant, rather arty place now, obviously much influenced by the estate (much of the town belongs to the Bedfords) and catering to an up-market tourist trade. There are several antique shops, and eating-places include the Woburn Wine Lodge, the Black Horse and the Bedford Arms. The drive across the park follows the road to Eversholt, through the Abbey gateway and a wooded area thick with rhododendrons, then out into the deer park itself. There was snow on the ground when I was last there, and the deer were etched dark against the skyline and the bare trees.

JUNCTION 13 BROGBOROUGH HILL & ASPLEY GUISE WOODS

Two other, much simpler attractions near junction 13 are worth mentioning. There is a county council picnic site – the **Brogborough Hill** site – ½ mile north-east of the motorway on the A421. Most of the land round here was once worked for clay to make bricks, and the landscape isn't very interesting. Its main feature vanished when the tall brickwork chimneys were demolished in the early 1980s. **Aspley Guise Woods** also make a pleasant walking and picnicking spot. Take the A4012 west from the motorway, turn right towards Aspley Guise, and then turn left along Wood Lane, shortly after going through the centre of this rather exclusive-looking village.

There is a path into the woods at the end of Wood Lane. This is private property, as a notice makes clear, but when I was there on a winter weekday morning there were several people exercising their dogs.

JUNCTION 14 MILTON KEYNES

Junction 14 is a study in contrasts. To the west there is Milton Keynes – a new city, as the planners and publicists hasten to tell you, not a new town. To the east, there are some rather more traditional attractions, with Chicheley Hall and the charming small town of Olney, built of lovely, mellow local stone. And, if you want a long break from the motorway, there is a lengthy diversion through pleasant country to junction 15. If you are travelling south, you can also leave the motorway here for Woburn Abbey (see junction 13, above); take the A5130 south through Woburn Sands.

The phrase new city is deliberate. **Milton Keynes** was designed as a self-sufficient city, not a satellite community as many of the earlier new towns were. The huge area, no less than 22,000 acres, was designated in 1967. Work began in the early 1970s, and over the next 10 years 23,000 houses were built, 30,000 jobs were created and the population more than doubled to 100,000. In many respects Milton Keynes is obviously a successful place. It has attracted a lot of industry and many commercial organizations; Central Milton Keynes has a large shopping centre, said to be the biggest in Europe, with a daily indoor market and an outdoor one twice a week, plus numerous department stores and specialist shops; and, it is claimed, there is a thriving community life.

I suppose my hesitations about the city, and they are purely personal, are because it is all so new: I long for something old, something settled and permanent. And that is certainly the feeling you get if you take the A509 west from junction 14. After 1 mile or so the main road runs along the southern edge of **Willen Lake**, and you can get to the shore by turning right along a signposted road, known as V10 in miltonkeynesspeak. Admittedly, I arrived in pouring rain, but I have rarely come across anything more glum and depressing in the several thousand miles I drove doing the research for this book: an uninviting, man-made stretch of water, with a flat view over factories, houses, building sites and the occasional old farmhouse. There are picnic and play areas here, and you can walk, sail, canoe and boat, and eat at a small lakeside cafeteria. Longer walks are possible on the **Redway**, a network of footpaths and cycleways throughout the city, claimed as the largest in Britain. Another possibility here would be to make for **Great Linford** village in the north of the city, where the manor grounds are an attractive area of parkland, and there is a picnic site overlooking the Grand Union Canal, with the possibility of towpath walks. Take the A509 west to the third roundabout, turn right on to Marlborough Street (V8) and carry straight on, following the signs to Great Linford village. But my advice, if you do come here, is simply to drive around and look – both at the central area and at the housing and landscaping.

Newport Pagnell is a pleasant old country town on the banks of the Ouse, less than 2 miles north-east of junction 14. It could hardly be a greater contrast with the new city, but there is nothing special to bring you here. The marvellously named Swan Revived is the main hotel in the town.

JUNCTION 14 CHICHELEY HALL

Chicheley Hall is about 4 miles east along the Bedford road. Take the A509 north and then turn right on to the A422. The house is a solid and handsome early 18th-century building, with some magnificent brickwork. The exterior, as the guide-book remarks, 'represents English baroque at its zenith', while the interior is all cool and restrained Palladianism. The tour takes in all the major rooms. High points include the main staircase, oak with beautifully carved balustrades, the lovely panelled Drawing Room, with a chimneypiece in white veined Carrara marble, and Sir John Chester's Library, in which virtually every panel can be swung open, revealing a shelved cupboard behind. Chicheley was built for Sir John Chester between 1719 and 1723, but it did not remain in the family long, at least in comparison with many other country houses. It was let for much of the 19th century, and its present owners, the Beattys, only bought it in 1954. Lord Beatty's Study has a collection of sea pictures and memorabilia of Admiral Beatty, commander of the British navy during much of the First World War; it was his son who purchased the Hall. The house is open on Sundays, Bank Holidays and Good Friday from 2.30 to 6.00 between Easter and the end of September. The Chester Arms pub in the village, at the corner of the main road and Bedlam Lane, looks good.

JUNCTION 14 OLNEY

For Olney, take the A509 north from the motorway. Just before it gets to Olney, with the fine 185-foot spire of the 14th-century church already well in view, the road runs along the edge of **Emberton**, a typical small local village, almost all the houses in the pleasing local stone. There is a craft gallery in the square, and the Two Brewers pub. Just off the main road **Emberton Country Park** runs down to the banks of the Ouse. You could picnic here, and there is dinghy-sailing, boating and fishing. You enter **Olney** across the

Ouse, past some lovely water-meadows, and the first impression is of an attractive and busy little town. Like Ampthill (see junction 12, page 12), it is a good-looking, self-confident place, not over touristified. You can spend a pleasant half hour wandering around, looking in the antique shops and visiting the church. Olney's most famous inhabitant was the poet William Cowper, who lived in Orchard Side on the Market Square for 18 years from 1768. The house is now the **Cowper Memorial Museum** (open from 10.00 to 12.00 and from 2.00 to 5.00 Tuesdays to Saturdays between Easter and October and from 2.30 to 5.00 the rest of the year; Sundays from 2.00 to 4.00 between June and September). Cowper suffered from occasional bouts of mania and depression, and his chief work at Olney was his contribution to the *Olney Hymns*, written with his friend John Newton, the evangelical curate of Olney, and published in 1779. Cowper's hymns included 'Oh! for a closer walk with God' and 'God moves in a mysterious way'. *The Task*, his long work in blank verse portraying country life (among other things), was written here; so too were some lighter poems, among them *John Gilpin's Ride*. The house is a charming little museum, with several rooms containing the poet's possessions and furniture, and also displays on local history. The house next door, where Cowper's servant lived, contains some lovely examples of the local Bedfordshire and Buckinghamshire lace, lace-making equipment, and displays on the history and development of lace-making in the area. Should you happen to come to Olney on Shrove Tuesday, you will be able to watch the annual Pancake Race, run by local housewives between the Market Square and the church. Contestants must toss a pancake in the air as they run, catching it in their frying-pan again, and the first person to reach the church without dropping the pancake wins a kiss from the bellringer and a silver salver. For more conventionally served food, there are the Cowper Tea Rooms, two wine bars and several pleasant pubs.

If you feel like a country drive, perhaps with a walk as well, take the side road through **Weston Underwood** (where the Cowper's Oak pub is in a lovely stone house) to the B526 at Stoke Goldington. Turn right here and then left after about 1½ miles into **Salcey Forest**, where there are plenty of attractive walks and good picnic spots. The direct route back to the motorway at junction 15 continues through the forest to the next crossroads; turn right here, then left in Quinton under the motorway and then right on to the A508. To get to the Waterways Museum at Stoke Bruerne (see junction 15, below), continue straight on at the crossroads and follow signposted roads through Hartwell and Ashton.

The Grand Union Canal

JUNCTION 15 STOKE BRUERNE

The principal attraction near junction 15 – and in my opinion one of the best along the entire M1 – is the **Waterways Museum** at **Stoke Bruerne**, 3½ miles south along the A508. Turn right about 1 mile after leaving Roade. The canal here is the Grand Union, and the Museum is housed in what used to be a mill building giving straight on to the towpath just above a lock. Stoke Bruerne is a mile or so south of the entrance to the Blisworth Tunnel – the towpath walk up to the tunnel mouth is well worth tackling – and in its heyday, the 40 or so years after the tunnel was opened in 1805, the village was a prosperous place. Some 70 or 80 boats a day passed through, it has been estimated, each with a horse and two men. The men and the horses needed feeding; the horses had to be shod; the men required clothes and other supplies; and ropes, tackle, candles and many other items had to be available for the boats. Leggers – men who worked the boats through the tunnel with their feet – were based at the lock as well. There was a lock-keeper too, of course, and several public houses. Competition from the railways started the long, slow decline of canal traffic, but the canal was still heavily used until the First World War and it was not until the early 1950s that commercial traffic almost entirely ceased. Today there is a minute amount still, although it is a special occasion when you see a working barge. Pleasure craft there are in abundance, however, and the lock is pleasantly busy, with a canal shop, the Boat Inn and the Butty Restaurant. The Museum itself covers every aspect of canal life and history, not simply the story of Stoke Bruerne and the Grand Union. The ground-floor exhibits are a general introduction, with engines, a traditional narrow-boat cabin, a boat horse and material on lifts and inclined planes. On the first floor the emphasis is on the engineers who planned the canals, the navvies who built them, and the boat-people, and their craft, who worked them. Painted ware, crockery, costumes and company seals are some of the many fascinating objects on display. Finally, on the top floor, the displays concentrate on canal structures (aqueducts, locks and so on), the problems of water supply, and on maintenance work. Many of the tools used in day-to-day maintenance are on show. There is an excellent and well-stocked shop next door to the Museum. The Museum is open daily from 10.00 to 5.30 between Easter and October, and daily except Mondays from 10.00 to 3.30 in the winter months. The small Rural Life Museum nearby is open during the Summer months only. Do try to come to Stoke Bruerne. I cannot recommend the Museum, and indeed the whole canal basin, too highly.

JUNCTION 15 NORTHAMPTON

Northampton lies east of the motorway between junctions 15 and 16. It is a busy town, not really suitable for a quick off-motorway diversion, unless you particularly want to see the **Museum of Leathercraft**, which is devoted to the history of leather. There are exhibits, some dating from 3500 years ago, from ancient Egypt, North America and Indonesia as well as from Great Britain and special displays on a number of themes, including saddlery and harness and glove-making. The Museum, in a former charity school in Bridge Street, is open daily except Sundays from 10.00 to 1.00 and from 2.00 to 5.30. The other museum is the **Central Museum and Art Gallery**, which has local geological and archaeological material, plus ceramics and footwear; its opening times are from 10.00 to 6.00 on Mondays to Saturdays. The town centre is just over 4 miles north of junction 15 along the A508.

A pleasant diversion through Salcey Forest and Olney south to junction 14 is described under that junction (see page 18).

JUNCTION 16 ALTHORP HALL

Junction 16 is about 5 miles west of central Northampton along the A45 (see junction 15, above). The best diversion here is not into the town but instead north through pleasant rolling country to Althorp.

Althorp Hall has become much better known in recent years, simply by virtue of the fact that it is the home of the eighth Earl Spencer, father of Diana, Princess of Wales. But, the royal connection aside, it is well worth visiting on its own account. The original mansion was built at the beginning of the 16th century, but there was a major restoration in the late 1780s, and the striking white bricks with which the exterior is faced were introduced then. The park and gardens were landscaped at the same time, not by Capability Brown himself, but by Samuel Lapidge, his chief assistant, although they underwent another improvement in the 1860s. The rooms are shown in rotation, and some are only open to the public on connoisseurs' days. The highlight of the house is undoubtedly the painting, although there is much interesting furniture, porcelain and so on. The Marlborough Room has magnificent portraits by Gainsborough and Reynolds, plus a spendid classical chimney-piece, while in the 115-foot Long Gallery – used in the earlier, Elizabethan, house for walks on wet days – there are works by Van Dyck and Lely. Althorp Hall is open from 1.30 to 5.30 daily and from 11.30 to 6.00 in July, August and September and on Bank Holidays. The house may be closed without warning for security reasons, and visitors should not arrive before opening time. Follow the A45 east from the motorway and take the second turn to the left, after about 1½ miles, towards Duston and Harlestone. Turn left at the crossroads on the edge of Duston and follow this road for approximately another 1½ miles, turning right on the edge of Althorp Park and then right again to enter the grounds. The route to Althorp is also signposted from junction 18.

Junction 17 is the junction with the M45, which runs west to Thurlaston and continues into Coventry (see junction 2 of the M6, page 217) on the dual carriageway A45. There is no access on to ordinary roads. You can join the M45 from the northbound carriageway of the M1, and leaving the M45 you can join the M1 going south.

JUNCTION 18 GUILSBOROUGH GRANGE WILDLIFE PARK

Rugby, 6 miles west of junction 18 along the A428, is described under junction 1 of the M6 (see page 216). To the east, the same road runs almost immediately into **Crick**, where there is the Wheatsheaf Inn for a pleasant, quick drink. Althorp Hall (see under junction 16, above) is also signposted from here. Crick is at the northern end of Crick Tunnel, on the Leicester arm of the Grand Union Canal, and as always the towpath offers good walks. You can get on to it from the A428 just beyond the village, or alternatively turn left along the side road towards Yelvertoft, which runs right next to the canal at one point. **Guilsborough Grange Wildlife Park** (open daily from 10.00 to 6.00 or dusk), 6 miles from the motorway, has over 500 animals and birds of 70 varieties, all living in 40 acres of beautiful parkland. This is one of the pleasantest of wildlife parks. There are some big animals – leopard, lion and puma among them – but for the most part the accent is on the smaller creatures, and there is a welcome friendliness and lack of commercialization about the place. Special features include a collection of birds of prey, some of which are shown daily, a pets corner, a collection of rare birds and monkeys, a children's playground and a large picnic area. There is a shop, and refreshments are available. From the motorway, take the A428 east to West Haddon, turn left on to the B4036 and then right on to a side road for Guilsborough village and the Grange.

JUNCTION 18 STANFORD HALL

The other attraction hereabouts is **Stanford Hall**, in the charming honeystone village of Stanford-on-Avon. Turn left in Crick along the side road to Yelvertoft, Clay Coton and Stanford (4 miles). The Cave family has lived at Stanford for over five and a half centuries, and Lady Braye, Stanford Hall's present owner, is a direct descendant of one Peter Cave, who came here in 1430. To begin with, the family home was in a house on the south side of the Avon, in Northamptonshire, but in the 1690s the decision was made to move north, on to the opposite bank and into Leicestershire, and work began on the present lovely mansion: a fine example of the William and Mary style. The tour of the house takes in all the major rooms, and there are numerous family portraits, antique furniture and family mementoes. The oak staircase and the lovely panelled Library are both worth a close look. The stable-block houses the **Pilcher Aviation Museum**. Lieutenant Percy Pilcher, R.N., the first person to fly in this country, was killed here at Stanford in 1899. The Museum contains a replica of Pilcher's *Hawk*, the flying machine in which he died; the aviator controlled the machine – or tried to – by swaying his body. There is also a large collection of motorcycles. Other attractions include a craft centre and a cafeteria serving home-made teas. The Hall is open at weekends and on Thursdays, and also on Bank Holiday Mondays and Tuesdays, from 2.30 to 6.00 between Easter and September. The grounds, cafeteria, Museum, craft centre and shop are open from 12.00 on Bank Holidays.

If you are travelling north, the quickest way back to the M1 is to junction 20. Take the Swinford road from Stanford, and then the Lutterworth road from Swinford. This brings you out on the A426 just south of Lutterworth. Turn right and then right again almost immediately on to the A427, and you are virtually on top of the junction.

Junction 19 is the junction at the start of the M6 (see page 213), and there is no access on to ordinary roads. You can only join the M6 from the northbound carriageway of the M1. Likewise, the M6 going south leads you straight on to the southbound carriageway of the M1.

Junction 20 is just south of Lutterworth, an undistinguished small town with nothing special to attract you. If you are travelling south, leave the motorway here for Stanford Hall (described under junction 18).

JUNCTION 21 LEICESTER

Junction 21 is the principal junction for Leicester, and also the junction with the M69, which runs south-west to meet the M6 at junction 2 of that motorway (see page 217). **Leicester**, 4 miles north along the A46, is not an especially inspiring place, and it is not really at all suitable for a break from motorway driving. There are, however, the usual city-centre amenities, and several interesting museums. The **Leicestershire Museum of Technology**, housed in the Abbey Pumping Station in Corporation Road, has beam engines and power and transport exhibits. **The Leicestershire Museum and Art Gallery** contains ceramics, English silver and glass, English drawings and paintings from the 18th century to the present day and a unique collection of modern German art, plus galleries on geology and natural history. Finally, and perhaps most interesting of all, there are the remains of Ratae Coritanorum, as Roman Leicester was known. The **Jewry Wall**, part of the *palaestra*, or exercise hall, of the public baths, stands an impressive 30 feet high, one of the largest upright structures surviving from Roman Britain. The nearby **museum** contains two stretches of wall-plaster, some lovely mosaic floors, and a milestone. All three museums are open on Mondays to Thursdays and Saturdays from 10.00 to 5.30 and on Sundays from 2.00 to 5.30, while the Jewry Wall is accessible at 'any reasonable time'.

JUNCTION 22 CHARNWOOD FOREST

Junction 22 is at the southern edge of Charnwood Forest. Like many of the forests that once covered much of the English landscape, most of Charnwood has long since vanished, although some stretches of woodland do remain. It is a curiously remote and undiscovered area, with lovely country and fine views: certainly a good spot for a brief rest from the motorway. **Groby Pool**, on the far side of the A50 from Groby village, is a 34-acre lake that provides a rich habitat for aquatic wildlife. Many species of duck are regularly seen here, and kingfishers have been spotted too. The pool itself is on private land, but there is a public car park nearby, and you can walk alongside the lake for a little way. Take the A50 south from the motorway for about 2½ miles and turn off left for Groby, turning right towards Newtown Linford at the end of the slip road. A place for enthusiasts, this, but worth visiting if you fall into that category.

JUNCTION 22 BRADGATE HOUSE & PARK

Of much more general interest is **Bradgate Park**, 800 acres of rocky outcrops and small woodlands with a mixture of heath, bracken and grass, all looking much as it must have done some 700 years ago, when Bradgate was established as a hunting area. The car park at Newtown Linford is the best place to make for. There is an information centre close by, and several good walks through the Park start here. One good route runs past the ruins of **Bradgate House**, built in about 1500 as the family home of the Greys (Lady Jane Grey, Queen of England for nine days in 1553, lived most of her life here), and then along the edge of Cropston Reservoir; swing west at the Hallgates car park up to Old John Tower, erected in 1786, and the war memorial, and then south back to the Newtown Linford car park again. Take the A50 south from the motorway and turn left on to the B5327 for Newtown Linford (2½ miles). If you are coming from Groby Pool, simply continue on the road north from the car park. There is the Bradgate pub in Newtown Linford, and the Grey Lady restaurant as well on the road towards Swithland.

JUNCTION 22 BEACON HILL

Two other small countryside attractions give you the option of a longer diversion through lovely rolling country – classic English shire land – returning to the motorway at junction 23. The first is **Beacon Hill**, 853 feet up and possibly the site of a Bronze Age fort. There are several walks in the surrounding woods, and wide views. One book of local walks claims first that one fifth of England can be seen from the summit; second that there is nothing between Beacon Hill and the east coast, and hence the continent too; and third – most incredible of all – that the next highest point due east is the Ural mountains in the USSR. Take the Swithland road out of Newtown Linford and the second left after leaving the village, just below Old John Tower; carry straight on at the next junction, on to the B5330, and then turn right on to the B591; the drive to the car park is soon on the left. Further along the B591, just before the village of

Woodhouse Eaves, you reach **Broombriggs Farm** on the right, where an interesting farm trail guides you round this mixed arable and stock farm. There are also picnic areas and several waymarked paths, and Windmill Hill can also be climbed. The trail boards are in position from April to October, but there is admission throughout the year, here and at all the other attractions mentioned.

From Broombriggs Farm you can return directly to junction 23 by retracing your tracks on the B591, turning right on to the B5330 and then right again on to the A512 (about 4½ miles). Alternatively, if you want to visit Loughborough and the Great Central Railway (see junction 23, below), continue on the B591 east, past Ye Old Bull's Head pub in Woodhouse and Quorn & Woodhouse Station on the Great Central, and turn left on to the A6; it is about 4 miles into the town centre.

JUNCTION 23 LOUGHBOROUGH
Loughborough, 3 miles east along the A512 from junction 23, is a solid, hard-working and prosperous town, whose character seems to speak out from its buildings. Wool was the dominant industry in the 15th and 16th centuries, hosiery in the 19th; today many well-known companies have their factories here, and there is also the world-renowned University of Technology, whose campus you pass on the way in from the motorway. One celebrated company is John Taylor's bell foundry, established in 1840. Their bells are in churches and cathedrals all over the world – and the **Loughborough Carillon** too, in Queen's Park, where there are no fewer than 47. The carillon – the only municipally owned one in the country – was built as a war memorial. The **Bell Foundry Museum** in Freehold Street, which forms part of the John Taylor plant, shows the evolution of the bell-founder's craft and describes the moulding, casting, tuning and fitting-up of bells. Opening times are 9.30 to 4.30 on Tuesdays to Saturdays and Bank Holiday Mondays. You can spend a pleasant half hour or hour walking through the town centre. **All Saints' Church** was built in the 14th century but heavily restored in the last, and there is a small **museum** in the Old Rectory, open from 10.30 to 4.30 on Saturdays.

JUNCTION 23 GREAT CENTRAL RAILWAY
The main attraction in Loughborough is the **Great Central Railway**. The original Great Central ran from Sheffield south through Nottingham, Leicester, Rugby, Banbury and Aylesbury, terminating at Marylebone Station in London. Opened in 1899, it was the last main line to be built into London, and elevated the Manchester, Sheffield & Lincolnshire Railway to the status of a national com-

pany, renamed the Great Central. Seven daytime expresses were operated in the line's heyday, and numerous cross-country services ran over part of the route. Competition from roads (including the new motorways) and rationalization within British Rail (all the major towns on the line were served by other routes) meant that the line was run down from the early 1960s, through expresses ceasing in 1966. For much of the 1970s, a group of dedicated enthusiasts struggled to revive steam-operated services on a small stretch of the line – and succeeded triumphantly. As soon as you reach the platform at the station in Great Central Road, you know you are back in the age of steam: the station buildings, the posters and noticeboards and timetables – and above all the smells – are just right. For those old enough, like me (but only just!), to remember the days when locomotives were *true* locomotives – not the anodyne, anonymous ones of today's network – the line is a marvellous trip back into the past. For those too young to remember, there is the chance to find out why everyone else is going on so. The special thing about the Great Central is that main-line steam is commemorated: most other preserved railways run over old branch lines. The 5-mile line runs from Loughborough south through lovely country to Quorn & Woodhouse Station (see also under junction 22, page 25) and then to Rothley. The round trip takes just under an hour, but you can get out at each station, explore the surrounding country or relax with a picnic, and return on a later train. A large number of different locomotives and rolling stock operate the services, and the company also undertakes much restoration work. Trains run at regular intervals at weekends throughout the year, and also on Wednesday afternoons between late May and mid-September. You can have an excellent lunch on board at weekends, and a luxury evening meal on occasional Saturday evenings. There is also an excellent shop at Loughborough Station, and light refreshments are available.

Junction 24 is a humdinger of a junction, with three attractions of national importance. At Donington there is the Donington Collection of Single-Seater Racing Cars. At Shardlow there is the inland port at the meeting-point of the river Trent and the Trent & Mersey Canal. And at Elvaston there is a lovely country park and the Elvaston Working Estate Museum, an absorbing and unusual look back at life on a big country estate.

JUNCTION 24 DONINGTON COLLECTION
The **Donington Collection** – over 200 cars at present and growing all the time – is the outcome of the efforts and inspiration of one man: Bernard Wheatcroft, known to everyone as 'Tom', a Leicester

builder and motor-racing enthusiast. Before the Second World War, Donington Park was Britain's principal motor-racing circuit, and in the mid- and late 1930s the young Tom Wheatcroft saw many races there, and many of the most celebrated drivers of the time too: 'B. Bira', Seaman, Ruesch, Rosemayer, von Brauchitsch, Nuvolari among them. With the war, the Park was requisitioned, becoming the largest military transport depot in the country. The military only moved out in 1956, and it was 15 years after that that Tom Wheatcroft bought the circuit. The museum was opened in 1973, and Tom's principal aim – to organize racing once again over the circuit – was achieved in 1977. Today, there are meetings most weekends between March and October, including many national and international car and motorcycle competitions.

There are cars in the collection from every famous marque in the history of motor-racing – and from many of the lesser-known ones too. The earliest is a 1911 Cottin et Desgouettes from France, the most recent the Brabham BT49 in which Nelson Piquet won the 1981 Formula 1 world championship. By and large, the cars fall into three main groups. First there are the early racers, those built before about 1932 with wide cockpits: the 1921 GP Sunbeam, for instance, and the 1931 Bugatti Type 51. These were superseded by the front-engined single-seaters that dominated racing in the 1930s, 1940s and 1950s. The 1934 Maserati 8CM and, post-war, the 1951 Ferrari Tipo 125 are typical; the Ferrari was the first car Tom Wheatcroft bought. The 1959 rear-engined Cooper Climax marked the change to a recognizably modern style of racing car, with wide tyres and often with aerofoils behind. Notable cars from the last two-and-a-half decades include the trend-setting 1962/63 Lotus-Climax 25, several four-wheel drive vehicles built in the late 1960s, and the 1973 Tyrrell-Cosworth 006/2. A number of other cars and motorcycles are also exhibited; many of Barry Sheene's motorcycles, including his modern Grand Prix machines, are here. A list of machines can hardly do justice to their real fascination. Behind each one lies a story of individual and collective endeavour – for motor-racing is at one and the same time dependent on the skill of the driver and the talents and expertise of his supporting team. And in many cases too the cars themselves were acquired in unusual circumstances.

The collection is open on weekdays throughout the year from 10.00 to 4.15, at weekends from 10.00 to 5.15. The route from the motorway is simple. Take the A453 west for about 4 miles, and turn right following clear signposts to enter Donington Park through a sham castle entrance. After about 1½ miles you pass the East Midlands Airport on the right: you can't miss it, because the planes

The Clock Warehouse at Shardlow

come in really low over the main road to land. In a corner of the air-field (turn right off the main road towards the airport building and then right again at the first roundabout) is the **East Midlands Aero-park**. Here you can enjoy a small exhibition on the history of avi-ation and a video on the operation of the airport. There is a children's play area, and refreshments are available during the summer. The viewing mound outside is the nearest the public can get to any civil aviation runway in this country; you can stand 150 metres from the runway and only 50 metres from the taxiway. Opening times are daily from 10.00 to 8.00 in June, July and August, 10.00 to 6.00 in April, May and September and 10.00 to 4.00 the rest of the year.

JUNCTION 24 SHARDLOW

Shardlow is 3 miles west of junction 24 along the A6. From the Don-ington Collection take the B6540 north through Castle Donington – there are restaurants and pubs here, but the remains of the early 12th-century castle are now part of Donington House – and then turn left on to the A6. In the canal era – roughly from the 1770s to the 1840s – Shardlow was the hub of water-borne trade in the Midlands. It all started with James Brindley, the engineer who built the Bridgewater Canal, the first true canal in this country (see junction 12 of the M62, page 261). He went on to plan a major project, intended to provide an inland link between the east and the west coasts, via the Trent and the Mersey rivers. Although work started in 1766, the complete route only opened in 1777 (Brindley having died in the meantime). It was a great success. Until the new railways started to compete, traffic was heavy on the Trent & Mersey Canal, all kinds of goods being carried – from iron, coal and stone to cheese, pottery and even Burton ales – and passengers as well. Shardlow's role in all this was crucial. Sea-going vessels could navigate the Trent as far as Gainsborough, and large barges could continue inland past Shardlow as far as Burton-upon-Trent. But, at some point, cargoes had to be transferred to narrow boats for the journey beyond Burton, and the spot selected for this was Shardlow. Wharves and warehouses were built, and the village soon became a major inland port, with all the ancillary services required: boat- and crane-building, rope-making, smithying, stables for horses and inns for the crews. Many of the buildings put up by this thriving community remain, and a fascinating trail leads you round most of them. The **Clock Warehouse** – so called because a clock once adorned the front – is well worth a visit. This lovely building, which dominates the western basin, the first one built here, was put up in 1780. The channels leading right underneath that enabled barges to unload and load easily can be seen. There is an excellent exhibition in the warehouse, with a lot of interesting material on the history and construction of canals. A reconstructed longboat with clothes, china and so on shows how canal folk used to live. There is also a well-stocked shop and a restaurant; boat trips on the canal start from here. The Clock Warehouse is open daily from 9.00 to 5.00 between April and October and from 10.00 to 4.00 on Saturdays and Sundays only during the rest of the year.

JUNCTION 24 ELVASTON CASTLE COUNTRY PARK

You get to **Elvaston Castle Country Park** by continuing west along the A6 from Shardlow for about 2 miles and then turning right on to the B5010 from where the Park is signposted. The Park entrance is then on the left in just under 1 mile. Quite remarkably, the gardens of Elvaston Castle were *not* designed by Capability Brown. He was asked, but turned the commission down, remarking that 'the place is so flat, and there is a want of capability in it'! Instead, it was William Barron who got the job. He planned a magnificent garden, shunning long vistas in favour of a series of smaller gardens surrounded by high hedges, and a number of short avenues with specimen trees at each end. The lake, with its artificial rock creations, is his too, and he also created the lovely topiary garden. Much of all this still survives, thanks chiefly to the efforts of Derbyshire County Council, who bought the Castle and the surrounding parkland in 1969, after it had been neglected for a long time. There is a replanting programme, a new rhododendron dell has been created, and in part of the old kitchen garden a lovely old English garden has been developed, with herbaceous borders, unusual climbing plants, a rose garden and a herb garden. A nature trail leads through woodland, where there are some superb mature trees: cedar and Japanese cedar, redwood, monkey puzzle, oak, beech and copper beech. The Castle is a magnificent Gothick early 19th-century creation with some marvellously extravagant decoration. None of this, unfortunately, can be seen by the visitor, since dry rot has taken hold, and an extensive repair programme is underway. What you should make time to visit, however, is the **Working Estate Museum** in the lower stable yard. Like many large country estates in the mid-19th century, Elvaston was virtually a self-sufficient community, employing craftsmen, labourers and tradesmen. An estate cottage with gardens, laundry and a dairy can be seen, and there are agricultural machinery, gipsy caravans, workshops – for blacksmith, cobbler, farrier, joiner, plumber and saddler – and original machinery for the preparation of timber. A fascinating glimpse back into an almost vanished past, and well worth your time. You can picnic and walk in the Park, and other facilities include a shop and the Parlour Tea Room. The Park is open daily throughout the year until dusk, and the Working Estate Museum from 1.00 to 5.00 on Wednesdays to Saturdays and from 10.00 to 6.00 on Sundays and Bank Holidays between Easter and October. If you are travelling north, the quickest way back to the motorway is to junction 25. Carry on north on the B5010 to Borrowash. At the crossroads keep straight on on the B5010 and then take the A52 east towards Nottingham and the motorway (about 5 miles).

Junction 25 leads on to the dual carriageway A52 which links Nottingham (7 miles east) and Derby (8 miles west). Leave the motorway here if you are travelling south and want to take a break in the lovely Elvaston Castle Country Park (see junction 24, above); the Country Park is signposted from the A52. Derby and Nottingham are both interesting places with quite a lot to offer, but rather distant and rather busy too for an off-motorway break. The Stanhope pub in Stanton by Dale (the Stanhopes owned Elvaston Castle) looks a good place for a relaxing drink. Take the side road north from the roundabout at the exit north through Risley for about 1½ miles.

JUNCTION 26 D. H. LAWRENCE BIRTHPLACE MUSEUM

Junction 26 is the start of a fascinating and rewarding literary pilgrimage. The word pilgrimage is used ironically. Pilgrims usually visit a shrine or a holy place dedicated to the worship of a saint or cult-figure. **Eastwood**, however, has for many years set its face solidly against its most celebrated son. In the rest of England, while he may once have been an unpopular author, his concerns and themes unwelcome, D. H. Lawrence now appears on the examination curriculum, and even *Lady Chatterley's Lover* has been freely available in paperback for over a quarter of a century. But here in Eastwood recognition has come very belatedly, and one senses continuing disapproval in some quarters. The principal shrine is No. 8a Victoria Street, the **D. H. Lawrence Birthplace Museum**. The rooms are furnished much as they would have been when the Lawrences lived here in the 1880s (David Herbert was born in 1885, the fourth child), and there are family photographs on the walls. It is a surprisingly large house on three storeys, with gas lighting throughout. Lawrence's father was a miner in a nearby colliery, while his mother, who supplemented the family income by running a small shop from her front parlour, had been a schoolteacher. According to one literary critic, 'the conflicting interests of his parents, his father's powerful working-class character and his mother's restless aspirations to refinement, coloured Lawrence's imaginative life'. Much of the vivid interest and fascination of the Museum is due to the crusading enthusiasm and hard work of its former curator, Mrs Enid Goodband, whose mother succeeded the Lawrences as tenants of 8 Walker Street (not open to the public), to which the Lawrences moved in 1891. Mrs Goodband told me that 'We should be proud of Lawrence.' But there has been real hatred for him locally, because he wrote of local people, and they have never forgiven him. Eastwood itself has changed, of course, since Lawrence's time – he left the area in 1914 when he married Frieda Weekly, the former wife of one of his professors at Nottingham University, and rarely returned – but not all that much. A town walk starting at the **library**, where there is a collection of first editions and letters, passes all the local places associated with Lawrence, including No. 28 Garden Road, to which the family moved from Victoria Street, and the Three Tuns Inn. These were immortalized as The Bottoms and The Moon and Stars in *Sons and Lovers*. The Birthplace Museum has leaflets describing three further walks in nearby villages. The local countryside had a profound impact on Lawrence, and occurs again and again in his writing. The Birthplace Museum is open daily from 10.00 to 5.00

between April and October and from 10.00 to 4.00 during the rest of the year. Eastwood is about 3½ miles west of the motorway at junction 26 along the A610. If you are travelling north, return to the motorway at junction 27. Turn right at the traffic lights at the end of Eastwood High Street (just past the top end of Victoria Street) on to the A608, the Mansfield Road, which reaches junction 27 in 4 miles.

JUNCTION 27 NEWSTEAD ABBEY

A different century, a different literary form, but there is more in common than one might think between D. H. Lawrence, junction 26's literary giant (there is a quick route to Eastwood from this junction, see above), and Lord Byron, whose family home was at **Newstead Abbey**, 3½ miles to the east of junction 27. Both spent much of their life abroad, Lawrence in New Mexico and then Italy, Byron in Italy and then Greece, in the cause of whose liberty he died. Both too explored and wrote about human passion and sexuality, although Byron's writing met a far better response than Lawrence's. The original abbey was built over 800 years ago, in 1170, for an Augustinian order, was converted into a family home for the Byrons after the Dissolution of the Monasteries in the mid-16th century, and underwent another major restoration in the 19th century. Byron lived here for several years from 1808, and requested in his will that he be buried in the gardens near his dog Boatswain, whose memorial bears a long epitaph by the poet; but the request was ignored. A number of rooms contain portraits and personal possessions of the poet, including the table on which *Childe Harold* was written. The gardens are magnificent. A Japanese garden reproduces the famous willow pattern design, and there is a rose garden, a lovely collection of old shrub roses, rock gardens, and banks of azaleas. The Abbey and grounds are open daily from 1.45 to 6.00 between Easter and September, last admission to the house is at 5.00. From the motorway, take the A608 east, turn left on to the A611, right on to the B6020, and finally right on to the A60. The driveway to the Abbey starts on the right in less than ½ mile (6½ miles from the motorway).

JUNCTION 28 MIDLAND RAILWAY CENTRE

The principal attraction near junction 28 is the **Midland Railway Centre**. Take the A38 west and turn left on to the A61 just beyond Alfreton. The Centre is on the A61 about 1 mile north of Ripley (about 4 miles from the motorway). The appeal of steam extends well beyond committed railway buffs, and virtually everyone will enjoy a visit here. What you can see now is just the beginning of an extremely ambitious and praiseworthy project that, according to the guide-book's slightly macabre forecast, 'may well not be finished within the lifetime of the present management'. It is the Midland Railway that is commemorated here, the third-longest system in Great Britain before the 1923 amalgamation and one of the best run in the world, it is claimed. Despite its name, the Midland's trains reached most parts of the country, Ireland as well; it built well-designed stations; and it was the first company to introduce third-class carriages, to upholster the seats in them, to abolish second class, and to operate Pullman cars. There are 3 miles of operational line, with no fewer than four stations, and the round trip, hauled by one of the many restored steam locomotives assembled here, takes just under 50 minutes. The original Butterley Station, where the trips start and finish, was demolished when the Ambergate to Pye Bridge line was closed, and the present building comes from Whitwell in north Derbyshire; volunteers took it apart stone by stone, brought it here and rebuilt it. Historic locomotives are displayed in the old goods yard. Over the level crossing there is a picnic area, and a footpath runs along the top of the cutting; this is an excellent spot for photography. Steam and water cranes, fire engines, dismantled signalboxes, a rail trolley and a turntable, all of which have seen 'active service' with the Midland, are on display at Butterley and at the 57-acre museum site at Swanwick Junction, the first part of which opens to the public in 1987. Future plans include a steam-driven workshop and material on road transport in the Midlands. The Centre is open at weekends and Bank Holidays between March and December; between four and six services run daily, depending on the time of year, between 10.00 and 4.00. There are also two Wednesday afternoon trains between late March and mid-July, while over Easter and during the late Spring Bank Holiday week and the school summer holiday trains run every day. Refreshments are normally available in the buffet car, and there is also a souvenir shop.

If you are travelling southwards, leave the motorway at junction 28 for Alton Towers (see page 228). The route is signposted from the motorway.

JUNCTION 29 HARDWICK HALL

Hardwick Hall, 2 miles from junction 29, is a grand Elizabethan country house. Nothing unusual in that, you might think. What makes Hardwick different is that it has scarcely been altered since then, and what restoration there has been is fully in keeping with the original style. No Adam or Barry came here to remodel the house, no Capability Brown or Repton to turn the gardens into a monument to 18th-century taste. Inside, the contents too are much as they

Hardwick Hall

were when the redoubtable Bess of Hardwick listed them in 1601. Bess was a local girl made good, the daughter of a local squire but brought up in much reduced circumstances. She outlived no fewer than four husbands, acquiring the Chatsworth estate on the death of her second. With her fourth, the Earl of Shrewsbury, she quarrelled violently; she moved back to Hardwick and set about transforming the Old Hall there into the magnificent house we see today. Well before work was completed, the Earl died, leaving his estranged wife a substantial fortune to add to her already considerable wealth, which came from farming, money-lending, her glass- and lead-works, and from the bequests of previous husbands. Fortunately for us, Bess's descendants chose to make Chatsworth their principal home, and so Hardwick has survived unscathed. Hardwick is a very English house; European influences are practically nil, and the building is a classic of the Perpendicular style. The façade is most impressive: a great expanse of glass ('Hardwick Hall, more glass than wall', the jingle runs) with striking symmetry, the height of the windows increasing from the ground floor up, giving a decidedly vertical emphasis, increased by the six towers. Inside, the two-storey Great Hall runs not lengthwise, as it did in medieval buildings, but at right angles to the façade. In contrast with most other contemporary houses, the state rooms at Hardwick were on the top floor, with excellent views, the private family rooms on the first, and the kitchens, offices and servants' quarters on the ground floor; in fact the servants probably ate in the Great Hall. There is a sequence of splendid rooms on the second floor. The high Great Chamber was Bess's presence chamber, where masques and other entertainments were given; a magnificent plasterwork frieze runs right round the room. The wall decorations in this room and in many others on this floor are exquisite Flemish tapestries, mostly depicting biblical stories. The Long Gallery, a majestic 166 feet, was used for exercise and has a series of interesting family portraits. There is lovely furniture in the Withdrawing Room, including a walnut draw-leaf table on 'sea-dog' supports, with an alabaster bas-relief of *Apollo and the Muses* over the chimney-piece. In tourism terms, Hardwick illustrates the problems of success. The house receives so many visitors that it is often uncomfortably busy, and the crowds make a leisurely visit impossible. In addition, we should realize that over-visiting can seriously damage the fabric of a house as valuable as Hardwick. So, if you have been here before, it might be best not to come again yet – and if you do come, be prepared to join a crowd! Take the A617 east as far as Glapwell, turn right and follow the clearly signposted road to the park entrance. The Hall is open on Wednesdays, Thursdays, Saturdays, Sundays and Bank Holidays from 1.00 to 5.00 between

April and October or sunset if earlier, the gardens daily during the same months from 12.00 to 5.30. The 300 acres of **Hardwick Park** surrounding the Hall are open daily throughout the year.

Bolsover, about 3 miles north-east of junction 29, lies along a high ridge of hills. It is a pleasant small town without any special attractions except the **Castle**. Put up in the 12th century, it was in ruins by the early 17th, when Charles Cavendish, one of Bess of Hardwick's sons, bought it and proceeded to improve it in mock-medieval fashion. The Castle opens at 9.30 on weekdays through-out the year, closing at 6.30 between mid-March and mid-October and at 4.00 in the winter months. On Sundays the Castle opens at 2.00 and closes at the same time as on weekdays. From the motorway, take the minor road to Palterton, and turn left there for Bolsover.

JUNCTIONS 29 & 30 CHESTERFIELD

Chesterfield is a handsome and well-cared-for town, 5½ miles west of junction 29 along the A617 and 6½ south-west of junction 30; take the A616 east from the junction and immediately turn right on to the A619. The centre is an attractive mixture of old and new buildings – and for once the combination works well. The market square is extremely attractive, with a lively bustle on market days, Mondays, Fridays and Saturdays. There is also a flea market on Thursdays. The handsome **Market Hall**, built in 1857, has recently been restored, and has a large number of indoor stalls, while the **Pavements Centre** is a brand-new shopping complex, far pleasanter than most of its kind. Chesterfield's best-known landmark is the crooked and twisted spire of **St Mary and All Saints'**, the parish church. It seems that the builders who put the spire up at the end of the 14th century were chiefly responsible. Unseasoned timber was used, and that, and the action of the sun on the lead cladding, caused the main contortion. When it was last measured in 1974, the spire had moved 9 feet 4 inches from true centre, and no fewer than 1½ feet in the previous 50 years. It is still moving, but we are assured that there is no danger of collapse. Naturally enough, over the years people have put forward many reasons why the spire should have settled into this curious shape. One legend has it that the Devil, on a long journey, found the spire a pleasant place to rest. When he went on his way, he left his mark behind him, and, so the story maintains, only the marriage of a virgin in the church will straighten the spire out again! The interior is lovely, chiefly 14th century, with an Anglo-Saxon font and three medieval screens. Take time too to visit the **Peacock Information and Heritage Centre** in a lovely restored building on Low Pavement, and stroll through **The Shambles**, an attractive maze of narrow streets.

JUNCTIONS 30 & 31 ROTHER VALLEY COUNTRY PARK
Junctions 30 and 31 are roughly equidistant from the **Rother Valley Country Park**. For the people of Sheffield, this new Park is a successful and increasingly popular area of open space, and a lot of leisure activities are catered for, including canoeing, rowing, sailing, sailboarding, grass-skiing and riding. For the motorized passer-by, there are walks and picnic possibilities, an attractive visitor centre at Bedgreave Mill, where there are working millstones and machinery, and a café. But don't expect too much in the way of good scenery. The area was for long a mess of old coal workings and a disused railway line. More recently there was open-cast mining, and now an ambitious, and continuing, reclamation programme has converted the former pits to lakes. The displays in the visitor centre (where there is also a café) explain the background to the project and how grass and wetland habitats for wildlife are being established; in time it is hoped that mallard, coot, moorhen, great-crested grebe and sedgewarbler will be attracted here. From junction 30, follow the A616 west, then take the second right, in just under ½ mile, towards Spinkhill and follow the road through the village and on to the junction with the A618. Turn left here, and the entrance to the Park is on the left in about 1½ miles (about 4 miles from the motorway). From junction 31, take the A57 west, turn left on to the A618, and the Park entrance is on the right shortly after you leave the tiny village of Wales.

Junction 32 is the junction with the M18, and there is no access on to ordinary roads.

JUNCTION 33 SHEFFIELD INDUSTRIAL MUSEUM
Junction 33 is the junction with Sheffield Parkway, the fast A630 straight into the city centre (about 4 miles). I don't normally recommend city centres for off-motorway breaks – after all, why add to the strain of a long drive? – but one museum in Sheffield is well worth the diversion, and the route there only touches the central area. This is the **Sheffield Industrial Museum** on Kelham Island. The island is in the middle of the river Don, and was created as long ago as the 12th century, when a mill race was built to drive a corn mill. The name Kelham comes from Kellam Homer, the town armourer, who owned a grinding workshop on the island in the middle of the 17th century. By the 18th century, there was a good deal of industrial development in and around the island, and in 1829 an iron foundry was established there. That building vanished at the end of

the century – although a bone-shaker bicycle made there is on display in the museum foyer – when Sheffield Corporation constructed a generating station for the city's new electric tramway. It is this building that now houses the Industrial Museum – and a fascinating place it is too, a loving tribute not only to the astonishingly diverse range of goods made in Sheffield but also to the people who manufactured them. It is vivid, living history, full of grandparents and parents remembering and telling their children what it was really like and what they did. The start of the Museum is a large display called 'Made in Sheffield' – not just the cutlery everyone thinks of but also machine tools, surgical instruments, sweets, tape measures and 101 other things. The most spectacular single exhibit is without question the enormous 12,000hp River Don engine, which from 1905 to 1978 powered a rolling-mill making armour plate. The engine, thought to be the most powerful working steam engine in any museum in the country, is steamed regularly, followed by a seven-minute film show. When I was there, the persistent thud-thud of a 150hp Crossley gas engine penetrated the entire Museum. A die-sinkers' workshop has been rebuilt, there is a model hand-rolling mill, and, most fascinating of all, there is the courtyard of 'Little Mesters' workshops. Little Mesters were specialist craftsmen, usually self-employed and with no more than a couple of assistants, making tools and cutlery. At first, a single craftsman made the entire piece, but as demand increased so did specialization. A Master Manufacturer would finance the entire production process and market the finished goods, sub-contracting the various intermediate processes to specialists, the Little Mesters. They might be blade-forgers, cutlers or grinders, and even these skills were in time sub-divided; thus there were razor-, scissor-, pen-blade- and table-blade-grinders, and so on. Mass production did finally replace this system, and all but a few of the hundreds of workshops disappeared. Not that the ones at Kelham Island are models, however: the craftsmen you see working here are true Little Mesters, and carry on their own businesses here in the Museum. The Museum is open from 10.00 to 5.00 on Wednesdays to Saturdays and 11.00 to 5.00 on Sundays, and there is a café and a shop selling Sheffield-made goods. From the end of the Sheffield Parkway at Park Square, take Castlegate which runs straight into Bridge Street. Bear right into Alma Street and turn right for the Museum. If you are travelling north, return to the M1 at junction 34. Cross the river from Bridge Street to Wicker, turn right into Savile Street and carry straight on along the A6109, which leads direct to the motorway (4½ miles from the motorway).

The two main museums in Sheffield are the **City Museum**, some way out of town in Weston Park, and the **Graves Art Gallery**. The Art Gallery (open from 10.00 to 8.00 weekdays and from 2.00 to 5.00 Sundays) has English watercolours and European paintings, and the Museum (open from 10.00 to 5.00 weekdays and from 11.00 to 5.00 Sundays, with an extension daily to 8.00 in June, July and August) has a good collection of cutlery and Sheffield plate, plus exhibits on local geology and archaeology and on the natural sciences.

JUNCTION 34 SHEFFIELD CANAL

If you are travelling south, leave the motorway at Tinsley, junction 34, for the Sheffield Industrial Museum at Kelham Island (see junction 33). The junction is directly above the river Don and the **Sheffield Canal**, and there is an interesting canalside walk among depressing scenes of industrial dereliction. The junction is in fact in two halves, one on each side of the narrow river valley. Travelling north you leave the motorway at the first half and join it at the second, the reverse if you are going south. Take the A630 east from the roundabout underneath the first half-junction coming from the south, and turn left almost immediately on to a side street. Park just by the canal, and walk in either direction. There are two flights of locks: one of four, just where you park, and the other of seven, a few hundred yards west towards Sheffield. You can follow the towpath right the way to the Canal Basin in Sheffield, through the 150-yard Attercliffe Cutting. The Don was made navigable as far as Tinsley in 1751, but the canal extension into Sheffield was only opened in 1819. Its heyday was brief in the extreme. The Sheffield to Rotherham Railway opened in 1838, and canal traffic fell rapidly, receipts with it: from £6428 in 1840/41 to £3776 in 1843/44. Within a decade the railway company took over the canal and, naturally enough, failed to maintain and promote it adequately. It was a long, slow decline, and commercial traffic finally ceased in 1970.

JUNCTION 35 WENTWORTH PARK

There is a pleasant country diversion from junction 35 to **Wentworth** and **Wentworth Park**. Take the A629 east and turn left almost immediately. Follow this side road straight through Thorpe Hesley (do not turn on to the B6086) towards Wentworth. The road runs along the edge of the Wentworth Park estate, and you could easily find a pleasant picnic spot at the edge of a field. There is a garden centre, and a right turn on to the B6090 takes you past the home farm, where produce is often sold, and the entrance to Wentworth Park. The house is part of Sheffield City Polytechnic, but there are public paths through the attractive grounds. Back on the

B6090 Wentworth village is small and charming, with attractive stone houses, an art gallery and coffee shop and the Rockingham Arms pub. The best way back to the motorway is at junction 36. Continue on the B6090 to Harley and then turn right on to the A6135 and then left on to the A61 immediately before the junction.

JUNCTION 36 WORSBROUGH COUNTRY PARK

From junction 36, it is 2½ miles north on the A61 to **Worsbrough Mill Museum** and the surrounding **Worsbrough Country Park**. A corn mill at Worsbrough is mentioned in the Domesday Book of 1086, but the oldest building you can see today – the watermill – went up in about 1625. The 19th century brought a period of rapid industrial growth in the area, and in 1843 a steam-powered mill was added on to the old watermill to meet the increased demand for flour and meal. In common with many stone-grinding mills, Worsbrough Mill went into decline from the beginning of this century as the milling industry changed. While the steam engine was scrapped in 1922, the watermill stayed in work until the 1960s – almost three and a half centuries after it was built. The mills have been sensitively restored to working order, and a rare 1911 Hornsby oil engine drives the once steam-powered millstones. You can usually see the watermill in operation, and there is always stoneground wholemeal flour for sale. The Museum is open daily except Mondays and Tuesdays. The 130-acre Country Park offers short walks through fields and woodland and around the banks of **Worsbrough Reservoir**, which was completed in 1804 to supply water for the Dearne & Dove Canal. Some paths follow the routes of old horse-drawn railways which were used to transport coal and iron from the local mines and workings to the canal wharfs. There are also interesting remains of metal-working industries. The hide on the west side of the reservoir is a good spot for observing the wealth of wildlife here. **Worsbrough** village is just behind the main road, on the opposite side from the Country Park: turn left as you leave the car park and then immediately right. Several pleasant-looking footpaths leave from the village green, and there is also the Edmunds Arms for liquid refreshment. **St Mary's Church** is 14th and 15th century, with a lovely and unusual memorial to Sir Roger Rockley, who died in 1553; the Rockleys owned the manor of Worsbrough. The figures and the framework of the memorial are both of oak; Sir Roger lies on the top tier, and beneath he is depicted as a skeleton placed in a shroud.

Worsbrough village and the Country Park are about 2½ miles south of Barnsley town centre on the A61. You can either return to the motorway at junction 36 or continue into the town centre and then take the A628 west to junction 37.

JUNCTION 37 CANNON HALL

Junction 37 is about 1½ miles west of **Barnsley**, which is at the centre of the Yorkshire coalfield. There is a pleasant old shopping arcade and a market three days a week (Wednesdays, Fridays and Saturdays), with an antiques market on Tuesdays. To the west of the motorway, reached by a slightly tortuous drive, is **Cannon Hall**, described as a 'country house museum'. The house is 17th century and was remodelled in the mid-18th, and there are 70 acres of lovely parkland all around. In 1957, when Barnsley Council opened the house as a museum, it must have been something of a pioneer; as a result, today the displays appear rather static. Nevertheless, there are some lovely things to see here, including superb collections of English furniture from the 17th to the early 20th centuries and of pottery from many celebrated factories such as Doulton, Wedgwood and Della Robia. The furniture is arranged in rooms according to period; the rooms overlooking the park contain rococo and neo-classical styles, while others are devoted to Regency, Victorian, Art Nouveau and Arts and Crafts pieces. Another interesting collection is of pottery and pewter made in about 1900, much of it for Liberty of Regent Street. The Regimental Museum of the 13th/18th Royal Hussars (Queen Mary's Own) is housed at Cannon Hall. The house is open from 10.30 to 5.00 on weekdays and from 2.30 to 5.00 on Sundays. Take the A628 west from the motorway, turn right after 2 miles in Silkstone for Cawthorne, turn left on to the A635 in Cawthorne and then right along a signposted road to Cannon Hall (about 4½ miles from the motorway). It is almost as quick to return to the motorway at junction 38. Take the A635 east, turn left into Cawthorne and take the side road to Kexbrough. Turn right in Kexbrough and then left on to the A637 just after crossing over the motorway. The A637 leads north direct to junction 38. Cawthorne itself is a pleasant stone hillside village with the Spencer Arms pub.

JUNCTION 38 BRETTON COUNTRY PARK

Junction 38 is just by **Bretton Country Park**, a few hundred yards north on the A637, and an excellent place for a short fresh air and picnic break from driving. There are three trails, 1½, 2 and 2¾ miles long, each starting from the information centre by the car park. Wildfowl can be seen on two lakes, which are a protected nature reserve; some 150 Canada geese are resident here, and there are also kestrel, curlew and willow warbler. The walks pass an old pump house from which water from the river Dearne was pumped to Bretton Hall and also to an iron works and corn mill downstream.

After less than 1 mile to the north along the A637 you come to what must be one of the most unusual and stimulating off-motorway attractions near the entire M1: the **Yorkshire Sculpture Park** in the grounds of **Bretton Hall**, a Palladian mansion now used as a college of higher education. It is the first permanent sculpture park in the country, opened in 1977, and the sculpture sits most impressively in the serene and mature Capability Brown landscape. Henry Moore, a native of Castleford a few miles to the north, has written that 'I would rather have a piece of my sculpture put in a landscape – almost any landscape – than in, or on, the most beautiful building I know.' The sculptures here, by Moore himself, Barbara Hepworth, who is a native of nearby Wakefield, and many others, triumphantly justify his claim. The Park is the only site outside North America where the full set of Hepworth's 'Family of Man' (nine bronze figures on a hillside) can be seen. The Park is open daily from 10.00 to 6.00 in summer and 10.00 to 4.00 in winter.

JUNCTION 39 NEWMILLERDAM COUNTRY PARK

Junction 39 leads into Wakefield from the south. The main route is along the A636, but a short diversion takes you to two interesting attractions. Take the A636 east from the junction and turn right almost immediately. When you reach the A61, turn right again, and after about ½ mile you reach the **Newmillerdam Country Park**, where there are attractive lakeside strolls and picnic spots, and woodland walks as well. It is a pleasant enough spot, but not, in my opinion, worth the diversion from the motorway unless your route happens to take you past in any case. Further north on the A61, towards Wakefield you come to **Sandal Castle**, described by one expert as 'one of the most fascinating castle excavations undertaken in the present century'. Photographs of the site before and after excavation show what has been achieved. In 1963 there were 6 acres of scrubland, dotted with the occasional stone ruin. Ten years later an elaborate and well-fortified structure had been uncovered, with a great tower, barbican and various other defensive features, all surrounded by a curtain wall. The original wooden motte and bailey here were built in about 1150; conversion to stone and alterations and improvements started in about 1200 and continued for most of the 13th century. Sandal was a royal castle from 1460 to 1566, then fell into ruins, was held by the Royalists in the Civil War and then slighted in 1645. A model of the structure as it must have looked when complete is on show in Wakefield Museum (see page 43).

JUNCTIONS 40 & 41 WAKEFIELD

Junctions 40 and 41 lead east to **Wakefield**, along the A638 and the A650 respectively. Here there is a smart, award-winning covered shopping mall known as the **Ridings**, very much of the late 20th century, and some pleasant older townscapes to admire. **St John's Square** is Georgian, dating from the very early years of the 19th century, and boasts some handsome town houses. The **cathedral**, set in an attractive precinct, is mostly 15th century, but was extensively restored towards the end of the 19th century. The lovely 14th-century **Chantry Bridge Chapel** on the Doncaster side of the city centre is one of the few bridge chapels in the country. The **Museum** concentrates mainly on local archaeology, history and natural history, while the **Art Gallery**, housed in a former Victorian vicarage, has a good collection of works by 20th-century artists, including Hepworth, Moore, Epstein and Sutherland. Opening hours of both the Museum and the Art Gallery are 10.30 to 12.30 and 1.30 to 5.00 Mondays to Saturdays.

Junction 42 is the junction with the M62, and there is no access on to ordinary roads. One of the best excursions in the area is to Temple Newsam House, 6 miles north of junction 30 of the M62 (see page 275), which in turn is 2 miles east of the motorway junction.

JUNCTION 45 MIDDLETON LIGHT RAILWAY

Junctions 43, 44 and 45 all lead off in quick succession into the southern suburbs of Leeds. Junction 45 is just by the terminus of the **Middleton Light Railway**. This is a privately owned, steam-powered line. But, unlike most preserved lines, it does not run through magnificent scenery, and it is not well placed to catch the tourist crowds. The Middleton is an industrial railway, as it has always been, its main purpose the carriage of goods, not people. Indeed, it still operates a freight run for a local firm. It was authorized as long ago as 1758, when an Act of Parliament permitted horse-drawn carriages to be run. In 1812, the line was converted to steam operation. Why, then, is not the Middleton Colliery Railway, rather than the Stockton & Darlington or the Liverpool & Manchester, proclaimed as the world's first railway? The steam locomotives certainly worked successfully, but they ran on a rack system. A gear-wheel on the locomotives engaged with toothed rails, just as happens today, in fact, on mountain railways the world over. John Blenkinsop, who built the track, was quite convinced that this system was the only one that would give adequate grip for traction. Like many pioneers, he got it almost – but not absolutely – right, and so the honours went to the Stephensons and the Liverpool & Manchester. The Middleton line itself was converted to the conventional system as early as 1835, only five years after the Liverpool & Manchester opened. About 3 miles of track are operated at present by a variety of industrial locomotives, and there are services at weekends and Bank Holidays between Easter and September. Junction 45 has restricted access, and you can only leave from the northbound carriageway. Turn right and follow the roundabout almost back to the motorway again, turning left for the railway.

JUNCTION 46 LEEDS INDUSTRIAL MUSEUM

Junction 46 is the final junction, a little to the south of Leeds city centre, and also at the junction with the M621 which runs southwest to join the M62 at junction 27 of that motorway. **Leeds** is a splendid city but not, to state the obvious, a good place for a quick and relaxing break. If industrial archaeology and history interest you, however, you will want to make for the **Leeds Industrial Museum** at Armley Mills, well worth the journey in my opinion. The site itself is fascinating, on an island between the Leeds & Liverpool Canal and the river Aire, where there has been a mill since about the mid-16th century. At the end of the 18th century a new fulling mill was built, powered by no fewer than five waterwheels. Then, after a fire, two huge waterwheels were installed, 28½ feet long and 18 feet in diameter, nicknamed Wellington and Blucher; these were some of the earliest suspension wheels ever built and could achieve about 70hp each, far more than any contemporary steam engine. They were removed in 1888, after a beam engine had been installed in the 1850s. The mills continued to operate until the late 1960s. Every aspect of Leeds's industrial history is covered here in vivid detail. There are displays on textiles and clothing, of course, as befits the Museum's home, and on leather, optics and the cinema, and printing and machine tools. There is a reconstruction of the Armley Palace Picture Hall as it was in 1912, in the very early days of cinema, plus cranes and locomotives made in Leeds, and a magnificent display of engines, powered by water, steam and petrol. Also of great interest is a large collection of models, including one of the first locomotives from the Middleton Railway (see junction 45, above). The Museum opens at 10.00 on weekdays except Mondays other than Bank Holidays, 2.00 on Sundays, closing at 5.30 betwen April and September and at 4.30 during the rest of the year. A fascinating 8¼-mile **Leeds Museum Trail** along the Aire valley links the four major city museums: the **City Museum, Armley Mills, Kirkstall Abbey** and the **Abbey House Museum** at Kirkstall, finishing at

Rodley village. The 2-mile stretch between Armley Mills and the City Museum in the city centre makes a fascinating walk. From the end of the M1, continue along the Leeds Urban Motorway and then join the A65. About 1 mile from the city centre turn left at traffic lights, the first set past the Yorkshire TV building, into Viaduct Road, and turn right into the Museum entrance just after crossing the canal.

The M11

Wanstead to Cambridge

INTRODUCTION

The M11, the motorway network's only incursion into East Anglia, links London's north-eastern suburbs with Cambridge. To begin with, the landscape is not especially distinguished. Then, after Bishop's Stortford has been passed, there is a pleasant, rather more varied stretch through gently undulating landscape near the river Cam before the road breaks out into the flat fenland plain, with its wide, windswept skies. This central section offers the best off-motorway excursion, if a rather lengthy one, to Audley End and Saffron Walden. Both are characteristically English. Audley End is the great house of a distinguished aristocrat, a royal servant and court favourite, while Saffron Walden is a perfect country town built by merchants grown prosperous in the wool trade. Near the northern end of the motorway, Duxford Airfield represents another important part of British history. From here, as from literally scores of other airfields throughout eastern England, took off the British and American pilots whose skills and courage in the sky did much to bring eventual victory in the Second World War.

Junctions 1 and 2 do not exist. The motorway begins at junction 3, at Wanstead in London's north-eastern suburbs, where there is nothing special to see.

Junction 4 is the junction with the dual carriageway North Circular Road, the A406. Access is restricted: travelling north, you cannot leave the motorway or join it from the westbound North Circular; travelling south, you cannot join the motorway, and there is no access on to the eastbound North Circular.

Junction 5 is also restricted: travelling north, you can leave the motorway but not join it; travelling south, you can join the motorway but not leave it. This junction leads to Loughton and then to Epping Forest, which is described under junction 26 of the M25 (see page 71).

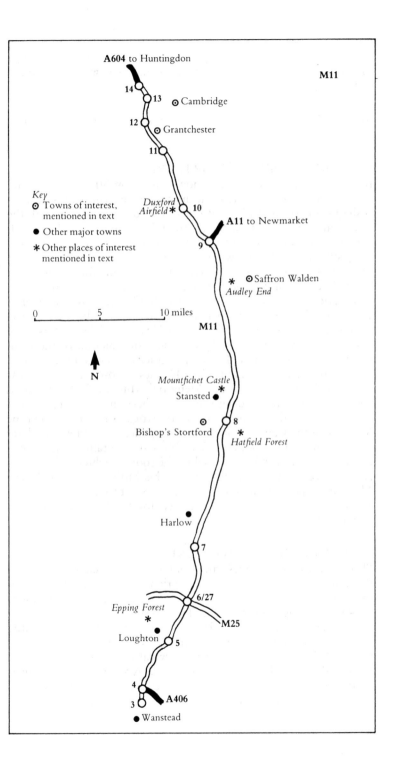

Junction 6 is the junction with the M25, and there is no access on to ordinary roads.

Junction 7 leads into Harlow; I would not advise leaving the motorway here.

JUNCTION 8 BISHOP'S STORTFORD

Junction 8 is the first recommendable junction off the M11 – and even here the highlights are some distance away. The nearest town is **Bishop's Stortford**, a pleasant but crowded market town with the usual parking difficulties; the centre is 2½ miles along the A1250 from the motorway. A Town Trail guides the visitor round the most interesting parts of the town, including the **Corn Exchange**, built in 1828 in a mixture of Grecian styles and, on the hill, the 15th-century **St Michael's Church**; the tall spire – one of Bishop's Stortford's landmarks – was added to the tower in 1812. There are a number of 16th- and 17th-century timber-framed buildings in the town centre, including the Black Lion, the Boar's Head, the White Horse, the Half Moon and the Star. **Windhill,** the continuation of the High Street beyond the church, has some attractive houses. Bishop Stortford's most celebrated son is Cecil Rhodes, whose father was vicar of St Michael's. The **Rhodes Memorial Museum** in South Road commemorates this adventurer, financier and statesman who became rich on the diamonds of South Africa, was appointed Prime Minister of the Cape Colony and first opened up the territory later named after him, Rhodesia. The Museum contains memorabilia and displays on Rhodes's life, while the room in which he was born is preserved as it was at the time of his birth in July 1853. The Museum's opening times are Mondays (except Bank Holidays) to Saturdays 10.00 to 4.00; it is closed for the first two weeks in August.

JUNCTION 8 HATFIELD FOREST

Pleasant walks and picnics can be enjoyed in **Hatfield Forest** east of the motorway along the A120. Turn right off this road after 2 miles in the little village of Takeley Street, and the entrance to the **Country Park** is on the right after ½ mile. The forest is one of the last remaining vestiges of the Great Forest of Essex that covered the entire county in Norman times and before. A royal hunting ground until the mid-15th century, it owes its survival first to one aristocratic family, the Houblons, who held it for two centuries until their estates were dispersed and sold in the 1920s, and then to Lord Buxton, who in 1923 bought the forest (it was later passed to the

National Trust), so saving it from destruction. It is a delightful spot. There are coppices of ancient oaks and hornbeams, stretches of scrub, and rides and chases to explore. The attractive lake (boating and fishing are available), half-hidden within the trees, was created in 1746. The area around the lake has been designated a Site of Special Scientific Interest; fallow deer, foxes and badgers are among the creatures that live here, and no fewer than 55 breeding species of bird have been recorded. The **Shell House** overlooking the water, built a few years after the lake, contains displays explaining how the National Trust operates the ancient system of coppicing, pollarding and grazing in the forest, and is the starting-point of a 1½-mile Nature Trail; there is a shop here as well, and refreshments are available. The forest is also the northern end of the **Three Forests Way**, a 60-mile footpath across Essex that links Hatfield Forest with Hainault and Epping Forests to the south.

JUNCTION 8 MOUNTFITCHET CASTLE

Have you ever wondered what it was really like to live in a medieval castle? What sort of food was cooked? What clothes were worn? How did you wash and keep warm? These are all questions that a visit to a conventional castle, however imposing the ruins may be, usually fails to settle. At **Mountfitchet Castle** in **Stansted** you should be able to discover some of the answers – for Mountfitchet is a brand-new Norman castle purpose-built to provide as authentic as possible an impression of life between about 1066 and 1086. The site is quite genuine. There once was a castle here, consisting of a small tower in the bailey, which was surrounded by extensive ditching and ramparts. It seems to have been dismantled during King John's reign, in the early 13th century, and probably belonged to one of the rebellious barons opposed to the King. For the reconstruction, every effort has been made to find authentic materials, such as the oak for the palisade and hazel coppicing for the walls of the buildings, and to discover, by means of a geophysical survey, where the original buildings stood; whenever possible, original construction methods have been used too. The entrance is grim: severed heads impaled on the gateway remind you how the lord of a castle dealt with attackers from outside and disobedience and rebellion within; and soldiers in the watch-tower look out for enemy forces. A medieval castle was a self-sufficient community. Here at Stansted you can see bread being baked in the bread ovens, skin-curing, and a forge being used; chickens, geese, sheep and goats, all of which provided essential food for the castle's inhabitants, roam freely around the enclosure and there are pigs in the pigsty; there is a loom for weaving cloth. The quintain was used for target practice; you had every incentive to be accurate – if not, the weight would swing round and unseat you from your horse. Baths were taken – not very often, probably not more than once a month – in a wooden tub, while the privy consisted simply of a wooden seat over a pit; sometimes the waste was carried away by an underground stream. Other buildings include the Kitchen, the Prison, the Church, its walls decorated with primitive murals, and the Great Hall, where, as at many other points throughout the Castle, an animated figure explains something about castle life. This 20th-century intrusion into a carefully researched recreation of life nine centuries ago can be rather disturbing, especially as, at least when I visited, the tapes were rather amateurishly made; but on the other hand they do help to personalize castle life. Mountfitchet Castle is open daily from 10.00 to 5.30 between mid-May and the end of November. Snacks are available, and Sinclairs coffee shop is only a short distance from the Castle entrance. From the motorway, take the A120 west, turn right at the first roundabout on to the B1383 and then right again in Stansted village into Chapel Hill; the Castle is at the bottom of this road, just the other side of Lower Street. Distance from the motorway is 3 miles.

JUNCTION 8 AUDLEY END

A lengthy but worthwhile excursion from junction 8 is north up the B1383 to Audley End and Saffron Walden. The B1383 is in fact the old A11, the main road to Cambridge before the motorway was built, and although this trip can be rather slow and time-consuming you can rejoin the motorway further north, at junction 10. **Audley End** is one of the great houses of England. It was built by Thomas Howard, first Earl of Suffolk and James I's Lord Treasurer, between 1605 and 1614, and was planned to provide accommodation in the proper style for a visiting monarch and his considerable entourage. The house the visitor sees today is a considerably altered and reduced version of the original structure. The great outer court was swept away in the 18th century along with part of the inner court, in order to make the house more manageable to live in. Robert Adam, the fashionable London architect and designer, was brought in to redesign the ground-floor reception rooms, while Capability Brown tackled the park. The result is a fascinating mixture of styles. The Great Hall, which was a central feature of all country houses until the early 17th century, has a magnificent wooden Jacobean screen carved with faces, fruit and animals' heads. The ceiling decorations are crests of families connected with the Howards. There then follows a sequence of exquisite Adam rooms. The Dining Parlour was painted green to continue the effect of the parkland outside. The

Tea House Bridge, Audley End

Great Drawing Room has silk wall-hangings and upholstery and lovely Adam furniture, all, if you look closely, slightly smaller than normal size; Adam found, when he came to create this room, that the ceiling was too low, and redesigned the furniture in proportion. The Little Drawing Room was where the ladies withdrew after dinner while the gentlemen remained at the dining table. The Lower Gallery has a fabulous collection of stuffed birds, the work of the fourth Lord Braybrooke, who owned Audley End in the mid-19th century. Several of the rooms in the north wing, including the State Dressing Room, still contain the original Jacobean plaster ceiling and friezes. One wonders what the huge state bed in the State Bedroom was like to sleep in; at least you could enjoy a fine view across the park to the Temple of Concord. Other interesting rooms include Lady Braybrooke's Sitting Room, full of late-Victorian clutter and mementoes, the cosy Library (did anyone ever read all those books?) with lovely fruit and foliage decorations on the ceiling, and the superb Saloon with its huge mid-Victorian ottoman that could seat 12 people in comfort. Outside the park invites you to walk; climb up to the Temple of Concord to get a good view of the entire estate. To the right is a column erected by Sir John Griffin Griffin (who owned the house in the mid-18th century and commissioned Adam) in memory of his aunt. The path to the far side of the lake leads over Adam's Tea House Bridge to the rose garden, stables and the kitchen garden. There is a pleasant tea room in what used to be the house-keeper's room, while the former kitchen now serves as a shop. The house is open daily except Mondays, but including Bank Holiday Mondays, between 1.00 and 5.00 from late March to early October; the grounds are open between 12.00 and 6.30 from late March to late October. The house is just off the B1383 11 miles north of junction 8. From junction 10, take the A505 east, turn right on to the A1301 and then, at the next roundabout, take the B1383 south. Distance from junction 10 is about 8 miles.

JUNCTION 8 SAFFRON WALDEN

Saffron Walden, 1 mile east of Audley End, is a handsome East Anglian market town, formerly a centre of the cloth industry and, for 300 years, of saffron cultivation, as its name suggests. There is hardly a pleasanter off-motorway place to stroll around, looking at the old houses and the antique and second-hand bookshops; the Weavers Tea Rooms serves an acceptable cup of tea. There are many timber-framed buildings, some of them with attractive pargetting (plaster decoration); one, the **Sun Inn** on Market Hill, depicts an old East Anglian legend according to which the Wisbech Giant was challenged to a fight and defeated by young Tom Hickathrift, a carter so mighty that he could lift a haystack on his fork. The names of the narrow rows running towards the Market Place indicate where, in the Middle Ages, the different traders had their shops. The **Market Place** itself is a predominantly 19th-century creation. The **Corn Exchange** was built in 1848, while the **Town Hall**, which has been aptly described as 'more magnificently Tudor than any 16th-century building in the town', is mere pastiche; it was built in the 1870s by Edward Burgess. **St Mary's Church** was rebuilt in the late 15th and early 16th centuries and richly decorated by the local merchants made wealthy by the wool trade; the present spire was erected in 1831. The **Saffron Walden Museum** concentrates on local history, and also has collections of ceramics and glass, furniture and toys. Opening times are Mondays to Saturdays 11.00 to 5.00, Sundays and Bank Holidays 2.30 to 5.00; closing time between October and March is one hour earlier. There are two unusual open spaces in the town. The **Common** has a rare earthen maze – that is, a maze created not with hedges but in two dimensions only, on the ground – while **Bridge End Gardens** has fine trees and an attractive rose garden.

Junction 9 leads into the A11 trunk road, which runs north-east towards Newmarket. There is limited access here; travelling north, you can only leave the motorway, while you can only join the southbound carriageway.

From junction 10 you can drive south on ordinary roads to Audley End and Saffron Walden (see pages 49–51).

JUNCTION 10 DUXFORD AIRFIELD

The entrance to **Duxford Airfield** lies a few hundred yards west of the motorway along the A505. From 1924, seven years after it was opened, until it was closed in 1961, the Airfield belonged to the RAF, except for a couple of years at the end of the Second World War when it was handed over to the United States Army Air Forces (USAAF). During the 1970s it was transferred to the Imperial War Museum, and it now houses the Museum's large collection of aircraft and military vehicles and artillery. What is fascinating about Duxford, however, is not merely the exhibits, varied though they are, but the very character of the place. The airfield itself is an almost perfectly preserved museum piece; as you walk around, it is easy to take yourself back to the Battle of Britain in 1940, when Duxford planes played a major role in defeating the Luftwaffe over southern England, or to 1943 and 1944, when fighters based at Duxford accompanied the American daylight bombing raids on Germany. Three of the original four First World War hangars are still standing, as are control towers, barrack blocks and so on; a video explains the history of the airfield. Added authenticity is given by the fact that Duxford is still an operational airfield; on most Sunday afternoons you can watch a fly-past, and perhaps even go for a spin yourself in a 1930s De Havilland Rapide. It is hard to decide which of the many famous aircraft on display to mention. There is an Avro Lancaster, the best-known and most successful British heavy bomber of the Second World War, which carried out the celebrated Dambusters raids on the Möhne and Eder Dams in May 1943, a P–51D Mustang fighter to represent the many that flew from Duxford over Germany in the Second World War, and a B–29A Superfortress, the most advanced bomber produced during the Second World War: it was a B–29A, *Enola Gay*, which dropped the first atomic bomb on Japan in 1945. More modern planes include a Dassault Mystère of the type used during the 1950s and 1960s by the French, Israeli and Indian Air Forces, and a Pucara, a light ground-attack aircraft of the Argentinian Air Force capture during the Falklands campaign and brought back to Britain. There is a fascinating exhibition on the US Eighth Air Force, the American bomber force that operated from Britain during the Second World War; among the old photographs is one of Bing Crosby entertaining airmen stationed at Duxford outside one of the hangars in 1944. The tanks and military vehicles include Montgomery's campaign caravans, which incorporated a map-room and a well-fitted bedroom with wardrobes and a bath; Montgomery is reported to have said that he would give up his accommodation to only two people, the King and Winston Churchill. The Dawn Patrol exhibit vividly evokes the atmosphere of the early days of military flying on the front in 1918. Part of the airfield is given over to the Duxford Aviation Society's collection of civil aircraft, some of which you can go inside; among the planes on display are a De Havilland Comet 4, a pre-production Concorde, a BAC Super VC10 and a Vickers Viscount 701. Visitors can also watch restoration and conservation work in progress. Duxford Airfield is open daily between mid-March and early November from 10.30 to 5.30 (or dusk if earlier); last admission is 45 minutes before closing time. A reasonably pleasant café serves snacks and light meals.

JUNCTION 11 GRANTCHESTER
Junction 11 is close to **Grantchester**, the pretty little village on the Cam outside Cambridge made famous by the poet Rupert Brooke, who lived for a time in the Old Vicarage.

> Stands the church clock at ten to three?
> And is there honey still for tea?

are the celebrated concluding lines of his poem 'The Old Vicarage, Grantchester'. The village remains quiet and secluded, but apart from the church, which has a 14th-century chancel, there is nothing special to see. The Orchard Tea Room serves afternoon tea during summer weekends, and there are two pleasant pubs, the Red Lion and the Green Man. There is a pleasant two-mile walk near the river into Cambridge, with the tower of the University Library and King's College Chapel clearly visible ahead. From junction 11 drive towards Cambridge on the A1309. Turn left in the village of Trumpington; Grantchester is about 1 mile along this country road.

JUNCTION 12 CAMBRIDGE
Junction 12 is the main exit for the centre of Cambridge, which lies 2½ miles east along the A603. In a brief off-motorway diversion you cannot possibly begin to tackle all the things the city has to offer. There are the colleges, each with its distinctive character and archi-

tecture, the inspiring **King's College Chapel** with Rubens' 'Adoration of the Magi', and lovely walks along the **Backs** (the college backs and gardens that run down to the river). Among the museums is, first and foremost, the **Fitzwilliam Museum**, with its magnificent collections of paintings, Egyptian, Greek and Roman antiquities, manuscripts, ceramics and arms and armour. There are also the **Folk Museum**, various academic museums arising out of University collections, and **Kettle's Yard Art Gallery**, which has a fascinating collection of modern art.

Grantchester can also be reached from junction 12 by taking the side road from the roundabout above the motorway for 1 mile.

Junction 13 brings you into Cambridge north of the city centre. This junction has restricted access. Travelling north, you can leave but not join the motorway. Travelling south, you can join it but not leave it.

Junction 14 is the junction with the dual carriageway A45 which bypasses Cambridge to the north. Travelling north, there is no access to the westbound carriageway of the A45. Travelling south, there is no access from the eastbound carriageway of the A45. The motorway finishes a few hundred yards further on, running straight into the dual carriageway A604, which leads to Huntingdon.

The M25

London Orbital Motorway

INTRODUCTION

The M25 is the London Orbital Motorway. Six lanes of highway, always busy and often jammed (at several spots the traffic-planners' estimates of traffic density quickly proved far too low), circle the built-up area of Greater London some 20 miles or so from the centre of the capital. For virtually its entire route the motorway runs through the Green Belt, the wide area of countryside around London protected by planning legislation from factory, office or housing development. The only significant stretches where the view is of an urban landscape are at the easternmost and westernmost extremities, near the crossing of the Thames and around Heathrow Airport, and these are quite short. The rest of the motorway passes through attractive and sometimes surprisingly remote countryside. To the south there are the chalk North Downs, remarkably steep in places, while in the north the road crosses the gentler slopes of southern Hertfordshire and Essex. There is a reasonable variety of places to visit within a few miles of the motorway, including some grand houses and gardens, as at Knole and Claremont, the lovely Norman abbey at Waltham Abbey, and the Roman villa at Lullingstone.

Junction 1 is the junction with the A226 to Dartford. There is nothing worth leaving the motorway for here.

Junction 2 is the junction with the fast A2 London to Kent road, which further east becomes the M2 (see pages 74–85). Again, I cannot recommend any off-motorway excursions.

JUNCTION 3 LULLINGSTONE ROMAN VILLA

Junction 3 is the junction with the beginning of the M20 to Maidstone and Folkestone (see pages 74–85). It is also the start of an excursion to one of the most interesting and complete Roman sites in southern England: the **Roman Villa** at **Lullingstone**. A remarkable amount is known about the history of the villa and about the sort of people who lived there. Originally, it was a quite modest farmhouse, the home of native British farmers who gradually became romanized. Then, towards the end of the 2nd century AD, there came a quite marked change. A new owner moved in – someone of status and substance, if not Roman himself then at least of Roman descent. Marble portraits of his ancestors adorned the walls, and coins and fine-quality imported pottery have been found, all of which suggest considerable wealth. Like all new house-owners, he soon began to improve his property, converting it into the luxury villa expected of someone of his importance. Baths were installed, with the usual sequence of cold, tepid and hot rooms, kitchens added (these are not on show to the public), and a series of cult rooms built. These beautifully decorated rooms were devoted to the worship of the local water goddesses; a lovely fresco depicting two water nymphs has survived. No one now knows for certain why the house was abandoned in about 200, after being occupied for only about 20 years. Perhaps its owner, who, it has been suggested, may have been a government official working in the capital, had to return to the continent because of some political crisis. At any rate, the house lay empty and derelict for the best part of a century. When it was reoccupied, it was as a farmhouse. The new owners carried out extensive repairs, built a large granary and then a temple-mausoleum (neither shown to the public) for the burial of a young man and a young woman, and later – for the villa remained in the same family for several generations – constructed the Dining Room and the Reception Room with their fine mosaics. In about 360 or 370, Lullingstone's owners were converted to Christianity and constructed a chapel in which to celebrate their new religion; one of the surviving frescoes depicts an early Christian at prayer. The chapel is unique in that it is the only private Christian chapel ever discovered on a Roman site in Britain. Farming may well have ceased towards the end of the 4th century, when it seems that the villa began to be used for worship alone. Then, some time in the early 5th century, all activity here came to an abrupt end when fire, its cause unknown, destroyed everything.

In contrast with some Roman sites, at Lullingstone it is easy to trace where the various rooms were situated. The stairs leading down to the bath-house can be seen, as can the furnace that heated the water and the various bathing chambers. The chapels, pagan and Christian, can be seen, and the living rooms too. The mosaics, vivid and remarkably well preserved, are the highlight of the visit. In the Dining Room, there is a scene from the abduction of Europa by the god Jupiter; Jupiter, transformed into a bull, is swimming from Asia Minor to Crete with Europa on his back. In the Reception

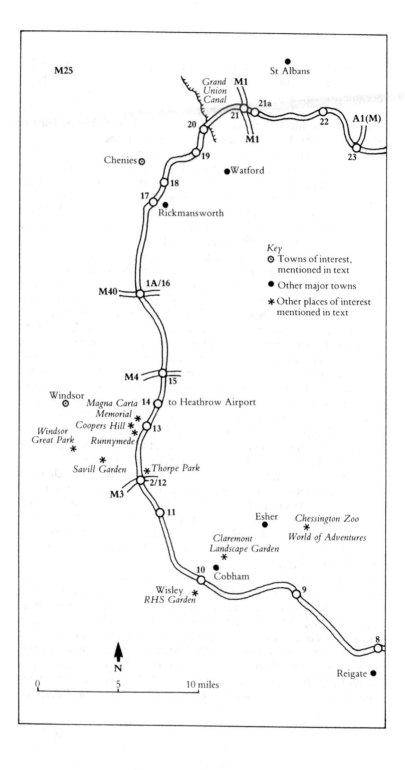

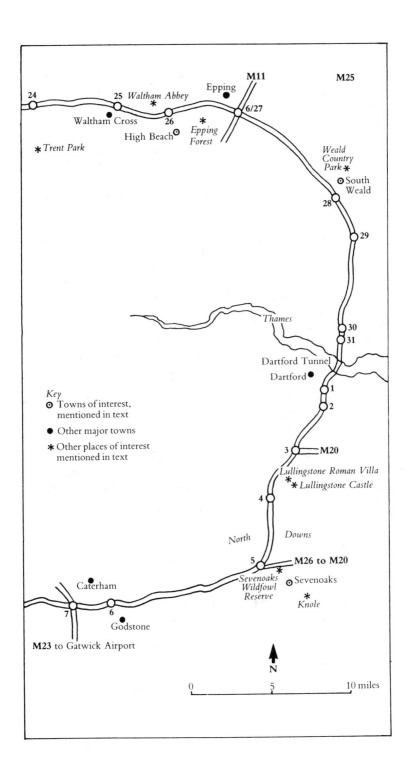

Room Bellerophon mounted on the winged horse Pegasus is depicted killing Chimaera with his spear. Also on show in the villa, which is protected from the elements by a wood and glass building, is pottery found on the site, and, perhaps most absorbing of all for those with a taste for the morbid, several skeletons. These include a hunting dog, geese and a human figure – his local nickname is George – wrapped in a shroud; a gaming board was found on the lid of George's coffin.

The Roman Villa is open on Mondays to Saturdays between 9.30 and 6.30, Sundays 2.30 to 6.30, from 15 March to 15 October; and from 9.30 to 4.00, Sundays 2.00 to 4.00, for the rest of the year. From the motorway, take the A20 (*not* the M20) east for 1½ miles, turn right on to the A225 towards Sevenoaks, and then right again in Eynsford villge. The villa is ¾ mile along this side road, past the ford and underneath the spectacular railway viaduct. Distance from the motorway is about 4 miles. Two pleasant-looking pubs in the village are the Castle and the Malt Shovel Inn. Also worth seeing in the village is **Eynsford Castle**, which is one of the earliest Norman castles in England built of stone – the first castles the conquering Normans erected in this country were made of wood. Parts of the severe curtain wall, almost 30 feet high, remain; garderobes – medieval lavatories – can be seen in the south-west angle of the wall. The undercroft of the hall (the main dwelling house) and of the solar (the private chamber of the lord) can be seen, as can the ruins of the forebuilding erected in front of the hall.

JUNCTION 3 LULLINGSTONE CASTLE
Lullingstone Castle, beyond the Roman Villa, is an originally 15th-century house with a fine collection of family portraits and armour; Henry VIII and Queen Anne were visitors here. Opening times are 2.00 to 6.00 on Saturdays, Sundays and Bank Holidays between April and October.

Instead of returning to junction 3, a pleasant alternative route back to the motorway is to make your way along side roads through the Darent Valley to junction 4.

Junction 4 is in attractive countryside at the foot of the North Downs, but there is nothing worth leaving the motorway for.

Junction 5 is the junction with the M26, the link motorway that connects the M20 at junction 3 (see page 88) with the M25, and with the dual carriageway A21 which runs south towards Tonbridge and the Weald, bypassing Sevenoaks. Note that this is a restricted junction. There is no access from the M26 on to the A21, from the M25 westbound on to the M26 or on to the A21, or on to the M25 eastbound from the A21.

JUNCTION 5 KNOLE

Sevenoaks is a pleasant but crowded commercial-cum-commuter centre. There are some attractive old houses in the town centre, especially along the upper part of the High Street. These include the mid-19th-century arcaded Market House and the narrow lanes of the Shambles behind it, the Red House, where Jane Austen visited her uncle, and the early 18th-century Manor House. But the real reason for turning off the motorway and making your way through the often overloaded streets of Sevenoaks is to visit **Knole**, the magnificent palace set in a 1000-acre deer park just to the south of the town centre. Originally, Knole was a simple medieval manor house. Then, in 1456, Thomas Bourchier, the Archbishop of Canterbury, bought it – for the princely sum of £266 13s 4d – and set about converting it into a palace fit for an archbishop. Less than a century later, Henry VIII took Knole into royal ownership, as was his wont. The improvements he organized were not the last, for in 1566 Elizabeth I gave Knole to her second cousin, Sir Thomas Sackville – and he began a mammoth programme of extensions and decoration. Some 300 Italian workmen were brought over, presumably to supply skills thought lacking in Britain; three long galleries, used, especially in inclement weather, for exercise, conversation and the admiration of the paintings hung there, were constructed instead of the customary one; seven courtyards, and, it is said, a staircase for every week in the year and a room for every day, were built. The Sackvilles held Knole for no fewer than 400 years – ownership was transferred to the National Trust in 1946 – and today the house looks much as it did when Thomas Sackville had finished his work. Inside there are superb collections of silver and antique furniture, tapestries and paintings, including works by Reynolds and Gainsborough. Beyond the formal 26-acre garden lies the lovely deer park, which offers enjoyable walks. The house is open from Wednesdays to Saturdays and on Bank Holiday Mondays from 11.00 and 5.00, and on Sundays from 2.00 to 5.00, between April and October; last admission is an hour before closing time. The park is open daily throughout the year. The garden can be visited on the first Wednesday of every month from May to September only, although glimpses can be caught of it from inside the house.

JUNCTION 5 SEVENOAKS WILDFOWL RESERVE

The **Sevenoaks Wildfowl Reserve** is an open space of a very different kind, and much nearer the motorway. Originally a series of worked-out gravel pits, the 135-acre Reserve was created to provide a sanctuary for wildfowl and to allow research into breeding and migration patterns. New islands and spits have been created, and reed and water plants, trees and shrubs have been planted. Many different species have been recorded here, including Bewick swan, gadwall, black and sandwich tern and osprey. There are two nature trails, one of which is designed especially with children in mind, and four hides from which the wildfowl can be observed. Part of the large visitor centre is devoted to exhibitions on the history and ecology of the area, and many mounted birds and animals are also displayed. The Reserve, which is open on Wednesdays, Saturdays and Sundays between 10.00 and 5.00, is halfway between Riverhead and Bat and Ball, north of Sevenoaks and just south of the motorway. From the M25, turn left on to the A25 at the first roundabout. After about ½ mile, turn left by some riding stables, from where the Reserve is signposted.

Junction 6 leads north to Caterham and south to Godstone, but I would not recommend leaving the motorway here.

Junction 7 is the junction with the M23, which runs south to Gatwick Airport and Crawley. There is no access on to ordinary roads.

JUNCTION 8 NORTH DOWNS WAY
Junction 8 lies on the very edge of the North Downs, just above Reigate and close to the **North Downs Way**, the long-distance footpath that runs the length of the Downs from Farnham in Surrey to the coast at Dover. For much of the way it follows the route of the old Pilgrims' Way, the ancient trackway used in the Middle Ages by pilgrims making their way from Winchester to the tomb of Thomas à Becket at Canterbury. The stretch to the west of junction 8 takes you through pleasant wooded countryside along Reigate Hill and then Colley Hill, and there are some fine views. A short, brisk walk here would do a lot to revive children tired and frowsty from a long car journey – but be warned that the path is often quite muddy, especially in wet weather. To the east, the path strikes through **Gatton Park** towards Merstham, but this stretch is not as pleasant as it keeps very close to the motorway. From the roundabout above the M25, take the A217 south towards Reigate. Turn left after a few hundred yards – before the main road starts to descend the hill. Now turn right immediately, and then right again straightaway. This will bring you out on to the brow of the Downs, where you can park and call at the 'tea bar' serving snacks and drinks. A little way down the A217 towards Reigate, the **Bridge House Hotel** is a rather plusher establishment.

JUNCTION 9 CHESSINGTON WORLD OF ADVENTURES

The main attraction near junction 9 is **Chessington Zoo**, which from 1987 is being turned into a theme park called **World of Adventures**. Here, it is claimed, you can experience 'mysterious and exciting lands, journeys that take you back in time, a voyage forward into a new dimension'. The destinations of these voyages of exploration include Calamity Canyon, a wild west town at the time of the Californian gold rush; the Mystic East, 'a mysterious oriental world of temples, palaces and pagodas'; Circus World, which offers the chance to try traditional circus skills; the Fifth Dimension, 'a journey of participation, suspense and adventure through a giant computer screen to the unknown dimension beyond...'; and an olde-Englishe Market Square, with a Norman castle, an old mill and a village pond, plus (and here someone's sense of history has gone rather awry) a parade of Georgian shops. After all this, it is something of a relief to learn that there does remain a place for the animals for which Chessington has long been famous. Many parts of the traditional zoo have been improved recently. Some of the inhabitants you can see are apes, monkeys and gorillas, alligators and snakes, elephants, giraffes and camels, polar bears, sea-lions and hippos, and smaller creatures such as maras (rodents rather like guinea-pigs), blackbuck (Indian antelope) and ring-tailed coati mundis. There is also a bird garden and a very popular children's zoo. A new Safari Skyway Monorail provides a panoramic bird's eye view of the park. Chessington is 2¾ miles north of junction 9 along the A243. There are several cafés and restaurants and a large picnic area. Opening times for World of Adventures are 10.00 to 5.00 daily from April to October only. The Zoological Gardens are open at the same times during the summer, and also daily throughout the winter from 10.00 to 4.00.

JUNCTION 10 CLAREMONT LANDSCAPE GARDEN

Junction 10 is for garden lovers. North of the motorway lies **Claremont Landscape Garden**, a lovely example of 18th-century landscaping – and so it should be, for no fewer than four of that century's most celebrated architects and designers helped to create it. The first two were Sir John Vanbrugh, who was responsible for the Belvedere (watch-tower) and some of the winding avenues through the woodland, and Charles Bridgeman, who built the huge grass amphitheatre and the round pond beneath it and planted avenues of trees. Then came William Kent. He transformed the pond into the present informal lake, created the island and built the pavilion on it. The last of this distinguished line (inevitably, one might be forgiven for remarking) was Capability Brown. He moved the Portsmouth road (the old A3 – now the A307) away from the lake and did away with all the remaining traces of the older, formal gardens. At Claremont, Capability Brown's talents were for once principally exercised on interiors rather than out of doors, for he designed the present Claremont House (now a school and not open to the public) in 1772 to replace the house built by Vanbrugh only sixty years before. As you enjoy the attractive walks, or gaze out at the lake from the top of the amphitheatre, it is pleasant to think of the varied cast of characters who lived at Claremont at one time or another and who must also have enjoyed this lovely landscape. Clive of India built the mansion, though he never lived here. In 1816 it was presented to Princess Charlotte, only daughter and only heir of the Prince Regent, and her husband, Prince Leopold, who later became King of Belgium. It is sad to relate that Charlotte did not enjoy her new home for long; she died the following year in childbirth at Claremont; a mausoleum, of which only the foundations remain, was erected at the top of the amphitheatre in her memory. Leopold stayed on at Claremont, where he was often visited by his

Claremont Landscape Garden

young niece Victoria. Victoria continued her visits here after she became Queen in 1837, no doubt accompanied by her beloved Albert. In 1848 Claremont became the last home of the exiled King Louis-Philippe of France, who fled to England disguised as plain 'Mr Smith' after being deposed in the 1848 Revolution; after he died here in 1850, his widow, Queen Marie-Amélie, remained at Claremont until her death 16 years later. After that the house became the home of the Duke of Albany, Queen Victoria's youngest son, and his wife. Gradually, the gardens fell into disrepair, overgrown by a dense jungle of undergrowth – some of the rhododendrons were no less than 30 feet tall, and the laurel ran riot, covering some 30 acres – obscuring every feature. Between 1975 and 1980, in a massive programme of horticultural archaeology, the Garden was fully restored by the National Trust – not to its appearance at any one moment in the past, but taking the best features from each period of its development. The result is a magnificent success: Claremont represents the true spirit of the English landscape garden. The Garden is open daily from 9.00 to 7.00 between April and October or sunset if earlier, and from 9.00 to 4.00 for the rest of the year. Last admission is half an hour before closing time. There is a refreshment kiosk. From junction 10, take the dual carriageway A3 north-east towards London. Leave the A3 at the first exit, and then take the A307 through Cobham village and on over the A3. The entrance to Claremont is on the right between Cobham and Esher. Distance from the motorway is 3¾ miles.

JUNCTION 10 ROYAL HORTICULTURAL SOCIETY'S GARDEN

The **Royal Horticultural Society's Garden** at **Wisley** lies south-west down the A3 towards Guildford from the M25. Reaching the entrance from the A3 is quite awkward. You take a slip road off the A3 just under 2 miles from the motorway and then return to the other carriageway before turning left for the Garden; the route is well signposted. Here are 300 acres filled with all the species of garden plants you have ever heard of – flowers, fruit, vegetables, shrubs and trees – and many more besides. As you would expect, the Garden is immaculately maintained. You can be sure of seeing lovely displays at almost any time of year – rhododendrons and azaleas, daffodils in spring, herbaceous borders, banks of heathers. The specialist gardens – for herbs, roses and wild plants – and the fruit gardens and glasshouses are especially interesting. What better way can there be of seeing unusual species growing and of picking up good ideas for your own garden? A great deal of experimental work is carried out at Wisley; research is in fact the Garden's principal purpose, and an advisory service is offered to members of the Society. The Garden is open daily from 10.00 to 7.00 or sunset, whichever is earlier, between February and October; and from 10.00 to 4.30 the rest of the year. There is a large shop, and you can buy plants at the well-stocked plant centre. The pleasant restaurant serves light refreshments and meals, or you can enjoy a picnic on the lawns or beside the lake.

Ockham Common is an attractive open space close to the motorway and the A3 and therefore rather marred by background traffic noise. Take the A3 towards Guildford, and turn left almost immediately. There are parking spots along this road, which runs beside a wide stretch of water known as **Bolder Mere.**

JUNCTION 11 THORPE PARK

Junction 11 is the exit to take for **Thorpe Park,** a large theme and amusement park built around a series of worked-out gravel pits, if you are travelling clockwise (i.e. at this point heading towards Heathrow) round the M25. Take the A317 east, turning left at the first roundabout. At the junction of the A317 and A320, take the A320 and follow this road until you reach the entrance to Thorpe Park. Thorpe Park offers all manner of thrills, from a History of British Architecture to the Phantom Fantasia Ride – or perhaps you would prefer the Roman Galley and Port or the Smirnoff Loch Ness Monster?! If you set to one side the more whizz-bang attractions here – and what, after all, is wrong with them, so long as people enjoy them? – there are in fact a number of interesting things to see; you could learn a great deal without having to make too much effort. Model World, for instance, illustrates at 1/36th size no fewer than 40 famous structures from throughout history, from the Colossus of Rhodes to the Sydney Opera House. There are replicas of famous fighter planes of the First World War, an exhibition entitled 'Our Heritage' illustrates by means of historical tableaux important episodes in British history, and Thorpe Farm recreates the atmosphere of a working farm between the two world wars. There are pleasant water gardens, including a nature trail and a bird sanctuary, and opportunities for water-skiing, board-sailing and swimming. The Park, which has plenty of cafés and restaurants, is open daily from 10.00 to 6.00 between late March and late September, with an extension to 9.00 during the second half of July and throughout August.

Junction 12 is the junction with the M3 (see pages 109–117), and there is no access on to ordinary roads.

If you are travelling anticlockwise (i.e. away from Heathrow Airport at this point), leave the M25 at junction 13 for Thorpe Park (see junction 11, above). Take the A308 east towards Staines briefly, and then turn right on to the A320.

JUNCTION 13 RUNNYMEDE

Runnymede, one of the most famous places in English history, lies just west of the motorway. Here came King John one June day in 1215 to start negotiations with his rebellious barons. For the King the situation was quite serious, for the rebels already held the capital. The two sides, each encamped on the meadow beside the Thames, talked for nine days. Finally, the King submitted to the barons' complaints, affixing his Great Seal to the preliminary draft of the Magna Carta (the Great Charter) that listed 49 specific grievances. This document – copies of the final draft were dispatched throughout the kingdom – came to form the basis of the English constitution. It would be too much to expect that some sense of history, some sign of those momentous negotiations seven-and-a-half centuries ago, would linger at Runnymede. But even so, the site is something of a disappointment. The meadow and riverbank, with gentle hills rising behind, are pleasant enough, but they are spoilt by the constant din of traffic on the main road and on the M25 a short way away and by the planes taking off from Heathrow. A little way up the hillside, the **Magna Carta Memorial**, in the form of a domed classical temple, fails to make any historical connections; it was erected by the American Bar Association in 1957. Nearby is Britain's memorial to President Kennedy of the USA, a rectangular seven-ton block of Portland stone. The Magna Carta Tea Room is a not especially pleasant café in the **Fairhaven Memorial Lodge**; this was built in memory of Lord Fairhaven, whose widow and sons gave 188 acres of the Meads, as the meadowland at Runnymede is known, to the National Trust in 1931. From the M25, take the A308 west for 1½ miles.

The **RAF Memorial** stands on top of Cooper's Hill above Runnymede, and gives splendid views over London. The memorial, consecrated in 1953, commemorates the 20,455 airmen who were killed during the Second World War and have no known graves. The Memorial is open daily from 9.00 to 8.00 or dusk, whichever is earlier; opening time on Sundays is 10.00. From the Magna Carta Memorial continue along the A308 towards Windsor, turn left up Priest Hill on the A328, and turn left again at the top of the hill.

JUNCTION 13 SAVILL GARDEN

Further west from the RAF Memorial, through the village of Englefield Green, you come to the **Savill Garden**. This is a lovely small woodland garden at the southern edge of Windsor Great Park, with rhododendrons and azaleas, camellias and magnolias, and many other flowering trees and shrubs. Although spring is undoubtedly the best time of year to visit it, the autumn colours, with every variation of brown, gold, red and green crowding on each other, are also spectacular. There is also a large temperate house. The Garden takes its name from Eric Savill, Deputy Ranger of Windsor Great Park earlier this century (the reigning monarch holds the post of Ranger), who developed the Garden from what had previously been bogland. The Garden is open daily from 10.00 to 6.00 or 7.00, or sunset if earlier. From the M25, take the A30 west along the Egham bypass, past Royal Holloway College, and then turn right into Wick Road. The car park for the Savill Garden is on the right. From here you can also walk through **Windsor Great Park**, perhaps along to the Obelisk Pond or down to Virginia Water.

Junction 14 leads to Heathrow Airport (see also junction 4 of the M4, page 125), and provides easy access to Terminal 4.

Junction 15 is the junction with the M4 (see pages 118–163), and there is no access on to ordinary roads.

Junction 16 is the junction with the M40 (see pages 164–173), and there is no access on to ordinary roads.

Junction 17 leads to the western edge of Rickmansworth. There is nothing worth leaving the motorway for here.

JUNCTION 18 CHENIES MANOR

Chenies Manor is a handsome brick-built 15th- and 16th-century manor house with a fortified tower set in the Buckinghamshire countryside 2¼ miles north of junction 18. The interior contains interesting furniture and tapestries, while outside there are lovely gardens, including a sunken garden and a physic garden. The house is open on Wednesdays and Thursdays (and also on the late Spring and late Summer Bank Holiday Mondays) from 2.00 to 5.00 between April and October. **Chenies** village has two pleasant-looking pubs, the Red Lion and the Bedford Arms. Take the A413 Amersham road north-west frm the motorway, and then the signposted country road to the right to Chenies.

Junction 19 leads to the western edge of Watford (see junction 5 of the M1, page 6). This junction has restricted access; travelling clockwise, you can leave the motorway but not join it, anticlockwise, you can join but not leave it.

JUNCTION 20 GRAND UNION CANAL

Junction 20, situated in scrappy countryside north of Watford and just south of Kings Langley, presents an interesting contrast for transport enthusiasts. Unceasing traffic on the M25, Britain's newest major motorway, roars overhead, while the valley below holds the main line north out of Euston, the tiny river Gade and the **Grand Union Canal**. The railway, built by Robert Stephenson, was the first main line out of London; the first trains ran between London and Birmingham in 1838. Extensions north were soon completed, and this line carried the first direct Anglo–Scottish trains 10 years later; electrification between London and Glasgow was completed in 1974. The canal, of course, is older still. In its heyday, in the late 18th and 19th centuries, coal, iron and manufactured goods from the factories and mines of the Midlands, and agricultural produce from its rich farmland, were carried south to London by barge along the canal, while traffic in the return direction might consist of luxury imported goods brought by ship to the London docks from the east and then transferred to barges for the final stage of their journey. The towpath is easy to reach. From the roundabout beneath the motorway, drive north on the A41, and then take the first turning to the right, signposted Home Park Industrial Estate. In a few hundred yards, the road crosses the canal, and a path leads down to the canal bank. Despite the nearby factories and motorway, the canal seems quiet and almost forgotten; there is a lock and a lock-keeper's cottage, and you can walk for as long as you want along the towpath.

Junction 21 is the junction with the northbound carriageway of the M1, and there is no access on to ordinary roads.

Junction 21a is the junction with the southbound carriageway of the M1 and with the dual carriageway A405 linking St Albans and Watford. For St Albans see junction 6 of the M1, pages 6–9.

Junction 22 leads to London Colney, where there is nothing worth leaving the motorway for.

Junction 23 is the junction with the dual carriageway A1 to the south, and the A1(M) running north to Hatfield and Stevenage.

JUNCTION 24 TRENT PARK

Trent Park, south of junction 24, offers pleasant country walks through an attractively landscaped area of mixed woodland and open fields. There is a farm trail, and inhabitants of the animal enclosures include pigs, goats and chickens. An obelisk on the east side of the Park commemorates a minor, but as it turned out signifiant, member of the royal family: Edward, Duke of Kent, the fourth son of George III. After the death of Princess Charlotte at Claremont (see page 63), the monarchy was left without a direct heir to succeed the future George IV. His younger brothers – most of whom had been living comfortably with their mistresses for years and had produced large families of natural children – were now required to enter into legal unions and produce legitimate offspring as rapidly as possible. The Duke of Kent obliged by marrying Victoria of Saxe-Coburg-Saalfeld. Their only child, also named Victoria, was born in 1819 and 18 years later succeeded to the throne. The Duke of Kent, his role in history now successfully completed, died in 1820 of a cold caught while sightseeing in Salisbury Cathedral. There is a refreshment room near the Cockfosters Road entrance, which is the one you will use if you are coming from the motorway. From junction 24 drive south on the A111; the entrance to the Park is on the left after about 2½ miles. The drive south from the motorway towards Trent Park illustrates a fascinating piece of social history. As you come over the brow of a hill and descend the other side, you will see in front of you, across a few fields of farmland, a row of 1930s villas. This marks the unplanned and undesigned end of London's suburban expansion – abruptly cut short when war broke out in September 1939. When building resumed after the war, planning legislation designated the countryside around London as Green Belt, protected from development for housing.

Junction 25 leads into Waltham Cross, where there is nothing to recommend.

JUNCTION 26 WALTHAM ABBEY

Waltham Abbey lies north of the motorway between junctions 25 and 26, but is most easily reached by driving west along the A121 from junction 26. The Abbey is a magnificent example of Norman architecture, and, although much smaller, is comparable with the greatest Norman cathedrals of that period. The Abbey was begun in about 1060 by Harold, the last of the pre-Norman kings of England, who lost his life at the Battle of Hastings, and it was extended during the 13th century. Three centuries later, only the townspeople's protests saved the entire Abbey from destruction during Henry VIII's

Waltham Abbey

campaign against the monasteries. What survives is almost entirely Norman, although the tower was built in the 1550s after the previous one collapsed. There are lovely decorative zig-zag patterns on the arches, and some of the columns are cut with spiral or zig-zag grooves. The ceiling painting, which dates from the 1860s, when the Abbey was extensively restored by the architect William Burges, represents the four elements, the past and the future, the signs of the zodiac and the labours of the months. The lovely 14th-century Lady Chapel is worth a few minutes' time. Look out also for two delightful tombs. That of Robert Smith, the 17th-century captain of a merchantman, depicts a ship in full sail, while the Denny tomb of 1600 has effigies of Sir Edward Denny and his wife and, beneath the couple, their 10 children (boys to the left, girls to the right) kneeling in prayer.

JUNCTION 26 EPPING FOREST DISTRICT MUSEUM

In Sun Street, at the other end of the town centre, the **Epping Forest District Museum** is housed in two restored timber-framed buildings dating from the 16th and 18th centuries. The displays concentrate on the history of the area and feature some magnificent oak panelling carved for the Abbot of Waltham's house in the 16th century. The Museum's opening hours are 2.00 to 5.00 on Fridays, Saturdays, Sundays and Mondays and 12.00 to 5.00 on Tuesdays; refreshments are available. Philpott's Tea Rooms, just off the pleasant little market square, is another good place for a snack or light meal.

JUNCTION 26 EPPING FOREST CONSERVATION CENTRE
Epping Forest lies east of junction 26, and it is only a short drive to **High Beach**, a small village on the edge of the forest where there are pleasant walks and you can visit the **Epping Forest Conservation Centre**. These 4000 acres of woodland, which form the largest forest of hornbeams in England and are home to a herd of black fallow deer, are the largest remaining tract of the forest that once stretched from the Thames to the Wash (see also Hatfield Forest, page 48). For several centuries, the monarch used to hunt here with his friends, often staying overnight at Waltham Abbey. While the king was a regular visitor, the forest laws were strictly enforced. But when, from the 17th century onwards, the royal pleasure was taken elsewhere, people started to enclose parts of the forest. As at **Burnham Beeches** (see page 164), the Corporation of London eventually intervened to save what remained of the forest as a place of recreation for east Londoners; the Corporation continues to administer the forest today. The Conservation Centre, it has to be said, is something of a disappointment. Although the teaching facilities for visiting schools are excellent, all the general public can see is a small exhibition area, which usually has displays on the history and ecology of the forest. The Centre is open between Easter and the end of October on Wednesdays to Saturdays from 10.00 to 12.30 and 2.00 to 5.30 or dusk, whichever is earlier; and on Sundays and Public Holidays from 11.00 to 12.30 and 2.00 to 5.00 or dusk. To get to High Beach, take the A121 east from the motorway, and after about ¾ mile turn right on to a side road signposted to the village. The King's Oak pub in High Beach serves food, as does another which looks rather nicer, the Woodbine, on the A121 just past the High Beach turning.

Junction 27 is the junction with the M11, and there is no access on to ordinary roads.

JUNCTION 28 WEALD COUNTRY PARK
The **Weald Country Park** is a large and attractive stretch of open country near junction 28 – and would be my choice, in preference to

Epping Forest, for a breath of fresh air and a walk near this section of the M25. There is a touch of sadness about this Park, for the estate once belonged to one of Essex's grandest stately homes, demolished after years of neglect in 1950. All that remains to remind you of the house, and of the elegance and wealth that once gathered here, is a single staircase that once climbed up from the garden front and nowadays seems to lead nowhere. Like many country houses, **Weald Hall** combined architecture from the 16th, 17th and 18th centuries; Robert Adam decorated the ceiling in the Dining Room and there was a splendid Georgian Great Hall, its exterior dominated by an Ionic portico. We may regret the house, but we can still enjoy the grounds, which were landscaped in the mid-18th century, although it is thought that the entire scheme, which was worked out by a French surveyor named Bourginion, was not carried out. There are avenues of oaks and chestnuts, a folly called the Belvedere Temple, and – perhaps most attractive of all – a trio of lakes (only two now lie within the Park boundaries) half-hidden in a gentle valley. The walks here are excellent; you can climb up to the Belvedere, admire the deer in the paddock and look at the exhibitions on local natural history and on the story of the house and park in the attractive visitor centre. From the roundabout above the motorway at junction 8, take the A1023 towards Brentford. Turn left after ¼ mile, just past the Post House Hotel, on to a minor road that crosses the A12 on a bridge and climbs a gentle hill to **South Weald** village, where the Tower Arms pub serves food. Turn left here, and there are two car parks on the right within a few hundred yards, the second of which serves the visitor centre.

Junction 29 is the junction with the A127 Romford to Basildon road, and there is nothing worth leaving the motorway for here.

The same has to be said of junction 30, which is on the A13 between Dagenham and Tilbury.

Junction 31, less than 1 mile from junction 30, is the last junction before the Dartford Tunnel. There is restricted access here. Travelling south (i.e. towards the river) you cannot leave the motorway, travelling north you cannot join it.

The M2

Strood to Faversham

INTRODUCTION

The M2 carries the motorist from the London side of the Medway estuary past the Medway towns' conurbation and on through the pleasant Kentish countryside of apple orchards and oast houses to beyond Faversham. The highlight of the journey is undoubtedly the crossing of the Medway on an elegant bridge high above the water; there are attractive views downstream towards Rochester Castle, where the keep is an imposing example of Norman defensive architecture. Immediately after the river crossing, the motorway runs through attractive country on the edge of the North Downs, and later there are occasional glimpses north towards the Isle of Sheppey. Rochester and Chatham, each with a long and distinguished history, supply the main off-motorway diversions, while further east Faversham can boast a remarkably unspoilt town centre, with a harmonious blend of buildings from several centuries.

The start of the motorway is simply a continuation of the three-lane A2 from London. The centre and right-hand lanes of the A2 become the motorway, while the A2 branches off in the left-hand lane. If you are travelling away from London and want to visit Rochester and Chatham, you can take the A2 here at junction 1, although the A229 from junction 3 is an easier and rather less busy route.

JUNCTION 1 COBHAM

A pleasant diversion before you reach the motorway is south off the A2 to **Cobham**. This attractive North Downs village has some interesting historic buildings. In the narrow main street, far more suited to the days of travel by horse and cart than to today's flow of cars and lorries, there is the timber-framed **Wealden House**, built in the early 15th century for use as a monks' visiting hall, or lodging house, and converted into shops in about 1840. Almost next door is the half-timbered **Old Leather Bottle** inn, frequented by the novelist Charles Dickens. One of his favourite walks was across the fields to

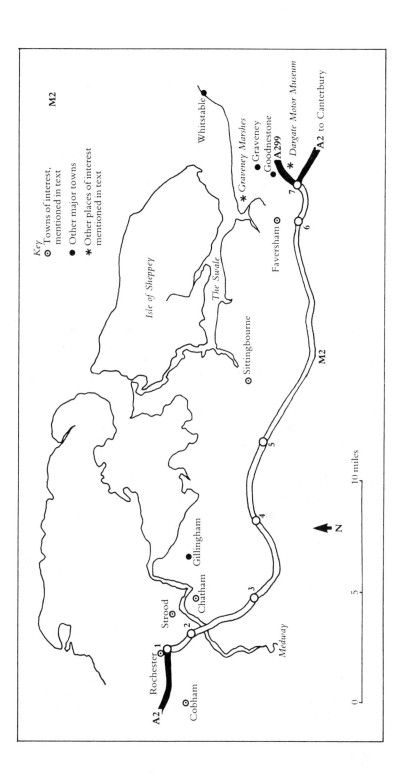

Key
⊙ Towns of interest, mentioned in text
● Other major towns
✳ Other places of interest mentioned in text

M2

Whitstable

Graveney Marshes

● Graveney
● Goodnestone

A299

Dargate Motor Museum
✳

7

A2 to Canterbury

6

Faversham ⊙

Isle of Sheppey

The Swale

⊙ Sittingbourne

5

4

N

Gillingham ●

Strood ⊙

2

Chatham ⊙

3

Medway

Rochester ⊙ 1

A2

⊙ Cobham

M2

0   5   10 miles

Cobham from his home at Gad's Hill near Higham, a few miles away, and the inn appears in *Pickwick Papers*. The 13th-century **church** has a fine collection of medieval brasses, all of them of the Cobham family and showing in vivid detail the costume of their period. The **almshouses** behind the church were originally part of a priests' college founded by Sir John de Cobham in 1362; suppressed by Henry VIII in 1537, the college was converted to its present use in the 17th century. **Cobham Hall** is a handsome late Elizabethan mansion; the central hall was rebuilt towards the end of the 17th century, and there were further alterations around 1800. Inside there is fine work by James Wyatt, Inigo Jones and the Adam brothers, while the park was laid out by Humphry Repton. The Hall is now a school, but it is open to the public over Easter and on Sundays, Wednesdays and Thursdays during late July and August. **Owletts**, at the far end of the village High Street, is a pleasant and unassuming red-brick house built by a local farmer in the late 17th century; there is a fine staircase and an attractive small garden. Opening times are 2.00 to 5.00 on Wednesdays and Thursdays from April to September.

To reach Cobham, turn off the A2 on to the B2009 about 2 miles east of the start of the M2. The entrance to Cobham Hall is near the junction of these two roads, while the village is 1 mile farther south on the B2009.

JUNCTION 2 TEMPLE MANOR

Temple Manor is a 13th-century house with 17th-century additions at each end that nowadays finds itself squeezed between a railway line and the small factories of an industrial estate in **Strood**, on the west bank of the Medway. The original house, which was built for the Knights Templars as a hostel for travellers on their way between London and the Channel ports and then became a farm, consisted simply of a large main hall in which visitors slept and ate. Lived in until the 1930s, the building was sympathetically restored to its original form during the 1950s by the then Ministry of Works; the outside porch and stairway are a modern copy of the original entrance. Temple Manor is open from April (or Easter, if earlier) to September as follows: Mondays, Wednesdays, Thursdays and Saturdays 9.30 to 1.00, 2.00 and 6.30; Tuesdays 9.30 to 1.00; Sundays 2.00 to 6.30. From junction 2, turn right on to the A228. After about 1 mile turn right immediately under a railway bridge, and then follow the signposted road through the industrial estate for about ½ mile.

JUNCTION 3 MEDWAY TOWNS

The **Medway towns** might well not be a first choice for an off-motorway break. The popular image is of a rather unattractive and traffic-filled group of towns without much to attract the visitor. Nowadays, nothing could be further from the truth. The city council is making a real, and on the whole successful, attempt to brighten the place up for visitors, and there is a remarkable amount to do and see – although you will need to spare an hour or two at the very least to get something out of your visit.

The easiest way to either Rochester or Chatham is to leave the motorway at junction 3 and then take the A229 north. Less than 1 mile from the motorway, you can either keep straight on the A229 for Rochester city centre or take the A230 to the right to the Historic Dockyard and Fort Amherst in Chatham. Another advantage of this route is that if you are driving out from London you get a fine view downstream to the Castle and the cathedral as the motorway crosses the Medway between junctions 2 and 3.

JUNCTION 3 ROCHESTER CASTLE

Rochester sits in a natural strategic position overlooking the Medway and halfway between London and the Channel ports. The Romans built a fortified camp here, which later grew into a walled city. After the Norman invasion, William quickly had a wooden

Rochester Castle

castle put up. The first stone fortifications were built soon after 1080 – **Rochester Castle** was among the earliest stone castles in the country – while work on the massive great tower began in 1127 and was completed within 10 or 15 years. Seventy feet square, 113 feet tall (rising to 125 feet at the corner turrets), and with walls between 10 and 12 feet thick, the tower remains an imposing sight eight-and-a-half centuries later. What a grim and impregnable citadel it must have seemed in the Middle Ages. The Castle was besieged twice. On the first occasion, in 1215, when it was in the hands of rebellious barons, King John managed to breach the walls by undermining the turret on the south corner, but even then the defenders held out for some time, making good use of the internal cross wall in the tower as they tried to throw back the King's men. In 1264, troops loyal to Henry III successfully held out against a siege by Simon de Montfort's army. The tower is well worth climbing, and not just for the views from the top. On the first floor you can see the original grand entrance from the forebuilding; grooves where the portcullis ran are still visible, while the recessed arches were designed to hold keys, lanterns and so forth. The Great Hall was on the second floor, and from the angle of the stairs between the second and third floors you can see the space it occupied. On the third floor, galleries run round what used to be the upper part of the Great Hall. The Castle's summer opening hours are daily 9.30 to 6.30; times in winter are Mondays to Saturdays 9.30 to 4.30, Sundays 2.00 to 4.30.

JUNCTION 3 ROCHESTER CATHEDRAL

The **cathedral** (open daily from 7.30 to 6.00) stands opposite the Castle. Rochester is the second oldest bishopric in England, and the first church here was founded in 604. The present building was started in 1080, and although it had to be repaired after damage during the Civil War and was worked over quite heavily by 19th-century restorers, a good deal of the lovely early work remains. Most of the nave is Norman, although towards the east end the arches and columns are Gothic; the monks set about rebuilding the nave in about 1300, but money ran out before they had got very far. The choir dates from the 13th century. Everywhere there are attractive decorations in stone. Look out for the remnants of the 13th- or 14th-century depiction of the wheel of fortune on the wall of the choir and for the Pilgrim Steps in the north choir transept, worn down by the knees of pilgrims praying at the shrine of St William of Perth, who was murdered in 1201. Behind the cathedral you can have a pleasant walk past the **Bishop's Palace**, where Henry VIII first met Anne of Cleves, the fourth and least loved of his wives, the monastic **cloisters** and **Prior's Gate**, the best of the three surviving 14th-century monastic gates, and then along **Minor Canon Row**. This handsome Georgian terrace is so called because the minor canons of the cathedral were formerly accommodated there. Then walk through the King's School, across a small green known as The Vines because it was once the monastery vineyard, and turn left down Crow Lane towards the High Street, past **Restoration House**, so called because, according to tradition, Charles II stayed there on his return to England from exile in 1660.

JUNCTION 3 DICKENS CENTRE

This walk brings you out into the **High Street**, where many of the buildings have been attractively restored and decorated and there are some interesting shops and eating places; two that look good are the Oliver Twist coffee shop and, just below the cathedral in College Yard, the Precinct Pantry. Turn right down the High Street for the **Dickens Centre**, Rochester's main tribute to one of its most famous sons, the novelist Charles Dickens. Dickens lived in Rochester from the age of five until he was ten or eleven, when the family moved to London. Those years gave him an abiding affection for this part of Kent, and in 1855, when he was an established and successful writer, he bought Gads Hill Place near Higham, a few miles outside the city, where he lived for the last 15 years of his life. His last four novels, all written at Gads Hill, are full of local references. Restoration House, mentioned above, is Satis House in *Great Expectations*, while Cloisterham in Dickens's final work, *The Mystery of Edwin Drood*, is closely based on Rochester. The well-laid-out displays in the Dickens Centre, which make use of early photographs, memorabilia and first editions to describe every aspect of the novelist's life and work, remind you just how energetic and vital a person Dickens was. He appears immensely warm and whole-hearted in everything he did, whether he was organizing amateur theatricals, campaigning for social reform or touring the USA giving Shakespearean recitations. 'Talking heads', including Dickens himself and Oliver Twist, and sound-and-light sequences, some of them based on scenes from the novels, help to bring Dickens' world to vivid life. From *Oliver Twist* you see Fagin teaching his boys to pick pockets and Nancy struggling, in vain, to escape as Bill Sykes murders her; while from *The Old Curiosity Shop* Quilp's grim death is recreated as, tied to a pole stuck fast in the Thames mud, he is engulfed by the rising tide. The Dickens Centre is open daily from 10.00 to 1.00 and 2.00 to 5.30; last admission is ½ hour before closing time.

Also worth seeing in Rochester is the **Guildhall Museum** in the High Street, which has displays of local history, archaeology and natural history, a fine collection of Victorian and early 20th-century dolls and toys, and arms and armour galleries. Opening times are the same as at the Dickens Centre.

JUNCTION 3 CHATHAM HISTORIC DOCKYARD

Chatham is a much younger place than Rochester. Nothing much happened here until the early 16th century, when Henry VIII established the Dockyard. The *Sunne*, a 56-ton pinnace with five guns launched in 1586, was the first of a line of nearly 500 vessels constructed at Chatham, among them HMS *Victory* (see also pages 104–105) and HMS *Achilles*, the first iron-clad built in a Royal Navy dockyard. By the 17th century, Chatham had become the Navy's principal building yard. The development of iron-clads in the 1860s, and the parallel replacement of sail by steam power, had a major effect on the Dockyard. A massive 300-acre extension (built by convict labour) was opened to the north of the original yard, and for the next century and a quarter, until the Dockyard was closed in 1984, most of the work was concentrated here – leaving the older workshops virtually unaltered. It is around this remarkable collection of 18th- and early 19th-century buildings that the **Chatham Historic Dockyard** is centred. Not that the area has been turned over exclusively to the past. Many of the buildings are still used commercially – among them the ropery, 47 feet wide and no less than 1140 feet long, and built for spinning yarn and making rope – and there are plans to establish more workshops as well as homes and offices. The old galvanizing shop has been converted into a visitor centre telling the story of the dockyard. An excellent audio-visual show sets the scene, and displays explain the details of ship-building and sail-making. The suggested walk round the yard passes the mast house and mould loft, where the ships' lines were laid down, the building slips, covered to protect ships' timbers from the weather and so continue the seasoning process, and the elegant Commissioner's House, built in 1703 and now the oldest intact naval building in England. It then moves on to the ropery, the hemp house and the lead and paint mill which now houses the dockyard museum. At this stage in its development, the Chatham Historic Dockyard is perhaps of most interest to naval enthusiasts and to people with an interest in 18th- and 19th-century architecture and industry; the walk through what remains in effect a working 19th-century dockyard is fascinating. The Historic Dockyard is open on Wednesdays to Sundays, and on Bank Holiday Mondays from 10.00 to 6.00 between April and October and from 10.00 to 4.30 on Wednesdays, Saturdays and Sundays only the rest of the year. There is a café in the Queen's Assistant Harbourmaster's Office on the waterfront. The Dockyard entrance is left off the A231 Chatham to Gillingham road ½ mile north of Chatham town centre.

JUNCTION 3 FORT AMHERST

Fort Amherst nearby is another project still in the course of development. As Chatham Dockyard expanded, and the Medway became one of the Navy's principal anchorages, official circles woke up to the realization that some form of defence was needed for this vital military area. Between 1755 and 1758 an initial line of earthwork bastions was dug behind the Dockyard. In 1770 these were extended and a complex of batteries and redoubts was created to form the strongpoint of the defensive lines, which were now more than 2 miles long. Further improvements were made during the Napoleonic Wars, including new magazines, barracks, gun batteries and guardrooms. But despite all the invasion scares in the years around 1800, Fort Amherst was never tested in battle – in fact the closest contact it has ever had with French forces, or with any other enemy troops, has been during recent 'invasions' staged at gala weekends by the local branch of the Napoleonic Association! – and by 1860 it had been officially declared redundant. The development of much longer-range weapons meant that both the Fort and the lines were now far too near the Dockyard – any invading force could easily launch an attack from much farther off, over the heads, as it were, of a garrison based at Amherst – and a new chain of more strategically positioned fortifications was erected along the Thames and south of the Medway towns. Technological advance proved to be the saving of Fort Amherst. While similar fortifications elsewhere have been expanded and rebuilt out of all recognition, Amherst has remained a rare, unspoilt example of 18th-century military building. A 10-year restoration programme is now gradually returning the Fort to its pre-1815 appearance – a massive task of military archaeology, since many of the surface ditches were filled with rubble and rubbish during the 1960s. The visit is great fun, and should appeal to people of all ages, even those without a special interest in military history. Once inside the Fort, you find yourself in a warren of brick-lined tunnels hewn out of the chalk, some of them natural, others perhaps the work of convicts and prisoners of war. One section of tunnel has been equipped as a Second World War Air Raid Precautions Centre; during that conflict mortar positions were set up in the Fort, while the Medway Civil Defence Headquarters were established in the tunnels. Further on in the tour you see the original ammunition shaft, down which powder and weapons were lowered for storing in the magazines, and the primitive latrines (only officers enjoyed the privilege of private cubicles) and washing facilities used by the garrison. Strategically sited defensive positions both inside and on the exterior ensured that, even if an invader did succeed in reaching the Fort, he would not last long. Future plans for Fort Amherst include the restoration of the magazine and a museum showing the development of fortifications in the Medway area. Fort Amherst, which is to the right off the A31 as it leaves Chatham for Gillingham, is open on Wednesdays, Saturdays and Sundays from 12.00 to 4.30 between April and October, daily during the school summer holidays. The Command House is a pleasant waterside pub and restaurant almost opposite the entrance to Fort Amherst and on the site of Henry VIII's original Dockyard.

JUNCTION 3 ROYAL ENGINEERS MUSEUM

Also in Chatham is the new **Royal Engineers Museum**, which is devoted to the history of military engineering, in particular to the story of the Royal Engineers. Uniform, weapons and scientific and engineering equipment are all on show; there are displays on the development of fortifications and siegecraft, models and sections on military diving, flying and transport. The models include one of the first known assault bridge, erected by Julius Caesar in 55 BC to cross the Rhône, and, in the Gibraltar Room, two depicting the Great Siege of Gibraltar in 1783 which were made shortly after the end of the siege. The work of General Gordon of the Royal Engineers is featured, and the First World War rooms include a full-size Nissen hut and a reconstruction of a trench system. The Museum is open from 10.00 to 5.00 on Tuesdays to Fridays and on Sundays from 11.30 to 5.00. The Museum is in the Royal Engineers' Brompton Barracks in Chatham. Take the A231 from Chatham past Fort Amherst and the Dockyard towards Gillingham. Turn on to the B2001 and the Museum is on the left-hand side.

Junction 4 is on the southern edge of Gillingham, where there is nothing special to see.

Junction 5 provides an interesting, if rather lengthy, diversion into Sittingbourne for two different types of transport enthusiast. Lovers of steam will head for the **Sittingbourne & Kemsley Light Railway**, while lovers of sail will find at the **Dolphin Yard Sailing Barge Museum** a fascinating glimpse into the now almost forgotten world of the Thames sailing barge.

JUNCTION 5 SITTINGBOURNE & KEMSLEY LIGHT RAILWAY

The railway is a narrow-gauge line (2 feet 6 inches) originally built in the 1930s to carry paper and other freight between the docks at

Ridham on the Swale estuary and the paper mills at Sittingbourne. Since the 1970s it has been operated by enthusiasts as a preserved line. Not all the original route has been saved, and today trains run through a mixed industrial and rural landscape only as far as Kemsley Down; the trip takes 12 to 15 minutes in each direction. The special interest of the line is its industrial origin; in contrast with many preserved routes, it never formed part of the national passenger network. Trains run on Sundays and Bank Holiday weekends between Easter and mid-October, and also on Wednesdays in August and around Christmas and the New Year. The Sittingbourne station is in Mill Lane (there is no road access to the station at Kemsley Down). From junction 5, take the A249 north to the junction with the A2. Then turn right on to that road. In the outskirts of Sittingbourne, turn left by a filling station into Stapleton Road; go straight on at the first roundabout, turn right at the second along the B2006, and then turn left along opposite the Bowater factory.

JUNCTION 5 DOLPHIN YARD SAILING BARGE MUSEUM

Throughout the 19th century, the flat-bottomed Thames spritsail sailing barge was a common sight not just on the Thames itself but also in the rivers and countless small harbours of the Kent and East Anglian coasts, even in the tiniest and remotest creeks. These flat-bottomed barges with their tall sails survived well into the 20th century. They carried all manner of cargoes from hay to the stock bricks manufactured along the Kentish coast and used to create the terraced suburbs of Victorian London, and were only displaced after the First World War when road transport became cheap and reliable. Over 500 barges were built at Milton Creek in Sittingbourne, which was one of the main centres of barge construction; at one time there were 11 ship- and barge-building yards there. Only one now survives: the **Dolphin Yard**, which has been converted into a fascinating working Museum. The main exhibits are housed in a former forge and carpenter's shop and sail loft; there are models, barge relics found in the quay, and old tools and equipment, while photographs and other historical material are used to explain the history and operation of the Thames barges. Outside, if you are lucky, there may well be several barges moored in the creek; the Museum offers facilities for private owners of the few surviving barges to do repair work. Two trails (each 2 miles each way) around Milton Creek guide you along old wharfs and past the remains of old brickworks (the Creek was an important brick- and cement-manufacturing area) and of wrecked barges. Both trails start at the **White Hart** pub in Crown Quay Lane, where there is a 'barge bar' with old photographs and souvenirs; the White Hart was a favourite haunt of bargemen. The Museum, which is reached along a ¼-mile footpath from Crown Quay Lane, is open on Sundays and Bank Holidays between Easter and mid-October. From junction 5, follow the directions given above into Sittingbourne, but continue into the town centre on the A2, and then turn left from the High Street into Crown Quay Lane.

If you are travelling towards London, the quickest way to reach Sittingbourne is to leave the motorway at junction 6 and drive east along the A2.

JUNCTION 6 FAVERSHAM

Junction 6 is a short way along the A251 from **Faversham**, an attractive and well-preserved small town with some handsome buildings, especially along Abbey Street and in the Market Place. The **Guildhall** in the centre is an early 19th-century replacement of the original Tudor building, of which the pillars and arches remain. There are several town walks around the most interesting parts of the town, details of which are available from the **Fleur de Lis Heritage Centre and Museum** in Preston Street. This excellent small exhibition about the town, run by the Faversham Society, is housed in an old pub in which, in 1547, a plot to murder Thomas Arden, the town mayor, was hatched. The story of Arden's death at the hands of his wife and her lover was turned by an unknown writer into a very successful play, *Arden of Feversham*, one of the earliest domestic dramas performed in England. (Feversham became known as Faversham about 200 years ago.) The Heritage Centre is open from 9.30 to 1.00 and 2.00 to 4.30 daily except Thursdays, Sundays and Bank Holidays between Easter and October; during the rest of the year the Centre opens at 10.00 and closes at 4.00. Near the town centre are the 18th-century **Chart Gunpowder Mills** – the oldest of their kind in the world – which supplied the powder used at celebrated battles such as Trafalgar and Waterloo; these have also been restored by the Faversham Society. The Chart Mills are open most Sunday afternoons between 2.30 and 4.30.

JUNCTION 7 WHITSTABLE & DARGATE MOTOR MUSEUM

Junction 7 is the end of the motorway. Faversham (see junction 6, above) is 2 miles west along the A2. To the south-east the A2, now a fast dual carriageway, leads towards Canterbury and Dover, while the A299 runs north-east towards **Whitstable**, a pleasant small seaside town and once an important oyster-fishing centre, where belated attempts are now being made to preserve and brighten up the town centre. Two miles from junction 7, the **Dargate Motor**

Museum has an interesting collection of old cars, commercial vehicles and automobilia, including a 1918 car vacuum cleaner still in its original box, petrol pumps, a 1920s police stop lamp and lots of intriguing little items such as oil cans, uniforms and signs. The vehicles include a 1903 Rambler from the USA, which still takes part in the annual London to Brighton run, a 1934 Ford Model B, a 1925 Bull Nose Morris and an early bubble car. The Museum is open daily from 10.00 to 6.00 between Easter and October. Turn right off the A299 about 2 miles from the end of the motorway, just before a Happy Eater restaurant on the left and by a service station on the right. Turn right again immediately, and follow this side road for about 1 mile through Dargate village; the Museum is at the end of the village on the left-hand side. The Dove pub nearby does food.

JUNCTION 7 GRAVENEY MARSHES
For what will most likely be a fairly wild and windswept walk on the Kent marshes, take the first left off the A299, turn immediately right, and drive through Goodnestone and Graveney to **Graveney Marshes**; the distance is about 5 miles from the motorway. You can walk along the shore towards Whitstable or, for an even more remote walk, take the path west along the **Swale**, the stretch of water that divides the Isle of Sheppey from the mainland. This is part of the **Saxon Shore Way**, a 140-mile path that follows the coast from Gravesend right to Rye in Sussex. It is named after the chain of forts built in the 5th century AD to guard England against a Saxon invasion.

The M20

Swanley to Folkestone

INTRODUCTION

The M20 is one of the motorways linking London and the Channel ports – though its usefulness is rather spoilt by the 14-mile gap between junctions 8 and 9. The first half runs through not especially attractive countryside from the outer rim of Greater London to the far side of Maidstone. There is, however, one dramatic moment where the motorway suddenly plunges down the scarp slope of the North Downs to the Medway valley below; the views from this stretch can be magnificent. The second half, which begins at Ashford, follows the line of the Downs as they run towards the coast. The countryside here is pleasanter, with the chalk hills rising up on one side and the remote flat land of Romney Marsh stretching out on the other. The motorway finishes not far from the sea on the unprepossessing outskirts of Folkestone.

The motorway starts east of Swanley on the border of Greater London and Kent as a continuation of the A20 trunk road from central London. The M20 and the M25 cross at junction 1 of the former motorway, junction 3 of the latter. For the Lullingstone Roman Villa, about 3½ miles south, see under the M25, pages 56, 57 and 60.

JUNCTION 2 TROSLEY COUNTRY PARK

Junction 2 is a staggered, partial junction midway down the scarp slope of the North Downs. Travelling east (i.e. away from London) you can leave the motorway, and you can join the northbound carriageway (i.e. towards London). Although much of the countryside immediately off the motorway is semi-urbanized, with straggly housing developments, there is some good walking through unspoilt landscapes from **Trosley Country Park**, 2¼ miles from the motorway. The Park itself is a mixture of woodland, scrub and open chalk downland with footpaths to explore and plenty of pleasant picnic spots; a visitor centre is open at weekends. The long-distance **North**

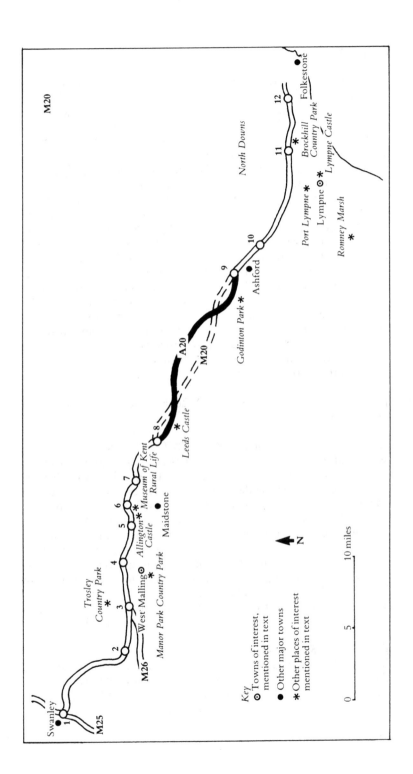

M20

Swanley

M25

M26

1

2

3

Trosley
Country Park

Manor Park Country Park

West Malling ◉

Allington ✱
Castle

Maidstone

4

5

6

7

Museum of Kent
Rural Life

8

Leeds Castle
✱

A20

M20

Godinton Park ✱

9

Ashford

10

North Downs

Port Lympne ✱

Lympne ◉
Lympne Castle ✱

Romney Marsh ✱

11

Brockhill ✱
Country Park

12

Folkestone

N

Key

◉ Towns of interest,
mentioned in text

● Other major towns

✱ Other places of interest
mentioned in text

0   5   10 miles

Downs Way, which runs the length of the North Downs from Farnham in Surrey to Dover in Kent, passes through the Park; the next stretch east towards the Medway offers good walking with fine views. This part of the North Downs Way uses the same route as the medieval Pilgrims' Way, the path used by pilgrims travelling from Winchester to the shrine of Thomas à Becket at Canterbury, which itself follows a prehistoric track. The chalk Downs, relatively easy to walk and ride on, have always provided a natural route for travellers. Three medium-distance circular footpaths start at the Park: the Trosley Ramble (3½ miles), the Coldrum Trail (6 miles) and the Harvel Hike (7 miles); leaflets describing each route are available from the visitor centre. The **Coldrum Stones** are one of at least seven Neolithic long barrows, used for burials 4000 to 5000 years ago, in the Medway area; four of the original 24 stones are still standing. To reach the Country Park from junction 2, take the A20 south for ½ mile, turn left on to the A227 towards Gravesend, and, after the road has reached the top of the Downs, turn right and then right again, following the signposts. If you are travelling towards London, take the M26 where that motorway and the M20 divide, leave the M26 almost immediately at junction 2a, and then drive north on the A20 to the junction with the A227.

Junction 3 is the junction with the M26, and there is no access on to ordinary roads.

JUNCTION 4 MANOR PARK COUNTRY PARK

West Malling, south of junction 4, has an elegant main street, its spaciousness spoilt by the flow of heavy traffic; the Swan Hotel is Tudor, and Ford House dates from the 14th century. South of the village on the A228 is **Manor Park Country Park** (open daily from 9.00 to dusk). The Park was originally created in the 18th century, and until recently formed part of the grounds of the manor house on the far side of the lake. While the Park is pleasant enough – there are trails to follow, you can fish in the lake, and four waymarked walks, each 3 to 4 miles long, start and finish there – my recommendation for a country break would be Trosley (see above under junction 2). To reach Manor Park from junction 4, take the A228 south through West Malling; the Park entrance is on the left beyond the village.

JUNCTION 5 ALLINGTON CASTLE

Junction 5 is a partial junction on the western edge of Maidstone; there is no access on to the eastbound carriageway of the motorway. **Allington Castle**, 2 miles east, commands a bend in the River Medway. A Norman motte castle was built here in the 11th century, but what you see now is an extensively restored and 'medievalized' version of a late 13th-century structure converted into a grand Tudor mansion and then destroyed by fire in about 1600. Wyatt's Rebellion, the uprising led by Sir Thomas Wyatt in protest at the marriage of Queen Mary to Philip II of Spain, is said to have been planned here. The restoration was done in the early years of this century by Lord and Lady Conway, who created as the focus of the Castle a magnificent Great Hall with an enormous chimney. Since 1951 Allington has been a Carmelite monastery and retreat house. Guided tours are available daily between 2.00 and 4.00. Take the spur road from the motorway, turn left at the roundabout on to the A20, and then left again after ¾ mile at the traffic lights. The Castle lies at the end of this road on the right after about 1 mile.

JUNCTION 6 MUSEUM OF KENT RURAL LIFE
Squeezed in a neck of land between the motorway and the Medway close to junction 6 is the **Museum of Kent Rural Life**. This is an excellent example of the new breed of museum that has been opening up all round the country during the last decade or so. Gone are the glass cases and the densely written captions; gone too is the focus on individual objects, no matter whether they are clocks or snuff-boxes or Roman remains. In their place has come an attempt to focus on ordinary life, to recreate what it meant to live and work in a particular part of the country at a particular moment in history. New as it is (1986 was the Museum's first season), the Museum of Kent Rural Life is succeeding admirably. The theme is the Kent countryside during the last two centuries. On the ground floor of a converted oast-house there is an introductory display and farm waggons are exhibited, while the drying floor upstairs, where the hops were dried before being sent to the brewery, is devoted to the history and cultivation of hops. There are fascinating photographs of East-Enders arriving at Kent stations for their annual holiday picking hops; by 1900 hop-growers had lists of reliable people who returned each year for the harvest. Outside, you can see hops growing in the hop garden, and agricultural equipment is displayed in the farm-yard, where there are also small exhibitions of harnesses and dairy equipment in the 18th- and 19th-century barns. A market garden has already been established with vegetables which were grown commercially during the 19th century; the orchard has been stocked with old varieties of apples, pears, plums and cherries; while the herb garden contains a variety of herbs used for cooking, dyeing and scent and as medicines. The Museum's livestock includes Sussex cattle and Romney sheep. Future plans include the erection of a hamlet with cottages, shops and workshops and an exhibition on

river transport based on the wharf alongside the Medway. During the summer various demonstrations and other events (e.g. bee-keeping, ploughing with vintage tractors, harvesting, hop-picking) are held at weekends. The Museum is open from April to mid-October; times are 10.00 to 4.30 on weekdays except Wednesdays, and 12.00 to 4.30 on Saturdays and Sundays. A small café serves light snacks and teas. Leave the motorway at junction 6 (take the second exit if you are travelling east, i.e. towards Folkestone), drive south on the A229 and then take the third left off the roundabout, called Forstal Road and signposted to Aylesford. Within ½ mile, turn left down Lock Lane; the Museum entrance is almost immediately on the right.

Junction 7 is another exit for Maidstone.

For the present, junction 8 is the end of the western section of the motorway; from here drivers heading for Ashford and Folkestone face a 14-mile stretch on the A20 trunk road before the motorway resumes at junction 9.

JUNCTION 8 LEEDS CASTLE
Barely ½ mile from the busy roads around junction 8 lies one of the

Leeds Castle

most tranquil and romantic spots in the whole of southern England; **Leeds Castle**. However often you visit Leeds, the walk from the car park to the Castle cannot fail to make you stop short in wonder. After a short stretch of woodland, you round a corner – and there a picture-book castle rises up from a wide lake. In summer, its walls seem to shimmer in the sun; in winter they reflect the grey of the scudding clouds above. Leeds is the quintessential fairy-tale castle of legend and of childhood imagination; surely it was here, if anywhere, that bold knights rode to rescue captive damsels of exceeding beauty. The first, wooden, fortifications on the site were built as long ago as the mid-9th century by Ledian, or Leed, the chief minister of Ethelbert IV, King of Kent. Although the Castle was acquired by the country's new Norman rulers after the Conquest, it was not until 1119 that the first stone defences were constructed; the nearby priory, begun at the same time and destroyed by Henry VIII four centuries later, offered hospitality to pilgrims making the journey to Canterbury.

Leeds's long royal associations began in 1278, when the Castle was presented to Edward I. He improved the defences, adding an outer bailey and strengthening the gate tower. Edward gave Leeds to his beloved queen, Eleanor of Castile, and later to his second wife Margaret, thus inaugurating the tradition whereby Leeds was the particular home of the queen and was kept by her during her widowhood. At least one royal romance was played out in these magnificent surroundings, when Catherine de Valois, the 21-year-old widow of Henry V, fell in love with Owen Tudor, the young Welsh courtier in charge of her dresses and jewels. The woods and parks of Leeds gave them the privacy they must have desperately craved. When their affair, for so it was thought to be, was discovered they were both imprisoned; in fact they had already married secretly. In the end, Catherine was released and Owen escaped from the Tower; it was their grandson who, as Henry VII, founded the Tudor dynasty. Leeds passed out of royal ownership in 1542: Henry VIII rewarded Sir Anthony St Leger, one of his most loyal ministers, by giving it to him.

The Castle was restored in the 1820s, when the park was laid out on the present design, and again by its last private owner, Lady Baillie, who lived here from 1926. With the help of skilled interior designers, she completely renovated the interior, producing the series of beautifully decorated and furnished rooms the visitor can see today and filling them with exquisite paintings, furniture, tapestries and ceramics from all over the world. Between the wars, Leeds became a fashionable centre of high society, with royalty, ministers and ambassadors all visiting, while during the Second

World War the Petroleum Warfare Department was directed from the Castle. It is thanks to Lady Baillie that the public can now visit Leeds, for on her death in 1974 she gave the Castle to the nation in perpetuity. A foundation now administers the Castle, which is used for medical research seminars and as a conference centre. Occasionally, high-level summit meetings of heads of state are held here, and then once again Leeds reverts to its original purpose as a secure and well-fortified stronghold.

The tour of the Castle takes in many of the main rooms. Les Chambres de la Reine ('the queen's rooms') are furnished as they would have been for Catherine de Valois. The enormous state bed, which looks far too large for comfort, would in fact never have been slept in; its purpose was simply to demonstrate the queen's importance – she herself slept in another room. In the Chambre de Retrait (the bathroom – literally, 'the retreating room'), the simple wooden bath-tub is draped with a fine linen curtain; the bath was filled with herb-scented water carried up from the kitchen. The Henry VIII Banqueting Hall has a magnificent ebony wood floor and carved oak ceiling, and the Thorpe Hall Room has a fine marble fireplace and wood panelling taken from Thorpe Hall near Peterborough. As you explore the Castle the constant glimpses of the lake caught through the small windows and arrow-slits remind you of Leeds's original defensive purpose.

Outside, there are some 500 acres of parkland to explore, as well as aviaries, with many unusual species of parakeet among the inhabitants, a duckery, a woodland garden and an attractive herb garden. A small Dog Collar Museum is housed in the gate tower. There is a restaurant, a well-stocked shop, and, in summer months only, a sandwich and snack bar. A nearby alternative for something to eat is the George Inn in **Leeds** village, ½ mile further along the B2163. The Castle's opening times are daily from 11.00 to 6.00 between late March and the end of October, and from 12.00 to 5.00 at weekends only during the rest of the year; last admission is one hour before closing time. The public entrance is left off the B2163 just south of the junction with the A20, which itself is ½ mile east of junction 8 of the motorway.

JUNCTION 9 GODINTON PARK

The motorway resumes at junction 9, on the western edge of Ashford. **Godinton Park** is a fine 17th-century mansion built on the site of a 14th-century house, part of the original roof of which survives. The finest feature of the house is the magnificent wooden panelling. There are scenes of hunting, pig-sticking and bear-baiting; a unique frieze depicts 17th-century militia drill movements and exercises;

while on the staircase heraldic beasts gaze out from the newel posts. The White Drawing Room, redesigned by Sir Reginald Blomfield at the turn of the century, makes a light and elegant contrast with the rest of the house. The park and gardens were landscaped in the 18th century; the formal garden, which has topiary and cypresses, formal paths and statues, was recreated in the 1890s and surrounded by a great yew hedge. Godinton Park is open on Easter Saturday, Sunday and Monday, and on Sundays and Bank Holidays from June to September, between 2.00 and 5.00. If you are travelling towards Ashford, turn right off the A20 at Potters Corner about 1½ miles before the motorway resumes; the entrance drive, which runs up to the house through fine parkland, is off this road.

Junction 10 is on the eastern edge of Ashford, where there is nothing special to be seen.

JUNCTION 11 PORT LYMPNE

Sir Philip Sassoon was an immensely wealthy socialite, Member of Parliament, collector of paintings and patron of artists, and enthusiastic and knowledgeable devotee of the classical world. **Port Lympne**, the house he built for himself immediately before and after the First World War on the side of the escarpment, with superb views of Romney Marsh, the Channel and across to France, is a rich and vivid reflection of all his cultural and artistic passions. Inside, the Tent Room, which evokes the atmosphere of a Bedouin tent, was created by the painter Rex Whistler; the Catalan painter Sert covered the walls of the Drawing Room with murals of African elephants, native boys and tropical trees and vegetation; and another creation was a Moorish patio of cool marble columns, tiles, fountains and orange trees. Outside, well-planted terraces descended the hillside, with a huge swimming-pool set in the south terrace, while the tennis courts were reached by the 125 steps of the grand Trojan Staircase set in the hillside.

High society visited Port Lympne throughout the 1920s and 1930s, and several peace conferences were held there. Philip Sassoon continued to lavish love and money on his house and gardens, constantly improving and rebuilding, until his death in 1939. Then Port Lympne's fortunes altered for the worse. The Sert murals were destroyed while Allied pilots were billeted in the house during the Second World War. A long period of neglect after the war was not terminated until the zoo-keeper John Aspinall bought the house and its estate in the mid-1970s. His primary purpose was to provide room for his expanding collection of wild animals, until then housed solely on his estate at Howletts, near Canterbury. But he also embarked on a substantial restoration of the house and gardens, now mostly completed, and commissioned the wildlife artist Arthur Spencer-Roberts to replace the Sert murals. The theme of these vivid and brilliantly executed new murals is the wildlife of south-east Asia in its natural environments.

The visit to the **Zoo Park** can take several hours if you want to see all the animals and follow the 2½-mile Zoo Trek path, which takes in all the enclosures. And walk you must, or take the safari bus; in welcome contrast with many safari parks, cars are not admitted. What you will be able to see depends to some extent on the mood of the animals themselves. In keeping with John Aspinall's philosophy of respect for animals – he writes that 'the animals are here for their own sake, to prosper and to reproduce their own kind' – they are kept in large paddocks or enclosures where, if they want to, they can conceal themselves from public view. Herds of deer, antelope, bison and wild horses make a fine sight in the Kentish countryside; among the other creatures here are lions, buffalo, rhinos, elephants, Indian and Siberian tigers, cats and wolves. If wild animals are to be kept in captivity – and all the evidence nowadays is that they must be for their very survival's sake – then the techniques used at Port Lympne seem among the best.

The house, gardens and Zoo Park are open daily from 10.00 to 5.00 or an hour before dusk. A café serves refreshments and light meals. From junction 11, take the B2068 south, turn right almost immediately on to the A20 and follow it for about 1½ miles, past Folkestone Racecourse on the right. Then turn left towards Lympne, and the entrance to the car park is in a little way on the right. Distance from the motorway is 2½ miles.

JUNCTION 11 LYMPNE CASTLE

In Lympne village you can visit **Lympne Castle**, originally built in the 1080s and replaced in the 14th century by the present building. The earlier stronghold was used by Archdeacons of Canterbury, among them Thomas à Becket. The Castle was restored in the early 20th century to its original plan of a central Great Hall with a tower at each end. There can hardly be a stronger or a more strategic position for a castle. The walls grow straight out of the sheer cliff, so steep and high that no invader could scale it, while from the top of the tower there is a commanding view over Romney Marsh and the Channel. The Castle is open from 10.30 to 6.00 between June and September. The Smugglers Tea Room near the Castle and the County Members pub both offer refreshment. **Lympne Church**, next to the Castle, has an early 12th-century tower. To reach Lympne from the motorway, follow the B2068 and then the A20 south for ½ mile, and then, where the A20 swings sharp right, carry straight on along the B2068 again. In Lympne village turn right and immediately left.

JUNCTION 11 BROCKHILL COUNTRY PARK

Brockhill Country Park, once part of a large country estate, would be a good place for a quick walk or picnic. There are paths through the woodland, a lake and streams and – an unusual feature, this – a outdoor game called Badger of Brockhill, which involves hunting the clues through the Park. Turn left on to the A20, and then almost immediately right. The Park entrance is on the right after about 1 mile, after you have passed Sandling station.

Junction 12 is on the northern edge of the Folkestone suburbs, where there is nothing worth leaving the motorway for. The motorway ends 1 mile further on, where it meets the A20 trunk road.

The M27

New Forest to Portsmouth

INTRODUCTION

This is the Solent motorway, linking the New Forest with Southampton and Portsmouth, the two great naval and commercial ports
of southern England. The sensation of history can hardly be escaped
on this route, from the inviting glades and tracks of the New Forest,
established as a royal hunting-ground more than nine centuries ago,
to the waterfront at Southsea where Henry VIII watched the *Mary
Rose*, the pride of his fleet, go under with all hands as she sailed out
to do battle with the French. Generations of soldiers have waited
here to sail to France: at Portchester they paused before Crécy and
Agincourt, and in June 1944 the entire Solent was lined with vessels
waiting to cross the Channel and begin the liberation of Europe
from Nazi oppression. In Portsmouth HMS *Victory* evokes vivid
memories of an earlier national hero, while the chain of fortifications on the hills to the north of the city bears witness to the perennial fear of invasion.

JUNCTION 1 NEW FOREST

The start of the M27 at junction 1 is simply a continuation of the
fast dual carriageway A31 which sweeps across the northern edge of
the **New Forest**, carrying a heavy flow of traffic to and from the
Bournemouth–Poole conurbation. Most of the interesting and
remoter parts of the forest, which has been 'new' since the time of
William the Conqueror, who afforested what had previously been
an area of infertile scrub land and turned it into a royal hunting preserve, are some distance away.

Two short but pleasant detours from the main road are north to
the Rufus Stone and south to the pretty village of Minstead. The
Rufus Stone marks the spot where William II, William the Conqueror's son, was killed while out hunting one day in 1100. The
fatal arrow was shot by Sir Walter Tyrrell, who, so tradition has it,
was aiming at a stag; the arrow glanced, struck the monarch's breast
and killed him instantly. Some historians dispute this innocuous ver-

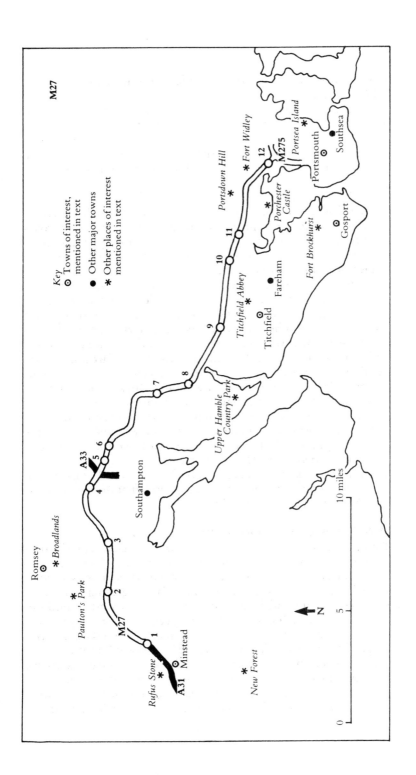

M27

Key
⊙ Towns of interest,
  mentioned in text
● Other major towns
✳ Other places of interest
  mentioned in text

sion of events, claiming that the 'accident' was no accident at all but deliberate murder.

To reach the Stone turn north from the A31 about 1 mile west of junction 1, and follow the side road towards Brook for a few hundred yards. There is a picnic spot opposite the Stone, with pleasant paths leading off through woodland. Sir Walter is commemorated in the name of a pub a short distance further on.

JUNCTION 1 MINSTEAD

Minstead is reached by turning south off the A31 (right if you are travelling east towards the motorway) and following country roads for a couple of miles. The most attractive feature of this pleasant village set in one of the more open parts of the forest is the lovely little **church**, the oldest parts of which date from the 12th century. There is an unusual three-decker pulpit; the lowest deck, entered from the nave, was used by the parish clerk, while from the two upper storeys, accessible only from the chancel, the scriptures are read and the sermon is preached. The fine classical gallery of panelled oak is also worth a look, with, above it, a second gallery added in 1818 in which the local charity school children used to sit. In the graveyard are the tombs of Sir Arthur Conan Doyle and his wife; as well as the celebrated Sherlock Holmes stories, Conan Doyle wrote romances, early science fiction stories and historical novels, one of which, *The White Company*, is set in the countryside around Minstead.

There are plenty of signposted footpaths round and about, while the village pub and the Honeysuckle Restaurant on the Stoney Cross road out of the village offer refreshment.

From Minstead the quickest way back to junction 1 of the motorway is to continue through the village, turn left at the next junction and then left again on to the A337.

JUNCTION 2 PAULTONS PARK

Paultons Park, the main attraction close to junction 2, really does seem to have something for almost everyone. Part of it is a conventional pleasure park, with such irresistible attractions as Captain Blood's Cavern and Kids Kingdom, a shooting gallery and coin-operated Ferraris and bikes. But there are also attractive bird gardens, with over a hundred different species on display, paddocks where grazing animals live, gardens, much of which were landscaped by Capability Brown, a lake fed by the river Cadnam, and attractive woodland. The animals include not only sheep, goats and deer but also more exotic species such as wallabies, llamas and guanacos, and capybaras. These last, which come from South America, are the world's largest living rodents; they look rather like outsize guinea-pigs, grunt a good deal, and enjoy swimming. Other attractions at Paultons include a Village Life display, where you can see a dairy, a wheelwright's and a carpenter's shop and a blacksmith's forge all recreated as they would have appeared at the turn of the century with the correct tools and utensils in place, and the fascinating **Romany Museum**. Here a number of Romany wagons are displayed with details about the Romany way of life. Interestingly, most Romany wagons were built between about 1875 and 1910; before then roads were so poor that Romanies found it more practical to walk from place to place, since then motor transport has taken over.

Paultons Park, which has been developed on part of the old Paultons Estate (the originally 17th-century house burnt down in 1963), is open from 10.00 to 7.00 daily except Christmas Day; last admission is at 5.00, earlier in winter. To do justice to the wide variety of entertainment available you will need to spend several hours here. Leave the M27 at junction 2 and follow the 1-mile spur motorway north; at its end turn left, and the entrance to the Park is on the right after ¾ mile. A variety of refreshments is available, from snacks to full meals; alternatively there is Mortimers pub and restaurant by the Park entrance.

If you are coming from the west, you should leave the motorway at junction 2 for Romsey (described under junction 3 below) and follow the A31 east for 3 miles from the end of the spur motorway.

JUNCTION 3 ROMSEY ABBEY

Romsey is 3½ miles north of junction 3 along the A3057. Although it is only just clear of the busy, over-developed Solent conurbation, Romsey is still very much a peaceful small country town, with some good shops and eating-places, including the Dolphin Hotel and Coffee House. **Romsey Abbey** is the third church on its site; the first, a structure of wood and wattle, was erected in 907 by King Edward the Elder. Work on the present abbey began in 1120 and took 130 years to complete. The south choir and the chancel, completed during the first wave of construction between 1120 and 1140, are glorious examples of late Norman architecture. Tiers of round arches stacked one on another carry the eye up to the roof, the plain stonework lightened by some lovely decoration. The abbey has many treasures worth seeing: they include the 16th-century painted wooden reredos above the north transept altar, a lovely modern embroidered curtain in the south aisle done in Byzantine style, and, behind the altar, a Saxon crucifix dating from about 1000 and depicting Christ as King and the cross as the Tree of Life. Outside, near the abbess's doorway on the south side of the abbey, is an 11th-century rood, or crucifix.

JUNCTION 3 BROADLANDS

Romsey's most famous recent inhabitant, Earl Mountbatten of Burma, first opened his home to the public in 1979, only a few months before his tragic assassination in Ireland; he is buried in the abbey. **Broadlands** is a magnificent Palladian mansion set in lovely parkland running down to the river Test. Among the finest rooms are the Saloon, decorated in a rich neo-classical style of white and gold, the Dining Room, where no fewer than four Van Dyck portraits look down from the walls, and the Wedgwood Room, so called because the decoration is done in the traditional Wedgwood blue and white. Throughout the house there are numerous mementoes of the Mountbatten family – Broadlands is now the home of Lord Romsey, Lord Mountbatten's grandson, and his family – and a stable block has been converted into the **Mountbatten Exhibition**. This is a fascinating audio-visual account of a remarkable career that began with two years at sea during the First World War and culminated in a series of major posts, as Supreme Allied Commander in south-east Asia towards the end of the Second World War, as the last Viceroy and the first Governor-General of India, then as First Sea Lord and, finally, Chief of the Defence Staff.

Broadlands is open daily except Mondays (but including Bank Holidays) from 10.00 to 5.00 between April and July and every day of the week in August and September. There is a self-service restaurant and a picnic area. The main entrance is on the A31 in Romsey, almost equidistant from junctions 2 and 3.

Junctions 4, 5, 6 and 7 all lead off into the Southampton suburbs, where there is nothing special to see. Junction 4 is also the junction with the dual carriageway A33 north to Winchester and the M3 (see pages 109–117).

JUNCTION 8 UPPER HAMBLE COUNTRY PARK

Junction 8 is just a short distance away from the Upper Hamble Country Park and the Hampshire Farm Museum. The **Country Park** is a pleasant area of woods and farmland bordering the river Hamble, just right for a relaxing break from long-distance driving. There are several picnic spots, and a network of pleasant footpaths criss-crosses the woods and runs down to the river. An information and catering kiosk at the **Barnfield picnic meadow** sells light refreshments and dispenses information about activities in the Park.

JUNCTION 8 HAMPSHIRE FARM MUSEUM

If you follow the road through the Park and out into the fields on the far side, you will eventually reach Manor Farm. Once, Manor Farm was a working farm like many others in this area of rich soil and fertile meadowland. Now it has been converted into the **Hampshire Farm Museum**, with the aim of recreating the agricultural way of life between about 1850 and 1950 and of demonstrating the enormous changes in farming methods that took place in those years. The first thing that strikes you is the smell – the authentic smell of an old-fashioned farmyard, where horses, chickens and cows all intermingle – and the human scale of everything. There is no high-tech machinery here, or any ugly prefabricated buildings. This is farming as it used to be, before the accountants and agricultural economists and Euro-experts made the land into big business. Barns and stables, most rescued from farms in and around Hampshire and re-erected here, round the farmyard contain well-designed exhibitions on different aspects of farming and display old tools and equipment. The original farmhouse was built in the 15th century from oak timbers with wattle and daub panels, some of which have been removed to display the method of construction. The farm garden is full of the traditional vegetables, herbs and flowers grown in a country garden in the first half of this century. There are geese and wildfowl on the farm pond, and you can walk down the lane to the old **church** just beyond, of which only the chancel remains.

This Museum, which is one of the most interesting places to visit near the M27, will be sure to keep an entire family amused, whatever their ages. Opening times are daily 10.00 to 6.00 during British Summer Time; during the rest of the year, the Museum closes at 4.00 until 31 January and at 5.00 from 1 February onwards. An attractive farm café serves light meals.

To reach the Country Park and Museum, turn west off the motorway, then go left and almost immediately right. The Museum is about 1½ miles from the entrance to the Country Park; simply follow the road right through the Park and out into the fields behind.

JUNCTION 9 TITCHFIELD ABBEY

Junction 9 leads to **Titchfield Abbey**. Ruined now, but still a noble sight, the abbey has a fascinating history. It was founded in 1232 as a Premonstratensian house. Three hundred years later, when Henry VIII dissolved the monasteries and handed out the spoils to his friends and courtiers, it came into the hands of Thomas Wriothesley, first Earl of Southampton and Lord Chancellor of England. He converted and extended the buildings into a mansion known as

Place House; the magnificent four-storey eight-sided Tudor gate-house dates from this time. The third Earl was Shakespeare's patron. It is claimed that Shakespeare wrote many of his sonnets here, and even that some of his plays were performed here for the first time. In 1647, Charles I spent the night at Titchfield on his way to captivity in Carisbrooke Castle on the Isle of Wight. The house was demolished in 1781. The abbey ruins are open from 9.30 to 1.00 and from 2.00 to 6.30 on Mondays to Saturdays, 2.00 to 6.30 on Sundays, although between 16 October and 14 March the abbey closes at 4.00. From junction 9 take the A27 south for ½ mile, then turn left at the roundabout along Segensworth Road and right at the end; the entrance to the abbey is almost immediately on the right. The Fishermans Rest pub opposite does meals and morning coffee. This route from the motorway runs past **Carron Row Farm Museum and Country Park**, where you can see old farm machinery, shire horses and farm animals and there is also carp fishing and a narrow-gauge railway; but the Hampshire Farm Museum at junction 8 is preferable, in my opinion. **Titchfield** village, on the far side of the A27, has an attractive Georgian square, and many older houses can be seen in the nearby streets.

Junction 10 is a supplementary exit leading into Fareham. You can join the motorway travelling east here, and leave it travelling west.

JUNCTION 11 FORT BROCKHURST

Junction 11 is the exit to take if you want to visit the **Submarine Museum** at Gosport (see pages 107–108) by road, rather than take the far nicer ferry trip across the harbour from Portsmouth. It is a long and uninteresting 5-mile drive through Fareham and scrappy suburbia-cum-countryside to the Museum, although on the outskirts of Gosport you do pass **Fort Brockhurst**, one of the chain of fortifications built to defend Portsmouth and the dockyards during the invasion alarms after the Crimean War. The Fort is a fascinating place, part medieval castle in atmosphere – you enter across a draw-bridge over a water-filled moat, and ramparts form an additional defence – part barrack-like, with a huge parade-ground in the centre. An exhibition tells the story of the development of Portsmouth's defences. The Fort is open from 9.30 to 1.00 and 2.00 to 6.30 Mondays to Saturdays, 2.00 to 6.30 on Sundays, from April to September inclusive.

JUNCTION 11 PORTCHESTER CASTLE

Much nearer junction 11 is **Portchester Castle**, which is clearly visible from the motorway between junctions 11 and 12. The original fortification on this site is Roman, one of the Forts of the Saxon Shore built along the southern and eastern coasts of England. Eight centuries or so later, the Normans simply built their own strongpoint within the Roman site, adding a fortified enclosure in one corner with a great tower, a moat on two sides and a strong gateway tower across it. The result is a magnificent Norman castle set within a Roman fortification, the original walls of which are still standing. The chapel in the south-east corner was originally part of a 12th-century Augustinian priory. Several monarchs stayed at Portchester Castle while visiting Portsmouth; Edward III assembled his troops here before setting sail for France and the Battle of Crécy, as did Henry V before the Battle of Agincourt. Centuries later, another invasion force of many thousands of soldiers came together along the Solent coast to launch the attack on German-occupied France on D-Day 1944. Such is the continuity of history. The Castle is open on Mondays to Saturdays from 9.30 to 6.30 and on Sundays from 2.00 to 6.30, but it closes at 4.00 between 16 October and 14 March. From junction 11 turn south towards Fareham; at the first roundabout turn left on to the A27, then turn right at the second roundabout and follow the signs to the Castle through small suburban roads (2½ miles). To return to the motorway at junction 12, drive straight through **Portchester** village, where the Cormorant pub offers light meals, and then turn right on to the A27; the junction is about 1 mile along the A27.

JUNCTION 12 PORTSDOWN HILL

High above the motorway, on **Portsdown Hill**, a chain of five forts was built in the 1860s to defend Portsmouth from invasion. They cost some £2 million to construct at contemporary prices, and none of them has ever been put into use; not one shot has been fired there in anger. Not for nothing were they nicknamed 'Palmerston's Folly', after the Prime Minister who promoted them. The fear was, as always, of invasion by France – a fear reinforced by two major technical developments that, at least in the minds of nervous military planners, made the garrisons and dockyards at Portsmouth particularly vulnerable. The first was the rifled cannon, which was more accurate and had greater penetrative power and a longer range (about 4½ miles) than any previous weapon. Although the new weapon was a British invention, there was no doubt that the French would soon develop the technology, enabling them to bombard the docks from a safe distance, well out of the way of retaliation from the existing defences. The second development was the steam-powered iron-clad warship, the first of which, the French *La Gloire*, was launched in 1859. These warships were far superior to the Bri-

103

tish fleet, which was in any case dispersed in far-flung seas around the world.

The particular fear in Portsmouth was, paradoxically, of a threat not from the sea but from the land. The French, it was thought, might land somewhere near Bognor Regis and then circle through the Sussex Downs to approach Portsmouth from behind. The idea seems faintly ludicrous now, and with the benefit of hindsight we can see that it was never a realistic possibility. But you need only stand on Portsdown Hill and see the city and the dockyard spread out before you too realize what damage an enemy force could do if it did manage to capture the hill. It was for this reason that the five forts along Portsdown Hill were designed to combat a land attack, with all their firepower concentrated not on the naval base to the south but on the countryside behind, to the north.

JUNCTION 12 FORT WIDLEY

One of the five, **Fort Widley**, is open to the public during summer weekends, and it is well worth making the slightly tiresome drive to it through suburban housing from the motorway. Any hostile French invader, or anyone else for that matter, approaching the Fort from the north (i.e. from the landward side) would have been in for a very nasty surprise. Advancing through what would have seemed quite ordinary fields he would first have found himself on the receiving end of fire from heavy guns mounted on the rampart, and then would have been stopped short at the edge of a steep-sided ditch nearly 40 feet deep and faced with knapped flint to give the maximum richochet. If he were so unwise as to descend into the ditch, more lethal fire from guns mounted in the caponiers and trained down the ditch awaited. All these features of the Fort, plus the network of tunnels built to carry ammunition from the central magazine to the various batteries, can be seen on the tour, which takes about 40 minutes; unaccompanied visits are not permitted.

Fort Widley is open on Saturdays, Sundays and Bank Holidays from 1.30 to 5.30 (the last tour starts at 5.00) between April and September. From junction 12, take the London road, turn left on to the A3 and then after about 1 mile turn left again along Portsdown Hill after passing the entrance to the Queen Alexandra Hospital.

Junction 12 is also the starting-point of the short M275, which carries traffic on to the western side of Portsea Island. From the end of this motorway it is a short and well-signposted drive to two of **Portsmouth**'s best-known sights, HMS *Victory* and the *Mary Rose*, well worth seeing if you have time for a fairly lengthy off-motorway diversion.

HMS Victory

JUNCTION 12 HMS *Victory*

Neither ship needs much introduction. *Victory* was the flagship of Lord Nelson, Commander-in-Chief of the Royal Navy, from 1803, and took part in a series of notable engagements against the French, culminating in the magnificent victory at the Battle of Trafalgar on 21 October 1805, at which the combined French and Spanish fleets were vanquished and 18 of their 33 ships were taken. But *Victory* was badly damaged, and Nelson himself was killed by a shot fired from the French *Redoubtable*. The tour takes in almost the entire ship, which has been restored to her appearance at the time of Trafalgar. You visit Nelson's quarters, relatively spacious in comparison with the cramped accommodation allowed for the crew, and also the cockpit. Normally used as the mess for senior midshipmen and master's mates, in times of battle the cockpit became a makeshift operating theatre. The ship's surgeon operated on the ordinary mess tables, which soon became stained with the blood lost during the frequent amputations necessary. It was here that Nelson was brought after he was shot, and here that he died, whispering his last words: 'Thank God, I have done my duty.'

JUNCTION 12 *Mary Rose*

The dramatic raising of the *Mary Rose* in 1982 from the bottom of the Solent, where she had lain embedded in mud for nearly 450 years, caught the public imagination – and deservedly so, for the operation was an amazing triumph of hope and determination allied with technological expertise. The raising was the culmination of many years of dedicated research by a team of divers-cum-underwater archaeologists, who had already brought to the surface a fascinating collection of over 14,000 artefacts that has compelled many experts on the Tudor period to revise their opinions and provides the visitor with a unique window into everyday Tudor life. The **Museum**, best seen before you visit the ship herself, contains a barber-surgeon's chest packed with jars, jugs, bowls and dressings – there is even an ointment jar with fingerprints in the ointment, as if someone had helped themselves only yesterday; gameboards, dice and a single domino (dominoes had only recently reached England); and book covers, quill pens and ink bottles. There are wooden combs whose fine teeth were designed to get rid of lice and fleas; the skeletons of a flea and of an officer's pet dog have been found; there is a single chamber pot. Among the musical instruments is one thought to be a shawm, an ancestor of the oboe; until this was brought up from the *Mary Rose*, no shawm had survived, although experts knew that there had been such an instrument. The mass of naval and military items – rigging, rope, netting, navigational equipment, arrows, gunnery equipment – is providing historians with vital new information about Tudor warfare.

After looking at the Museum, you move on to the *Mary Rose* herself. The Ship Hall is kept at a constant temperature of 5°C and at 95 per cent humidity, and chilled water is sprayed on to her hull to prevent it drying out and disintegrating. The ship is a magnificent sight, her port side rearing up tall and proud. So real and lifelike is she that it is easy to transport yourself back 400 years and see her proudly sailing up the Solent to meet her French rivals.

The third attraction in the Dockyard complex in Portsmouth is the **Royal Naval Museum**, whose galleries recount naval history from Tudor times to the Falklands campaign in 1982.

Opening times for the *Mary Rose* are 10.30 to 5.30 daily, closing at 5.00 between October and March; last admission is 1 hour before closing time. HMS *Victory* is open on Mondays to Saturdays from 10.30 to 5.30, on Sundays from 1.00 to 5.00; closing time from November to February is 5.00. The Royal Naval Museum's times are 10.30 to 5.00 daily. There is a not especially pleasant café in the dockyard complex.

JUNCTION 12 HMS *Warrior*

In 1987, a third ship is due to join the *Victory* and the *Mary Rose*.

HMS *Warrior*, the world's first ocean-going iron-clad battleship and the only surviving iron-clad in the world, will arrive in Portsmouth. The pride of the Royal Navy when she was launched in 1860, she became obsolescent within 10 years, so rapid was the pace of technical change. She then served periods as a coastguard ship and a storage hulk before becoming a floating jetty in Pembroke Dock, Wales, for warships taking on fuel oil. In 1979 she was rescued and towed to Hartlepool, on the north-east coast, where she has undergone a complete restoration.

JUNCTION 12 D-DAY MUSEUM & SOUTHSEA CASTLE

There are many other museums and places of interest in **Portsmouth** and **Southsea**, although most are only reached after a drive through busy streets. Certainly worth seeing is the **D-Day Museum** on Clarence Esplanade, which is open daily from 10.30 to 5.30. The centrepiece is the magnificent Overlord Embroidery, a stunning visualization of the story of the preparations for the invasion and of D-Day itself commissioned by Lord Dulverton and created by a team of embroideresses from the Royal School of Needlework. There is also an excellent audio-visual programme, and the displays in the rest of the Museum, which are rather cramped and noisy and not particularly easy for children to understand, fill in more details of the D-Day story. Almost next door to the Museum is **Southsea Castle**, built by Henry VIII as part of his defences against invasion by France or Spain. Inside there are displays of military history and local archaeology. Opening times for the Castle are daily from 10.30 to 5.30. On the other side of the D-Day Museum is a marine attraction called **Sea Life**, which offers a full-scale simulation of a ship's bridge, 'touch pools' which you can dip into to examine the starfish, sea urchins, etc. and an ocean reef, where you can see all kinds of exotic sea creatures. Sea Life is open daily and also has a restaurant that can be used without visiting the exhibition.

JUNCTION 12 ROYAL NAVY SUBMARINE MUSEUM

Possibly the most unusual excursion from Portsmouth is to take the ferry across the harbour to Gosport and visit HMS *Alliance* and the **Royal Navy Submarine Museum**. Ferries run every 15 minutes from Portsmouth Harbour Station, a short distance from the Dockyard, and the brief trip provides a good view of shipping in the harbour and of HMS *Foudroyant*, the oldest British warship still afloat, which is used nowadays as a training ship. From the Gosport landing-stage, follow the waterside path to the left, turn left across the bridge and left again into the naval base, following signposts to the Museum entrance; the walk from the ferry takes 10 to 15 minutes. The highlight of the Museum is undoubtedly the tour of HMS *Alliance*, which takes 30 to 45 minutes. *Alliance* was completed in 1947 and remained in service until 1973. The atmosphere inside is dank and airless, with pipes and dials everywhere and the insistent glare of artificial lighting. Accommodation for the crew is minute – a series of narrow bunks stacked along the companionways – and that for the officers is not much better, while it is hard to believe that meals were cooked and bread was baked for 65 men in the tiny galley. Imagine living in *Alliance* while she remained underwater for as long as two months. The rest of the Museum contains interesting displays on the development of submarines and their role in wartime. The Royal Navy's first-ever submarine, HM *Submarine No. 1* can also be visited. Built in 1901, she was the prototype on which all later submarines have been based; her simple and unsophisticated interior makes a fascinating contrast with *Alliance*. The Museum is open daily from 10.30 to 4.30 between April and October, closing at 3.30 for the rest of the year; a small café serves refreshments and also 'Original Possers Rum as served to the Royal Navy'.

The M3

Sunbury to Winchester

INTRODUCTION

The M3 runs from London's outer suburbs to the edge of the historic city of Winchester, which was for a long time England's capital. The journey falls into four distinct stages. First there is the crowded and characterless land on the edge of London to get through. Then comes a long stretch through the heathlands of Surrey and northern Hampshire, where the atmosphere is distinctly military, as an excursion from junction 4 to Aldershot will prove. Next the motorway briefly touches the high Hampshire Downs near Basingstoke, before it descends to the lush, green scenery of the Itchen valley near Winchester.

JUNCTION 1 HAMPTON COURT PALACE

The motorway begins at Sunbury in the outer suburbs of London. The nearest place of interest is **Hampton Court Palace**, a few miles south-east along the A308. The Palace itself can be visited, together with the attractive gardens and park, and you can also try to find your way out of the celebrated but rather shabby and disappointing maze. Thomas Wolsey, soon to be appointed Cardinal and Henry VIII's Chancellor, began building here in 1514; what was ostensibly a private residence soon became one of the grandest mansions in the land. Within 15 years, Wolsey had fallen from favour. The King appropriated Wolsey's property, and set about creating what became the finest and most elaborate of all the royal palaces. The turreted and battlemented Great Gatehouse seen as you approach from the main entrance is of one of the finest examples of Tudor architecture in the country. Henry, who used Hampton Court as a country hunting retreat, came here with five of his six wives in turn. The arms of Anne Boleyn are worked into the decorations that embellish the roof of the Great Hall – although by the time work had finished on this most elaborate and richly decorated chamber Anne had been beheaded and her place, both at the king's side and in

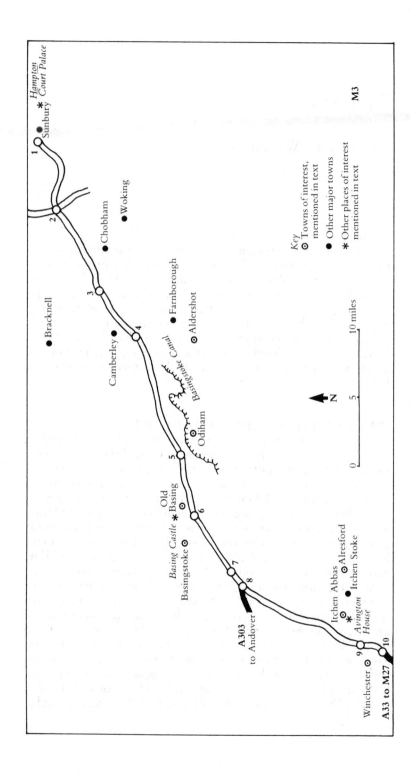

M3

his bed, had been taken by Jane Seymour. A second major wave of rebuilding took place at the end of the 17th century, when William and Mary commissioned Christopher Wren to create new State Apartments. The best exterior view of these splendid rooms in classical French renaissance style is from Fountain Court. The last monarch to live in Hampton Court was George II. Since then it has been used for 'grace-and-favour' apartments – lodgings offered to deserving people in some way connected with the Crown – and since the mid-19th century it has been open to the public: an early tourist attraction for people from the capital enjoying a day out along the Thames. The fire in summer 1985 destroyed several rooms in the Palace, but these are undergoing restoration. Outside you can see the magnificent Great Vine, first planted in 1769 by Capability Brown; enjoy the formal gardens, most of which date from the 18th century, although some parts are recreations of the original Tudor gardens; and stroll through the park and along the river bank. There is a pleasant café in the gardens. Opening times are 9.30 to 6.00 Mondays to Saturdays, 11.00 to 6.00 Sundays, between April and September; winter times are 9.30 to 5.00, 2.00 to 5.00 on Sundays. The gardens are open daily throughout the year from 7.00 until half an hour before dusk; the maze is open from March to September.

Junction 2 is the junction with the M25, and there is no access on to ordinary roads.

Junction 3 leads to Woking, Chobham, Camberley and Bracknell (for Bracknell see page 131, and there is nothing worth leaving the motorway for.

JUNCTION 4 ALDERSHOT
Junction 4 is the junction for military buffs. That is no surprise at all, since **Aldershot** lies 3 miles to the south. Perhaps rather more surprisingly, you may find you enjoy visiting Aldershot even if you are not an enthusiast for things military, or do not have an army background. As well as the Museum, there are a number of interesting Victorian buildings to see, and it is possible to get some sense of what army life was like in the 19th century. The **Military Museum** in Queens Avenue sets the scene. The Army selected Aldershot as a summer training camp in 1855; the sandy soil was ideal for exercises and manoeuvring, and men and *matériel* could easily be rushed to the south coast in the event of an invasion. The summer camp soon became the country's major military base; Aldershot is the only complete military town built in England since the Roman occupation. Living quarters remained makeshift for some time, and gen-

erations of soldiers and their wives had to put up with some pretty uncomfortable living conditions – the first huts were neither wind- nor rain-proof – as well as strict discipline and the regular round of manoeuvres, reviews and tattoos that were the main ingredients of military life in the 19th century. The Military Museum recreates the early years of the military camp, shows in detail the grand recon- struction that took place in the 1880s and 1890s, when brick bar- racks, schools, a hospital, gas works, reservoir and many other amenities were built, and recounts the later history of the town. There is a fascinating recreation of a barrack room in about 1900. Regulations current at that time provided for each soldier to be issued with a paliasse every three months and a clean sheet every month; food was brought over from the kitchen in pails and eaten, at best lukewarm, at a table in the barrack room. It was during the late 19th century that the Military Town acquired its own by-laws and came under the control of the Military Police – who continue to exercise considerable powers, as large signboards at the boundary of the military area make clear. The Military Town was rebuilt once again in the 1960s, when most of the Victorian quarters were replaced by what may well be more convenient and comfortable offices and housing but are certainly less visually interesting. A Town Trail guides visitors around what remains of the Victorian Military Town, including the Cambridge Military Hospital, the Prince Consort's Library and the Royal Garrison Church. The Mili- tary Museum is open daily from 10.00 to 5.00 between March and October, closing at 4.30 for the rest of the year. Take the A321 south from the motorway, and almost immediately turn right on to the A325 through Farnborough towards Aldershot. At the edge of Aldershot turn left on to the A3011 and then right down Queens Avenue.

There are many other smaller, specialist museums in the Alder- shot area. These include: Airborne Forces Museum, Gurkha Museum, Royal Corps of Transport Museum, Royal Army Medical Corps Museum. Royal Army Ordnance Museum, Royal Army Dental Corps Museum, Army Physical Training Corps Museum, Queen Alexandra's Royal Nursing Corps Museum. Further details are available from the Aldershot Tourist Information Centre, Queens Avenue, Aldershot (telephone Aldershot (0252) 20968).

JUNCTION 5 BASINGSTOKE CANAL

Junction 5 offers a complete contrast, in the form of the peaceful, not to say virtually forgotten, **Basingstoke Canal**. Built in the late 18th century to carry agricultural produce from the fertile farms of north Hampshire and Surrey to London, the canal linked Basingstoke with the river Wey, which is itself a tributary of the Thames. The canal prospered for a few decades, but by the middle of the 19th century the railway had become an unchallengeable competitor, offering a far quicker (a few hours instead of several days) and more efficient route to the capital. The last barge to travel west from Aldershot took no fewer than three months to make its way through the weed-infested canal. That was in 1914, and after that decay continued unchecked. Now, however, all that has changed, and after a mammoth restoration project that has already lasted nearly 10 years and should be completed by the end of the 1980s all but the western seven miles of the canal have been restored, and are used for fishing, walking, boating and many other recreational activities. The blockage at the western end is caused by **Greywell Tunnel**, nearly ¾ mile long, which has collapsed beyond repair. The tunnel, which has been designated a Site of Special Scientific Interest, is now home to a large colony of bats, thought to be about 500 strong; winter is the time to come if you want to see them, and also other wildlife which find the tunnel a comfortable and warm place (the temperature is a constant 54°F) for hibernation.

JUNCTION 5 ODIHAM

There is a pleasant walk along the towpath from the tunnel, which is only about 1 mile from the motorway. Drive west towards Odiham along the A287 and almost immediately turn right on to a side road signposted to Greywell. Soon you will reach a T-junction by the Fox and Goose pub. Park near here, walk back to the junction and take the narrow footpath to the left a short way down the side road to **Odiham**. This reaches the towpath in a couple of hundred yards; when I was there, one warm autumn afternoon, the birds were singing and I felt I had stumbled on some magical, half-hidden, world. The towpath walk to Odiham passes **Odiham Castle**, of which the shell of the great tower remains. This was one of King John's favourite castles, and it was from here, one day in 1215, that he set out to ride to Runnymede, where he signed the Magna Carta.

Another pleasant canal-side spot is at **Odiham Wharf**, just beyond the attractive Georgian town centre, where there are some pleasant little shops and good eating-places, including the Raffles coffee house and the George pub. For the Wharf, turn left off the far end of the High Street, drive past the Water Witch pub, over the canal and into the car park. There are picnic areas for outdoor eating, or you can buy a sandwich in the pub and sit on the edge of the canal; unfortunately the atmosphere is somewhat spoilt by the noise of traffic on the nearby bypass. From the motorway, take the A287 towards Odiham, turn right at the first roundabout on to the

A32, continue on the same road at the next roundabout, and then turn left into the High Street.

JUNCTION 6 BASINGSTOKE

Junction 6 leads to **Basingstoke**, which is a busy shopping and commercial centre. The **Willis Museum and Art Gallery** in New Street, about 200 yards from the main shopping centre, is an excellent local museum, concentrating on the natural history, geology, archaeology and history of the area, and also boasts an interesting collection of clocks and watches; Basingstoke used to be an important watchmaking centre. Two of the Museum's curiosities are the curved tusk of a woolly mammoth found near Odiham and the country's first post-box. Opening hours are Tuesdays to Sundays 10.00 to 5.00.

JUNCTION 6 BASING CASTLE

Rather more suitable for a relaxing off-motorway break are the ruins of **Basing Castle**, roughly 2 miles from the motorway. The earliest parts of the Castle were built soon after the Norman Conquest, although archaeologists have found evidence of much older settlements. Over the centuries Basing expanded to become one of the largest private mansions in the country. In its heyday in the 16th century, when it was the property of William Paulet, a courtier who served several monarchs, it covered no fewer than 8 acres and was more extensive and more grandiose than many royal palaces. Then came the passions and turmoil of the Civil War. In an epic siege Basing held out for three years in the Royalist cause. Ultimately resistance was in vain, and Cromwell's forces destroyed almost all the buildings. A well-laid-out display recounts the history of Basing, and visitors can explore the medieval earthworks and the remains of the Tudor mansion excavated by archaeologists. Also open to the public is a magnificent 16th-century **tithe barn**, said to be one of the finest in the country; this was almost the only building on the site to survive the siege. A pleasant path leads from the Castle car park, which is signposted from junction 6, to the Castle itself alongside the river Lodden and past ancient fishponds. During June, July and August the Castle is open on Tuesdays, Wednesdays, Fridays and Saturdays from 2.00 to 6.00, and on Sundays and Bank Holidays from 11.00 to 6.00; in April, May and September opening times are 2.00 to 6.00 on Saturdays, Sundays and Bank Holidays. The tea room (open on Sundays and Bank Holidays only) offers refreshments, while in the pleasant village of Old Basing there is the Crown pub and near the car park are the Millstone pub and Bartons Mill Restaurant.

Junction 7 leads to the western edge of Basingstoke, where there is nothing worth leaving the motorway for.

Junction 8 gives access on to the fast dual carriageway A303 that leads to Andover, southern Wiltshire and Dorset.

JUNCTION 9 WINCHESTER

Junction 9 is immediately east of **Winchester** town centre, which is well signposted from the motorway. There is plenty to see in this historic city, which is an ideal place to stroll around, admiring the

The west window of Winchester Cathedral

many historic buildings and enjoying the shops. The lovely **cathedral**, the second longest medieval building in the world, was built over three centuries and contains the work of some of the finest craftsmen of the Middle Ages; there are also the tombs of many monarchs, while Izaak Walton and Jane Austen are among the other famous people buried here. Look out for the carvings on the 12th-century black marble font – a boy being rescued from drowning and decapitated heads being restored to their bodies are among the legends from the life of St Nicholas which are illustrated – and the lovely chantry chapel of William of Wykeham. It was William of Wykeham who founded **Winchester College** in 1382; the pupils are known as Wykehamists to this day. A walk through the attractive cathedral close and then across College Street brings you to the College, where some of the oldest buildings, including the chapel and the 15th-century chantry and cloisters, can be seen on the guided tours laid on daily between April and September. **Castle Hall** (open daily), all that remains of the original castle and now sandwiched in the middle of Victorian and late 20th-century buildings, is one of the finest surviving medieval halls in the country; in 1603 Sir Walter Raleigh was tried here and condemned to death. The great table, 18 feet in diameter, that originally stood in the Hall and now hangs on one of its walls may be known as 'King Arthur's Round Table' but has, it has now been conclusively established, no connection whatsoever with King Arthur and his knights; it was made almost 1000 years after that legendary monarch is said to have lived. Other museums in Winchester are the City Museum, Westgate Museum, and three separate regimental museums, of the Royal Green Jackets, the Royal Hampshire Regiment and the Royal Hussars.

JUNCTION 9 ALRESFORD
Alresford, 7 miles east of junction 9 along the A31, is a pleasant alternative diversion from the motorway. There are in fact two Alresfords: Old and New. The original old village lies on the far side of what used to be an episcopal reservoir, created in the 12th century to make the river Itchen navigable, and is now merely a large pond. The new village, which itself dates back to before the Conquest, straddles the A31. There are two spacious main streets with elegant 18th-century houses and some good shops and eating-places; Tiffins is an attractive place to have tea. Alresford is also the western terminus of the Mid-Hants Railway – nicknamed the Watercress Line after the extensive watercress beds hereabouts. The line, which first opened in 1865, remained a typical country branch route throughout its life, finally closing in 1973. It was not long before local enthusiasts were putting forward plans to reopen the line with steam haulage; after the usual lengthy negotiations with British Rail trains ran again in 1977. At first the new company operated from Alresford to Ropley only, but since 1985 trains have been running the 10 miles through to Alton, where there is a connection with British Rail. A variety of steam engines and rolling stock is in operation. A regular timetable is worked on Saturdays, Sundays and Bank Holidays in March, April, May, September and October, daily except Mondays in June and July, and every day during the school summer holidays. There are also weekend trips during December.

JUNCTION 9 AVINGTON HOUSE

A pleasant back route to Alresford avoiding the busy A31 is to leave the motorway at junction 9, drive briefly north on the A34 and then the A33 and then turn right on to the B3047 which runs along the Itchen valley through Itchen Abbas and Itchen Stoke to New Alresford. A right turn by the Plough Inn in Itchen Abbas brings you to **Avington House**, which is predominantly 18th century, although some parts are older. The State Rooms can be seen (Avington's celebrated visitors include Charles II and his Nell Gwyn and, a century and a half later, the Prince Regent and his Mrs Fitzherbert), and there are long walks to be taken in the park. Opening times are 2.00 to 6.00 on Wednesdays to Sundays in August only; teas are available.

Junction 10 leads directly into the dual carriageway A33, which after about 8 miles meets the M27 at junction 4 of that motorway (see page 100).

The M4

Chiswick to Cross Hands

INTRODUCTION

The M4 is a motorway of contrasts: contrasts both in the surrounding landscape and in the places to visit nearby. From west London the route follows the over-populated Thames valley west to Reading. There is higher ground next, the Berkshire and Wiltshire Downs and the southern flank of the Cotswolds, then the descent to cross the river Severn. Up to this point the motorway passes through what must be one of the most prosperous parts of Britain. Berkshire is one of *the* counties for the well-heeled motorized commuter. If there were a record for the number of sleek Rovers, Volvos, Audis and Mercedes carried per minute, the M4 would surely hold it. The towns near the motorway – Maidenhead, Reading, Swindon – have all done pretty well for themselves too. The countryside reflects this general well-being. Warm, soft and mellow are the descriptions that come to mind. It is a gentle, embracing land, not a challenging one, and the sights off the motorway – principally country mansions and Roman remains – also have an air of settled civilization.

The contrast when you cross the Severn is a telling one. In many ways Wales is still a separate nation, and certainly a land with its own very definite, individual identity. It is poorer and more rugged, and its landscape has conspired against the people, resisting rather than aiding their efforts to win a livelihood. The motorway keeps to the coastal strip, confined between the sea and the mining valleys and barren hilltops behind. The evidence of past industrial exploitation, and present industrial decline, is clear. The off-motorway attractions are more varied than in England: castles built by the Norman invaders to meet resistance stronger and more prolonged here than almost anywhere else in the kingdom; magnificent forest and foreshore walks; and some interesting sites from the Industrial Revolution.

The start of the M4 at junction 1 is simply a continuation of the A4, which leaves London along the Cromwell Road and over the

Hammersmith flyover. There is a bunch of remarkable attractions in the immediate surroundings here. If you want a break at the start or end of a long motorway haul, this is definitely the place to take it, because the next few exits all lead to pretty uninteresting areas.

HOGARTH'S HOUSE & CHISWICK HOUSE

About ½ mile before the official start of the M4, the main road swings right at the roundabout under the Chiswick flyover, so flimsy-looking it always reminds me of a fairground rollercoaster. Here, ignored by the incessant traffic, is a reminder that Chiswick once knew more pastoral days: **Hogarth's House**. This was not Hogarth's town house but his country residence. What a shocking contrast there must have been 200 years ago between the orchards and fields here and the London the artist portrayed with such savage humour and anger. Many of his engravings are on display in the House, which is open daily except Tuesdays from 11.00 to 6.00 (Sundays from 2.00 to 6.00), closing between October and March at 4.00. The House is closed from the first Monday in September for two weeks, and also around New Year and on Good Friday.

Hogarth was a fierce moralist who lived in a plain, unassuming house. Richard Boyle, third Earl of Burlington, his immediate neighbour at **Chiswick House**, was not and did not. The House, designed by the owner himself and the architect William Kent, has been described – surely correctly – as the finest Palladian building in Great Britain. The downstairs rooms are restrained and classical, the upstairs ones splendidly exuberant. In the gardens statues and follies, vistas, lakes and cascades abound. The whole place is a wonderful vision of Italy amid inter-war suburbia and the noise and aggravation of the road west. Opening times are daily from 9.30 to 6.30 between mid-March and mid-October and in winter from 9.30 to 4.00 Wednesdays to Sundays only. The most convenient entrance is in Burlington Lane: carry straight on at the roundabout if you are coming from central London, turn right if you are travelling east.

JUNCTIONS 1 & 2 KEW BRIDGE STEAM MUSEUM

Junction 1 is only for traffic making the direct A4/M4 link in either direction. Traffic from other roads has to use junction 2, at which you can join the westbound carriageway and leave the eastbound one. In Green Dragon Lane, on your right immediately after Kew Bridge station on the A315, you reach the **Kew Bridge Steam Museum**, identifiable by its stand-pipe tower. A fascinating steam museum is housed here – not railway steam, but magnificent steam engines that were used to pump much of London's water supply during the last century, and well into the present one too. Six large

M4

Ealing

Ealing

Osterley Park
Syon House
Kew Gardens
Richmond

Feltham

Thames

1
2

Slough

M25

Heathrow
Airport

Windsor

Bourne End
Marlow

Cliveden

Maidenhead

Cookham

Courage Shire
Horse Centre

Bracknell

Wokingham

Wellington Country Park

Stratfield
Saye House

Silchester

Dinton Pastures
Country Park

Reading

Kennet & Avon Canal

Pangbourne

Newbury

Snelsmore
Common
Country Park

Donnington Castle

Ridgeway Path

Littlecote
House

Hungerford

Swindon

Coate Water
Country Park

Lydiard Country Park

Malmesbury

Liddington Castle

Barbury Castle

Sheldon
Manor

Chippenham

Castle
Combe

Key
⊙ Towns of interest,
   mentioned in text
● Other major towns
✳ Other places of interest
   mentioned in text

N

0   5   10 miles

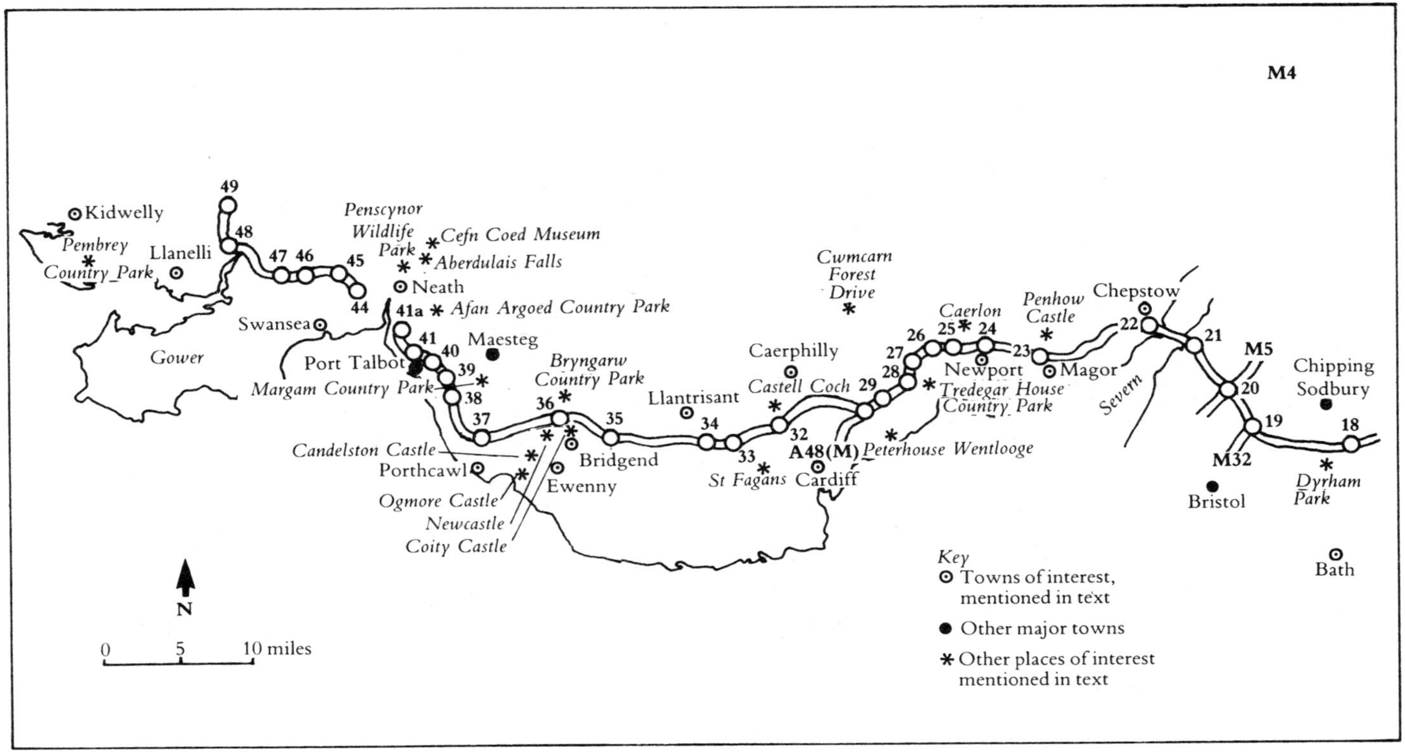
M4
Kidwelly
Pembrey Country Park
Llanelli
49
48
47
46
45
44
Gower
Swansea
Penscynor Wildlife Park
Cefn Coed Museum
Aberdulais Falls
Neath
41a
Afan Argoed Country Park
41
40
39
38
Port Talbot
Margam Country Park
Maesteg
Bryngarw Country Park
37
36
35
Candelston Castle
Porthcawl
Ogmore Castle
Newcastle
Coity Castle
Bridgend
Ewenny
Llantrisant
34
33
32
St Fagans
Caerphilly
Castell Coch
Cumcarn Forest Drive
A48(M)
Cardiff
Peterhouse Wentlooge
29
28
27
26
25
24
Caerlon
Newport
Tredegar House Country Park
23
Penhow Castle
Magor
Chepstow
22
Severn
21
M5
20
19
M32
18
Bristol
Chipping Sodbury
Dyrham Park
Bath
Key
Towns of interest, mentioned in text
Other major towns
Other places of interest mentioned in text
N
0
5
10 miles

engines are run regularly, including three Cornish beam pumping engines. The Museum has five of these in all, a quarter of the world's total population, plus a number of other smaller stationary steam and internal combustion engines. Other items of interest include a forge and a 2-inch narrow-gauge railway, and an exhibition of items to do with London's water supply. The Museum is open daily, except the week before Christmas, from 11.00 to 5.00; the engines are in steam at weekends and on Bank Holiday Mondays. There is a shop and a tea room. Just a little further along the A315 is the **Musical Museum**. Its home is a Victorian church, nicknamed, for obvious reasons, St George's by the Gas Holder. Every imaginable type of automatic musical instrument is displayed here – and some you will never have imagined! Among them are the Wurlitzer Theatre organ, 10 re-enacting pianos played from paper rolls, a self-playing violin· and a race-horse piano, music boxes, barrel organs and pipe organs; many are the only working examples left in the world. The Museum is open from 2.00 to 5.00 at weekends between April and October for two conducted tours of 1½ hours each, during which some of the instruments are demonstrated. The Watermans Arts Centre a little further along Brentford High Street does meals and light refreshments.

JUNCTIONS 1 & 2 ROYAL BOTANIC GARDENS

Over Kew Bridge on the South Circular Road (the A205), turn right immediately for the **Royal Botanic Gardens**, Kew. How can one possibly do justice to their 300 acres? There are exotic species from virtually every country in the world to admire. You can stroll along formal walks, or across the lawns and through the tree plantations to the lake and the river beyond, with Syon Park majestic on the far bank. There are glasshouses to visit: the Temperate House, the new Princess of Wales Conservatory, which in 10 computer-controlled environments houses a fascinating diversity of tropical plants and has exciting habitat displays with mangrove swamp, aquaria, a Namib Desert area, cloud forest and tropical dry forest, and many more. My favourite spot is the Queen's Garden behind Kew Palace, a handsome mansion in 17th-century Dutch style that must surely be the jolliest and most comfortable of all London's royal palaces. The garden is laid out as it would have been in the 17th century, gravel walks leading between neatly clipped and trained herb bushes, with an elegant little gazebo perched on a tiny knoll. The Gardens open daily at 10.00 (the glasshouses at 11.00) and close between 4.00 and 8.00 according to season; times for Kew Palace are 11.00 to 5.30. There is a Refreshment Pavilion and a Tea Bar; outside, there are a number of restaurants near Kew Green, including the Maids of Honour tea shop on the Kew Road. If you want something stronger, cross Kew Bridge and turn sharp right along the embankment. This is **Strand-on-the-Green,** a tiny village all but submerged between the river and the incessant traffic behind. But it manages to preserve its own pleasant rather twee atmosphere, and does have two excellent pubs, the City Barge and the Bull's Head.

JUNCTIONS 1 & 2 SYON HOUSE
There are numerous other excursions hereabouts. **Richmond** is only a couple of miles to the south. There are excellent shops and the huge royal park is one of the few places in London where you can almost feel yourself to be in the country. On the north bank of the Thames, take the A315 through **Brentford** village until you reach the canal. The towpath here makes a good walk, and although you pass right under the elevated section of the motorway there is a country feel about it. Beyond the canal, a left turn brings you to **Syon House,** already seen from Kew. The interior could not present a greater contrast with the severely Tudor exterior. It is Robert Adam at his most expansive and brilliant: five rooms of dazzling virtuosity, among the most magnificent in England. The gardens are the work of another master, Capability Brown, who created wide lawns and tree and shrubbery areas. The walks here are lovely, almost irrespective of the season, and Charles Fowler's Great Conservatory, the inspiration for Paxton's Crystal Palace, houses plants, an aviary and an aquarium. There is a 6-acre rose garden and a huge garden centre as well. The House is open from 12.00 to 5.00 on Sundays to Thursdays between April and September, and on Sundays only in October. The gardens are open from 10.00 throughout the year, closing at 6.00 between March and October and at dusk the rest of the year. Syon is also the home of the London Butterfly House, where butterflies from all over the world fly freely in a vast tropical house, and a Motor Museum, where more than 90 vehicles are on display. The Motor Museum opens at 10.00 and closes at 5.30, 4.00 between November and February. The Butterfly House is open from 10.00 to 5.00 from mid-February to November, 10.00 to 3.30 during the rest of the year.

JUNCTIONS 1 & 2 OSTERLEY PARK
One more attraction beckons before we set off west: **Osterley Park.** Drive west along the A4, the Great West Road, and turn right up Thornbury Road just before Osterley underground station (a classic example of 1930s London Transport architecture). Once upon a time, and not so long ago either, the Great West Road was a living example of the wonderfully flamboyant art deco style, and the

The garden entrance at Osterley

factory and office buildings here were decorated with classical columns, baroque ironwork and vivid colours. It is all rather sad and run-down now. Most tragic of all, the Firestone Building – which would not have looked out of place on a Hollywood set – was demolished, only days before it was due to be listed for preservation. Osterley is another Robert Adam remodelling of a 16th-century original. There are some splendid rooms, notably the Eating Room, the Library and the Drawing Room, all richly and elaborately decorated. The grounds are flat and uninteresting, and walks there are rather spoilt by the M4, which runs straight through in a cutting. The stables and clock tower from the original house, and two 18th-century summer-houses, are worth a look. The house is open daily Tuesdays to Sundays and on Bank Holidays from 11.00 to 5.00. There is a pleasant tea room, open in the summer only.

Now we finally get on our way, hurrying past a succession of uninteresting junctions. Junction 3 leads north to Hayes and south to Feltham, and there is nothing to recommend at either. You can get to Osterley Park (see above) by leaving the motorway here, driving south on the A312 and then turning left on to the A4.

JUNCTION 4 HEATHROW AIRPORT

Heathrow Airport lies south of junction 4, along a 1½-mile motor-way spur ending at junction 4a. The airport is the fifth largest in the world in terms of total passenger traffic; some 31.5 million passengers used the four passenger terminals in 1986. If you want to join them, and the 47,000-plus people who work at the airport, there is a spectator viewing area, open daily from 9.30 to dusk. From here the majority of the average 776 daily aircraft movements can be seen.

Between junctions 4 and 5, the M4 and M25 (see pages 56–73) cross at junction 15 of the M25.

My hope was, when I researched junction 5, to find a nice, quiet canal walk along the Grand Union, just to the north of junction 5. No such luck. Access to the towpath is difficult, and the country is nondescript.

Junction 6 brings some relief. To the north there is Slough and beyond the town Burnham Beeches, described under junction 2 of the M40 (see page 164). Take the A355 north to Farnham Common (about 4 miles).

JUNCTION 6 WINDSOR

To the south a short drive along the A332 and then left at the first roundabout brings you to the centre of **Windsor**. I arrived early one autumn morning and stopped the car by the Thames. It was magical: mist rising off the river, branches slowly dripping the morning dew, and a hint of sun in the air. There is a pleasant walk along the river, with gentle water-meadows opposite. Everywhere you go in Windsor, the **Castle** dominates. As one of the Royal Family's homes, it is inevitably a No. 1 tourist attraction, and very crowded. Not all the Castle, which William the Conqueror built soon after 1066 as part of a ring of fortifications around London, can be seen. But normally the Precincts, State Apartments, St George's Chapel, Queen Mary's Dolls' House and the exhibition of drawings are open to the public. Of these, the chapel and the State Apartments are undoubtedly the most interesting. Ten kings and queens are buried in the Chapel, which is one of the finest ecclesiastical buildings in the country and a masterpiece of the late Perpendicular style: 'visually thrilling', Pevsner calls it in his *Buildings of England*. Every June, on Garter Day, the 26 Knights of the Most Noble Order of the Garter gather here to worship in the presence of the Sovereign of their Order, Her Majesty the Queen. Their banners hang above the choir stalls, and above them great heraldic badges are set in the roof. The State Apartments are magnificent rooms, with stunning views north across the Thames. And so they should be. George IV, the last of five monarchs to remodel them, spent no less than £1 million on them – and that was in the 1820s. A dolls' house is not that unusual, but an architect-designed one is something different – and Queen Mary's Doll's House was the work of Sir Edwin Lutyens, the great establishment architect of the early 20th century. Inside there are books for the dolls written by contemporary authors, and the plumbing and electric light are fully functioning. The exhibition of drawings is a changing selection from the Queen's large and priceless collection. Holbein and Leonardo da Vinci are among the artists represented.

Opening times for these attractions are complicated, and if you are especially anxious to see something ring the tourist office on Windsor 852010 beforehand. The precincts always open at 10.00. In the winter (broadly speaking late October to late March) they close at 4.15; between late March and the end of April and in September and most of October at 5.15; and in the summer at 7.15. The Chapel is open in summer from 10.45 to 4.00, Sundays 2.00 to 4.00; in winter closing time is 15 minutes earlier. The State Apartments, dolls' house and exhibition of drawings all open at 10.30 on weekdays, closing at 3.00 between late October and late March, and at 5.00 for the rest of the year; on Sundays from 1.30 to 5.00 between May and late October only. *But* note that the State Apartments are always closed when the Queen is in residence: usually between mid-March and early May, the end of May to near the end of June, and most of December. They may well be shut at other times too, during a state visit, for instance.

Apart from the royal sights, Windsor is an excellent place for an hour or two's window shopping, with good boutiques, antique shops and so forth, plus a full range of eating-places. One of the best is the Country Kitchen Restaurant in King Edward Court, which offers salads, wholefood and hot dishes. Other attractions in the town are the **Household Cavalry Museum**, which has a comprehensive regimental collection (open Mondays except Bank Holidays to Fridays from 10.00 to 1.00 and 2.00 to 5.00 and on Sundays from May to September to 4.00); and the **Royal Mews Exhibition**, which contains a collection of royal carriages and coaches, a display of state harness and of driving and riding bits, and a three-stall stable with horse models; opening times are the same as at the dolls' house. Although **Windsor and Eton Central Station**, with its imposing approach road, is still a British Rail station, most of the building has been taken over by the **Royalty and Empire Exhibition**, which recreates in elaborate detail the scene when Queen Victoria met guests here as they arrived for a state visit. A fire burns in the waiting-room grate, the station-master hovers anxiously, troops are lined up waiting to be inspected. There is also an audio-visual presentation on Queen Victoria's reign entitled 'Sixty Glorious Years'. Opening times are 9.30 to 5.30 from Easter to the end of British Summer Time, 9.30 to 4.30 the rest of the year.

The best way to see Windsor and enjoy its very special atmosphere is on foot. The **Royal Windsor Walk** is a good introduction to the town: it includes most of the sights already mentioned and introduces some interesting lesser-known ones as well. A short stroll across the Thames brings you to **Eton**. Eton College can be visited between Easter and the end of September. Times are 2.00 to 5.00 during term and 10.30 to 5.00 during school holidays. The highlights are School Yard, where one building, the Lower School, completed in 1445, is still in use today, and the chapel, a glorious example of 15th-century architecture with some magnificent stained glass.

South of the town **Windsor Great Park** offers plenty of opportunities for walking, picnicking and relaxing. From junction 6 you can avoid Windsor town centre by staying on the A332 for about 3 miles to Queen Anne's Gate.

JUNCTION 7 BURNHAM

Junction 7 leads into a short spur motorway terminating just over ½ mile north on the A4. A left turn here, and then a right almost immediately, eventually brings you to **Burnham**, which is still a pleasant village with some handsome houses, despite the trappings of the prosperous Thames valley. The Garibaldi Inn is a good place for a stop. Burnham Beeches is about 2 miles north, but the best route there is direct from junction 6 (see page 125).

JUNCTION 7 DORNEY COURT

Dorney Court is a fine Tudor mansion in the middle of uninspiring countryside south of the M4. To get there, turn left on to the A4 and left again on to the B3026, about 2½ miles in all. One family has owned the house since 1600, and care and love show everywhere. There is fine furniture, an interesting collection of family portraits, lovely panelling and, above all, a splendid Great Hall. Home-made cream teas are served, and there is a farmhouse shop. The house is open on Sundays from Easter to mid-October, and also on Mondays and Tuesdays between June and September, from 2.00 to 5.30.

JUNCTION 7 CLIVEDEN

If you are travelling west, leave the motorway at junction 7 for

Cliveden, one of the most famous of all the English country houses. The house, a grandiose mid-19th-century creation built by Sir Charles Barry for the Duke of Sutherland on the site of several earlier mansions and partly remodelled by two subsequent owners, was for over 70 years the home of the Astor family and, during the 1930s, became the focal point of the so-called Cliveden Set. This was the name bestowed on the right-wing politicians and journalists entertained by Viscount Astor and his wife Nancy, who had in 1919 become the first woman MP to take her seat in the House of Commons; historians have differed about the Cliveden Set's importance, but the latest opinion is that it had little significant influence on events. Although the house is now in use as a hotel, three rooms are open to visitors. But what makes the journey from the motorway worthwhile are the magnificent grounds, with their impressive collection of classical statuary, most acquired by the first Viscount Astor, and the elaborate terraces and staircases on the south front. The Main Avenue leads from the Fountain of Love, where three life-size female figures are attended by cupids, past a series of eight classical Roman sarcophagi to the north front of the house. From the south front, where there are magnificent views over the Thames, you can descend the double staircase to the parterre, a formal garden of lawns and geometrically shaped beds, and walk on through lovely woodland to the yew tree walk and then to the river beyond. From the parterre, look back at the Borghese Balustrade carved in 1618–19 for the Villa Borghese in Rome and erected here in 1896. Other parts of the grounds you might like to visit include the long garden, which is full of 18th-century Venetian statues, the rose garden and the water garden, where a charming pagoda occupies the island. The house is open from 3.00 to 6.00 on Thursdays and Sundays between April and October. The grounds are open daily from 11.00 to 6.00, or sunset if earlier, from March to December. There is a shop, and a restaurant serves morning coffee, teas and light lunches. From junction 7, take the A4 west, turn right on to the B3026 and then right again on to the B476. Cliveden can also be reached from junction 8/9 (see page 129) and from junction 2 of the M40 (see page 164).

JUNCTION 8/9 MAIDENHEAD
Maidenhead is the main centre near junction 8/9, which leads straight on to two spur motorways. One, the A308 (M) is only ½ mile long and terminates at the A308 about 1 mile south of the town. The other, the A423 (M), runs west of the town for 3 miles, ending at the junction with the A4.

Maidenhead wouldn't be my choice for a rest from the M4. It is busy and crowded, and parking can be a hassle. And for me at least the riverside is a big disappointment. The Thames here is prettified and sophisticated, and the tarmac walks are nothing like as pleasant as a water-bank stroll in the middle of the countryside. And then, throughout the summer, and at winter weekends too if the sun is shining, there are often large crowds to contend with. If you do decide to come here, make for **Boulters Lock**, about ½ mile upstream from the bridge. This is the longest, deepest and busiest lock on the entire river, and there should be plenty of craft to watch. From the lock cross to Ray Mill Island, where there are some lovely public gardens and a good view of the weir and the woods of the Cliveden estate upstream.

There are three walks round the town: one in the town centre, one near the river, and the third around the elegant Edwardian streets of Castle Hill and Boyn Hill. At the **Henry Reitlinger Bequest** in Guards Club Road, just west of the bridge, there is a fine collection of prints, paintings, medieval Italian pottery and works from the Far East, plus a display mounted by the local historical society. Opening times are Tuesdays and Thursdays from 10.00 to 12.30 and 2.30 to 4.30 and also the first Sunday of every month from 2.15 to 4.30, all between April and September. To reach Cliveden (see page 127 from junction 8/9, turn left at the end of the A308(M) and then right on to the A4 in the town centre. Cross the river and turn left after about ¼ mile on to the B476. The Stanley Spencer Gallery at Cookham, described under junction 3 of the M40 (see pages 167–168), can be reached along the B4447 from Maidenhead town centre.

JUNCTION 8/9 COURAGE SHIRE HORSE CENTRE

The **Courage Shire Horse Centre** lies in rolling parkland on the A4 a few hundred yards west of the end of the A423(M), and, hardly surprisingly, there is a Courage pub, the Shire Horse Inn, right next door. Bar food is served, and there is also a restaurant. The Centre is a celebration of that most typically English creature, the heavy horse. These gentle giants stand about 18 hands high (a hand is about 4 inches) and weigh about 1 ton. Sixteen horses live here, but usually at least one team of four is away, competing at a horse show or taking part in a carnival, pub opening and so on. You can admire the horses at close quarters when they are brought out into the yard, and can watch them being fed, groomed and shod. A farrier comes two or three times a week, carefully beating the iron shoe to the exact contours of the horse's feet. (A shire horse needs new shoes every three to six weeks.) In the display room there are magnificent show harnesses, all burnished metal and gleaming leather, and hundreds of prize rosettes. Old photographs recall the days before tractors and heavy goods vehicles, when heavy horses pulled ploughs and drays. Besides the horses, there are also enclosures for small animals and birds, a tea room and some pleasant picnic spots. The Centre is open daily from 11.00 to 5.00 between March and October.

JUNCTION 10 READING

Junction 10 is the junction with the A423(M), which leads to **Reading**, a lively commercial centre with some interesting things to see, although you may well have to cope with some heavy traffic to get to them. The town centre can also be reached along the A33 from junction 11. The principal attractions are the ruins of the **abbey** and the magnificent **Forbury Gardens**; the **Museum and Art Gallery** in Blagrave Street, which has many finds from Silchester (see page 133); and two unusual museums, the Museum of English Rural Life on the University campus in Whiteknights Park, and Blake's Lock Museum on the banks of the river Kennet. The **Museum of English Rural Life** is a pioneering collection of agricultural and craft equipment, one of the best in the country and a fascinating record of rural domestic and working life. **Blake's Lock Museum** is devoted to Reading's waterways, trades and industries. There are reconstructions of a printer's workshop, a bakery and a gentleman's hairdresser, displays on local brick- and cycle-making, sauce and mineral water manufacturers and on shops such as pharmacies and confectioners, plus material on navigation and on the town's riverside life. The Museum and Art Gallery is open from 10.00 to 5.30 on Mondays to Fridays, and until 5.00 on Saturdays, but not on Bank Holidays. The Museum of English Rural Life is open on Tuesdays to Saturdays from 10.00 to 1.00 and 2.00 to 4.30. The campus is best reached from junction 11. Take the A33 north and then the A327; it is well signposted. Blake's Lock is open from 10.00 to 5.00 on Wednesdays to Fridays and from 2.00 to 5.00 on Saturdays and Sundays.

JUNCTION 10 DINTON PASTURES COUNTRY PARK

Dinton Pastures Country Park would be my choice for a break near this part of the M4. To get there, take the A329(M) north from junction 10, and leave the motorway at the first exit, following the signs to Winnersh. Then take the A329 towards Wokingham, and finally turn left on to the B3030. The Park entrance is on the left after ¾ mile, just after the bridge over the motorway. Formed from old sand and gravel workings, the Park is based on no fewer than seven lakes, and the river Loddon and Emm Brook flow along its boundaries. All this water provides ample opportunity for fishing and water sports, and there is also good walking and a golf course. The Park's 230 acres include various habitats: hedgerow, scrub, meadowland, river bank and open water. More than a hundred species of bird have been recorded, and every autumn and spring migrating duck and geese visit. The Park is open daily from dawn till dusk throughout the year. The Country Park Centre, in a converted Edwardian farmhouse, has a café (you can sit out in the garden in good weather), a shop and a small exhibition area.

From junction 10 (which has no access on to ordinary roads) the A329(M) runs south-east for 3 miles to Amen Corner, on the A329 half-way between Bracknell and Wokingham. **Wokingham** is a pleasant town with some fine red-brick houses and a handsome old town hall. **Bracknell** was one of the eight new towns sited around London after the Second World War, and construction work has continued until very recently. There are nine residential areas, each with its local shops, and a large modern centre with everything you would expect. Bracknell is where they make our weather. The Met Office is one of the commercial and government organizations that have moved out here.

JUNCTION 11 WELLINGTON MONUMENT & STRATFIELD SAYE HOUSE

The main attraction south of junction 11 is **Stratfield Saye House**, 6 miles on the A33, which is mostly fast dual carriageway. Shortly before you get there, the road passes the enormous **Wellington Monument**. The Iron Duke himself gazes out from the top over his estate. The inscription reminds us that: 'He was honoured abroad for in all the might of conquest he was ever just, considerate and humane' and also that 'he was beloved at home for he had great power and ever used it well. He was firm in friendship and his hand was ever open to the poor.' You learn as well that the monument was paid for by the second Duke of Wellington and the estate tenants – which might just have affected their judgement of the first Duke's character. After Wellington's triumph at Waterloo, a grateful Parliament voted him £600,000 to buy a country house and estate. All things considered, Stratfield Saye was quite a modest establishment. The Duke's plans to demolish the house, already two hundred years old, and build a grand mansion on the scale of Blenheim, foundered for lack of cash, and the Duke simply added a conservatory and the two outer wings and introduced water-closets and central heating: both unheard-of comforts in those days. The visit takes in all the principal rooms. For me at any rate, their interest lies chiefly in their association with the Iron Duke and his descendants. Many of the books in the Library are from Napoleon's personal collection. Next door is the Music Room, misnamed since it commemorates Copenhagen, the Duke's favourite charger whom he rode all day at Waterloo. Copenhagen's grave is in the grounds, inscribed:

God's humbler instrument, though meaner clay
Should share the glory of that glorious day.

The Duke is best remembered for that single day in 1815. But he lived for nearly 40 more years, and twice served as Prime Minister. Outside, in part of the stables, the Wellington Exhibition tells the story of his life, aided by a profusion of memorabilia – including the first Wellington boots – and the Duke's huge and elaborate (and in my view very ugly) funeral carriage designed by Prince Albert. The extensive gardens include the pleasure grounds, where among many rare and interesting trees are a group of fine wellingtonias, named for the Iron Duke when they were introduced to this country in 1853, the year after his death. Exotic duck and geese can also be seen in the Wildfowl Sanctuary. The house is open daily except Fridays between late April and September from 11.30 to 5.00, and refreshments are available.

JUNCTION 11 WELLINGTON COUNTRY PARK

This is very much Wellington country, and we have not finished with the Iron Duke yet. Some 3 miles north of Stratfield Saye, back towards the M4, is the **Wellington Country Park**. (From junction 11, take the A33 south, turn left after about 4 miles at the first roundabout, and then left again at the next.) The main feature of the Park is a large lake, with meadows and woodland around it. You can sit and relax, go for walks or follow one of five nature trails. Two of these pass through the deer park; a herd of spotted fallow deer was introduced here in 1984. By following the Thames Valley Time Trail you can trace the development of the world over 4500 million years and look at various models, including the iguanadon, one of the earth's inhabitants 71 million years ago, an eohippus, the forefather of today's horse, and Neanderthal Man, who lived a mere 350,000 to 100,000 years ago. Other amenities include an adventure playground, children's animals, and so on. The **National Dairy Museum** is also here, where you can find out all about milk, its quality, distribution and processing. Most interesting is the old equipment, such as a 'milk pram', the predecessor of today's electric milk float. It was pushed by hand, and the roundsman and his boy ladled milk from the churns straight into the customer's own jug. Despite all these attractions, the Park is something of a disappointment: rather more commercialized and less genuinely rural than Dinton

Pastures (see page 130), which remains my first choice; Dinton is free as well. The Wellington Country Park is open daily between March and October from 10.00 to 5.30 and also at winter weekends.

JUNCTION 12 BASILDON PARK

Pangbourne is about 5 miles north of junction 12. This is one of the prettiest Thames-side villages and, as you might expect, often very crowded. (The precise route is west on the A4 and then right on to the A340.) There are attractive 17th- and 18th-century houses, and a river bank path runs along the Thames in both directions from the centre. **Basildon Park**, a few miles outside Pangbourne on the A329 to Streatley, is a fine classical 18th-century house built by John Carr of York overlooking the Thames. Beyond the handsome Palladian facade of the west front you pass through the Hall and the Dining Room, both with richly patterned plasterwork, and on to the Octagon Drawing Room with its Italianate ceiling and three great windows giving views over the river and the woods beyond. Other noteworthy rooms are the Green Drawing Room and the Shell Room, so called because it contains a large collection of land and sea shells. The house the visitor sees today is remarkable not only as a superb example of 18th-century style but also as the product of 20th-century conservation. Thirty uninhabited years from 1910, followed by 12 years' use by soldiers and prisoners of war, had left Basildon little more than a shell and in urgent need of drastic repairs. It is thanks to the dedication of Lord and Lady Iliffe, who bought the house in the early 1950s, that Basildon has not only survived but has been restored and furnished with such success. The house is open between April and October from 2.00 to 6.00 on Wednesdays to Saturdays and from 12.00 to 6.00 on Sundays and Bank Holiday Mondays; closed Good Friday and the Wednesday following Bank Holidays. A tea room offers teas and, at weekends, light meals.

JUNCTION 12 SILCHESTER

A more unusual excursion is to **Silchester**, or Calleva Atrebatum, as its Roman inhabitants knew it. The site is quite complicated to find, and when you do get there it is not as immediately spectacular as some of the well-known Roman remains. But it is worth the effort, all the more so if you are interested in ancient history. From junction 12, the easiest route is along the A4 for about 4 miles until just before the junction with the A340 to Aldermaston. Turn left on to a side road towards Padworth. In Padworth, turn left and then right and follow this road through woodland as far as you can go. Turn left again and then right through Mortimer West End. This road stops at a T-junction with the road running round much of the perimeter of the old city; turn left for the church, right for the museum. From Stratfield Saye House (see page 130), it is a reasonably simple drive through Stratfield Saye village following the signposts to Silchester.

Silchester remains a hidden city. There were extensive excavations in the second half of the 19th century, but now they are covered with grass and soil again. Had you visited the site at the right moment in the 1890s, however, you would have seen a forum with a basilica at its centre, baths, temples and houses: all the amenities and trappings, in fact, of a sophisticated and civilized city of the Roman Empire. Today the imposing wall is the major visible remnant. The best place to start is in the churchyard, behind which there is a substantial 15-foot high stretch of **wall**. It can be followed round to the west gate of the city, where a footpath leads you straight across the buried city back to the church. The northern half of the wall can be seen from the road (aptly named Wall Lane), but the land on which it stands is private property. The most recent excavations have been at the **amphitheatre**, north of the church at the corner of Church and Wall Lanes. There is also a tiny **museum**, in what looks no more than a tin shack, but with interesting and well laid-out displays. These help to put flesh on the bare bones of what you can see outside. They portray Calleva as it must have been in its heyday: a busy administrative centre and market town, with shops, workshops, public buildings and homes for about 4000 people. Virtually all the objects found on the site are in the Silchester Collection at Reading Museum (see page 130), and a trip there is essential for enthusiasts.

From Silchester there is a long route on country roads through Heath End and Brimpton to Newbury (see page 136), from where it is 4 miles north on the A34 to junction 13. The most notable thing about this detour is the culture shock it involves. From the peace of Silchester, with its almost tangible feel of the past, you move to the worst aspect of the late 20th century, for this route runs past the Greenham Common airbase, a screeching jungle of concrete and violence.

The long section of motorway between junctions 12 and 13 (12 miles) introduces quite a different type of landscape. You move out of the rather featureless Thames valley into high downs with wide views and good walks enclosing fertile valleys scattered with pleasing towns and villages.

JUNCTION 13 RIDGEWAY PATH

Leave the motorway at junction 13 for one of the best walks near the entire M4. Drive north on the fastish A34 until the turning left for West Ilsley. Take that, and then turn right in West Ilsley (1½ miles) and follow the road up to **Bury Down**. The **Ridgeway Path** runs along the tops here. This route has been a well-trodden path since long before Roman times, and it is now an official long-distance path. You can walk for as long as you want to up here. There are marvellous views north, to Harwell in the foreground and then to the Midlands and beyond. The best walks go west, to East Hendred Down, Scuthamer Knob and, about 4 miles from Bury Down, to the B4494 near Wantage. **Scuthamer Knob**, which is concealed in a small wood, is thought to be the burial place of Cwicchelm, a West Saxon monarch who died in 593. Just before the B road you pass an obelisk in memory of Lord Wantage, who died in 1901. Keen walkers could do this walk in both directions (it took me a little over two hours one brisk winter's day), or alternatively they could be dropped at Bury Down while a driver follows the side roads through West Ilsley and Farnborough and north on to the B4494 to pick them up by the monument.

JUNCTION 13 SNELSGROVE COMMON COUNTRY PARK

There is more sedate walking, and nearer the motorway too, at the **Snelsgrove Common Country Park** – and to get there you pass one of the best pubs near this part of the M4, Ye Old Red Lion in Chieveley. Take the A34 north, but turn left almost immediately into Chieveley. Then turn left in the village, carry on for just under 1 mile, swing sharp left with the road and turn left on to the B4494. The entrance to the Park is on the right after about 1½ miles. Snelsgrove is one of the nicer and simpler country parks: woodland, a few benches and picnic tables, and pleasant paths – ideal for a relaxing hour off the motorway.

Another 1½ miles south on the B4494 brings you to **Donnington** village, which has pretty thatched cottages and, the purpose of the visit, some impressive castle remains. **Donnington Castle** dates from the 14th century. But it is most remembered for a siege three centuries later, when Royalist forces held out against Cromwell's troops for 20 months, which makes it one of the last castles to see active service. Only the three-storey gatehouse stands now, some 65 feet tall. But it is easy to appreciate the strategic importance of the Castle, built high on a spur commanding major routes in all directions. The country round about is rolling wooded land, and several footpaths are signposted. In the village the Donnington Castle pub is also worth a visit.

JUNCTION 13 NEWBURY

Newbury is a pleasant market town with a variety of pubs and cafés, including the Bricklayers Arms and, near the museum, the oddly named Hatchet. There is a pleasant municipal park by the Kennet & Avon Canal, whose towpath also makes a good walk. Start near the museum, where there was once a wharf, and walk past the attractive bridge, one of the oldest on the canal, through the tunnel under W. H. Smith's and up to the lock and West Mills swing bridge. The museum has produced an architectural trail round the best parts of the town, although it does help to emphasize how much redevelopment has damaged its character. The **museum** itself is in two historic buildings: the 17th-century Cloth Hall and a granary built in the 18th century. There are fascinating displays on local history from the Inkpen Beaker, dated to 1750 BC, to the present day. Also housed here is the George Parker History of Photography Collection, which has cameras, accessories and other photographic apparatus. Opening times between April and September are from 10.00 to 6.00 on Mondays, Tuesdays, Thursdays, Fridays and Saturdays, from 2.00 to 6.00 on Sundays and Bank Holidays. In winter, opening times are 10.00 to 4.00 on Mondays, Tuesdays, Thursdays, Fridays and Saturdays only.

JUNCTION 14 HUNGERFORD

Junction 14 is one of the best in the English part of the M4, simply because it leads to a classic small English country town and to a classic stately home. The countryside is lovely rolling downland. In the main street of **Hungerford**, south of the motorway along the A338, there are plenty of antique and tea shops plus the Bear Hotel for large meals, and it is a delightful place for a quiet stroll: handsome houses, interesting shops, few tourists. At the top (north) end of the High Street the road crosses the canal – the Kennet & Avon again, which runs along the Kennet valley, linking the Bristol Avon and the Thames – and there is a tiny basin. From Hungerford it runs west through delightful country to Crofton pumping station. Not all the canal is navigable as yet, and considerable restoration work is still needed; but the section around Hungerford is open, and trips on motor- and horse-drawn barges are available.

JUNCTION 14 LITTLECOTE

If you are driving from junction 14 direct to **Littlecote**, there is a pleasant back-lane route via **Chilton Foliat**, a nice village with some good-looking houses and the Wheatsheaf Inn. Turn right off the A338 about 2½ miles south of the motorway. At the first road junction in Chilton Foliat, turn sharp left, then right again almost immediately, and the entrance to the estate is shortly on the right.

The house at Littlecote is an extremely attractive Tudor mansion, its south side faced in a lovely, mellow red brick. During the English Civil War, the Popham family, who owned Littlecote from 1580 to 1922, were staunch supporters of the Parliamentary cause, and it is said that the footsteps of the Cromwellian troops quartered here can still be heard in the house. But by the end of the 1650s, Colonel Alexander Popham had seen which way the wind was blowing, for he assisted General Monk in restoring Charles II and later received a royal pardon. Final amends were no doubt made when the King, on a royal progress to Bath, was served a 'costly dinner' at Littlecote.

The tour of the house takes you back in time to one day in July 1642, shortly before the start of the Civil War, when Colonel Popham had just returned to Littlecote with a troop of 60 armed cavalrymen and his wife Katherine was preparing to leave her home for a safer refuge elsewhere. In the Troopers Room two soldiers are relaxing while another two prepare for guard duty, and in the Upper Oak Room Katherine Popham is seen hastily packing her things for her journey. Beyond the Dining Room her husband is deep in discussion with his two brothers Edward and Hugh, who are to escort his wife. Two rooms are the highlight of the tour: the Chapel and the Great Hall. The former is the only surviving Cromwellian chapel; there is no altar, and a pulpit stands in its place. The impressive Great Hall, 46 feet by 24 and 25 feet high, contains the Littlecote armoury. This, the only surviving private armoury of the 17th century (it is now owned by the Royal Armouries), consists of the arms and armour the Pophams acquired for their cavalrymen to use during the Civil War. There are buff-coats made of cow-hide, breastplates, pistols, carbines and muskets, cavalry and infantry armours and one heavy armour used in siege warfare – all of which have remained in the house since Colonel Popham and his men returned home victorious at the end of the Civil War.

Outside, there is a wealth of things to see. On the Littlecote farm, which is a working establishment, ancient breeds of sheep and cattle – the ancestors of the creatures seen on today's farms – are kept. A team of heavy horses pulls the plough, there are Tamworth pigs and old English goats, and several breeds of sheep, including the horned Hebridean sheep and, from nearer to home, the Wiltshire horn sheep and the Cotswold sheep. Another historical feature is a recreation of a traditional English village, while jousting and falconry displays are regularly staged. The lovely grounds include a herb garden, a rose garden and knot gardens, and there are pleasant walks and picnic areas, horse-drawn wagon tours and a steam railway.

The Orpheus Mosaic at Littlecote

I have left what, for me at least, is the best part of Littlecote until last: the Roman villa with its lovely mosaic. There was a large villa here, plus outbuildings, such as a workshop, barns and a bakery – almost a small village, and certainly big enough to support a farming community. A medieval village was built on top of the old Roman settlement, and when the present Littlecote house went up, that in turn was grassed over to make the deer park. The mosaic itself – it represents Orpheus playing his lyre surrounded by four female figures who may be the four seasons – was discovered in 1729 by the Littlecote steward. He drew the mosaic: a drawing that turned out to be crucial to its present reconstruction. Then, almost unbelievably (but maybe not so unbelievably, considering the way we nowadays allow important archaeological sites to be treated), the site was lost and trees were planted right over the mosaic. It was exacavated between 1978 and 1980, and the restoration of the damaged parts in modern terracotta was only possible because of that drawing made 250 years ago. Most non-experts will find it difficult to judge where the original ends and the restored sections begin. The end result is a work of lyrical beauty and marvellous craftsmanship. Interestingly, although the mosaic dates from the late Roman Empire, long after the Empire's official conversion to Christianity, it formed part of a pagan chapel. The period to which it has been dated, the early 360s, was the moment of a brief revival of the old pre-Christian religions under the Emperor Julian, nicknamed 'the Apostate'. Littlecote is open daily from 10.00 to 6.00 between Easter and October. There is a restaurant and the Popham Arms Tavern as well.

JUNCTION 15 LIDDINGTON CASTLE

South of junction 15, the Downs and the Ridgeway Path (already met at junction 13, see page 134) are very close. There are two possibilities: Liddington Castle, on the hill of the same name, and Barbury Castle, round which a country park has been developed. Keen walkers with cooperative drivers could walk between the two on the Ridgeway Path. The best view of **Liddington Castle** is the one you are least likely to get: from the air. Aerial photographs show an almost perfect hill-fort on the edge of the scarp, with wide views to the north. It was almost certainly here that King Arthur defeated the Saxons in about 500, at the battle of Mons Badonicus. The hill-fort, which dates back to the Iron Age, was originally faced with chalk and flint blocks, and timber was added later. The best route from the motorway is south on the A345 for about 1 mile to just beyond Chiseldon. Turn left here on to the road that runs along the side of Liddington Hill.

JUNCTION 15 BARBURY CASTLE

Barbury Castle is slightly more elaborate than Liddington, and has two defensive banks and ditches; traces of sarsen stone have been found in the facings. The interior is large – 11½ acres. When I was last here a cruel wind and a lowering sky helped the imagination to leap back to the 6th century (the battle of Beranbyrig was fought here in 556) and beyond to the Iron Age. There were of course periods of peace too, as the agricultural implements found on the site in the 19th century indicate. There are some interesting information panels about the Castle, prehistoric life, hill-forts, local agriculture and geology, and nature conservation, plus sections on the essayist and novelist Richard Jefferies and on Alfred Williams, a labourer who composed poems and essays, both of whom loved the area. The route to the Castle from junction 15 is south on the A345, right on to the B4005 in Chiseldon and then left after 2 miles. From here it is about 2½ miles to the Castle, past a large hospital on the right. My choice between Liddington and Barbury would probably be the former, simply because it is nearer the motorway.

JUNCTIONS 15 & 16 SWINDON

Swindon town centre is about 4 miles north of junction 15, slightly less from junction 16. On the way into Swindon from junction 15 you pass near the **Coate Water Country Park**, whose centrepiece is a large lake. You can swim, sail and fish, and there is a pitch and putt course. It's pleasant enough, and if I lived nearby I'd certainly take an evening stroll there. But since there is a choice here between real country (see junction 15 above) and a man-made leisure park, for me the answer is obvious – as I suspect it is for most people. Also in Coate is the **Richard Jefferies Museum**, in the farmhouse in which he was born. Jefferies and Alfred Williams are both commemorated, and there is also a collection of horse-drawn agricultural equipment from the late 19th century to about 1940. Opening times are Wednesdays, Saturdays and Sundays from 2.00 to 5.00.

It is difficult to decide whether to recommend a trip into **Swindon** – although if you do go there be prepared for heavy traffic. At first sight the town is exactly what I complain of so often in this book: a Victorian centre overlaid with an ill-fitting modern development. At second glance, though, the picture isn't quite so clear. Some of the streets are pinched, mean terraces, others marvellous examples of early Victorian cottage architecture, while on top of the hill in the Old Town there are some fine 18th-century houses. The new centre itself is high-tech architecture at its most gloriously brash, a revel in steel and concrete and tubing. Somehow it manages to look good and feel fun, while feebler imitations elsewhere are just plain ugly. The **Brunel Centre** in particular – where there are no fewer than 5½ hectares of traffic-free shopping – has an American zappiness and energy about it. The name Brunel gives the clue to the major factor in Swindon's history: the Great Western Railway. When Brunel built his famous line east from Bristol and west from London the two halves met just outside Swindon in 1835. Seven years later the locomotive works were opened, and Swindon's career as a railway centre was really launched. More lines were built, and at their peak the works covered 320 acres and employed over 12,000 people. The **Great Western Railway Museum**, which records this glorious past, is well worth a visit. Several GWR locomotives are displayed in the main hall. There are paintings and prints, models and railwayana of all kinds, as well as a gallery devoted to Brunel himself. The GWR was something of a model employer. The Museum was once a lodging-house for railway workers and stands in the middle of a model village built in the 1840s for employees. There are 300 homes, arranged in six rows on each side of a central square with a church, library, park and Mechanics' Institute. Redevelopment plans once threatened the village, but a reprieve was granted, and the houses are now beautifully restored. In one, No. 34 Faringdon Road, you will find the **Railway Village Museum**. The cottage is furnished as it would have been in the late 19th century. Gas and oil lamps are the only lighting, there is a range and copper in the kitchen, and the table is laid in the parlour. Both these museums are open at the same time: weekdays from 10.00 to 5.00, Sundays from 2.00 to 5.00.

The **Town Museum** in Apsley House has much local material – geological, botanical, historical, archaeological and on local customs and folklore – plus, less predictably, a large collection of 20th-century British paintings, including works by Augustus John, Henry Moore, L. S. Lowry, Ben Nicholson and many others. Opening times are from 10.00 to 6.00 weekdays and from 2.00 to 5.00 Sundays.

JUNCTION 16 LYDIARD COUNTRY PARK

Lydiard Country Park, on the western edge of Swindon, 2 miles from junction 16, offers the chance of a relaxing break from the motorway in pleasant countryside. There are pleasant walks through pastureland and woodland, and the visitor centre, where refreshments are available, contains material on the natural history and wildlife of the area. Several rooms in Lydiard Mansion can be seen, with an interesting collection of period furniture. **St Mary's Church, Lydiard Tregoze**, nearby has lovely and unusual 17th-century memorials to the St John family, who once owned the big house. From the motorway, take the A3102 east towards Swindon, turn left at the first roundabout along Whitehill Way, and left again along Hook Road at the second; the Park entrance is on the right after ⅔ mile. The Link Centre is another nearby leisure complex, to use the current jargon, where there is swimming, snooker, ice-skating, a health suite and countless other varieties of keep-fit and sport. Continue along Whitehill Way and turn right at the third roundabout from the motorway.

JUNCTION 17 MALMESBURY

The A429 runs north from junction 17 to **Malmesbury**, which, although it is 6 miles from the motorway, is well worth the diversion. Driving over the Avon and then steeply up to the town centre always makes me think I am arriving at a little French hill-town. Malmesbury's charter was granted in 880, which makes it the oldest borough in the country. Settlement started long before that, first as a hill-fort, and then, when the **abbey** was founded in the 7th century,

Malmesbury Abbey

as a Christian centre. The present magnificent building dates from the mid-12th century and was substantially restored two centuries later. The south front is superb, in particular the biblical stories carved in stone. The parvise (the room above the porch) contains a rich collection of treasures, including illuminated bibles and a silver penny minted in the town during the reign of Edward the Confessor: there was a mint here from about 950 to 1150. A visit to the abbey, and to the Cloister Gardens established in 1980 on the site of the old monastic cloister to celebrate the 1100th anniversary of the town, and then a stroll through the town to look at the antique shops, is my idea of a relaxing break from a long drive. The Old Bell Hotel, next to the abbey, always serves a good pot of coffee. There is also a pleasant river walk at the foot of the town.

JUNCTION 17 SHELDON MANOR
South of junction 17, the A429 leads to Chippenham, which is fairly industrialized and not especially interesting. **Sheldon Manor**, on the A420 just west of the town, is a 700-year-old medieval manor. Take the A429 south from the M4 to the northern edge of Chippenham, turn right on to the A350 and then right again on to the A420. After about ½ mile turn left on to a side road and the entrance to the house is on the right (5½ miles). Although there have been restorations and additions in later centuries, the core of the Manor – the great porch and the massive walls behind it – dates from the late 13th century. Inside there is a beautiful oak staircase and much

lovely early oak furniture, outside rare trees and shrubs, a water garden, old-fashioned roses and an orchard. The house is open on Thursdays, Sundays and Bank Holidays from 12.30 to 6.00 between the Sunday before Easter and the first Sunday in October. There is a gift shop, and excellent home-made teas and buffet lunches are served.

JUNCTION 17 CASTLE COMBE

From here you can either return to junction 17 or continue to Castle Combe and then along side roads to junction 18. **Castle Combe** (about 4 miles along the B4039 through Yatton Keynell from the A4020 west of the turning for Sheldon Manor) is the ultimate tourist village, with lovely mellow Cotswold stone houses and beautifully tended gardens. It must have featured on a thousand calendars and chocolate box tops – and doesn't it just know it! There is not a blade of grass out of place, not a weed unplucked or a sweet paper uncollected. As far as I am concerned, its looks kill it. It is just too good to be true. You may disagree, and in any case the church, the arched bridge and the ancient market cross are worth a look. If you want to continue to junction 18, follow the B4039 to Acton Turville, turn left just beyond the village on to the B4040 and then turn left on to the A46.

JUNCTION 18 CHIPPING SODBURY

Chipping Sodbury is 4 miles north-west of junction 18, north along the A46 and then left on to the A432. It is a pleasant Cotswold market town with some handsome houses along the wide main street and a 16th-century market cross at the top end. But, given the attractions south of the motorway, I can't especially recommend a visit.

JUNCTION 18 DYRHAM PARK

South from the motorway on the A46 you reach **Dyrham Park** after 2 miles, an extremely fine National Trust property. There was once a Tudor mansion here, but all that survived the rebuilding in the 1690s by William Blathwayt, William III's Secretary of State, is the Great Hall, and even this is furnished in the style of the late 17th century. And it is the furniture, together with the paintings, tapestries, pottery and *objets d'art* of that time, that are most interesting. Admire the magnificent collection of blue and white Delftware and the two fine staircases, in walnut and cedar. There is a sober Dutch look about the house and its contents: hardly surprising, since the monarch himself was from Holland and William Blathwayt often travelled there on official business. Originally the gardens were built

The terrace and parish church at Dyrham Park

in the formal Dutch style, with parterres and terraces and elaborate waterworks on the hillside, including an astonishing cascade of no fewer than 224 steps. All that remains is a Neptune fountain, dry now for almost two centuries, and two fishponds: the formal gardens were replaced by a landscaped park in about 1800, in which there is pleasant walking, with good views towards the Severn and the Welsh hills. The Park is open daily from 12.00 to 6.00 or dusk if earlier, the house daily except Fridays from 2.00 to 6.00 or dusk between April and October. (There is Thursday closing in April, May and October as well.)

About 8 miles further south, the A46 reaches **Bath**. No city could be less suitable for a book dedicated to brief off-motorway breaks. It is worth a long, leisurely visit. Highlights are the Roman baths, the abbey, the Pump Room and Assembly Rooms, numerous museums and magnificent Georgian terraces. Shopping, eating and drinking are all excellent.

Junction 19 is the junction with the M32 which runs south almost as far as central Bristol. There is no access to ordinary roads here. Junction 1 on the M32 is less than ½ mile off, but there is no reason to turn off there.

Junction 20 is the junction with the M5, and there is no way off the motorway, although junction 16 on the M5 is less than ½ mile away.

JUNCTION 21 SEVERN BRIDGE

Junction 21 comes immediately before you reach the river Severn and, alas all too often, long queues to get through the tollbooths and on to the **Severn Bridge**. The bridge is a spectacular sight, and a spectacular engineering achievement too. It took five years, four months to build (the Queen opened it on 8 September 1966) and it cost a mere £16 million. This sum included both bridges (what we loosely call the Severn Bridge is in fact two, one bridge over the Severn and the other over the Wye), the approach motorway, and all road surfacing, lighting and signs. That a bridge was needed had been self-evident for decades before officialdom stirred itself. Thomas Telford, who built the Menai Straits suspension bridge, suggested a crossing here in 1824, and after that the idea was rarely off the agenda. The opening of the railway tunnel in 1886—itself an extremely complex piece of engineering which took 12 years and involved digging under 'the Shoots', a 50-foot gully in the river bed—relieved pressure for a while. In the 1920s, motor traffic increased rapidly, and public demand for a bridge along with it. But construction only started in 1961, and in November of that year the Minister of Transport, Ernest Marples – remember Ernie Marples! – buried a canister at the foot of the main tower at Beachley on the west bank. The canister contained coins, newspapers, a photo of the Minister and a note he himself wrote wishing 'the best of luck to whoever finds this'. What a discovery for archaeologists in the year 4000! At the time of its completion, the bridge was for its length and loading the lightest ever built. The main span is 3240 feet long, the two side spans 1000 feet each; the two superstructure towers are each 400 feet high and weigh 1300 tons.

There is a good view of the bridge from the service station just by junction 21. But so much more could have been made of its splendid position. All the facilities seem to have been built with their back to the river. Most of the time you only get the occasional glimpse of water and wide skies. However, there is a grassy terrace outside for picnics. A path leads across a footbridge over the motorway and then down on to the pedestrian walkway across the bridge. It is a 10 to 15 minute walk to the centre.

For a far more interesting view, leave the motorway at junction 21, take the B4461 south and turn right immediately on to the B446. Readers who regularly drove to south Wales before 1966 should prepare for a sudden wave of nostalgia – for this is the road to **Old Passage** and the landing-stage for the now discarded ferry across to Wales. Park the car and walk along the foreshore towards the bridge. The old jetty is still there, slowly rotting in the mud but nevertheless recognizable, and the shell of the booking office too.

You realize here just how turbulent the river is. The tides can run at 9 knots and rise over 40 feet, and there are countless rocks and sandbanks.

JUNCTION 22 CHEPSTOW CASTLE

Across the bridge, road signs in both Welsh and English immediately remind you that you are in a different land. In fact it takes quite some time to reach a Wales that is recognizably Welsh, and **Chepstow**, about 1½ miles from junction 22 along the A466 and then right on to the A48, seems quite English. It is a charming, rather traffic-filled town, and one of the nicest spots for a break on this stretch of the motorway. Its chief interest is the **Castle**, overlooking the river Wye, along with Caerphilly (see page 153) one of the most impressive castles near any motorway. The first building here was the great tower, erected by William FitzOsbern almost immediately after the Conquest and the first stone tower constructed in these islands. You need little imagination to see how oppressive it must have appeared nine centuries ago, a potent symbol of the new rulers' power. During the next two-and-a-quarter centuries a thick curtain wall was added, followed by the barbican, the upper bailey and two gatehouses – making Chepstow an almost complete catalogue of castle development; there are even 17th-century gun loops. Despite, or maybe because of, all these elaborate defences, the Castle was never attacked: at least not until the 17th century, when Parliamentary forces besieged it twice. After the Castle – which ought to be top of your list here – make for the **museum**, housed in **Gwy House**, a handsome 18th-century house just opposite the Castle car park. This is an interesting local museum where the main focus is on the working life of the town over the centuries. The port and its trades in timber, corn and wine are shown, as is the river life, with displays on traditional salmon-fishing methods. Industry is represented, including ship-building, engineering and bridge-building, and commerce too; a Victorian shop-front, a wine merchant's vault and the entrance to Chepstow's Victorian 'Old Bank' are all recreated. Another room has material on local sports and entertainments, a third concentrates on the history of Gwy House, which has served as a hospital, a school for young ladies and a private house, while the print room features 18th- and 19th-century prints of the Castle. More of Chepstow's history can be seen along the town trail, which starts at the museum. The first stop is the lovely cast-iron bridge over the Wye. This should be a glorious piece of industrial archaeology – but it still carries the A48 Gloucester to south Wales road. There were traffic jams here as early as the 1920s, almost before the

146

term had been invented. The **Riverside Gardens** are a good picnic spot, while for a meal or a snack you can try the Willow Tree restaurant on the river bank or the Castle View Hotel next to the museum. The Castle is open daily from 9.30, closing at 6.30 from mid-March to mid-October and at 4.00 on weekdays in winter. Sunday times in winter are from 2.00 to 4.00. The museum's times are weekdays from 11.00 to 1.00 and 2.00 to 5.00 and Sundays from 2.00 to 5.00 between March and October.

There are good walks on the neck of land between the estuaries of the Wye and the Severn, directly beneath the Severn Bridge. Although the M4 runs above this fascinating area of mudflats and saltmarshes, access is difficult. From Chepstow cross the Wye on the A48 and then turn right on to the B4228 through Sedbury to Beachley. Keen bird-watchers will certainly want to come here, but the trip takes a good deal of time. **Offa's Dyke Path**, the long-distance path that criss-crosses the border north to Rhyl, on the north Wales coast, starts at Sedbury Cliffs.

JUNCTION 23 MAGOR

Junction 23 is interesting, which is not what you might expect from the map. To the north there is Penhow Castle, to the south a good foreshore walk. And close to the junction there is **Magor**, a pleasant village with an attractive main square and worth visiting simply to get a quiet half hour away from the traffic. There are two pubs, the Wheatsheaf and the Golden Lion, both of which serve food. Beside the large church stands the ruin of the 13th-century **Procurator's House**. The Procurator was a tax-collector, and the job was held by an abbot from central Italy. To reach the walk, drive south over the railway line, turn left and then left again after about ½ mile into a cul-de-sac. Park by the entrance to the sewage farm. The footpath starting there brings you out on to the foreshore after about ½ mile, and there are walks in each direction with good views of the shipping in the Bristol Channel.

JUNCTION 23 PENHOW CASTLE

Penhow Castle dates from the early 13th century, with 15th-century alterations and a 16th-century wing. The Great Hall has a lovely minstrels' gallery, and one room is furnished as a Victorian housekeeper's parlour. The Castle advertises itself as the 'cradle of the Seymour family' – it was Sir William St Maur who started to build here, and it seems that gradually, over the centuries, his name changed into Seymour – and a special welcome is extended to all Seymours! The Castle is open daily except Mondays and Tuesdays from 10.00 to 6.00 (last admission 5.15) between Good Friday and September. From Magor take the side road north. Turn right about ¼ mile after going under the M4 and continue on this road until it meets the A48. Turn left and the Castle entrance is almost immediately on the left. If you are coming from the west, leave the M4 at junction 24 and take the A48 east for about 5 miles.

JUNCTIONS 24–28 NEWPORT
The M4 loops round the north of Newport, and junctions 24 to 28 lead off in rapid succession to routes into the town centre. **Newport** isn't ideal for a motorway break: the streets are busy, and it can take quite a while to work your way in from the motorway. Apart from the usual pubs, restaurants, cafés and shops, there is the **Museum and Art Gallery** (open Mondays to Thursdays 9.30 to 5.00, Fridays 9.30 to 4.30, Saturdays 9.30 to 4.00), which has works by leading Welsh artists as well as a collection of English watercolours, St Woollo's Cathedral, and the **transporter bridge** over the Usk. There are only four such bridges in the world (this one was opened in 1906); the transporter supports a moveable platform for cars and pedestrians. There is a **castle** too, mostly a 15th-century re-working of 13th-century buildings. It fronts on to the river, and at high tide small vessels could pass through a watergate and moor at a quay at the rear of the tower.

JUNCTION 25 CAERLEON
Junction 25 is 2 miles from one of the most interesting diversions off the Welsh section of the M4: **Caerleon**, headquarters of the Second Augustan Legion of the Roman Empire. The two major features here are the **amphitheatre**, described by Roger Wilson (whose book *Roman Remains in Britain* ought to accompany everyone at all interested in Roman Britain) as 'still the only completely excavated example in Britain', and, in the centre of the present-day village, the baths used by the 6000 or so men of the garrison stationed here. What makes the arena so absorbing is that you can really see how it functioned: the seat of honour, the elaborate entrances, the rooms where performers waited to make their entrance. At Caerleon, the performers, Wilson believes, were probably soldiers taking part in military exercises and displays, whereas at larger amphitheatres in less obscure and distant parts of the Empire gladiators and wild beasts would frequently appear. The amphitheatre was built in about AD90, only a few years after the fortress itself was established, and has been silent ever since the garrison departed. Precisely when they left is uncertain, but certainly well before 300. The **baths**, which were built shortly before the amphitheatre as a Roman ver-

sion of today's leisure and sports complexes, are among the largest yet discovered in Britain. As well as the massive cold, warm and hot rooms, each almost 50 feet high, where the sweat and dirt of military exercises and parades could be washed away, there was swimming in the long pool and opportunities for games and athletics, as well as refreshments and gaming and board games. The recently excavated remains of the open-air swimming pool, a heated changing-room and part of the *frigidarium*, the cold room, can now be seen, together with an informative exhibition recreating the atmosphere of the baths. The newly opened **Legionary Museum** near the baths contains many of the finds that have helped archaeologists to build up a detailed picture of life at Caerleon – bones of mutton joints and chicken legs eaten at the baths, for instance, and a lovely collection of engraved gemstones lost one day the best part of 2000 years ago at the baths. Perhaps slightly less interesting, because they require a real effort of imagination to invest these stone remnants with life, are the remains of the **legionary barracks** opposite the amphitheatre. The amphitheatre, baths and barracks are open daily from 9.30 to 6.30 between mid-March and mid-October, and from 9.30 to 4.00 on weekdays, 2.00 to 4.00 on Sundays, during the rest of the year. Times for the Museum are weekdays 10.00 to 6.00, Sundays 2.00 to 6.00, between mid-March and mid-October; 10.00 to 4.30, Sundays 2.00 to 4.30, during the rest of the year. Caerleon itself is a pleasant, spacious village, with several eating and drinking places, including the Priory Hotel, the Drovers Arms and the Ship on the banks of the Usk. The route from junction 25 is simple. Take the B4596 north-east and turn left on to the B4326 just before the river. The amphitheatre is well signposted in the village.

JUNCTION 27 FOURTEEN LOCKS PICNIC SITE

From the archaeology of the Roman invasion to that of the early Industrial Revolution, less than 1 mile from junction 27. The **Fourteen Locks Picnic Site** is centred on a staircase of 14 locks on the western arm of the now disused Monmouthshire Canal. (A staircase is an inter-connected succession of locks. The front gates of one lock also act as the rear gates of the next, and so on.) There is an excellent Interpretation Centre, with full information on the history of the canal, and a short waymarked trail leads you to the most interesting spots. The 14 locks raised the canal 168 feet in only ½ mile, and to keep water losses as low as possible a complicated system of ponds, channels, tunnels and weirs was built. Several longer waymarked walks start at the visitor centre, and the towpath north to Risca can also be followed. The Interpretation Centre is open daily except Tuesdays and Wednesdays from 10.00 to 5.30 between Easter and

September. The site itself is open all the time and makes a delightful picnic spot. Alternatively there is the Tredegar Arms pub ¼ mile or so further north on the main road. Drive north from the motorway towards Risca, and turn right after ½ mile along the road signposted Henllys. (Take care, as the turning is easy to miss.) The Centre is ¼ mile further on this road.

Seven miles north of junction 28 on the A467 brings you to the start of the Forestry Commission's 7-mile **Cwmcarn Forest Drive**, which runs through mixed coniferous woodland, with stupendous views over the Bristol Channel. The drive is lovely, and from the highest part of the forest there are fine walks along the open hilltops. A visitor centre has displays on the history of forestry in the area. Turn right off the A467 just beyond Crosskeys and follow the signposts.

JUNCTION 28 TREDEGAR HOUSE COUNTRY PARK

Another attractive setting for rural relaxation, and closer to junction 28, is **Tredegar House Country Park**. The House was once the home of the Morgans of Tredegar, and, as so often has happened, was several times remodelled in line with current tastes and to display the current generation's wealth and power. The present building chiefly dates from the rebuilding in the 1660s, when a glittering sequence of lavishly decorated state rooms was built, and the 19th century, when the servants' quarters were enlarged. Outside, there are pleasant landscaped grounds for strolls and picnics. These date from the 1790s, and only one of the majestic avenues of oak, walnut and chestnut planted in the 17th century survives. Several estate buildings still stand, including a magnificent 17th-century stable block and orangery. Others house a restaurant and bar, craft workshops and a visitor centre. The woodland walk is especially lovely in early summer when the rhododendrons are in bloom. The House is open between Good Friday and September, the grounds daily throughout the year (tours of the House every half hour from 12.30 to 4.30 on Wednesdays to Sundays and Public Holidays); the gardens and grounds are open daily from dawn to dusk. The Park entrance is on the B4239, which you reach by taking the A48 east and turning right almost immediately.

JUNCTION 28 PETERSTONE WENTLOOGE

There is another good coastal walk here, with a distinctly Dutch feel about the wide views. The ships on the horizon are no more than dots, and the sea, sky and mudflats merge gently and imperceptibly. Follow the B4239 past the entrance to Tredegar Park and on through the magnificently named St Bride's Wentlooge to **Peterstone Wentlooge**. Park the car by the church, and follow the footpath alongside the churchyard and across a couple of fields. The sea wall looms up in front of you, and you scramble up to find an expanse of mud and water suddenly revealed. You can walk along the sea wall – known as Peterstone Great Wharf – in both directions. To the east it takes you back to St Bride's Wentlooge, where a side road runs right up to the shore from the B4239, and beyond along the banks of the Ebbw river until the path peters out near Tredegar Park (about 7 miles). To the west it takes you to the mouth of the Rhymney river and then inland to the edge of Rumney, on the far outskirts of Cardiff (about 5 miles). The Six Bells pub opposite the church in Peterstone Wentlooge will serve you a well-deserved drink or two. As far as scenery is concerned, this walk and the one near Magor (see page 147) are similar. I prefer this one, but either makes an excellent break from driving.

If you are travelling west into Wales, do not try to regain the motorway at junctions 29 or 29a, but return to junction 28, either along the B4239 or via the A48 at Castleton. If you are going east towards England, an alternative is to turn left half-way between Peterstone and St Bride's Wentlooge and make for the A48 at Castleton. The Port O'Call pub here looks nice, and the Wentlooge Castle Hotel does 'Welsh teas'. For junction 29a and the eastbound M4, turn left along the A48. For junction 28 and the westbound M4, turn right.

Junction 29 has no access on to ordinary roads and leads straight into the A48 (M), a short spur motorway which ends at junction 29a, where it meets the A48. You can only get on to the A48 (M) from the M4 if you are travelling west, from Newport. And the A48 (M) only leads on to the eastbound carriageway of the M4, towards Newport. But there is nothing to leave the M4 for anyway.

The next junction is 32: and this is neither printer's error nor author's aberration. Nos. 30 and 31 do not exist. Junctions 29 and 32 both provide fast routes into **Cardiff** – which offers shops, museums, and the Castle – along the A48 and the A470 respectively.

JUNCTION 32 CASTELL COCH
But with two such magnificent castles as Castell Coch and Caerphilly only a short drive from junction 32, who could possibly want to tackle Cardiff's crowds and traffic? You get a clear view of **Castell Coch** from the motorway, proud and dominant on the hill-

side, and, it appears at first sight, the home for centuries of some ancient aristocratic line. Quite the contrary! For all its 13th-century appearance, the castle is scarcely a hundred years old and the whole thing is an artifice – an artifice, mind you, of the highest craftsmanship and skill. The building is the work of William Burges, an architect whose work exemplifies what is often called 'high Victorian' verve: 'a unique blend of scholarly historicism and archaeological exactitude on the one hand with a total immersion in Romantic fantasy on the other', to quote one expert. Burges's exteriors were extremely accurate. While working on Castell Coch he studied a large number of medieval castles in Britain and Europe, and took many of his ideas from the Château de Chillon on Lake Geneva. Inside, however, he gave free rein to his wildest fantasies. 'If we could reincarnate a Welsh warrior from the thirteenth century, he would ride into Burges' Castell Coch, thunder across the drawbridge and dismount in the courtyard without a trace of surprise. Only when he entered what Burges called the "Castellan's Rooms" would our Welsh rebel suffer a total mental and nervous collapse.' And the castle entrance is extremely impressive, with a dramatic approach through beech trees and then the castle suddenly rising up in front of you. Inside, the courtyard, all red-painted wood and with a wooden gallery running along three sides, is almost like a theatre in the round. I half-expected to be met by a minor character escaped from a Shakespeare play. The main rooms are full of luxuriant colour and gilt, vivid wall decorations (the paintings in the Drawing Room depict Aesop's *Fables*, with a wealth of mythical and real beasts and birds) and extraordinary furniture. The wash-stand in the Marchioness's Bedroom is decorated with two crenellated towers, one each for the hot and cold water tanks. It is a make-believe and romanticized medieval world and I loved it. The castle is open on Mondays to Saturdays from 9.30 to 6.30, Sundays from 2.00 to 6.30, between mid-March and mid-October; and from 9.30 to 4.00 on weekdays, 2.00 to 4.00 on Sundays, during the rest of the year. The quickest route from junction 32 is along the A4054 north from the motorway into Tongwynlais and then right in the middle of the village. The castle entrance is soon on the left.

If you are making from the motorway straight to Caerphilly, follow the A470 dual carriageway north to the junction with the A468, and turn right on to that road. From Castell Coch there is a pleasant back route. From the castle entrance follow the road away from Tongwynlais through attractive woodland (inviting paths suggest a short stroll) and turn right at the Black Cock Inn. On the far side of Caerphilly Common turn right, then left, and a steep hill descends into the centre of town.

JUNCTION 32 CAERPHILLY CASTLE

Caerphilly Castle has been described as 'one of the most spectacular military ruins in the world' – and surely correctly. A marvellous example of a concentric castle, it was the first in these islands to be designed as such. The main stronghold is the central block, surrounded by a curtain wall with a twin-towered gatehouse at the western end and two gatehouses with single towers at the eastern end. But before an attacking force could get anywhere near this redoubt, they had to face not only elaborate water defences, consisting of an inner and an outer moat and two lakes, but also, to the west, a large outwork and, on the east, a long platform between the two moats. Like many people I find castles confusing: however carefully I study the plans, I find it difficult to visualize what was supposed to be and to happen where. For once, here at Caerphilly, this is not the case, and it is worth looking at all these defensive features in some detail. The irony is that all this sophisticated planning was done almost in vain. The great threat to English dominance in Glamorgan during the late 1260s was Llywelyn ap Gruffydd, Prince of Wales, and it was to resist him that Henry II permitted Gilbert de Clare, Earl of Gloucester and Hereford, to build such a substantial work. Llywelyn attacked in 1270, when part of the Castle had been built, and burnt it, and again in 1271, when he was beaten off. But by the time the Castle was completed the main Welsh threat had vanished. This is probably the best castle mentioned in this book, and it is well worth the journey from the motorway. An exhibition entitled 'Castles in Wales' in the Lady Tower tells the story of castle-building in Wales. The Castle is open on Mondays to Saturdays from 9.30 to 6.30, Sundays from 2.00 to 6.30, between mid-March and mid-October; and from 9.30 to 4.00 on weekdays, 2.00 to 4.00 on Sundays, during the rest of the year. The Court House pub and restaurant opposite the Castle is a good place to eat, and especially to sample the Caerphilly cheese made in the small dairy on the premises, the first Caerphilly to be made in the town since the late 1960s.

JUNCTION 33 WELSH FOLK MUSEUM

The **Welsh Folk Museum**, at **St Fagans**, a few miles south of junction 33, is a fascinating memorial to the now almost vanished cultural heritage of rural Wales. Over the last 40 years, a collection of some 30 buildings – homes, workshops, farm buildings, chapels and many more – from every part of the land have been re-erected around the 100-acre site. There is, for instance, a tannery from Rhayader, the last oak-bark tannery to operate in Wales, a 19th-century water-powered corn mill, a blacksmith's shop, a moorland long-house, occupied by the family at one end and cattle at the other, a Unitarian chapel and a schoolhouse, where all the pupils, from 5- to 14-year-olds, were educated in a single classroom. Most of the buildings contain the furniture and equipment their earlier inhabitants would have used; the detail is authentic, and all the more interesting for that. It is easy to spend as much as a long afternoon here, simply walking around, or watching expert craftsmen at work: flour and wool are produced in the Museum, horses are shod and tools are fashioned by a blacksmith, and, at the appropriate season, sheep-shearing and hedging take place. **St Fagans Castle** is a late 16th-century building set in attractive gardens; the interior is furnished to show life in the 17th century. The Museum's indoor galleries contain a large selection of objects illustrating the domestic, social and cultural life of Wales – including Welsh dressers and other furniture, musical instruments, kitchen and laundry equipment, firearms, etc. – costume, and agricultural equipment and vehicles. The Museum is open on Mondays to Saturdays from 10.00 to 5.00 and on Sundays from 2.30 to 5.00; there are several cafés and restaurants. Take the A4232 south from the motorway, turn left on to the A48 and then left again almost immediately. This road runs through the pleasant countryside of the Ely valley to St Fagans village.

JUNCTION 34 LLANTRISANT

Llantrisant, 3 miles north of junction 34, is best known nowadays as the home of the Royal Mint, which lies in a wooded valley behind the town. Unfortunately, tours of the Mint are no longer available. However, the town centre, perched on the top of the hill, is worth a quick visit if you are a connoisseur of out-of-the-way, non-touristy places. If it isn't quite as dramatic as a Provençal or Tuscan hill town, it is a good imitation. You turn left off the A473 Pontypridd road and climb steeply through narrow streets, the houses clinging to the hillside. Once you are at the top of the town, there is little to do but come down again: but I don't regret my visit, and would certainly go again, if only for the lovely views. On the **Bullring** a curious statue seems at first sight to commemorate a character from mythology or legend. On closer inspection you find that in this case historical fact is quite as vivid as legend. Dr William Price – his normal dress was green coat and trousers and a foxskin cap with tails – was a surgeon, Chartist, healer and self-styled Druid. Marriage being one of the many institutions he despised, he lived with a young woman by whom he had a child at the age of 83. The child (whom his father had named Iesu Grist – Jesus Christ) died, and Dr Price cremated him, much to the horror of the local inhabitants. He was pursued by an angry mob, arrested, tried – and acquitted. This acquittal changed the law and made cremation legal. Small wonder, then, that Dr Price's statue has been erected by the Cremation Society and the Federation of British Cremation Authorities.

JUNCTION 36 COITY CASTLE

Junctions 35 and 36 are for castle enthusiasts, but not really for anyone else. There are two interesting castles a short way off – Newcastle and Coity – while a longer diversion takes in two more, Ogmore and Candleston, plus Ewenny Priory and an attractive stretch of coast. Bridgend, the town nearest the exits, is a pretty uninspiring place, made worse by a tricky one-way system.

Newcastle overlooks the river Ogmore on its west bank in Bridgend, and was built in the mid- or late 12th century to a polygonal design, with no fewer than nine unequal sides. Of rather greater interest, and certainly my choice if I only had time for one, is **Coity Castle.** Leave the motorway at junction 36, take the A4061 south and then turn left on to the side road for Coity village. Ruined though it is, the Castle is still impressive, with a large curtain wall, great tower and moat. It was built in two stages, in the late 12th and early 14th centuries, and successfully withstood a siege by Owain Glyndwr in 1404. Opening times at both Newcastle and Coity are Mondays to Saturdays from 9.30 to 6.30, Sundays 2.00 to 6.30, between mid-March and mid-October; weekdays 9.30 to 4.00, Sundays 2.00 to 4.00, during the rest of the year.

JUNCTION 35 EWENNY PRIORY

The diversion mentioned above starts at junction 35 and wanders through Ogwr, the stretch of land between Bridgend and the sea. The first stop is **Ewenny Priory**. Take the A473 west from the motorway, turn on to the A48 west at the second roundabout and then left on to the B4265 to Ewenny. Once you have crossed the river, turn left and the priory is reached after about ½ mile. The priory was founded in 1141 and, according to one expert view, can 'claim to be the best example of Norman ecclesiastical architecture in Wales'. The defensive walls were built in the 13th century, and in the south transept the founder, Maurice de Londres, is buried. In the attractive little village there are two potteries, one of which, the **Ewenny Pottery,** was established in 1610 and has been run by the same family ever since. Ewenny ware is still sold and you can see it being made by methods that have changed little over the centuries. The pottery is open daily from 9.30 to 5.30 (Sundays from 2.00 to 5.30) between Easter and the end of September, and in the winter on Mondays to Fridays from 9.30 to 5.30 and on Saturdays from 9.30 to

12.30. The **Claypits Pottery**, also in the village, is open at similar times.

JUNCTION 35 OGMORE CASTLE & MERTHYR MAWR WARREN

On now to **Ogmore Castle**, about 1½ miles further down the B4524 towards the sea. This Castle guarded a crucial ford across the river, and stepping stones lead from the outer bailey across the river. The earliest earthworks were begun here in the early 12th century, but by the end of the century a great stone tower had been built, the first of a succession of works that added a cellar building, a gateway, an enclosing curtain wall and a two-storey hall. A moat on three sides and the river on the fourth provided additional protection. The Castle is open on Mondays to Saturdays from 9.30 to 6.30, Sundays 2.00 to 6.30, between mid-March and mid-October; and from 9.30 to 4.00, Sundays 2.00 to 4.00, during the rest of the year.

The next port of call is **Merthyr Mawr**, hardly any distance away in miles but a long way by road. Retrace your tracks to Ewenny, take the B4265 out of the village but turn left almost immediately, and then left again after about ¾ mile. The village has attractive thatched cottages set in lovely woodland, but it is the area beyond the village that is of greatest interest. The road peters out after ½ mile at **Candleston Castle**, a 14th-century structure in which a polygonal courtyard enclosed a square tower. Beyond it is **Merthyr Mawr Warren**, a wild and dramatic area of sand dunes bounded on one side by the sea, on the other by the estuary of the Ogmore river. Part of the warren is designated a Site of Special Scientific Interest: Neolithic tumuli have been found here. By now you are quite some way from the motorway, and to regain it you must return on the same road until it meets the A48. Then, if you are making for the west, turn left and follow the A48 to junction 37.

JUNCTION 36 BRYNGARW COUNTRY PARK

A much more accessible excursion close to junction 36 is to **Bryngarw Country Park**, only a couple of miles from the motorway. The Park occupies the grounds of Bryngarw House, now converted to flats, and as a result offers pleasantly contrasting walks around the formal gardens and lawns – including an ornamental lake and a Japanese garden with many exotic plants – and then through pleasant woodland and along the bank of the river Garw. There is a small visitor centre, and refreshments are available. Take the A4061 north from the motorway, turn left on to the A4065, and the Park entrance is on the right, shortly after the junction with the A4064.

JUNCTION 37 PORTHCAWL & KENFIG NATURE RESERVE

Porthcawl, 3 miles south of junction 37 on the A4229, must surely have seen better days. When I was there, there was something indefinably run-down about it. All the amenities of a major seaside resort are present and correct – beaches, paddling pools, amusements, funfairs, Grand Pavilion – but without any real conviction. The holidaymakers who spent a week or two here in the 1950s are off to Spain or Greece now – or at least their children are – and one wonders who will replace them. That said, if you like resorts you will find it pleasant enough. Rest Bay, west of the centre, is becoming known as a mecca for surfers.

There is a much more interesting trip from junction 37 to the **Kenfig Pool and Dunes Local Nature Reserve,** to give it its full title. The Reserve – which consists of sand dunes, wet 'slacks', a freshwater pool and associated habitats – is tucked into a curious no-man's-land between Porthcawl and Port Talbot, the sea, the railway and the motorway. There is some excellent walking from the visitor centre: just over ¼ mile each way to the 70-acre pool, and a longer trek (1½ miles and up to 45 minutes each way – the path can be very muddy) to the beach. A wide variety of flowers and plants can be seen: more than 580 species have been recorded. The area is especially noted for orchids; the first to appear each year, in May, are the marsh orchids. As might be expected, the Reserve is a haven for birds, and over 180 species have been recorded, including many wintering migrants. When I was there, pintail, spotted redshank and lapland bunting were among the recent sightings. The wind was whistling, the clouds were low: a fine and lonely place. There is access to the Reserve itself at all times, but the visitor centre – which has displays on the ecology, history and wildlife of the area – is only open at weekends and Bank Holidays from 2.00 to 5.00. It is about 2½ miles from junction 37. Take the North Cornelly road from the motorway and then follow the signs to Kenfig. The Reserve also contains the site of the medieval borough of Kenfig, overwhelmed by sand in the 15th century, part of whose castle has now been excavated.

JUNCTION 38 MARGAM COUNTRY PARK

Junctions 38 and 39 are not even standard half-junctions. You can do everything at junction 38 except join the westbound carriageway. For that you have to continue on the A48 to junction 39. Margam Country Park, close to these two junctions, and Afan Argoed Country Park, high in the hills behind junction 40 (see page 158, are both inspired examples of countryside planning. I strongly recommend a visit to at least one.

Margam Country Park is a remarkable place. There is a wide range of unusual things to do – genuinely something for everyone – and yet it isn't over-commercialized and it doesn't lower its standards. And its popularity suggests that this approach pays off. The Park is based on Margam Castle, a huge 19th-century pile built by Christopher Rice Mansel Talbot, the Talbot of Port Talbot and one of the largest landowners and wealthiest men in Glamorgan. For all its rich display of wealth both inside and out – the exterior is decorated with battlements, turrets and pinnacles, while inside there was marble, stained glass, gilded plasterwork and carved panelling – the Castle's career as a grand mansion was short-lived. Almost exactly a century after its completion, the Second World War broke out, the Castle was requisitioned and became home, of a sort, for thousands of British and American troops. Since then it has lain derelict, and it is now no more than a shell. The lovely orangery, where almost two hundred years ago a large collection of orange, citrus and lemon trees bloomed, has been restored, however, and part of it is open to the public. The best place to start a visit is at the elegant visitor centre in the Castle courtyard. There is a well-laid-out display here on the history and ecology of the Park, plus a well-stocked shop. The Coach House Theatre nearby regularly shows two films on the Park: *Heritage of Margam* and *Margam through the Seasons*. After that the choice is wide open: boating, fishing and riding; an adventure playground and an area devoted to rare animal breeds; picnics in the Park, where there is a large herd of fallow deer, believed to be descended from a herd brought here in the 15th century, and a smaller herd of the extremely rare Glamorgan cattle, which until a few years ago were thought to be completely extinct. There are several quite lengthy walks through the grounds, with opportunities to see many different species, including buzzard and kestrel and, if you are lucky, kingfishers beside the streams. The Park is also at one end of the **Coed Morgannwg Way**, a 26-mile walk through Glamorgan. The Park is rich in history: **Mynydd-y-Castell** is an Iron Age hillfort, its massive bank and ditches enclosing almost 7 acres, and, in the far west of the Park and certainly not to be missed, lies **Margam Church**. There was a Cistercian abbey at Margam for four centuries from 1147, although after the Black Death the number of monks fell, and there were a mere nine when the abbey was dissolved in 1536. The present church is based on part of the abbey nave; the remains of the fine 12-sided chapter house can also be seen.

I have left the two most unusual features of Margam Park – for me the most interesting as well – until last: the maze and the sculpture park. The maze is quite amazing (sorry, the pun was irresistible) – reputedly the largest and most complicated in the world. It is one of the newest too since it was laid out only in 1982. The trees, principally gold-coloured conifers mixed with a dark green variety, have already reached their planned height of five feet. The 40 or so sculptures carefully placed around the Park include works by sculptors such as Barbara Hepworth, David Kemp and Brenda Oakes. I am not a sculpture specialist, and I shall not attempt an appreciation of the individual works. But it is well worth spending some time looking at the different pieces – examining them from different angles, seeing how they fit into the landscape, even touching them.

Margam Country Park is open daily from 9.30 to 7.00 (last admissions at 5.00) between April and October; daily except Mondays and Tuesdays from 9.30 to 5.00 (last admissions at 3.00) during the rest of the year. The entrance is only ¼ mile from both junctions 38 and 39.

JUNCTION 40 AFAN ARGOED COUNTRY PARK & WELSH MINERS MUSEUM

Around junction 40, the hills descend sharply to the sea and the motorway is squeezed into a tiny coastal strip, just above the port and steel works at **Port Talbot**. There are excellent industrial views here. In the immediate neighbourhood, there is nothing to suggest a worthwhile break, but just 6 miles away, and 15 minutes' driving at worst, you can be in an entirely different world. **Afan Argoed Country Park** is less sophisticated than Margam, and you have to find your own pleasures here. But even if you only sit and rest, drinking in the majestic forest scenery, the diversion will be worthwhile. For the more energetic there are a number of walks, including two longish forest trails, the Michaelston and Argoed (5 and 3 miles respectively). Both these run through wonderful country and also pass interesting mining and agricultural remains. The **Coed Morgannwg Way** also passes through the Park (the countryside centre is the halfway point), accompanying each of the trails mentioned. The countryside centre, which is on the A4107, the road up from the M4, has a small shop and displays on local history and ecology. There is also the **Welsh Miners Museum,** a detailed and fascinating record of mining in this part of Wales from 250 years ago almost to the present day. Documents and pictures, reconstructions of a coalface and domestic interiors bring the miners' way of life home in vivid, intimate detail. This Park is certainly worth the longish detour from the motorway. (The Park is open all the time. The visitor centre and the Museum are open daily from 10.30 to 6.00 between April and October, and at weekends only for the rest of the year from 11.30 to 5.00.)

Junction 41 is a quarter-junction, almost on top of junction 40 in any case. All you can do here is join the westbound carriageway of the motorway.

Logically, you would expect the next junction to be no. 42. It isn't. Shortly after junction 41, the motorway stops, and the next 5 miles past oil refineries and across the estuary of the river Neath have to be covered on ordinary roads. The route is well signposted.

ABERAVON SANDS

For **Aberavon Sands**, turn left at the roundabout at the end of the motorway. The route through a large council estate is badly signposted, but if you press straight on towards the sea you cannot go far wrong. The sands are beautifully golden, an excellent place for children and dogs – and adults too – to get a quick burst of fresh air. There are hardly any amenities here, except a small amusement park and a couple of cafés at the southern end of the sands. If you drive down this end, you can regain the motorway west by making for the centre of Port Talbot and junction 41.

NEATH ABBEY

Neath is the main town near this motorway 'gap', but the centre has little to attract visitors. On the opposite side of the river valley and the main A465 north, **Neath Abbey** is rather incongruously situated in the middle of a small industrial estate. The abbey was founded in 1130 and joined the Cistercian order 17 years later, but the present building – or what remains of it – dates from 1280 to 1330. It must have been an impressive sight then, with accommodation for 25 monks and double that number of lay brothers. Now, sadly, only the outer walls are standing, which makes the visit really worthwhile only for abbey enthusiasts. After the Dissolution of the Monasteries in 1536 the abbey's fabric gradually disappeared. The abbot's house was converted into a country mansion, much of the stone was used to build new housing in the 18th century, and – an unusual fate for an ecclesiastical building – by the 1720s copper smelting was being carried on close to the abbey ruins. The abbey is open on Mondays to Saturdays from 9.30 to 6.30 and on Sundays from 2.00 to 6.30 between mid-March and mid-October; and from 9.30 to 4.00 on weekdays, 2.00 to 4.00 on Sundays, during the rest of the year. The best route to the abbey from the main road is to turn north up the A465 and then left at the first roundabout, from where the abbey is signposted.

PENSCYNOR WILDLIFE PARK

It is worth continuing on the A465 up the valley as there are several attractions of greater family appeal. The first to be reached is the **Penscynor Wildlife Park**. The proclaimed philosophy of its founder, a former wildlife photographer, is that 'animals have as much right to this planet as have we human beings', and a particular effort is made 'to keep each animal in as free an environment as possible'. Fine words, and most people would agree with them. But I'm not sure how far this ambition is realized at Penscynor. On my visit, the place seemed a little sad, its inhabitants not very lively, the space available to them rather restricted. That said, there is a lot to see, especially since the emphasis, happily, is on small creatures. There are monkeys, chimpanzees and marmoset, which are now enjoying life in their new house built in the forest; flamingoes, sea-lions and numerous species of waterfowl; a walk-through aviary, plus macaws, birds of prey and many others. Other attractions include a lake fed by a 40-foot waterfall, a pets corner and, for those less taken with wildlife, a chair-lift and alpine slide. There is a shop and a café, and also the Tree Tops Restaurant. The Park is open daily from 10.00 to 6.00. To get there, take the A465 north to the Cilfrew turning, from which signposts show the way.

ABERDULAIS FALLS & BASIN

Just north of Penscynor some fascinating pieces of industrial archaeology at Aberdulais Falls and at the junction of the Neath and Tennant Canals are well worth visiting. Until the late 16th century, all our refined metals were imported. Then the Mines Royal, with the Earl of Pembroke at its head, was organized to start refining in Britain, and **Aberdulais Falls** was chosen as a site. The reason? The Earl of Pembroke owned a good deal of land around Neath, and the falls had plentiful coal and timber, plus water power for the bellows. Within a hundred years Neath was the most important centre of copper and lead refining in Wales, and the industry was spreading throughout the country. The remains of this pioneering activity are now being restored, and visitors can see the wheel pit and bastion, furnaces and chimney stack, and can also enjoy a pleasant riverside walk; there is also a visitor information centre. The site is open on Mondays to Fridays from 9.00 to 5.00 and at weekends and Public Holidays from 11.00 to 6.00 between April and October; times during the rest of the year are daily 11.00 to 4.00. Just a few hundred yards away you jump two hundred years or so to **Aberdulais Basin**, where the Neath Canal (1795) and the Tennant Canal (1824) met at a graceful skew bridge. Both canals were used to transport coal from the upper Neath valley to the ports at Neath and Swansea. The basin now makes a pleasant picnic spot, and towpath walks along both canals start from here with good views of the

Neath and Dulais rivers. To get to the basin, turn right off the A465 towards Tonna and then almost immediately left. There are two pubs here, the Railway Inn and the Dulais Rock Hotel.

CEFN COED COAL & STEAM MUSEUM

The final attraction in the Neath valley is the **Cefn Coed Coal and Steam Museum**, which is rather a long way from the M4 but certainly worth the trip. When the two huge steam winding-engines at Cefn Coed Colliery were shut down in 1975, it was decided to preserve and restore one of them as well as the six boilers that provided the steam, together with pithead gear, winders and a compressor. There is also an exhibition with displays on the equipment and local history of coal mining. All this is interesting, but what really conveys the feel of work underground is the simulated mining gallery, 30 metres long and two below the surface. The Museum is on the A4109 2 miles north of the junction with the A465, which in turn is about 5 miles from the motorway. The Museum is open daily from 11.00 to 6.00 (last admissions at 5.15) between April and October.

JUNCTION 44 SWANSEA

The motorway resumes at junction 44 and loops round **Swansea** to the north. Access is easy from junctions 44, 45 and 46, but 46 is another half-junction, at which you can only leave the westbound carriageway and join the eastbound one. There are several interesting museums in Swansea – notably the new **Maritime and Industrial Museum**, which includes a fully operational woollen mill and the lively Maritime Quarter, where there are arts workshops and a marina – and good shops and eating places, but the city is too busy to recommend for a quick break.

Gorseinon is the nearest village to junction 47, but there is nothing special here.

JUNCTION 48 LLANELLI

From junction 48 it is a 4-mile drive along the A4138 to **Llanelli**. The town has a pleasantly airy feel about it, perhaps because of the contrast with the narrow valleys and tightly packed houses only a little way behind on the M4. There is a largish pedestrianized shopping centre, and a covered market too. **Parc Howard** is an attractive municipal park just behind the town centre, and the **Mansion House** there has a display of Llanelli or South Wales pottery, including the well-known 'seaweed' design (open from 10.00 to 6.00 on Mondays to Saturdays, 2.00 to 6.00 on Sundays, between March and November).

JUNCTION 48 PEMBREY COUNTRY PARK

Pleasant though Llanelli is, it isn't worth turning off for – unless, that is, you are making for Carmarthen and beyond. In this case, the A484 from Llanelli through Burry Port and Kidwelly and north to Carmarthen is an excellent alternative to the last stretch of the M4 and the A48. This route is a long rather than a short cut (but not much longer, 23 miles as against 19 on the M4 and A48), but in terms of scenery and things to do it is far more interesting. From Llanelli the road runs along the coast to Burry Port and then past **Pembrey Country Park** (open daily, dawn to dusk) to Kidwelly. At the Park there are nature trails, woodland, adventure and play areas and a magnificent seven-mile stretch of sandy beach. The **Welsh Motor Sports Centre** on the old Pembrey Airfield stages regular weekend events including motor and motorcycle racing, sprinting and karting. The imposing Castle at **Kidwelly** overlooking the estuary of the Gwendraeth Fach was started in 1270, work continuing until well into the next century. Opening times are weekdays from 9.30 to 6.30, Sundays 2.00 to 6.30, between mid-March and mid-October; and 9.30 to 4.00, Sundays 2.00 to 4.00, during the rest of the year. Also worth seeing here is the **Kidwelly Industrial Museum**, which occupies the remains of a disused tinplate works. Production of tinplate is thought to have begun here in 1737, and it continued until the 1940s. The entire tin-making process can be followed, from the heating of metal bars in the hot rolling mill through pickling and annealing to coating with tin and finally cleaning and polishing. Other features of the Museum are industrial locomotives and a steam winding engine and pithead gear, together with industrial machinery and tools. Opening times are 10.00 to 5.00 on weekdays, 2.00 to 5.00 at weekends, between Easter and September.

The M4 ends at junction 49 in some not especially attractive countryside. There is a service station at the junction with the A48, which continues through Cross Hands and Carmarthen to the magnificent inland and coastal scenery of western Pembrokeshire.

The M40

Uxbridge to Oxford

INTRODUCTION

The M40 is the Chilterns motorway. From the edge of the rather dreary western outer London suburbs, it runs past Beaconsfield and High Wycombe and then – the single dramatic moment of the journey, this – descends the scarp slope in a steep cutting in the chalk, with fine views ahead towards Oxford and the south Midlands plain. Although the countryside to each side of the road is not especially attractive, a diversion of a few miles in each direction brings you to some pleasant spots. To the south there is Burnham Beeches, and then the Thames-side villages of Cookham, birthplace of the artist Stanley Spencer, and Marlow. To the north there is Jordans, an early centre of the Quaker movement, and then two grand but very different country houses, Hughenden and West Wycombe. Hughenden, home of Benjamin Disraeli, the founder of the modern Conservative Party, is predominantly 19th century, while the house, park and village at West Wycombe are all creations of the most exquisite and learned 18th-century taste.

The motorway starts at junction 1, on the edge of the built-up area of Greater London, just west of Uxbridge and Ruislip. There is nothing worth leaving the motorway for.

Junction 1a is the junction with the M25, and there is no access on to ordinary roads.

JUNCTION 2 BURNHAM BEECHES

Burnham Beeches lies a couple of miles south along the A355 from junction 2. Turn right off the A355 after 1.8 miles along a local road signposted to Egypt, just past the Yew Tree Inn, which would be a good place for a drink and a light meal. A drive into the forest leads off to the right after about ½ mile. These 500 acres of surprisingly remote woodland, which manage to remain uncrowded even at the busiest times, offer plenty of pleasant walks and picnic spots.

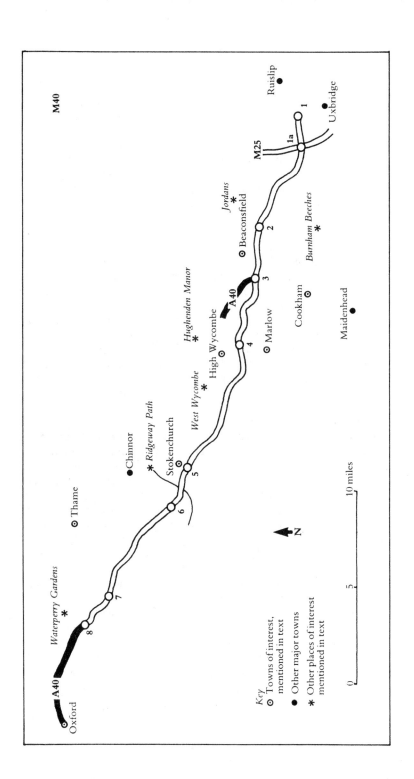

Key
⊙ Towns of interest, mentioned in text
● Other major towns
∗ Other places of interest mentioned in text

M40

Ruislip
Uxbridge
1
1a
M25

Jordans
∗
Beaconsfield ⊙
2
Burnham Beeches
∗
3
Cookham ⊙
Marlow ⊙
Maidenhead ●

Hughenden Manor
∗
A40
High Wycombe ⊙
4

West Wycombe
∗

Ridgeway Path
∗
Stokenchurch
Chinnor ●
⊙
5

Thame ⊙
6

Waterperry Gardens
∗
7
8
A40
Oxford ⊙

N

0   5   10 miles

Autumn, when the leaves are showing every shade of green, yellow and brown, is a specially good time to come. As you will see from the maps and signboards conveniently posted around the forest, Burnham Beeches is run, perhaps somewhat surprisingly, by the Corporation of London, which took the forest over in 1880 to preserve it as an open space for the ever-increasing population of London. In the Middle Ages the land was scrub and common used by peasants for grazing cattle. It escaped enclosure and gradually, over the centuries, reverted to woodland; some parts are over 400 years old.

JUNCTION 2 JORDANS

North of junction 2 there is an excursion through pleasant countryside to **Jordans**, an historic centre of the Quaker movement. From the motorway, take the A355 north, turn right on to the A40 almost immediately, and then take the first left off the A40; Jordans is 1 mile along this road. The first building you come to is the **Meeting House**, on the right. This simple building of local materials was erected in 1688, the year when James II's Declaration of Indulgence put an end to the persecution and imprisonment which the Society of Friends and other nonconformists had suffered for their unwillingness to subscribe to the Church of England. The meeting room itself is plain and unadorned, with simple wooden benches facing in towards a central table; the window furniture and glass are mostly original. Among the headstones in the graveyard outside are those of several active early Quakers, including William Penn and his two wives, Gulielma and Hannah. Penn founded Pennsylvania in the USA as a 'holy experiment' in government intended to establish freedom of conscience and peace among both Indians and white settlers; he became the first Governor of the colony. (The Meeting House is open on Mondays from 10.00 to 1.00; on Wednesdays to Saturdays from 2.00 to 6.00 or dusk if earlier; on Sundays from 12.00 to 6.00.) Up the gentle hill behind the Meeting House are the Mayflower Barn and Old Jordans. Originally a farm, **Old Jordans** is now a Quaker guest and retreat house; morning coffee, lunch and tea are served to non-residents, and non-Friends are given a warm welcome. Regular meetings for worship began to be held at Old Jordans in 1659. At that time religious toleration was practically non-existent – the Conventicle Act of 1664 forbade religious meetings or more than five people and the following year nonconformist ministers and preachers were prohibited from living within 5 miles of a town – and many meetings at Jordans were broken up by the justices, the Friends being carted off to prison. After the Meeting House was built in 1688, the farm passed out of Quaker hands until 1910, when it was bought and converted into a guest house. The **Mayflower Barn** on the far side of the garden from the farmhouse is a well-preserved example of a timbered Buckinghamshire barn. It is said, although there is no absolute proof, that the ships' timbers used to build the barn came from the *Mayflower*, the ship which carried the Pilgrim Fathers to America in 1620. The barn, which is open throughout the day, is now used for concerts, lectures, receptions and many other cultural and community events. On the left just beyond Old Jordans is Jordans village, a self-governing garden village community founded and built by Friends in 1919.

JUNCTION 2 BEACONSFIELD

Beaconsfield is a prosperous country-cum-commuter town a little way west of junction 2 along the A40. The main attraction here is **Bekonscot Model Village**, where a miniature community – complete with houses, shops, streets and lakes – is laid out in an attractive garden. Opening times are daily between 10.00 and 5.00 from March to October. From the motorway, take the A355 north, turn left on to the A40, right again very soon back on to the A355, and then left again in about 1 mile after crossing the railway. At the end of this road turn left into the B474, and then left again almost immediately.

JUNCTION 3 COOKHAM

The main excursion from junction 3 is south to **Cookham** and the **Stanley Spencer Gallery**, which is housed in the former Methodist chapel where the artist worshipped with his family as a child. Spencer lived in Cookham for most of his life, and the attractive Thames-side village features in many of his paintings: 'The Resurrection, Cookham', for instance, now in the Tate Gallery, and the *Christ Preaching at Cookham Regatta* series, two of which hang in the Gallery at Cookham. But the visitor should not expect conventional landscape views. Spencer was a religious visionary, a painter who, in the words of one commentator, took as his theme 'the wonder of life that is compounded of love and joy'; Spencer himself wrote that 'only goodness and love and Christian and other benign beliefs are capable of creative works'. The Gallery contains a collection of Spencer's major works, including several landscapes, paintings of Englefield House – home of Gerard Shiel, one of Spencer's patrons – 'The Last Supper' and 'Sunbathers at Odney'. Other items include letters, memorabilia and, perhaps best-known of all, the perambulator Spencer used to carry his easel and paints on painting expeditions. The Gallery is open daily from 10.30 to 6.00 between Easter and October and from 11.00 to 5.00 at weekends and Public

Holidays the rest of the year. There are several pleasant eating-places in Cookham including the Ferry Inn, on the riverside by the Victorian cast-iron bridge that crosses the Thames. From junction 3 take the A40 briefly towards Beaconsfield, then turn left on to the A4094 under the motorway and through Wooburn and Bourne End to Cookham. Distance from the motorway is just under 5 miles. Cookham is equidistant from junction 7 of the M4 (see page 129). Drive west along the A4, cross the river in Maidenhead, and then turn immediately right on to the A4094. Distance is 5 miles.

JUNCTION 4 MARLOW

Marlow is a pleasant Thames-side town 3½ miles south of junction 4. Drive south on the A404 and then turn right on to the A4155. The suspension bridge over the river was built in 1831; the river life – swans, boats, fishermen, the weir – is always enjoyable to watch, especially from the Compleat Angler inn on the south bank. A riverside path runs along the north bank both up- and down-stream. There are some attractive old houses in the town, especially in the High Street, and the **Crown Hotel** is another hostelry; Dick Turpin is said to have drunk here.

JUNCTION 4 HIGH WYCOMBE

High Wycombe, 1½ miles north of the motorway along the A404, is a busy shopping and business centre where parking is not always easy. But if you are prepared to do battle with the traffic, there are a couple of places well worth visiting. The first is the **Wycombe Chair Museum** in Priory Avenue, just north of the town centre and near the station. Chairs may hardly seem a likely subject for a museum, but High Wycombe has for long been a major furniture-making centre and this is one of the most interesting and friendly local museums I have visited. Downstairs the emphasis is on chair-making and other local crafts. Apart from many different types of Windsor chair, more than one ever thought existed, wood-working tools are displayed and there are features on the history and making of chairs. The Chiltern Room contains displays on associated crafts such as cane-seating and rushing and, most fascinating of all, on traditional Buckinghamshire pillow lace. A lace pillow with its bobbins is shown, and there are old photographs of lace-makers at work. The three upstairs rooms are all linked with celebrated local people who achieved national fame. The Hampden Room, named after John Hampden, the Buckinghamshire Parliamentarian who opposed the imposition by Charles I of ship money, contains 16th- and 17th-century furniture, including a lovely pine staircase and a beautiful silk-embroidered jewel case. The 18th-century Dashwood

Room (see Wycombe Park, below, for the Dashwoods) has Chippendale, Sheraton and Hepplewhite pieces, while the 19th-century Disraeli Room (see also Hughenden, below) contains the Champion Chair made for the Great Exhibition of 1851 and portraits of the Prime Minister and his beloved Queen Victoria. At the back of the Museum in the old stables is a fascinating bodgers' hut – bodgers were chair-leg turners who worked in the Chiltern woods around High Wycombe – and a framers' workshop dating from the 1880s. The Museum's opening hours are 10.00 to 1.00 and 2.00 to 5.00 on Mondays (but not Bank Holidays), Tuesdays, Thursdays, Fridays and Saturdays. Also worth seeing in Wycombe town centre is the **Heritage Exhibition** (open Mondays to Saturdays 10.00 to 5.00) in the attractive 18th-century Guildhall.

JUNCTION 4 HUGHENDEN MANOR
One-and-a-half miles north of the town centre on the A4128 is the entrance to **Hughenden Manor**. For 33 years this was the home of Benjamin Disraeli, still one of the most celebrated Tory leaders. By the force of his personality and his successful novels, and as a result of the reforms he initiated as Prime Minister from 1874 to 1880, he modernized his party's attitudes and thinking and laid the foundations for its continued electoral success in the 20th century. Disraeli and his beloved wife Mary Anne bought the house in 1848, thinking it appropriate for a rising Tory politician to acquire a country estate, and spent as much time here as Parliamentary and social duties in London would allow. Under their guidance, the inside of the house, which had originally been a farmhouse and was converted into a gentleman's residence in the mid-18th century, was 'Gothicized' according to contemporary fashion. The Jacobean exterior, with its parapet and pinnacles in an attractive red brick, is their work too. The gardens were redesigned as well, and Mrs Disraeli commissioned the monument to Disraeli's father Isaac that stands on the hill top on the south-west edge of the grounds. Inside the house, which was quite considerably altered by Disraeli's nephew, who inherited it from his uncle, are many Disraeli relics including his furniture, pictures and books. There is the Wycombe chair made to chair him after the 1832 election but never used as he failed to be elected, while the paintings represent a fascinating portrait gallery of 19th-century notables. The room in which the visitor feels closest to Disraeli is undoubtedly the study – his 'workshop' – which still looks today much as it did when he died; black-edged notepaper, always used by Disraeli after his wife died in 1872, lies on his writing table, and there are editions of his novels on the shelves. The house is open between April and October on Wednes-

169

days to Saturdays from 2.00 to 6.00, on Sundays and Bank Holiday Mondays from 12.00 to 6.00, and on Saturdays and Sundays in March only from 2.00 to 6.00; last admissions are half an hour before closing time. Tea and biscuits are sometimes available.

JUNCTION 4 WEST WYCOMBE HOUSE

West Wycombe, a short distance west along the A40 from High Wycombe, is a remarkable survival from the 18th century and a remarkable memorial to the enthusiasms and vision of one man, the second Sir Francis Dashwood. Sir Francis was a polymath. He was interested in everything, and especially in architecture, theology and the ancient world; he travelled widely, undertaking five long tours of Europe and reaching as far afield as Russia and Asia Minor; he was a politician who held high office, briefly and unsuccessfully as Chancellor of the Exchequer, with great success as Postmaster-General; he had a taste for the exotic and the adventurous; and he was a collector and builder *par excellence*. Perhaps his greatest memorial is **West Wycombe House** and park. For nearly half a century, from his return from Greece and Asia Minor in 1735 until his death in 1781, he worked on remodelling the plain Queen Anne house he had inherited from his father. Every 18th-century style is

Music Temple and cascade, West Wycombe

represented inside – baroque, ornate rococo, classical Greek, neo-classical Roman – while outside each of the four fronts is adorned with porticoes or colonnades. The rooms are full of paintings, sculpture and furniture collected by Sir Francis on his travels, or bought specially for the house, many from Italy. The decoration, again done in a variety of styles, is magnificent. Classical scenes adorn the hall and staircase; there are tapestries and wonderful examples of marquetry, handsome chimney-pieces (for instance in the Saloon and in the Music Room, where a frieze depicts Cupid and Psyche set amid flowers, foliage and birds), and elaborate rococo plasterwork. The park was laid out in the 1730s and extensively remodelled in a more informal style in the 1770s. A number of temples and follies are scattered about the landscape, including the Temple of Apollo, a gigantic stone and flintwork arch and a cascade.

JUNCTION 4 HELL-FIRE CAVES

Sir Francis was a leading light in a mysterious semi-secret society known as the Knights of St Francis of Wycombe, whose members all came from the circle of friends around Frederick, Prince of Wales. (Frederick was the son of George II; he never came to the throne, dying in 1751, none years before his father.) From 1763 the Knights met in the Hell-Fire Caves at West Wycombe, becoming known as the Hell-Fire Club. Little is known of their activities, though a good deal of ceremonial seems to have been involved and wine and women certainly came into things somewhere. The **Hell-Fire Caves**, which were originally a chalk quarry and were extended by Sir Francis as part of a building programme intended to relieve local unemployment, are now open to the public. The winding passages run for ¼ mile through the Knight's Cave and the Labyrinth and on to the Treasure Chamber, across the river Styx – the river that, in classical legend, separates the world from the underworld – to the Inner Temple at the very end of the caves. It is said that secret chambers and passages may still lie hidden in the cliff. The caves, which at their deepest are 300 feet underground, now contain scenes with life-size members of the Hell-Fire Club.

JUNCTION 4 DASHWOOD MAUSOLEUM

A short but stiff climb up the hill from the entrance to the caves brings you to **St Lawrence's Church** and to the **Dashwood Mausoleum** next to it. (You can drive up if you want to, and park at the top of the hill.) Sir Francis rebuilt the church in the 1750s and early 1760s, and like West Wycombe House it reflects his catholic taste in art and architecture. The design of the nave is based on a late Roman temple of the sun erected at Palmyra, in what is now Syria, while the tower imitates the Customs Building in Venice. The golden ball on top of the tower was clearly a favourite spot for Sir Francis; there were seats for eight inside, from which not only the splendid views across Buckinghamshire could be enjoyed, but also the alcoholic refreshment Sir Francis provided – John Wilkes recalled singing bawdy songs there once with Lord Sandwich and their host. The impressive six-sided Mausoleum, which was built in 1765, is modelled on the Arch of Constantine in Rome; inside there are numerous niches and urns along the walls, and monuments to members of the Dashwood family and to friends of Sir Francis Dashwood. Opening times are as follows. House and Park: 2.00 to 6.00 Mondays to Fridays in June, July and August and also on Sundays and Bank Holidays in July and August. Caves: Mondays to Fridays 1.00 to 6.00, early March to early April; Mondays to Fridays 1.00 to 6.00 and Sundays 11.00 to 6.00, early April to late May; daily, 11.00 to 6.00, late May to early September; daily, 1.00 to 5.00, early September to the end of October; Saturdays and Sundays 1.00 to 5.00 November to March. There is a restaurant, and the Swan, the George and Dragon and the Plough in the village all offer refreshment.

From the roundabout above the motorway at junction 4, take the minor road north (not the A404), take the third right off this, and then turn left on to the A40 after about 1 mile. West Wycombe is just over ½ mile west along the A40. Distance from the motorway is 3 miles.

Junction 5 leads to Stokenchurch and the A40. If you are travelling towards London and want to visit West Wycombe, take the A40 east from here for 5 miles.

JUNCTION 6 RIDGEWAY PATH

Junction 6 brings the opportunity for a walk on the **Ridgeway Path**, the long-distance path that runs along the Wiltshire and Berkshire Downs and across the Thames to the Chilterns. But it has to be said that this is not the most spectacular stretch of countryside. To the south-west, the Ridgeway Path runs under the motorway in a specially built tunnel and then continues almost at the foot of the hills, beneath Pyrton Hill and Shirburn Hill. In the other direction, the route is across fields towards **Chinnor**, where there is a large cement works. From junction 6, drive north-east on to the B4009 towards Chinnor, and almost immediately turn right on to the A40. The Ridgeway Path crosses the A40 in about ½ mile. Note that there is little or no parking space along the A40.

JUNCTION 7 THAME

Thame is a pleasant little market town 4 miles east of junction 7 along the A329. There is a wide main street with buildings of all ages ranged happily along it, creating a well-proportioned and agreeable environment. Even the most recent buildings blend in appropriately – a good example of how, with a little care and imagination, new and old can work well together. Some buildings worth looking at are the Almshouses and old Grammar School and a fine tithe barn nearby off the lower end of the High Street. The **Town Hall** with its clock tower forms the focal-point of the High Street, and to the left is **Hampden House,** where John Hampden (see also page 168) died after being wounded in the Battle of Chalgrove in 1643. There are several inns and cafés in the town.

WATERPERRY GARDENS

The motorway ends not at a junction but simply by merging with the dual carriageway A40 running west to Oxford. **Waterperry Gardens**, some 4 miles north by road (though much nearer as the crow flies), were developed in the 1930s as a horticultural training school for women. Although that has now closed, the county council still runs courses here, and visitors can enjoy walking in the lovely gardens and looking at the wide variety of plants, shrubs and fruit that are grown. There is an old walled kitchen garden, a rock garden, a small area of woodland, a rose garden, shrub borders and an alpine nursery, and a walk alongside the little River Thame where a formal garden is being created with a herb border, a knot and a simple parterre. The parish church close by Waterperry House can also be visited. All the plants grown in the Gardens are on sale, which makes the walk round that much more purposeful; there is also a tea room. The Gardens are open daily from 10.00 to 5.30 on Mondays to Fridays, and 10.00 to 6.00 at weekends, between April and September; and from 10.00 to 4.00 the rest of the year. From the motorway, continue along the A40, and leave it at the first exit, signposted to Aylesbury and locally to Wheatley. Turn left immediately, then right after 0.7 miles. After 1.5 miles on this road, turn right at the crossroads; you will reach the Gardens after about ½ mile through the village.

The M5 and M50

West Bromwich to Exeter/
Strensham to Ross-on-Wye

INTRODUCTION

Scenically, the M5 starts badly. The early junctions are all in one of
the more dispiriting parts of the West Midlands conurbation. But
the off-motorway attractions more than compensate, especially the
Black Country Museum, which is a fine introduction to the life of
this part of the world. If you want to make rapid progress, however,
it is annoying to find that quite substantial sections of this busiest
stretch of the motorway only have two lanes.

The countryside off the first half of the motorway, which follows
the Severn valley south to the Bristol Channel, is flattish and un-
dramatic, pleasant without being especially interesting. It is an in-
between sort of area, with the Cotswolds to the east, the Malverns
and the Welsh hills to the west. (For convenience the M50, which
runs through a much more attractive landscape, is dealt with in this
chapter, on pages 186–190.) But to make up for this the man-made
sights are splendid: most notably the two glorious cathedrals of
Worcester and Gloucester and the Regency elegance of Cheltenham.
The bridge over the river Avon, between junctions 18 and 19, signals a rapid change of scenery. The motorway is soon deep in some
lovely Somerset and Devon countryside, warm and welcoming and
luxuriantly green. There are plenty of country diversions, with good
walking and picnicking. Then, at the very end of the motorway, you
reach the entrance to a very different West Country, less domestica-
ted, wilder and more open, with the tang of the sea and the high
moorland.

The M5 starts at junction 8 of the M6, in a no-man's land between
West Bromwich and Walsall. There is no access to ordinary roads,
but junctions 7 and 9 of the M6 are 1 and 2 miles away respectively.

Junction 1 is in the middle of an equally nondescript area, and there
is nothing worth leaving the motorway for at this point.

174

JUNCTION 2 DUDLEY ZOO & CASTLE

Junction 2 is on the eastern edge of Dudley, and it is a 3-mile drive along the heavily used A4123 west to Dudley Zoo and Castle. (Bear left at the roundabout 2 miles from the motorway on the A461, carry straight on and the Zoo entrance is on your right.) **Dudley Zoo** is among the best-known in the country, and deservedly so, with a large and varied collection of wildlife. There are Himalayan and polar bears, cats of all kinds (not the domestic sort, of course, but lions, tigers, leopards, lynx and caracal), giraffe and gazelle, cassowary and penguin, bison and zebra, African elephants and many others. There is a collection of insects and spiders, and houses for monkeys, apes and reptiles. Although this is a zoo of the traditional kind, not a safari park, the grounds are a spacious 40 acres of attractive woodland on the slopes of **Dudley Castle**, stretching right up to the ruins of the keep. The aquarium is housed in the crypt of the early 14th-century chapel, which must count as one of the oddest uses of an ecclesiastical building ever. You can picnic in the Castle courtyard amid lovely floral displays and enjoy the water garden just outside the enclosing curtain wall. Most of the Castle dates from the late 13th and early 14th centuries, although the manorial buildings on the north-east side of the courtyard are 16th-century. A Royalist stronghold in the Civil War, it surrendered in 1646 after two sieges and was slighted the following year. A century later fire destroyed the 16th-century buildings, and the Castle lay derelict until the Zoo was opened in 1937. Other attractions here include a chair lift up the Castle mound, a children's corner with lots of domestic animals, an amusement park and several restaurants and cafés. The Zoo is open on weekdays from 9.00 to 6.30, on Sundays from 10.00 to 6.30.

JUNCTION 2 BLACK COUNTRY MUSEUM

Rather further from the motorway, but certainly worth the trip if you have enough time, is the **Black Country Museum** on the Tipton road north out of Dudley. To get there follow the A4123 north for about 4 miles, turn left on to the A4037 and the Museum is on the right. This is one of the newish breed of museums that has abandoned static objects neatly arranged in glass cases. Its aim, in which it succeeds brilliantly, is to celebrate the work and workers of Britain's industrial heartland in about 1900, the time of Britain's greatest prosperity. The 26-acre site is on an island between two canal arms, and numerous buildings have been re-erected here to create a typical Black Country community. There is a chemist's shop, a bakery in which traditional crusty loaves are still baked, a

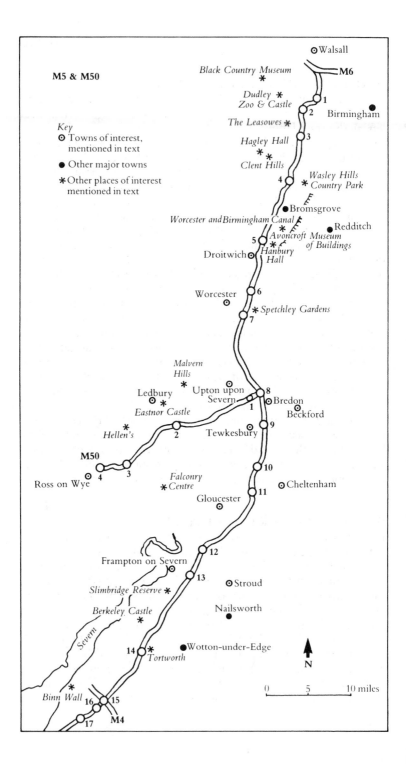

M5 & M50

Key
⊙ Towns of interest,
   mentioned in text
● Other major towns
∗ Other places of interest
   mentioned in text

⊙ Walsall

Black Country Museum
∗

M6

Dudley ∗
Zoo & Castle

1

2   Birmingham ●

The Leasowes ∗

Hagley Hall
∗
∗
Clent Hills

3

4

Wasley Hills
∗ Country Park

● Bromsgrove

Worcester and Birmingham Canal
∗
∗

● Redditch

Avoncroft Museum
of Buildings

5   ∗

Droitwich ⊙   Hanbury
Hall

Worcester
⊙

6

7   ∗ Spetchley Gardens

Malvern
Hills
∗   Upton upon
Ledbury   Severn
⊙ ∗

Eastnor Castle

8

1   ⊙ Bredon
⊙
Beckford

9

Hellen's
∗
2   Tewkesbury

M50

4   3

Ross on Wye
⊙

Falconry
∗ Centre

10

11   ⊙ Cheltenham

Gloucester
⊙

12

Frampton on Severn

13

Slimbridge Reserve ∗

⊙ Stroud

Berkeley Castle
∗

Nailsworth
●

Severn

● Wotton-under-Edge

14   ∗
Tortworth

N

Binn Wall
∗

16   15
17   M4

0   5   10 miles

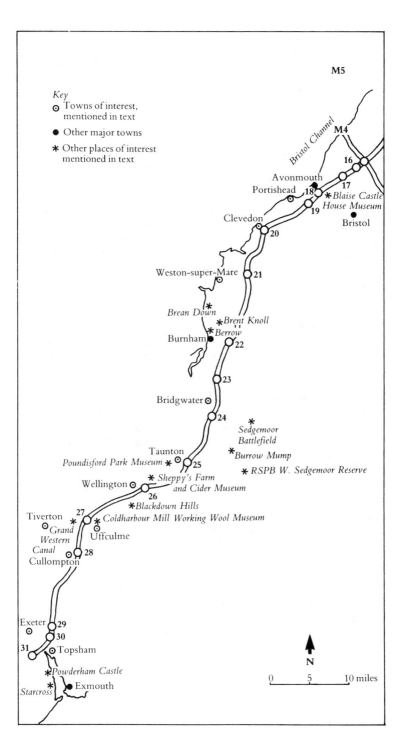

Key
⊙ Towns of interest,
  mentioned in text
● Other major towns
✱ Other places of interest
  mentioned in text

M5

Bristol Channel

M4

16

Avonmouth
Portishead   18   17
                       ✱ Blaise Castle
                         House Museum
                  19

Clevedon
              20   Bristol

Weston-super-Mare   21

       ✱
  Brean Down
            ✱ Brent Knoll
            ✱ Berrow
Burnham
                 22

              23

Bridgwater ⊙
              24
                    ✱
                  Sedgemoor
                  Battlefield
                 ✱ Burrow Mump
Taunton
Poundisford Park Museum ✱ ⊙ 25   ✱ RSPB W. Sedgemoor Reserve

            ✱ Sheppy's Farm
Wellington ⊙   and Cider Museum
              26
          ✱ Blackdown Hills
       27 ✱ Coldharbour Mill Working Wool Museum
Tiverton ⊙
  ⊙ Grand   Uffculme
  Western
  Canal   28
Cullompton ⊙

Exeter   29
  ⊙   30
31   ⊙ Topsham
  ✱ Powderham Castle
      ✱ ● Exmouth
Starcross

                    N

        0   5   10 miles

Methodist chapel, the Bottle and Glass pub (open to the public during midday licensing hours), and a chainmaker's house with the chainmaking shop in the yard. An electric tramway runs across the Museum site. As so often, it is the small details that count, helping to evoke the smells and sensations of the past. At Gregory's store, transplanted from its original site in Old Hill, cow heel and pigs' trotters were sold, and home-made faggots on Wednesdays. There are frequent demonstrations of Black Country crafts, and you can watch nail- and chain-making and glass-engraving. From the canal basin, where 19th-century narrowboats are on display, the Dudley Canal Trust runs short trips into the **Dudley Tunnel**. This is one of the most amazing tunnels in the entire national canal network. Vast caverns, created in the 18th century to provide limestone for the new and rapidly expanding iron-making industries, alternate with low passages, so low that only small boats can pass through, and even these must either be 'legged' or use electric power (as the Trust's boats do). Legging involved the crew walking their legs against the tunnel walls – not to be recommended. The climax of the trip is the spectacular Singing Cavern. The Museum is open daily from 10.00, closing at 5.00 between March and October and at dusk during the rest of the year. The canal trips are operated between March and November.

JUNCTION 3 THE LEASOWES
Junction 3 brings you into a sort of half-countryside on the edge of the built-up area. The nearest attraction is also the most unusual, and the most interesting too: **The Leasowes**. This is the garden created by the 18th-century poet, essayist and landscape gardener William Shenstone. Shenstone believed in nature pure and simple, in natural and picturesque beauty – unlike his celebrated near-contemporary, Capability Brown, who did not hesitate to make wholesale improvements on what nature had provided. Shenstone loved ruins, views and water and made them a feature of his landscape. A historical trail leads visitors round much of his estate. Marker 7 on the trail is at the site of a 150-yard cascade, now sadly almost dry, but once decked with ferns, mosses and flowering waterside plants. At marker 12 Shenstone and his visitors could enjoy the view to the Wrekin, obscured in 1792, less than 50 years after the estate was landscaped, when the embankment of the Dudley No.2 Canal was built, from an octagonal seat surmounted by an urn inscribed with an old Shropshire toast 'All friends round the Wrekin'. At marker 22 we can still enjoy the view today, to the Shropshire hills and the distant Welsh mountains. Shenstone scattered ruins, urns, benches and seats all over his estate, many

inscribed to his friends (one was even dedicated to his publisher, a Mr Dodsley!). The trail starts at Mucklow Hill on the A458 north-east of Halesowen. The quickest route from junction 3 is west along the A456 to the first roundabout, then right on to the A459 and right again at the next roundabout on to the A458 (about 2½ miles).

JUNCTION 3 HAGLEY HALL

The house and park at **Hagley Hall** have been described as 'among the supreme achievements of 18th-century English architecture and landscape gardening'. And with every justification. Like many of his aristocratic contemporaries, the first Lord Lyttelton, who built Hagley Hall, looked to Italy in matters of taste and style. The exterior of his handsome Palladian mansion is plain and unadorned. Inside, the contrast could hardly be greater, with every room opulently decorated. In the White Room there is magnificent plasterwork and sculpture and a carved stone chimney-piece supported by almost life-size figures. In the Library fronds of palm and laurel wind through the plasterwork frieze, while in the Dining Room it is winged putti that fly amidst the clouds on the ceiling. The Drawing Room and Gallery are also fine rooms. Hagley Hall remains the home of the Lyttelton family (the present owner is the eleventh Viscount Cobham, the Cobham title having come into the family in 1889), and it is a mark of their love for their home that a disastrous fire in 1925 led, not to the abandonment of the Hall, but to the faithful restoration of the damaged rooms. The magnificent park also dates from the mid-18th century, and is notable for a series of 'eye-catchers' – constructions intended to catch the eye and provide both visual and intellectual interest to a stroll in the grounds. There is a Gothick ruined castle, a Doric temple, an Ionic rotunda and many smaller urns, seats and so on. The stable block and the parish church were also deliberately designed to form a picturesque group. Hagley Hall is roughly equidistant from junctions 3 and 4 and is open daily except Saturdays from 2.00 to 5.00 in July and August and also on Bank Holiday Sundays and Mondays from Easter. A restaurant serves teas, and there is a shop. A number of special events are held throughout the spring and summer. From junction 3 take the A456 west to Hagley village (about 6 miles) and turn left, following the signposts, for the Hall.

JUNCTION 3 CLENT HILLS COUNTRY PARK

West of junction 3, the A456 runs along the northern edge of the Clent Hills, where the 523-acre **Clent Hills Country Park** offers pleasant walks through an attractive, wooded landscape. Fox and fallow deer have been seen, and a variety of birds too. There are four standing stones at the summit of Adam's Hill. But don't be deceived into thinking these are evidence of occupation by some group of ancient Britons. They stand witness instead to the 18th-century taste for the mock antique, and were erected by the Lytteltons of Hagley Hall. The newest part of the Park is High Harcourt Farm, which will be run along traditional lines; a countryside interpretation centre there will provide background information. For the moment, there is a snack bar and a small information centre at Nimmings on Hagley Wood Lane. The **North Worcestershire Path** links four country parks in this area, and the 4-mile stretch between the Clent and Waseley Hills (see junction 4, below) would make a pleasant walk if you had a driver prepared to meet you at each end.

JUNCTION 4 WASELEY HILLS COUNTRY PARK

The **Waseley Hills Country Park** has the great advantage of being not much more than 1 mile from the motorway, and the corresponding disadvantage of being within earshot of the traffic. There is little else to say about it. The 148-acre Park is a pleasant but rather uninspiring piece of country open space, with Windmill Hill as its main feature. (A toposcope on the 94-foot summit identifies the main features in the surrounding landscape.) Most of the wildlife is found in and near Segbourne Coppice on the west of the Park. There is a visitor centre at which light refreshments and light lunches are also available. The best route from the M5 is along the A491 west from junction 4. Take the first turning right on to the B4551, turn right again at the pleasant-looking Manchester Inn, and right yet again to cross over the motorway to the Park entrance on the right.

The Clent Hills County Park (see junction 3, page 179) is also easily accessible from here, and in any case is a much pleasanter stretch of countryside. Take the A491 north-west from the motorway and turn right through Clent village after about 4 miles. The A491 continues to Hagley village, where you turn right for Hagley Hall (see page 179).

JUNCTION 4 WORCESTER & BIRMINGHAM CANAL

To the east of the motorway, Bromsgrove lies 3 miles south of the junction down the A38, but there is nothing special here to justify a visit. The A448 Redditch road crosses the **Worcester & Birmingham Canal** 3 miles east of Bromsgrove. The famous flight of locks here – the longest in the country – is best reached by turning right off the main road in Tutnall, just before Tardebigge. The New Engine House is a smart restaurant and club in the restored canal pumping-station; morning and afternoon refreshments are served as well as formal meals.

If you visit Bromsgrove, you can return to the motorway at junction 5, taking the A38 south from the town centre. This route passes the entrance to the Avoncroft Museum of Buildings (see junction 5) at Stoke Heath.

Junction 4a is the junction with the western end of the M42. There is no access on to ordinary roads.

JUNCTION 5 AVONCROFT MUSEUM OF BUILDINGS

Junction 5 is the turn-off for Droitwich. I found this little spa town rather a disappointment, and if you do want a break here I recommend the **Avoncroft Museum of Buildings**, 3 miles north-east on the A38. Like the Black Country Museum (see junction 2, page 175). Avoncroft consists of dismantled buildings painstakingly reconstructed with every attention to detail. In my view at least, it suffers slightly in comparison. At the Black Country Museum you get a definite sense of time and place, a real feeling of the past. Here at Avoncroft the buildings, while individually extremely interesting, come from a variety of places and periods and sit together less well. To be fair, the aims of the two museums do differ, and Avoncroft makes it clear that its 'primary aim' is to 'rescue buildings from destruction'. It all started in the early 1960s, when a lovely late 15th-century timbered merchant's house in Bromsgrove was threatened with demolition. Local attempts to save it failed, but the timbers were rescued. Five years later the newly reconstructed house became the Museum's first exhibit, and it remains one of the most attractive buildings on site: a fine fire was burning in the hearth when I visited on one rather cold and rainy day. Buildings here span a period of over six hundred years, from the roof of the Guesten Hall, built in 1320 next to Worcester Cathedral to accommodate the prior's guests, to a fully-furnished 1940s prefab; a new Guesten Hall incorporating the original roof is currently being built. Other buildings include a Shropshire ice house, removed here because it was in the path of the M54, an early 17th-century Staffordshire dovecote and a toll house from Little Malvern built around 1800. Local industry is well represented, with an Industrial Revolution nail shop and chain shop, and agriculture too, with stables, a wagon shed, granary and barn. A miller is employed to operate the mill, which is one of the only three surviving post-mills in the Midlands, and the Museum also employs a wood-turner and a shire horse. A blacksmith sometimes works in the forge, and occasional demonstrations of chain-making are given. There is a practical use for some of the buildings. The Museum's excellent shop is housed in the String of Horses from Shrewsbury, which started as an inn in 1576 and became a Co-op store in 1912, and offices occupy the forge cottage. The Museum has a small tea room and there is a large picnic area. The Museum is open between March and November. Times are as follows: June, July and August, daily 11.00 to 5.30; April, May, September and October, daily except Mondays (but including Bank Holidays) 11.00 to 5.30; March and November, 11.00 to 4.30 on Tuesdays, Wednesdays, Thursdays, Saturdays and Sundays.

JUNCTION 5 DROITWICH SPA

Droitwich, 2 miles south of the motorway on the A38, has been known for its salt since before the Roman occupation. But it was only in 1830, when the local brine was used to good effect against an outbreak of cholera, that it began to develop as a spa. The moving spirit behind the town's expansion was John Corbett – nicknamed the Salt King – who built several hotels and, for his French-educated wife, the amazing Château Impney, a late Victorian version of a French château, now a luxury hotel. The spa's appeal was principally to sufferers from rheumatism, whose treatment combined hot brine with hydrotherapy and physiotherapy. If you come in summer and swim in the **Lido** you can literally get a taste of it, as it is diluted there to the strength of sea water. A new brine bath opened in 1985 on the site of the old St Andrew's Brine Bath in the town centre, and here you can wallow in the amazingly salty and buoyant water (brine is 20 per cent more buoyant than fresh water) to your heart's content, or sit in the rest and relaxation areas. The Brine Bath is open to the public from 12.00 to 8.00 on weekdays, 10.00 to 5.00 on Saturdays and 9.30 to 4.00 on Sundays. But be warned that the admission charge is very high. In the town centre there are half-timbered buildings along the High Street, where you can get a traditional tea in Bullocks Café, and imposing Victorian hotels in and around Victoria Square. The 1920s mosaics in the **Church of the Sacred Heart and St Catherine**, itself modelled on a Roman court of justice, are said to be among the finest outside Westminster Cathedral.

JUNCTION 5 HANBURY HALL

There are two alternative routes to Hanbury Hall, an attractive National Trust property which was the home of the Vernon family for more than 250 years. From Droitwich take the B4090 east and turn left just past Gallows Green, following the signs (2½ miles). From junction 5, take the A38 north and turn right almost immediately. Then turn left and immediately right on the edge of Wychbold and follow the road over one railway, under another and over the canal near the Astwood flight of locks before turning right just past the church in Hanbury village. **Hanbury Hall** was completed in 1701, a substantial, handsome red-brick house, very much the home of a successful professional man. (Thomas Vernon, who built it, was a chancery barrister.) The hall and painted staircase are its most interesting parts. There is a fine ceiling in the hall, and one of the murals (done by James Thornhill shortly after 1710) on the staircase depicts a Dr Sacheverell about to be attacked by the Furies. The doctor was a high-church parson who preached a Tory sermon in St Paul's, was accused of sedition and found guilty. The fine 18th-century pieces on show throughout the house are not the original contents, which were auctioned in 1790 when the marriage between Emma Vernon and Henry Cecil broke up, but have been assembled by the Trust; the Long Room has a lovely collection of English porcelain figures and flower paintings. Unusually, the Long Gallery is detached from the house, and the fine orangery can also be visited. The original formal garden was replaced at the end of the 18th century by the wide lawns we see today. Hanbury Hall is open from 2.00 to 6.00 on Wednesdays to Sundays between May and September and also on Bank Holiday Mondays. In April and October opening times are from 2.00 to 5.00 at weekends and on Easter Monday.

In Hanbury village the **Jinney Ring Craft Centre** is a group of craft workshops where you can watch potters, wood-carvers and wood-turners, weavers, jewellers, glass-blowers and many other craftsmen and women at work. There is also a shop, gallery and café.

JUNCTIONS 6 & 7 WORCESTER
Junctions 6 and 7 lead into **Worcester**, from the north (west along the A449 and then left, about 4 miles) and the south (3 miles along the A44) respectively. First stop for every visitor must surely be the **cathedral**, which dominates the skyline wherever you are in the city. The floodlighting in the evening is spectacular. The crypt and the lovely chapter house are the oldest parts, dating from 1084. Most of the rest of the building dates from the 13th and 14th centuries, although there were extensive restorations in the 19th. The Early English choir, in which King John was buried at his own request, is exquisite, with Purbeck marble columns and beautifully carved foliage. The whole cathedral is well worth a lengthy visit. Prince Arthur's Chantry is a beautiful piece of stonework – and also a place to contemplate the accidents of history. Arthur, who died in 1502 at the age of 16, was Henry VII's first son, and thus his heir. In 1501, following an arrangement made when he was still a baby, he married Catherine of Aragon. What, one wonders, might have happened had he lived, and had his brother, whom we know as Henry VIII, not succeeded him . . . ? There is a gift shop and a refreshment

room in the attractive cloisters. The cathedral is open daily from 8.00 to 7.30 between May and August, 8.00 to 6.00 in March, April, September and October, and 9.00 to 6.00 in winter.

After the cathedral, my next two priorities would be a walk round the attractive precincts, in particular College Green, and then a visit to the **Royal Worcester works**. Under one name or another, the Worcester Royal Porcelain Company, as it is properly known today, has been producing fine porcelain since 1751 and today manufactures some of the finest tableware and limited-edition figures (of birds, cattle, horses, etc.) in the world. Examples from every period and style of the firm's output are on show in the **Dysons Perrins Museum**, part of the factory complex and well worth a visit. I find case after case of china somewhat daunting and thought the tour of the factory rather more interesting – definitely to be recommended. (Tours operate between 9.55 and 11.45 and 2.00 and 3.45, 2.30 on Fridays. Advance booking is essential: contact Dysons Perrins Museum, Severn Street, Worcester WR1 2NE; telephone (0905) 23221.) It is fascinating to see how the most up-to-date technology and traditional hand processes are combined to produce these exquisite pieces: small wonder that the limited editions, each of which is carefully painted by hand, appreciate in value so rapidly. There is a seconds shop, a retail shop, and also a restaurant, and the Potters Wheel pub is just opposite the factory gate. The Museum is open on Mondays to Fridays from 9.30 to 5.00, on Saturdays from 10.00 to 5.00, and on Sundays between early May and early October only from 10.00 to 5.00.

Much of Worcester's central shopping area has been pedestrianized, and the modern shops do not clash too badly with the older parts of the town. The **Guildhall** in the High Street is one of the finest 18th-century guildhalls in the country (open Mondays to Fridays from 9.30 to 4.00). Also in Friar Street, there is the **Tudor House Museum** (open daily except Thursdays and Sundays from 10.30 to 5.00), a 16th-century timber-framed building with exhibitions on domestic and social life in Worcester from Elizabethan times onwards. Two pleasant eating-places are Hodson's Coffee House and Patisserie, near the entrance to the shopping precinct opposite the cathedral, and Inglenook's English Tearoom on the corner of Edgar Street near the cathedral.

There is an attractive riverside walk alongside the Severn below the cathedral and opposite pleasant water-meadows. Running south the path comes to Diglis Basin, where the Worcester & Birmingham Canal joins the Severn, and there are docks and transit sheds. Turn north up the canal and you will soon reach the **Commandery**. Founded in 1085 as the Hospital of St Wulfstan to care for the sick and poor of the city (St Wulfstan was bishop of Worcester and started work on the present cathedral), the present lovely building dates largely from 1500. The Great Hall has a magnificent but much restored hammer-beam roof and a minstrels' gallery. During the Civil War Worcester was a Royalist stronghold – the first city to declare for the King and the last to surrender. Charles II held a council of war at the Commandery before the decisive Battle of Worcester in 1651 – and today the building houses a Civil War Centre which uses all the latest techniques of audio-visual presentation to show the course of the battle, examine strategy and recount the defeated King's flight into exile after his final defeat. Four reconstructed workshops – cooper's, cobbler's, forge and glove-maker's – give a vivid picture of the city's industrial history, while in the gardens are a herb garden and a picnic area. A Civil War Trail starts from here. The Commandery is open from 10.30 to 5.00 on Mondays to Saturdays and 2.00 to 5.00 on Sundays.

JUNCTION 7 WORCESTER WOODS COUNTRY PARK
Worcester Woods Country Park consists of two large stretches of ancient woodland within the Worcester city boundary. Parts of Perry Wood may never have been cleared; the earthworks there are thought to have been the work of Parliamentary forces encamped outside the city during the Civil War. In Nunnery Wood traces of medieval ridge and furrow farming suggest that arable crops were grown here in the Middle Ages. The Worcester Countryside Centre next to Hereford and Worcester County Hall on the A422 contains an exhibition hall, an information desk and a snack bar. From the motorway, take the A44 towards Worcester, and then take the second exit from the Spetchley Road roundabout on to the A422 east. County Hall and the entrance to the Country Park are on the left in about ½ mile.

JUNCTION 7 SPETCHLEY GARDENS
Further east along the A422, **Spetchley Gardens** are a must for garden enthusiasts. Generations of the Berkeley family (of the castle described at junction 14, page 199), which has owned Spetchley since the early 17th century, have contributed to the Gardens. Probably the most influential were the present owner's father, grandmother and great-aunt, and the Gardens reflect the tastes and fashions of the early 20th century. There is a melon garden, a kitchen garden surrounded by a series of borders, a rose lawn with 17 central beds, and a cork lawn. From the garden pool there are views of the Malvern and Bredon Hills, and the copse is especially colourful in spring. Spetchley Gardens are open from 11.00 to 5.00 on

Mondays to Fridays and on Sundays from 2.00 to 5.00 between April and October; closed Saturdays. Plants and shrubs can be bought in the garden centre.

Junction 8 is the junction at the start of the M50, which runs west through lovely country for 22 miles to Ross-on-Wye. There is no access to ordinary roads, but junction 1 of the M50 is only 2 miles away.

Junction 1 of the M50 is 3 miles south of **Upton upon Severn**, reached along the A38 and then left across the Severn on the A4104. It is a pleasant town with some lovely old buildings, including the timber-framed Anchor Inn on the High Street, which dates from the early 17th century: an attractive place for a short stop, but not quite worth the 5-mile diversion from the main motorway. Tewkesbury, 3 miles south of the junction also on the A38, is described under junction 9 of the M5 (page 190).

JUNCTION 2 MALVERN HILLS

From junction 2 of the M50 you can make one of the best long excursions off the entire Midlands-to-Devon route, and certainly the best in the northern half. The eventual destination is Ledbury. But on the way there is some fine countryside with good walking possibilities and also, at Eastnor, a magnificent mock medieval castle to visit. From the motorway follow the A417 towards Ledbury (the town is only 5 miles off if you want to drive there direct) and then take the first right towards Broomsberrow and Chase End. The winding road immediately plunges into a delightful, well-wooded landscape at the southern end of the Malvern Hills, running round the side of Chase End Hill to Chase End itself, a tiny hamlet sunk in the middle of lush country. After Chase End take the next left, which brings you after about ½ mile to the A438, where you should turn left again. There are plenty of picnic spots along these quiet lanes, and short field and woodland walks too. But the best walking comes in less than 1 mile west along the A438, where, just below Midsummer Hill, the road meets the end of the main north-south Malverns path. It is a fine striding route up Midsummer Hill and then on north towards **Herefordshire Beacon** (2 miles), 'one of the finest examples of a contour fort in Britain', according to one expert, and topped with a 12th-century castle mound. From here the path continues north towards **Worcestershire Beacon**, at 1394 feet the highest point of the range, stretching wide and inviting, one of the finest walks in this part of the country. Walk for as long as you have time and inclination, and then continue west along the main road to Eastnor (2 miles).

JUNCTION 2 EASTNOR CASTLE

Despite its appearance, **Eastnor Castle** is the creation not of those centuries when the borderland between England and Wales was disputed territory but of the early 19th century, when a highly romanticized view of the Middle Ages was in fashion. The finest rooms in the Castle, built between 1812 and 1814, are the Great Hall and the Gothic Drawing Room. The former is no less than 60 feet long, 30 wide and 55 high, and contains a magnificent collection of arms and armour. The Drawing Room was designed and furnished by A.W.N. Pugin in 1849 and is a masterpiece of intricate and colourful flamboyance. Throughout the house, and especially in the Long Gallery, there are fine carvings, pictures and tapestries. The grounds contain an interesting collection of specimen trees and also offer fine views towards the Malverns. The Castle is open at Easter and on Sundays and Bank Holidays between late May and September and also on Wednesdays and Thursdays in July and August, from 2.15 to 5.30. Light refreshments are available. **Eastnor** village is a tiny estate village with black-and-white cottages grouped around a lovely green. The parish church, originally Norman, was almost entirely rebuilt by George Gilbert Scott between 1849 and 1852.

JUNCTION 2 LEDBURY

From Eastnor it is less than 2 miles west along the A438 into Ledbury. **Ledbury** is a jewel. There can hardly be a pleasanter place in the country to potter for a relaxed hour or two. The most celebrated of its many magnificent timber-framed buildings is the **Market House**, built as a corn market during the first half of the 17th century. A market is still held in the open ground floor, and public meetings take place in the enclosed hall on the first floor. For many years the 16 stout timber pillars that support the first floor were also used to display public notices; thousands of tack and nail marks can still be seen. Of the many other timber-framed houses, the Feathers Hotel in the High Street and the Old Talbot Inn in New Street are both worth a look. Church Lane is a gem, leading to the **Old Grammar School**, built between 1480 and 1520 and recently restored as an excellent Heritage Centre (open daily from 11.00 to 5.00 between the Spring Bank Holiday and September). The *Ledbury Walkabout* published by the local council and available at the information office guides you to virtually every house of interest in the town and is well worth following if you have the time (about 1½ hours). The publication is a model of its kind, with detailed explanations and high-quality line illustrations. Two good places to eat

The Market House, Ledbury

are Clark's Coffee House and Restaurant, near the car park and information office, and the smartly painted Market Hall Coffee Shop next to the Market House.

If you are travelling north or south along the M5, the quickest way to regain the motorway is along the A417 to junction 2 of the M50. If you are travelling west, to Ross-on-Wye and beyond to Wales, take the A449 south-west out of Ledbury towards Ross. This brings you after 8 miles to the end of the M50 at junction 4, where it meets the A40 to Monmouth and Abergavenny. The A449 passes close to Hellen's at Much Marcle (see junction 3, below).

JUNCTION 3 HELLEN'S
Junction 3 of the M50 is in lovely country, and is a good point for turning off to find a picnic spot. North of the junction, a side road (first right off the B4221 going west) brings you after about 4 miles to **Much Marcle** and **Hellen's**, an ancient manor house begun in 1292. The Great Hall contains a stone table at which the Black Prince dined. Queen Mary slept here in 1554. There are pictures, tapestries, furnishings, armour and carriages on view. The house is open from 2.00 to 6.00 on Wednesdays, Saturdays, Sundays and Bank Holiday Mondays between Easter and September. Locally brewed cider can be bought in the village. A few miles east, the little village of **Dymock** was the home, in those last Indian summer days before the First World War, of a group of poets: Rupert Brooke, Edward Thomas and the American Robert Frost among them.

JUNCTION 3 FALCONRY CENTRE
The main attraction at **Newent**, 4 miles east of junction 3 along the B4221, is the **Falconry Centre**. Turn right at the crossroads in the centre of Newent, following signs to Huntley, take the road to Cliffords Mesne between the BP garage and the car park, and carry straight on at the staggered crossroads. The Centre is on the left 1½ miles out of Newent. In the days before shotguns were invented, falconry was not simply a sport but also an efficient means of obtaining food. The Centre commemorates this ancient and noble pastime. The most important part of its pioneering work consists of conservation and breeding. Over 50 birds of varying species are bred each year, and in spring and summer visitors can see eagles, owls, buzzards, vultures, kites, falcons and many others rearing their young in the breeding aviaries. Free-flying demonstrations are held several times a day, weather permitting: spectacular displays that are the highlight of a visit. The Centre is open daily except Tuesdays from 10.30 to 5.30 (dusk if earlier) between March and October. In the village you can watch craftsmen at work in the **Cowdy Glass Workshop**.

JUNCTION 4 ROSS-ON-WYE

Ross-on-Wye, 1 mile beyond junction 4 at the end of the M50, is a busy, hilltop market town running down to the banks of the Wye. There are pleasant walks along the river bank, and a town trail takes you to all the interesting historic buildings. The most notable of these are the lovely red sandstone 17th-century Market Hall and St Mary's Church. Behind the church is a fine walled public garden, the **Prospect**: as its name suggests, it has excellent views over the town and the Wye. The Prospect was established by John Kyrle, who lived in Ross from 1660 until his death in 1724 and became its most generous and public-spirited benefactor. Among his other good works were the restoration of St Mary's spire and the introduction of a water supply to the town. If you are passing on the A40, the town is worth a visit, but I don't recommend a special diversion down the M50.

JUNCTION 9 TEWKESBURY ABBEY

Back on the M5, junction 9 is the turning for **Tewkesbury**, a little more than 1 mile west on the A438. This is a pleasant small town, just right for a quick break from the steering-wheel. The numerous restaurants include the Riverside, the Bell, the Abbey Tea Rooms, the Black Bear (Gloucestershire's oldest inn), the quaintly named Ancient Grudge and Telfords. (It was Thomas Telford who built the iron bridge across the Severn.) Inside **Tewkesbury Abbey**, the atmosphere is wonderfully quiet and cool, and the great plain columns of the nave (said to be the tallest Norman pillars in England) stretch out before you. The choir is 14th-century, with six chapels and magnificent stained glass. Look out for the chantry of Richard de Beauchamp; the fan tracery in the lower canopy at the west end of the chapel is exquisite. Almost opposite the main entrance to the abbey is another interesting but very different place of worship: the Old Baptist Chapel. Now restored to its 17th-century appearance, the building, which started life in the 15th century, is thought to be the first Baptist chapel established in southern England. The Avon and Severn meet at Tewkesbury, and there is a lovely riverside walk along the Avon in the town and also opposite on the Severn Ham, a large grassy water-meadow between the two rivers, reached by the Quay Street bridge. Another enjoyable walk is the Alley Trail, which begins at the abbey gates and takes you through some of the surviving 30 alleyways; about 90 were built originally. These tiny passageways leading back from the main streets were first constructed in the late 17th century as a result of increasing demand for housing and restricted land supply. The **John Moore Countryside Museum** in a medieval cottage in Church Street commemorates the local journalist and novelist, who wrote many books on the countryside and conservation, and has interesting displays on rural history and conservation. The Museum is open between Easter and October on Tuesdays to Saturdays from 10.00 to 1.00 and 2.00 to 5.00, and also Bank Holidays and some Sunday afternoons. The little museum next door but one, at No. 41, is furnished as it would have been five hundred years ago, when a medieval merchant occupied the newly built cottage.

JUNCTION 9 BREDON HILL

Four miles north of the junction, **Bredon** is a delightful riverside village with the lovely St Giles's Church and its graceful 160-foot spire. The 14th-century barn has fine porches, one of which has an unusual stone chimney cowling. It is open from March to the end of November on Wednesdays, Thursdays, Saturdays and Sundays from 10.00 to 6.00 or sunset if earlier, at any other time by prior appointment with the National Trust Office, Tewkesbury; closed on Good Friday. From the motorway, take the A438 east and then turn left on to the B4079 at Aston Cross. The B4080 is a direct road from Tewkesbury to Bredon. North-east of the village lies **Bredon Hill**, 961 feet high, with spectacular views. A large number of paths lead up to the summit, where a well fortified hill-fort was constructed in about 300BC and twice extended, in about 150 and 100BC. The hill-fort was attacked and destroyed towards the beginning of the first century AD, and 60 of its defenders were brutally slain, their bodies cast aside by the entrance and their skulls displayed on poles. The best routes up this side of the hill are from Kemerton and Overbury, reached on side roads from the B4079 between Aston Cross and Bredon.

JUNCTION 9 BECKFORD SILK MILL

A visit to **Beckford Silk Mill** provides a fascinating opportunity to watch the hand screen-printing of lengths of silk and to ask the printers and their assistants about the production process, textile design, screen engraving and so on. The Mill specializes in producing silk ties, scarves and other garments. The Mill is open from 9.00 to 1.00 and 2.00 to 5.30 on Mondays to Saturdays. Beckford is on the southern slope of Bredon Hill, and is reached along side roads through Kemerton and Overbury (see above). The direct route from junction 9 is east along the A438, branching left towards Evesham along the A435, and then turning left after about 1 mile to Beckford village at the Beckford Inn.

There is restricted access at junction 10, 4 miles north-west of

The Pittville Pump Rooms, Cheltenham

Cheltenham along the A4019. You can leave the southbound carriageway and join the northbound one only.

JUNCTION 11 CHELTENHAM
Junction 11 is the main junction for Cheltenham, and for Gloucester as well. To **Cheltenham** first, 3½ miles along the A40 – and a marvellous place for a shopping expedition. But take care to have plenty of spending money, unless you can make do with window-gazing. The Promenade, Montpellier, Suffolk Road and the High Street are the main shopping streets, and there are antique shops, high-fashion boutiques for both women and men, jewellers and gift shops – plus wine bars, coffee bars and restaurants. Even sceptical shoppers like myself enjoy Cheltenham: the town simply invites you to stroll and take your ease, just as it must have done in Regency days, when high society first came here to take the waters. **Lansdown Crescent** and **Suffolk Square** are perhaps the most elegant and attractive streets, and **Pittville Park** stands out among the town's many lovely parks

and gardens. And of course you can still take the waters here, either in the splendid Edwardian **Town Hall** or in the Regency **Pittville Pump Room**, said by some to be the handsomest building in all Cheltenham (I'm not sure I agree). The water here is the only natural alkaline water in the entire country. Its effect, so the local guide claims, is 'mainly physiological. Its chief action is antacid, mildly diuretic and laxative'. Try it at your own risk! The three main museums are the **Art Gallery and Museum** in Clarence Street, the **Pitville Pump Room Museum** and the **Gustav Holst Birthplace Museum** in Clarence Road. The first has a rich collection of material on Cheltenham's history, in particular its heyday as a spa in the first half of the 19th century, together with paintings, pottery and furniture from the 17th century onwards. Special attention is paid to the early 20th-century 'Cotswold School' of furniture-makers and metalworkers centred on Ernest Gimson. The Pittville Pump Room Museum, on the upper floors of the Pump Room, is largely a gallery of fashion, with displays of costumes, textiles and accessories from the 1760s to the present day, together with displays on the history of the town and a valuable collection of jewellery. The Holst Museum commemorates the composer, who was born in the town in 1874. Opening times at the Museum and Art Gallery are Mondays to Saturdays from 10.00 to 5.30; at the Pittville Pump Room 10.30 to 5.00 Tuesdays to Sundays and Bank Holiday Mondays between April and October, 10.30 to 5.00 Tuesdays to Saturdays during the rest of the year; and at the Holst Museum 12.00 to 5.30 Tuesdays to Fridays, 11.00 to 5.30 on Saturdays.

JUNCTION 11 GLOUCESTER

The high spot of **Gloucester,** west along the A40 and then south into the town centre, is without question the magnificent cathedral. It stands in **College Green,** an elegant, peaceful precinct with an air of calm, almost Trollopian seclusion. I have to confess that, arriving at College Green, my attention was diverted from the cathedral by a sign to the tiny **House of the Tailor of Gloucester.** This, it turned out, was the very house that Beatrix Potter drew to illustrate her tale. Page 39 of her book shows Simkin the Cat leaving the tailor's front door at midnight on Christmas Eve, the moment when all the animals are said to be able to talk. The house is now a Beatrix Potter centre, with a small museum of memorabilia upstairs and a pleasant shop on the ground floor. All the Peter Rabbit books are stocked, in foreign translations as well, and a wide range of Peter Rabbit pottery, greetings cards and so on, all illustrated with scenes from the stories. Across College Green again and inside the **cathedral,** the Norman nave sweeps up to the glorious Perpendicular choir. The

Gloucester Cathedral

choir was originally built in 1090, at the same time as the nave, but was completely transformed in 1330, when the clerestory and the lovely, intricate roof were added. The magnificent east window was installed 20 years later, 78 feet by 38, commemorating those who fought at Crécy and Calais. In the Norman tribune galleries off the north transept there is an interesting exhibition on the history and construction of the cathedral. For me, the most moving and welcoming place was the cloisters, originally Norman but decorated in the second half of the 14th century with some exquisite fan vaulting, the earliest in the country. When I sat in the monastic garden there on a warm November day, writing the notes for this book, the busy life of the city was scarcely more than a gentle hum in the background, and it was hard to tear myself back to the 20th century. There is an excellent refectory off the cloisters serving home-made food, and a well-stocked shop.

Other eating-places near the cathedral include two in College Street. The College Green restaurant serves fairly formal meals, and the Comfy Pew does teas, morning coffee and snacks. Just round the corner in Westgate Street, you can get delicious-looking salads, cakes and filled rolls and sandwiches at a pleasant café called Butties. The best way to see the rest of the city is from the **Via Sacra Walkway**, along the old city walls from the cathedral. The route passes through part of the large pedestrianized shopping centre, although for interesting antique and clothes shops rather than the standard chain stores Cheltenham is the place to visit (see page 192). Behind the cathedral you can work your way down to the Severn, past the **Folk Museum** in Westgate Street (open Mondays, except Public Holidays, to Saturdays from 10.00 to 5.00), a timber-framed house with exhibits on Gloucester life and history, including a Double Gloucester dairy and a wheelwright's shop.

Exciting things are happening in Gloucester Docks. All the modern buildings have recently been demolished, leaving 13 fine Victorian warehouses, most of which were in regular commercial use until a few years ago. The area, which is one of the best Industrial Revolution areas of dockland in the country, is now being converted to an interesting variety of uses. The North Warehouse has become the City Council's civic headquarters, while the Albert Warehouse houses a museum called 'The Pack Age Revisited' and the Llanthony Warehouse forms part of the National Inland Waterways Museum, shortly due to open. It is well worth taking time to wander round the docks. Look out for the tiny Mariners' Church, still in regular use, the Tall Ships, shortly moving to Bristol (the docks have been used to film *The Onedin Line* among many other films and TV programmes), and for the neo-classical Weighbridge House. The **Gloucester Antiques Centre** has found yet another use for a former warehouse. Here some 65 dealers have their own shops selling every kind of antique and 'collectable', to use the trade jargon, you can imagine. There are several attractive restaurants and pubs in the Docks, including Onedins, the City Barge and the Whitesmith Arms.

Pack Age is Britain's first museum of packaging and advertising. Its initial appeal is, of course, nostalgic: here are the long-forgotten biscuit tins, sweet wrappers, medicine jars of our childhood, as well as posters and leaflets, advertisements and TV commercials. Then you realize that all these ephemera, all this 'junk' that we throw away every day without a moment's thought, together form a vivid and unusual social history of Britain. We can trace the disappearance of the servants who did all the hard domestic tasks and the introduction of labour-saving materials and equipment to make household cleaning quicker and less of a grind; we can follow the development of branded goods and the retailing revolution that began in the early 1950s when the first supermarkets were opened; and we can see the rapid growth of convenience and fast foods. The museum is open on Tuesdays to Sundays and on Bank Holiday Mondays from 10.00 to 6.00.

When it is finished, the **National Inland Waterways Museum** will provide a comprehensive picture of the history, technology and current uses of the canal network. The outdoor exhibition area, due to open in summer 1987, will include historic craft, and visitors will be able to see craftsmen undertaking restoration work such as painting and rope-making. A dockside cottage will recreate the social life of the canals. Inside the Llanthony Warehouse will be working models, displays on different aspects of canal life and, most exciting of all, a 'walk-through' lock running from the ground to the first floor. This part of the Museum is due to open at Easter 1988. Nearer the time, the Gloucester Tourist Information Centre – telephone Gloucester (0452) 421188 – will have more detailed information.

Junction 12, on the southern outskirts of Gloucester, has limited access. You can leave the M5 if you are travelling north and join it if you are driving south. If you are making for Gloucester from the south, leave the motorway here. It is 5 miles along the A38 (some of it dual carriageway) into the city centre.

JUNCTION 13 FRAMPTON ON SEVERN

Junction 13 is ideal if you want to leave the motorway for a pleasant picnic or a quiet country drink. Take the A419 west, turn left on to the A38, and then almost immediately right on to the B4071 towards **Frampton on Severn**. At the village you turn a corner and suddenly emerge on to a long wide green, fronted with attractive houses and with a welcoming pub at each end. There are some fine trees, all a rich golden brown when I was there in autumn. At the far end of the village, beyond the green, the road narrows and eventually reaches the Gloucester & Sharpness Canal. There are good field and towpath walks, many signposted, and beyond, across a wide and muddy field, the expanse of the river Severn. The view back across the canal to Frampton Church has an East Anglian feel about it.

Five miles east along the A419 from the motorway brings you to **Stroud**, a pleasant enough town with some handsome houses and built on a series of steep hills. It has long been an industrial centre, and drew most of its early prosperity from cloth mills, some 150 of which were operating in the 1820s (Stroud scarlet is still used for military uniforms). But there is nothing special to bring you out of your way here.

Frampton on Severn

JUNCTION 13 SLIMBRIDGE RESERVE

Whether you are a wildlife enthusiast or not, a visit to the Wildfowl Trust's **Slimbridge Reserve** – the oldest of seven now scattered throughout the country – is virtually essential. There are two main parts to the Reserve. Over 2500 birds of 180 different kinds live in a 100-acre enclosure, among them all six of the world's varieties of flamingo, tropical species such as humming birds and tanagers and many species of duck, goose and swan. Beyond the pens and the tropical house is a far larger reserve, a vast area of tidal mudflats at the mouth of the Severn, only to be viewed from observation hides. This is the regular wintering-ground of thousands of white-fronted geese and Bewick's swans from the Soviet Arctic, and in the winter months the sight is spectacular, the sky often full. In summer, when the migrants have departed, the grounds are dotted with downy cygnets, goslings and ducklings. It is worth spending some time in the carefully designed Research and Education Centre. The displays there make it clear that the Trust's most important long-term work is in research and conservation: in particular the breeding in captivity of reserve stocks of threatened species. The Ne-Ne or Hawaiian goose is one early and extremely successful example. In 1950 there were fewer than 50 individual birds surviving. Three were sent to Slimbridge, and from these, and four later arrivals, more than 1100 birds have been reared, 200 of which have been returned to Hawaii. There is an excellent restaurant and a well-stocked shop. The Reserve is open daily from 9.30 to 6.00 (dusk if earlier) throughout the year. Slimbridge is 5 miles from junction 13. Take the A38 south and turn right, following clear signposts, at the crossroads just out of the tiny village of Cambridge. Junction 14 is equidistant, so if you are making for Bristol or the West Country continue south on the A38.

JUNCTION 14 TORTWORTH

Tortworth Church, not much more than 1 mile from junction 14, is a pleasant 15th-century building, heavily restored in the last century but without any damage to its appearance. But what makes the brief diversion there worthwhile are the magnificent trees in and around the churchyard: in particular the Tortworth Chestnut, a splendid spreading Spanish chestnut. It was described as a 'notable tree' in the reign of King Stephen – and that was from 1135 to 1154! A chestnut takes at least 250 years to reach maturity, and so the Tortworth specimen is probably not far short of 1100 years old. There are also cedars of Lebanon, one of the largest silver-leafed limes in the country, a wellingtonia, an American hickory that still bears nuts, and tulip trees. Take a look also at the **preaching cross** (15th-century except for its top), a focal point of village life in the Middle Ages. It was garlanded on holy days, the parish clerk read news and proclamations from its steps, and vestry meetings were called there to discuss grievances. At a meeting held here in 1830 it was even proposed to set fire to the rector's tithe barn! To get to Tortworth, take the B4509 east from the motorway, towards the Cotswold foothills, and then the first turning left along the edge of a small wood.

JUNCTION 14 BERKELEY CASTLE

If you are travelling north, leave the motorway here for the Wildfowl Trust's Slimbridge Reserve (see junction 13, page 198). This is also the junction for **Berkeley Castle**. There was a wooden castle here from shortly after the Norman Conquest, but the earliest parts of the present building date from shortly after 1153, when Henry II granted the Castle to one Robert FitzHarding. His descendants have lived there ever since, and the present owner represents the twenty-fourth generation.

The most notable event in Berkeley's history is surely also its most gruesome: the murder of Edward II in 1327 in what is now known as the King's Gallery. The tour of the Castle takes in the Picture Gallery, the Game Larder, Buttery and Kitchen, the splendid Great Hall, a magnificent staircase and the Long Drawing Room. The Picture Gallery has sea pictures by Willem van de Velde; many of the ships portrayed were captained by members of the Berkeley family. The gardens are delightful; be sure to look at the lily pond and the lovely bowling alley. The Castle is open between May and August from 11.00 to 5.00 on Tuesdays to Saturdays and all Bank Holiday Mondays and from 2.00 to 5.00 on Sundays. In April and September opening times are from 2.00 to 5.00, and in October Sundays only from 2.00 to 5.00. Refreshments are available and there is a shop. An additional attraction is the Butterfly House, where you can see free-flying tropical and British butterflies in close-up. To get to Berkeley, take the A38 north from junction 14 and turn left after just over 1 mile in Stone on to the B4509. Turn right at the crossroads in Berkeley and the Castle driveway is on your right. If you are travelling north, it is quicker to return to the M5 at junction 13. In the village, the **Jenner Museum** commemorates the famous medical scientist and naturalist who was born in Berkeley and spent most of his life there, working as a country doctor. Although he is most famous for his development of a vaccine against smallpox, Jenner did a great deal of research work. He recorded one of the first accounts of hypothermia, studied the hibernation of hedgehogs, helped to launch a hydrogen-gas balloon, and studied the natural history of the cuckoo. This last project gained him membership of the Royal Society, although it was another 140 years before his observations were finally corroborated by photography. The Museum is housed in the Chantry, Jenner's favourite home, where he died in 1823. Both the house and gardens, including the Temple of Vaccinia, a small thatched hut in which Jenner used to vaccinate the poor free of charge, are open daily from 11.00 to 5.15 except Mondays, but including Bank Holidays, between April and September.

Junction 15 is the junction with the M4, and there is no access on to ordinary roads.

Junction 16 is midway between Almondsbury and Patchway, but there is nothing in either place to draw you off the motorway. The Almondsbury Interchange Hotel (what an original name!) is a little way north up the A38.

JUNCTION 17 SEVERN ESTUARY
There is a fine blowy sea-wall walk at New Passage on the Severn estuary, 4 miles from junction 17. Take the B4055 north-east from the motorway through Pilning – where the Cross Hands Inn is a good place for a drink and a sandwich – to the shore at the New Passage Hotel. (There's no longer a hotel here, trade having vanished when the Severn Bridge replaced the ferry crossing.) It is about 1 mile south along the **Binn Wall** to Severn Beach, and the foreshore path continues most of the way to Avonmouth.

The **Blaise Castle House Museum** at Henbury, once a delightful little village but now submerged in suburban Bristol, has interesting material on rural and urban social life, and there are pleasant walks in the woodland near the House. The Museum is open from 10.00 to 1.00 and from 2.00 to 5.00 on Saturdays to Wednesdays. From the M5, take the A4018 south and turn right at the first roundabout, from where it is about ½ mile into Henbury. The Blaise Inn near the Museum looks good.

Junction 18 leads off to Avonmouth, now the major port for Bristol, and there is nothing to justify turning off here. You can reach the centre of Bristol reasonably quickly from each of the last three junctions, but the A4 along the banks of the Avon and under Brunel's elegant Clifton Suspension Bridge, 245 feet above the Avon gorge, is probably the most interesting and attractive.

JUNCTION 19 PORTISHEAD
From junction 19, the A369 runs 3 miles west to **Portishead**. This is a curious little place, half a resort, half a not especially attractive working dockyard. There is a pleasant front with all the usual seaside

entertainments and a really fine outlook over the Bristol Channel. The deep-water channel passes just off Battery Rock, and so the shipping can be seen at close quarters. While there is little to be said against Portishead, if you want a seaside resort my advice would be to continue to junctions 20 (Clevedon) or 22 (Burnham-on-Sea and Berrow). There is a fine cliff-top walk along the old Mariners' Path from Portishead past Redcliffe Bay to Clevedon (about 5 miles): well worth doing if one of your party is happy to drive the car round to meet you. The parallel coast road runs along the side of Weston Down, where there are some attractive walks as well.

JUNCTION 20 CLEVEDON
Clevedon, just west of the motorway at junction 20, is a beautifully preserved Victorian and Edwardian resort. There are attractive rows of substantial villas leading back from the sea-front, and it is quite easy to imagine their residents coming down for a modest bathe from the bathing-machines that once lined the beach, and then, perhaps, taking a stroll on the pier. You can still bathe here (though it was pretty muddy when I went in), but for the moment at least the lovely slender Victorian pier is out of bounds. Two spans sank to the bottom in a storm some years ago, and after a prolonged fight to prevent demolition, repair and conservation work is now underway. There are good walks along the front and north to Ladye Bay and Ladye Point and on to Portishead (see page 200). South of the main beach a fine 2-mile walk runs past St Andrew's Church and round Wain's Hill; part of the route follows Poet's Walk, so called because of the many writers who visited the ancient church.

JUNCTION 20 CLEVEDON COURT
Just outside the town, and literally only two or three minutes' drive from the M5, is **Clevedon Court**, an outstanding National Trust property. The house is a rare survival. Built in 1320, its basic form has scarcely been altered since, and it gives us an excellent picture of how a medieval knight, his family and his servants lived. A screens passage running down the centre of the house divided the servants' quarters from the Great Hall and the lord's living rooms. Clevedon Court came into the hands of the Elton family in 1709, and descendants of Abraham Elton, a prosperous Bristol merchant, have lived there ever since. It is a distinguished line. Sir Charles Abraham Elton (1778–1853) knew many celebrated men of letters and brought Lamb, Tennyson, Thackeray and many others to stay at his home. Sir Edmund Harry Elton (1846–1920) was chairman of the local council and fire brigade, and a mechanic and inventor. The Elton–Stephens automatic gas lighter and the Elton instantaneously

detachable dress-guard, which kept ladies' skirts out of their bicycle wheels, are both his work. As well as all that, he was a potter, and invented Elton ware, which in its time won world-wide acclaim. A large collection of pieces can be seen in the museum at the house. Refreshments are available, and the house is open from 2.30 to 5.30 on Wednesdays, Thursdays, Sundays and Bank Holiday Mondays between April and September. From the motorway junction, take the main road towards Clevedon, turn right on to the B3133 and almost immediately right again on to the B3130. The entrance is on the left, just before the bridge under the motorway.

JUNCTION 21 WESTON-SUPER-MARE

Weston-super-Mare is a traditional resort on a grand scale, conveniently close to junction 21 (3½ miles). There are two long piers – Birnbeck and the Grand – miles of golden sands (plus, unfortunately, a good deal of mud at low tide), funfairs and a model village, cricket and fishing, tennis and golf, and the attractive Winter Gardens. The **Woodspring Museum** has fascinating displays on local natural history, archaeology and history – and in particular on seaside life in Victorian Weston. **Weston Woods**, the headland to the north of the town, has some lovely walks. The big and inevitable disadvantage is that the town is very crowded, especially in summer, and for that reason I don't particularly advise an off-motorway break here. The Museum is open from 10.00 to 1.00 and 2.00 to 5.00 Mondays to Saturdays. There is a shop and a café.

Cheddar Gorge and the caves are about 8 miles east of the motorway on a rather winding and indirect route, and for that reason – and again because they get extremely busy – I don't recommend a visit.

JUNCTION 22 BRENT KNOLL

Junction 22 could not be a greater contrast. There is a good walk within five minutes of the motorway, and a lovely stretch of sandy beach only a little further off. The walk is up **Brent Knoll**. Take the A38 north from the motorway, and turn left almost immediately into Brent village. The path starts at the church. The 137-metre summit, from which there are fine views over the Bristol Channel and to Wales, was once an Iron Age hill-fort, and Roman coins and pottery have been found there. From Brent it is about 2½ miles on to the fine sands at **Berrow**, good for letting children and dogs loose. Continue to the end of the village and turn left on to the B3140. In Berrow follow the footpath by the Berrow Inn (which looks a good place for a drink and a snack) across the dunes to the beach. Coming to the beach here at Berrow means that you avoid the crowds and traffic in Burnham. Four miles north of Berrow, along the coast road, you come to **Brean Down**, a headland owned by the National Trust. Sea birds nest here. There are also the remains of an ancient fort and of more recent fortifications, manned during the Napoleonic campaigns and both this century's world wars.

JUNCTIONS 23 & 24 BRIDGWATER

Junctions 23 and 24 are for Bridgwater: junction 23 is 3 miles north of the town along the A38 and junction 24 is 1½ miles south along the same road. **Bridgwater** is a pleasant surprise, and should not be judged by the rather dingy approaches or the crowded inner ring road. Penetrate to the centre of town and you find a good small shopping centre – Oliver's Food Hall is an excellent delicatessen and coffee shop – and some elegant 18th-century merchants' houses along the banks of the river Parrett. This mixture of water and solid prosperity gives something of the feel of a Dutch provincial town. St Mary's Church is also well worth visiting. The **Admiral Blake Museum** (open on Mondays to Saturdays from 11.00 to 5.00, with an extension to 8.00 on Wednesdays, and on Sundays from 2.00 to 5.00) is housed in the cottage where the celebrated admiral was born. It was he who maintained British naval supremacy over the Dutch throughout the 1650s. The Museum also contains exhibits on the Battle of Sedgemoor and the town's history.

The battlefield is on the edge of the village of Westonzoyland, 4 miles south-east of Bridgwater on the A372. Sedgemoor was the last battle fought on English soil, and marked the end of the Duke of Monmouth's Western Rebellion of 1685 against the Roman Catholic King James II, who had recently succeeded his brother Charles II. Monmouth was cornered in Bridgwater with only 3000 men. Planning a surprise night attack on James's forces, they missed their way and a pistol shot revealed their position. They fought bravely but in vain. The King's revenge was brutal: many of the rebels were shot as they tried to escape, and 500 were locked in Westonzoyland Church until they appeared before the Bloody Assizes.

JUNCTIONS 23 & 24 SOMERSET LEVELS

If you have time to spare, a long excursion runs from Bridgwater to Westonzoyland and then through the southern part of the **Somerset Levels** to Othery, Athelney and back to the M5 at junction 25, just outside Taunton. The Levels are a strange, remote area of fenland – at 250 square miles the largest on the west coast of Britain – into which drain the rivers and streams of the Quantocks and Mendips. For the most part the Levels are open grass, interrupted only by basket-makers' withy beds, countless drainage channels and the occasional low hill. The ecology and wildlife of the area is fascinating, and there is a constant clash of interest between those who want to preserve this unique area and farmers who want to drain and plough the fields. Low-intensity farming in which meadows are grazed or kept for hay presents no problem; the difficulties arise when a more substantial return is sought through pump drainage schemes, ploughing and reseeding. From Westonzoyland continue on the A372 as far as Othery, and turn right on to the A361. At Burrow Bridge, over the Parrett, **Burrow Mump** crowns the landscape, visible from miles off. Nothing remains of the Norman castle that once stood at the summit, which is now topped by the ruins of an unfinished 18th-century chapel. The aptly named King Alfred pub here is worth a visit. Turn left just after crossing the river, and then right fairly soon towards Athelney. Alfred the Great set out from here in 878 for his great victory over the Danes at Ethandun, and later founded a monastery. A small monument, reached by crossing a field, commemorates him. Continue straight on in Athelney towards Stoke St Gregory, where you should turn right for North Curry and the A378, just before the junction with the A358. Turn right here and the main road leads straight to junction 25. The RSPB's (Royal Society for the Protection of Birds) West Sedgemoor Reserve lies about 1½ miles east along the A378, near the village of Fivehead. The habitat consists of low-lying wet meadows which contain a large heronry. Numerous species can be seen, among them godwits, redshank, curlew, snipe, lapwing, mallard, widgeon, teal and golden plover. The woodland birds include buzzard, blackcap and nightingale. The entire diversion runs through lovely country, past the workshops of basket- and hurdle-makers, and is well worth your time.

JUNCTION 25 TAUNTON

Close to junction 25, **Taunton** is the busy shopping and commercial centre for a wide area. But there is nothing special to see, and as traffic can be heavy I don't recommend a visit.

JUNCTION 26 SHEPPY'S FARM & CIDER MUSEUM

If junction 25 was something of a disappointment, junction 26, in the middle of the lushest Somerset countryside, more than makes up for it. There is a good selection of things to do. For me the highlight is the longish drive up to the Wellington Monument and then on through the Blackdown Hills to Culmstock, the wool mill at Uffculme and junction 27. But first to some attractions rather nearer at hand. Junction 26 lies just south of the fast A38, and a right turn on to that road brings you after about 1 mile to **Sheppy's Farm and**

Cider Museum at Bradford-on-Tone. The Museum is on the main road itself (on the right-hand side travelling north), not in the pleasant little village, where the White Horse Inn is worth a stop. All stages of cider-making are clearly explained in the Museum and antique equipment is displayed. Outside there are cider orchards where all the best cider apples are grown, including varieties with such magnificent names as Kingston Black, Stoke Red and Tremlett's Bitter. The agricultural machinery includes a thatcher's iron and a thatcher's womble: say no more. Several types of cider made on the premises are sold – the draught scrumpy I bought was excellent – and there are equally delicious local Cheddar cheeses. Monday to Saturday opening hours are as follows: 8.30 to 8.00 in June, July and August, 8.30 to 7.00 in April, May and September, and 8.30 to 6.00 during the rest of the year; on Sundays opening hours are 12.00 to 2.00 only between Easter and Christmas.

JUNCTION 26 POUNDISFORD PARK
Poundisford Park is a lovely Tudor country house, built in 1546 in what used to be the deer park belonging to Taunton Castle and scarcely altered since then. There are some fine period ceilings, and interesting furniture, paintings, porcelain, costumes and so on. The simple Tudor garden has lovely views towards the Quantocks and the Blackdown Hills. The house is open Wednesdays, Thursdays and Bank Holiday Mondays from the beginning of May to mid-September, and also on Fridays in July and August, from 11.00 to 5.00. Light lunches and teas are available. To get to Poundisford Park, continue on the A38 towards Taunton from the Farm and Cider Museum and turn right on the edge of town for Trull. The house is off the country road between Trull and Blagdon Hill and is signposted from Trull.

JUNCTION 26 WELLINGTON
Wellington, 2 miles south-west of junction 26 along the A38, is a pleasant country town with some quite good shopping and several cafés and restaurants. Try the Blue Mantle Hotel, Mario's or Polly's Pantry. The Iron Duke took his title from the town, and his victory at Waterloo is commemorated by the Wellington Monument, a commanding 75-foot obelisk, clearly visible from the motorway, on the Blackdown Hills south of the town. Entering Wellington on the A38 from junction 26, turn left at the crossroads in the centre of the town and then left and immediately right on the edge of the town, along roads signposted to Hemyock. The narrow country road climbs steeply up to the central ridge of the Blackdowns, where there are plenty of pleasant picnic spots and footpaths. When you reach

the summit, turn right on to the ridge road for the **Wellington Monument**. A small plaque at its foot records its erection in 1817, and there are fine views from it over the Tone valley and the town to the long line of the Quantocks beyond. The noise of traffic on the M5 below is rather irritating, though. At the summit of the Blackdown Hills, you can instead turn left for an attractive small area of National Trust land. To continue to junction 27, turn right along the ridge road from the path leading to the monument, and then take the first left down Culm Davy Hill to the tiny hamlets of Culm Davy and Whitehill in the valley of the river Culm. Turn right in Whitehill and follow the side road to Culmstock (2 miles) and then the B3391 west to Uffculme.

JUNCTION 27 COLDHARBOUR MILL WORKING WOOL MUSEUM

There are interesting things to see on both the east and west sides of junction 27. To the east, the first place you reach is **Uffculme** (2 miles). The main attraction here is the **Coldharbour Mill Working Wool Museum**: a fascinating glimpse into the industrial past, and in my opinion the single most enjoyable and interesting attraction off the entire M5. Serge, flannel and worsted yarn were manufactured here until April 1981, and the Museum started not long after that. Some of the original machinery remains, and other equipment has been brought in from nearby mills. As a result, the place has an authentic feel about it. What you see is not a sanitized reconstruction but a genuine workshop much as it was decades ago. There are three levels. On the first, the combing shed, you see a magnificent circular combing-machine, nicknamed the Noble Comb, which straightens out the fibre and separates long and short wool. Drawing and spinning take place on the second floor, wool-processing on the third. In the gallery, there are six Hattersley power looms, each capable of about a hundred picks – crossways movements of the shuttle – per minute. You can also see the water-wheel, which powered the machinery in the combing shed until 1979, and the magnificent 300-hp steam engine that powered most of the rest of the factory. The water-wheel is 18 feet in diameter and 14 feet wide. Visitors are encouraged to watch the machinery working, and to talk to the machinists as well. The Mill's fine products are on sale in the well-stocked shop, along with garments knitted by Devon people. Also of interest are the steam gallery and a steam-powered carpenter's workshop. There is an excellent restaurant and a lovely picnic area near the river. The Museum is open daily from 11.00 to 5.00 between Easter and October, and from 11.00 to 5.00 on Mondays to Fridays only during the rest of the year. From the motorway,

Coldharbour Mill, Uffculme

take the A38 north-east towards Wellington, and turn right almost immediately on to the B3181 towards Uffculme, following signs to Uffculme and the Mill. The main feature of **Uffculme parish church** in the centre of the village is the lovely early 15th-century rood screen, at 67 feet the longest in Devon. From Uffculme it is 3 miles east along the B3391, through the delightful **Culm Valley**, to Culmstock, where you can pick up the drive to the Blackdown Hills and the Wellington Monument described under junction 26 above.

JUNCTION 27 GRAND WESTERN CANAL

A little way west of the motorway, the **Grand Western Canal** winds through pleasant countryside, and would be a pleasant spot for a quick walk and picnic. The 11-mile route barely merits the over-ambitious description its sponsors gave it, and the Grand Western is a supreme example of the over-optimism of the canal-building boom at the end of the 18th century. The original idea was to link the English and Bristol Channels along a route from Topsham on the Exe estuary to Taunton and Bridgwater, and then along the river Parrett. Most of the route between Tiverton and Bridgwater got built one way or another, but the link to Topsham was never started, and the middle section, between Lowdwells and Taunton, was built on the cheap. The effective life of the Grand Western – the Tiverton to Lowdwells part of the route – was little more than a century. As often happened, the local railway company bought the canal so as to stifle competition. Today, there is a fine towpath walk through lovely country along the entire canal, and a lot of interesting canal architecture can be seen. The first access point is just before Sampford Peverell. Follow the dual carriageway A373 west from the motorway, and take the first exit left to Sampford Peverell. Turn right and then right again almost immediately; the road crosses the canal after less than ½ mile. For the second access point, follow the road through Sampford Peverell and on towards Halberton; you cross the canal shortly before reaching Halberton.

JUNCTION 27 TIVERTON

In **Tiverton**, 6 miles west of the motorway along the A373, you can reach the canal basin by turning left at the roundabout as you enter the town and then taking the second left. The basin is the starting-point for horse-drawn barge trips along the canal. Services operate twice a day most days between the end of May and early September, and also at weekends and Bank Holidays at each end of the season, between Easter and early October. There is a pleasant picnic area at the basin and also a small souvenir shop. Tiverton town has an appealing main street spoilt, as all too often happens, by some ugly shopfronts. Are there no architects, planners and developers with a sense of the scale and sweep of a street? There are two town trails, which between them take in most of the town's notable buildings – in particular St Peter's Church, the Chilcot School (founded in 1611) and Waldron's and Slee's Almshouses – and the excellent, award-winning local **Museum**. Of special interest in the Museum are galleries devoted to railways (including a GWR locomotive) and textile machinery, an industrial gallery with exhibits on the Grand Western Canal, a Victorian laundry, a costume gallery and two water-wheels. Opening times are Mondays to Saturdays 10.30 to 4.30 betwen February and December. The Museum is closed from 24 December to 31 January each year. The earliest parts of the **Castle** date from 1106, and the interior offers an international clock collection, a Joan of Arc gallery and the Chapel of St Francis, not to mention the more usual furniture and pictures. Opening times are from 2.30 to 5.30 daily except Fridays and Saturdays between Good Friday and late September.

JUNCTION 28 CULLOMPTON

Cullompton, literally just west of the motorway at junction 28, has a pleasant main street with some handsome buildings and a good selection of eating-places. My choice would be the elegant Manor House Hotel. The most notable and visible landmark in Cullompton is the 100-foot red sandstone tower of **St Andrew's Church**. Inside the church is marvellously light and airy. There is a beautiful rood screen and, most unusual, an additional aisle on the south side. This is known as Lane's Aisle, after John Lane, a local clothier, who built it. He died in 1528, before work on his aisle was complete, and is buried with his wife at the east end. Look out for the Tudor figures in niches on the piers dividing Lane's Aisle and the south aisle. There is a handsome oak Jacobean gallery too, one of the longest in Devon, and an elaborate wagon roof. In an early public relations exercise, the Great Western Railway inserted iron tie-rods in the roof in 1859, as it was feared that vibrations from the railway in the valley below might damage the building.

There is restricted access at junction 29. You can leave the motorway travelling north and join it to go south.

JUNCTION 30 EXETER

Junction 30 is the main turn-off for Exeter. But if you only have limited time to spare and simply want a quick break, I suggest a drive 2 miles south to **Topsham**, a pretty little village on the Exe estuary. Take the A3052 east from the motorway and turn right almost immediately. There are some lovely riverside houses in Topsham, among them a 17th-century Dutch-gabled one whose sail-loft now houses the local **museum**, which has interesting exhibits on local history and trade. Opening times are from 2.00 to 5.00 on Mondays, Wednesdays and Saturdays. Mistress Meg's in the main street would be a good place for a light meal, and there is also the Salutation Inn. Further down the estuary, **Lympstone** is an interesting village with some good shops and several pubs, including the Globe Inn. There is a good walk along the estuary into Exmouth. Lympstone is about 5 miles from junction 30. Turn east along the A3052 and then right on to the A376.

There is of course plenty to do in **Exeter**, but the city merits at least a day's visit. High spots include the **cathedral**, built between 1260 and 1394, with magnificent rib-vaulting and a lovely minstrels' gallery; the **Maritime Museum** (open daily from 10.00 to 5.00, until 6.00 in July and August) where over a hundred veteran steam and sail vessels from all over the world are on display; the **Museum of Costume and Lace** in Rougemont House (open Mondays to Saturdays from 10.00 to 5.30, with an extension to 7.30 on Wednesdays in July and August, and from 2.00 to 6.00 on Sundays in July and August); and the celebrated medieval **underground passages** (tours Tuesdays to Saturdays 2.00 to 4.00), built to provide the city with a constant supply of fresh water. It's a marvellous city to stroll about in. Interesting areas include the Quay, where the 17th-century Customs House is one of several fine buildings, the cathedral close and the Georgian terraces of Southernhay just to the south.

JUNCTION 30 POWDERHAM CASTLE

Powderham Castle and the Brunel Atmospheric Railway at Starcross are both on the west side of the estuary, and should strictly speaking be dealt with under junction 31. But that junction leads straight into two major trunk roads, and there is no convenient route from them south down the estuary. Instead, leave the motorway at junction 30 and cross the river and the Exeter Canal on the A379, and then, at the roundabout on the west bank, turn left (south) on the same road down the estuary. For **Powderham Castle** (4 miles) turn left off the A379 about 1½ miles out of Exminster, and the Castle entrance is on the right after about 1 mile. The Castle, which has a fine view over the estuary, was built between 1390 and 1420 – very late for an English castle, and its design suggests a manorial residence as much as a fortified stronghold. It was damaged in the Civil War, however, and much restored in the 18th and 19th centuries. The tour takes in the Marble Hall, where there are delicately worked 17th-century Brussels tapestries, the Music Room, with a lovely Wyatt ceiling, and the lavish 18th-century plasterwork of the Staircase Hall. The Castle is open daily except Fridays and Saturdays between late May and mid-September from 2.00 to 5.30. There is a picnic area and garden and souvenir shops, and cream teas are available.

JUNCTION 30 ATMOSPHERIC RAILWAY

Starcross, about 1 mile south of Powderham Castle on the A379, is the site of what must be one of the country's most curious railway relics: one of the pumping houses of Isambard Kingdom Brunel's **Atmospheric Railway**. Unlike many of Brunel's projects, the atmospheric railway was a complete failure right from the start, and with hindsight even its theory was ill-conceived. An atmospheric railway ran without locomotives. Power was provided by a combination of partial and atmospheric pressure. Stationary engines in a series of pumping houses – there were to be seven on the 52-mile line from Exeter to Plymouth – pumped air along an iron pipe laid between the rails. This created a vacuum in front of a piston in the pipes. The leading carriage was attached to the piston, and the vacuum enabled atmospheric pressure building up behind the piston to propel the train forwards. The operational problems encountered when services were started in 1847 were immense, and the line never got further than the 20 miles to Teignmouth. Costs were much higher than anticipated – Brunel had claimed that this was a very cheap form of transport – the trains ran late (and often had to be pushed by third-class passengers), and the vital leather flap that connected the train and the piston got eaten away. In 1848, only a year after services had begun, Brunel himself recommended that the line be converted to conventional steam operation. The pumping house at Starcross, on the main road just beyond the railway halt, was opened as a museum in 1983, mainly through the efforts of one local enthusiast. It is a fascinating place. There is a model of the train (powered by vacuum cleaners!), and also one of the pumps Brunel designed, plus interesting displays on the history of the line. In time it is hoped that the museum will extend its scope to cover all Victorian science and invention. Refreshments are available, and there is a shop. Opening times are daily from 10.00 to 6.00 (last admissions 5.00) between Easter and the end of October.

From the end of the motorway at junction 31 at Shillingford St George there is direct access only to the A30 and the A38. These fast dual carriageways lead to Okehampton along the northern edge of Dartmoor and to Plymouth along the southern edge respectively, and continue for several miles without an exit. There is an alternative back route to Powderham and Starcross (see under junction 30, above) from the first exit off the A38 at Kennford. Make your way on country roads through the village to the tiny hamlet of Kenn. Keep straight on here and you will reach the A379 just south of the turning for Powderham. For Powderham turn left and then first right. For Starcross turn right down the main road.

The M6

Rugby to Carlisle

INTRODUCTION

The M6 is primarily an industrial motorway. It runs through the heart of the country's industrial regions, through the great West Midlands conurbation and north to the Black Country, then on the edge of Merseyside and Greater Manchester. Traffic is consistently heavy, with numerous trucks. Even in the northern sections, in north Lancashire and Cumbria, where you might expect to leave the traffic behind, the motorway is well used – a reminder that the M6 is one of the two principal routes to and from Scotland.

Despite all this, there is plenty to do and see off the M6. True, in the industrial areas you may have to look fairly hard to find something worth leaving the motorway for, but elsewhere it is quite the opposite. In Staffordshire, there is some fine country at Cannock Chase, and then a great deal of interest in and around Stoke-on-Trent. In Cheshire, the motorway misses the best countryside, which lies some miles both east and west, beyond the reach of this book. Nevertheless, there are country houses, museums, canal walks – even, at Jodrell Bank, one of the world's largest radio telescopes. In the far north, the motorway skirts the Lake District, but many of the most celebrated lakes and peaks are only a few minutes away, and even if you stay on the motorway there is plenty of rugged scenery. (It is rugged driving too in the winter, and this stretch of the M6 is often snowbound.)

But for me, the highlight of the route – perhaps because it came as such a surprise – was in north Lancashire, in particular the junctions south of Lancaster and north of Carnforth. The landscape may not be as dramatic as in the Lakes a little to the north, but it is a fascinating area, quiet and remote, with a wealth of interesting things to tempt you off the motorway.

The M6 starts at junction 19 of the M1, in the not especially interesting north Northamptonshire countryside. There is direct

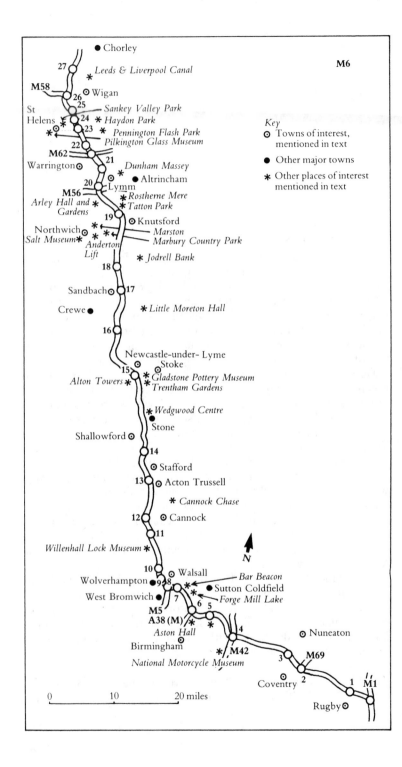

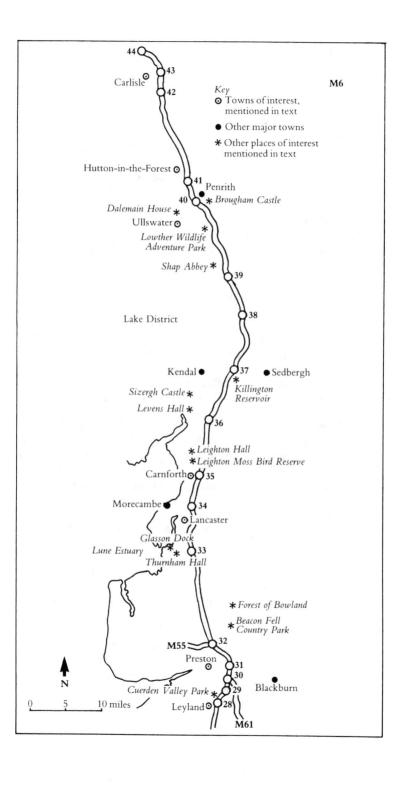

44

43

Carlisle ⊙

42

Key
⊙ Towns of interest, mentioned in text

● Other major towns

✳ Other places of interest mentioned in text

M6

Hutton-in-the-Forest ⊙

41 Penrith ●

40 ✳ *Brougham Castle*

Dalemain House ✳

Ullswater ⊙

✳

Lowther Wildlife Adventure Park

Shap Abbey ✳

39

38

Lake District

Kendal ● **37** ● Sedbergh

✳

Killington Reservoir

Sizergh Castle ✳

Levens Hall ✳

36

✳ *Leighton Hall*

✳ *Leighton Moss Bird Reserve*

Carnforth ⊙ **35**

Morecambe ● **34**

⊙ Lancaster

Glasson Dock

Lune Estuary ✳ **33**

Thurnham Hall

✳ *Forest of Bowland*

✳ *Beacon Fell Country Park*

M55 **32**

Preston ⊙

31

30

Cuerden Valley Park ✳ **29** Blackburn ●

Leyland ⊙ **28**

M61

↑
N

0 — 5 — 10 miles

access on to the M6 from the northbound carriageway of the M1, and likewise direct access from the M6 on to the M1 going south; but you cannot drive straight from the M1 going south on to the M6, nor from the M6 on to the M1 going north. For most people the M69 provides a suitable alternative. If you do want to make the link, however, you can use junction 20 of the M1, just south of Lutterworth, and junction 1 of the M6. The intervening few miles are done on the A426, and the route is well signposted. There is no way off the motorway on to ordinary roads from junction 19.

JUNCTION 1 RUGBY

Rugby is the main town hereabouts, some 2 miles south of junction 1 on the A426. The name strikes all kinds of chords – **Rugby School**, the great Dr Arnold, *Tom Brown's Schooldays*, Rugby football – but the place itself is a bit of an anti-climax. The School dominates the town architecturally, but although you may be able to take a quick, unofficial look at the Close through the tower gateway on Lawrence Sheriff Street, officially the School is open to the public on only two or three days a year. (Write to the Bursar at the School for details.) As at many public schools, there are a lot of fine Victorian buildings, quite a number by the famous architect William Butterfield. He was also responsible for the town's parish church. 'Although not one of Butterfield's best works', says the town guide, the church has 'much character' – and a prominent, 182-foot spire. It was the building of the railway in the 1830s that made Rugby an industrial centre (the London to Birmingham line was the first main line out of London), and the handsome railway station just outside the town centre shows that Rugby was a major junction. The **James Gilbert Rugby Football Museum** in St Matthews Street is housed in the premises of Gilbert Rugby Footballs Ltd, who have been making footballs here since 1842. Two Gilbert footballs were shown at the Great Exhibition in 1851, and as soon as the Rugby Football Union was formed in 1871 Gilbert balls began to be exported all over the world. The Museum contains photographs, programmes, magazines, balls and equipment mainly from the years 1920 to 1960, although the collection is growing all the time. Among the items on display are the six- and eight-panel balls used during the first half of this century until the present four-panel ball was adopted. The Museum is open from 10.00 to 1.00 and 2.00 to 5.00 on Mondays to Saturdays. Otherwise, there is not much of interest here, except for an attractively laid-out, covered shopping mall with all the usual chain-stores. There are two trendy-looking eating places: Peppers in Sheep Street, where they serve excellent wholemeal scones, and Crumbles in Chapel Street.

JUNCTION 2 COVENTRY

From junction 2, the A46 takes you straight into **Coventry** city centre on a dual carriageway. There's plenty to see here, of course, but a detour is inadvisable unless you've time to spare and are happy to do battle with inner-city traffic, multi-storey car parks and the like. First and foremost are the **cathedrals** – the ruins of the old one, destroyed in the Second World War, and, next to them, the new one, designed by Basil Spence. Together they are an impressive and poignant reminder of the horror of war, especially forceful in this age of nuclear lunacy. There are several splendid works of art – Graham Sutherland's altar tapestry, John Piper's baptistry window, and Jacob Epstein's statue of St Michael and the Devil – but everyone will find something to move them, some spiritual sustenance.

JUNCTION 2 MUSEUM OF BRITISH ROAD TRANSPORT

The rest of the city has a remarkably dated air about it. Coventry suffers from having been rebuilt at a time when inner ring roads were in vogue and shopping centres were turned out uniformly dull. But in Spon Street something of the medieval city remains. Several of the street's original medieval buildings have been restored, and others have been moved here from elsewhere in the city. **The Museum of British Road Transport** in St Agnes Lane is one of the country's most important transport museums – fittingly, since Coventry in particular and the West Midlands in general have been so closely connected with the British motor industry; legendary names such as Daimler, Jaguar, Hillman, Rover, Singer, Standard and Triumph all hail from Coventry. The Museum contains more than 150 motor cars, 90 motor cycles and 200 cycles (the earliest bicycles were also made in Coventry). Among the exhibits are Queen Mary's 1935 Daimler, King George VI's 1947 Daimler State Landaulette, the earliest surviving Standard (1906) and Hillman (1908), Field Marshal Montgomery's 'Victory Car', the Rover/BRM jet racing car, and Thrust 2, the car that in 1983 set a new world land speed record of 1019.44 km an hour on the mudflats of the Black Rock Desert, Nevada, which is displayed in an exciting audio-visual auditorium. The social history of transport is not neglected. Three interesting displays that take visitors back to the early days of motoring are 'Memory Lanes', 'Royalty on the Road' and 'History of the Cycle'. From April to October the Museum is open on Mondays to Fridays from 10.00 to 4.00, on Saturdays and Sundays from 10.00 to 5.30. In winter opening hours are Fridays from 9.30 to 4.00, Saturdays and Sundays from 10.00 to 5.00. There is a Museum shop.

The M69 runs north from junction 2, linking with the M1 at junction 21 for Leicester. If you want to travel north on the M1 from the M6, this is the route to take.

JUNCTION 3 NUNEATON

South from junction 3 the A444 also runs into Coventry. Going north, the dual carriageway bypasses Bedworth on its way to **Nuneaton** (4¾ miles). There is little to detail you here, unless you want to make a George Eliot pilgrimage. The novelist was born near here in 1819, spent all her childhood in a house on what is now the A444, and set many of her novels in the area. The Nuneaton Library has a George Eliot collection, and wards in the local hospital are named after her characters.

JUNCTION 3 ARBURY HALL

Arbury Hall, west of Nuneaton, was originally an Elizabethan house with late 17th-century additions, including a porch by Sir Christopher Wren, one of the very few works he designed outside London. But today Arbury Hall is most celebrated as a magnificent example of the Gothick Revival style. Extensive alterations were made during the second half of the 18th century. The most interesting rooms are the Drawing Room, where the barrel-vaulted ceiling is decorated with groining and the design of the elaborate chimney-piece is based on a 13th-century tomb in Westminster Abbey, and the Dining Room, where there is another high chimney-piece and classical statues stand in niches around the walls beneath spectacular fan-vaulting. Like the house, the attractive gardens were also created in the second half of the 18th century. Opening days at Arbury are Sundays and Bank Holiday Mondays from Easter to the end of September, and Tuesdays and Wednesdays in July and August, from 2.00 to 5.30 (last admission 5.00); the park and gardens remain open until 6.00. From the motorway take the A444 north towards Nuneaton. Turn left off the Bedworth bypass on side roads to Astley and then right on to the B4102, from where the entrance to the park is signposted.

JUNCTION 4 COLESHILL

Junction 4 marks the start of the built-up West Midlands, and from now until junction 11, 23 miles away, opportunities for off-motorway relaxation are few and far between, with the honourable exception of the Beacon Regional Park near junction 7. **Coleshill**, right off the A446 north from the motorway, just manages to preserve its independent identity, separate from the surrounding Birmingham sprawl, and there are some handsome houses and several pubs on the pleasant main street. The countryside nearby is classic Midlands land, fertile and undulating (it is only a few miles to Meriden, the centre of England), but there are few opportunities for walks or picnics.

JUNCTION 4 NATIONAL EXHIBITION CENTRE

This is also the junction for the M42 and the **National Exhibition Centre**. The M42 runs along the south-eastern rim of Birmingham, joining the M5 (see pages 174–212) at junction 4a of that motorway, and north to Appleby Magna in Leicestershire. Opened in 1976, the NEC, which is reached from junction 6 of the M42, is the country's largest exhibition area; its six halls are as big as London's Olympia and Earls Court put together. The Exhibition Centre office specializes in issuing mind-blowing statistics. There are 111 miles of structural steel tubing in the roof. The roof of the complex covers 27 acres. There are almost 32 miles of drains on the site. And, finally, you could accommodate over three thousand double-decker buses in the exhibition area – always supposing, that is, you had three thousand to spare!

JUNCTION 4 NATIONAL MOTORCYCLE MUSEUM

Even closer to junction 6 of the M42 is the **National Motorcycle Museum**, which contains a comprehensive collection of British motorcycles – and so also stands as a memorial to a once great but now almost entirely defunct British industry. The hundreds of machines on show here are sensibly arranged to enable visitors to make the most of the story. The first exhibition hall, called 'Sixty Glorious Years', contains one machine for every year between 1901 and 1961. The second and third are devoted to motorcycles under and over 500cc, while the fourth houses competition motorcycles of every kind, trials bikes, scramblers, sprinters, road racers and record breakers. As well as the machines themselves (every famous make is represented, plus many long-forgotten ones), photographs and other memorabilia help to create the atmosphere. The Museum, which is open daily from 10.00 to 6.00, is almost directly beneath junction 6 of the M42; take the A45 east towards Coventry.

Junction 5, at Castle Bromwich, has restricted access. You can leave the motorway going north, and get on it going south. But there is nothing worth stopping here for anyway.

JUNCTION 6 SPAGHETTI JUNCTION & GAS STREET BASIN

Junction 6 is **Spaghetti Junction** – which isn't half as horrendous in reality as it is in reputation. In fact, unless you take the trouble to turn off here, you'll hardly notice it. From a car, the best view of the junction is from the A5127 going towards central Birmingham (*not* from the A38(M), which is the quickest route into the centre). Ironically, however, the junction is most impressive seen from the canal towpath. Three canals meet underneath it – the Grand Union, the Tame Valley and the Birmingham & Fazeley – and the junction rears up steeply above the water. It is quite difficult to park anywhere near the junction, and if you do manage to it can be difficult to find a way on to the towpath. Instead, if you have the time and feel like an industrial canalside walk, take the A38(M) into the centre and make for **Gas Street Basin**. This is one of the centres of the Birmingham Canal Navigations, as the network is known: it's hard to believe, but there are more canals in Birmingham than in Venice. The towpath walk takes you right underneath the city centre, past the Post Office tower, the **Museum of Science and Industry** and the **Farmers Bridge locks**. It is about 4 miles to Spaghetti Junction – 4 miles in a world quite remote from the busy, high-tech life of central Birmingham. For canal and urban history enthusiasts, this is a must.

JUNCTION 6 BIRMINGHAM

From the M6, **Birmingham** city centre is only 3 miles down the A38(M) – and not many minutes more, unless you happen to hit the rush hour. In the centre there is plenty of well-signposted parking. There are all the amenities you would expect: excellent shopping; the **Museum and Art Gallery**; two **cathedrals**; and large numbers of cafés, restaurants and pubs. There are two fascinating town trails round the narrow streets of the **Jewellery Quarter**, just north of the city centre, both of which feature the elegant 18th-century St Paul's Square. In its heyday, just before the First World War, some 30,000 people were employed in the gold, silver and allied trades in Birmingham.

JUNCTION 6 ASTON HALL

There is not much open space hereabouts, but if you are desperate, a trip to **Aston Hall** (open April to October) might be worth the effort. Follow the A5127 south from junction 6 towards central Birmingham and take the first main road right. After this has worked its way underneath the A38(M), Aston Hall is straight in front of you. You reach the driveway by turning right at the traffic lights and then immediately left. The Hall was built between 1618 and 1635. There is period furniture of the 17th, 18th and 19th centuries on display, plus a fine Jacobean oak staircase, large Jacobean chimney-pieces, intricate plasterwork and a panelled Long Gallery. The pleasant gardens with their formal lawns offer wide views over Birmingham.

Aston Hall is open from 10.00 to 5.00 on Mondays to Saturdays, 2.00 to 5.00 on Sundays.

JUNCTION 7 BEACON REGIONAL PARK

Part of the **Beacon Regional Park**, a 12-mile-long park being established along the urban fringe of the West Midlands, lies close to junction 7. There is a variety of landscape here: woodlands and open fields, scrappy wasteland, ponds and canals, farmland, conventional municipal parks and so on. Two interesting spots near the motorway are Barr Beacon to the north and Forge Mill Lake and the Nature Centre nearby to the south. To get to Barr Hill, where there are fine views and pleasant picnic spots, follow the A34 north towards Walsall and then take the first right past the Post House Hotel towards Aldridge. The long-distance footpath that runs across the entire Park passes here. Forge Mill Lake in the Sandwell valley is fed by the river Tame. Geese and other wildfowl can be seen here, and there are more walks and picnic spots, plus sailing on the lake. Take the A34 Walsall road south from the motorway (away from Walsall), and then turn right on to Hamstead Road.

Junction 8 is the start of the M5, and there is no access to ordinary roads.

JUNCTIONS 9 & 10 WALSALL

Roads north-east from junctions 9 and 10 bring you into the centre of **Walsall**. Both are usually pretty crowded, but the route from junction 10 along the A454 is slightly better. There is a town trail round central Walsall, and the **Museum and Art Gallery** has an important collection of work by the sculptor Jacob Epstein. Paintings by Picasso, Matisse and Reynolds are also on show, as well as exhibits of the town's traditional trades, leather-working and saddlers' ironmongery. (Opening hours are Mondays to Fridays from 10.00 to 6.00, Saturdays from 10.00 to 4.45.) One fine building in the town centre is the **Guildhall**, built in 1867 as magistrates' courts and now converted into a shopping mall. The nearby **market**, established in the town in 1219, is said to be one of the best in the West Midlands; if you are here on Mondays, Tuesdays, Fridays and Saturdays look out for fabrics, seconds of Staffordshire pottery and crockery, and fresh fruit and vegetables. A boating holiday – no matter how chaotic – along the Thames is not something one would normally associate with Walsall. But the connection is very real, for Jerome K. Jerome, author of *Three Men In A Boat*, that most celebrated acount of such a trip, was born in the town. The small **Jerome K. Jerome Birthplace Museum**, in a handsome town house in Bradford Street where Jerome was born in 1859, contains an exhibition about his life and works, with several first editions, and a reconstructed parlour of the 1850s. The Museum is open from 10.00 to 5.00 on Tuesdays to Saturdays. Beyond the town centre **Walsall Arboretum** offers peace and quiet and tree-lined walks. The famous Walsall Illuminations take place in the Arboretum every autumn, from the last Friday in August to the first Sunday in October. Opening times are dusk until 10.00, and if you do come here then you will enjoy the lakeside walks festooned with hundreds of coloured lights and the tableaux of childrens' television characters.

JUNCTION 10 LOCK MUSEUM

West of junction 10 the A454 brings you after 2 miles into Willenhall, the traditional centre of the lock trade. The **Lock Museum**, housed in a former lock-maker's house and workshop in New Road, contains a fascinating collection of locks and keys, padlocks and lock-making equipment, and there are opportunities to watch skilled lock-makers at work. The gas-lit rooms are furnished as they would have been at the turn of the century. The Museum is open from 1.00 to 5.00 on Mondays to Fridays and from 10.00 to 5.00 on Saturdays.

Junction 10a is the junction with the M54, which starts here and runs west to Telford and Wellington. There is no access on to ordinary roads.

JUNCTIONS 11 & 12 CANNOCK CHASE

With junction 11, you emerge from the urban mass of the West Midlands, and there is at least a hint of fresh air and green fields. But don't be too optimistic. The traffic is still heavy, and much of the landscape is 'straggly urban' – small estates and factories scattered about, apparently at random. And, worst of all, the genuine attraction of the area – Cannock Chase – lies on the far side of Cannock town.

Cannock itself is just under 3 miles from junction 11 along the A460 and just over 3 miles from junction 12 on the A5. The town has nothing special to recommend it – but equally I'd find it hard to say anything against it. There is a pleasant wide main street centred on the market place, with the usual number of shops, pubs and cafés you find in a small town.

The southernmost part of **Cannock Chase** lies about 3 miles north of Cannock. Take the A460 north-west from Cannock to beyond Hednesford, and then take the Brindley Valley Road to Brindley Heath, the Chase and the Marquis Drive visitor centre. Now you are right in the Chase itself: it is high, wild forest and heathland country, extensive enough to feel really lost in. There are superb walks among the heather, silver birch, pine and oak, and plenty of places for a quiet picnic. Most of the main visitor facilities – the Chase is now a Country Park run by the County Council – are on the southern side of the Chase, which is really quite a long way from the M6. These include a Forest Centre and Museum at Ladyhill, 2 miles west of Rugeley, and the County Council's visitor centre at Marquis Drive, from where forest trails and natural history trails lead through the Chase; an Iron Age fort at Castle Ring; three forest trails and another three natural history trails. If you are lucky, you may see fallow deer on one of these walks: a herd several hundred strong roams the Chase, as it has for almost a thousand years now, ever since the area became a Royal Forest.

If time is short, stick to the road that runs near the western edge of the Chase from Pye Green north to **Brocton**, where it rejoins the A34. It is magnificent country, with good walking in the woods and good views from the Glacial Boulder. This road also passes near the **German Military Cemetery** – burial place for prisoners of war who died in captivity in both world wars – the **Commonwealth Cemetery** and the **Katyn Memorial**, which commemorates the thousands of Polish officers massacred at Katyn. Cannock Chase was the last home billet for many who fought and fell in France in the First World War, and a **Great War Trail** (which has to be done by car and on foot) links all the relevant sites.

From Brocton you can return to the M6 via Acton Trussell to junction 13 or to junction 14 through Stafford.

JUNCTION 13 ACTON TRUSSELL

Junction 13 is the best exit for the northern part of Cannock Chase. Take the A449 north towards Stafford, but turn right for **Acton Trussell** almost immediately. This pleasant village lies the other side, first, of the river Penk and, second, of the Staffordshire and Worcestershire Canal. From Acton Trussell it is about 3 miles along country roads to Brocton.

JUNCTION 13 STAFFORD

Junction 13 is also the turn-off for **Stafford** if you are coming from the south. It is a pleasant market town and administrative centre, with some 17th- and 18th-century buildings and the timber-framed **Ancient High House** in the main street, built in 1595 of local oak; Royalists were jailed here during the Civil War. A history trail runs round the town. Despite all this, and the **Castle** (open during daylight hours), a 19th-century reconstruction of a mid-14th century castle built on the site of a motte and bailey castle erected in about

1070, I wouldn't especially recommend the town for an off-motorway diversion.

JUNCTION 14 IZAAK WALTON'S COTTAGE

Junction 14 leads into Stafford from the north. About 4 miles north of the junction, in the village of Shallowford, is **Izaak Walton's Cottage**. Izaak Walton was a native of Stafford. In his lifetime he was best known for his biographies, not *The Compleat Angler*, which seems to have been compiled as a leisure activity and which had to be rescued from obscurity in the mid-18th century by Dr Johnson, another Staffordshire man. The cottage (which you reach by taking the A5013 north and then turning right in Little Bridgeford) forms part of a farm which he owned, and is now a museum. Its aim, according to the hand-out, is 'to show a typical late 17th-century domestic interior such as Walton would have known'. There are exhibits illustrating Walton's life, and the history of angling and of the cottage, and a period garden in which herbs are grown. The museum is open daily except Wednesdays and Thursdays from 12.30 to 5.30 between mid-March and the end of October, and from 12.30 to 4.30 at weekends during the rest of the year.

From Shallowford, it is probably best to retrace your way to junction 14 – there is a 12-mile gap between junctions 14 and 15 – unless you want to go on to the Wedgwood Visitor Centre at Barlaston. To do that, continue on the road through Shallowford, turn right on to the B5026 and then left on to the A34 on the edge of Stone. The turning for Barlaston is 3 miles further north, in the village of Tittensor.

JUNCTIONS 14 & 15 WEDGWOOD VISITOR CENTRE

For the **Wedgwood Visitor Centre** at **Barlaston**, leave the M6 at junction 14 if you are travelling north, at junction 15 if you are coming south. From junction 14, it is about 8 miles north on the dual carriageway A34 to Tittensor and the turning for Barlaston. Coming south from junction 15, it is about 4 miles. You take the A500 east from the motorway and then turn right on to the A34.

Whichever way you come, the Centre is certainly well worth the journey. Following the signs from Tittensor, you cross the railway and then turn left in Barlaston village to enter the grounds of a large estate. This is the estate that the Wedgwood Company bought in 1937 when their original factory at Etruria – itself once a country idyll – was threatened with pollution and subsidence. The factory's rural surroundings make a startling contrast with other potteries in and around Stoke. The nice thing about the Centre is that it is right in the middle of a genuine, productive factory. At other 'working' museums, the work is done primarily for the benefit of visitors. Here

The Trent in Staffordshire

visitors are a welcome but almost incidental part of the day's routine: all the work is for real.

The visit starts with a short film. Then you move into the beautifully laid-out museum, which tells the story of the Company, and in particular of the work and achievements of its founder Josiah Wedgwood. There are examples of the three ceramic bodies he invented – Queen's ware, Black Basalt and Jasper – and literally thousands of pieces of every type, style and period of the firm's production. I especially liked the early 19th-century fine bone china. A recreation of Josiah Wedgwood's workshops at Etruria, Georgian and Victorian table settings and an art gallery containing works by painters such as Reynolds, Stubbs, Wright, Romney and Singer Sargent are among the other interesting features. In the Craft Demonstration Hall you can talk to craftsmen working on every stage of production – many of the traditional hand processes are still in use today – and you can linger for as long as you like to see how they are done. There is a large souvenir shop with a wide variety of gifts and tableware, and a refreshment lounge as well. The Centre is open from Mondays to Fridays from 9.00 to 5.00 and on Saturdays from 10.00 to 4.00; the Centre is closed for two weeks over Christmas and the New Year.

JUNCTION 15 TRENTHAM GARDENS

The nearest attraction to junction 15 is **Trentham Gardens**. The formal Italian gardens were designed by Capability Brown, and must have been magnificent in their heyday – some 50 gardeners were required to tend them. In the 1830s Trentham Hall was remodelled on a grand scale, the architect Sir Charles Barry creating a stunningly splendid house, with a Sculpture Gallery, State Bedroom block and a Clock Tower. Although the sculpture block and Clock Tower remain, the house itself was demolished in 1911. At the beginning of this century, Trentham Gardens was one of the Midlands' most famous pleasure and entertainment centres. Nowadays, there are pleasant walks to enjoy through the Gardens and across park and woodland, plus a small children's play area. The Gardens are open all year round from 9.00 to dusk, the attractions only from 10.00 to 5.00 from Easter to the end of September. To get to Trentham, take the A500 east from junction 15, and then turn right on to the A34. The entrance is fairly soon on the right.

There is plenty to see in the **Stoke** area. But beware. Traffic is heavy, so the further you get into Stoke the longer it will take to extricate yourself. It is worth remembering that the A500 runs straight through the centre of the city, linking junctions 15 and 16 and making a good escape route.

Newcastle-under-Lyme is the nearest town to junction 15 (some 2½ miles along the A519). Newcastle isn't part of Stoke, and it preserves a definite sense of identity. There is a bustling market in the attractive main street on Mondays, Fridays and Saturdays, and some pleasant houses to look at. Two town trails can be followed and the **Museum and Art Gallery** in Brampton Park can be visited. Opening times are Mondays to Saturdays 9.30 to 1.00 and 2.00 to 6.00 and Sundays between May and September from 2.00 to 5.30.

JUNCTION 15 GLADSTONE POTTERY MUSEUM

If you have limited time to spare, the place that will tell you most about the Potteries is the **Gladstone Pottery Museum**. It's in Longton, one of the famous 'Five Towns' that make up Stoke. (In fact there are six – Tunstall, Burslem, Hanley, Stoke, Fenton and Longton – but the novelist Arnold Bennett, whose works portray the area and its people so vividly, chose to call them five.) The Museum is on the A50. The best way to get there from junction 15 is to follow the A500 to where it meets the A50, turn right, and follow the signs.

Gladstone is a fascinating place and tells you everything you want to know, and more, about the history of pottery and how it is made. The centrepiece of the Museum is the Yard, with four bottle kilns: pottery has been made here for over two hundred years. Off the Yard there is a decorating shop, the 'Potter at Home' gallery, tile and sanitary galleries (this last has a working replica of the first water closet ever made, in 1590, not to mention numerous later loos), a reconstruction of a slip house and another of a potter's office, an engine shop and the potting shop. A great deal of pottery is actually made here, including many commemorative items for schools, clubs and so on; some of the Museum's production is on sale in the well-stocked Museum earthenware and china shops. The Museum suggests you leave an hour and a half to look round. Once, when I had plenty of time to spare – and was lucky enough to visit with a friend who works as a potter – I spent nearer two and a half. In any case, there is a pleasant and very welcome teashop. Opening hours are from 10.30 to 5.30 Mondays to Saturdays, from 2.00 to 6.00 Sundays and Bank Holidays (last admission an hour before closing time). The Museum is closed on Mondays from October to March inclusive.

You can visit many other famous factories – Spode, Coalport and Crown Staffordshire (who also have a craft and historical centre) and Royal Doulton among them – but advance booking is essential, and often children under 14 are not admitted. For full details contact the Tourist Information Centre, telephone Stoke (0782) 411222. Stoke's **City Museum and Art Gallery**, now housed in a handsome new building in Bethesda Street, Hanley, has a fine collection of English pottery and porcelain, with the emphasis, naturally enough, on Staffordshire ware. There is also a local history exhibition and a gallery devoted to a 1944 Supermarine Spitfire; R. J. Mitchell, who designed the Spitfire, came from Stoke. The Museum is open from 10.30 to 5.00 on Mondays to Saturdays and from 2.00 to 5.00 on Sundays.

JUNCTION 15 ALTON TOWERS

If you are travelling from the south, leave the motorway at this junction for **Alton Towers**, a British version of Disneyland, claimed as the nation's 'only world-rated leisure park'. There are attractive gardens and nature trails, rides on whizz-bang attractions such as the Sky Ride and the Grand Canyon Rapids Ride, lots of live entertainment and much, much more. The route to Alton Towers is signposted from the motorway.

Junction 16 is the exit to take for Alton Towers (see above) if you are travelling from the north.

JUNCTION 17 SANDBACH

With junction 17, you finally reach a stretch of consistent, proper countryside – almost the first since the start of the motorway. Even now, it is not a particularly exciting landscape, though pleasant enough. **Sandbach** lies 1 mile west of junction 17 on the A534, an attractive place for a short stop. Its greatest claim to fame is its two Saxon crosses that stand in the cobbled Market Square. There are some handsome enough buildings in and around the square and the parish church, but the square is marred by parked cars and a large and very ugly new post office. Two good pubs for a sandwich and a beer are the Market Tavern and the Lower Chequer.

Going east from junction 17, the A534 brings you after 6 miles to Congleton, where there are some elegant houses near the town centre, including a few half-timbered buildings, but little else to detain you.

JUNCTION 17 LITTLE MORETON HALL

The chief attraction round here, and one well worth the journey, is **Little Moreton Hall**, a National Trust property situated on the A34, 4 miles south of Congleton and 6 miles from junction 17. Take the A534 east from junction 17 for about 3½ miles and then turn right on to a side road to Brownlow (the pub has the unoriginal name of the Brownlow Inn) and continue until you reach the A34. Turn right and Little Moreton Hall is on your left after less than 1 mile. From

Little Moreton Hall, Congleton

junction 16 you can take the A500 until it meets the A34 and then travel north.

The Hall is a marvellous half-timbered building, the best in the country, so some experts claim. It looks almost like a crazy house out of a child's picture book, with leaning walls and sagging roofs. But looks deceive. It's as sound as the day it was completed, four hundred years ago or more. Inside, there is hardly any furniture. Not that this matters: there is simply all the more space to appreciate the skill of the craftsmen who worked here, creating magnificent panelling and ceilings. The Withdrawing Room and the Long Gallery are perhaps the most impressive rooms, but the entire house is most attractive – and surprisingly light and airy for a building of its age. From the gardens you can look up to **Mow Cop**, another National Trust property, a rocky 1000-foot hill, on top of which a sham castle perches, built in Gothic style in 1750. In 1807 a 12-hour open-air prayer meeting held here marked the start of the Primitive Methodist movement.

The Hall is open daily except Tuesdays from April to September between 1.30 and 5.30; in March and October it opens on Saturdays and Sundays at the same time, and on Bank Holiday Mondays it opens from 11.30 to 5.30. There is a gift shop, and home-made afternoon teas are served.

JUNCTION 18 JODRELL BANK

If junction 17 took you back to the 16th century, junction 18 returns you firmly to the late 20th, in the shape of the University of Manchester's Nuffield Radio Astronomy Laboratories – or, more familiarly, **Jodrell Bank**. You can hardly miss the huge circular bowls of the two telescopes – the Mark IA, 250 feet in diameter, and its smaller elliptical neighbour, the Mark II, 125 feet by 83 – as you drive north-east from Holmes Chapel on the A535. The Science Centre (open daily from 10.30 to 5.30 from Good Friday to 31 October, and on Saturdays and Sundays from 2.00 to 5.00 the rest of the year) provides a lucid explanation of modern astronomy. For many, myself included, it seems mind-boggling stuff, but the exhibition tries hard to make it seem simple: and to a large extent succeeds. There is an introduction to radio astronomy which explains how radio telescopes work; a replica of the main control desk which monitors the movements of the Mark IA telescope; an exhibit monitoring radio output from the sun; and displays on planets, galaxies and satellites. Other exhibits enable you to experiment yourself with forces in the universe. For instance, you can spin yourself round on a 'gyro chair' and discover, by moving your arms and legs, how angular momentum works. A planetarium gives presentations every 45 minutes, and from the upper terrace of the Exhibition Building you can get to within a few feet of the Mark IA telescope. Outside there is a 25-foot radio telescope – tiny in comparison with its big sisters, but you can steer this one yourself and pick up radio waves from the sun – and a 21-foot Satcom telescope, which receives signals from geostationary satellites (satellites in constant orbit round the Earth).

To get a good idea of what goes on here, you should allow at least an hour and a half for your visit. Refreshments – and you will certainly need them after all this mental stimulation – are available in the restaurant. A picnic area adjoins the car park. A final feature is the **Tree Park**, which covers 35 acres and has over 20 thousand trees and shrubs, including some national collections. There are a number of trails to follow.

Jodrell Bank is 5 miles from the M6 at junction 18, through Holmes Chapel, a small village with the Old Red Lion pub.

JUNCTION 19 NORTHWICH

Very occasionally, you reach a junction with a cornucopia of things to see and do. Junction 19 is one such. To the west there is Northwich, with the Salt Museum, the Anderton Lift and Marbury Country Park, and also Arley Hall and Gardens, which lie midway between junctions 19 and 20. Then, to the east, there is Knutsford, with its unique Italianate architecture, the nature reserve at Rostherne Mere and two National Trust properties, Tatton Park and Dunham Massey.

First, west to Northwich, on the A556 to begin with and then into the town on the A559 (5 miles). The centre need not detain you long. There is a small modern shopping centre, more pleasant than many, some attractive timber-framed buildings and the first electrically-operated swing bridge in the country, opened in 1889 and still working today. What is worth making for is the **Salt Museum**, a little way out of the town on the London road. If you are coming direct from the motorway, you can avoid the town centre by continuing on the A556 bypass and then turning right towards the town on the A533. Salt has been produced in Cheshire since Roman times, and this Museum, housed in an elegant building dating from 1837, tells the story of the industry, emphasizing its heyday in the 19th century. There are four exhibition galleries. The first explains what salt is: its chemistry, world resources, salt beds, extraction techniques and its numerous uses. The second looks at brine supply and rock-salt mining, the third at the open-pan process and at working conditions in the 19th-century salt industry. Finally, the business is put in its social context: the lives of the workers and the salt proprietors are examined, and the problems of environmental pollution highlighted. There is also an audio-visual presentation and a small shop. The Museum is open on Tuesdays to Sundays and Bank Holiday Mondays from 2.00 to 5.00; on Tuesdays to Saturdays in July and August the Museum opens at 10.00.

JUNCTION 19 ANDERTON LIFT

From the salt industry to the transport system that, for a short time at least, carried its products. Northwich is at the heart of the Cheshire canal network, and just outside town boasts an astonishing example of Victorian canal engineering: the **Anderton Lift**. To get there, take the A533 north-west out of the town for about 1 mile. Then turn right on to a road that runs through the middle of an ICI works, cross the river and turn right immediately. The road climbs uphill, crossing the canal. Access to the canal towpath is easy, and it is only a couple of hundred yards along to the lift.

The lift makes the junction between the river Weaver below and the Trent & Mersey Canal, 50 feet above. People had long wanted to build a flight of locks, but problems of water supply defeated them. Then, in 1875, an engineer named Leader Williams thought of the answer – a vertical lift that would carry craft between the two waterways. Going down, for instance, you take your boat along a short aqueduct from the canal and into an electrically operated caisson, or tank of water. The gates are closed behind you, the lift descends, the gates open again, and off you go. The perfect engineering solution: simple and neat. The lift was fully operational until recently, and although at the time of writing (late 1986) it is out of use and awaiting major repairs there are plans to restore it and to open a visitor centre nearby.

JUNCTION 19 MARBURY COUNTRY PARK

Half a mile or so further on the same road you reach **Marbury Country Park**, set in the grounds of Marbury Hall, which was demolished in 1968. There are picnic and barbecue facilities, hides from which to watch the bird life on Budworth Mere, and fine walking in parkland and avenues of trees. The canal towpath at Anderton is another walking possibility too. From Marbury Country Park you can retrace your steps to junction 19 via Great Budworth, where there is the George and Dragon Hotel. I made a detour here to Pick Mere: obligatory for anyone named Pick, but not worth it for the rest of you!

JUNCTION 19 ARLEY HALL AND GARDENS

Arley Hall and Gardens is an excursion of another, more traditional, kind. Leave junction 19 on the A556 towards Northwich, but turn right almost immediately on to the B5391 and follow the signposts. The present Hall was built in the 1830s and 1840s in what the architect called the Queen Elizabethan style: according to the excellent guide-book, 'every architectural feature ... had to have a model in some existing Elizabethan building'. The whole thing is a classic example of the Victorian mania for rebuilding. The owner, Rowland Egerton-Warburton, first had the east, north and west wings of the old house demolished, and then, a decade later, the old south front came down. In their place arose an imposing structure with brewhouse, bakehouse, laundry, dairy and poultry yard. Above stairs, there were imposing ceilings, fine panelling, a Gothic chapel and a grand staircase, the latest in plumbing and even hot water in the bathrooms (quite a rarity in those days). The Gardens were laid out, including one of the earliest double herbaceous borders established in England and yew hedges, avenue of limes and of ilex and a new formal drive up to the house. On the estate, woods were planted and a village school built for the tenants' children.

The Warburton family has lived at Arley since the 15th century and owned property there for at least three hundred years before that. They continue to make improvements, and in 1984 a woodland walk was introduced. The Hall and Gardens are open between early April and early October, from Tuesdays to Sundays inclusive, and also on Bank Holidays. Opening times are from 12.00 to 6.00 in June, July and August, and from 2.00 to 6.00 in April, May, September and October. There is a tea room in part of the stable block.

JUNCTION 19 KNUTSFORD

Knutsford lies 2 miles east of the motorway: take the A556 towards Northwich and then turn left on to the A5033. To many people, the town's more familiar name is Cranford – the Cranford of Mrs Gaskell's celebrated novel by that name, a lively and loving portrait of the town in which she grew up in the 1810s and 1820s. No. 17 Gaskell Avenue, where the novelist lived as a child (the road has been renamed to commemorate her), is not open to the public. But you can see a memorial tower in King Street in the centre of town (this is one of Knutsford's nicest streets, with some attractive shops). She is buried in the graveyard of the Unitarian Chapel in Brook Street, along with her husband and two of her daughters. The other interesting feature of the town is its architecture: in particular the houses designed at the turn of the century by Richard Harding Watt. What must the prosperous, solid Edwardian merchants and professional men who lived in these extraordinary Italianate concoctions have thought of them? The best examples of Watt's unique style can be seen in Drury Lane and Legh Road, and also in La Belle

Epoque, which serves evening meals. (Other eating places in the town include the Cross Keys Hotel, Ye Angel Hotel, the Rose and Crown Hotel and several wine bars.) Take a look also at the Ruskin Rooms at the end of King Street, which Watt built in 1902 as a recreation and reading room for the townspeople. Half tumbledown a few years ago, it has now been sympathetically renovated as offices.

JUNCTION 19 TATTON PARK

If you are tackling the long haul north or south on the M6, **Tatton Park** is one of the best places for a break. The publicity leaflets claim that 'There's nowhere like it in Britain' – and for once they may be right. It isn't simply another stately home, albeit an extremely grand and impressive one. The life of an entire family, the Egertons, and their estate is brought to vivid life, with, refreshingly, as much emphasis on the mundane, daily routine of domestic service and farm work as on the grand life in the big house. And if it is fresh air and exercise you feel in need of, there are attractive walks and views to enjoy – or you can even hire a bicycle to tour the 1000-acre deer park.

The house itself (which is the original of Mrs Gaskell's Cumnor Towers in *Wives and Daughters*) is the grandest of neo-classical mansions, completely remodelled between the 1770s and 1820s. There is a Grecian Entrance Hall, coldly classical with Ionic columns, and, in stark contrast, an ornate, ostentatious Drawing Room, with two Canalettos and a Van Dyck on the walls. The visit includes the Card Room, the comfortable Library and the Yellow Drawing Room, and, upstairs, the Chintz, Lemon and Silk Bedrooms. Below stairs, you can see the Kitchen and the huge Tenants' Hall (156 feet by 48), where the last Lord Egerton displayed his collection of curiosities brought home from his travels. To mark the visit of the Prince and Princess of Wales to Tatton in 1887, the mansion is being 'Victorianized' in 1987, and the cellars will be restored to their former use.

At some stately homes, it can be difficult to get a sense of how people *really* lived, perhaps because their lifestyle is so remote from ours. However, if you are lucky, you may find scenes of country-house life being performed by the Tatton Living History Society; the 'Egertons' and their servants tend to be in residence at weekends rather than on weekdays. And at Tatton Dale there is a vivid and loving display of life on the home farm 50 years ago. Tatton Dale was the heart of the huge Egerton estate, the place from which the affairs of nearly a thousand tenant properties in the county were run. In the Estate Yard there was a smithy, which provided work for three blacksmiths, and a joiner's shop; off the Middle Yard were the stores and the bothy for the men employed in the building department (no fewer than 39 of them!). There is farm machinery too from the 1930s, the farm animals kept in their original setting.

Old Hall is another major attraction at Tatton Park, and a visit there will give you a good idea of the long span and continuity of Tatton's history. The Hall was the original manor house, and the culmination of the visit is a vivid re-creation of the Great Hall as it would have been in 1475. Out of doors there are the gardens, where you will find a fernery and an orangery, a pinetum, a small beech maze, and, most remarkable of all, an authentic Japanese garden built in 1910 by Japanese workmen specially brought to England for this purpose. In the park, which was designed by Humphry Repton, perhaps this country's most celebrated landscape architect after Capability Brown, you can walk and picnic more or less anywhere. There are also several trails, including one round the site of a medieval village pulled down when the park was landscaped. There is riding as well, and you can swim from the eastern side of Tatton Mere.

Opening times at Tatton Park are extraordinarily complex, and if you are planning a visit in advance you would do well to check by telephoning Knutsford (0565) 54822. On summer afternoons you will find everything open – house, farm, garden, park and Old Hall. During winter (that is, November to Easter) the house, farm and Old Hall are closed; the park is open daily from 11.00 to 4.00, the garden from 1.00 to 4.00 (12.00 on Sundays). Note too that there is an admission charge for cars entering the park and separate additional charges for admission to the house, garden, farm and Old Hall. The stable block near the entrance to the gardens has extensive refreshment facilities. From junction 19, take the A556 north to the A5034, turn right, and then left along the edge of the estate. The entrance is just below Rostherne village.

JUNCTION 19 ROSTHERNE MERE NATIONAL NATURE RESERVE & DUNHAM MASSEY

If Tatton Park has something for everyone, the **Rostherne Mere National Nature Reserve** is quite the opposite. There is no admission for the general public – and rightly so. The Mere is an undisturbed refuge for waterfowl, and many thousands of birds find sanctuary here each year. You can, however, get reasonable – and perfectly legal – views of the Reserve from several places along the surrounding lanes. Rostherne is reached by turning right off the A556. Winter is the time to come. Mallard and teal are the most numerous inhabitants then – January is the most crowded month – but there are usually wigeon, shoveller, pochard and tufted duck as well. The Mere is also a major roost for black-headed and herring gull in winter, and their numbers often reach 20,000.

Continue yet further up the A556 north towards Manchester, past junction 7 of the M56. Follow the A56 towards Manchester, and after 1 mile turn left on to the B5160. After another mile you will reach the car park for **Dunham Massey**. Like Tatton Park, this house was extensively remodelled during the 18th century. The exterior is pleasantly homely, in a plain red brick, and could almost be called modest, were it not for the sheer size of the place. Inside, however, the style is of the early 20th century rather than the 18th. In 1905 the Stamford family moved back to Dunham Massey and the ninth Earl set about a substantial programme of renovations. The Great Hall, Grand Staircase and Great Gallery are all particularly fine, and the Salon is, as the guide-book rightly says, 'an unusually complete and rare example of the work of the finest Edwardian decorators and upholsterers'. The curious feature of Dunham Massey – the thing that makes its collections, particularly of textiles and of Huguenot silver so precious and rare – is that the tenth Lord Stamford (on whose death in 1976 the house passed to the National Trust) was the most zealous housekeeper and conservator. He lived in only a few rooms, closed many of the others and carefully cleaned and stored the textiles. The result is an unusually well-preserved collection, which, naturally, the Trust takes care to maintain.

Outside, you can visit the kitchen and laundries, much of whose original equipment has been preserved, and the handsome stable block, completed in 1721. The gardens chiefly date from the second half of the 17th century and the first half of the 18th, and the park is medieval in origin. There are fine walks, and plenty of opportunities to observe the deer, although the constant hum of traffic in the background can be distracting. The 17th-century corn mill, used as the estate saw mill during the 19th century, has now been fully restored. The park is open all year round. The house is open daily except Fridays from April to the end of October from 1.00 to 5.00, the garden, restaurant and shop from 12.00 to 5.30.

Between junctions 19 and 20 the M6 meets the M56, at junction 9 of that motorway. There is no access to ordinary roads.

JUNCTION 20 BRIDGEWATER CANAL

After this run of top-quality junctions, with more than enough to improve a tedious journey, there follows a succession of less promising possibilities. Lymm is the nearest place to junction 20, about 1½ miles away, reached by taking the A50 east from the junction and turning left almost immediately on to the B5158. It is a small, smart town, chiefly interesting because it is on the **Bridgewater Canal**. This was almost the first true canal in the country, and certainly the one that initiated the canal-building mania in the late 18th century. There are interesting towpath walks – in fact the towpath here is part of the 97-mile Cheshire Ring Canal Walk that runs alongside no fewer than six different canals in the county. But, given the attractions of junctions 17 to 19, I wouldn't especially recommend a stop here.

If you are travelling south, you can use junction 20 to get to many of the places described in the entry for junction 19. For Arley Hall and Gardens, to the west of the M6, take the A50 going west from the junction, and almost immediately turn left on to the B5356 as far as Appleton, where you should turn left again on to side roads to Arley. For Tatton Hall, take the fast A50 east and turn right on to the A556. For Rostherne Mere and Dunham Massey take the A50 east and turn left on to the A556, and then follow the directions given on page 235. You can also reach Dunham Massey by a back route from Lymm, by following the A6144 north-east and then turning right on to the B5160.

Between junctions 20 and 21 the motorway crosses the **Manchester Ship Canal**, and you will get a good view as you drive past. But there is nothing to entice you off at junction 21, unless, conceivably, bridge design interests you. There is a good view of the motorway bridge from the A57 going east. Going west, the A57 takes you into central Warrington.

Junction 21a is the junction with the M62, and there is no way out on to ordinary roads. For an interesting open-air break, you might consider a quick diversion east along the M62 for 2 miles to **Risley Moss**, at junction 11 (see page 260).

Junction 22 is another way out into the flat and featureless plain between the Manchester and Merseyside conurbations, and I have found nothing to recommend it.

JUNCTION 23 HAYDOCK PARK

In terms of landscape, junction 23 is almost as bad as 22. But there is good reason to take a break here, for there are some unusual walks and, in St Helens, a fascinating museum of the greatest interest (see below).

Haydock Park racecourse lies just ½ mile north of the junction on the A49. Meetings are held here on 28 days a year, when admission is charged. On non-race days, you can get into the racecourse free, but there is little to go for, except – if it is drink and bar food you want – the Chasers Bar, furnished in comfortable Edwardian style. The bar keeps normal pub hours. The Posthouse Hotel is just outside the racecourse entrance.

JUNCTION 23 PENNINGTON FLASH COUNTRY PARK

To the east, **Pennington Flash Country Park** is about 3½ miles away, along the A580 and then left on to the A572. This seems an unpromising place at first, on the edge of a straggly 'rurban' area, but the Park is a mecca for birds – the handbook calls it one of the 'premier ornithological resorts in the country', and for once does not exaggerate – and it also has a fascinating history. The land here was mined for many years, subsidence and flooding resulted, and refuse was dumped. The whole area became semi-derelict. After years of work, an attractive 1000-acre park has been created, centred on the Flash itself, a 170-acre expanse of water. Over two hundred species of resident and migratory birds can be seen from specially built hides. There is angling, sailing, boating and pony-riding, and a developing network of footpaths. The visitor centre has a small exhibition on the history and ecology of the area and tells the story of the Park's creation. The Park is open daily in daylight hours. In good weather it can become very crowded; the car park was packed when I was there on a chilly but sunny late October afternoon.

JUNCTION 23 SANKEY VALLEY PARK

Going west along the A580 from the motorway, and then turning left on to the A58, you come into the suburbs of St Helens. A sharpish right turn, following the main road, brings you to one of the visitor centres of the **Sankey Valley Park**. This is imaginative use of what was until fairly recently urban wasteland, mainly the haunt of local lads on their motorbikes. The Park stretches for several miles along the old **St Helens Canal**, and there are good canalside walks, with, if you have time to spare and can go further, woodland and open farmland as well. The visitor centre has an interesting small exhibition, and the Ship pub is nearby.

JUNCTION 23 PILKINGTON GLASS MUSEUM

The Sankey Valley Park might be a good place for a quick breath of fresh air on the way to the **Pilkington Glass Museum** in St Helens. It is attractively designed, and besides exhibits on the history and processes of glass-making, and a display on mirrors, there are some exquisite individual pieces on display. You start with a section called 'What is Glass?', and very soon you are with the Romans, who made the crucial discovery that glass can be blown, and hence manipulated into more or less any shape desired. There are examples of rich blue glass and of the many techniques used to decorate glassware, and there is also a display on the development of window glass. On the lower floor, things are more practical and industrial. Individual exhibits guide you through the uses of glass in optics, science and technology and transport, bringing you right up to date with the latest technologies, such as photochromic glass, which darkens in sunlight and fades as brightness decreases. All in all, it is a fascinating exhibition on a versatile and vital material.

The Museum, which is signposted from St Helens town centre, is on the A58 (the Prescot road). If you are coming from junction 23 on the M6, follow the directions to the Sankey Valley Park above and continue on the same road. Access is also easy from junctions 6 of the M62 and 1 of the M57, via the A58, and a visit to the **Prescot Museum of Clock and Watch Making** can also be included (see page 258). The Glass Museum, which is situated in the grounds of Pilkington's head office, is open on Mondays to Fridays from 10.00 to 5.00 (9.00 on Wednesdays from March to October) and on weekends and Bank Holidays from 2.00 to 4.30.

Junctions 24 and 25 are half-junctions leading to Ashton-in-Makerfield. At junction 24 you can leave if you are travelling south and join if you are going north. At junction 25, where a short spur leads straight to the A49, you can leave the northbound carriageway and join the southbound one. There is nothing to recommend here, although junction 25 is a quick route into Wigan from the south.

JUNCTION 26 WIGAN PIER

Junction 26 is the junction for the M58 going west. This joins the M57, which in turn meets the M62, thus forming a motorway box around Merseyside. To the east, Wigan (about 3 miles along the A577) is the nearest town. **Wigan** is most famous for its **pier** – made famous as a music-hall joke by George Formby long before George Orwell adopted it as a symbol of the poverty and deprivation of the north in the 1930s. Contrary to belief, the pier does exist – not as a seaside pier, of course, but as a landing-stage on the Leeds & Liverpool Canal, just west of the town centre. A railway ran to the pier from several pitheads, and a coal tippler mounted on the pier was used to drop coal from each wagon into the barge below. (Interestingly, the railway was operated by self-acting inclines and horse haulage until as late as 1878, when locomotives took over.) The tippler has long since gone, but a number of handsome industrial buildings remain around the nearby canal basin. These have now been converted into a fascinating and ambitious heritage area. The centrepiece of the complex of canalside buildings along Wallgate is 'The Way We Were', an exhibition that recalls Wigan as it was in the years around the turn of the century. The aim is 'to recreate the feel, smell, pace of life in this part of Lancashire as it was then'. All the latest techniques of museum display are used to re-create the everyday events and scenes of that world: the brief Wakes Week respite enjoyed on the front at Blackpool, the fatigue of work at the coalface and the horror of the Maypole colliery disaster, work in the factories and mills and life at home and at school, and the all too brief escapes from the harshness of the real world provided by the pub and the music hall. This world – so different from ours, and yet so close, for it is the life that our grandparents and great-grandparents experienced – is made yet more real and vivid by actors/interpreters, who bring the exhibition's re-creations to life. After seeing the exhibition, you can take a waterbus along the canal to the Trencherfield Mill Engine at the other end of the site. Built in 1907 and now in full steam once again, this is the world's largest working mill steam engine; it has an enormous flywheel and rope run. The **Mill at the Pier**, next to the engine, is a concert hall and exhibition and conference centre. There are pleasant gardens, an information centre, a shop, and a pub and restaurant. Open times are daily 10.00 to 5.00. Elsewhere in Wigan there is a 13th-century parish church and some attractive Victorian shopping arcades, plus an excellent market.

JUNCTION 27 STANDISH

From junction 27, the A5209 leads east through the village of **Standish**, where the medieval market cross, stocks and dipping well have all survived. If you take the B5239 east from the village, crossing the A5106, you will come to the Leeds & Liverpool Canal. There are towpath walks and a pleasant canalside pub, the Crawford Arms. Distance from the M6 is only about 3 miles, but the roads are winding, with a fair amount of traffic.

JUNCTION 28 BRITISH COMMERCIAL VEHICLE MUSEUM

Junction 28 is the turn-off for Leyland, the town that gave its name to Leyland commercial vehicles and cars. Where better to develop the new **British Commercial Vehicle Museum**? The Museum occupies one of the few remaining buildings on the South Works site, which the company vacated in 1980. About 40 vehicles are on display, and there are plans to increase the size of the collection. I must confess to a prejudice: I don't find displays of vehicles, gleaming, polished and static, very interesting, and prefer to learn more of their social context. But for those who *are* interested – far more, I am sure, than those who share my reaction – the collection is not to be missed. It starts in 1896, with one horse-drawn and two steam-propelled vehicles from that year, and finishes with the most up-to-date models. There are buses, trucks, vans and fire engines, including the celebrated Morris T commercial van, whose long and successful production run started in 1924, and the well-known Leyland fire engine from the 1920s. Also on show is the Popemobile, the special vehicle built for the Pope's visit to Britain in summer 1982. You will recall the Pope standing in a large central area, so that he could be seen by as many people as possible. In fact he was seated on a little seat, shaped rather like the seat of a shooting-stick – a thoughtful touch. There is a small café and shop in the Museum, which is open from 10.00 to 5.00 daily except Mondays between April and September, and on Saturdays and Sundays in October and November at the same times. It is also open on Bank Holiday Mondays. To reach the Museum, take the B5256 west from junction 28, turn left at the roundabout and then left again almost immediately, following the signposts to the Museum.

JUNCTION 29 CUERDEN VALLEY PARK
Junction 29 leads to a rather scrappy area just south of Preston. There is not much to leave the motorway here for, unless you feel in need of a quick walk in the conveniently placed **Cuerden Valley Park**. Take the A6 west from the motorway, and turn left on to the A49 at the traffic lights. A car park is signposted left off the A49 about 200 yards from the traffic lights. Most of the Park is still farmland, but there are no fewer than nine miles of footpaths, woodland and a lake, part of which has been roped off to provide a wildlife sanctuary. It is pleasant, undulating countryside, nothing spectacular but OK for an injection of fresh air and a chance for the children to let off steam. The Park covers 700 acres, so it is possible to escape the constant hum of the motorway if you are prepared to walk far enough.

Junction 30 is the junction with the M61, which runs south to Chorley and Bolton, meeting the M62 between junctions 14 and 15 on the northern outskirts of Manchester. There is no access to ordinary roads here.

JUNCTION 31 PRESTON
Junction 31 is the main exit for **Preston**, along the A59. Preston has some handsome Victorian and Edwardian buildings and a fine old open market, but inner ring roads and a lot of rather uninspired modern office blocks rather spoil its integrity. There is also a fien-

dish one-way system. The **Harris Museum and Art Gallery** specializes in British paintings of the 19th and 20th centuries and has a remarkable collection, including works by Turner, Samuel Palmer, William Blake, Holman Hunt and Alma Tadema. There is also a substantial collection of ceramics, glass and costume well worth seeing, and also displays of social, local and natural history. The Gallery is open daily, from 10.00 to 5.00, except Sundays and Bank Holidays.

JUNCTION 32 BEACON FELL COUNTRY PARK

Junction 32, just north of Preston, is the junction with the M55 west to Blackpool. Strictly speaking, there is no access to ordinary roads here, but on the M55 junction 1 is reached in less than half a mile. The terrain has definitely changed now. Although the motorway runs through low-lying country, just a few miles to the east are the hills of the Forest of Bowland: wild and inhospitable land, a foretaste of the Cumbria stretches of the motorway ahead. The Forest of Bowland (not a forest at all, in fact, but a lonely stretch of moorland fells) is too far off, and the walking there too difficult, to recommend for a motorway break. The **Beacon Fell Country Park**, on the other hand, is easily accessible from this junction (4½ miles), and quite exhilarating enough for a quick stopover. To get there, turn north on to the A6 from junction 1 of the M55, past the smart Broughton Park Hotel on the right, and take the B5269 right towards Goosnargh. The road goes under the motorway and you then turn left on to a country road which climbs slowly towards the fells through the little village of Inglewhite, where you might choose to stop at the Green Man pub. Beacon Fell is a sort of geological outpost, an isolated 873-foot hill of rough country rising out of the surrounding plain, with commanding views east to the main ridge of fells and west towards the coast. There are forest and moorland walks here, and plenty of good spots for picnics, plus facilities for wayfaring and barbecues. Light refreshments are usually available at the information centre. On your way back to the motorway, make a diversion to the village of Goosnargh to buy some Goosnargh cakes at the post-office-cum-general-store. Sprinkled with caraway seeds, they have a deliciously savoury taste.

JUNCTION 33 GLASSON DOCK

The last time I travelled this stretch of the M6 I was with my wife and daughter, and junction 33 was unanimously voted one of the best in the entire northern half of the motorway. The attraction is **Glasson Dock**: a genuinely busy dock with working as well as pleasure craft, and with wide views over the Lune estuary. Ignore the signs for Glasson Dock pointing south down the M6 as you leave the motorway. Instead, turn right (north) and then left in Galgate. Just past the railway, turn left again and follow this winding side road for about 3 miles to the A588. Shortly after Galgate the road crosses the Lancaster Canal, where the towpath makes a pleasant walk. Turn left on to the A588 and then immediately right on to the B5290, which leads straight into Glasson.

This is an area for those who, like me, are drawn by the end-of-the-world feelings that estuaries evoke – water, mud and sand imperceptibly merging, so that you barely notice the difference, and seabirds wheeling overhead in a wide blue sky. Glasson Dock came into being because silting in the Lune made access to Lancaster difficult. In 1787, the harbour had room for no fewer than 25 merchantmen. But in 1819 the Lancaster Canal was built south to the Ribble estuary. This drew trade away from Glasson. Things got worse when Preston Docks opened in 1892. Even the railway from Lancaster to Glasson, which had opened nine years before, could not reverse the trend.

JUNCTION 33 LUNE ESTUARY

The railway (closed to all traffic since 1964) is now a fine 3½-mile path along the **Lune Estuary footpath** from Glasson Dock to Aldcliffe. There is a picnic site at Conder Green, on the A588 just north of the Glasson turn-off, and the Stork is a nice pub nearby. The estuary is a Site of Special Scientific Interest and has the largest wintering and passage population of wading birds in Great Britain; there are also numerous wildfowl. There is another trail, this one prepared by the Lancashire Naturalists' Trust, from the picnic site to Glasson Dock, then along the Glasson branch of the Lancaster Canal to Thurnham Mill and back over the river Conder to Conder Green. The saltmarsh and saltpans between the picnic site and Glasson are especially interesting.

From Glasson, you can either return to the M6 at junction 33, or, if you are travelling north, follow the A588 north into Lancaster and regain it at junction 34.

JUNCTION 34 LANCASTER

Junction 34 is the principal route into **Lancaster** from the M6 along the A683. The dominant feature of the town is the imposing, rather forbidding **Castle**. Most of the present building dates from the early 15th century, although there was a castle here for at least three hundred years before that, and there were substantial renovations and extensions in the 18th century. Unlike most castles in this country, Lancaster is still functioning: the Crown Court sits here, and it is also used as a prison. Visits are possible daily between Good Friday and the end of September, from 10.30 to 4.00, when the Court is not sitting; part tours are available when it is in session. Grouped around the Castle entrance, rather in the manner of a cathedral close, are some lovely 18th-century houses, from the days of Lancaster's greatest prosperity.

There are several interesting museums in Lancaster. The **Judges' Lodgings**, in Church Street just down the hill from the Castle, is three museums in one. There is the building itself, which is the oldest house standing in Lancaster and dates from the first half of the 17th century. From 1826 to 1975 it was used to provide lodgings for judges visiting Lancaster for the Assizes held in the Castle. Then there is the **Gillow Furniture and Town House Collections**, which occupy the ground and first floors, and the **Museum of Childhood**, which is housed on the top storey. On the ground floor the parlour is furnished as it would have been in about 1700, and the servants' hall in about 1800. Gillow – the name remains in today's high streets as part of Waring and Gillow – was established in Lancaster in the 18th century, and the firm made most of the beautiful furniture on the first floor; the last room contains a collection of their post-1830 pieces, including a marvellous 'medieval' sideboard from about 1870, with carvings of the heads of Robin Hood and Maid Marian. One room on this floor is a fascinating butler's pantry of about 1825, complete with all the tools of the butler's trade: crumb tray, linen press and wine-cooler among them. The top floor – the Museum of Childhood – has Edwardian day and night nurseries and a schoolroom from about 1900. School parties can even have a lesson taught here! Kindest note of all: the Museum's information sheets make it clear that in these rooms anything within a child's reach is there to be touched. There are also collections of tin toys, dolls and baby wear, prams, dolls' houses and so on. The Lodgings are open in July, August and September on Mondays to Fridays from 10.00 to 1.00 and 2.00 to 5.00, Saturdays and Bank Holiday Sundays from 2.00 to 5.00; in May and June on Mondays to Saturdays and Bank Holiday Sundays from 2.00 to 5.00; and in October to April on Mondays to Fridays from 2.00 to 5.00.

JUNCTION 34 MARITIME MUSEUM

The **Maritime Museum**, housed in the handsome recently restored Palladian Custom House on St George's Quay, commemorates the days when Lancaster was a major port, importing rum, sugar, cotton and mahogany from the West Indies. The principal displays concentrate on the history of the port and on the old fishing communities of Morecambe Bay; shrimps, cockles, mussels and wet fish have all been traditionally caught in the area for generations. There are several reconstructions: of the office of the Collector of Customs in about 1800, of an 18th-century warehouse, of the 19th-century fast canal packet boat *The Water Witch*, and of a cottage kitchen of a fishing family in the mid-1920s. More up-to-date subjects include the Morecambe Bay Gas Field and a section about crossing Morecambe Bay Sands. The Museum is open daily from 11.00 to 5.00 between April and October, and daily from 2.00 to 5.00 during the rest of the year; there is a cafeteria.

A town trail runs through the city centre, taking in the Priory Church and the City Museum. The Market Hall is also worth seeing; there are plenty of pubs and cafés nearby.

JUNCTION 34 ASHTON MEMORIAL
Lancaster's latest attraction is centred on the newly restored **Ashton Memorial**, on the edge of the city centre and clearly visible from the motorway. Described by Pevsner as 'the grandest monument in England', it was erected by Lord Ashton, the Lancaster linoleum millionaire and politician, as a memorial to himself and his family. The climb inside leads to an exhibition on the life and times of Lord Ashton and another presentation on the Edwardian era, which is based on one man's recollections of those seemingly halcyon years before the First World War, entitled 'Endless Summer', and to the external balconies. From there are excellent views: west to Morecambe Bay and, on a fine day, to the Isle of Man, north to the hills of the Lake District and east to Ingleborough in the Yorkshire Dales. The Memorial is situated in Williamson Park – James Williamson was Lord Ashton's father – where there is a fine Victorian palmhouse and a Butterfly House with a collection of more than four hundred exotic butterflies. There is also a cafeteria. Plans are under way to create a Victorian and Edwardian theme park based around the Memorial. The Memorial is open daily from 11.00 to 5.00 between Good Friday and the end of September, and on Saturdays and Sundays from 2.00 to 5.00 during the rest of the year.

JUNCTION 34 HORNSEA POTTERY
Just outside town, on the Wyresdale Road, is the west-coast factory of **Hornsea Pottery**. There is a large leisure complex here, and besides touring the factory you can visit the children's farmyard and, most interesting of all in my opinion, a rare breeds survival unit. This consists of about 19 acres of grassland set aside for a collection of farm animal in danger of extinction. Among them are White Park and Highland cattle, Herdwick sheep, Golden Guernsey goats and Bronze turkeys. There is also a seconds shop, plus a gift shop, cafe-

teria and picnic area. The Pottery is open daily from 10.00 to 5.00; in the winter months closing time is brought forward to 4.00.

JUNCTION 35 STEAMTOWN

Carnforth is the nearest place to junction 35 – or, to be really pedantic, to junction 35a, since from junction 35 a tiny spur motorway, less than 1 mile long, carries you on to the A6 just north of town. The only attraction here – but it is a considerable one – is **Steamtown**, the largest mainline operating steam locomotive depot in the country. Drive into town from junction 35a, turn right at the first set of traffic lights, and follow the signs. The focal point of the collection is the large engine shed. This was one of the last used by British Rail for steam operation, and now it houses a collection of 30 mainline and industrial locomotives from this country and the continent. Every steam buff will have his (sometimes her) own favourites, but *Leander*, *Lord Nelson* and, above all, the *Flying Scotsman* must be mentioned; the *Flying Scotsman* is based at Steamtown but is often away working excursions in different parts of the country. Visitors can wander among the locomotives and coaches, and water columns, a signal box, a turntable, a working coaling plant and workshops are on show as well. There is the chance too at Steamtown to relive the experience of steam in motion: a standard-gauge line runs for about 1 mile through the 37-acre museum complex. The 00-gauge model railway is housed in an old road coach which contains an astonishing collection of models of a railway, road transport, trolley buses and town life, even down to a building on fire and a model fire brigade putting it out. Other amenities include picnic areas, a gift shop, a well stocked Collectors' Corner where lamps, signs, badges, signals and the like can be bought, and a café. Steamtown is open daily from 9.00 to 5.00 between Easter and October and from 10.00 to 4.00 during the rest of the year. Steam rides are available every Sunday between Easter and October and daily during July and August. The Lancaster and Morecambe Model Engineers also have a site at Steamtown with its own track; they give rides every Sunday between Easter and October and also on Wednesdays in July and August.

North-west of Carnforth the neck of land stretching out into **Morecambe Bay** is an isolated and little-known piece of lovely country. When I was there on a crisp and sunny autumn day the colours were wonderful: every shade of brown and orange, with still a little green left on the trees. If you have time to spare, there is an enjoyable diversion to be made here, with several interesting places to visit.

JUNCTION 35 LEIGHTON MOSS BIRD RESERVE

First stop is the Royal Society for the Protection of Birds' Reserve at **Leighton Moss**, near Silverdale. Take the road past Steamtown out of Carnforth, turn left and go round the foot of **Warton Crag** (there are fine coastal views here) towards Silverdale Station. Turn right for the Reserve shortly before you reach the station. There is a fascinating variety of habitat in the 321-acre Reserve – 'all stages of natural succession from open water through fen vegetation to mature woodland', according to the Society's leaflet. Most important of all are the reedbeds, which occupy about 200 acres. No fewer than 207 species have been seen at Leighton Moss in recent years, and 74 of these have bred. The accolade of most distinguished inhabitant must be given to the 10 or 11 pairs of nesting bitterns, the only regular breeding pairs in the north of England (the total British population is only about 50 pairs). They tend to skulk in the reeds a lot, and the best time to see them is in May and June, when the young have to be fed and the adults are therefore more active. There are also reed warblers, water rails and bearded tits, plus, of course, a large population of waterfowl. As at all the Society's reserves, the visitor is well catered for. There is a well-marked route round the Reserve, a public hide with good views over one of the main meres, and an extremely well-stocked shop in the visitor centre. The sight of the natural world going about its business undisturbed by humans is impressive and moving: I recommend a visit.

Now there are several alternatives: you can make a complete circuit back to the M6 at junction 35 on country roads via Yealand Redmayne, calling in at Leighton Hall if you want to; or, if a longer diversion through more of this delightful country appeals, take side roads to Beetham and then continue north on the A6 to Milnthorpe. The return to junction 36 is either along the B6385 from Milnthorpe or via Levens Hall and Sizergh Castle (see junction 36, page 248). The Wheatsheaf Hotel in Beetham looks a good place for a snack or a meal.

JUNCTION 35 LEIGHTON HALL

The approach to **Leighton Hall** is astonishing. The road descends, and there before you lies the white Gothic façade of the house, rather like an elaborate stage set, the hills of the Lake District forming the backdrop. The construction of the façade in 1800 was in itself a piece of theatre: it was simpily superimposed on an Adam-style house built 40 years before. Once the country seat of the Gillows of Lancaster (see page 242), the house contains a great deal of Gillow furniture, including some exceptionally fine pieces from the late 18th century. There is also a collection of early French and

English clocks. Apart from the obvious things such as paintings and antiques, I find family mementoes intriguing: they tell you a lot about the sort of people who lived in a house. Here there is the Studio belonging to the late Mrs J. R. Reynolds (the mother of the present owner), which contains many of the paintings she produced as a professional portraitist. On the staircase are moose and wapiti heads; these animals were shot by the present owner's great-great-uncle in Canada in 1892, at which time the wapiti was the largest of its kind known in the world. Other attractions at Leighton Hall are pleasant gardens to stroll in and a woodland walk with dramatic views. Teas can be bought in the converted brew houses, and there is also a gift shop. Especially not to be missed is the collection of birds of prey, which are flown every afternoon. Also on show is an exhibition of remarkably lifelike miniature figures, all done solely with threadwork; not a single piece of cloth has been used. Leighton Hall is open from May to September on Sundays and Tuesdays to Fridays from 2.00 to 5.00 and also on Bank Holiday Mondays at the same times. Distance from the M6 is 3 miles.

JUNCTION 36 LEVENS HALL & SIZERGH CASTLE

Junction 36 is the main route into the southern Lakes, and the A591 is a fast dual carriageway for about 8 miles to a little north of Kendal. But even before you get there, there are two interesting sights well worth turning off the motorway for: **Levens Hall** and **Sizergh Castle**. Both can also be reached from the south along the A6, and a long diversion from junction 35 is described on page 247.

While most of England was united and secure relatively early in its history, the northern counties remained under constant threat of attack from Scotland. For local landowners security was as important an aspect of their homes as comfort. Both Sizergh (which has been inhabited by one family, the Stricklands, since 1239) and Levens started life as pele towers, the one in about 1350, the other some 50 to 100 years earlier. A pele was a substantial tower, usually with three storeys, thick walls (the ones at Sizergh are 7½ to 9½ feet thick at the base) and few windows, and thus easy to defend. Both, too, were considerably improved and extended as raids from the north dwindled and life began to take on a more settled and comfortable feel. In about 1450 a Great Hall was added at Sizergh, itself later twice remodelled; wings were added in the 16th century. At Levens Hall, the great remodelling dates from the reign of Elizabeth. Inside, while each house has its particular family heirlooms and portraits, the great glory is the Elizabethan panelling and plasterwork. The Drawing Room at Levens contains a magnificent overmantel dated 1595, richly carved and decorated, and there is a second in the

The Topiary at Levens Hall

Small Drawing Room. At Sizergh there are no fewer than five chimney-pieces, all dating from before 1580 and all exquisite examples of the woodworker's art.

And at both houses too the gardens are well worth a visit. At Sizergh they were created between the second half of the 18th century and the early years of the 20th. There are attractive terraces and a lake with parkland beyond, and also a magnificent rock garden with pools, streams and dwarf conifers, together with the national collection of ferns. At Levens the design for the gardens and park has remained unaltered since 1690. Colonel Grahame, Levens' owner, gave the commission to Monsieur Guillaume Beaumont, a French landscape architect trained by Le Nôtre, who created the gardens at Versailles. Beaumont's masterpiece was – and is – the topiary garden. Here there are birds, animals, pyramids, castellated towers – all beautifully shaped in yew and box. In the park beyond there is a herd of black fallow deer and a small herd of 'Bagot' goats (the Bagots are the present owners of Levens), and also a fine collection of steam engines, mostly dating from 1820 to 1920, including beam engines, table engines, hot air engines and horizontal engines.

Levens Hall and gardens are open on Sundays to Thursdays from 11.00 to 5.00 between Easter Sunday and the end of September, the steam collection from 2.00 to 5.00; there is also a plant centre, woodland play area, picnic area, gift shop and tea rooms. At Sizergh, the shop and gardens open at 12.30, the Castle at 2.00 on Sundays, Mondays, Wednesdays and Thursdays from April to October; last entries to the Castle are at 5.15. There is a tea room. Levens Hall is about 1 mile south of the A591 on the A6. For Sizergh, turn right almost immediately after joining the A6 from the A591. The Strickland Arms pub is just by the start of the driveway to the Castle.

Now the motorway runs deep through the Cumberland Fells, and there are majestic views wherever you look. At junction 37, Kendal is only 6 miles along the A684, and to the east the pretty little town of Sedbergh, on the borders of the Lakes and the Yorkshire Dales, is just 4 miles away. Kendal is very crowded throughout the summer, and if you want just a quick taste of the Lakes before hurrying on follow the suggestions under junctions 39 and 40, rather than turn off here.

But if a pleasant place for a picnic is all you need, do turn off. Take the A684 east from the junction and then turn immediately right on to a side road by **Killington Reservoir**. There are several good picnic spots here, all with good views.

Junction 38 is in lower, rather uninteresting country, with nothing special to leave the motorway for.

JUNCTION 39 SHAP ABBEY

If I could break my journey only once in this northernmost part of the M6, it would be here at junction 39, for a visit to **Shap Abbey**. Turn right on to the A6 from the motorway and head north for about 1½ miles to Shap village, where there are shops and a few cafés, and turn left at the far end of the village. Now a real surprise awaits. The narrow road to the abbey descends sharply, and in front of you, well secluded in a tiny valley, stands the tall ruined tower of the abbey. There is a millpond (the mill itself has vanished long since), and the cool, clear river Lowther is crossed by a lovely old bridge. You could picnic on the grass amidst the ruins, reflecting on what life must have been like here in the Middle Ages for the abbey's community of a dozen or so canons. The overall layout of the abbey, endowed in the late 12th century and a prosperous foundation with extensive land in Westmorland, is clearly visible. Decay set in after the Dissolution under Henry VIII, and it must have been some time after that that stones were removed from the abbey to construct the farm buildings in the far corner.

JUNCTION 39 LOWTHER PARK

From Shap you can return to the motorway at junction 39, or, if you are travelling north, take the A6 (which is reasonably fast at this point) for 9 miles or so to junction 40, just outside Penrith. On the way, you pass the entrance to **Lowther Park**. The best thing to be said about this, so far as I am concerned, is that if you like this sort of thing, then it is the sort of thing you will like. The attractions include jousting tournaments, a big top circus, a boating lake and miniature railway, a Tarzan Trail assault course, an aerial cableway, and many different rides and sports. There are also walks and nature trails through attractive woods and parkland, where you may be able to see the herd of red deer. There is a gift shop, a bar and a cafeteria. The Park is open during Easter school holidays, at weekends in May and on May Day Bank Holiday, and daily from late Spring Bank Holiday to mid-September 10.00 to 5.00.

Rather than continue on the A6, there is a pleasant diversion along a side road to **Askham** (2 miles). The road winds through a tiny estate village with model cottages for farm workers and past the parish church, situated in a grand but remote position in the estate parkland, with a large family mausoleum in the churchyard. The Lowthers are a great Westmorland family, and forebears of the present Earl of Lonsdale have lived in the area since the time of Henry II.

The present estate runs to no less than 72,000 acres. Once you are off the estate, there are walks along the river Lowther and views ahead to the Lakeland peaks. Askham itself is a pleasant village with wide streets and the Queen's Head pub. From here you can take the road straight back to Penrith or follow a side road (turn left off the Penrith road just outside the village) through Celleron to the B5320. Turn left here, and you will soon come to the top of Ullswater at Pooley Bridge (see junction 40).

JUNCTION 40 ULLSWATER

For a quick taste of the Lakes without using too much time and petrol, leave the motorway at junction 40 and take the fast A66 west towards Keswick, turning left on to the A592 towards Pooley Bridge (4½ miles). **Ullswater** is one of the most beautiful lakes, and even in the height of summer when, on the main roads at least, it seems as if you will never escape the crowds, its magical appeal remains intact. There is boating, fishing, canoeing, water-skiing and sailing on the lake, and a steamer service runs from Pooley Bridge to Glenridding between Easter and the end of September. Further down the lake on the A592, footpaths lead from a large car park to **Aira Force**, a spectacular 65-foot cascade.

JUNCTION 40 DALEMAIN HOUSE

On the A592, on the way to Ullswater, you pass **Dalemain House**. Like many big houses round here, it is a pleasing mixture of styles and periods. It started life as a Norman pele tower, had a medieval hall built on, was changed into a manor house, acquired two side wings in the Elizabethan period and, last of all, an early Georgian façade in about 1750. Especially interesting rooms in the House include the Chinese Drawing Room, which has chairs of a Chinese Chippendale design and 18th-century Chinese wallpaper, the Fretwork Room, so called because of its plaster ceiling decorated with Tudor roses, fleur-de-lys and acorn bunches; and the Nursery, with a mid-18th-century dolls' house. There is a small museum devoted to the Westmorland and Cumberland Yeomanry in the base of the pele tower. Outside, the garden contains many rare trees and unusual, old-fashioned plants; the knot garden, with low-clipped boxwood hedges, was planted in Elizabethan days. There are two small museums. One, a countryside museum, has stuffed birds, birds' eggs and other country exhibits. The other has displays on the local fell ponies, plus old agricultural implements and dairy and household utensils. There is a gift shop, and lunches and teas are available in the medieval Old Hall where, except in the very hottest weather, a large open log fire always burns in the fireplace. The House and gar-

dens at Dalemain are open on Sundays to Thursdays from 11.15 to
5.00 between Easter and mid-October.

JUNCTION 40 PENRITH

If you are stopping at junction 40, the excursion to Dalemain and
Ullswater described above is probably your best choice. In Penrith
itself, there is the Castle, now surrounded by a municipal park, but
little except the walls remains, and it is hardly worth the effort. The
Penrith Steam Museum is in an old iron works, the Castlegate
Foundry, which belonged to a firm of agricultural engineers. On display are steam traction engines, vintage farm machinery, a working
blacksmiths' shop, a furnished Victorian cottage and a collection of
steam models. Engines are in steam most days. The Museum is open
at Easter weekend and then daily except Saturdays, but including
Bank Holiday Saturdays, from 10.00 to 5.00, Sundays 12.00 to
5.00, between the late Spring Bank Holiday and the end of September. Light refreshments are available. Otherwise, the town isn't very
inspiring; there is a fine Georgian church and the usual selection of
shops, cafés and pubs.

JUNCTION 40 BROUGHAM CASTLE

Travelling away from the Lakes, some 1½ miles east from junction
40 on the A66, you come to **Brougham Castle**. This is in a delightful
setting on the banks of the rippling river Eamont, and there are
excellent picnic prospects. The site has been of strategic importance
for centuries: Agricola probably built a fort here in the first century
AD, and several Roman roads met here. The present keep was built
in about 1170, and later an inner and an outer gatehouse, plus a
passage building, were added, making the Castle one of the
strongest and most formidable of its period. That so much of the
Castle remains, and in such good condition, is thanks to Lady Anne
Clifford (1590–1676), whose family owned no fewer than five
castles in the north-west. She spent her time overseeing her estates,
and did much rebuilding and restoration work here at Brougham – a
17th-century forerunner of today's conservationists.

JUNCTION 41 HUTTON-IN-THE-FOREST

Three miles north of junction 41 on the B5305 you come to **Hutton-
in-the-Forest**, where the basic house is a 14th-century pele tower,
with substantial later additions. An interesting collection of paintings, tapestries and furniture is on display, and the gardens and terraces are delightful; there is also a 17th-century dovecote. Beyond
them stretches parkland and woodland with a fine collection of
specimen trees. The house is open on Thursdays, Fridays, Sundays

and Bank Holiday Mondays from 1.00 to 4.00 between mid-May and mid-September; the grounds, gardens and forest walk are open all year. Home-made teas are available in the Cloisters.

JUNCTIONS 42 & 43 CARLISLE

Junctions 42 and 43 both lead into **Carlisle** along the A6 and A69 respectively. Most people won't want to take a quick off-motorway break here, since it is a fairly big town with a lot of traffic, and once you get into the centre it may take you some time to get out again. I did make the effort however – and was well rewarded, especially by the charming little **cathedral**. The immediate impression is of a curiously squashed building, and then you discover that six bays of the nave were destroyed by Puritan forces in 1646 to strengthen the Castle defences. There is a lovely choir, with carved stalls and a painted roof, and a great east window. Elsewhere in the city centre a good deal of historical interest remains, and a City Trail guides you past the Old Town Hall and the Guildhall, through the delightful cathedral precincts and on to **Abbey Street**, where there are fine 18th- and 19th-century houses, and finally to the Castle. The **City Museum and Art Gallery** in Abbey Street has a lot of material of local interest and a large collection of English porcelain. Not surprisingly, given its position right on the border of England and Scotland, the **Castle** has had a turbulent history. Edward I, Robert the Bruce, Mary Queen of Scots and Bonnie Prince Charlie are some of the famous people associated with it – all of them recalled in a special exhibition of the Castle's history. There is also a labyrinth of vaulted passages, chambers, staircases and towers to explore. The cathedral (which has a café and bookstall) is open daily from 7.30 to 6.30 between October and April, and until 9.30 in the summer months. The Castle's hours are as follows: May to September, daily 9.30 to 7.00; March, April and October, Mondays to Saturdays, 9.30 to 5.30, Sundays 2.00 to 5.30; November to February, Mondays to Saturdays, 9.30 to 4.00, Sundays 2.00 to 4.00. Opening times for the Museum are 9.00 to 7.00 Mondays to Fridays and 9.00 to 5.00 Saturdays between April and September; and 9.00 to 5.00 on Mondays to Saturdays between October and March. It is also open from 2.30 to 5.00 on Sundays in June, July and August and at the Spring and August Bank Holidays.

Junction 44 is literally the end of the road. Ahead, if you are driving north, lies the A74 dual carriageway which eventually turns into the M74 south of Glasgow. If you are heading north-east, towards Edinburgh, the road to take is the A7. To the west there is the wild Solway Firth and, at Bowness-on-Solway, the western point of

Hadrian's Wall, of which, unfortunately, virtually nothing remains here. Near Burgh-by-Sands, Burgh Marsh is a remote National Trust property.

The M62

Broad Green, Liverpool to North Cave

INTRODUCTION
The M62 is the trans-Pennine motorway. It bisects the country, from the outskirts of Liverpool in the west almost as far as Hull in the east, skirting the Manchester and the Leeds/Bradford conurbations. It is a curate's egg of a route. The good parts are very good indeed – principally the Pennine range, which the motorway crosses at one of its highest and most desolate points, and rugged, individual Pennine hill towns such as Rochdale and Halifax. The eastern end of the motorway, a remote and compelling area of water, wind and skies, is fascinating in a different way. In its bad parts, the M62 is truly awful. The plain between Liverpool and Manchester is featureless and depressing, and often wet as well, and for the most part the towns are unprepossessing and undistinguished. On a practical note, be prepared for bad weather in winter: snow often blocks the Pennine sections of the route.

JUNCTION 4 LIVERPOOL
Junctions 1 to 3 do not exist, and the motorway starts at junction 4 in Broad Green, just south of the celebrated Knotty Ash (yes, it is a real place!). It is about 3½ miles into the city centre, but there is so much to do in **Liverpool** that it hardly qualifies as a place for an off-motorway break. There are the two cathedrals, the Maritime Museum and the entire waterfront, including **Albert Dock Village** in the restored Albert Dock, where there are shops, wine bars and a marina. The **County Museum** has an aquarium, vivarium and planetarium along with a space gallery and sections on local and transport history. **The Walker Art Gallery** is justly famous, with Rembrandt, Stubbs and Cézanne well represented among sculpture and paintings from many periods. **Beatle City** commemorates four of the city's most famous sons; the exhibition contains over a thousand items of memorabilia, and you can see the celebrated group on film and video and listen to their music.

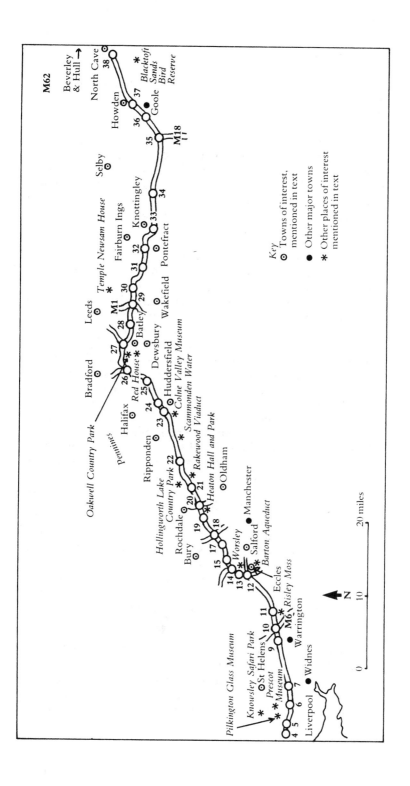

M62

Beverley & Hull →
North Cave 38
* Blacktoft Sands Bird Reserve
Howden 37
36 Goole
35 M18
Selby
Knottingley
Temple Newsam House *
Fairburn Ings
31 30 32 33 34
Leeds M1 29 Pontefract
28 Wakefield
Batley
Bradford Dewsbury
27 * Huddersfield
Red House * * Colne Valley Museum
26 25 * Scammonden Water
Halifax 24 * Rakewood Viaduct
Pennines 23 *
Oakwell Country Park
Ripponden 22 * Heaton Hall and Park
Hollingworth Lake 21 *
Country Park 20 Oldham
Rochdale 19
Bury 18 Manchester
17 Salford
15 Worsley
14 Barton Aqueduct
13 12 Eccles
11 Risley Moss
M6 *
10 Warrington
St Helens 9 Widnes
Knowsley Safari Park *
Prescot
Museum *
Pilkington Glass Museum
* 7 6 5 4
Liverpool

N
0   10   20 miles

Key
◎ Towns of interest, mentioned in text
● Other major towns
* Other places of interest mentioned in text

Junction 5 leads off to Huyton, and there is nothing to recommend here.

Junction 6 is something of a lifeline for those desperate to break their journey. Close by there are two attractions – the Knowsley Safari Park and the Prescot Museum of Clock and Watch Making – both different enough to suit a variety of tastes, and a third, the Pilkington Glass Museum in St Helens, is only a little further off. Junction 6 is also the junction with the M57, which runs north-west to Aintree, where it meets the M58, which in turn links with the M6 at junction 26, near Skelmersdale.

JUNCTION 6 KNOWSLEY SAFARI PARK
The best route to the **Knowsley Safari Park** is along the M57 to the first exit (marked junction 2). Take the A57 from here and then the A58, following the signs to the Safari Park. Elephants, lions and tigers on the outer edge of Liverpool might seem a contradiction in terms, although no more so perhaps than at many other zoos and safari parks. In fact, there is a longer history here of zoology and animal-collecting than one might expect. The thirteen Earl of Derby – the modern Safari Park is owned by his direct descendants – started a menagerie here in the early 19th century, collecting creatures from all over the world. In 1832 he invited a successful landscape artist to Knowsley Hall to paint and draw the animals and birds in his collection. This turned out to be none other than Edward Lear, who not only produced a series of lovely and lively drawings but also invented, for Lord Derby's grandchildren, limericks and nonsense verses – the eventual contents, in fact, of his *Book of Nonsense*. Today's inhabitants include bison, camels, white rhinoceroses, zebra, wildebeest and monkeys, as well as the almost obligatory elephants, lions and tigers, plus many species of birds. They can be seen at close quarters on a winding 5-mile drive through the Park. (My advice is to leave at least an hour for a visit.) Other attractions include a pets corner and a children's amusement park, together with souvenir shops, a cafeteria and a picnic area. The Safari Park is open daily from 10.00 between March and October, and to give yourself enough time to see everything you should arrive well before 4.00.

JUNCTION 6 PRESCOT MUSEUM OF CLOCK & WATCH MAKING
You will find the **Prescot Museum of Clock and Watch Making** in a plain but handsome house in the centre of Prescot, obviously once a separate small town with its own identity but now rather submerged

in Merseyside suburbia. Prescot was the centre of the south Lancashire clock and watch industry, and the displays show the manufacturing techniques used and also something of the lives and conditions of the clock-makers themselves. During the 18th century, and for a good part of the 19th too, the time business in Prescot was a classic example of early industrialization. There were no clock and watch factories at all. The timepieces were produced by a series of individual craftsmen working in their own workshops, helped at most by a few apprentices and assistants. There were specialists who made the springs, others who worked on the balances and still others on the hands or on the screws that held all the parts together; and there were toolmakers as well. All kinds of beautiful and extremely accurate timepieces were produced in this way, and some lovely examples are on show in the Museum, still keeping time to the second. But production by this method was time-consuming, and as soon as mass production began in the USA and Switzerland Prescot's products began to lose out. The Lancashire Watch Company was established in Prescot in 1889 to try to meet this competition, and for the first time complete watches, and later clocks as well, were made in the town under one roof. By 1900 the factory was turning out some five hundred watch movements and cases per day. In the end, though, the Company failed, and its tools and equipment were auctioned in 1911. This was the virtual end of clock and watch production in the area, although trade did continue in a small way until the 1960s. As well as many individual timepieces, including up-to-date quartz and digital watches, there is a reconstruction of a traditional local watchmaker's shop and also, to point up the contrast between cottage and factory production, part of the Lancashire Watch Company's factory. There is also material on local history in general, and, interestingly, a horological workshop where conservation work is undertaken. The Museum is open on Tuesdays to Saturdays from 10.00 to 5.00 and on Sundays from 2.00 to 5.00. To get there from the M62, take the M57 to junction 2, turn on to the A57 east towards Prescot, and follow the signs for the Museum.

To reach the **Pilkington Glass Museum** in St Helens (described under junction 23 of the M6, page 238, follow the A58 east from junction 1 of the M57 towards St Helens. You pass the entrance to the Pilkington Works, where the Museum is housed, on the right after about 4 miles. The diversion is well worthwhile, and the Museum an excellent one.

Junction 7 leads to Widnes to the south and to Rainhill and Prescot to the north, but the route to Prescot via junction 6 and junction 1 of the M57 (see above) is quicker. In 1829 the directors of the Liverpool & Manchester Railway held the celebrated Rainhill Trials here to determine the best locomotive to use on their line. The route was the first proper railway in this country: the first, that is, to carry fare-paying passengers on a regularly timetabled service operated entirely by steam locomotives. Robert Stephenson's *Rocket* won hands down, reaching a speed of 24.1 mph with a full load. Unfortunately – but hardly surprisingly – nothing remains to commemorate the occasion.

Junction 8 does not exist.

Junction 9 is a little way north of Warrington, where there is nothing to recommend a diversion.

Junction 10 is the junction with the M6, at junction 21a of that motorway (see page 237), and there is no acess on to ordinary roads.

JUNCTION 11 RISLEY MOSS
Junction 11 is at Risley, a large overspill village with modern estates on the edge of Warrington. You might justifiably think that there is nothing to warrant a diversion here: but you would be wrong. **Risley Moss** is all that remains of the large peaty bog that once covered almost all the land between Warrington and Manchester. It is a fascinating place to wander or picnic for half an hour or an hour, starting at the visitor centre, which has interesting exhibitions. There are woodland walks to enjoy. Perhaps the most interesting spots of all are the Cruden Observation Tower, which has good views over the mossland, and the mossland hide itself, in the middle of the moss and reached only on guided walks. A great deal of work is done to conserve this ecologically sensitive area of acid wetland, and an interesting variety of wildlife can be seen. This is not dramatic countryside, and you must look carefully for its pleasures and unusual features. But if you do spend time, the rewards are great. To get to the visitor centre, take the A574 south from the motorway, turn left, and follow the signs to Risley Moss. Risley Moss is open daily except Fridays. Between April and September opening times are from 9.00 to 5.00 Mondays to Thursdays, 8.00 at weekends. In the winter, opening times are from 8.30 to 4.30 Mondays to Thursdays and 9.00 to 5.00 at weekends. The visitor centre opens half an hour later than the park and closes half an hour earlier.

JUNCTION 12 SALFORD
Junction 12 is the junction with the M63, which starts here and runs

round the western edge of Manchester through Urmston and Sale to meet the M56 near Cheadle. In addition, a short spur motorway, the M602, takes you east towards **Salford**. Traffic is normally heavy in Salford, but if you do decide to break your journey here there are some interesting things to do. The highlights are two museums – the Museum of Mining and the Museum and Art Gallery. The **Museum of Mining** has underground scenes from different periods and also a reconstruction of a working drift mine of the 1930s. Equipment on show includes a horse gin, a coal-cutter and a pit cage and wheel, and there are displays on many aspects of miners' working and domestic life. All this is a far cry, one might imagine, from the calm seclusion of an art gallery. Not so in Salford, where the centrepiece of the **Museum and Art Gallery** is the largest publicly owned collection of works by L. S. Lowry in the country. The painter lived in the borough at Pendlebury for 40 years. His marvellously evocative paintings and drawings commemorate day-to-day life and people in a Salford now almost entirely vanished, though no doubt well remembered still. There is marvellous detail in his works, and they repay considerable study. The Art Gallery also has a strong collection of Victorian paintings, sculpture and decorative arts, and in the Museum on the ground floor there is 'Lark Hill Place', a reconstructed typical 'northern' street, with a pawnbroker's, clogger's, public house, chemist's and corner shops, all with fixtures and fittings rescued from demolished local houses and shops. The Museum and Art Gallery is in Peel Park, opposite the handsome houses of the Crescent and near pleasant walking by the river Irwell. Opening times are Mondays to Fridays from 10.00 to 5.00 and from 2.00 to 5.00 on Sundays. The Museum of Mining, in Buile Hill Park on Eccles Old Road, is open from 10.00 to 12.30 and 1.30 to 5.00 Mondays to Fridays and from 2.00 to 5.00 on Sundays.

Close to the M602 in **Eccles, Monks Hall Museum** is housed in the oldest secular building in the area, parts of which date back to 1500. There is an interesting toy collection here, together with industrial exhibits of local interest, including machine tools, a Gardner gas engine and a Nasymth steam hammer, and pleasant gardens. Leave the M602 at junction 2, turn left and then left again into Wellington Road. The Museum is open from 10.00 to 5.00 on Mondays to Fridays, and from 2.00 to 5.00 on Sundays.

JUNCTION 12 BARTON AQUEDUCT

For waterways enthusiasts, the **Barton Aqueduct** is a must. Take the M63 south to junction 2, turn on to the A57 east towards Salford, and then soon turn right on to the B5211, which crosses the Manchester Ship Canal directly next to the aqueduct. The structure we see now is the second aqueduct to be built on the site, and this one, a swing bridge that pivots on a central pier, went up when the Manchester Ship Canal was opened in 1894. The first was the work of the Duke of Bridgewater, whose story deserves a moment or two of our time. Francis Egerton, third Duke of Bridgewater, was a mineowner – an unusual occupation for a duke, but then he was an unusual man. The coal mined in his underground workings at Worsley, just by junction 13 (see below), found a ready sale in Manchester. But there was one problem: transport. How best to bring the coal cheaply and quickly from Worsley to Manchester? The answer, when Bridgewater hit on it, was simple: an artificial waterway. So it was that the first canal in this country was constructed – the first waterway that did not simply bypass an awkward stretch of river but ran on an entirely artificial course. The original intention was to end the canal at the river Irwell, from where boats could travel directly into central Manchester. But the river authorities, thinking they were on to a good thing, proposed enormous charges. The Duke objected, and in another imaginative leap of lateral thinking decided that his canal would cross the Irwell on an aqueduct. This solid brick-built structure immediately seems to have become a popular tourist attraction. It would certainly have got a glowing write-up in some 18th-century equivalent of this book: *Off the Turnpike*, maybe! Its successor is also worth your time, especially if you are keen on canals. Water is carried in two troughs, one on each side of the central pivot. Boats on the Bridgewater Canal pass directly across, while to allow vessels on the Manchester Ship Canal below to pass, the whole structure, still full of water and sealed by gates at the ends of the troughs, is swung sideways. If you have turned off here, you will also want to visit Worsley, the Duke's home and the site of his mines, directly by junction 13 and best reached from the aqueduct by taking the B5211 north (about 2½ miles).

JUNCTION 13 WORSLEY

Worsley, just east of junction 13 on the A572, was the home of the Duke of Bridgewater, whose story is told under junction 12 above. His home, Worsley Old Hall, is now a restaurant (turn left off the A575 just north of the junction), and the Delph, the entrance to the underground workings, can still be seen, together with the Packet House, where packet-boat passengers alighted. The Duke's boatyard was at the Green, and there are dry docks, built in the 18th century and still in use for boat repairs, between the Green and the canal. This junction offers a fascinating glimpse into the industrial past, and a peaceful change from the landscape of the industrial present elsewhere along this part of the M62: thoroughly recommended.

Junction 14 – on some maps called 14 and 14a – is a complicated double junction with access to the M61 and on to the A580 at Swinton. There is unrestricted access between the M62 and the M61, which runs north-east past Bolton and Chorley to join the M6 at junction 30, just south of Preston, but restricted access to and from the A580.

Junction 15 is yet another half-junction. There is access on to the A666 from the westbound carriageway of the motorway, and you can join the motorway going east. But there is nothing worth turning off for here in any case.

Junction 16 does not exist.

JUNCTION 17 HEATON HALL & PARK
Junction 17 serves Whitefield to the north and Prestwich to the south, but neither has anything suitable for an off-motorway break. There is **Heaton Park**, however, which is mid-way between junctions 17 and 18. This is a relatively early example of conscientious municipal benevolence, for Manchester City Council bought the 650-acre estate, with **Heaton Hall** at the centre, from the fifth Earl of Wilton as long ago as 1902. The house is a handsome neoclassical building designed by James Wyatt in about 1772, with some magnificent plasterwork, a collection of late 18th-century inlaid English furniture and French Empire furniture, and paintings by Reynolds, Gainsborough and Romney. The Samuel Green organ built in 1790 is still played, and occasional Sunday afternoon recitals are given. (For details telephone 061–773 1231.) There is also an audio-visual introduction to the Hall and the Wilton family, and displays on the architecture of the house. The gardens were landscaped at about the same time by William Emes, a pupil of the ubiquitous Capability Brown, and replanned in the early 19th century by John Webb, and there are plenty of pleasant walks, although with a rather organized feel about them. The Dell, a riot of colour at rhododendron time, is a particularly attractive spot. My advice would be to make for the interpretation centre just behind the Hall, where there are displays on farming techniques, and a hatchery and farm machinery can be seen. There are also many farm animals, including Highland cattle, St Kilda sheep and an apiary. Other attractions include a boating lake, pony trekking, golf and miniature golf, a pets corner and children's play area, and – most unusual

touch of all – vintage bus and tram transport. Two 1914 trams – one from the Blackpool & Fleetwood Tramway Company, the other from Manchester Corporation – operate over a 300-yard stretch of track from an 'electric car depot', as it was called in 1904, the year it was built. The track, in the south-west corner of the Park, near the Middleton Road, was formerly part of the municipal tramway network. There is also a museum display. The vintage buses run a regular service to most parts of the Park from the tram depot, whose designer disguised it to look like a summer-house. To reach Heaton Park from junction 17, take the A56 south, turn left on to the A6044 and then left again on to the A576, and the entrance is on the left (about 2¾ miles). Slow down, as it is a narrow and sharp turn through the gates. The Park is open in daylight hours, the Hall on Mondays and Wednesdays to Saturdays from 10.00 to 6.00, and on Sundays from 2.00 to 6.00, between April and September. The tram service operates on Sundays from 12.00 to 5.00 between early April and early October, on weekdays from 11.30 to 4.00 between late June and the end of August and on Bank Holiday weekends from 12.00 to 5.00. The bus service runs on Sundays and Bank Holidays from May to September. Refreshments are available in the gardens.

JUNCTION 18 EAST LANCASHIRE RAILWAY

Junction 18 is the junction with the M66, and there is no access to ordinary roads. Going south, the M66 runs alongside Heaton Park, ending after 1 mile. Turn right here on to the A576, and the park entrance is almost immediately on the right. To the north, the M66 reaches Heywood, Bury and the A56 just north of Ramsbottom (10 miles). Bury is the terminus of the **East Lancashire Railway**, the latest privately operated enthusiasts' railway to open in Britain. The original East Lancashire Railway, opened in 1846, ran from the Manchester to Bolton line some miles south of Bury through Radcliffe and Bury and on north to Ramsbottom and Rawtenstall. The line managed to survive the Beeching cuts of the early 1960s, but the section north of Bury was closed to passenger traffic in 1972, although freight services continued until 1980; south of Bury the line continues to be operated by British Rail. Already waiting in the wings when the northern section of line closed was the East Lancashire Railway Preservation Society, which initiated the long and arduous negotiations with British Rail, local authorities and the Railway Inspectorate for permission to re-open the line and the equally lengthy programme of restoration and maintenance work. The final go-ahead was given in February 1986 in the form of a Light Railway Order, and the first trains are due to run as far as Ramsbottom, 4 miles north of Bury, in June 1987. It is hoped that services will be running through to Rawtenstall by 1989. The line runs along the valley of the river Irwell through a mixed urban and rural area, and past the cotton mills, now almost all closed, that stand testimony to this area's former industrial strength and prosperity. There is a short tunnel – the faces decorating the north face are thought to be of the original directors of the East Lancashire – before the station at Ramsbottom, another mill town, is reached. Most of the trains will be steam-hauled, although as well as four former main-line steam locomotives the Preservation Society owns five former main-line diesels and several steam and diesel industrial locomotives. Trains will operate every Saturday and Sunday between June and mid-October; seven or eight services will be run each day, and the round trip to Ramsbottom will last about 1 hour. The Bury Transport Museum next to the Bolton Street Station has static exhibits, including preserved road vehicles; its opening times are 11.00 to 5.00 at weekends.

Junction 19 leads north to Heywood, south to Middleton, and I don't recommend turning off.

JUNCTION 20 HOME OF CO-OPERATION

Junction 20 is the junction with the A627(M), and there is no immediate access on to ordinary roads. To the north, the motorway ends after 1 mile, and it is another 1½ miles or so along well signposted roads into the centre of **Rochdale**. Despite the roundabouts and inner ring roads that have been carved out of the town, much of the old Rochdale of steep cobbled streets remains, and I immediately got a sense of a friendly, no-nonsense place. There is a standard but smart 20th-century shopping centre, and a large covered market with stalls piled high with delicious-looking fruit and vegetables. You can spend a pleasant 20 minutes or half hour wandering around the shopping streets – I bought some excellent parkin – and there are a number of cafés, several of which look much better than the usual.

The highlight of the town, and definitely not to be missed, is the original Co-operative store in Toad Lane: the **Home of Co-operation,** as the Co-operative Movement now describes it. The Rochdale Equitable Pioneers Society was not the first co-operative ever established. But while earlier ventures may have flourished briefly and then failed, the Rochdale store developed and grew into today's world-wide movement, with 500 million members in 70 countries. The original business was founded with the tiny capital – tiny even for 1844 – of £28, and at first only a few items were sold (tallow candles, sugar, oatmeal, butter and flour) in a sparsely furnished, whitewashed front room. Before trading began, the pioneers, each of whom bought a £1 share in the concern, established their objectives and rules, and it was thus that the celebrated Co-op 'divvy' was really launched: the scheme whereby members were paid a dividend based on the amount they spent at the store. Other important principles and aims included the democratic running of co-operative societies on a one member one vote basis; dealing in pure and unadulterated goods; and the provision of education in the co-operative ideal. Success was rapid. By 1850 membership had increased to six hundred and capital to £2300, a newsroom and library were provided, and drapery, tailoring, butchery and footwear had been added to a much extended range of groceries and dried goods. The museum in the Toad Lane shop tells this story, and that of the movement's subsequent expansion, in detail. There is a reconstruction of the original shop, and fascinating documentation on Robert Owen, the social reformer whose ideas inspired the original pioneers, on the pioneers themselves, and on later leaders of the movement. Interestingly, the pioneers were not labourers but mostly skilled artisans motivated at least as much by idealism and the vision of a better social order as by hunger and poverty. The upstairs room, originally used by the pioneers as a library and classroom, has now been converted to a meeting-room. The museum is open from 10.00 to 12.00 and 2.00 to 4.00 on Tuesday to Saturdays and from 2.00 to 4.00 on Sundays. What remains of Toad Lane – most is now buried under the new shopping centre – is now a conservation area, unfortunately looking a bit like a set for a TV series. There is an 1866 post-box, and next door to the Co-operative shop there is a 'Victorian wine bar': one wonders what the pioneers would have made of that.

JUNCTION 20 TANDLE HILL COUNTRY PARK

Going south, the A627(M) reaches the outskirts of Oldham after 3 miles. Despite the loss of many fine buildings in recent years, this remains the classic Lancashire mill town. Take the exit to the A663, signposted Royton. On the left is the **Elk Mill**, in 1926 the last mill built in Lancashire using spinning 'mules'. On the other side of the road, the **Manor and Kent Mills** stand out. These are fine examples of the mill-building boom of 1906–08, when rural spinning firms competed with each other to get into production. Their names are picked out in white brick on the towers. These are not only decorative but house huge water tanks that feed sprinklers in case of fire. Turn left on to the A671, signposted Rochdale. After about 1½ miles a road on the left, Tandle Hill Road, leads to **Tandle Hill Country Park**. This is an excellent place for a picnic, and the walks through thick woodland lead to summit views over the mills of Oldham to the south and the Pennines to the east.

JUNCTION 21 HOLLINGWORTH LAKE COUNTRY PARK

The motorway climbs towards the high Pennines now, and there are excellent walking prospects ahead. Junction 22 is the junction nearest the summit, but, although you can get to the Pennine Way close by, junction 21 offers a greater choice of walks to suit all energies and inclinations. The place to make for is the **Hollingworth Lake Country Park**. Take the A663 north from the motorway and turn right on to the B6225. The road climbs out of Milnrow across high moorland to Smithy Bridge, where a right turn and then a left almost immediately brings you alongside the lake, looking almost Alpine with the high hills behind. To reach the attractive visitor centre, follow the B6225 past the Beach Inn, the Trattoria del Lago pizzeria and the little marina as far as the Fish Inn (which would be my choice for a drink). Turn right here following the signs to Rakewood (2½ miles from the M62). The visitor centre has displays and a slide show on the Country Park, fishtanks, a mural done by a local artist, Walter Kershaw, and temporary exhibitions, plus a café. The centre is open from 10.30 to 7.00 on weekdays, 10.30 to 8.00 at weekends and on Bank Holiday Mondays, between April and September, and from 11.00 to 4.00 on weekdays, 10.30 to 5.00 or dusk at weekends, during the rest of the year. As soon as the lake was created in 1798 – its purpose was to supply water for Rochdale's canal system, and three dams were constructed – it became a popular spot for outings. Weighver's Seaport was its 19th-century nickname. There was a Swiss-style Lake Hotel with pleasure gardens and outdoor dancing on the promontory on the southern shore. In those days you got to the hotel on a paddle-steamer which plied across the lake, and today a motor launch, the *Lady Alice*, provides the same sort of service. That and the children's playground apart, however, the Country Park's attractions are rather more sober, and none the worse for that. The easiest walk is the 2½-mile circular trail around the shore, which starts at the visitor centre and crosses all three dams. Another walk goes to Bib Knowl on a circular route; the name is derived from Bible Knoll, so called because Dissenters met there in the 16th and 17th centuries. Yet other, rather tougher walks take you further out into Pennine country. There is also interesting wildlife around the lake, and the marshy area just before the promontory is designated as a nature reserve, to which the general public is not admitted. Great-crested grebe are among the regular inhabitants.

For a less organized taste of the Pennines, turn south from the motorway on the A663 and then turn left on to the A640. The road climbs rapidly, and after about 1 mile you turn left on to Ogden Lane; take care as the road has only a tiny nameboard, and you may well shoot straight past. The road leads up to no fewer than five reservoirs, and there are plenty of footpaths, both unofficial and signposted, official ones. (Swimming is not permitted.) A little way farther along the A640 brings you to two restaurants, the Moorcock on the left and the accurately described Alpine on the right; both have grand views.

The motorway stretch between junctions 21 and 23 is the grandest of all, the **Rakewood Viaduct** one of the route's most impressive engineering achievements. (You can get a good view of the viaduct on the Hollingworth Lake to Bib Knowl walk described under junction 21, above.) The viaduct is 840 feet long and 140 feet above the valley bottom, and the valley itself had to be widened to ensure a suitable gradient for the viaduct. Twenty massive steel-reinforced concrete columns support it.

JUNCTION 22 PENNINE WAY
South from junction 22 the A672 almost immediately crosses the **Pennine Way**, the first, one of the longest and certainly the most challenging of the country's long-distance paths. This is really desolate country, wild and inhospitable. You can walk in either direction, of course, but unless you are prepared for a really long walk you will have to retrace your steps the way you came. Going south the path swings east and meets the A640. You can turn right here on to the main road, then strike right after about ⅓ mile on to another path running along the southern edge of Readycon Dean Reservoir to the A672, and finally turn right along that road back to your car (about 5 miles). To the north the Pennine Way crosses the motorway on a footbridge and then proceeds along Blackstone Edge to the Aiggin Stone, at the junction with a stretch of old road, thought to date from the Middle Ages; there is no circular route here, and you will have to return the way you came. This area is criss-crossed with drovers' routes dating back to the Middle Ages and earlier. The road here has 16-foot wide kerbs with a central channel that was probably planted with turf to enable horses to get a good foothold. Even if you are contemplating only a mile or so's walk along the Way, don't set off in bad weather, or even in fair weather that looks as if it might turn bad. Mists, fog and rain can descend very quickly. And make sure you have proper walking boots and are warmly dressed.
The A672 continues south to the Junction Inn at Denshaw. Turn right here on to the A640, which takes you past the Moorcock and

Alpine restaurants and, eventually, via the A663, back to the motorway at junction 21 (see page 267).

JUNCTION 22 RIPPONDEN

North of the motorway the A672 slowly descends through magnificent country with good views. You reach the Turnpike Inn after about 3 miles (its name commemorates the 18th-century turnpike that ran here). Opposite, the car park overlooking **Boothwood Reservoir** would be a pleasant place for a quick picnic. You see trees again as you descend into **Ripponden** (5 miles from the motorway), an attractive stone village whose centre is now a conservation area. A small farm museum in a 19th-century farmhouse is worth visiting if you happen to be around during its very limited opening hours (from 2.00 to 5.00 at weekends and Bank Holidays between March and October). There is old agricultural equipment and a kitchen and dairy. From Ripponden return to the motorway at junction 22 if you are travelling west. If you are going east, take the B6113 east to Elland, turn left on to the A6025 and then right on to the A629, which brings you to junction 24 (about 5½ miles).

JUNCTION 23 SCAMMONDEN WATER

Junction 23 has restricted access. You can leave the motorway from the eastbound carriageway and enter it on the westbound one. There are fine views and good walking back along the A640 at Scammonden. Take the A640 west, and turn right after about 3½ miles for **Scammonden Water**. There are good views of the reservoir and Calderdale beyond it from the car park. From here you can take the footpath past the monument commemorating the day the Queen opened the reservoir, through a small tunnel under the motorway and down into the pleasant Black Brook valley. From here there are easy connections with the network of footpaths that runs through Calderdale.

JUNCTION 23 COLNE VALLEY MUSEUM

South of the motorway, the Colne valley is an intriguing mixture of the industrial (with many factories and mills sadly now derelict) and the rural (small farms clinging tightly to the hillside). It was the cloth industry that brought this area its prosperity, and it was the industry's eventual collapse that undermined its well-being. **Golcar**, a small steep-sided village perched high above the Colne, was for centuries one of the most important centres of wool weaving in England. In 1830 no fewer than 101 independent clothiers from Golcar were selling their pieces in the Huddersfield Cloth Hall. Industrialization – in the form of powered looms and other machinery situated in large mills and worked by employees – came relatively late to the woollen industry, and as late as the mid-19th century most cloth was manufactured by independent producers working in their own homes.

In Golcar three weavers' cottages house the **Colne Valley Museum** and offer a fascinating glimpse back into domestic and working life in the mid-19th century. The weaver's parlour on the ground floor is furnished as it would have been in about 1850, and it takes little imagination to re-create the family life of the Taylors, who lived here. William Taylor was 34, so the 1851 census tells us, and a woollen waste dealer, his wife Ann 26, and they had three young daughters. Ten years later husband and wife were using the top-floor workshops as a loom chamber, assisted by their three eldest children, another daughter and two sons having been born in the meantime. This room is among the last domestic loom chambers to be built in England. There are eight mullioned windows on the south side, to give as much light as possible for the looms, and a wide taking-in door on the north side. Two looms are on display here, a four-shaft treadle loom and a witch loom. Next door, in the spinning room, you can see how yarn was made on spinning wheels in the 17th and 18th centuries. By the 1850s, spinning had already moved to the mills, where it was done on power-driven spinning mules. The clogger's shop is arranged as it would have been in 1910, when almost everybody in the Colne valley wore clogs. Clogs kept feet warm and dry no matter the weather and protected them on roads made up with broken stones. If you are lucky you will see demonstrations of the machinery and old skills during your visit, and you can talk to the weavers, spinsters and clog-makers on duty. The Museum's latest addition is a modern replica of a spinning jenny, made largely from materials saved from mill closures and mechanical parts rescued from scrap mules and looms; although the basic proportions of the jenny have been maintained, its dimensions have been reduced to allow it to fit into the restricted space available in the Museum. Invented by Robert Hargreaves in about 1764, the spinning jenny enabled yarn to be produced on no fewer than 16 spindles at a time, instead of on the previous one. (There are two theories about the origin of the name 'jenny'; one has it that the word is a corruption of 'engine', while according to the other the machine was named after Hargreaves' daughter Jenny.) Although Hargreaves himself made hardly any money out of his invention, jenny-spinning revolutionized yarn production, helping to transform the process from a cottage industry to one based on large mills. By the end of the 18th century, jennies were already being used in mills, although they continued in use in individual cottages as well for the best part of another century. The Museum is open at weekends and Bank Holidays from 2.00 to 5.00, and there is also a shop. The Weavers' Hall restaurant is nearby. Take the A643 west from the motorway at junction 23 and then the first right off the main road, after about 1 mile. Take the fifth turning left off this road in just under 1 mile at a sharp quarter-left turn, and follow the road round to Golcar Church. The Museum is just down an extremely steep and narow lane opposite the church.

JUNCTION 24 HUDDERSFIELD

To get to the Colne Valley Museum at Golcar (see junction 23 above) from junction 24, take the A643 west parallel to the motorway as far as junction 23, and then follow the route already described. **Huddersfield** is the main town south of the motorway here, 3 miles along the A629 from junction 24. The centre is a fine example of Victorian town architecture, with St George's Square as the focal point. The masterpiece here is the **station**. And it really is a masterpiece, often described as one of the finest stations in England, with a magnificent Palladian façade with Corinthian columns. At one time, British Rail wanted to demolish the forebuilding but the local council bought it, and it is now used for meetings and exhibitions. Also in St George's Square are the George Hotel, built at the same time as the station in 1850, Lion Chambers and the offices of the Huddersfield and Bradford Building Society, all grand buildings and worth a look. The **Art Gallery** (open Mondays to Fridays from 10.00 to 6.00, Saturdays from 10.00 to 4.00) has a collection of British paintings, sculpture, drawings and watercolours from about the mid-19th century onwards, with works by Lowry, Spencer, Moore and Ruskin. Take a look too at the late 19th-century cast-iron and glass market building in Brook Street, now superbly restored (general markets are held on Mondays and Thursdays, bric-à-brac markets on Tuesdays and Saturdays) and at the splendid town hall. The office section was opened in 1879 and the concert hall – home of the internationally renowned Choral Society – three years later.

JUNCTION 24 HALIFAX

But for a really magnificent Victorian townscape – probably the best Victorian town (as opposed to city) centre in Great Britain – you should turn north from the motorway at junction 24 for 4 miles along the A629 to **Halifax**. It's a fine place to walk about in, with good shops, some pleasant eating-places (Watson's coffee shop is a traditional establishment, selling numerous different types of parkin and all manner of bread, cakes and buns) and a lively atmosphere. The single most interesting building, in my opinion at least, is the

Piece Hall, so called because weavers from all over Calderdale came here to sell their lengths, or pieces, of cloth. Opened in 1779, it is now the last surviving manufacturers' hall. Classical arched and colonnaded galleries give access to the merchants' rooms – no fewer than 315 of them – in which the business was transacted. In the centre there is a large grassed and cobbled quadrangle, site today of a bustling market every Friday and Saturday. Many of the merchants' rooms now house specialist craft and antique shops, and there is also an industrial textile museum, plus an excellent tourist information centre. Also within the Piece Hall is the **Pre-Industrial Museum**, which is devoted to life in farms and cottages before the age of mills. Displays show domestic spinning, weaving and cloth preparation. Next door is an art gallery which puts on regular temporary exhibitions. Plan to spend some time here as the shops are great fun to browse in – you can buy curios, cloths, glass, clogs, ceramics, books, linen and lace, and all kinds of antiques. The Piece Hall is open from 10.00 to 7.00 on Mondays to Saturdays and from 10.00 to 6.00 on Sundays. The Pre-Industrial Museum and the art gallery are open daily from 10.00 to 6.00 between April and September, 10.00 to 5.00 during the rest of the year.

Next to the Piece Hall is the **Calderdale Industrial Museum** (open 10.00 to 5.00 on Tuesdays to Saturdays, 2.00 to 5.00 on Sundays). The focus here is on local industry: textiles, including carpet manufacture, wire-drawing and – perhaps most interesting of all – sweet-making. John Mackintosh started making US-style toffee in Halifax in 1894, and the firm is still going strong; it is now part of the Rowntree Mackintosh confectionery empire. Reconstructions help to bring factory work to life, and there is also a good display of steam engines, two of which are steamed daily, and material representing the social life of Halifax in about 1850. An unusual feature of the Museum is its smell! Small gadgets creating authentic smells have been installed, so that, for instance, you experience a strong aroma of toffee as you tour the Mackintosh exhibits.

The town trail, which, conveniently, starts and finishes at the Piece Hall, is the best way of seeing the rest of the town. Allow about 45 minutes if you follow the short route, and up to 2½ hours for the long route if you want to stop and look at everything in detail. The highlight of the walk is without question the magnificent **Town Hall**, built between 1859 and 1862 by Sir Charles Barry, architect of the Houses of Parliament, and his son E. M. Barry. The town trail booklet (obtainable from the tourist office at the Piece Hall) sums it up well. 'The style is officially described as North Italian cinquecento, but much elaboration has been added, and it may perhaps best be described as Victorian extravaganza.' The elaboration outside consists of carvings and sculpture, including four carved figures, one on each side of the spire, representing Europe, North America, Africa and Asia. Inside, the well-preserved central galleried hall is well worth a look. Make sure too that you wander round the 1890s glass and iron market, where there is some lovely cast-iron work and a good range of stalls selling clothes, meat, fruit and vegetables and so on. The Halifax Building Society's new headquarters building, with its window walls of bronze aluminium and bronze tinted glass panels, is controversial locally, though acclaimed worldwide by architects, it is said. (I wonder how easily they got a mortgage on that!) North-east of the town centre on the A58, and hence a good distance off the motorway, is **Shibden Hall Folk Museum of West Yorkshire**. The half-timbered Hall, which dates back to the early 15th century, contains period rooms of the 17th and 18th centuries showing what life was like in a prosperous household. Outside you can see horse-drawn carts and other vehicles in a 17th-century Pennine barn, and an early 19th-century village has been created in the cobbled courtyard. The Museum is open between April and September on Mondays to Saturdays from 10.00 to 6.00 and on Sundays from 2.00 to 5.00; in October, November and March from 10.00 to 5.00 on Mondays to Saturdays and 2.00 to 5.00 on Sundays; and on Sundays only in February from 2.00 to 5.00; closed in December and January. Refreshments are available.

At junction 25 you can turn off north-west for Brighouse and south east for Mirfield, best known as the home of the Community of the Resurrection. But there is nothing suitable in the way of off-motorway breaks here.

JUNCTION 26 RED HOUSE

There are two attractions near junction 26 – the Red House at Gomersal and Oakwell Hall in Birstall, which now forms the centre-point of a small country park. Neither is all that special, although interesting and pleasant enough in their own way. The **Red House** was built in 1660 by William Taylor, and generations of Taylors continued to live there until 1920. In the 1830s, Charlotte Brontë often visited and based her novel *Shirley*, published in 1849, on the House and the family, changing the House's name to Briarmains and the family's to Yorke. Today the House is a lively museum, with displays on local history and rooms furnished as they would have been in about 1820. The House was packed with schoolchildren when I was there, filling in worksheets, looking at the exhibits really carefully and enthusiastically and generally thoroughly enjoying themselves – just what a museum should be. The Red House is open from 10.00 to 5.00 on Mondays to Saturdays and 1.00 to 5.00 on Sundays. From the motorway take the A638 south to Cleckheaton, turn left on to the A643 and then left again on to the A651 (2½ miles).

JUNCTION 26 OAKWELL HALL & COUNTRY PARK

Oakwell Hall, not much more than ¾ mile away from the Red House, was built in stone in 1583 on the site of an earlier timber building. Remodelled internally in the 17th century, it has changed little since. There is attractive Elizabethan furniture, and in the Great Hall a lovely fireplace and a beautifully carved screen. Oakwell too appears in *Shirley*, as Fieldhead, and the Parlour downstairs contains Brontë memorabilia. The 87 acres of **Oakwell Hall Country Park** surrounding the house and bordered to the north by the motorway include a herb garden, an arboretum, formal gardens and a wildlife garden, an equestrian arena, picnic sites, bridleways, a nature trail and an adventure playground. The visitor complex contains temporary exhibition galleries, craft studios, and a shop and a café. The Hall is open from 10.00 to 5.00 on Mondays to Saturdays, 1.00 to 5.00 on Sundays, while the Country Park's times are dawn to dusk daily throughout the year. From the Red House continue north to the A651, turn right on to the A652 and then left, following the signposts to the Hall. If you are travelling east, return to the motorway at junction 27. Continue south on the A652, turn left on to the A643 and almost immediately left again on to the A62.

Junction 26 is also the junction with the M602 which runs north for 2 miles to the southern edge of **Bradford**. This is a fine city, with plenty to do, but crowded and not especially suitable for a quick off-motorway break. Walk around the handsome town centre, with the **Victorian Wool Exchange** and the great wool warehouses in 'Little Germany', or visit the **Industrial Museum** at Eccleshill on the northern side of the city (open Tuesdays to Sundays and Bank Holiday Mondays from 9.00 to 5.00). The **National Museum of Photography, Film and Television** in Prince's View contains no fewer than six floors of exhibits covering both the history of photography and current and future developments. Opening times are Tuesdays to Sundays and Bank Holiday Mondays from 11.00 to 7.30.

Oakwell Hall Country Park, described under junction 26 (see above), is just as accessible from junction 27. The junction is also the junction with the M621, which runs north-east to Leeds, meeting the northern point of the M1 (see pages 1 to 45), just south of the city centre.

Junction 28 leads to Morley to the north and Dewsbury to the south. Again, there is nothing to recommend here.

Junction 29 is the junction with the M1 and there is no access on to ordinary roads.

JUNCTION 30 TEMPLE NEWSAM HOUSE
One of the finest attractions on the eastern half of the M62 lies 6 miles north of junction 30, well worth the slightly tortuous drive to get there: **Temple Newsam House**. The publicity leaflet issued by Leeds Corporation, which bought the House in 1922, calls it 'the Hampton Court of the North'. Rather an extraordinary description, this, for why should a northern house need comparison with one in the south? Temple Newsam is quite magnificent and quite historic enough to merit praise on its own account. Begun some time before 1521 by Lord Darcy, who was beheaded by Henry VIII after the Pilgrimage of Grace, the unsuccessful northern uprising against the Dissolution of the Monasteries, it has been several times extended and remodelled. Only the central block remains from the original severely handsome Tudor mansion. The two side wings were added in the 1620s, along with the grand entrance porch and the famous inscription around the balustrade of the roof: 'All Glory and Praise be Given to God the Father the Son and Holy Ghost on High Peace on Earth Good Will towards Men Honour and True Allegiance to our Gracious King Loving Affection amongst his Subjects Health and Plenty be within this House' – all in stone capital letters. Finally, in 1796, the south wing was converted to two storeys. Inside, few of the original features remain, and the finest rooms were created in the 1740s, among them the Grand Salon, with magnificent plasterwork, richly carved door cases and handsome chimney-pieces. Further improvements in the 1790s included the stone staircase, the neo-classical chimney-piece in the Great Hall and the bedrooms and dressing rooms in the south wing. Finally, a century after that, the oak staircase, modelled on an Elizabethan example, was installed. The tour of the House is fascinating. There are family portraits and paintings by Vasari, Stubbs, Reynolds and many other well-known artists; extensive displays of English silver, porcelain, pottery and wallpaper; magnificent furniture, including many pieces by Chippendale and almost all the original pieces from the Long Gallery, upholstered in a lovely floral needlework. Outdoors, a fascinating variety of things to do and see awaits you. There are walks in the grounds, part of which were landscaped by Capability Brown, including a nature trail and a rhododendron walk and the lovely rose garden. The **Home Farm** has agricultural exhibits and rare breeds, and the stable block has been converted into an extremely at-

tractive centre with an information room, exhibition galleries, a restaurant and the estate shop. There is even an adventure playground: something, in fact, for everyone. Temple Newsam is open from 10.30 to 6.15 or dusk from Tuesdays to Sundays and on Bank Holidays (with an extension to 8.30 on Wednesdays between May and September). To get there from junction 30 of the M62, take the A642 north, and turn left on to a side road just after the main road crosses the Aire & Calder Navigation and the river Aire. Continue on this road for as long as you can, turn left on to the A63, bear left at the roundabout and finally turn left in the middle of Whitkirk, following the signs to the house.

JUNCTION 30 WAKEFIELD

The A642 south from junction 30 brings you after 2½ miles to the centre of Wakefield, described under junctions 40 and 41 of the M1 (see pages 42–43).

JUNCTIONS 31 & 32 FAIRBURN INGS NATURE RESERVE

Junction 31 leads south to Normanton and north to Castleford, which is also served by junction 32. The only attraction here is the Royal Society for the Protection of Birds' reserve at **Fairburn Ings**. Take the A656 north from Castleford and turn right near Allerton Bywater on to a side road signposted to Fairburn. Ings is a Viking word meaning a riverside water-meadow. About one third of the 618 acres of the reserve is now under open water, and other types of habitat are provided by spoil heaps (the National Coal Board still tips colliery spoil here, although it is careful not to damage wildlife) and by low-lying farmland with flashes caused by subsidence. No fewer than 240 species have been recorded; 170 to 180 are identified annually, and some 70 breed. The number of rarities, 60 or 70, is unusually high, but the reserve lies on a migration route along the Aire valley through the 'Aire gap' in the Pennines and along the Ribble valley to the Lancashire coast. Wildfowl and waders are most common, and mallard, teal, shoveler, gadwall, tufted duck and pochard all breed. Mute swans and Canada geese come here for the midsummer moult and 30 to 50 whooper swans in most winters. In spring the easterly winds often bring large numbers of tern, chiefly Arctic but with some of the common and black species as well. Large flocks of gull are common in winter. There is an information centre and hide along the side road leading east from the A656 to Fairburn; opening times are from 10.00 to 5.00 at weekends. A path, Cut Lane, runs from Fairburn village to the eastern end of the reserve and is open at all times. Fairburn itself is a pleasant stone village. If you are travelling east, the return to the motorway is best made at junction 33. Continue through Fairburn towards the A1 (there are good views looking down on the reserve here, and also the Bay Horse pub), and then turn right on to the A1. Junction 33 is reached after 4 miles.

JUNCTION 33 PONTEFRACT CASTLE

The Fairburn Ings Nature Reserve, described under junctions 31 and 32 above, is equally accessible from junction 33. Otherwise, the main attraction here is **Pontefract**, about which there is not much to be said. To the casual visitor, the **Castle** would be a lot more interesting if it had not been so thoroughly demolished in 1649, at the end of the Civil War. In its day it must have been an impressive sight, even if not quite as impressive as the majestic, many-towered structure depicted in a fanciful 17th-century painting on show in the Pontefract Museum. The first Norman castle-builders took advantage of a large natural mound of rock nearly 40 feet high, and succeeding generations extended and improved the original wooden motte-and-bailey. The chief work took place after about 1311, and a series of flanking towers was added, along with an improved gate tower, kitchens, the west barbican and the great tower. Pontefract became the principal royal castle in the north of England, and Richard II was imprisoned and then died here in about 1400: 'bloody Pomfret', Shakespeare called it. A Royalist stronghold in the Civil War, it was besieged no fewer than three times between 1644 and 1649 and then pulled down, apparently at the petition of the townspeople – who were perhaps fed up with being the centre of attention. Today there is very little to see. The mound is a rather uninspiring public garden, made worse when I was there by building and excavation works, and a stretch of the inner bailey wall can be seen. Elsewhere in the town there are some fine 18th- and 19th-century buildings around the Market Place, and a butter cross dating from 1734. To get to Pontefract, turn north on to the A1 at junction 33, and then left very soon on to the A645. For the Castle turn right at the traffic lights about halfway up the gentle hill into town and then right again almost immediately following a not very prominent sign. The **Museum** is in an art nouveau building in Salter Row, and there is a small but well set out display on local history and the Castle. Opening hours are from 10.30 to 12.30 and 1.30 to 5.00 on Mondays to Saturdays; closed on Bank Holidays.

At junction 34 you reach a flat watery landscape with wide views and scudding clouds, quite unlike anything so far on the M62. The not very jolly-looking Jolly Miller pub is ½ mile north on the A19, and you could have a rather windy walk, quite likely wet as well, along the towpath of the nearby **Aire & Calder Navigation**. The canal is quite heavily used by commercial traffic, so don't expect the normal sort of canalside walk through lush countryside and past quaint locks. **Selby** with its magnificent abbey and elegant market square is 7 miles north along the A19. Quite large ships can navigate the Ouse as far as Selby, and there is an attractive small dock there.

Junction 35 is the junction with the M18, and there is no access on to ordinary roads.

JUNCTION 36 BLACKTOFT SANDS BIRD RESERVE

Goole, close to junction 36 (the unique skyline, visible from the motorway, of church spire, water towers, cranes and boat hoists set amid flat agricultural land has even been described as the 'Venice of the North of England'), is Britain's most inland port; it lies no less than 50 miles from the sea. Public access to parts of the dock area is allowed, and shipping movements at tide time can be observed from the Ocean Lock and Lock Hill. **St John's Church**, built in 1838 by the Aire & Calder Navigation Company, who were responsible for creating the port when they cut the Navigation to link the Aire and Calder rivers with the Ouse, has memorials to ships as well as to seamen.

The Royal Society for the Protection of Birds' reserve at **Blacktoft Sands** is about 8½ miles from the motorway: a visit will certainly repay the time it requires. Take the A614 east from the motorway, and then turn right on to the A161, following it through Old Goole and Swinefleet. Turn left here on to the side road that runs along the southern bank of the Ouse as it widens out to meet the Trent. The entrance to the reserve is just when the road turns sharply south. Visitors are allowed only as far as two hides close to the car park and also to the river embankment close by (remember to walk at the bottom of the bank so as not to disturb the birds), but there are no restrictions on when you may come. The reserve occupies 460 acres at the confluence of the Ouse and the Trent – a fascinating mixture of reedswamp (one of the largest expanses in the country) and salt-marsh, with patches of couch grass and a small mudflat as well. At the western end areas of higher, grassy land are being converted into lagoons with islands. The water is brackish, a combination of salt water from the Humber estuary and fresh water from the two rivers. About 150 species of birds are seen here regularly, and another 50 have been spotted since the reserve was established in 1973. There are wildfowl and waders in winter. In summer some four hundred pairs of reed warbler nest in the reed beds, along with water rail and bearded tit; at times up to 10 per cent of the entire British population of bearded tit can be found here. Many species pause at Black-toft in May and June *en route* to their summer homes, and as early as July and August again on the return trip. The winter visitors include a spectacular number of teal, often as many as 1500.

JUNCTION 37 HOWDEN
Howden, close to the motorway at junction 37, has been described as the old East Riding's 'second best but least appreciated market town'. (The best is undoubtedly Beverley, of which more under junction 38, on page 281. Much of the old East Riding, by way of explanation to non-Yorkshiremen, is now Humberside, although in hearts and minds it remains Yorkshire.) Least appreciated is certainly an apt description. Howden was a small but thriving commercial centre – its annual horse fair was famous, and in the early 19th century was probably the biggest in the country – until a long, slow decline began in the mid-19th century, a decline only now very slowly going into reverse. Not until 1971 did the town's population exceed that recorded in the 1861 census. The benefit of this is that much of the character and buildings of the 18th- and early 19th-century centre has been preserved relatively unchanged, and you can spend a pleasant half hour or more strolling through the winding narrow streets. The disadvantage is that, until recently at least, nobody has seemed to care much. Some of the buildings have been left dilapidated and badly in need of repair; 20th-century alterations and 'improvements' are generally unsympathetic and out of character; and in 1975 the local council even went so far as to encourage the demolition (fortunately prevented) of the Bishop of Durham's **Manor House,** a listed building and the most important domestic building in the town. Things are at last gradually beginning to improve in the town, and local people are realizing the value and interest of the fabric of their town, and the importance of spending money on it. The Bishop's Manor House has been fully restored, repairs are being made to the ruined part of the minster and to some of the other buildings of historic interest in the town, and some of the attractive winding streets in the town centre have been resurfaced with traditional setts and York stone paving.

Although there was a Norman church on the same site, the present **minster** dates from the late 13th century. The north and south transepts and the choir were built in about 1270, the nave some 10 years later. Then, so wealthy was the church, the choir had been rebuilt by 1330, and the octagonal chapter house went up towards the end of the century. Being a college of priests, the church escaped the Dissolution of the Monasteries in the 1530s, only to get caught in the dissolution of collegiate churches late in the following decade.

Howden Minster

From then on, wealth gone, things went from bad to worse. The choir was closed off in 1609, the roof and spire of the chapter house collapsed in 1750, and the tower and chancel were badly damaged in a fire in 1929. The condition of the ruined choir continued to deteriorate, although since it was taken over by the Department of the Environment in 1970 it has been tidied and repaired. Inside, the nave sweeps forward majestically towards the magnificent west window. There is a beautiful 15th-century statue of the Virgin Mary in the Lady Chapel, a dove, symbol of the Holy Spirit, perched on her left shoulder, and handsome tomb effigies in the Saltmarshe Chapel. Dooggles restaurant opposite the minster is passable, and Bowman's an acceptable alternative.

East of Howden there is a fine walk along the north bank of the Ouse and then the Humber (as the Ouse and Trent are called after they meet). One particularly good stretch is between Yokefleet and Blacktoft, more or less opposite the RSPB reserve mentioned under junction 36 (see page 278). Take the B1230 east from Howden and turn right for Yokefleet after 4 miles. Walk here for as long as you like – there is normally plenty of traffic on the river, and four vessels passed in as many minutes when I was last there – and return to the main road via Blacktoft and then north to Gilberdyke. The Hope and Anchor pub at Blacktoft looks rather uninviting, the White Horse on the main road at Gilberdyke rather better. From Gilberdyke it is about 2½ miles east along the B1230 to junction 38.

JUNCTION 38 HULL & BEVERLEY

Junction 38, just outside the pleasant little village of North Cave, is the end of the motorway, although you will hardly notice it, as the M62 merges into the dual carriageway A63. **South Cave** has a handsome main street with some attractive houses and a couple of good pubs; continue on the A63 for 2 miles and then turn left on to the A1034. Hull (13 miles along the A63) and Beverley (11 miles – left on to the A1034 and then right after South Cave on to the B1230) are the nearest towns. **Hull** is a much and unfairly maligned place by those who have never been there. It is a fine city, still an important port, with a tangible taste of the sea in the air. There is an excellent **Town Docks Museum**, the **Ferens Art Gallery** with a good collection of maritime paintings, a transport museum, and the birthplace of William Wilberforce, the philanthropist and campaigner for the abolition of slavery. The Old Town is pleasant to walk round and has some good restaurants. On the way into Hull, the road runs underneath the northern edge of the **Humber Bridge**, opened in 1981 and the longest single-span suspension bridge in the world. It is well worth walking at least some of the way across the bridge on

The Humber Bridge

the walkway: the views are superb. Turn off the main road for the car park by the bridge – but don't get muddled up with the traffic crossing the bridge. The road on into Hull runs parallel with the Humber, giving interesting views of the river and dockland. **Beverley** must be mentioned for two reasons. First, because it is an exquisite town, with two fine churches – St Mary's and the minster – and some lovely 18th-century buildings. And second because it is my wife's home town, and I met her there.

The M9

Kirkliston to Dunblane

INTRODUCTION

You might well dismiss the M9 at first as nothing more than a quick route to and from the central Highlands. What could there possibly be to tempt you off it? In fact, even though the route may seem unpromising at first sight, and even though it does pass through some not especially attractive industrial areas, there is a surprising variety of things to do, and some lovely countryside to enjoy, only a few minutes' drive from the motorway. In addition, there is the bonus of Edinburgh and Stirling – two of Scotland's most historic cities – at each end of the motorway. It is also interesting to realize that the motorway cuts straight across one the earliest centres of the industrial revolution in Scotland. The area's extensive ironstone and coal deposits have been intensively worked for several generations, and in many cases are now exhausted. (The motorway crosses the river Carron, which gave its name to the carronade, a famous artillery piece.) The area's other significant natural resource was oil. The cannel-coal and oil-shale refineries established here in the mid-19th century (the reddish 'hills' visible at the Edinburgh end of the motorway are the relics of that early industry), later led to the growth of oil-refining at Grangemouth.

Described on paper, the start of the M9 some 8 miles west of central Edinburgh seems rather complicated. Driving along it, it all becomes much simpler. The M9 and the M8, which goes west to Glasgow, share their junction 1. The two motorways simply run together, and except for the signboards there is nothing to show that you are leaving one and joining the other. From junction 1 there is no immediate access to ordinary roads, and a spur motorway less than 1 mile long takes you on to the A8000 just north of Kirkliston. Access to and from this spur is restricted to the M8. You can get on to it if you are coming from the M8; likewise, coming from the A8000 you can only join the M8.

To cut a long story short, then, if you are making for the M9 from

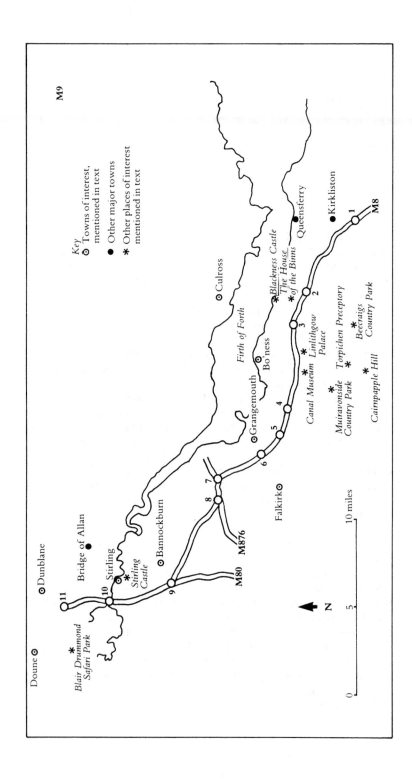

the M8, just continue driving. If you are coming from central Edinburgh, take the A8 out of the city to junction 2 of the M8, and join the northbound carriageway of that motorway. If you have come over the Forth Road Bridge, take the sliproad left immediately after the tollbooths and turn right at the roundabout on to the A904. After about 4 miles turn left on to the B8046, and junction 2 of the M9 is immediately on your right.

After all this, it is something of a comedown to report that junction 1 is in the middle of flat land on the western fringes of Edinburgh. There are good views towards Edinburgh, however, with Arthur's Seat frequently visible and often the distinctive outline of the Pentland Hills behind as well. Ahead, you may get occasional glimpses of the two Forth bridges, road and rail. Two grand houses round here – Dalmeny and Hopetoun – are both well worth visiting. But they are easier to reach on the way to the M90, and so are dealt with on pages 298–300.

JUNCTIONS 2 & 3 THE HOUSE OF THE BINNS
Junction 2 is yet another half-junction. Traffic from the north (Stirling) can leave the motorway, and northbound traffic can join it. Junction 3, about 2 miles further on, is the exact opposite: eastbound traffic can join, northbound can leave.

Whichever junction you use, the most interesting place to visit is **The House of the Binns**, a fascinating National Trust for Scotland property with roots deep in Scottish history. It was Thomas Dalyell, an Edinburgh butter merchant, who founded the Dalyell family fortune and built The House of the Binns – or at least the present core of it, since the House has been much remodelled and extended since his time early in the 17th century. But today it is Thomas's son Tam who is most remembered. (Interestingly, the Dalyell who currently occupies the house with his family is another Tam, the local Labour MP.) The 17th-century Tam was a larger-than-life figure, round whom numerous legends have grown up. When Charles I was executed in London, Tam, a staunch Royalist, swore never to have his hair cut or his beard trimmed until the Stuart dynasty was restored. He joined Charles II when that monarch was crowned in Scotland in 1651, was caught and imprisoned in the Tower of London, escaped, and then went off to serve in the Russian army, where he was promoted general and made a noble of Russia. Once Charles II had become King, Tam returned and, in charge of the King's forces in Scotland, suppressed the Covenanters with 'stern measures', as the guide-book to The House of the Binns puts it, rather ambiguously. Nevertheless, Tam seems not to have been a man without feelings; he spared some of the women and children following the covenanting forces, and later resigned his commission in disgust when they were executed. At home, he carried out experiments in gardening and arboriculture and added a west wing to his House.

The House itself has an interesting collection of furniture, paintings and objects from three centuries, including, in the Blue Room, a good collection of ceramics. This same room also contains a portrait of General Tam with his hair uncut. Outside there are walks in the grounds, and the hill behind the House affords commanding views over the Firth of Forth. The tower here cost £26. 10s. when it was built by James Dalyell (1774–1841) – money James won in an after-dinner wager! It could be, too, if you linger long enough in the grounds, that you will see the ghost of General Tam riding on a white charger across the ruined bridge over Errack Burn and up to the House.

The entrance to The House of the Binns is on the A904 just over ½ mile west of junction 2. From junction 3 turn right on to the A803 and then right again on to the A904 almost immediately, and it is about 1½ miles. The park is open on Easter Saturday, Sunday and Monday and then daily between May and September from 10.00 to 7.00, the House daily in the same months except Fridays from 2.00 to 5.00 (last admissions 4.30).

JUNCTIONS 2 & 3 BLACKNESS CASTLE

Immediately next to the entrance to The House of the Binns, the B9109 leads off the A904 north towards the Firth and **Blackness Castle**. The Blackness Hotel is at the corner of the two roads. The Castle stands on a rocky outcrop in the Firth of Forth – a strategic position commanding traffic in the Firth. The great rectangular tower was built in the 15th century, and in the 16th was surrounded by a courtyard shaped rather like a ship, with another tower and a triangular bastion. Blackness is certainly worth a visit if you are a castle devotee. If not, and you simply enjoy an occasional stroll round one, I suggest waiting until junction 3 and Linlithgow Palace. Blackness is open on weekdays from 9.30 to 7.00, Sundays from 2.00 to 7.00, between April and September; and from 9.30 to 4.00 on weekdays except Monday afternoons and Tuesdays, and from 2.00 to 4.00 on Sundays, during the rest of the year.

JUNCTION 3 BO'NESS

Nearest to junction 3, but equally accessible from junctions 2 and 4, is the little coastal town of **Bo'ness**. From junction 2, you simply follow the A904 all the way; from junction 3, take the A803 right and then join the A904 almost immediately; and from junction 4 take the side road to Polmonthill and then turn right on to the B904;

this soon meets the A904 and brings you into Bo'ness from the west.

Two centuries ago Bo'ness (or Borrowstounness as it was originally known) was the third most important port in Scotland. It was Glasgow's east-coast harbour, and 17 brigantines and eight sloops sailed out of the port. But the opening of the Forth & Clyde Canal in 1790 put paid to its prosperity. As always, improvement was two-edged: the canal ended at Grangemouth, and so that town's prospects grew, while Bo'ness's suffered. After nearly two centuries of decline, Bo'ness is now beginning to revive. A Town Trail around the centre takes you past some fine 18th-century buildings, including the **Tobacco Warehouse** in **Scotland's Close**, one of the best-preserved streets in the town. The recently-formed Heritage Trust has plans to develop features in the town focusing on the area's involvement in salt, fireclay, timber, whaling and maritime trade.

Well worth visiting in Bo'ness is the **Bo'ness & Kinneil Railway**. Although many preserved steam railways have opened in England in the last 10 years or so, they are much rarer north of the border. As yet operations at Bo'ness are on a relatively modest scale. The plan is ultimately to run services from Bo'ness inland for 4¾ miles to Manuel near Whitecross – the entire length of the original Slamannan & Borrowstounness Railway, opened in 1851 and used to transport coal from the Monklands coalfield to the port at Bo'ness. For the moment, however, the Scottish Railway Preservation Society, which owns the railway, has bought two miles or so of track and operates services at weekends over most of it. The terminus is on the foreshore at Bo'ness, just east of the town centre. The SRPS has a large and impressive collection of carriages, wagons and steam locomotives, some of which work the railway, and there are a number of interesting historical items. The station building originally came from Wormit, at the south end of the Tay Bridge, the footbridge from Murthly, on the Highland main line, and the 1842 train shed from Edinburgh Haymarket. A 'visitor trail' now operates around the station site. Refreshments are available at the station or alternatively you can eat your own food in the picnic area, and there is a book and souvenir shop.

A little way out of town west on the A904 – and past some depressing scenes of industrial dereliction, including a closed colliery (this area has suffered badly from the decline in traditional heavy industries) – you come to **Kinneil House** and the **Kinneil Museum**. The House, the seat of the Dukes of Hamilton in the 16th and 17th centuries, has lovely wall paintings and decorated ceilings. The cottage in the grounds is where James Watt experimented on his steam engine; the first was installed at a local colliery in 1765. The Museum is housed in a beautifully reconstructed 17th-century stable block, and there are well laid out displays on the history of the town and its industries, including coal, salt, pottery and iron. Upstairs there is more on the 200-year-old Bo'ness pottery industry (sadly, nothing remains in operation today), and a fascinating section on the discovery nearby on the Kinneil Estate of an Antonine Wall fortlet. (The Wall marked the furthest point of the Roman advance in these islands; built in about AD 142, it was held for only a few years before the Romans withdrew to Hadrian's Wall again.) Between April and September the House is open on Mondays, Wednesdays, Thursdays and Saturdays from 9.30 to 7.00, on Tuesdays from 9.30 to 1.00 and on Sundays from 2.00 to 7.00; during the rest of the year the times are 9.30 to 4.00 on Mondays, Wednesdays, Thursdays and Saturdays, 9.30 to 1.00 on Tuesdays and 2.00 to 4.00 on Sundays. Times for the Museum and fortlet are 10.00 to 5.00 on Mondays to Saturdays between May and September.

JUNCTIONS 3 & 4 LINLITHGOW PALACE

If I had time for only a single stop off the M9, it would be at **Linlithgow**, where the **Palace** is a scenic and historic must. Access is easiest from junction 3 (turn left on to the A803), but if you have time carry on to junction 4, as the motorway gives you a superb view of Linlithgow Loch and the Palace on the far side. If you are travelling from the north, use junction 4 in any case, as you can't get off at junction 3. The route from junction 4 is simple: turn east on to the A803 and you will reach the town in just under 4 miles.

The present Palace (by no means the first building on the site) has been described by one expert as 'a fine mix of the best contemporary residential appointments with up-to-date fortifications'. It was started by James I of Scotland in 1425, and no less than £4500 was spent in the next decade. James certainly seems to have got his money's worth. It is a handsome structure, imposing and formidable from wherever you look at it. Inside, one of the most remarkable rooms is the Great Hall, or Lyon Chamber, on the first floor. This occupies the whole of one side of the Palace, running from the north-east corner tower to the south-east one. The royal table was placed on a dais at the south end of the Hall. It was here that the Scottish Parliament met in 1585. Subsequent monarchs carried out extensive improvements and additions – the elaborate King's Fountain in the courtyard was commissioned by James V in the 1530s – and three Kings, James IV, James V (who, like his daughter Mary Queen of Scots, was born here) and James VI lived at Linlithgow for quite long periods. After the Union of England and Scotland, royal visits decreased (although Oliver Cromwell spent much of the winter of 1650/1 here), and in 1746 troops quartered in the Palace acciden-

Linlithgow Palace and the Loch

tally started a fire. The building was gutted, leaving the stark and impressive ruin you see today. The Palace is open on weekdays from 9.30 and from 2.00 on Sundays. Closing time is 7.00 between April and September and 4.00 during the rest of the year.

Linlithgow is a pleasant place to spend an hour or so, and a town trail takes you past some of the town's historic architecture. Good places to eat include the Four Marys in the High Street and the Coffee Neuk, just by the path up to the Palace from the High Street. There are also good towpath walks beside the **Union Canal**, which runs just south of the town centre. The canal was built in 1818 to link Edinburgh to the Forth & Clyde Canal and can boast three handsome aqueducts. The small **Canal Museum** at Linlithgow, which occupies a stable used by barge horses, has interesting displays on canal ecology and history and also on the construction and operation of the canal. The packet-boat *Victoria* operates regular trips from the canal basin by the Museum. Despite her name, the boat was built in 1974, although her design faithfully follows that of a Victorian steam packet. The Museum's opening hours are from 2.00 to 5.00 on Saturdays and Sundays from Easter to September. The Museum is signposted from the east end of the High Street. Turn sharp right under the railway, then left over the canal bridge and immediately right.

JUNCTIONS 3 & 4 BEECRAIGS COUNTRY PARK

South of Linlithgow some pleasant hilly country offers walking possibilities. In the **Beecraigs Country Park** there is canoeing, sailing, archery, rock-climbing, orienteering and – perhaps most important of all for the casual visitor – some excellent walks. The best is probably up to the top of Cockleroy Hill, where a view stretching north from the Bass Rock off North Berwick to the peaks of Ben More and Ben Vorlich awaits you. If a climb seems too much of a good thing, plenty of other paths and marked trails criss-cross the 500 acres of woodlands here. Two unusual features are a trout farm and a deer park. The trout farm is open to the public on most Sundays from 10.00 to 4.00; on some summer days table trout can be bought direct from the farm. The large herd of red deer can be seen from a pedestrian walkway and viewing platform. The best way to reach the Park is to take the Preston road south from Linlithgow. If you are coming from the Palace, turn left at the west end of the High Street, opposite the junction with the A706. Leaving the houses of Linlithgow behind you, drive on for about 1 mile until you reach Beecraigs Wood. Bear right for the car park for Cockleroy, keep straight on for the Balvormie car park in the middle of the woods, or turn left for the loch car park, the Park Centre and the deer park and trout farm. The Park Centre, housed in a distinctive log cabin, contains exhibitions on the Park and information about all the various activities there. Its opening times are as follows: summer months, 9.00 to 5.00 Mondays to Thursdays, 9.00 to 4.00 Fridays, 1.00 to 6.00 Saturdays and 10.00 to 6.00 Sundays; winter months, 9.00 to 5.00 Mondays to Thursdays, 11.00 to 4.00 Sundays (closed Fridays and Saturdays).

If the landscape appeals, continue straight through Beecraigs Wood from the Balvormie car park. Emerging from the forest, take the first right and then the first left (this is a very sharp turn) for **Cairnpapple Hill**. From the lay-by on the road it is a short, breezy walk to the top of this 4000-year-old burial place. No fewer than three separate groups of ancient peoples buried their dead here over a period of some two thousand years. From here the quickest way back to the motorway is along side roads to Torphichen, then north on the B792, briefly left on to the A706, and then right on to the A801, which leads direct to junction 4. Apart from passing through some attractive country, this route also takes you near **Torphichen Preceptory**, the only Scottish house of the Crusading Knights of St John of Jerusalem; the tower and vaulted transepts survive. Opening times are Mondays to Saturdays 9.30 to 7.00, Sundays 2.00 to 7.00, between April and September; 9.30 to 4.00, Sundays 2.00 to 4.00, during the rest of the year.

JUNCTION 4 MUIRAVONSIDE COUNTRY PARK

If time were limited, but I still wanted a quick stop for some fresh air, I would leave the motorway here at junction 4. My goal? The **Muiravonside Country Park**, about 3 miles off. Take the A801 south from the junction, and then turn left on to the B825, back towards Linlithgow; the Park entrance is on the right after a mile or so. This is the best kind of country park. There are no sophisticated amenities – and certainly none of the over-commercialized sort of attractions you often get in privately run establishments. The Park is simply an attractive area of country, some 170 acres, in which you can relax in whatever way you want to: bird-watching, looking for interesting plants, walking – or simply sitting back and letting the rural peace sink in. The land once belonged to Muiravonside House, and the estate has changed relatively little since the 18th century. The plan is to keep it that way, and the facilities that have been introduced for visitors – a visitor centre in the home farm, a barbecue site and children's play area, car parks, etc. – are all discreetly and sensitively designed. A disused mine shaft, old limekilns, a mill lade (or stream) and other industrial remains are a particularly interesting feature of the Park, and just outwith its boundaries, but still within easy walking distance, is the Union Canal and the aqueduct on which it crosses the river Avon. All in all, well worth the short detour from the motorway. The visitor centre is open daily from 10.00 to 6.00 during the summer, at weekends only from 10.00 to 4.00 during the winter.

Junctions 5 and 6 are half-junctions leading west to Falkirk and east to Grangemouth. Leave the motorway at junction 5 if you are coming from the south, at junction 6 from the north. To join it, use junction 5 if you want to go south, junction 6 if you are northbound.

JUNCTION 5 CALLENDAR PARK
Callendar Park is the principal outdoor attraction in Falkirk. There are pleasant walks – especially attractive in spring when the daffodils are out and a couple of months later when the rhododendrons and azaleas are in full bloom – and all the usual park activities, such as boating, pitch and putt, children's play areas and so on. Callendar House is a striking mansion built in the style of a French château. A small section of the Antonine Wall can also be seen in the Park, together with a slightly longer stretch of the ditch. The ditch, which is 6 to 10 feet deep, runs west from the College of Education for about ½ mile. The wall, about 1½ feet high, is slightly to its south, between two lines of trees. (Enthusiasts for Roman Scotland should not fail to visit **Rough Castle**, near Bonnybridge, off the B816, 6 miles west of Falkirk; the nearest motorway exit is junction 1 of the M876. This is the best preserved Antonine Wall fort, and the ramparts and ditches can be seen clearly.) To get to the Park from junction 5, turn left on to the A905 and then right on to the A803; the Park entrance is on your left after about ½ mile. From junction 6, turn right on to the A905, right again on to the A904 at the roundabout, and right for a third time on to the A803 in the centre of Falkirk. The Park entrance is now almost immediately on the right. Callendar Park is open daily throughout the year. Other attractions in Falkirk include the **Coasters Arena**, a major events centre which is also the largest roller-skating arena in the country (times for roller-skating are Friday, Saturday and Sunday evenings and Saturday afternoons), and the **Mariner Centre**, which is an exotic swimming pool with all the latest in palms, tropical areas, chutes and so on. Places to eat in the town include the Cladhan and the Art Nouveau Heatherley Restaurant.

JUNCTION 7 CULROSS
Junctions 7 and 8 are junctions with the M876 and between the two the motorways run in tandem. From junction 7 the M876 runs

north-east for 2 miles to the junction of the A905 and the A876. If you cross the Firth of Forth on Kincardine Bridge (the A876) and turn right on to the coast road, the B9037, you come after about 4 miles to the royalburgh of **Culross**, a National Trust for Scotland property described as a 'unique survival, a town which time has passed by; the most complete example in Scotland today of a burgh of the 17th and 18th centuries'. Culross is a fascinating place, with a lengthy trail to guide visitors round everything of interest: certainly worth a visit.

Junction 8 is the link with the M876 going south towards Cumbernauld. There is restricted access. You can join the M876 from the northbound carriageway of the M9, and you can drive from the M876 on to the southbound carriageway of the M9, going towards Edinburgh.

JUNCTION 9 BANNOCKBURN

Junction 9 is rather a disappointment. The motorway signs read 'Bannockburn', and as soon as you leave the motorway there are clear signposts to the **visitor centre** 1 mile along the A872 towards Stirling. But when you get there, you may find it something of a letdown: at least that was my reaction. The visitor centre is an elegant building and attractively laid out inside, to the same high standards that many National Trust for Scotland projects achieve. The exhibition traces the history of Robert the Bruce from the period before Bannockburn through the battle itself to the events immediately following, and also includes a section called 'The Kingdom of the Scots' which highlights characters and events in Scottish history between the Declaration of Independence and the Union with England in 1707. The importance of Bannockburn in the history of Scotland cannot be over-emphasized. The battle (as the audio-visual presentation in the centre explains) was the culmination of Robert the Bruce's eight-year War of Independence to rid his kingdom of the English occupation. Thereafter Scotland became an independent country again, and remained one for the next four hundred years. The English under Edward II were routed. The King himself survived, but only by fleeing ignominiously and hotly pursued to the coast at Dunbar, where he found a small rowing-boat to take him to Berwick. Almost all the English footsoldiers and archers were killed or captured, seven hundred cavalry were left dead and many nobles were taken prisoner and held to ransom; the spoils of victory, principally the English supplies, were valued at £200,000 even then. Most of the battlefield has now vanished – covered by 20th-century housing estates – and the rest had to be bought before it went the same way. What remains is a flat and rather featureless piece of land, hardly improved by a huge, and in my opinion very ugly, bronze equestrian statue of the Bruce. The statue is set in the middle of a rotunda, built to focus on the English approach route from Falkirk and on Stirling Castle to the north, which they were trying to relieve. The visitor centre is open daily from 10.00 to 6.00 between April and October.

JUNCTION 10 STIRLING CASTLE

The motorway is now crossing the glacial flood plain of the river Forth. There are fine views all around, to the Gargunnocks behind, the Ochils to the north-east and the distant Highlands in the north. In the foreground, sentinel-like and dominating the surrounding land, stands a huge isolated mass of volcanic rock, with the looming mass of **Stirling Castle** at its top. Junction 10 is the one to take for Stirling, although if you have been to the visitor centre at Bannockburn it is quicker to continue into town on the A872. Another excellent view of the Castle may be gained from the motorway between junctions 10 and 11.

The first records of a castle here date from the early 12th century, which is fairly late for a site of this strategic importance, overlooking a vital crossing-place on the river Forth. It seems almost certain that a castle was here well before that, however, and probably prehistoric fortifications as well. In the late 13th and early 14th centuries the Castle was taken and retaken by the Scots and the English as Scotland struggled for independence. However the structure we see today dates not from that time but from several centuries later. James IV and V built prodigiously here, converting a rough-and-ready castle into a great palace fit for kings and quite as grand and splendid as any of the renaissance palaces going up on the continent at the same time. James IV built the great defensive forework across the entire width of the Castle rock, laid out the magnificent Upper Square and constructed the imposing Great Hall. James V was responsible for the magnificent palace, also on Upper Square, a building that the guide-book rightly describes as 'of outstanding historical and architectural importance' and as one of the earliest attempts to create a classical façade in Britain. Later monarchs continued to improve and adapt, most notably James VI, who reconstructed the chapel. After 1603, when James accepted the English crown, the Castle's importance as a royal seat diminished, and by the 18th century it was used merely as a military headquarters and barracks. It remained such, in one form or another, until as recently as 1964, and only since then has it become possible to wipe out the signs of military occupation and restore the buildings to their former full grandeur.

The north entrance, Stirling Castle

The tour of Stirling Castle must count as one of the major highlights of the M9. If you are in a hurry, restrict your visit to the major buildings – the ones mentioned above, plus the King's Old Building. If you have plenty of time, the north gate and the nether bailey, the kitchens, the Elphinstone Tower and the outer defences are all worth a look. From the wall walks there are majestic views. There is an excellent shop and visitor centre, where a multi-screen audiovisual show provides a dramatic introduction to the story of the Castle. The Castle is open from 9.30 to 6.00 Mondays to Saturdays and from 11.00 to 6.00 on Sundays between April and September; and during the rest of the year from 9.30 to 5.05 on Mondays to Saturdays and from 12.30 to 4.20 on Sundays.

The **Top of the Town**, as the streets around the Castle are known, is well worth exploring. There are grand 16th- and 17th-century houses, built by the Scottish nobility for their residence near the court, and the 13th-century Church of the Holy Rude, where James VI of Scotland and I of England was crowned. These streets form the backdrop for frequent medieval markets and fairs and similar events, and in **Old Town Prison and Court** in Broad Street there is a laser and hologram show and an exhibition on the history of Stirling. Also worth seeing in the lower part of the town is **Stirling Bridge**, on the A9 going north. Built in about 1400, the bridge was for centuries the lowest crossing-point over the Forth. **Cambuskenneth Abbey**, 1 mile east of the town, is the ruins of an Augustinian abbey founded in 1147; Robert the Bruce held his Parliament here in 1326. Opening times are Mondays to Saturdays 9.30 to 7.00, Sundays 2.00 to 7.00, between April and September, and 9.30 to 4.00, Sundays 2.00 to 4.00, during the rest of the year.

Another landmark visible from miles off – and, like the Castle, especially striking when it is floodlit at night – is the **Wallace Monument**, built in 1870 to commemorate Sir William Wallace, hero of the Scottish resistance to English rule. Wallace defeated the English at the Battle of Stirling in 1297, when he captured the Castle, but was defeated the following year at Falkirk by Edward I, and was eventually captured and hanged. The Monument stands 300 feet up on the Abbey Craig: it is a stiff climb up (there are 242 steps), but the effort is more than repaid. Outside, the views are stunning, and there is a statue of Wallace on the side of the tower. Inside the Monument there are three rooms. In the Wallace Sword Room, which contains the famous painting 'The Battle of Bannockburn' by Sir William Allan and stained-glass windows depicting the Scottish crown and regalia and Scottish arms, two audio-visual presentations are given, one on the history and wildlife of the Forth valley, the other on Wallace himself; it is said that Wallace directed his forces during the battle from the top of the Abbey Craig. Upstairs, the Hall of Arms contains a collection of medieval and later weapons and more stained-glass showing, among other things, the Scottish lion. The Hall of Heroes on the second floor has busts of a varied collection of Scottish heroes. Among their ranks are Robert the Bruce, John Knox, Allan Ramsay, Robert Burns, Adam Smith, James Watt, Sir Walter Scott, Thomas Carlyle, David Livingstone and W. E. Gladstone. Another dramatic audio-visual presentation focuses on each hero in turn and sets his life and deeds in the context of Scottish history. The Monument is open daily from 10.00 to 6.30 between May and August, daily from 10.00 to 5.30 in April and September, and daily except Wednesdays and Thursdays in February, March and October. There is a shop and a tea room.

Junction 11, 1 mile or so south of Dunblane, is the northern point of the M9. Ahead, there are various routes north into the Highlands or west across to Oban and the lovely west-coast islands. **Dunblane** itself is a pleasant little town. Most of the **cathedral**, set in a small square, dates from the 13th century, the oldest part from about 1100. After the Reformation the nave stayed roofless for 300 years, and the church was restored at the end of the 19th century. There are some interesting shops in the town, including an excellent silversmith's.

JUNCTION 11 DOUNE

Doune, 4 miles west of junction 11 along the B824, boasts an extremely well-preserved **Castle** built in the late 14th century and much restored in the 19th and 20th centuries. The front of the Castle is a massive rectangular block of stone, designed as a formidable stronghold against attack. Behind it lies a large quadrangle enclosed by a curtain wall. About 1 mile north-west of the town centre, on the A94, you come to the **Doune Motor Museum**. The Museum houses Lord Moray's personal collection of thoroughbred cars, both vintage and post-vintage. Many of the most celebrated names of motoring are here: Lagonda, Hispano Suiza, Rolls-Royce, Morgan, Maserati and so on. Opening times are from 10.00 to 5.00 daily. There is a picnic area, a shop and a cafeteria.

The M90

Rosyth to Perth

INTRODUCTION

The M90 runs between the Firth of Forth and Perth and the Grampians. Unlike the M9, which is chiefly in low-lying country and merely hints at the grandeur of the Highlands ahead, the M90 passes straight through some spectacular landscape. From junction 4 northwards, the route is among the most impressive stretches of motorway in the country. There are plenty of things to do off the motorway as well, with variety enough to suit all tastes.

Junction 1 is barely noticeable. Having paid your toll at the southern end, you cross the Forth Road Bridge on the A90, the main road north out of Edinburgh. There is about 1 mile of dual carriageway on the north bank and the A90 simply becomes motorway, without any fuss or bother on your part.

But even before you cross the Forth, there are two grand houses and a shoreline walk. Each is well worth breaking your journey for, and each, incidentally, is as easily accessible from the M9. The houses are Hopetoun and Dalmeny, the seats of two great families, the Hopes and the Roseberys. The walk is from South Queensferry round Hope Point and then down to the coast to the ferry at Cramond.

JUNCTION 1 HOPETOUN

Hopetoun must be one of the most splendid and impressive houses (or mansions – the word 'house' implies something far too small) described in this book. The approach makes it seem yet more magnificent. From the A90 take the junction for the A904 just south of the toll booths, and drive west towards Bo'ness. Signs for the house then direct you along the shore road, from where there are fine views across to Fife and beyond the two bridges, road and rail, towards the open sea. (A tiny point jutting out into the water would make a good picnic spot.) A drive to the left leads gently uphill through woodland towards the house. And here a tiny trick of the

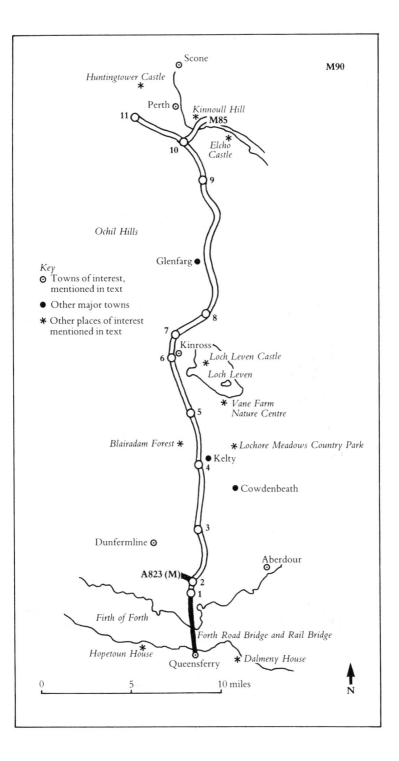

landscape creates a stunning visual effect. You emerge from the trees on to formal, well-manicured lawns, expecting to see the house laid out before you. But no. The land rises slightly, and the house sits in the dip beyond, revealing itself slowly, from the roof and chimney downwards. When eventually you do see it all, it is glorious – a perfect example of what, for me at least, is a perfect style.

William Adam was responsible for the house as it now appears, along with his two sons Robert and John who did the interior decoration after their father's death in 1748. But the original house, which chiefly survives in the west side of the main block, is 50 years older than that, having been built between 1699 and 1703 by Sir William Bruce, who designed Holyrood Palace in Edinburgh. The tour takes in all the finest rooms, and includes the best work of both architects. The Entrance Hall is classical, with marble reliefs and a marble chimney-piece, while the Garden Room has fine, warm oak panelling. The staircase is superbly decorated; fruit, flowers, wheat-ears and peapods are everywhere, on the panelled walls, on borders, friezes and cornices. The State Apartments include the Yellow Drawing Room with its fine ceiling, the elaborately rococo Red Drawing Room, and the State Dining Room. There are paintings by Gainsborough, Teniers, Canaletto and Raeburn, and a museum with family papers, china and so on. Outdoors, red deer and the rare four-horned black St Kilda sheep roam in the parkland. There are walled gardens to walk in, and a splendid avenue of limes too, plus a nature trail, a wildlife exhibition and an information centre. In short, Hopetoun is a must. The house is open daily from 11.00 to 5.00 at Easter and from May to mid-September, the walled garden centre all year from 10.00 to 5.30. Refreshments are available, and there is a shop.

JUNCTION 1 DALMENY HOUSE

From 18th-century classical to 19th-century Gothic at **Dalmeny House**. The House was built in 1815 and set the style for the numerous baronial mansions scattered throughout Scotland. Inside there are paintings, furniture, tapestries, porcelain in abundance – most notably some of the best pieces from Mentmore, formerly the Roseberys' English home in Buckinghamshire. In the Napoleon Room a collection of Napoleonic memorabilia includes paintings, the Emperor's shaving stand from Malmaison, items used in his St Helena exile and (perhaps perversely in a room dedicated to his long-standing foe) the red leather campaign chair Wellington used in the Peninsula Wars and at Waterloo. In the Dining Room there are busts and portraits (among them works by Gainsborough and Reynolds) of many famous 18th-century figures, including Admiral

Hopetown House, West Lothian

Rodney, Dr Johnson, Edward Gibbon and Charles James Fox. Outside, you can walk in the enclosed garden and the garden valley behind it, where the rhododendrons and azaleas make a good show in early summer. The House is open Sundays to Thursdays from 2.00 to 5.00 between May and September, and home-made teas are served. To get to Dalmeny from Edinburgh turn right off the A90 on to the B924 about 2 miles before reaching the Forth Road Bridge. If you are coming across the bridge from the north, take the slip road left just after the toll booth, turn left at the roundabout on to the A800 and then immediately left again down into Queensferry. When you reach the shore, turn right on to the B924 and follow the road under the Forth Rail Bridge until you reach the entrance to the House.

The 4½-mile **shore walk** runs through Dalmeny Woods and there are fine views everywhere. Hound Point takes its name from the ghostly dog said to howl shortly before the death of each laird of Barnbougle, the old castle (now restored as a private house) on the shore almost in front of Dalmeny House. The walk finishes at the ferry across the mouth of the river Almond at Cramond; the ferry runs daily except Fridays from 9.00 to 1.00 and from 2.00 to 7.00 (4.00 in winter). Dogs and picnicking are not permitted on the walk, which begins just beneath the Forth Rail Bridge, where the B924 strikes inland from the shoreline.

Everywhere here the two bridges intrude on the view, and down on the shore at Queensferry (where there are a few cafés and pubs but not much else) you feel positively dwarfed by them. The Firth was first crossed in 1851, by a 'floating railway' that carried goods trains on large flat steamers. Then the **Forth Rail Bridge** was opened in 1890 and, eventually, after decades of pressure, the **Forth Road Bridge** in 1964. The cantilever rail bridge is over 1½ miles long, and at the time of construction the two spans, each of 1710 feet, were the longest ever built. The central span of the Forth Road Bridge, the largest suspension bridge in Europe when it was built, is 3300 feet, the two side spans 1340 feet.

JUNCTION 1 ABERDOUR

On the north side of the Forth, there is little to recommend except a diversion east along the A921 to **Aberdour**, 5 miles off. Many of the **Castle's** buildings date from the 16th and 17th centuries, and not much remains of the original 14th-century great tower. You can have a pleasant stroll in the streets around the harbour and along the jetty, and the bathing off the long sandy beach is excellent. According to the local tourist leaflet, 'the clear water, the sparkling waves, the sandy beach itself, are temptresses which should not be refused'. I couldn't have put it better myself!

JUNCTION 2 DUNFERMLINE

From junction 2, the A823(M) – a tiny spur motorway no more than 1 mile long – takes you on to the A823 just south of **Dunfermline**. The town centre is equally easy to reach from junction 3, along the A907. Dunfermline is associated with some of the most famous names of Scottish history, both medieval and modern. Robert the Bruce is one of seven monarchs buried in **Dunfermline Abbey,** and the town was the birthplace of Andrew Carnegie, the handloom weaver's son who emigrated to the USA and made a multi-million dollar fortune as an ironmaster. Your first stop will surely be the majestic, greystone abbey, which is well worth a visit. The fine nave is late Norman and was built in the 12th century, while the Gothic choir was finished by 1226. It was not until 1818, in the midst of reconstruction work, that the Bruce's grave was located for certain. There was a bizarre reason why the experts knew it was his: the breast bone had been neatly cut and the heart extracted. The King had left instructions for his heart to be removed and taken on crusade to the Holy Land. This duly happened, although the heart was eventually returned to Melrose, in the Borders. South of the abbey are the ruins of the Benedictine house founded in the 11th century by Queen Margaret.

Memorials to Andrew Carnegie are scattered throughout the town. There is the **Carnegie Library**, the first of the 2500 or so public libraries he endowed throughout the world. There is the 76-acre **Pittencrieff Park,** just to the west of the abbey, which you enter through some imposing gates named after Louise Carnegie, Andrew's wife. Carnegie bought Pittencrieff House and its grounds for £45,000 and at the same time endowed its trustees with several million dollars to use to provide 'sweetness and light for the toiling masses of Dunfermline'. There are fine walks in the grounds, which boast an aviary and pets corner, a formal garden and a floral hall and greenhouses, and the house itself can be visited. A visitor centre occupies the ground floor, and there are costume displays on the first. The house is open in the summer months daily from 11.00 to 5.00 except Tuesdays. One of the best places to eat in Dunfermline is here at the centre of the Park, where there is the Peacock Restaurant and also a cafeteria if you simply want a cup of tea or a snack. Also in the Park are the remains of **Malcolm Canmore's Tower,** the stronghold of Malcolm Canmore, one of the earliest kings of Scotland. It was Malcolm, you may remember from your school Shakespeare, who killed Macbeth, who had himself slain Malcolm's father Duncan. The weaver's cottage in Moodie Street where Carnegie was born is now the **Andrew Carnegie Birthplace Museum**; displays tell the story of his life and how he made all those millions. Opening hours are from 11.00 to 5.00 on Mondays to Saturdays (with an extension to 8.00 on Wednesdays), 2.00 to 5.00 on Sundays, between April and October, and 2.00 to 4.00 daily during the rest of the year. More energetic homage to Carnegie can be paid in the **Carnegie Centre**, in Pilmuir Street, where facilities include a fitness room and gymnasium, turkish and areatone baths and a traditional swimming-pool.

The 7½-mile drive from junction 3 to **Lochore Meadows Country Park** (described below) is longer but probably just as quick as the route from junction 4. Take the A907 east to Crossgates, and then turn left on to the A910 to Cowdenbeath and Lochgelly, where you turn left on to the B920.

JUNCTION 4 BLAIRADAM

With junction 4 you reach some really fine countryside and what in my opinion is the best picnic and walking spot on the entire motorway: **Blairadam Forest**. Take the B914 west from the junction and turn right after about ½ mile. The small forest road winds slowly downhill towards the tiny visitor centre, with good views to Benarty Hill and Loch Leven beyond. You can walk and picnic anywhere you like in these 300 acres of lovely country; when I was there in mid-autumn the colours were delightful. Refreshingly, the Forestry Commission makes no attempt to provide sophisticated facilities. There are no guided trails or routes, hides or observation points, picnic benches and tables – simply the chance to use your senses. There is much animal and bird life here. Look out in particular for roe deer and, for a pleasant change, both red and grey squirrel.

JUNCTION 4 LOCHORE MEADOWS COUNTRY PARK

Blairadam is so magnificent, and so conveniently close to the motorway, that it rather overshadows the **Lochore Meadows Country Park** 5 miles to the east. This is a shame, because in its own rather more specialist way the Park is very interesting. Once there was slurry and waste here, subsidence and flooding. Now, in what is claimed to be the largest land reclamation scheme yet undertaken in Britain, rolling countryside has replaced the dereliction of the coalfields. The loch is the focal point of the Park, and there is sailing and canoeing and fishing. You can play golf, walk and study the wildlife which is gradually returning to the area. The visitor centre has an interesting display on the Park's history and ecology, and recounts in fascinating detail the pioneering land reclamation techniques used here, which included the planting of some 200,000 young trees. At the entrance to the car park are the ruins of the 12th-century Lochore Castle, and, what I found most moving, the renovated winding-gear of the Mary Pitt: a monument to the generations of men who worked the difficult Fife coalfields. The route from junction 4 is east along the A909 to just short of Cowdenbeath, then left on to the A910, and left again in Lochgelly on to the B920. You can get to Cowdenbeath from junction 3 as well (see above), and the Park can also be reached via junction 5 (see below).

There are some good choices at junction 5. If it is a meal out you want, take the B9097 west along the foot of the Cleith Hills, and the Nivingston House Hotel is reached on your left after about 1¾ miles. (Reservations are advisable, as the restaurant has an excellent reputation.) The country is pleasant here, and there are plenty of opportunities for walks and picnics. If these are your aim, take the B9097 east, turn right almost immediately on to the B996 and then left again after about ½ mile. This road runs along the side of Benarty Hill through lovely scenery, and there is the possibility of walks up to the summit. (But beware: the map marks a danger area at the extreme west of the range.) You can go on to the Lochore Meadows Country Park (see page 304) by following the road through Ballingry and turning right on to the B920.

JUNCTION 5 VANE FARM NATURE CENTRE
But for most people the obvious attraction here is **Loch Leven** – and, in particular, the RSPB's **Vane Farm Nature Centre** on the southern shore. (Take the B9097 east from the motorway.) The whole of the loch – 3946 acres including the seven islands and land adjacent to the shore – is a national nature reserve. As such, humans must take second place. The loch is primarily a sanctuary for birds, although some research work is permitted. Visitors such as you and I can use the public access areas at Findatie (at the south-east end of the loch) and Burleigh Sands, in Kirkgate Park in Kinross and on Castle Island. But my recommendation is to avoid these and make for Vane Farm, where there is an observation room equipped with high-powered binoculars, a nature trail over the hillside, a hide (restricted opening to the general public) and, as so often at RSPB reserves, an excellent shop with some really high-quality goods.

About 130 species of bird visit or live on the loch. Ducks and geese are the most numerous. About a thousand pairs of duck nest here in summer, mostly on St Serfs Island, and in winter numbers go up to as many as ten thousand. Tufted duck are the most common (about 10 per cent of the entire British community live here), and

305

there are also mallard, wigeon, gadwall, shoveler, teal and many other species. In October, spectacular flights of geese – principally pink-footed, but with many greylag as well – arrive from Greenland and Iceland, to rest and feed after their long journey. Some stay here all winter, others eventually move south. Canada, barnacle, brent and white-fronted geese have also been seen recently. On land, in the woodland behind the visitor centre, there are kestrel, rook, carrion crow and woodpigeon among many others, and peregrine, sparrow-hawk, buzzard and merlin have been seen.

Between April and Christmas the Vane Farm Nature Centre is open daily from 10.00 to 5.00; in January, February and March opening hours are from 10.00 to 4.00 on Saturdays and Sundays. From the Centre you can return to the motorway at junction 5, or continue to Kinross and junction 6 along the B996 (see below). The circuit of the loch can be made by road, and there are some fine views from the B9097 further east along the southern shore. After that, as you turn north on the B920 and then the A911, it is less interesting than you might expect. There is a pub and restaurant, the Balgedie Toll Tavern at Wester Balgedie (lunches and dinners are served). The return to the M90 can be at junction 7 or 8, or you can complete the entire circuit via Kinross.

JUNCTION 6 LOCH LEVEN CASTLE

At junction 6, **Kinross** is a pleasant small loch-side town with a reasonable selection of eating-places. Among them are the Bridgend Hotel, the Green Hotel and the Salutation Hotel. The main sight is **Loch Leven Castle** on Castle Island in the loch. A ferry (daily services throughout the summer) takes you across, and the trip is well worth making. The present Castle started life in the 14th century as a simple tower, almost square and with five storeys; two centuries later, a curtain wall was added to form an enclosure. The event for which the Castle is most famous – the moment when it hit the headlines of history – took place in May 1568, when Mary Queen of Scots escaped after 11 months of imprisonment on the island. The person who helped her was Willy Douglas, a young page-boy. While waiting at table, he managed to steal the keys to the Great Hall, locked the assembled company in and rowed Mary across the lake, having thrown the keys in: the keys were found three hundred years later. In Kinross, which is really little more than one long main street, there is a mill shop, and a pleasant lakeside beach, which would be a good spot to picnic. **Kinross Museum** has local collections, and the gardens of **Kinross House** (designed in 1692 by Sir William Bruce, whom we have already met at Hopetoun) are open daily from 2.00 to 7.00 between May and September. Yew hedges, rosebeds and herbaceous borders are the features for which it is particularly noted.

JUNCTIONS 7 & 8 BURLEIGH CASTLE

Junctions 7 and 8, west and east of Milnathort, have limited access. Travelling north, towards Perth, you can leave the motorway at junction 8 and join it at junction 7. Southbound, you leave at junction 7, and join at junction 8. There are several hotels in the village, including the Royal, the Thistle and the Jolly Beggars. If you have time, it is worth leaving the motorway here and taking the old road through Glen Farg to Bridge of Earn, returning to the motorway at junction 9. The circuit of Loch Leven can start or end here (see page 307), and ½ mile or so outside the village the A911 going east passes close to **Burleigh Castle**, which is complete except for its roof. This is a typical Scottish tower-house – basically simply a tower with a corbelled caphouse (chamber) at the top – and interestingly enough was built in about 1500. In England castles were hardly being built at this time, and comfortable country mansions were preferred. But in Scotland internal conflict lasted longer and was sharper, and fortified residences continued to be put up until well into the 17th century.

JUNCTION 9 ELCHO CASTLE

The next 10 miles on the M90 are a splendid route through the **Ochil Hills**, with plenty of dramatic scenery and views. Rather than take the motorway or the A90 straight on into Perth, there is a good excursion to be had on the side road round Moncrieffe Hill to **Elcho Castle**. Turn right at the north end of the village, just after crossing the bridge, and follow the road along the banks of the Earn and then back along the north-eastern side of the hill. Just before the tiny hamlet of Rhynd, there is a turning right on to a barely made-up track leading down through a farmyard to Elcho Castle. This is well worth a visit on two accounts: its commanding position on the river Tay and the inherent interest of the building itself. Recent restoration has left the Castle in a splendid state of repair. Its basis is a five-storey rectangular tower-house, to which no fewer than four towers, all slightly different shapes, have been added in apparently haphazard fashion. From Rhynd it is 2 miles along the same road to junction 10. The Castle is open on weekdays from 9.30, Sundays from 2.00. Closing time is 7.00 between May and September, 5.30 in March, April and October and 4.00 in winter months.

Junction 10 (which is also convenient for Elcho Castle, see above) is at the centre of some contorted motorway planning. Strictly speaking, what happens is this. The M90 swings left (north-west, that is) and continues 3 miles to the western edge of Perth, where it meets the A9. Another motorway – the M85 – swings right (north-east) high across the Tay on a very striking bridge and after 2 miles meets the A85 dual carriageway north to Dundee. This all sounds much more complicated than it really is, and the M85 is such a minute motorway (all of 2 miles, with no intermediate exits!) that it isn't even named on many maps. But the signposting at the approach to junction 10 is very clear, and you have enough time to decide what to do.

JUNCTION 10 PERTH

The easiest way of getting into **Perth** is to leave the M90 here at junction 10 and follow the A90 for 2 miles or so to the centre. I have always enjoyed visiting Perth. Maybe the river is the reason, maybe the lovely hills to the north rising to high mountains behind, but there is a sparkle about the city. The buildings are another reason, and the Perth Civic Trust has published several short walks around the town. (Details are available from the Tourist Office, itself housed in a notable building, the Round House, on the corner of Marshall Place and Tay Street.) Probably the most interesting walk is called 'Georgian Elegance in Perth'. Highlights are Rose Terrace, handsome enough to rival those in Edinburgh, and Barossa Place, Melville Street and Atholl Street. Plays were staged at the old Perth Theatre in Atholl Street, before the building became a warehouse and clothing factory in 1845. John Knox preached in **St John's Kirk** at the beginning of the Reformation in Scotland. The church, founded in 1126, is a fine example of mid-16th-century Gothic architecture. The **Museum and Art Gallery** has a particularly strong section on local history. (Opening times are Mondays to Saturdays from 10.00 to 1.00 and from 2.00 to 5.00.) The mid-19th century **St Ninian's Cathedral** in North Methven Street is the first cathedral built in Scotland since the Reformation; the architect was William Butterfield. I'm not all that an enthusiastic gardener, but I shall certainly return to **Branklyn Garden** on the Dundee Road, described as 'the finest two acres of private garden in the country'. Dwarf rhododendrons are a speciality here, and there are also conifers, Japanese orange-skinned birch and numerous beautiful small-leaved plants. The Garden is open daily from 9.30 to sunset between March and October. Eating places in the city are numerous (the Tourist Office has a full list), as are interesting shops; Scottish crafts and knitwear and Caithness glass are all available.

Just outside the city, but still within only a short distance of the motorway, are several attractions. Best of all, in my opinion, is

Kinnoull Hill on the north bank of the Tay. If you cross by the Perth Bridge, turn right at the far side on to Gowrie Street, and then left up Bowerswell Road. If you use Queen's Bridge, go left at the end along Dundee Road, and Bowerswell Road is on the right. There is a nature trail on the hill, but for most people the impressive views over Perth and to the mountains will be enough.

JUNCTION 10 SCONE

Scone, 2 miles north of Perth on the A93, is one of Scotland's most historic places, and was the capital of the ancient Pictish kingdom. The celebrated Stone of Destiny – the stone upon which all kings of Scotland were crowned from the mid-9th century onwards – was stolen from here by Edward I of England and taken to Westminster Abbey. It has never been returned. The present Palace, the most recent of several on the site, dates from the very beginning of the 19th century and has fine collections of furniture, ivories, clocks, china and needlework. The grounds, which run down to the banks of the Tay, are very attractive, and when I visited in autumn were a riot of browns, golds and oranges. Scone Palace is open from 9.30 to 5.00 on Mondays to Saturdays, 1.30 to 5.00 on Sundays (10.00 to 5.00 in July and August) between Good Friday and mid-October.

Three miles' driving west of Perth on the A85 brings you to **Huntingtower Castle**, starting-point in 1582 of the Raid of Ruthven, one of the oddest episodes of Scottish history and still surrounded by mystery. A group of nobles kidnapped the young James VI, but nobody is certain why. The Castle itself is a substantial one, on the banks of the river Almond with views to the Grampian Hills behind; worth a visit for castle enthusiasts, but less appealing for others. Opening times are Mondays to Saturdays 9.30 to 7.00, Sundays 2.00 to 7.00, between April and September, and 9.30 to 4.00, Sundays 2.00 to 4.00, during the rest of the year.

Index

ISBN 978-0-282-99431-0
PIBN 10874989

This book is a reproduction of an important historical work. Forgotten Books uses
state-of-the-art technology to digitally reconstruct the work, preserving the original format
whilst repairing imperfections present in the aged copy. In rare cases, an imperfection in
the original, such as a blemish or missing page, may be replicated in our edition. We do,
however, repair the vast majority of imperfections successfully; any imperfections that
remain are intentionally left to preserve the state of such historical works.

PROCEEDINGS

OF THE

𝔏iverpool 𝔊eological 𝔖ociety.

SESSION THE SIXTEENTH,

1874-5.

(The Authors having revised their own papers, are alone responsible for the facts and opinions expressed in them.)

PART I—VOL. III.

LIVERPOOL:
COURIER PRINTING WORKS, VICTORIA STREET.

1875.

PROCEEDINGS

OF THE

𝕷iverpool 𝕲eological 𝕾ociety.

SESSION SIXTEEN TO NINETEEN,

1874-78.

EDITED BY THE HON. SECRETARY.

(The Authors having revised their own papers, are alone responsible for the facts and opinions expressed in them.)

VOL III.

LIVERPOOL:

C. TINLING & CO., PRINTERS, VICTORIA STREET.

—

1878.

S+

212948

TABLE OF CONTENTS.

PROCEEDINGS

OF THE

𝕷𝖎𝖛𝖊𝖗𝖕𝖔𝖔𝖑 𝕲𝖊𝖔𝖑𝖔𝖌𝖎𝖈𝖆𝖑 𝕾𝖔𝖈𝖎𝖊𝖙𝖞.

SESSION THE SIXTEENTH,

1874-5.

(The Authors having revised their own papers, are alone responsible for the facts and opinions expressed in them.)

PART I—VOL. III.

LIVERPOOL:

COURIER PRINTING WORKS, VICTORIA STREET.

1875.

OFFICERS, 1874—5.

President.
T. MELLARD READE, C.E., F.G.S.

Vice-President.
ROBERT A. ESKRIGGE, F.G.S.

Honorary Treasurer.
ALFRED MORGAN.

Honorary Secretary.
GEORGE H. MORTON, F.G.S., F.R.G.S.I.

Council.
THOMAS J. MOORE, Cor. Mem., Z.S.

HUGH F. HALL, F.G.S.

ROBERT BOSTOCK.

WILLIAM SEMMONS, F.G.S.

CHARLES RICKETTS, M.D., F.G.S.

THE PROCEEDINGS

OF THE

LIVERPOOL GEOLOGICAL SOCIETY.

SESSION SIXTEENTH.

OCTOBER 13TH, 1874.

THE PRESIDENT, ISAAC ROBERTS, F.G.S.,
in the Chair.

ALLEN GREEN was elected an Ordinary Member.

The President read the Annual Address.

PRESIDENT'S ADDRESS.

ONE of the most important subjects that is now prominently occupying the attention of geologists, is the investigation of the superficial deposits that are scattered far and wide, and (at first sight) without any apparent order, over large portions of the surface of the globe.

The study of the rock formations upon which the deposits here referred to rest, has been diligently and successfully pursued for more than half a century, by energetic and zealous workers, and they have furnished us with elaborate memoirs and carefully prepared treatises concerning the several divisions and sub-divisions into which those rock formations have been classified. But the systematic study of the superficial deposits has been reserved chiefly for the present time; and we have, since the close of our last Session, been presented by Mr. James Geikie, F.R.S.E., F.G.S., with a thick volume of matter, by the aid of which we may place ourselves in an advanced position for understanding the difficult and complex phenomena which those superficial deposits present to those who attempt to investigate them.

GLACIAL DRIFT is the name given to most of those loose, incoherent materials which cover large areas in this and other countries. The Glacial Drifts are, (like the rock formations,) found to represent several long successive intervals of time and conditions of climate during their deposition. Their faunæ at one time indicate a severe arctic climate. That was followed by a temperate, if not a tropical climate; later still, the land was submerged beneath the sea; again it rose, under a mild climate, was clothed with vegetation, inhabited by animals, man probably being amongst the number. The mild climate was succeeded by another arctic climate, which, in its turn, gave place to the existing order of things. But I intend to deal moderately on this occasion with speculation, and present to you instead, as far as the very brief time at my disposal will permit, some of the evidence upon which the inferences I have just stated are founded.

I therefore propose to describe some of the beds which are generically termed the Glacial Drifts; and, after examining some of their physical properties, pass on to cold, and arctic, and antarctic regions, to describe the forces of Nature which are now in operation, producing phenomena similar to those which we can trace in the Drifts. We will examine the Drifts in the order of super-position which the experience of many geologists in this and other countries has now assigned to them; but we must not assume that this arrangement of super-position is final, for as the work of examination and co-relation proceeds, probably modifications will be made in both the order and number of the beds.

Mr. Geikie, in his "Great Ice Age," says that in Scotland are found good typical examples of successive Glacial Deposits, and these he co-relates with the Drifts of other countries. The lowest or oldest of the deposits is the TILL, and is described by him as "Usually a firm, tough, tenacious, stony clay. So tough, indeed, does it often become, that engineers would much rather excavate the most obdurate rocks. Hard rocks are more or less easily assailable with gunpowder, and the numerous joints and fissures by which they are traversed enable the navvies to wedge them out, often in considerable lumps. But Till has neither crack nor joint; it will not blast, and to pick it to pieces is a very slow and laborious process. Occasionally, however, the clay becomes coarser and sandier, and when this is the case water soaks through it. It then loses consistency, and is ready to 'run' or collapse as soon as an excavation is made. Sometimes the stones in the Till are so numerous that hardly any matrix of clay is visible. This, however, does not often happen. On the other hand, they occasionally appear more sparsely scattered through the clay, which may then be dug for brick-making; but this occurs still less frequently. As a rule, it is hard to say whether the stones or the clay form the larger share percentage of the deposit, in a mass of typical Till. Generally speaking, however, the stones are most numerous in the Till of hilly districts; while at the lower levels of the country the clayey character of the mass is, on the whole, more pronounced; but to this there are many exceptions.

"The stones vary in size, from mere grit and pebbles up to blocks several feet, or even yards, in diameter. These last, however, do not occur so commonly as smaller stones; indeed boulders above four feet in diameter are comparatively seldom met with in the Till. Stones and boulders alike are scattered higgledy-piggledy, pell-mell, through the clay, so as to give to the whole deposit a highly confused and tumultuous appearance. There is something very peculiar about the shape of the stones. They are neither round and oval, like the pebbles in river gravel, or the shingle of the sea shore, nor are they sharply angular, like newly-fallen débris at the base of a cliff, although they more closely resemble the latter than the former. They are, indeed, angular in shape; but the sharp corners and edges have been invariably smoothed away. Each is smoothed, polished, and covered with striæ, or scratches, some of which are delicate as the lines traced by an etching-needle, others deep and harsh as the scores made by a plough upon a rock; and, what is also worthy of note, most of the scratches, coarse and fine together, seem to run parallel to the longer diameter of the stones; which, however, are scratched in many other directions as well."

The Till is quite local in character; for in districts where sandstone occurs most abundantly, the stones in the clay likewise consist almost exclusively of sandstone. And, similarly, in regions where hard volcanic rocks prevail, the overlying Till is invariably crowded with fragments of the same. Not only the stones, however, but also the colour and texture of the clay itself, are influenced by the character of the rocks in whose neighbourhood the Till occurs. Thus, in a district where the rocks consist chiefly of dark shales, clays, and thin sandstones, with occasional seams of coal, the overlying Till is usually hard and tough, and its prevailing colour a dark, dingy grey, or dirty blue; while in a region of Red Sandstone it is tinted red or brown, and commonly shows a more open or sandier texture. Remains of the great woolly elephant, or mammoth, and the reindeer, and fragments of various kinds of trees, such as pine, birch, and oak, have occasionally been found in the Till, in which they appear precisely in the same manner as stones or boulders; but not a single *trace of any marine organism* has yet been detected in true Till.

It is in the lower lying districts of the country where the Till appears in greatest force. Wide areas of the central counties are covered with it continuously, to a depth varying from two or three feet up to one hundred feet and more, and it is distinctly *un*stratified; it is a homogeneous mass from top to bottom. But, although this is the invariable character of the Till itself, it nevertheless contains, here and there, more or less regular beds of gravel, sand, silt, mud, and brick-clay, and occasionally similar deposits underlie the Till, and separate that deposit from the subjacent solid rocks.

The next deposit above the Till is the Boulder-clay. This appears to be limited to maritime districts. In many respects, the composition of the Boulder-clay. resembles that of the Till so closely that it is difficult, if not impossible, to distinguish one from the other. But, unlike the Till, it presents in parts distinct bedding. It also differs from the Till, in having the contained stones and boulders more rounded, less scratched, and smaller in size. It also frequently contains marine shells, generally in a broken state.

There are, in and around Liverpool, very extensive

areas covered with Boulder-clay; and, from the frequent opportunities afforded for examining them in excavations for foundations of buildings, trenches for sewers, tanks for gas-holders, docks, and cliffs fifty or sixty feet in height, along both sides of the River Mersey, its characteristic features have been studied by several members of this Society; and the results of their investigations have from time to time been published in the "Proceedings" of the Society.

I bring before you this evening specimens of the Boulder-clay in its natural state, and also separated into its constituent parts.

The microscope slide marked A shows that portion of the clay which, when washed with water, remains for a very long time in suspension, giving the water a slightly turbid appearance. Viewed under the microscope, it is resolved into transparent globules or crystals, some of which are probably lime and alumina. The next slide, marked B, contains what is shown on slide A, together with rocky matter, in a very finely divided state. The next slide, marked C, shows the clay separated into an impalpable powder, and also into grains of sand which are just visible to the eye. The next slide, marked D, shows the clay separated into coarser grains of sand, which show the characteristic features of the various rocks which have been ground down to form the Boulder-clay. In the drawer on the table are larger specimens of the same rocks, some of which show striæ; but the great mass of the Boulder-clay of this locality seems to be composed of the ground-up Keuper shales and Bunter sandstones.

In the drawers which are now before you are specimens of the shells which have been picked out of the Boulder-clay; and you will observe that the shells of the species *Turritella communis* form by far the larger proportion of the shells found in the clay. Many of them are in a very perfect state, with the point of the shell as sharp as the point of a bodkin.

The whole of the shells in these drawers were picked from two excavations made in the Boulder-clay, each about 150 feet in diameter and 33 feet in depth below the surface. They may be considered roughly to represent the relative proportions, varieties, and numbers of the shells found in the Boulder-clay, in the neighbourhood of Liverpool, and might be adopted as a rough basis for calculation of the number of shells that might be found in any given similar area and depth.

I have already described the shells here referred to before this Society, and for further details refer you to the Proceedings for Session 1870-71. I have also found similar shells to these at Wavertree; on the shores of the Mersey; at Toxteth Park, New Ferry and Egremont. I would also refer you to the list of shells given by Mr. Morton, F.G.S., in the "Proceedings" for last Session, and one by Mr. T. Mellard Reade, F.G.S., in the "Quarterly Journal of the Geological Society," vol. 30.

Mr. C. E. de Rance, F.G.S., who, in the "Quarterly Journal of the Geological Society" (vol. 26, page 1), has given a slight sketch of the bank of clay at Egremont, has divided it into upper and lower Boulder-clay, with middle Drift-sand between. But, after examining wide areas of Boulder-clay in and around Liverpool during a period of more than twenty years, and with many opportunities of seeing excavations for wells and other purposes made deeply into and through the Boulder-clay, I have failed to discover any conclusive evidence that the Boulder-clay of this neighbourhood is geologically divisible into upper and lower, with Drift-sands between.

I have frequently seen local patches of sand imbedded in the Boulder-clay; and, if these can be proved to be the lowest remnants of Middle Drift Sands, which were deposited, and then denuded, leaving only these patches as evidence of that deposition, Mr. de Rance's statement would be established; but I think we require clearer evidence than we yet possess, to establish the theory.

The sandstone rocks which underlie the Boulder-clay in places where they have been exposed to view, are found to be planed to a comparatively even surface, and that surface is distinctly grooved and striated.

Mr. James Geikie* gives several sections of the Boulder-clay, as it is seen in Scotland. The following, at Lewis, will serve as an example:—

1. Boulder-clay.
2. Sand, gravel, and coarse shingle, with rolled and angular fragments of shells.
3. Dark bluish brown clay and silt, with shells, many of them mere fragments.
4. Boulder-clay, with broken shells.

The Boulder-clay is sometimes partially stratified; at other times it contains beds, bands, and layers of sand, gravel, and clay, in which shells, or fragments of shells, are not unfrequently detected. Again, it passes into a regular stony clay, which it is difficult, or even impossible to distinguish from the Till of the interior.

The period which succeeded the deposition of the Boulder-clay, is marked by large accumulations of sands, gravels, and erratic blocks, widely scattered over the surface of the country, and often occurring at heights of more than 1,000 feet above the level of the sea. These accumulations are found resting sometimes on bare rock, sometimes on the Till, sometimes on the Boulder-clay, and

---

" The Great Ice Age," p. 211.

sometimes the erratic blocks are found in and upon the mounds or "kames" of sand and gravel.

Time will not permit me to trace in detail the deposits which are of more recent origin than those already described. We shall, therefore, pass on to the regions of great ice and snow, to see how far the forces of Nature which are now in operation there, can be shown to be producing phenomena similar to those which we have already noted in the Drifts.

There we shall see that most of the phases presented to us in studying the Drifts, can be accounted for, without having recourse to cataclysms and other irregular interference with what we observe to be the laws of Nature.

The chief difficulty that meets us at the threshold of our investigation is, how to realise to ourselves the magnitude of the changes that are constantly in progress by the action of snow and ice, such as now exist, in the Arctic and Antarctic regions. But to help us in this difficulty, I refer you to three drawings, which are exhibited on the wall, and marked respectively A, B, and C, and also the photographs in the book. The drawing marked A is an enlarged sketch of one published in Sir J. C. Ross' voyage to the Antarctic regions, in 1839–43. It represents a barrier of ice, or end of a *mer de glace*, which probably covers the whole of those regions as far as lat. 60° to 65° S. It was traced in an unbroken wall for a length of 450 miles, and it is at least 1,000 feet in average thickness, and 180 feet above the level of the sea.

The drawing marked B is enlarged from a sketch by H. M. Skae, in Mr. Geikie's work, "The Great Ice Age," and represents one of the Greenland glaciers; one of which, called the Humboldt Glacier, is 60 miles in breadth at its termination, and its seaward height measures 300 feet ; its depth is unknown, but, assuming that it is immersed to the extent of seven-eighths its height, that being the approximate proportion of iceberg flotation, its total thickness would be 2,400 feet.

The drawing marked C is an imaginary sketch of the end of a glacier, when it has proceeded so far out to sea that its buoyancy is sufficient to snap off the end, to form icebergs. That takes place suddenly, and is accompanied by sounds like the roar of cannon, and by extensive disturbance of the sea for considerable distances. The photographs in the book called "The Oberland and its Glaciers" show the general appearance of inland glaciers, and their terminal moraines.

It is only a few years since the discovery was made that glaciers are not inert accumulations of snow and ice ; and still more recent is the discovery of the cause of glacier motion; and that it is a powerful force contributing largely to the physical changes that modify and re-arrange the surface of the Earth.

It is now known that glaciers move by the combined energies of heat, gravitation, and crystallisation. Heat dissolves the snow or ice on the surface of the glacier ; the water, thus liberated from the crystalline state, shrinks in volume and finds its way to a lower level in the mass of the glacier by the influence of gravity. There it is re-crystallised, and expands in volume, exerting at the same time a pressure on the adjoining particles of ice ; these are forced to move, so as to make room for the new crystals; and thus, throughout the length, breadth, and thickness of the glacier is the alternate solution and re-crystallisation of the molecules of water, made the power by which the glacier is forced to move, even along a level plain.

The work done in grinding and removing the floor

upon which the glacier moves will be proportional to its depth or weight, its rate of motion, the yielding nature of the floor, and number of pieces of hard rock attached to the underside of it, which act as grinders or rubbers.

In order fully to realise the extent of the changes effected by glacier action in the present time, it is necessary to visit the Arctic and Antarctic regions ; and, furtunately for us, many bold navigators and scientific men, amongst whom I will mention Ross, Parry, and Franklin, have already done so, and have furnished us with data and vivid descriptions of what they have seen, from which we may draw inferences. The icefields of the temperate zones have also been carefully studied, and the results laid before us. From all these sources we may form an idea of the gigantic operations which are constantly being performed under the influence of alternate heat and cold, in breaking up, grinding, selecting, and re-distributing the rocks and materials which form the surface in those regions.

The whole of the land within and beyond the Arctic Circle, which is covered with snow and ice, is subjected to the grinding process of a heavy, slow-moving continent of ice, which, with its imbedded stones, scours even the hardest rocks into gravel, sand, and impalpable mud, which the running water of dissolved snow and ice carries to the sea from beneath the glaciers, and which the sea distributes far and wide, and arranges according to the size and weight of the respective particles, and force of the currents and waves.

From beneath the ice continents and glaciers, which cover the Arctic and Antarctic regions, as indicated by the paper caps which are placed on the globe before you, flow immense rivers of water, formed by the ice and snow, which been have melted by the heat of the sun in summer, and by the heat of the rocks beneath. These rivers are turbid, or muddy, with the spoil of the rocks which have been ground by the ice in motion. At last the mud reaches the sea, and is distributed in a gentle slope over the sea-bottom.

Along with the mud the moving ice pushes stones of all sizes, striated and rounded, which it has used as rubbers to scour down the rock-bed upon which it slides, but which rubbers it had not time to use up entirely in the process of grinding. They are, therefore, ejected at the foot of the ice, and form a sub-marine *moraine*; and, as the foot of the ice advances and retreats for many miles with the alternations of the winter and summer temperatures in the regions of the ice and snow, the stones of the *moraines* are, in like manner, pushed along the sea-bottom over the deposits of fine mud; and thus they get mixed with the mud, as we see by examination was done during the deposition of the Boulder-clay of this and other localities.

This is not the only mode in which Glacial deposits are now distributed, for we find in cold climates that the margins of the seas are frozen in winter, and in summer these margins break up and float away to sea, carrying, with the materials which have been frozen to the underside of them, vast quantities of *débris* which have fallen upon their surface from the cliffs which form the boundaries of the shore margins. There are also Glacier rivers which carry immense quantities of mud out to sea.

Thus we arrive at the present state of our knowledge concerning the Glacial Drifts, and we may now be able to follow and appreciate the inferences which have been drawn from the study of those Drifts.

I have already, in describing the Till, referred to

several beds of gravel, sand, silt, mud, and brick clay, which are intercalated, or deposited, in the Till at different horizons. These beds are accounted for by the theory that, during the deposition of the Till and Boulder-clay, which indicate a severe Arctic climate, with great confluent glaciers stretching far out to sea, there were intermediate periods of mild climate, when corresponding floræ and faunæ flourished. During the Boulder-clay period the land would appear to have stood lower, relative to the sea, than it does now ; but what was the extent of the submergence we cannot tell, the upper limits of the Boulder-clay not having been precisely determined. No Boulder-clay, however, has yet been noticed higher than 200 or 260 feet above the sea, and generally it occurs at much lower levels.

The climate and condition of the glaciers during the deposition of the Boulder-clay, may be considered as somewhat similar to the conditions that now prevail at Greenland. " Great Glaciers reached the sea and presented steep faces of ice to the swell of the Atlantic ; but between the glacier valleys were long stretches of rocky coast line, fringed with a thick shelf of ice like that which flanks the shores of many regions that border on the dreary Arctic Ocean."

Coast ice and bergs floated about, and the bottom of the sea was tenanted by Arctic Mollusca.

During the deposition of the morainic gravels and stones, which succeeded the Till and Boulder-clay periods, the intense Glacial climate was ameliorating, and the British Islands were elevated above the sea and joined to the Continent.

At that time Mr. Geikie fixes the age of the cave deposits, river gravels, with flint implements imbedded. After the period of the morainic gravels the land was submerged to a depth of about 2,000 feet below the sea, and the high level beaches were there formed.

Following this was another Arctic climate, but less severe than the former, when the valley moraines, dilluvium, of the south of England, sand, and brick-clay were deposited. After that the land was again elevated, with a cold, temperate climate, following which there was another partial submergence of the land, when the ancient forests were destroyed and peat-beds formed, in which are found relics of man. After the partial submersion I have just referred to, there was another partial re-elevation, which brings us to the existing state of the northern hemisphere.

The question may now be asked, How came England to be involved in an Arctic climate? Mr. Darwin,* who visited South America in 1834, will help us to answer. He describes immense glaciers which flow to the sea from Tierra del Fuego, where the mountains in the interior are only some 4300 feet in height, and the latitude is only as far south as the Cumberland Hills in this country are north. At St. Cruz, in the Cordillera, similar glaciers are met with, and the latitude is only as far south as the southern extremity of Cornwall is north.

If, then, we could find a cause that would transfer the present climate of the southern hemisphere to the northern, we should have the climate of Britain like that of Greenland. and if the cold were a little more severe than that, we should have the coldest period of the Glacial Drift. If a few degrees of cold were transferred from the southern hemisphere to the northern, all the glacial conditions would be attained. That this has been accomplished again and again we have strong evidence to show, and that even Greenland has had a temperate

* "Surveying Voyages to South America," 1839. Vol. 3., p. 280 285.

climate its buried floræ and faunæ show. We also have
ample evidence that the climate of England has changed
more than once from tropical to Arctic and from Arctic
to temperate again; but it would occupy too much of
your time on the present occasion to discuss at large
the causes which may have brought about the great
changes of climate that I have referred to. I shall,
therefore, only refer very briefly to one or two of the more
striking theories which have been propounded to account
for these.

Sir Charles Lyell thinks that the changes in the
relative distribution of land and sea would account for
the phenomena. We know that the land is constantly
being degraded by the action of the various forces of
Nature, and spread out again under the sea, and then
uplifted by volcanic agencies. Consequently, the continents shift their position, and when there is much land
within the tropics, much heated air would result and
pass away in great volumes towards the poles, and so
ameliorate the polar climates. On the other hand,
when there is much land in the temperate zones and at
the poles, and less within the tropics, the polar climates
would be more severe, and the severity would extend to
the temperate zones. But although these theories are
supported by so great an authority, their acceptance is
only partial. They do not carry conviction to the mind
by fully accounting for the phenomena.

The other theory to which I will refer is the astronomical, and the expounders are Mr. Adhémar and
Mr. Croll. It is an astronomical fact that the orbit of
the earth is an ellipse, the sun being in one of the foci.
It is also a fact that in our time the southern hemisphere of the earth is turned towards the sun, and
traverses that part of its orbit which is nearest the sun

B

during our winter months; but in 10,500 years hence the reverse of this will be the case, for then the northern hemisphere will be exposed to the same conditions as the southern is now; and in 21,000 years hence the northern hemisphere will be just in the same relative position that it is in now. The effects of these changes, which are caused by the precession of the equinoxes, will be, it is inferred, that in 10,500 years from this time the climate of the northern hemisphire will be as severe as the climate of the southern hemisphere is now; and that England, if it should then be known by that name, will be undergoing another glacial climate.

It is also inferred that the precession of the equinoxes and eccentricity of the earth's orbit would, at their maximum, produce great caps of ice at the poles alternately; and that these would displace the earth's centre of gravity, and so cause the waters of the seas to rise higher towards the poles. This, in effect, would be the same as a depression of the land, which appears to have occurred more than once during the deposition of the Glacial Drifts.

In considering the temperate and polar climates, we must not omit to take into account the effects produced by the great ocean currents, such, for instance, as the Gulf stream, and there are others equally great. These streams convey a large amount of solar heat from the tropics towards the poles, and in their course materially modify the climate in many countries which are contiguous.

I hope that I have now said enough to induce those who have not hitherto studied the phenomena of the Glacial Drift to induce them to turn their thoughts into this prolific and profitable field of enquiry.

NOVEMBER 10TH, 1874.

THE VICE-PRESIDENT, R. A. ESKRIGGE, F.G.S.,
in the Chair.

JAMES PATERSON, THOMAS HATHAWAY, C.E., EDWARD
W. B. M. HANCE, L.L.B., GEORGE JEVONS, Jun., JAMES
KERSHAW, and THOMAS DIXON were elected Ordinary
Members.

The following communication was read:—

OBSERVATIONS ON THE GEOLOGY OF THE CHESHIRE SHORE, WITH REMARKS ON THE SUBJECTS NOTICED BY THE MEMBERS OF THE SOCIETY DURING THEIR LAST VISIT.

BY CHARLES POTTER.

DECEMBER 8TH, 1874.

THE PRESIDENT, T. MELLARD READE, C.E., F.G.S.,
in the Chair.

JAMES L. McCLAY was elected an Ordinary Member.

The following communication was read:—

THE GLACIAL AND POST-GLACIAL DEPOSITS OF GARSTON AND THE SURROUNDING DISTRICT, WITH REMARKS ON THE STRUCTURE OF THE BOULDER-CLAY,

BY T. MELLARD READE, C.E., F.G.S.

IN my paper on "The Post-Glacial Geology of Lancashire," published in our Proceedings, Session 1871-72,
there is a section of a brook disclosed by the dock

excavations at Garston.* Since this section was drawn I have made frequent visits to the excavations, and propose now to describe the results of my observations.

BASE OF THE DEPOSITS.

The whole series of deposits rest upon a floor of rock (Bunter Pebble Beds), shelving at a gradual inclination westward, the *strike* of this slope being approximately parallel with the direction of the River Mersey at Garston. Considering that it is cut out of beds dipping 18° W of N, this floor is remarkably regular.

Ground Moraine.—Resting upon this base is a bed of rocky *débris*, varying from a few inches to two or three feet thick, consisting of red sand ground out of the bed rock, with embedded masses of rubble. This bed, I have elsewhere stated, I consider to be the ground moraine of the great Ice Sheet, representing the maximum intensity of the Glacial Period and the equivalent of the true Scotch Till.† It is a local deposit, varying with the rock it rests upon, and never containing travelled stones. In the section of the Liverpool Extension Railway, disclosing deposits continuous with those bared by the dock excavations, it was also to be seen where the rock was reached, and the Widnes borings also proved it at a depth of 140 feet below ordnance datum in the ancient bed of the river.‡ From the nature of the rock, no groovings or striations were to be met with, and I invariably find them absent where the rock is covered by this deposit.

Erratic Blocks.—Upon the preceding bed erratic or travelled stones and pebbles frequently rest ; and, in some cases, large blocks. These do not differ, either in the

---

* Plate 4, Sec. No. 24.
† "Quarterly Journal of the Geological Society," February 1874.
‡ "Buried Valley of the Mersey."—*Pro. Liverpool Geol. Soc.*, 1872-73.

character of the rocks, or appreciably in the proportions in which they occur, from those distributed through the overlying Boulder-clay. Many blocks of Granite, Syenite, and Greenstone resting upon this sand were to be seen in the railway cutting near St. Mary's Road. Nearer to Warrington the Carboniferous rocks become more frequent. The larger number of these blocks, both in the dock and railway cutting, showed signs of glaciation; and, from the manner in which many were planed, polished, and striated, had evidently been shaped in the Glacier bottom. Coast ice would be incapable of shaping them. I should estimate the largest blocks at about two tons. Where the over-lying Boulder-clay is denuded, as at Stanley Road, near Miller's Bridge, these blocks are frequently met with.

The Low Level Marine Boulder-Clay and Sands.— Super-imposed upon the ground moraine, or, where that is absent, the rock itself, is the deposit I have ventured else-where to term the " Low Level Marine Boulder-clay and Sands." It is a series of continuous deposits, reaching in the Buried Valley of the Mersey under the town of Widnes to a maximum depth of 163 feet below the surface, and to 169 feet in a well-sinking at Hooton Station, in Cheshire.* As a rule, the deposit I estimate to range from 10 to 50 feet thick over a large area of the country; though in places it is denuded to a few feet, and in some, such as rocky knolls, absent altogether. The bottom beds of the deposit are often hard and coherent, having incorporated with them a large proportion of the red sand from the bed below. In other cases, resting upon the smoothed surface of the rock, it differs little from the mass of the brown-red clay forming the bulk of the deposit above, and familiar to us all as the brick-making

* The depths of these deposits are given in my paper on the "Buried Valley of the Mersey," before referred to.

clay of the neighbourhood. In other instances yellow
sand occurs sometimes, as at the Hooton Well, of considerable thickness, and interstratified with gravel. In
portions of the dock excavations good examples of
current-bedded sands and gravels of limited thickness
were observed and sketched by me at the time. Occasionally the red sand from below occurs in veins included
in the clay itself, but always near the base. One of the
advantages of watching excavations over an extended
area is, that parallel sections can be obtained showing the
variations in the beds laterally, from which we may form a
good notion of the horizontal boundaries of the deposits.
Single vertical sections, such as are exposed in a railway
cutting, are often misleading. In one of the sections
referred to, recorded in my note-book, the ground
moraine of red sand and rubble fills up saw-like notches
in the rock below, the serrations probably arising from
the crushing of the upturned edges of the beds, which,
as before stated, dip at an angle of 18°. Above this is a
layer of the red sand ; then current-bedded yellow sand
and gravel ; and above that, clay and gravel mixed. In
another section a bed of "book leaf" clay from half-
an-inch to one inch thick, thinning out to nothing in each
direction, occurs in the clay near the base; and, above
that again, with a couple of feet of unlaminated clay
between, is a mass of Boulder-clay in laminations about
two inches thick and when dry, splitting up into flaggy fragments, the whole being studded with the usual erratics.
While in some cases the clay appeared to be quite
unstratified, in others divisional planes were very
perceptible. Decomposed granite and greenstone boulders
were of frequent occurrence and, in one spot especially
thick with them, looked like almonds in a pudding, being
cut in twain by the navvies' pick, and showing as sections

in the clayey mass. Divisional planes are characteristic of the Boulder-clay of the neighbourhood, and are to be seen in the cliffs above Garston; but the most remarkable instance of persistence in a bed of this kind was one disclosed in the railway cutting at Farnworth, where a bed of sand and gravel not more than from three inches to six inches thick divides the deposit in two, sweeping over in a curve approximately concentric with the rock below for a distance of five-eighths of a mile. Extensive included beds of laminated sand and gravel showed in the cutting west of Hunts Cross Station, and very curious instances of cross laminations and curved laminated beds occurred nearer to Garston. Weathering brings out these laminations very distinctly, forming connecting stalactitic drops of clay between. There are also pot-holes of sand, and barren unlaminated beds of sand containing neither shells nor stones.

The nature of the clay itself varies within certain limits, the bottom and oldest beds being generally the hardest and most compact, and, as a rule, containing the most stones. In the Widnes borings, as I have before described, the clay, especially towards the bottom, is of a fine unctuous character, like some of the beds at Bootle Lane Station.

Shell Fragments.—Included in the clay generally, and sometimes in laminated seams of sand, are shell fragments proving the whole to be a Marine Deposit. I found representatives of the following species:—*Mya truncata, L., Tellina balthica, L., Venus gallina, L., Astarte borealis Chem, Cardium Edule, L., Littorina litorea, L., Turritella terebra, L., Purpura lapillus, L., Buccinum undatum, L.* As I have elsewhere* developed this portion of my subject, I will not repeat it here.

---

* "The Drift Beds of the North-West of England."—*Quarterly Journal of the Geological Society*, 1874, p. 281.

Proportion in which Erratic Fragments occur.—I have not at Garston estimated the proportion in which the various formations are represented; but at Great Crosby in a similar deposit, I carefully estimated them; they were as follows :—

1. Granites, Syenites, and Porphyries... 23
2. Greenstones, Felstones, and Tuffs, many being Porphyritic 31
3. Old Red Sandstone....................... 1
4. Cambrian and Silurian Grits and Slates, &c. 28
5. Carboniferous Limestones.............. 8
6.   ,,   Sandstones 8
7. Triassic Sandstones and Marls 1

        100

I also found, in one instance, the proportion of stones to the mass of clay to be one in 1200, while in another instance it rose as high as one in 130. Probably the average would be about one in 900. These proportions were estimated by measuring the excavations and the heap of stones taken out, and, of course, are only approximate.

Striated Stones.—If the molluscous fauna of the Boulder-clay does not indicate the intense conditions of cold one would expect, there are indisputable records of severe ice action in the planed and striated boulders, pebbles, and blocks profusely embedded in the whole series of deposits. The proportion of striated stones among those mentioned was as follows :—

No. 1.........None were properly striated, being mostly rounded and subangular.
,, 2.........13 were striated.
,, 4.........26   ,,
,, 5......... 8   ,,
,, 6.........None were distinctly striated.

Thus, out of 100 stones 47, or nearly half, bore marks of ice action. I consider this excellent evidence of the existence of Glaciers at the time the Marine Boulder-clays were being deposited.

Parent Rocks.—It will be observed that 83 per cent. are of such rocks as can only be derived from the Cumbrian or Welsh mountains; and, after much trouble and care, I have succeeded in identifying—in addition to the Eskdale Granite first discovered in the Drift by Mr. Mackintosh—the Syenite of Buttermere, which also occurs plentifully scattered over the Macclesfield Hills in the form of large blocks. Is not this presumptive evidence of the former existence of Glaciers in the mountains from which most of these rocks were torn, especially if taken together with the ice markings so sharply cut in them, and freshly preserved to the present day?

Evidences of Tidal Action.—From an extensive series of observations, I am of opinion that none of the deposits described are of littoral origin, excepting in so far as they have been swept from the shores to the deeps; and that the current-bedded sands and gravels, the laminated sands, the divisional planes, the finely laminated beds of clay, were all formed below low water by Tidal Action, and often at considerable depths. I have shown that the tide-wave acts at the bottom of the sea even at the greatest depths,* and that it is capable, in many instances, of considerable erosive action. The almost universal prevalence of shell fragments, of only a small size, also leads to the belief that they have been sorted by the tidal current, as I find that dredgings in the silts of the estuary of the Mersey show a preponderance of small shell fragments.

---

* "Tidal Action as a Geological Cause."—*Proc. of Liverpool Geo. Soc.*, 1873-4.

Post-Glacial Beds. — These deposits occurred in a gulley cut in the Boulder-clay, and in level lay between high and low water. The sequence of beds was well borne out in the several sections across the whole width of the dock, and confirmed my determination of them in the section before referred to in my "Post-Glacial Geology of Lancashire and Cheshire." They are instructive, as showing conclusively a Post-glacial downward movement of the land by physical evidence altogether apart from inferences drawn from the submerged forests.

The deposits lay invariably in the north side of the gulley, the opposite side being apparently denuded by the inrush of the tide up the Mersey; and they widened out as they approached low-water mark, as also did the gulley itself. A reference to the original section will show that Deposit No. 3, coarse flesh-coloured sand, and No. 4, yellow sand, are coloured as equivalents of the Washed-Drift sand; but further down laminated silt occurred, leading me to suppose that the upper beds were re-arranged and contemporaneous with the Formby and Leasowe Marine Beds. Peat Bed No. 5, I found, occurred with stools of trees in situ in a patch on the floor of the gulley, resting upon a thin bed of silty sand. Bed No. 6, undoubtedly recent, contained *Scrobicularia piperata* in situ, and showed an interesting example of cross laminations arranged at all angles with partings of comminuted peat. This, as occurring in *mud*, was instructive; and, no doubt, due to the eddying tidal currents created by the gulley.

In conclusion, I may point out that it is not often we can get a complete series of deposits, such as these, contained in one section, exhibiting beds from the commencement of the Glacial Period down to the present time; and, in addition, so disposed as to throw considerable light on several physical questions of successive subsidences and re-elevations, which I have on other occasions called your attention to. Within the limits of this short paper it has been impossible for me to do much more than describe facts, but they are such as I believe to be fully worth recording, and therefore, it has been with much pleasure I have laid them before you. The very means through which such information is obtained involves the destruction of the record itself. I wish that this reflection would induce those who have the opportunity not to omit to record, or to let others profit by observations of a similar nature.

JANUARY, 12TH, 1875.

THE PRESIDENT, T. MELLARD READE, C.E., F.G.S.,
in the Chair.

CONYERS KIRBY, C.E., and BRICE M. WRIGHT, F.R.Hist.S., were elected Ordinary Members.

The following communication was read :—

THE CARBONIFEROUS LIMESTONE AND MILL- STONE GRIT OF THE COUNTRY SOUTH OF LLANGOLLEN.

BY GEORGE H. MORTON, F.G.S.

The publication of this paper is unavoidably post-poned until next year.

FEBRUARY 9TH, 1875.

THE PRESIDENT, T. MELLARD READE, C.E., F.G.S.,
in the Chair.

The following communications were read :—

THE METALLIC ORES OF CORNWALL—GROUP 1:

TIN, COPPER, IRON, AND LEAD.

By William Semmons, F.G.S.

Perhaps no district in the United Kingdom of similar extent has yielded so many combinations of the various metals as the mining district of Cornwall. Of some metals it furnishes our total British supply, while of almost all of them it appears to furnish marketable quantities.

Tin.—First in importance stands the ores or rather ore of Tin, the value of which as an object of industry may be estimated by the fact that in 1873 no less than 14,885 tons "Black" Tin were sold from Devon and Cornwall, producing £1,056,835. The production in Devon is but a small part of this quantity, and from these two counties all our British Tin is obtained. The Tin mines are scattered over the whole of Cornwall. but are chiefly confined to the Granite ridge, which traverses it from N.E. to S.W.; and a very large proportion of the yield is extracted from an area which might be comprised in a circle having a radius of $1\frac{1}{2}$ mile. From two sets of veins, the one running along the north and the other along the south side of Carn Bré Range, about one third of the present production is obtained. Carn Bré forms the northern limit of a large exposure of Granite, the whole of which is probably stanniferous; and along its flanks rests the clay slate or killas, which covers so large a portion of the low lands of the county.

Cassiterite, Sn. O_2, the ore which furnishes the exclusive supply of this metal, is usually found associated with Chlorite, Quartz, and other minerals. Although this mineral crystallises in the Pyramidal system, which admits of but few variations compared with some of the other systems, one conversant with the locality can generally pronounce with certainty the district from which a specimen has been raised, so exquisitely poised are the forces which regulate the deposition of these crystals. The average produce of the Tinstuff raised is probably less than 5 per cent.; and the extraction of the ore from its matrix, in consequence, becomes a matter of prime importance to the miner. This is principally effected by washing, advantage being taken of the high specific gravity of the mineral. Roasting has to be resorted to, in order to get rid of the Arsenic in Mispickel, which is a frequent companion of Cassiterite. Wolfram, with which it is sometimes associated, requires a more complicated process for its extraction.

Stannine, a mineral now usually considered a Sulpho-stannate of Copper and Iron, is found mixed with other ores, generally those of Copper.

Copper.—The number of combinations which Copper enters into with other elements is very great, and a very large proportion of these is found in Cornwall. Perhaps no less than 30 Copper ores of well-defined composition are met with in addition to several others, which help to fill the cabinets of mineralogists.

In a native state, it is found in the Granite, Clay Slate, and Serpentine Rock.

Combined with Oxygen we have—

Cuprite .... $Cu_2 O$

Melaconite .... $Cu O$

Cuprite has been found occasionally in large quantities. It is often crystallised, even when it occurs in masses. The capillary variety Chalcotrichite is rare.

In Carbonates—

Azurite............ $2 Cu C O_3, \ Cu H_2 O_2$

Malachite......... $Cu C O_3, \ Cu H_2 O_2$

The Cornish Malachite is not so compact as the Australian and Russian varieties, and consequently is but little used for ornamental purposes. Specimens are sometimes met with showing crystals of Cuprite partially converted into Malachite, similar to those met with at Chessy.

Chrysocolla a silicate, $Cu\, Si\, O_3 + 2\, H_2\, O$, found also in small quantities, appears to be a product of decomposition of other Copper ores.

Condurrite, $Cu_8\, As$, a rare mineral is, I believe, the only combination with Arsenic found here.

The Sulphides are represented by—

Redruthite...............	$Cu_2\, S$
Covellite	$Cu\, S$
Bornite	$3\, Cu_2\, S\, ,\ Fe_2\, S_3$
Towanite	$Cu_2\, S\, ,\ Fe_2\, S_3$

Redruthite has been found in large quantities; and some of the crystals, particularly the Nail-headed variety, are remarkable for their size and brilliancy.

Bornite is a very common ore. A noticeable fact about this mineral is, that crystals of it are confined to so few localities.

Covellite is only found in small quantities.

Towanite, which is in Cornwall as in most places the principal ore of Copper, is found in almost every mine where Copper has been extracted.

A most interesting group of minerals, showing the interchangeability of Sulphur, Arsenic, and Antimony, is composed of Fahlerz, Bournonite, Tennantite, and Polybasite.

The Cornish crystals of Bournonite are perhaps the finest that have been raised, whilst those of Fahlerz, with their almost invariable covering of Towanite, are interesting from showing pauses in the act of deposition, and a change in the character of the deposit. Atacamite represents the oxychlorides of Copper. Those compounds which represent the decomposition of other ores are well represented—In the Sulphates we have Cyanosite, Langite, and Brochantite, which represent various stages of hydration; while no less than ten minerals are found in the group of Arseniates and Phosphates.

Lead.—The ores of Lead are comparatively few; those of commercial importance are very few. They are well represented in Cornwall.

Plumbic Ochre, a rare mineral here, represents the oxides.

The Carbonate, Pb CO_3, Cerussite, is frequently met with here, though not in large quantities. Some crystals of great size and beauty have been found in one or two localities.

The principal source of Lead here, as in most localities, is Galena, Pb S. This mineral is found in veins, of which it is the sole or main constitutent, and also associated with ores of Tin, Copper, and Iron.

A rare combination Chloride and Carbonate is illustrated by the mineral Cromfordite Pb CO_3, Pb Cl_2, of which a few specimens have been found.

Several minerals, of which Pyromorphite and Mimetite are the most common, represent the Phosphates and Arseniates.

We may note here the frequent occurrence of Plumbic Chloride, in combination, in the ores of Lead; although, distinct, it has, I believe, only been found two or three times.

The Sulphate Anglesite is a rare mineral here, as is also the Cupreous Sulphate, Linarite; while the Antimonates are represented by Bleinerite.

The percentage of Silver in the Cornish lead ores is much greater than the average of the United Kingdom.

Cornish lead ores average 40 ounces per ton, while the average of the whole of the British mines is slightly under 10 ounces per ton.

Iron.—The value of the Iron ores raised in the county is at present but small; not, however, through lack of quantity, but from lack of development.

Magnetite $Fe_8 O_4$ is only found in small quantities.

Hematite $Fe_2 O_3$ is present in almost every mineral vein, and associated with the ores of other metals.

Goethite, $Fe_2 O_3, H_2 O$, is found in several mines. The Restormel mines have yielded some remarkable specimens.

Limonite, $2 Fe_2 O_3, 3 H_2 O$ is found in great abundance. Gossan, an ochreous deposit seen on the out-crop of the Cornish veins, is largely composed of this mineral.

Chalybite, $Fe C O_3$, is found in many places. Some of these rhombohedral crystals have their extemities so truncated as to resemble octohedrons of the cubic system, and are therefore of great interest.

The Sulphur compounds are well represented.

Pyrrhotine, $Fe_7 S_8$, the magnetic variety, is found but rarely.

The Ferric dissulphide is found in both its dimorphic forms, Pyrite and Marcasite.

Pyrite occurs in crystals presenting every modification of the cubic system, and is very abundant.

Marcasite, in its varied forms, is also a common mineral. The occurence of these minerals immediately superimposed on each other lends some support to the theory of deposition from solution, a change in conditions causing a change in form.

Mispickel, $Fe As S$, is found abundantly; and, from its high specific gravity is one of the impurities which cannot be extracted from Cassiterite by washing. The roasting of this mineral, and the consequent formation of Arsenious anhydride, constitutes a considerable source of income to some mines.

Lencopyrite, Fe As$_2$, found in small quantities only, shows the complete replacement of Sulphur by Arsenic.

The Arseniates and Phosphates are comparatively rare, but are represented by Vivianite, Pharmacosiderite, Scorodite, and Pitticite.

The Silicates are represented by those rare minerals Chloropal and Cronstedite, while Melanterite represents the Sulphates.

Wolfram, Fe W O$_4$, frequently occurs mixed with Tin ore.

During the past few years the workings on the Iron lodes in Cornwall have assumed quite another aspect to their former appearance. Large sums of money have been spent on their development, and it seems certain that in the course of a short time this branch of metallic mining will be one of great importance. One of these lodes, known as the Perran Iron lode, is in some places no less than 100 feet wide; consisting at the surface of Brown oxide of Iron, passing as we descend into Chalybite. The Chalybite is remarkably free from Phosphorus and Sulphur, and is of the description required for the manufacture of Bessemer Steel. In some places they have sunk through the Chalybite, and there find the lode to contain Blende, Galena, and Towanite. This deposit of Iron, therefore, appears to be a gigantic Gossan on the back of a Copper or Lead lode, and most miners think the amount of mineral beneath will be very great.

The foregoing minerals are obtained from two sources:—Stream works and Vein mining.

The Stream works are confined to alluvial deposits, in which Cassiterite is found, and occasionally other heavy minerals; as for instance, though but rarely, Gold. This method of obtaining minerals would naturally occur in the first instance to a rude people; but, as this source would be soon exhausted, they would be driven to work on the veins from which the alluvial deposits were derived.

Vein mining is therefore of ancient date, particularly for Tin. Most authorities are now agreed that the Ictis of Diodorus, from whence the Tin was shipped by the Phœnicians, was one of the islands on the Cornish coast.

Copper mining appears to have been developed at a more recent date, for we read of Sir Walter Raleigh reporting to Queen Elizabeth that the Copper ores of Cornwall were of little value.

The Cornish veins may be divided into two classes :—

1.—E. and W. veins—containing Tin, Copper, Iron Gossan, and but little Lead.

2.—N. and S. veins—frequently comprised of Clay, containing sometimes Lead ore and Iron.

The contra veins are intermediate in their direction. For a description of these veins I would refer to— W. J. Henwood's great work, also to papers by Carne— *Trans. Royal Geol. Soc.*, Cornwall.

The direction of a vein appears in many cases to affect its productiveness. Charles Thomas, a man of great practical experience, in his little work gives an instance where the relation between them is well shown viz.,—in the lode at Alfred Consols Mine.

The "dip" of lodes is extremely variable, and the same lode is generally more inclined in some places than in others. Not only is this the case, but, frequently on a shaft being sunk, the lode is found to dip on both sides of the perpendicular in the course of 100 fathoms. This variation in the direction and dip of lodes gives rise to numberless intersections, the result of which appears more to increase than diminish their productiveness, though instances could be given of both effects.

A peculiar fact with regard to N. and S. lodes containing Lead is that, when they are crossed by E. and W. lodes, the Lead ore becomes richer for Silver. At Wheal Ludcott the Lead lodes at these intersections produced native Silver and Silver ores. The great Perran Iron lode intersects several Lead veins. In one place at Treskerby Green the Galena yielded over 3,000 ounces of Silver per ton; in another, Wheal Peru, a large mass of native Silver was found.

This fact, taken in connection with Robert Were Fox's researches on the electrical condition of veins, tends much to support the theory of deposition from solution. The numerous cases of pseudomorphism show that chemical change is ever at work; while endomorphs give undoubted evidence of lapse of time and change of conditions during the filling up of the veins.

The following are the writers who have described the district:—De la Beche, F.R.S., R. Were Fox, F.R.S., W. W. Smyth, F.R.S., W. J. Henwood, F.R.S., J. Garby, R. Pearce, F.G.S., J. H. Collins, F.G.S., and others. Mr. Collins' work is an invaluable guide.

SPECULATIONS ON THE PROBABLE DISTRIBUTION OF LAND AND SEA DURING THE DEPOSITION OF THE MARINE BOULDER-CLAYS AND SANDS.

By T. Mellard Reade, C.E., F.G.S.

It is, I believe, to Lyell the credit is due of first conceiving and clearly stating the changes of climate that may result from a given distribution of land and sea. Since he gave his views to the world there has, however, been an increasing tendency to attribute the cold of the Glacial Period to astronomical rather than to geographical causes. While not disposed to undervalue the effect which a change in the eccentricity of the earth's orbit might produce, or of a change in the inclination of the earth's axis to the ecliptic—of which, however, astronomers say they have no evidence—it may be as well if we revert to the effect of known causes, and keep clearly in view what agencies now at work are capable of effecting.

Assuming that the axis of the earth was practically at its present angle to the ecliptic in the comparatively recent period of the Marine Boulder-clays of the N.W. of England, it follows that an extension of cold into lower latitudes would not create the same climatic conditions as a similar mean degree of annual temperature in higher latitudes. If the extension of cold towards the Equator only affected one portion in longitude of the circumference of the globe, the summer Isotherms would vary less in latitude than the winter Isotherms; while, if the Glacial conditions were equally distributed, the summer and winter Isotherms might be nearly parallel in direction. On the other hand, it is quite·evident, from the altitude of the sun in summer, the heat might then be great, though the winter temperature were exceedingly low.* Through speculations of this kind, it has occurred to me, that the puzzling mixture of a few southern or Lusitanean, with the prevailing northern forms of the testaceous fauna of the Boulder-clay, may be due to these variations of the seasons. Such conditions would, I think, be likely to produce currents of varying

---

* A reference to the Isothermal lines of the globe will show how they are affected in this manner now.

temperature, and the proximity of such currents to each other would have the effect of bringing the Southern and northern forms into close proximity.

As regards the degree of cold indicated by the fauna of the Boulder-clay, we have only to turn our attention to the present condition of the North American Continent to see that present causes are quite competent to produce sea conditions fitted for such an assemblage of molluscs.

It is true that there are now no Glaciers in North America in this latitude, but, if the land were more mountainous and the prevailing wind blew from the east instead of the west, it is quite possible that the hygrometrical conditions would be such as to create a great fall of snow such as we know takes place at Tierra del Fuego, lying on the southern parallel corresponding to the northern one on which the deposits in question lie ; and, therefore, Glacial conditions may have prevailed without the sea being necessarily of a very low temperature.

Lyell and Forbes have pointed out that there must have been a littoral or shore connection between the Continent of America and Europe in Post-tertiary times to account for the similarity of the testaceous fauna on both sides of the Atlantic. It does not follow, however, that this connection was at any one time *continuous ;* a very slow wave of upheaval of the land would be sufficient to carry the fauna from one continent to the other. It is thus presumable that there was, during the Glacial Period, a preponderance of land towards the North Pole, and these successive and wave-like subsidences and upheavals are probably connected with the Icelandic Volcanic system.

The oscillations of level of the land, which are proved

to have taken place during the Glacial Period, increasing northwards from a zero line from London to Bristol to 2,000 feet in Wales, and possibly more in Scotland, show that the disturbing causes—deep-seated, no doubt—must have been situated in the far north. It is also not improbable that a depression of 2,000 feet may have been preceded by a rise to a similar or greater extent; and this in itself would be sufficient to intensify, if not to produce, Glacial conditions.

Thus, if we find an alteration in the distribution of land and water—such as we have good reasons for supposing actually took place—competent to produce the effects we see in the Marine Drift, it seems unnecessary for our purpose to invoke, in addition, the aid of astronomical causes. And, further, if the cold at this period was not due to other than geographical causes, it is quite evident that though the isothermal lines would at that time trend further south in Europe than they do now, the summers might be very hot, and the winters very cold.*

This is exactly what takes place, perhaps in a lesser degree, in the same latitudes in North America; and we find, according to Forbes and others, that the Arctic and the American representatives of the Lusitanean Province meet and actually intermingle at Cape Cod in lat. 42°. Southern shells are there dredged up with Arctic species.

It is not, then, a very violent supposition to ascribe, as I have suggested, the presence of southern forms, such as *Venus chione, Cardium rusticum, C. aculeatum,*

---

* A reference to the concluding paragraphs will show that, the opposite of this takes place in Tierra del Fuego—that the summer temperature is there very low. This is a local condition, but one eminently fitted to produce glaciers, when combined with the high temperature of the inflowing waters heated in adjoining seas.

and *Arca lactea* found in the Lancashire Drift, along with a great preponderance of Arctic forms to the extremes of cold and heat, peculiar to a low latitude under Glacial conditions.

It may, perhaps, be urged that in the case of the Boulder-clay this is invoking too great a machinery to account for the presence of only *one* southern shell, viz :—*Venus chione.* There are, however, other circumstances to be considered. We know that some forms are far more persistent than others, and adapt themselves to changed conditions more readily. We also know that several shells common to the crag have since retired into Arctic or northern seas.* If, therefore, shells ranging further south, when warmer conditions prevailed, have since retired north, there is no violence in supposing that a southern shell retired further south, even after living through the Glacial seas in these localities. The apparent anomaly remains to be accounted for in some way, and, as the course of the erratic boulders contained in the clay shows that the Drift-ice was from the *north*, the shells could hardly be travelled ones from the south, unless brought up by tidal action, of which there is an absence of evidence. The frequency of the occurrence of *Venus chione*, at Macclesfield and Edge Hill, is also strongly confirmatory of its being a local shell.†

The beds in our neighbourhood lie midway between the 53rd and 54th parallels of latitude; and, though now a comparatively mild and equable climate prevails, Liverpool is as far north as a considerable portion of the

---

* *Astarte borealis* among the number.

† The presence of Lusitanean Forms is not peculiar to the Drift of Lancashire, *Cardium aculeatum* and *C. pygmæum* occurring in the Scotch clays. See A. Geikie " On the Phenomena of the Glacial Drift."—*Tran. of Glasgow Geol. Society.*

ungenial coast of Labrador, the extreme northern point of which is on the same parallel as the Shetland Isles. If we contrast the climates of the two places, we shall have less difficulty in understanding how readily a change in the distribution of land and sea, and consequently marine currents, might re-introduce a condition of things indicated by the Drift-beds of Lancashire. We have seen that the Arctic and southern faunas on the opposite side of the Atlantic meet, and actually intermingle at Cape Cod in latitude 42°, or over 11 degrees further south than Liverpool, and that these two places are about on the same Isothermal line of mean summer temperature. Doubtless, this meeting of the southern and Boreal fauna is due to the impinging of the cold currents of the north upon the warmer ones from the Gulf of Mexico; and the sharp line of division also probably results from the same physical causes, combined with the separation of the two streams by this Cape. It is instructive, as bearing upon the question before us, to notice the wedge-like thinning out of the southern and Boreal areas on the east coast of America in this latitude; and will help, as before pointed out, to explain the otherwise anomalous appearance of southern forms in the Drift that now do not range so far north.*

During the Glacial Period, so far as we know, no more northern forms than *Cyprina Islandica*, *Mya truncata*, *Panopea Norvegica*, and *Buccinum undatum*, which are found in the Cicilian beds, reached to the Mediterranean, or 4 degrees further south than Cape Cod. There is, however, in the Glacial beds, so far as at present known, no sharp line of division showing a northern

---

* Forbes notes the discovery by Captain James of *Turritella incrassata*, a crag fossil, a southern form of *fusus*, and a *mitra* allied to the Spanish species, in the Wexford gravels.

assemblage of shells in contiguity with those of a southern type, such as would be exhibited to us were the land about Cape Cod elevated and the beds exposed. Though we find a sprinkling of southern shells in the Glacial beds, the general evidences are that the conditions of the sea favourable to the northern species were more diffused, wide-spread, and embraced a larger area than what we see in America. In estimating the relative intensity of cold prevailing now in North America, as compared with the former cold of Europe, we must also not lose sight of the configuration of the land, and the changes it would produce in the currents from the north or south. Thus, though the Mediterranean during the Glacial Period were connected with the Atlantic on the one hand and the Red Sea on the other, it would be out of the line of the great northern currents, consequently an intense cold would be unlikely to prevail.

In the more northerly parts of America we find that the climate of the more sterile regions of the Hudson's Bay territory is much colder even than Greenland under the same latitude. At Winter Island, 66° 11" N. lat., 83° 30" W. long., the mean annual temperature does not exceed 7° Fahrenheit, the maximum of heat observed being 54° and the minimum—42°. At Fort Franklin, about 230 feet above the sea, and only one degree further south, viz., 65° 12" N. lat., but in longitude 132° 13" W. and situated in the Mackenzie Valley, the mean annual temperature is 17°, the maximum of heat is 80°, and the minimum—58°. The mean annual temperature at Fort Chippewa, on the banks of Lake Athabasca, 58° 43" N. lat., does not rise above freezing point, or 30°.*

It is thus seen that proximity to the Arctic currents, through Baffin's Bay and the archipelago of islands

* English Cyclopædia—Article, "Hudson's Bay Territory."

dividing North America from Greenland, makes a difference of 10° mean annual temperature between Winter Island and Fort Franklin; which, being 48° 43" to the westward, is subject to the ameliorating influences of the Pacific Ocean and the eastward extension of the Japanese current. On the other hand, to the eastward the mean annual temperature of Greenland, to some extent open to the influences of the North Atlantic, is much higher. The American pole of *relative* cold* is in lat. 65° N., long. 96° W., near Wager Inlet, at the northeast coast of Hudson's Bay, where the mean deficit of annual temperature over a normal climate due to the same latitude is—13°. The American pole of *actual* cold is situated about 11° further north on the same meridian. Quebec is affected with a mean deficit of 6½°, and New York by 4°. When we consider that the line of permanent ground frost includes most of Labrador, we can form some conception of the influence of cold currents. Turning our attention to the continent of Asia by way of contrast, it is instructive to find intense cold produced by a different set of causes; for at Yakutsk, the Siberian focus of relative cold, there is a mean annual deficiency of—15°, referable to the extension across Asia of lofty mountain chains between the 30th and 40th parallels, which increase the rigour of the winter to the countries north of them by intercepting the south-west anti-trade, and obliging it to deposit its moisture on their summits; thus draining it of its latent heat, which would otherwise be given out to the plains beyond in rain or snow.† In

---

* The pole of relative cold is that focus where the temperature falls the most below what would be due to the latitude in which it is situated, on the supposition of a normal climate. The pole of actual cold is the focus of the absolutely greatest cold.

† The soil at Yakutsk is frozen to a depth of 630 feet—Sir J. Herschell's "Physical Geography," p. 235.

one case the distributor of temperature is the *sea* and atmosphere, in the other *solely* the atmosphere. Is it not, then, quite evident from these facts that the distribution of land and sea, their physical configuration, together with the direction of currents either of water or air, are competent to produce the conditions of cold shown in the marine drift-beds of Britain?

Marine Evidences of intense Cold on the East Coast of Britain.—It is a remarkable fact that the east coast of Britain presents us with a much more northern fauna as characteristic of the earlier drift-beds than those of the west.

At Elie, in Fifeshire, and Errol, in Perthshire, the Rev. Thos. Brown found shells pronounced by Dr. Otto Torrel to be the exact representatives of those now living in front of the great Glacier of Spitzbergen.[*] The Bridlington beds on the coast of Yorkshire are also shown by Mr. Searles Wood, junr., to indicate more arctic conditions than any of those found either in Lancashire or in the Clyde laminated clays. Mr. Wood also offers very good evidence in favour of the greater age of these east coast beds;[†] in which opinion, from a variety of considerations, and not trusting entirely to the *facies* of the several assemblages, I am inclined to concur. If this be so, it is then quite evident to me, after closely inspecting the base of the clay beds at every available point in this district, that the *conditions on the west coast were subaërial at the time those on the east were submarine.* If this were so, the amelioration of the climate set in before the Lancashire plains were sub-

---

[*] Tran. of the Royal Soc. of Edin., vol. 24, p. 627.

[†] "Quarterly Journal of Geological Society," 1869, p. 97.

merged,* and it would be quite conceivable that if the
German Ocean were flanked by a considerable extension
of land to the westward, and also to the eastward, under
glacial conditions, the then channel would be under
somewhat similar physical conditions to that portion of
the Hudson's Bay territory near to Winter Island.

The absence of Tertiary beds on the west coast lends
further probability to this supposition. The red and
coralline crags occurring only on the south-east angle of
England—unless equivalent deposits have been denuded
from the west coast, of which I am not aware there is
any evidence—show that seas existed then on the site of
the German Ocean. It is considered by Lyell[†] and
Prestwich, that even during these periods floating ice
must have existed from the "presence of huge irregular,
quite unrounded chalk flints, retaining their white
coating, and 2 feet by 1 foot 6 inches, in beds, worked
for phosphatic nodules at Foxhall, four miles south-
east of Ipswich;" and the occurrence of a large block of
Porphyry at Sutton in the base of the coralline crag.
We thus have evidence of a succession of marine deposits
on the east coast, dating from the coralline crag, which
are absent on the west coast. If we combine this fact
with presence of Arctic species in the Drift on the east
that are not found on the west coast, underlying a Drift
—such as that of Caithness, described by Mr. Jamieson,
and seemingly precisely similar to our low-level Boulder-
clay—it is difficult to resist the conclusion that there
was an extension of land to the westward during the
more severe part of the Glacial Period.

* The more I extend my inspection of the base of the Boulder-clay
in the north-west of England, the more clearly it appears to me that
there is a great break in *time* between the period of the rock groovings
and that of the marine clays.

[†] Lyell's "Students Elements of Geology," pp. 176-7.

When we find a difference of relative level occurred during the later stages of the Glacial Period, between the Bristol Channel and Snowdon, of 2,000 feet, forming a gradient of 1 in 330—a wave of elevation, in fact—it is readily conceivable that such difference of relative level, or flexure of the earth's crust, may have, propagated itself also westward and eastward; and an elevation of 600 feet at the 100-fathom line on the west coast of Ireland, shading off into nothing as it approached the east coast of England, giving a gradient of about 1 in 4,400, would, during the prevalence of cold and the existence of land to the northward, now submerged, together with a simultaneous submergence of the northern part of Africa, which we know happened in Post-pliocene times,* produce the conditions that prevailed at the time the Bridlington and other extreme Glacial-beds of the east coast were laid down.†   Until I deal comprehensively with the stratigraphical portion of my investigations, it will, however, be impossible to correlate the Lancashire beds precisely with those so carefully and elaborately worked out by Mr. Searles Wood, junr.   The great submergence, culminating in 2,000 feet in Wales and Scotland, must have had considerable local climatic effect; and would, one is inclined to suppose, of itself, independently of what was taking place elsewhere, tend to raise and equalize the temperature.   It is, however, clear that the Moel Tryfaen shell list shows a rather more northern *facies* than that of the Lancashire clays, and still more than that of the

* See Mr. Maw's Paper.   "Notes on a Journey from Algiers to the Sahara."—*Quart. Journ. Geol. Soc.*, vol. xxx, page 121.

† To enable us to draw a map of the relative amount and distribution of land and sea, it would be necessary to ascertain the synchronisms of the submergences.   From what I suppose to have been the wave-like characters of the earth movements, this synchronism would be a very difficult problem to work out.

Macclesfield cemetery beds. There is, however, nothing at Moel Tryfaen in the constitution of the beds themselves to suggest any greater severity of climate; and I am inclined to think that the difference arises mainly from the spot being in proximity to the mountain district generating the glaciers, though at that time Snowdonia would form an assemblage of small islands.

Having now pointed out the competency of Geographical causes to produce the later stages of the Glacial conditions, and the probability that such a distribution of land and sea did prevail, I may at the same time express my opinion that there appears to have been in the northern hemisphere such an uniform extension of cold southwards round the circumference of the globe, as to lead to the belief that at an earlier period a general or cosmical cause co-operated with the agencies I have mentioned; and it is quite probable that the astronomical effects graduated into geographical effects. It is also evident to me that the intensest period of cold cannot be paralleled by anything we see now; therefore, I am not inclined to ascribe the Glacial Period solely to geographical causes, but rather to astronomical, *re-inforced* by suitable geographical conditions.

The archipelago of Tierra del Fuego, lying between 52° 30'' and 56° S. latitude, has an extremely cold climate. Cloudy weather, rain, and wind prevail throughout the year, and fine days are rare. In the mountainous part of King Charles' Southland, the largest of the islands, Glaciers descend into the sea from almost every valley. Notwithstanding this, the surface of the sea in the Straits of Magalhaens is never lower than 45° Fahrenheit; though the coasts exposed to the influence of the open ocean probably possess a colder climate, as they are in the winter surrounded by large fields of ice. The mean winter temperature is $2\frac{1}{2}°$ above freezing point, though it occasionally descends to $12\frac{1}{2}°$ of Fahrenheit. The snow line is often 3500 to 4000 feet. The existence of Glaciers is probably largely due in this case to the low mean summer temperature and the warm current of water to the inflow from the west coast of South America. The prevailing winds are westerly, and those traversing the Antarctic current will be reduced in temperature. No season is, in fact, quite free from frost; even in February, corresponding with our August, the thermometer descends occasionally a few degrees below freezing point. The climate is altogether peculiar, as fogs are extremely rare; but thick rainy weather prevails, and strong winds. The sun shows itself but little, the sky, even in fine weather being generally overcast and cloudy. A clear day is a very rare occurrence.

The prevalence of winds seem to point to variations of temperature, probably produced by the mingling of air of different temperatures from the north and south, and this would also account for the precipitation of rain and snow. That the atmosphere is drained of its moisture is shown by the level portion of King Charles' Southland, to the eastward of the mountainous district, suffering from want of moisture.

It follows from this example that an extension of cold into lower latitudes is favourable to the creation of currents of water of a temperature different to that of the atmosphere at the same place; for though in this case the summer days are seldom very hot, from the sky being continually overcast, the water heated in adjoining seas flows in to restore the balance of temperature. A warm current would also supply the evaporating surface for the production of moisture, and hence snow. The colder air would get super-saturated; and, expanding as it rose into a higher stratum, when ascending the mountain range, would re-deposit its moisture either as rain or snow. A low mean summer temperature would also be favourable to glacial conditions. The presence of southern forms in the Boulder-clay would rather lead us to think that geographical causes were then more potent than astronomical; at the same time, we have also at Tierra del Fuego indications from old moraines of a former extension of Glaciers. It is the cumulative evidence, both in the south and north, at almost every locality that has been examined, of a former extension of cold towards the Equator, that leads irresistibly to the belief that it was in its intensest form due to cosmical causes. It seems hardly probable that the changes of land and sea could have so uniformly affected the globe this way, even if we consider the existence of the cold as successive, and not synchronous. There is, in fact, no point now on the earth's surface in which we have conditions of cold as intense in the same parallel as during the Glacial Period.

North America.—As showing that the Glacial period was really a "period," and not the mere localisation of cold in Europe, I may point to the extension of Glacial deposits to the 42nd parallel in North America. Lyell describes a train of erratic blocks, rounded on the top, which occurs in the State of New York, thus showing that the cold affected that continent *proportionably;* for no similar example occurs in Europe in so low a latitude, though there is evidence that the southern range of the Reindeer extended to the south of France and the Lake of Geneva, and may have extended further. The southern limit of the Reindeer in North America now is the 50th parallel, or about the same distance south as the Land's End.

MARCH 9TH, 1875.

THE VICE-PRESIDENT, R. A. ESKRIGGE, F.G.S.,
in the Chair.

Dr. JAMES CAMPBELL BROWN, F.G.S., was elected an
Ordinary Member.

The following communication was read :—

THE CAUSE OF THE GLACIAL PERIOD WITH REFERENCE TO GREAT BRITAIN.

BY CHARLES RICKETTS, M.D., F.G.S.

SOME who consider that the Glacial Period was dependent on extreme cold, caused by the winters occurring
when the earth was in aphelion, with a greatly increased
eccentricity of its orbit, have deduced inferences which
do not appear to accord with present physical conditions.

With great glacier systems, such as existed in North
America and in Europe, the air would have had almost
the whole of its moisture condensed out of it by the cold
long before it reached the Arctic Circle; consequently
glaciers could not then have existed on the water slope
of the land surrounding the Arctic Ocean, any more than
they do now; and, so far from there being an "ice-
cap" covering the Arctic regions, there would not have
been sufficient moisture left to form in it ice-floes so great
or extensive as at present.

The increased accumulation of snow now taking place
in Greenland is accompanied by subsidence of the land,
whilst elevation is at the same time rapidly occurring in
Norway and Spitzbergen; it is, therefore, not requisite

to attribute "the invariable occurrence of submergence along with glaciation, to change in the centre of gravity of the earth." The cause of the present subsidence in Great Britain during the Glacial Period was ascribed to the effect which an increased weight of snow would have in forcing downwards the crust of the earth into its fluid substratum.

Previous to the Glacial Period, that is during the Tertiary Period, the Gulf of Mexico extended as far north at the junction of the Mississippi and the Ohio; Florida was submerged; and an extensive belt of land on the east coast of the United States was covered by a sea having a tropical temperature. Such alterations in the coast lines must have induced a condition of climate nearly approaching, if not similar to, that which is indicated by the beds of plant-remains found in Greenland, Iceland, and Spitzbergen.

Dr. Carpenter has demonstrated that the North Polar "set" or current (commonly called North-East Branch of the Gulf Stream) is dependent on diminution of temperature in the Polar regions, causing displacement by sinking of the surface sea-water rendered denser by cooling, and the consequent influx of lighter, that is, warmer water, to supply its place. Increased severity of the winter in the north would therefore augment the volume and velocity of this current, and, *cæteris paribus*, thus render milder that of Britain. This appears to be in accordance with the persistent increase of cold in Greenland and Iceland, simultaneously with recession of the glaciers in Norway, and the occurence of milder winters in Britain; and also with changes which occasionally take place of a more temporary character, as the occurrence in America of winters of exceptional severity, whilst the same seasons were remarkable for their mildness on the eastern shores of the Atlantic, and *vice versâ*.

Not only has the Gulf of Mexico extended far up the valley of the Mississippi, but a former depression of the land has occurred in the West Indian Islands—to 2,000 feet, and even to 5,000 feet. Raised sea beaches occur on the west coast in California, and the Gulf of California is but an extension of the Colorado Valley, which has been submerged. Subsidence to so great an extent on each side would in all probability affect the Isthmus in a similar manner. If such a depression took place in certain areas to the extent respectively of 134 and 300 feet only, it would enable the waters of the Atlantic to flow into the Pacific Ocean.

The fauna has been considered to afford indications of a former inter-communication of the two oceans; by the identity or similarity on each side, of many of the Mollusca (Mr. P. P. Carpenter; British Association Report, 1846), and also of the Echinodermata ("Depths of the Sea," page 14). It is thus more than probable that a passage for the Equatorial Current has been afforded at Panama and Nicaragua. If it occurred to a considerable extent, the North Polar Current would have had no higher temperature than that which it could derive from the Temperate Zone. Such a removal of the Gulf Stream is by most, if not all, considered sufficient to reduce the temperature to so great an amount as to cause the formation of glaciers in Britain; but, though the intense cold would condense the atmospheric moisture and cause extensive ice-floes between Greenland and Norway, there would under such circumstances have been but little remaining to be precipitated in the Arctic Ocean.

It was contended that the succession of Glacial Periods, having intervening times characterised by a mild, or even genial, climate, as demonstrated by Professor and Mr. James Geikie, might have been caused by successive depressions and upheavals of the Isthmus of Central America. To obtain positive proof of this supposed change in the direction of the Equatorial Current, it is requisite that investigations, with this object in view, be made in Nicaragua and other parts of Central America.

MEMBERS

OF THE

LIVERPOOL GEOLOGICAL SOCIETY.

◆

HONORARY MEMBERS.

A. C. RAMSAY, F.R.S., F.G.S., London.
JOHN MORRIS, F.G.S., London.
S. J. MACKIE, F.G.S., F.S.A., London.
WILLIAM PENGELLY, F.R.S., F.G.S., Torquay.
EDWARD W. BINNEY, F.R.S., F.G.S., Douglas, Isle of Man.
WILLIAM BRYHAM, Wigan.
HENRY HICKS, F.G.S., M.R.C.S.E., London.
W. KING, D. Sc., Queen's College, Galway.

MEMBERS.

ABRAHAM, J., Riverham, Grassendale Park.
  87, Bold Street.
ARCHER, F., B.A., Boundary Cottage, Crosby.
  14, Cook Street.
ARNOTT, T. R., Bramshill, Harlesden Green, London.
  6, Mersey Chambers.
BEASLEY, H., Gateacre.
*BOSTOCK, R., 8, Grange Lane, Birkenhead.
BREWSTER, C., Rev., 115, Huskisson Street.
BROWN, C. H., Low-wood, Alexandra Road, Southport.
BROWN, J. CAMPBELL, D. Sc., F.C.S., 10, Clare Terrace, Marmaduke
  Street.

CLEGG, T., 28, Wentworth Street.
DAVIES, C., 8, Kinglake Street, Edge Hill.
DAWBARN, W., Elmswood, Aigburth.
         The Temple, Dale Street.
DIXON, T., 27, St. James's Road.
DODD, J., 2, Derby Terrace, Rock Ferry.
ECCLES, J., F.G.S., Springwell House, Blackburn.
*ESKRIGGE, R. A., F.G.S., Fir Cottage, New Brighton.
         18, Hackins Hey.
FOSTER, E., 7, Newstead Road, Smithdown Lane.
FITZPATRICK, M., 62, Seel Street.
GOLDSWORTH, W., Prescot.
GREGSON, S. L., Aigburth Road.
         Slater Court, 5, Castle Street.
GREEN, A., York House, Old Chester Road, Rock Ferry.
         9, Canning Place.
GRIFFITHS, J., 27, Castle Street, Chester.
*HALL, H. F., F.G.S., Green Heys, Grove Road, Wallasey.
         17, Dale Street.
HANCE, E. W., LL.B., Municipal Offices, Dale Street.
HATHAWAY, T., C.E., The Mount, Bangor, North Wales.
*HIGGINS, H. H., Rev., M.A., Rainhill.
HILES, J., Sefton Villas, Rice Lane, Walton.
JEVONS, G., Jun., 5, Chapel Street.
JONES, T., Top Lane, Wallasey.
         Orange Court, Castle Street.
KEEN, R. J., 85, Edge Lane.
         17, South Castle Street.
KERSHAW, J., Nevill Street, Southport.
KIRBY, C., C.E., Newport, Monmouthshire.
LOBLEY, J. L., F.G.S., 59, Clarendon Road, Kensington Park,
    London, W.
McCLAY, J. L., Spring Bank, Church Road, Higher Tranmere.
M'KAIG, W. R., 30, Queen Buildings, Dale Street.
*MARRAT, F. P., 21, Kinglake Street.
MAYER, J., F.S.A., Pennant House, Lower Bebington.
*MOORE, T. J., C.M.Z.S.L., 21, Fitzclarence Street, Everton.
         Liverpool Museum.
*MORGAN, ALFRED (Honorary Treasurer), 2, Rathbone Terrace,
    Wellington Road, Wavertree.   Office, 126, London Road.
MORTIMER Captain, Liverpool.
*MORTON, G. H., F.G.S., F.R.G.S.I. (Honorary Secretary), 21, West
    Derby Street.   122, London Road.
MOTT, C. G., Sunnyside, Cavendish Road, Birkenhead.
PARIS, T. J., 68 and 70, Lord Street.
         Rake Lane, Liscard.

PATERSON, J., Palmyra Street, Warrington.

PEARSE, W., Green Bank Farm, Wavertree.

*PICTON, J. A., F.S.A., Sandy Knowe, Wavertree.
      4 and 5, Queen Buildings, Dale Street.

*POTTER, C., 101, Miles Street.

PEARSON, J. E., Golborne Park, near Newton-le-Willows.

*READE, T. M., F.G.S., Heath House, Blundellsands.
      Canning Chambers, 4, South John Street.

*RICKETTS, C., M.D., F.G.S., 22, Argyle Street, Birkenhead.

*ROBERTS, I., F.G.S., 26, Rock Park, Rock Ferry.
      39, Gardener's Row.

SHONE, W., F.G.S., 86, Watergate Street, Chester.

SEMMONS, W., F.G.S., 20, Canning Place.

STRONGITHARM, G., 77, Whetstone Lane, Tranmere.

WASON, J., 26, Hamilton Street, Birkenhead.
      4, Harrington Street.

WILSON, W. H., St. Michael's Hamlet, Aigburth.
      31, Wapping.

WESTWORTH, R., 31, King Street.

WHALLEY, E., London and Lancashire Insurance Company, Queen Buildings.

WRIGHT, B. M., F.R. Hist. Soc., 37, Great Russell Street, Bloomsbury, London.

WARD, T., Northwich, Cheshire.

*Have read Papers before the Society.

PROCEEDINGS

OF THE

iverpool Geological Society.

ESSION THE SEVENTEENTH.

1875-6.

he Authors having revised their own papers, are alone responsible for the facts and opinions expressed in them.)

PART II.—VOL. III.

LIVERPOOL:

COURIER PRINTING WORKS, VICTORIA STREET.

—

1876.

SIDE-CAÑON OF THE COLERADO.
AFTER LIEUT. J. C. IVES, U.S.

PROCEEDINGS

OF THE

𝕷𝖎𝖛𝖊𝖗𝖕𝖔𝖔𝖑 𝕲𝖊𝖔𝖑𝖔𝖌𝖎𝖈𝖆𝖑 𝕾𝖔𝖈𝖎𝖊𝖙𝖞.

SESSION THE SEVENTEENTH.

1875-6.

(The Authors having revised their own papers, are alone responsible for the facts and opinions expressed in them.)

PART II—VOL. III.

LIVERPOOL:
COURIER PRINTING WORKS, VICTORIA STREET.

———

1876.

OFFICERS, 1875—6.

President.
T. MELLARD READE, C.E., F.G.S.

Vice-President.
ROBERT A. ESKRIGGE, F.G.S.

Honorary Treasurer.
ALFRED MORGAN.

Honorary Librarian.
EDWIN FOSTER.

Honorary Secretary.
GEORGE H. MORTON, F.G.S., F.R.G.S.I.

Council.
FREDERICK P. MARRAT.

HENRY BEASLEY.

HUGH F. HALL, F.G.S.

WILLIAM SEMMONS, F.G.S.

ROBERT BOSTOCK.

THE PROCEEDINGS

OF THE

LIVERPOOL GEOLOGICAL SOCIETY.

SESSION SEVENTEENTH.

OCTOBER 12TH, 1875.

THE PRESIDENT, T. MELLARD READE, C.E., F.G.S.,
in the Chair.

ERNEST L. FLEMING, F.C.S., was elected an Ordinary
Member.

The President read the Annual Address.

PRESIDENT'S ADDRESS.

SINCE I last had the pleasure of presiding over a
meeting of this Society, a giant intellect has passed away.
In the late Sir Charles Lyell were combined all the
qualities necessary for the formation of an inductive
philosopher of the very first rank. The position he
occupied in Geological science you are familiar with.
Yet, if I may be allowed to be critical with the critics,
I think that his labours have not been justly appreciated :
no notice of his life that I have seen appears to fully
realise the extent to which modern Geology is indebted
to him, to say nothing of the influence—the silent
influence—his writings have had upon the philosophical
thought of the age. It will take years before the focus
of distinct vision is reached ; and then, if I mistake not,
Lyell will be recognised as the founder of the philosophy
of Geology—the science of Geology in its widest aspects

and relations. In the light of the work of such practical geologists as William Smith, Sir Roderick Murchison, Sedgwick, Buckland, and De la Beche, probably many will think my views exaggerated; and it may also be said that Hutton and Playfair laid the foundations of the uniformitarian view of inorganic creation long before Lyell had directed his attention to the subject. These are names which, together with those of many eminent geologists now living, I need hardly say, I hold in the very highest estimation; but their work was of a different order: they were great and earnest workers in discovering new *facts*, while Lyell was systematising the science of Geology as a whole, and dropping down each into its exact place in his system, the facts as discovered by them and other investigators all over the civilised globe. Great geologists, of the type of Murchison and Sedgwick, distinguished themselves by their labours and perspicuity in working out the relationship of the various formations. I have heard those who can only appreciate that class of work say that Lyell was not a discoverer; never was there a profounder mistake. As I stood, at the commencement of this year, in Westminster Abbey upon the great man's grave—with the wreath by which Her Majesty intimated the estimation in which she held his name lying faded upon it—I could not help saying to myself: "This was the man to whom it was first given to clearly apprehend the relations of the natural phenomena of the earth as a whole." If the correct reading of the history of the earth is not a discovery, then Lyell is no discoverer; or, if it be argued that this history could not have been revealed to him without the labours of others, then, we may reply, neither could Sir Roderick have discovered the Silurian system without the assistance of other earnest workers in the rocks. What Murchison and Sedgwick did for the Cambrian and Silurian systems, Lyell did for Geology. The key-note which he struck is not the doctrine of uniformitarianism, of which too much is made, but the doctrine of slow change: the building up of the earth's crust by small accretions, in opposition to the tremendous cataclysms which geologists in his early days resorted to so freely to explain difficulties. Whatever my hearers may think of the truth or otherwise of Dr. Darwin's particular evolutionary hypothesis, it is— though represented by no less an authority than Mr. Geikie as striking at the root of Lyell's uniformitarianism—to my mind but the natural off-shoot of the principles he enunciated so well. Lyell does not start with the assumption that nature has been uniform throughout all time; but that, so far as inorganic nature is concerned, as shown by the science of Geology, we have no reason for considering it otherwise than practically so. This, to my mind, is an *induction*—not an hypothesis. Lyell, evidently, was not fond of hypotheses: he knew too well how the early geologists had been misled in this way; and there are, I rather regret to see, certain signs of a relapse in favour of *à-priori* reasoning—or, a putting of hypothesis in place of fact— which we shall do well to guard against. The truth is, no mind was more open to new light than Lyell's, but he would not accept crude theories, even though they might tell in favour of his view; hence his earnest combating of the Lamarkian hypothesis in the early editions of his "Principles." Hence, also, a feasible explanation of a phenomena by reference to actual fact had more weight with him than a possible explanation by an assumption. The latter *might* prove the true explanation, but sound principles led him to prefer the former until it was disproved. In such a tone of mind, let us trust, the great problems of Geology and Life will continue to be approached by others, and that Lyell may not have lived his life in vain.

Having now briefly referred to the labours of the author of the "Principles of Geology," and attempted to estimate the place he will occupy in the history of Geological science, I cannot render a fitter tribute to his memory than in the subject I am about to bring before you—to adhere to that true and safe mode of investigation of which he was the able and eloquent expounder. What I have said of Lyell will, I trust, form a fitting introduction to the subject matter of this address, viz: a comparison of what is known of the Geology of the EARTH, with what we can infer of the formation and history of the MOON from her surface configuration.

In looking over Professor Ramsay's memoir on the Geology of North Wales, and then reading the remarks of Sir Roderick Murchison in "Siluria"—in which he politely hints his disbelief in the ancient forms of the Snowdon range as depicted by sweeping anticlinals in Ramsay's diagrams*—it struck me that, if, as astronomers say, there is no appreciable atmosphere and no water in the moon, a comparison of the forms of the lunar surface with that of the earth would be sure to yield some interesting and instructive information. Fortunately for my purpose, Messrs. Nasmyth and Carpenters' work afforded a considerable amount of information of the kind required regarding our Satellite; and, without further preface, I will now proceed to lay before you the conclusions the comparison has led up to.

It is hardly necessary for me to call your attention to the fact that, by far, the greater proportion of rocks

---

* Siluria, pp. 498-9.

exposed at the surface of the earth are what is called sedimentary—that is, they have been formed by the disintegration of other rocks by atmospherical, chemical, or mechanical forces, and removed, conveyed, distributed and aggregated by aqueous action, either fresh or marine. These rocks have, I believe, been variously estimated as having an aggregate thickness of from 14 to 17 miles; but, from various causes, this thickness is very difficult to calculate.

In the first place, no system possesses the same thickness in any two places; therefore, if we add up the maximum thicknesses of the various formations—from the Laurentian upwards—we may over-estimate the thickness of the sedimentary crust of the earth, while, on the other hand, it is impossible to predicate, as Lyell so forcibly points out, that the Plutonic rocks underlying the sedimentary are not melted sediments themselves. Thus, in an attempt to estimate the part that water has played in the former history of our globe, we are met by a twofold difficulty; and the question is still further complicated by our limited knowledge of the earth's surface, that knowledge being solely confined to the continents and islands—many hardly yet explored— occupying but one-fourth of the surface of the globe. Again, as the later sedimentary rocks are principally derived from preëxisting rocks of the same character, the denudation of the one must be co-extensive with the formation of the other, denudation and deposition forming a physical equation. Thus, as you are well aware, it is only by continual upheavals and subsidences and fractures of the crust that the earth has been so uniformly covered with sediment as we find it. That these movements—consisting partly of slow variations of level over large areas, unaccompanied, so far as we know, with rupture of the crust, and partly of movements due to earthquake shocks faulting the rocks in the way we are familiar with, and causing vertical displacements of, in some instances, thousands of feet—are due to volcanic forces, there can, I think, be no reasonable doubt.

It is not, however, my immediate object to discuss whether this action is deep-seated in a central fluid nucleus; or whether it arises from chemical action in the crust of the earth itself; or whether it be due to the secular cooling of the earth and the reproduction of heat by the falling in of the crust—a conversion of simple mechanical force into heat—as lately ingeniously maintained by Mr. Robert Mallet. From whatever cause it may arise, we know that volcanic forces—heat energy—still exists in sufficient quantity, according to Lyell, to account not only for recent changes, but for those which have taken place through the long course of Geological time, without pre-supposing that these agents were present in greater energy than now. This is what has been called by the awkward name (invented first, I believe, by Professor Huxley) "uniformitarianism." As I have before stated, Lyell never has committed himself to any statement of the *absolute* uniformity of nature : only *practical* uniformity. That these views are fully justified by our present knowledge of Geology, has been questioned lately by Professor Prestwich in his late valuable address on the "Past and Future of Geology"—but, in my opinion, without disturbing Lyell's position. Whether or not we believe that the forces of nature were more energetic or not in early geologic ages, that they were the same in *kind*, I think no one now disputes. That the centres of volcanic action shift their places over the surface of the globe, is also an admitted axiom in the mechanics of Geology. To go no further than North Wales or the

Cumberland mountains, we there find some of the earliest instances of volcanic *centres*, Silurian in age, though the cones and craters—but not lava streams—have long since been removed by that great agent, denudation, of which more anon. Then, again, we have in the Basalts of Antrim and Fingal's Cave the remains of volcanic action in the Tertiary age, with the cones and craters removed; and, as is so admirably shown in a late paper by Mr. Judd "On the Ancient Volcanoes of the Highlands, and the Relations of their Products to the Mesozoic Strata," the Granitic and Syenitic cores or bases formed originally deep down in the bowels of the earth, traversed by extensive masses of gabbro, displayed to the eye in all their complicated anatomy by nature's scalpel denudation.* Again, in the classic region of Auvergne, in the South of France, volcanic cones, pronounced by Professor Hull to be Tertiary and of the same age as the Antrim Basalts, exist almost as perfectly formed as when first built up from the ejecta of the volcanoes, though, at the same time, their enormous age is indicated in the valleys by the denudation which has since taken place.†

---

* Speaking of the Island of Mull, Mr. Judd says:—"The group of mountains occupying the central portion of the Island is clearly the greatly denuded core of an immense volcanic pile—the great accumulation of scoriæ and lavas which formed the bulk of this mountain mass having been to a great extent removed, and what now remains to our study being little more than the skeleton or framework of the vast pile formed by the consolidation of the springs of liquefied rock which rose through its mass."—*Quar. Journ. of Geo. Soc.*, vol. xxx, p. 248.

† Professor Hull says, in his Address to the Geological Section of the British Association, Belfast, 1874:—"But the most remarkable result of the denudation, as bearing upon the subject before us, is the complete obliteration of the volcanic cones which, we may well suppose, studded the plateaus. Some of these cones, at least, were contemporaneous with those now standing upon the granitic plateau of Central France, and which are but little altered in elevation since the fires which once burst forth from them became extinct."—p. 72.

Thus, we see, through the different action to which these volcanic rocks of the North of Britain and Ireland, and those of the South of France, have been exposed, we might, if we did not keep true to Lyell's safe mode of reasoning, infer from those in the North a greater activity and energy of the denuding agents of nature in the Tertiary times, and from the cones in the South of France but little energy of denudation from the time they were formed unto the present.

If we examine the Silurian formation in the neighbourhood of Ludlow, we not only find that the various divisions of Siluria up to the Llandovery beds occur successively without a break, but that they also lie conformably on the Cambrian rocks of the Longmynd. Mr. Hicks has also shown this to be the case with the Silurians at St. David's Head, in Pembrokeshire, and that "the sequence of rocks, of which these form a part in the promontory of St. David's, is a perfectly continuous one, from the base of the Longmynd or Harlech group to the Llandeilo group, and that in this section there are no lines of division stronger than what would naturally occur in a great series deposited over a sea-bottom becoming gradually depressed and subject to the ordinary physical influence which must have prevailed during such a change."—*Quar. Jour. Geo. Soc.*, vol. xxxi, p. 181.

The total thickness of the British Silurian rocks is 26,000 feet. They contain, in Shropshire, millions of fossils—mollusks, crustaceans, and, lastly, fish-bones, in regular order and sequence, laid down in quiet waters in undisturbed sediments, containing, about Ludlow, not even a boulder or pebble, so far as my personal examination has gone. Is it, then, not a legitimate inference that, while the volcanoes of Wales and Cumbria were active through ages longer than it is possible to calculate, sediments were being laid down in the Silurian seas lasting over a still more lengthened period: a period long enough for one species to be succeeded by another, and to be replaced, again, by a third; so that the geologist's estimate of the time required for the sediments to be deposited over the immense area occupied by these rocks, thousands of feet thick, is reinforced by arguments drawn from Paleontology. There is nothing whatever known to me to show that these sediments were formed under physical conditions differing, in any respect, from what can be paralleled upon the earth now. The immense length of time involved in the creation of these rocks is so stupendous as to defy the human mind to grasp.*

If, then, such early rocks took so long to form, what becomes of the supposed superior energy of the forces then existent?—where is the evidence or the necessity for it? That they were formed under quiet conditions is known; for Ramsay has shown that the Silurian sediments, with their included Ash-beds, Porphyries, and Traps of the Snowdon district, were bent, plicated, compressed, and contorted by a distinct set of internal forces, long after the volcanoes giving birth to the Ash-beds and Porphyries became extinct.†

Again, to argue from another class of facts, there is hardly an instance known of a cliff produced by a fault. A writer in "Nature,"‡ describing an excursion of the

---

* Professor Ramsay says, in the discussion of the Rev. O. Fisher's paper on Mallet's theory of volcanic energy:—"In that sense, the Laurentian rocks are not of extreme antiquity; for the sediments of which they were formed were derived from pre-existing continents composed, as at present, of stratified and igneous rocks."—*Quart. Journ. Geo. Soc.*, vol. xxxi, p. 477.

† Ramsay's Geo. of North Wales—Memoirs of the Geo. Survey.—p. 234.

‡ Vol. xii, p. 93,

Geological class of the University of Edinburgh, has pointed out that the great fault—of unascertained displacement—traversing Scotland from Stonehaven, on the east coast, in a straight line to Arran, a distance of 170 miles, is undistinguishable on the surface, being crossed by all the rivers and some of the lakes which emerge from the southern side of the Grampians;* and this is not a solitary but a common fact. I ask, is this not another proof that Lyell was right in attributing these great faults and dislocations to repeated shocks acting in the line of least resistance, rather than to enormous catastrophes? I think it is; else the obliteration of the work on the surface should not have been so complete. In dealing with my subject so far, I feel that I have been merely stating elementary principles. There are, however, a class of deductive reasoners rather in the ascendant at present, who, arguing from two or three simple principles, demonstrate mathematically, to their own satisfaction, that such and such things *ought* of necessity to happen, and, therefore, *did* happen; to enquire whether their notions square with known facts being quite unnecessary. A knowledge of Geology would tend to make such reasoners less sure, and compel them to ask of Nature if such theories were confirmed by her records. Any theory of the earth that does not stand the geologic test—the test of reference to the earth itself—is valueless, except as a warning against hasty generalisation; and it

---

* Mr. Judd points out the striking instance of denudation since the Miocene afforded in the great fault of Morven, where a mass of Lias is unconformably overlain by upper Cretaceous; and this, again, by Miocene basalts, let down about 2000 feet, against the contorted gneissic rocks of the Lower Silurian.—*Quar. Journ. Geo. Soc.*, vol. xxx, p. 231,

is pleasant to find that rising geologist, **Mr. Judd,** insisting on the importance of adhering to the safe principles Lyell was the first clearly to expound. *

To revert again to the subject of the shifting centres of volcanic action or subterranean force, we may instance the Swiss Alps, mostly composed of Tertiary rocks; of the great Plateaus of Thibet, 14,000 feet above the sea also containing Tertiary fossils; and, lastly, what we have evidence of nearer home—the submersion of the whole of Great Britain and Ireland to a maximum depth of about 2,000 feet below the sea level, during the comparatively recent Glacial period.

Without citing further instances, it is quite clear that the earth is covered all over with signs of volcanic action, most of which is only disclosed to us by the denuding action of rain, rivers, and the sea. If we could pare off the crust of the earth, we should find them still more numerous, the roots of ancient volcanoes ramifying through the strata of various ages. Mr. Scrope, in his classic treatise on volcanoes, conceived in the truest geological spirit, states it has been variously estimated there are at the present time from 200 to 400 volcanic cones in existence, most of which are active, or have been within the historical age.† Others, we know, have been denuded, and their remains buried among the sedimentary rocks, or entirely obscured by them.

It is perfectly clear that the whole of the present continents have been not once, but often, immersed beneath

---

* Mr. Judd says, in his paper on "Volcanoes" (*Geological Magazine,* New Series, vol. ii, p. 3):—"In some of the latest researches on Vulcanology—to which I have referred at the commencement of this article—however, a tendency is shown towards abandoning those safer methods of enquiry based on the doctrine of Uniformity, and reverting to the earlier methods: in effect, to the substitution of Cosmogony for Geology."

† p. 11—Second Edition.

the sea, and (as is fair to assume, from the forms of the sea as displayed by soundings) that which is now sea has been not once, but often, dry land.*

It is a well-established fact that the islands of the Pacific have formed, at one time or another, vast continents. This is proved, not only by their faunas and a consideration of the geographical distribution of animals, but by the known subsidence of the bed of the Pacific, first demonstrated by Darwin in his theory of coral atolls. Not only so, but the valleys and mountains now forming the bottom of the sea, disclosed by soundings in various parts of the world, bear the impress of their sub-aërial origin; their formation, in many cases, by rain, rivers, or ice. Again, the West Coast of Ireland and Scotland, and the fiords of Norway, are further proofs of subsidence, the irregular coast line being formed by the partial submergence of valleys excavated by sub-aërial influences; and, in my opinion, the great trough, or valley, from the Cattegat to the North Cape, from 100 to 300 fathoms deep, following the coast of Norway and receiving these tributary valleys, is, in all probability, in its origin the same. To multiply instances would take up too much time; but I can refer you to my paper on the "Distribution of Land and Sea during the Glacial Period" for some further evidences.

If we consider that during the historical period Vesuvius and Etna have served as vents for the subterranean forces of Europe; that—excepting the blowing up and shivering of one cone and the building up of another within it, or the repetition of this on several occasions—the two mountains remain substantially now

---

* Ramsay seems to hold the view that the present continents have existed, as such from very early geological times.—*Quar. Journ. of Geo. Soc.*, vol. xxxi, p. 478.

what they were at the time of our earliest records; that it is probable they have existed as vents, before this, for a length of time immense but difficult to estimate; and that the volcanoes of Iceland may not improbably have existed since the Tertiary era: we may form some conception of the time it has taken for the volcanic energies to have travelled over the whole surface of the globe. The distribution of volcanoes in *time* would prove an interesting and fruitful investigation, and throw considerable light on the history of Geology.

In the short space of this address, it has been impossible to give more than the salient features of the Geology of the Earth from the standpoint that I have chosen; but I trust sufficient has been said to bring clearly to your minds the antithisis existing between the earth and its satellite, which I am now about to describe.

If now we turn our attention to the Physiography of the Moon, we find, from the admirable views and photographs of models made by Mr. Nasmyth of her surface,* that the side which is turned towards us presents what

---

* It must not be forgotten that the moon is but $\frac{1}{3663}$ of the diameter of the earth, and the force of gravity at the surface but $\frac{1}{6}$ that of the earth; and this may assist to account for the absence of signs of violent ejection, as the ejective forces must be commensurate with the resistance met with. If the rocks are of a compactness at all similar to those of the earth, it is also evident that a greater mass might be built up with a smaller force, as the "hydraulic head" of the molten fluid would be practically only $\frac{1}{6}$ of that on the earth volcanoes. The density of the moon is also 0.62 that of the earth. I subjoin the table of data given by Nasmyth and Carpenter:—

Diameter of the Moon ....2,160 miles.. $\frac{1}{3663}$ that of the Earth.
Area ....14,657,000 sqr. miles.. $\frac{1}{13434}$,,
Area of the visible hemisphere, 7,328,500 ,, ..
Solid Contents..5,276 millions of cubic miles.. $\frac{1}{49186}$
Mass ....73 trillions of tons.. $\frac{1}{80}$
Density ....3.39 (water=1).. 0·62   ,,
Force of Gravity at the Surface .... $\frac{1}{6}$,,
    Mean distance from Earth ....238,790 miles.

has not inaptly been termed a Phlegreian field of volcanoes—so named from the *Campi Phlegræi*, the volcanic
district about Naples. Instead of mountain ranges,
valleys, and other irregularities such as we are familiar
with on the Earth, we have the so-called lunar volcanoes
in ring after ring, almost incalculable in numbers, and in
sizes varying from a mile to 200 miles in diameter.
This is usually considered indisputable evidence of long
continued volcanic activity, such as, apparently, cannot
be paralleled by anything we have experience of here.
There is also this difference from the earth, *inactivity*,
inasmuch as astronomers who have watched the moon
say that the whole of her volcanoes are now extinct.
There is also a decided general difference in the section
of the rings to the volcanic cones existing on the earth;
but this I will presently speak of more in detail.

To give you a general conception of the physiography
of the lunar surface, I must now ask your attention to
the picture map of the moon, and index map, enlarged
from those prepared by Nasmyth and Carpenter. The
class of features observable are four in number, and
consist of crater rings—with or without central cones—
the largest of which have been called walled plains;
mountain chains, with occasional isolated peaks; smooth
plains called "seas," with more or less irregularity of
surface; cracks or fissures, occasionally forming cliffs,
one valley, and bright radiating streaks. Nasmyth
and Carpenter say "a higher telescopic power
shows us that not only do these craters exist
of all magnitudes within a limit of largeness — but
seemingly with no limit of smallness—but that in their
structure and arrangement they present a great variety
of points of difference: some are seen to be considerably
elevated above the surrounding surface—others are

basins hollowed out of that surface, and with low surrounding ramparts; some are merely like walled plains, or amphitheatres, with flat plateaus, while the majority have their lowest point of hollowness considerably below the general level of the surrounding surface; some are isolated upon the plains—others are aggregated into a thick crowd, and overlapping and intruding upon each other; some have elevated peaks, or cones, in their centres, and some are without these central cones, while the plateaus of others, again, contain several minute craters instead; some have their ramparts whole and perfect, others have them breached or malformed, and many have them divided into terraces, especially on their inner sides.

In the plains, what, with a low power, appeared smooth as a water surface, becomes, under greater magnification, a rough and furrowed area: here gently undulated, and there broken into ridges and declivities, with now and then deep rents or cracks, extending for miles, and spreading, like river beds, into numerous ramifications. Craters of all sizes and classes are scattered over the plains; these appear generally of a different tint to the surrounding surface, for the light reflected from the plains has been observed to be slightly tinged with colour. The tint is not the same in all cases: one large sea has a dingy greenish tinge, others are merely grey, and some others present a pale reddish hue. The cause of this diversity of colour is mysterious; it has been supposed to indicate the existence of vegetation of some sort; but this involves conditions that we know do not exist.

The mountains, under higher magnification, do not present such diversity of formation as the craters, or, at least, the points of difference are not so apparent; but they exhibit a plentiful variety of combinations. There are a few perfectly isolated examples that cast long shadows over the plains on which they stand, like those of a towering cathedral in the rising or setting sun. Sometimes they are collected into groups; but, mostly, they are connected into stupendous chains. In one of the grandest of these chains, it has been estimated that a good telescope will show 3,000 mountains clustered together, *without approach to symmetrical order*. The scenery which they would present, could we get any other than 'the bird's-eye view' to which we are confined, must be imposing in the extreme, far exceeding in sublime grandeur anything that the Alps or the Himalayas offer; for while, on the one hand, the lunar mountains equal those of the earth in altitude, the absence of an atmosphere, and, consequently, of the effects produced thereby, must give rise to alternations of dazzling light and black depths of shade; combining to form panoramas of wild scenery that, for want of a parallel on earth, we may well call unearthly." With reference to the radiating bright streaks from some of the more conspicuous centres, it is proved that they do not arise from any difference of level, as they show most plainly when the sun is shining perpendicularly upon them. It is not improbable these may be dykes of a more highly reflective rock than that of the mass they have cut through. "Whatever may be the cause that produces this brightness of certain parts of the moon, without reference to configuration of surface, this cause has not been confined to the formation of the radiaing lines; for we meet with many isolated spots, streaks, and patches of the same bright character. Upon some of the plains there are small areas and lines of luminous matter possessing peculiarities similar to those of the radiating streaks, as regards visibility with the high sun, and invisibility when the solar rays fall upon them horizontally. Some of the craters also are surrounded by a kind of aureole of this highly reflective matter. A notable specimen is that called Linné, concerning which a great hue-and-cry about change of appearance and inferred continuance of volcanic action on the moon was raised some years ago. This object is an insignificant little crater of about a mile or two in diameter, in the centre of an ill-defined spot of the character referred to, and about eight or ten miles in diameter. With a low sun, the crater alone is visible by its shadow; but as the luminary rises, the shadow shortens and becomes all but invisible, and then the white spot shines forth. These alternations, complicated by variations of atmospheric condition, and by the interpretations of different observers, gave rise to statements of somewhat exaggerated character, to the effect that considerable changes of the nature of volcanic eruptions were in progress in that particular region of the moon."

The following is a list of some of the principal craters:—

Crater	Diameter	
Companion to Hell	1¾ miles diameter.	
Companion to Tibit	2¾ ,,	,,
Small crater inside "Walter"	4 ,,	
Companion to Parot	11 ,,	
Herschel	17 ,,	..
Godin	22 ,,	
Vitello	24 ,,	
Delambre	26 ,,	
Campanus	27 ,,	
Agrippa	30 ,,	
Eratosthnes	33 ,,	
Werner	38 ,,	
Copernicus	46 ,,	
Tycho	50 ,,	
Theophilus	64 ,,	
Alphons	70 ,,	
Petavius	78 ,,	

It must be remembered that, through the moon revolving on her axis exactly in the same time that she accomplishes her orbit, we see but half of her surface; but through what are called her "librations," this is increased to about four-sevenths of her surface; still leaving ample room for those who try, to imagine what her *other side* is like.

Now, what is the first idea that a consideration of these facts impresses on the mind? Probably that the moon is, in the largest sense, a "used-up" world—that, as Mr. Lockyer in one of his lectures in this town startlingly said, "the moon is dead, the earth is dying." A little investigation from the geological point of view will, however, I think, show that the "situation" he depicted is more dramatic than true, and that the inhabitants of this planet have some few crumbs of comfort left! I have shown you that volcanoes have been active on the earth through all geological time—that they are active still we all know—yet the evidences of their former profusion are not patent to every one, but must be sought for. The cones have been removed, cut down, covered up, and their bases again disclosed by denudation. The thickness of the sedimentary deposits accumulated proves that the time required to effect all these changes in the earth's surface must have been enormous. If, then, the external forms of these ancient volcanoes have been destroyed on the earth and volcanic cones are limited to particular areas, how is it that the moon's surface remains dotted all over with rings, presumably volcanic? To me the answer is obvious and clear:—In the moon there is *no atmosphere* and *no water*, and consequently no denuding agencies to remodel her surface; so that the inferences of astronomers as to the physics of the moon are strangely borne out by geological considerations. If we are to assume, on the other hand, that, though non-existent now, there *were formerly* seas and an atmosphere to the moon, which in process of time have become dried up, withdrawn into cavities and fissures in her surface, or through her peculiar form have gravitated to the opposite side to that which we see, or in fact have done anything to escape observation—and all these hypotheses have from time to time received support from one or. another eminent scientific man—I ask, where are the geologic evidences of the former existence of a sea or an atmosphere? So far as we can judge from the physiography of her surface, I answer that there are none; and that, if we are to assume their previous existence, we must be also prepared to believe that they have not only been entirely obliterated by volcanic action since, but that the volcanic action, after entirely extinguishing them, has lasted long enough to destroy all vestiges of the denuding agencies which would be at work while the water and the atmosphere existed! Let us now revert to our own world, and consider what sort of a surface she would have presented had she also had no sea or atmosphere. Here you will say we are at once involved in hypothesis, and so we are; but I think, if we agree that water and the atmosphere are the great destroy-ers as well as renovators of our earth—the only denuders we know of — we may safely assume that, the volcanic activity remaining as before, the earth's surface would now present a series of rings and truncated cones not altogether dissimilar to that of the moon. There is, however, one thing to be considered which complicates the reasoning: if there were no water there would be no steam, and no ejecta from the volcanic vents. This undoubtedly is the great difficulty we have to face in the comparison; but I think there are reasonable evidences

to show that steam, which, as beautifully explained
by Scrope, plays so important a part on mundane volcanoes, may have been absent—nay, that there is every
probability it was absent in the moon, even when her
volcanoes were in full activity. When we know, from
spectroscopical observations, now so scientifically carried
out, that the elements of the sun and planets are identical
with those of the earth, and also from meteorites (supposed fragments of asteroids), we infer that the mineral
composition of planetary bodies does not materially differ
from those we are acquainted with, it seems difficult to
understand why the moon should be devoid of water and
an atmosphere. As my object is not to suggest reasons
or hypotheses, but rather to deal with facts, I must confine myself to the thesis that the geologic evidences are
at one with the physical observations; and not only rein-
force the truth of their declared non-existence, but also
tend to prove that they never did exist. A careful study
of the moon's physiography shows no instances of denu-
dations such as we find on the earth, where, as is
acknowledged by all our leading geologists, its contours
of hill and dale, as we see them, are due to denuding
agencies; or, to use a simile to better express the idea,
the volcanic forces have provided the *blocks*, but the
denuding agencies have carved them into shape. Had
water at any time existed on the moon in the form of
seas, most of the rings and cones would have been
levelled and destroyed; vapours would have been raised
by the sun's rays, and again precipitated in the form of
rain: such rain would have cut gorges and valleys dissimilar to anything we see on the moon's surface. It
would have corrugated the mountains, and through great
rivers have carried the detritus washed from the decomposing rocks, to spread it evenly over the sea or lake

bottoms; which being in after ages upheaved, would have been again exposed to the denuders and carved into those endless forms of beauty the true lover of landscape so delights to depict: it would, in fact, instead of being a desolate mass of scoriæ and volcanic rocks, have been an earth in miniature.

What lends greater force to this reasoning, is the fact that from the revolution of the moon on its own axis only taking place monthly, the extremes of temperature of the surface exposed and that hidden from the sun's rays are intense, estimated as ranging from 200° below zero, or the supposed temperature of space, to twice that of boiling water. Is it not likely that storms of great violence, tremendous downpours of rain, and the not less destructive influence of frost arising from a range of 500° of heat, would have destroyed most of the rings and cones, and carved the surface of the moon much more rapidly. than anything we see taking place upon the earth? That the volcanoes were successive and not synchronous is clearly proved by the superposition of one ring upon another, and by the numerous parasitic cones existing upon the rings themselves. If the volcanoes had emitted steam, such steam would have condensed into rain, and we should see the effect of it now on the physiography of the surface.

Again, had there been seas, the tides would have been greatly higher than those on the earth. Sir George Biddell Airy, the Astronomer Royal, to whom I have been more than once indebted for valuable assistance, informs me that the height of a tide in the moon, due to the earth and sun would be 36·18 times the height of a tide on the earth, due to the moon and the sun. This would have given a considerable amount of shore between high and low waters exposed to the tremendous extremes of temperature named, and would have left its beach-marks permanently on the moon. It is true that the tides taking place twice a month instead of twice a day would not have possessed the momentum the earth tides have, and consequently not the same destructive force; but it is probable the revolution of the moon on her axis was at one time greater than now; and had it at any time been in the same period as the earth, though the temperature would have approached the equableness of the earth, the mere mechanical force developed by the tides would have been appalling. If, however, as Sir William Thompson and some other eminent mathematicians consider, the friction set up by tides in the particles of the fluid body act like a brake, even while the moon was in a molten state—assuming it to have been once so—its motion on its own axis would soon have been retarded, and the destructive agencies modified.

Having now given you a general conception of the differences of the earth and her satellite, geologically considered, I will, in further illustration of my meaning, consider the differences of physical configuration of their surfaces in detail.

To revert to Murchison's scepticism as to the correctness of Ramsay's outlines of the mountains of Wales in Silurian times, it is clearly demonstrable that, even were they never at any one time exactly in the form pourtrayed by Ramsay, *that material to the same extent has been removed*, and this is the main fact at present interesting us. Believing as I do that the tremendous anticlinal folds were not due to sudden and vast upheavals, but to forces acting in the same direction throughout a great length of time—vertical being converted into horizontal movement—it is quite evident that the denuding agencies, while the upheavals were taking place, would have time to produce great results; consequently it were impossible to reproduce now, with accuracy, their exact appearance at any one stage of their formation.

To enable you to understand more clearly my meaning, I reproduce on an enlarged scale Ramsay's section from the Menai Straits through Snowdon to Arran Mowddy; showing the Cambrian grits and slates exposed by the denudation of the Merionethshire anticlinal, and also clearly proving, by reasoning based on facts and observations, and not *on à-priori* hypothesis, that no less than 20,000 feet of solid rocks, consisting of Cambrians and Silurians, with inter-bedded ashes and porphyries, up to the horizon of the Bala Limestone, have been removed before such exposure could take place. That these solid rocks were once above the Cambrians is easily understood, although the actual working out in the field of the complicated anatomy of the strata so clearly displayed in the section, required great penetration and a very comprehensive and practical grasp of geology. It is plainly seen that the whole of the rocks are conformable throughout the series—that is, they have been originally deposited in apparently horizontal planes, though now so contorted and folded. That the inter-bedded ashes and lavas are contemporaneous, Professor Ramsay has fully satisfied himself; consequently it follows that these anticlinal folds have been the result of a second series of earth movements, long after the original volcanoes had belched forth the ash beds and welled out the liquid lava enclosed between the Lingula and Llandeilo beds. Of the denudation of all the rocks between the Cambrians and the Bala Limestone the evidence is indisputable; but there is every probability that the foldings took place deep in the bowels of the earth, when the rocks were covered with a much greater series of other rocks than any we find representatives of here. "When that contortion occurred and was finished, the mountain tops, for instance, of the Cader Idris and the Snowdon ranges were still buried deep under many thousands of feet of higher Bala beds; and at a later period, I believe, by an immense thickness of Upper Silurian Strata."—*Memoirs of the Geological Survey,* vol. iii, p. 287, Professor Ramsay also shows that the whole of Wales suffered extreme denudation before the formation of the Upper Llandovery Rocks.

The Bala Fault is estimated by Ramsay to have a throw of 11,000 feet.—p. 36, *Memoirs.*

To give another instance of denudation of a more simple character, I exhibit a section of the Wigmore Valley, near Ludlow. Without further explanation, it is quite clear that the valley occupies the site of an anticlinal, and that what is now the axis of the valley was formerly the axis of a hill. If we admit the original horizontality of the sedimentary rocks of which the flanking hills are composed, the inference of the valley being entirely due to the excavating power of rain and rivers is obvious.* I have inspected this part of the country with great interest, and not the least noticeable feature is a deep gorge at Downton, which the river has

---

* Sir Roderick Murchison argues.—"Siluria," p. 492—that only "very powerful currents of water could have removed every fragment of the débris that must have resulted, whether at one or several points of elevation, from the destruction of all the once superposed arches of rock, and have scooped out all the detritus arising from such destruction, from the circling depressions, the central dome, flanking ridges, and former cover of these Silurian Strata"—forgetful of the fact that a result of slow atmospheric degradation is the gradual carrying away of the waste of the rocks, either in solution in water or in the mechanical form of alluvium.—The nature of the rocks in this locality rendering them peculiarly liable to this species of dissolution.

worn through. That this ravine was formed gradually as the great mass of the anticlinal was decomposed and worn away, I am fully satisfied.

It is, of course, impossible to draw any section of the strata of the moon; but we can, I think, draw one sufficiently true in its salient features to compare its surface configuration with the typical sections of the earth strata I have just described. The section I exhibit is on the same scale as those of Snowdon, and is of the crater "Eudoxus," 35 miles in diameter and 11,000 feet deep.

A section across any portion of the moon's surface would show combinations of very similar outlines, excepting where the mountain ranges occur, such as the "Alps" and "Apennines;" and I have compared it with the usual surface configurations of the earth rather than with that of a volcanic district, to show the great difference which exists between the geology of the moon and the earth.

Without at present entering upon the controverted question of how the lunar volcanoes were formed, I ask, is it not, as I have previously pointed out, evident from the preservation of the ring-like form and the truncated cones in so many thousands of instances on the moon, and their comparative absence on the earth, that those on the moon have not been exposed to similar denuding agencies? Nasmyth and Carpenter consider that they have discovered portions of the rings of these lunar craters which have broken down and fallen into the craters; but it is just as likely that these "benches," as they are described, may have been produced by the welling up of the molten material, its consolidation at its edges in the form of "beaches," and its gradual sinking down by contraction.

One of the distinctive peculiarities of the lunar volcanoes is the depth of the crater, the floor of it being generally far below the surface of the surrounding surface. The absence of denuding agencies may assist also to account for this phenomenon; for if the building of the surrounding surface was continually going on by successive lava flows, and the large cauldron of molten rock rose and welled over its edges on the cooling of the fluid nucleus below, these craters' hollows would naturally result from contraction. In one case—that of "Wargentin," 53 miles in diameter—the molten matter seems to have welled up to its brim, and there consolidated in a form resembling a thin cheese. The general sinking down of the floors of the volcano beneath the general surface is no doubt also connected with the immense diameter of the crater hollows; for were we to make a section of an earth crater extended to the dimensions of a lunar one, setting the edges of the encircling rim proportionately to the diameter at the same elevation only above the general surface, we should find that the bottom of the crater would in that case be far below the general surface. If, as I have suggested, there has been an absence of denudation answering to what we are acquainted with on the earth, it is evident that the exudation of the lava on the surface would build up from the innumerable centres or vents strata upon strata of volcanic rocks. The absence of those potent carrying agents, the rain, rivulet, torrent, and river, and of that great distributer, the ocean—even though conditions of decomposition did exist—would leave the lava flows and ejecta intact, excepting to the extent that gravitation could affect the materials in distributing them as taluses to the higher slopes.

That these successive outbursts have taken place, covering the moon's surface with a stratified crust of volcanic rocks—not possessing, however, the regularity of our sedimentary deposits—seems strengthened by the fact of the existence of what appears to be partially submerged rings, such as we see in the neighbourhood of "Wargentin." It is also not at all clear that the great surfaces (or seas, as they were formerly called) are not in all cases covered with vents which are too minute to be distinguished with the telescope.* In what are called the Lunar Apennines the ring-like vents exist in considerable numbers; and these groups of mountains have most probably been built up by long-continued exudation from numerous cracks and fissures.

A more instructive lesson than a comparison of these lunar mountains with our earth-mountains could not be found. I reproduce Nasmyth and Carpenter's plate. You will observe that there are no continuous main valleys with ramifying branches like those which the denuding power of water has traced upon our earth—no distinguishable lines of watershed and lines of drainage, such as we see so well in the shaded ordnance sheets of the Cumbrian mountains I place before you. There is no reason to suppose that these mountains—the Apennines —described as "a confused mass of broken peaks and pinnacles," are not very ancient in the moon's history; and I point to them as confirming me in my views of the absence of water on the moon at any time since they began to be formed. Out of the lips of many of the crater-like rings there appears to have been a considerable and lengthened flow of lava in one or more directions. There are also ridge-like corrugations of the surface of a very roughened aspect. There are cliffs and fissures —the latter of late origin. Many of the larger rings are

* A crater hollow less than 1 mile in diameter is indistinguishable by the telescope.

broken into by those of later date, creating "overlapping craters;" but the singular persistence of these crater-like rings is one of the most remarkable facts we have to deal with; for, had they been on the earth, even in the absence of denudation, the contortions to which the crust has been subjected would have tilted, bent, and broken them up, and entirely destroyed their symmetry.

There appear to have been cracks and fissures, but no foldings of the crust at all comparable to those which have taken place from the earliest times to the latest in the earth's geology, where strata have been, in some cases, tilted completely over, the under surface becoming the uppermost, as in the Silurians of Sibyl Head, in Ireland. Had such been the case, even without denudation, the moon would not have possessed the "pitmarked" appearance it does. So far as we can judge, not one of the rings appears to have been disturbed by internal force further than what is caused by the breaking through of other crater-like rings, and a few large fissures. This, again, seems to show that, notwithstanding her rugged aspect, the moon has been subjected to forces more regular in their action than earth volcanoes. Nasmyth and Carpenter themselves say: "We scarcely accept Scrope's term 'basal wrecks' (of volcanic mountains that have had their summits blown away) as applicable to the craters of the moon, for the reason that the lunar globe does not offer us any instance of a mountain comparable in extent to the great craters, and whose summit has *not* been blown away." Had the rings been built of ejecta thrown out of a vent, cones would assuredly have been built up of a size surpassing those of the earth, as the moon's gravitating force falls below it.

Two of the illustrations I exhibit, reproduced in the frontispiece by the aid of photography, have been chosen

as shewing the characteristic differences of the geology
of the moon and the earth. That of the "Normal Lunar
Crater" is from Nasmyth and Carpenter's work and the
"Side Cañons of the Colorado" from the report of
Lieutenant J. C. Ives, U.S., the commander of the Ives'
expedition. In these copies, executed in Paynes grey,
my object has been to show—though the scales are vastly
different—the two scenes under the same effects of light
and shade. In that of the moon we see, as I have
described, the result of volcanic or fire action only. In
the cañon one of the most remarkable examples of denudation the earth can present us with, in which sedimentary rocks of Carboniferous and older Paleozoic age
are cut through to the granite base, and frequently 500
or 600 feet into it by aqueous action. Dr. Newberry
attributes these profound gorges to river erosion, and his
views are generally accepted. For 200 miles the river
Colorado runs between nearly vertical walls of rock
from 3000 to 6000 feet high. What a striking contrast
does this not present to the surface of the moon where,
as I trust I have shewn, there exists neither sedimentary
rocks nor traces of aqueous denudation.

My remarks have already far exceeded in length what
I originally contemplated, so, unexhausted as my subject
is, I must draw them to a close. Without starting from
a single hypothesis and building thereon a full-blown
theory, I think we may legitimately draw the following
conclusions from observed facts:—First, that the
geology of the moon differs greatly from that of the
earth, in possessing no sedimentary rocks; that, in the
conformation of its surface, whether in mountain or
crater, there is no evidence of denudation such as we see
upon the earth, and that combinedly—for the one fact is
strictly complimentary to the other—the evidence of the

non-existence *now* of an appreciable atmosphere or of water is not only confirmed by Geology, but that, from all we see, we may legitimately infer *that they never did exist;* that, if there was no water, there was also no steam—that active principle of earth volcanoes—and this inference is further strengthened by the fact that the ring-like craters could not have been built up of ejecta,* but rather by liquid lava welling up in huge cauldrons solidifying at its edges, and occasionally overflowing them; that there are no evidences of the folding and contortions of strata, such as we are familiar with on the earth, and that the fissures—admittedly of a late date— are due to secular shrinkage; that, in fact, the moon behaved as if subjected only to molten conditions, and that the explosions and earthquakes to which we are even now subjected had no counterpart in the moon. That there has been denudation or breaking of the rocks —due to the extremes of cold and heat to which the moon's surface is subject—may assist to account for its rugged exterior. These, I think, are all inferences probable in themselves, and not in the nature of hypothesis.

To look at the question in another aspect, the study of the lunar surface throws light upon the geology of the earth, and, by contrast, shows the correctness of geological reasoning on the subject of denudation. It also assists to prove the accuracy of Professor Ramsay's sections, even in opposition to so great an authority as Sir Roderick Murchison. There are, however, a wider set of inferences—mere suggestions, it is true, but, still, well worthy the attention of the philosopher no less than the geologist. It appears tolerably clear that the moon,

---

* I cannot accept Nasmyth's force of "expansion on consolidation" as capable of ejecting molten rock to the distances or with a regularity necessary to produce the rings.

in one sense, is a "spent" satellite—that her internal heat force is exhausted. Will it not, then, be said that this is a blow to the uniformitariansm of Lyell? Properly considered, I think not; for, independently of the greater length of time it would take for a planet having the mass of the earth to cool, the conservative agencies of the water and atmosphere must not be lost sight of: the heat even of the volcano is not lost by radiation into space, for the steam imparts its heat to the clouds and atmosphere, and they again impart it to the earth in refreshing showers, while the sediments accumulating from age to age must act as a non-conducting envelope; while the sea remains a distributer of heat as well as material. The moon has "run down," but we cannot legitimately infer from that that the earth will do likewise—the conditions differ. Geology tells us that the earth has existed, in a condition differing little from what she is now in, for countless myriads of years; the process of "dying" is, at all events, very slow; and, what is pretty clear, if life does become extinct and our planet dead, it will be in a way differing vastly from that of the moon.

According to geologists, volcanic action is the conservative force which retains for us our continents; and were it to cease and the earth to become rigid and inflexible, denuding agencies would level both isle and continent, and the earth would become, not without form, and void, but one uninterrupted, monotonous sea; but life—aquatic life—might still exist, so long as the earth preserved the present rate of revolution on her axis, and the sun his present heat. These may all pass away; but to contemplate such a remote and ideal picture is pure speculation, hardly within the province of the essentially common sense science of geology.

NOVEMBER 9TH, 1875.

THE PRESIDENT, T. MELLARD READE, C.E., F.G.S.,
in the Chair.

THOMAS LEA, RICHARD M. FOSTER, ARCHIBALD McMILLAN, EDMUND SPARGO, SAMUEL ATKINSON, JOHN J. FITZPATRICK, J. R. WARD, and CHARLES FABERT were elected Ordinary Members of the Society.

The following communications were read:—

THE CARBONIFEROUS LIMESTONE AND MILL-STONE GRIT OF THE COUNTRY SOUTH OF LLANGOLLEN.

BY GEORGE H. MORTON, F.G.S.

This Paper forms a portion of the Author's communication on "The Carboniferous Limestone and Millstone Grit of the Country around Llangollen," which will be found at the end of the volume.

THE FOSSIL FERNS.

BY FREDERIC P. MARRAT.

DECEMBER 14TH, 1875.

THE PRESIDENT, T. MELLARD READE, C.E., F.G.S.,
in the Chair.

CORNELIUS SHERLOCK was duly elected an Ordinary Member of the Society.

The following communications were read:—

A NOTE ON THE THEORY OF METALLIFEROUS DEPOSITS IN VEINS, &c.

BY ALFRED MORGAN.

ON former occasions I have brought before this Society the theories that have been propounded with a view to the explanation of the phenomena associated with those metalliferous deposits termed lodes or veins.* Two constants appear to have been established in relation to the observed phenomena of such deposits: one is the uniformity of general direction of the productive lodes in any given district, and the other is the influence of the surrounding rocks upon the contents of the veins or fissures.

With respect to the theories themselves, that least generally adopted is that the deposits have a purely igneous origin and are the resultants of sublimatory processes which have operated, perhaps, at great depths. Another view is that the fissures and other cavities now filled with metalliferous deposits were at one time the vents through which thermal waters found their way to the surface, and that in so doing they deposited layer after layer of mineral matter against the walls of the cavities and cracks through which they passed. Mr. J. A. Phillips states that this process can be actually observed in California, where highly silicious waters are forced through rents in the rocks, in which they deposit their silica, usually in the gelatinous condition; and also, he states, in this soft silica are to be found particles of iron pyrites, and even gold. The third theory (and the one, I think, most generally adopted), supposes the water to have penetrated from above; and that, in passing through the rock fissures which were the natural channels of aqueous circulation, they deposited, under what Sir H. De la Beche in the "Geological Observer" calls "rock-conditions," and what Mr. Robert Were Fox and M. Becquerel refer to electrical action, those metallic and earthy matters forming veins and other ore-deposits. Whichever theory may be held, it appears certain that

---

* On the Formation of Metalliferous Veins."—*Proc.* xi, 1869-70, p. 37. "Observations on Metalliferous Deposits."—*Proc.* xii., 1870-1, p. 45.

the metalliferous deposits are the resultants of the circulation of waters through fissures and cavities—which may have been natural joints or not, but were at all events originally formed—and that in passing, whether from above or below, they held in suspension the minerals that have crystallised in the metalliferous veins.

These mysterious "rock-conditions" have been called in to the aid of theories which have required of them results which, combined together as a general factor, they would appear to be unable to accomplish. Though we know little of the nature and action of these occult forces, we are led to infer that electrical energy is the directing power that regulates the deposition of metalliferous deposits as regards their localisation. This will, I think, be generally granted.

I have therefore read with much pleasure a paper by Robert Hunt, F.R.S.,* in which he details some experiments which go to show that, without calling in such aids, there exists a power capable of producing the phenomena observed. While believing in electrical energy as a powerful agent in directing the place of deposit, &c., Mr. Hunt desires to afford "evidence of the existence of a vast power common to all matter, capable of producing all the phenomena of mineral lodes." Mr. Hunt continues:—"Capillary attraction has long been known. Exosmose and endosmose action have been made tolerably familiar to us. The influences of cellular bodies in condensing fluids within them, and the absorbent powers of porous masses, such as spongy platinum, charcoal, and the like, have been repeatedly shown. It is only lately, however, that we have become acquainted with the facts, that a certain thickness of silicious sand will separate salt from its solution in water, and that agricultural soil

---

* Trans. Roy. Geol. Soc. of Cornwall, vol. ix, part i, p. 22.

deprives the water percolating through it of the organic matter dissolved in it. M. Edmond Becquerel has lately shown that if two plates of glass are so arranged that by touching at one end and being kept slightly open at the other, so as to show the capillary curve of attraction, and if between these plates we pour a solution of some mineral salt in water, that the surface force will separate the metal from its chemical combination and attract it to the surface of the glass, on which it will be deposited as a metallic film."

Acting upon this suggestion, Mr. Hunt made a few experiments, with the idea that if he could produce a state of unstable equilibrium in the chemical solution, the metalliferous deposit might be induced to take place upon surfaces widely separated. He says:—"By adding to a solution of cyanide of silver a very small quantity of an hyposulphite, quite insufficient to produce a precipitation, the surface action of the sides of a pint bottle was sufficient to produce this deposition, in the form of a coat of sulphate of silver.

"Aldehyde and grape sugar have a similar power; with porous vessels this condition can be most readily established, and most beautifully so, by the action of charcoal. By putting a piece of freshly-burnt charcoal into a solution of nitrate of silver we obtain in a little time very beautiful crystals of silver, which are entirely due to the influence of the surface force, distributed over the molecules of carbon arranged to form the cells of the carbonised wood."

Though experiments are yet required to determine the extent to which this surface force may be brought into action, we have afforded by these experiments a clue, perhaps, to the unravelling of some of those secrets which, notwithstanding the student's earnest questionings, Nature still holds in her inexorable grasp.

NOTES ON THE RELATION BETWEEN THE MINERAL FLINT AND THE COUNTY OF FLINT.

By George H. Morton, F.G.S.

The occurrence of chert in the Carboniferous Limestone is well known, though, perhaps, the difference between chert and flint is not generally understood. Chert is an impure flint, and usually contains lime. It also differs from flint in breaking into square splintery pieces instead of a conchoidal fracture. An analysis of this very common mineral, found near Holywell and Flint, in North Wales, proved it to be flint rather than chert, and much of it is certainly flint in appearance, but only certain portions of it. That the mineral flint should occur most abundantly in the county of Flint is very remarkable, but it is equally remarkable that Mold (mould) should occur in Flint. But the question is, whether there is any connection between the mineral flint and the name of the town and county, or whether the latter was so named by chance without any object; which, however, is unlikely. We may safely conclude that flint the mineral and Flint the name are one and the same word. The Saxons probably gave the name to the county, for the word flint is of Teutonic origin; although some authorities have referred it back to the Greek. The German is *flintenstein,* or fire-stone, so that so far as the origin of the word is concerned it is possible enough. There might have been some difficulty if there had been a Welsh word *fflint* meaning something quite different to flint, but there is no such word in the language. The subject has evidently attracted attention before now; for Pennant, in his "Travels in North Wales," says:—

"I cannot assign any derivation of the word; our country is totally destitute of the fossil usually so called. I can only remark that it is purely Saxon; and, notwithstanding it is not mentioned in the Domesday Book, was called so before the Conquest." It is strange that Taylor, in his "Words and Places" the best book on the subject—does not mention Flint. However, in Charnock's "Local Etymology," the following occurs:—"Flint, the county town of Flintshire, N. Wales. Pennant remarks that this town had an early origin, and although not mentioned in Domesday, that the name is Saxon, and that the spot was so called anterior to the Conquest; but as the country produces none of those accompaniments of chalky strata denominated flints, he is at a loss for the derivation. Upon which a later writer [*no reference given*] observes that when Flint was made one of the four N. Wallian counties, in the time of Edward I, the statutes were promulgated in barbarous Latin, and the county was in some instances called Comitatus de Flint, which was probably a translation or various mode of expressing in writing Comitatus de Silici, or the silicious territory; chert, which the ancients designated both by the name of *silex* as well as *petrosilex*, being a predominant feature in the geology of this district. He suggests also that it may be the Brit. *fflwyn*, a shred, a severed part; a name the independent Britons would naturally give it after the inhabitants had submitted to the Roman yoke, which, from historical documents, they appear to have done long prior to the other subdued parts of Cambria." The question, therefore, is—Whether the mineral occurs in such abundance that the town or county would be likely to be so named in consequence. It can scarcely be considered to be remarkably abundant, so that I am inclined to think it might be rather on account of its relative abundance; for on Halkin Mountain flint is actually quarried from regular beds ten feet in thickness, and sent to the Potteries, where it is largely used in the construction of grinding floors. According to Pennant, it was used for the same purpose in his time. The locality is three-quarters of a mile W. of Pentre Halkin, which is two and a-half miles from Flint, and the same distance from Holywell; and there can be no doubt that the silicious strata were much more conspicuous before they were worked along their outcrop. However, chert or flint occurs in the upper beds of the Carboniferous Limestone throughout the whole length of Flintshire, though more fully developed in the locality described. Certainly the mineral occurs in other Welsh counties, but I have never seen any deposit at all to be compared with the silicious strata near Flint. If flint was in request for any particular purpose in Saxon times, if only used as a means of obtaining a light, and was far more abundant in the hills along the side of the Dee than in other places, it seems likely that the county might have been named Flint in consequence. It may be difficult to prove that it was so, but it will be just as difficult for any one to disprove it. It is curious, too, that if Flint be a Saxon name, it is the only Welsh county that has a Saxon one. but this is not a strong objection against it, for there are many places about the town of Flint the names of which are undoubtedly of Saxon origin; and it is not more extraordinary that Flintshire should have a Saxon than Beaumaris should have a Norman one. Though I am not altogether inclined to adopt this origin of the name of the county, it appears to me that it is very likely, and that the subject is worth further consideration. Probably the foregoing observations may elicit additional information.

THE LOWER LIAS OF STREET, SOMERSET.

By T. Mellard Reade, C.E., F.G.S.

The County of Somerset presents a striking contrast in its scenery to that of Lancashire, and both are instructive as shewing how intimately related landscape is to Geological structure. To one who has worked at the Trias in this neighbourhood it is doubly interesting, for in addition to the striking contrast between the paleontological barrenness of the New Red rocks of Lancashire and Cheshire, in which the only fossils are the imprints of the Cheirotherium footsteps, and the wonderful richness of the ammonite beds of the Lower Oolites (or, as some will have it, the Upper Lias), in Dorset, on the borders of Somerset, at Bradford Abbas and Sherbourne, we have in Somerset the connecting links between the Trias and the over-lying fossiliferous rocks.

In a cutting in the Somerset and Dorset Railway, between Midsumer Norton and Shepton Mallet, I had the good fortune to see the passage beds between the New Red Marl and the Lower Lias, consisting of the Rhætic Clay and Shales, with the *Avicula Contorta* bed well exposed and overlaid by the Rhætic White Lias, containing the Landscape Stone so well known to collectors, and again by the Lower Lias. In a descending order also were the grey and red marls of the Trias, the Dolomitic conglomerate hitherto classed with the Trias, but uncommonly like Permian, containing great fragments of the Carboniferous Limestone, with most interesting hollow nodular concretions lined with quartz crystals, splendidly-coloured pink, by a hematitic iron deposit on their surfaces. The base rock of the whole, the Carboniferous Limestone could also be studied with advantage.

In the neighbourhood of Street, a village about one and a half miles south-west of Glastonbury, there are several quarries in the Lower Lias, and the section of one of these it is my present object to describe. I have seen the Lower Lias at Lyme Regis on the south coast, and at Watchet on the Bristol Channel, and there is, without pretending to trace the individual beds, a striking lithological persistency in the character of the rocks. They are remarkable for thinness, regularity, and parallelism. At Watchet, where the beds dip towards the Bristol Channel, a large expanse on the shore looks more like masonry in the regularity of its main jointing planes and the "breaking joint" of its cross jointing.

The bottom of the quarry must be pretty close to the Rhætic beds, though they are not actually reached, as the Red Marl shows on the other side of the hill to the south, not far off. The stone is quarried for "paving," or what we call here "flags," and it seems, from the regularity with which it splits, well adapted for the purpose. A good many Icthyosaurian remains have been taken out of the quarry and carefully put together and cleaned-up by the proprietor, Mr. Josiah Seymour. Among these not the least interesting is the *Icthyosaurus Communis*, which I obtained for the Liverpool Museum, remarkable as possessing perfect, even the small terminal vertebra of the tail. This specimen, together with most of the others, was obtained from what is called the Principal Shale, 8 inches thick only, not far from the base of the quarry. The following is a description of the section which gives one a good idea of the stratigraphical character of the Lower Lias, consisting as it mostly does of beds of Blue Limestone, with partings of Shale, and beds of Argillaceous Shale :—

	Ft. In.
Clay and Soil	1·9
Yellow Stone	0·9
Clay (Reptiles, *Icthyosaurus*, &c.)	3·0
Top Rock (in 4 beds), Building Stone..	2·6
White Stone	0·6
Creams	0·4
Red Livers	0·3
Black Stone	0·4
Six inches	0·6
Four-inch Bed	0.4
Blue Clay	0·11
Principal Shale (*Icthyosaurus Communis*)	0·8
Grey Clay	0·9
Blues (2 beds)	0·8½
Top Fires	0·4½
Bottom Blues	0·4
Thick Fires	0·8
Shale	0·9
"New-found-out," Fish, *Cycads*, Rain drops, thickness not stated.	
Total	15·5

REMARKS ON THE COUNTRY AROUND THE WREKIN.

By Charles Ricketts, M.D., F.G.S.

In directing attention to the country around the Wrekin, it is not intended to give a detailed account of the Geology of a district already so well known, nor am I aware that I shall be enabled to bring forward any new facts; my desire is rather to place phenomena observed there in a different light, and, comparing them with those of other districts, to use them for the illustration of principles—some not as yet generally accepted—which I have had occasion to bring before the notice of the Society on various occasions.

The Wrekin, which rises a conspicuous object above the surrounding country to the height of 1320 feet, consists of a volcanic mass which has, in its passage through a rent formed in the Caradoc rocks, converted the sandstone strata into quartzite. It extends in a direction from N.E. to S.W. for about three miles; being, independently of the hardened quartz rock flanking its sides, a quarter of a mile wide at its greatest breadth, but becoming narrower at other places to less than an eighth of a mile. The character of the rock varies, being hard and compact where a little stream has cut for itself a channel dividing the hill into two parts, and through which the road to Wellington passes; whilst at its northern extremity, at Ercal Wood, it forms large rounded masses of a red colour, which, by weathering, separate in concentric coats, these again breaking into small pieces make a good substitute for gravel, in place of which it is extensively used.*

---

* "A similar rock forms the nucleus of Primrose Hill, at the southwestern extremity of the range."—"Notes on the Geology of North Shropshire," by Charlotte Eyton, p. 18.

If the direction of the longer axis of the Wrekin is extended for about nine miles, the line will pass very nearly into the eruptive rocks of the Lawley and Caradoc Hills. This "long line of dislocation and faults extends for 65 miles, from Coalbrook Dale, S.W., to the neighbourhood of Gladestry, in Radnorshire."* So that, as modern volcanos occur along definite lines, their "great trains of vents, indicating the existence of extended fissures or lines of dislocation across the earth's crust, through which subterranean igneous matter has for a vast series of ages been habitually protruded," † it may be presumed that these ancient ones have been situated along similar lines of weakness; but, as now, so also then, the fissures along which the vents have occurred did not permit the molten rock to pass entirely through the earth's crust, from the interior to the surface, along its whole length, otherwise a dyke would have extended the whole distance between the different foci of eruption.

There is no evidence remaining to indicate the period when the volcanos near Church Stretton—the Lawley, the Caradoc, and Cardington Hills—were in a state of activity; every trace of the accumulation of ashes and lava which once issued from these volcanic vents has been removed by denudation, which occurred previous to the subsequent deposition of any stratified rock now remaining. With respect to the Wrekin, it is different. Extending parallel to it for nearly its whole length, but separated by a space of from half a mile to a mile, there are displayed on its eastern side the remains of a succession of bands of basalt and volcanic ash; the latter, by the innumerable volcanic bombs with which it is studded, seen along the road as it approaches Little

---

* Professor Ramsay.—"Horizontal Sections of the Geological Survey,", sheet 54; Explanation, p. 1.

† "Volcanos," p. 258.—G. Poulett Scrope, F.R.S.

Wenlock, indicates the near vicinity of the crater from which they had been ejected; and the irregular and unstratified manner in which they lie embedded, with no stratified deposits intervening between the beds, proves that the eruption had been subaërial. The bombs are extremely like, both in size and appearance, many of those ejected during the progress of making steel by the Bessemer process. At Harris' Coppice is another ash-bed, apparently near to if not forming the base of the eruptive rocks, containing an abundance of small grains and lapilli; it has a bed of basalt resting upon it, both being overlaid by Millstone Grit.

These eruptive rocks lie successively on the eroded surfaces of the Caradoc and of the basement beds of the Upper Silurian strata, that is, upon the May Hill Sand-stone and Conglomerate, and the Wenlock Shale; so that not only did the eruption take place after the deposition of the Old Red Sandstone, and the exertion of that power which has resulted in the tilting up, at a considerable angle, of it and the underlying strata, but also subse-quent to the denudation by which even then the whole series, from the summit to the base, were displayed in this neighbourhood within an area of five or six miles. It is, in fact, to causes which were in action prior to the deposit of the Carboniferous strata, that the more pro-minent features in the present contour of this district are chiefly due.

Though the displacement and upheaval of the older stratified rocks occurred previous to the intrusion of what is now the Wrekin, the presence of this hard and unyielding mass appears, upon the occurrence of subse-quent changes, to have had influence in determining the foldings which exist in the Carboniferous rocks of Coal-brook Dale, causing them to take place in a direction parallel to that of its longest axis.

Resting upon the lava and ashbeds is a bed of limestone, quarries of which have been opened in different places along the outcrop, extending from Little Wenlock in a northerly direction for about two miles; the occurrence in great abundance of *Productæ*, characteristic corals, and other fossils, refer it to the Carboniferous Limestone series. At its southern extremity, in Oldfield Quarry near Little Wenlock, the strata lie horizontally; but at Hatch they dip to E.S.E. at 22°, and at a higher angle further north. The limestone proper is, at the southern portion of the area, only 20 to 25 feet thick; and at Steeraway, further north, the vertical section of the Geological Survey makes it 40 feet; so that, compared with other districts, the thickness of this limestone is remarkably small. With the exception of a small area at the northern extremity of the Coalbrook Dale coal-field, and at the Titterstone Clee Hills (to be referred to hereafter), the nearest place at which the Carboniferous Limestone exists is Llanymynech, 30 miles distant to the north-west; Mr. G. H. Morton, F.G.S., calculates that its thickness there is about 400 feet, and has informed us that nine miles further north it gradually dwindles down to about 100 feet.[*] It again increases to 1,000, and even to 1,500 feet, in Denbighshire.[†] At Llanymynech it must have been deposited in a hollow formed in the older rocks—I should consider it to have been in a submerged valley—situated between the Breidden Hills and the extension of the Longmynd northwards on the one side, and the hilly country north of Llanfyllin on the other. A subsidence of all this land has taken place gradually and progressed simultane-

[*] Proceedings of the Liverpool Geological Society, 1875-76.
[†] "The Coal-fields of Great Britain."—Professor E. Hull. Second Edition, p. 99.

ously with the deposition of the limestone strata; the area about Llanymynech having been submerged, as is shown by the greater comparative thickness of its limestone, ages before that of its own extension northwards, or before the area of Little Wenlock reached the sea level; whilst the higher hills must have formed promontories, and some perhaps small islands, situated in a Carboniferous sea.

The limestone passes upwards into beds of sandstone and carbonaceous shale, having together about the same thickness as it. This estuarian deposit consists of materials such as might have been derived from the disintegration of the older rocks of the neighbourhood, and is referred to the Carboniferous Limestone series. Though at Oldfield Quarry these deposits are from 40 to 50 feet thick, there is nothing to represent them at Harris' Coppice, at a mile distance to the south on the Little Wenlock road, unless it be a band of muddy sediment not more than an inch in thickness; beds of conglomerate (Millstone Grit) lying immediately on the basalt and ash-beds. Bosses of igneous rock rise through the Millstone Grit at various places, whilst "others have been discovered in the deep workings."* So that the intrusive and erupted volcanic rocks, which had even then suffered much denudation, will have appeared above the level of these sedimentary deposits; and, if not forming islets during the deposition of the Carboniferous Limestone, they would at a later period, when the land was further depressed, during that of the Millstone Grit, in a manner similar to the small islands formed of volcanic rock situated in the Firth of Forth.

* "Geology of Coalbrook Dale," by Joseph (now Professor) Prestwich.—*Proc. Geol. Soc.*, vol. ii, p. 403.

The transition is sudden from the strata which have been referred to the Limestone Series to that of the Millstone Grit, the basement beds of which are conglomerates composed of rounded quartz pebbles. At one place the shales upon which they rest had rootlets passing from its upper surface perpendicularly downwards *in situ* as they had grown; so that this then surface of low-lying land must have subsided below the sea level, possibly was also partially denuded, thus permitting the deposition of materials which had been derived from a different and distant source. I traced the Millstone Grit of this district to its farthest extent southwards at Barrow, a farm two miles due east of Much Wenlock, where it overlies respectively the Upper Ludlow Shales, and the Old Red Sandstone; whilst near the Wrekin, at Harris' Coppice, where the Carboniferous Limestone does not exist, it rests upon the erupted matter which has issued from the volcano of the Wrekin.

These grits and conglomerates are eighty feet thick at Steeraway and form the base upon which the measures of the Coalbrook Dale Coalfield rest. Their margin indicates the extreme limits of a bay which the Carboniferous Sea occupied; the Longmynd, the Stiper Stones, and the Breidden Hills constituted a promontory separating it from the Oswestry district, where the Millstone Grit is, according to Mr. Morton, about 560 feet thick; whilst Wenlock Edge and its overlying Ludlow rocks and Old Red Sandstone formed an isthmus, dividing it from the bay in which was deposited the Limestone and Millstone Grit of the Titterstone Clee Hill. But in South Staffordshire the Coal-measures rest directly on Upper Silurian strata, so denuded that they overlie the whole series from the base of them, or May Hill Sandstone, near Barr, to the Aymestry Limestone at Sedgley; it therefore

D

seems certain that this land extended to the eastward by Dudley and Walsall, through Warwickshire to Leicestershire, and, though depressed to, or even below, the sea level, was never submerged during the Carboniferous period.*

The Clee Hills, situated on the southern side of this ancient isthmus, consist of several detached patches of Carboniferous rocks, resting upon Old Red Sandstone, which have been preserved from destruction by cappings of basalt. The more northern of these areas consist of Coal-measure strata only, whilst the Titterstone Clee Hill is composed also of marine beds of the Carboniferous series—Carboniferous Limestone and Millstone Grit. The Limestone differs most materially from any found further north, being characterized by an oolitic structure which, in a quarry to the north-east of Knowl, extended through its whole thickness, 25 feet; the shells contained in it having been broken into such small fragments that it was impossible to identify any. This oolitic character, common also in the Bristol area, indicates a great difference in physical conditions during the deposition, between what was here a submerged area forming a shallow bay and the sunken hilly districts farther north.† The Limestone of the Titterstone Clee Hill, was overlaid by about 60 feet of Carbonaceous Shale prior to the deposition of the Millstone Grit.

* The fact of this ridge existing during the Carboniferous period as a division between two seas, was demonstrated by the late Professor Jukes in "Memoirs of the Geological Survey—South Staffordshire Coalfield," preface, page xiii; and by his successor in the Geological Survey of Ireland, Professor E. Hull, in "The Coal-fields of Great Britain," page 108, and in *British Association Reports*, 1870, page 75, where he also shewed that the northern boundary of the Coal formation to the north of this central barrier was formed by the Cambro-Silurian rocks of the Lake-district and portions of the "southern uplands" of Scotland.

† Mr. Morton informs me that some of the beds of limestone in the Llanymynech district are oolitic in structure.

The land which, at the commencement of the formation of the Coal-measures, was, near Coalbrook Dale, the boundary of the Carboniferous sea, rose from its shores to a considerable elevation above its level, as at Benthal Edge, Wenlock Edge, the Longmynd, and towards the Breidden Hills; a marine plain formed of the conglomerates and sandstones of the Millstone Grit being the base upon which they were deposited. During the earlier period of their formation the accumulation was neither very great, nor the subsidence considerable, when compared with other coalfields, the partings between the lower or workable beds of Coal being thin, and the deposit chiefly consisting of a fine ferruginous clay. Taking the section at Lawley as given by the Geological Survey* (and it very nearly coincides with other sections, and with information derived from workmen) the strata in which the profitable Coals lie, from the Top Coal to the Little Flint Coal, is 180 feet thick, containing thirteen beds of Coal amounting to 40 feet in thickness, and the measures to 140 feet, being a marked contrast when compared with those of other districts. Professor Hull states that in Denbighshire the Middle Coal-measures, which are the only ones worked, have in a thickness of 800 feet of strata an aggregate amount of from 27 to 30 feet of workable Coal, the lower measures, about 1000 feet thick, having several seams varying from 2 to 8 feet, but are little sought after in the presence of the thick seams of the middle series.† Professor Hull states that in the St. Helens district the strata from the Lyons Delf to the Arley Main Coal is 1807 feet, with an aggregate of 59 feet 6 inches of Coal,‡ and observes that

---

* Vertical Sections, Sheet No. 32.

† *The Coalfields of Great Britain.*—By Professor Edward Hull, Second Edition, pages 99 and 100.   ‡ Page 124.

"there is a general thickening of the sedimentary materials, as sandstones and shales, to the N.N.W. Thus the same coal-seams are farther apart at St. Helens than at Prescot, and at Wigan than at St. Helens."[*] The Lower Coal-measures or Gannister beds are 1800 feet with 6 or 7 seams of coal, seldom of greater thickness than 2 feet for each.[†]

Professor Jukes has conclusively proved that the *Thick or Ten-yard Coal* of South Staffordshire, which, in the neighbourhood of Dudley, consists of thirty feet of coal without any or with but very thin partings, is, five miles to the north of Bilston—at Essington and Wyerley —represented by ten beds of coal and interposed shales and sandstones, amounting together to the thickness of 300 feet. The aggregate thickness of the coal is the same, the increase being entirely due to the amount of sedimentary materials between the beds.[‡] It may, I consider, be inferred that at the southern portion of the district, near the summit of the ridge previously referred to, the land, during the period of the growth of the enormous amount of vegetation forming the "thick coal," continued persistently stationary; whilst towards the north, that is, somewhat nearer the source of the sedimentary deposits, there was a gradual and progressive subsidence, which proceeded in a greatly increased ratio further northwards.

Where the Measures in Coalbrook Dale are situated above the Millstone Grit, they contain many valuable beds of coal, whilst those formed later and upon old land surfaces, extending southward to the Forest of Wyre and from Caer Caradoc by Shrewsbury to Alberbury, are of a comparatively "valueless nature," containing at the most

---

* Page 123.   † Page 127.
‡ "Memoirs of the Geological Survey—South Staffordshire Coal-field."

only "two or three coal-seams not of sufficient value to induce mining operations far from the outcrop." "The strata belong generally to the higher part of the coal series which throughout England is but sparingly enriched with beds of coal."* The contrast between the different coal-fields is remarkable; the one studded all over with numerous shafts, the other with but here and there evidence that coal has been "gotten," and that generally consisting only in the bank of a deserted colliery.

It has been shown that, prior to the eruption of a subaërial volcano (whose vent is now represented by a portion of the igneous rock which constitutes the Wrekin), the Old Red Sandstone, the Upper Silurian and the Caradoc strata had been upheaved and extensively denuded; and that remains of the materials ejected are distributed on the eroded surfaces of the two older formations. The northern extremity of Wenlock Edge and of the Longmynd constituted higher ground encircling this area, which by depression formed a bay; these same hills became an isthmus separating it from another bay situated a few miles southward, its most northerly extension being the Titterstone Clee Hill. The erupted rocks had undergone a considerable amount of denudation previous to their depression beneath the sea. That this subsidence was gradual, and occurred towards the termination of the period of the formation of the Carboniferous Limestone, is indicated by its being much greater in thickness at Llanymynech, and especially farther north, compared with its small amount here, where it is at the utmost eighty feet, and thins out entirely within a very short distance.

---

* *Idem*, pp. 91–92.

There are in various other places indications of the Carboniferous Limestone having been deposited in areas which had previously been more ancient valleys, as in Anglesey, near Denbigh and Llangollen, and in Cumberland, where the base of the Carboniferous series is not unfrequently represented by what has been erroneously designated Old Red Sandstone, now recognised by the staff of Her Majesty's Geological Survey as "Carboniferous Basement Beds;" "they contain fragments derived entirely from rocks which are seen in the immediate neighbourhood,"* and the limestone lies conformably upon them; whilst, in the different districts, it may ·be seen within a short distance resting on the eroded surfaces or edges of older rocks. It is more than probable that these conglomerates and sandstones are situated in the bottoms of ancient valleys, and were deposited near the mouths of their rivers. As depression progressed these strata were overwhelmed by the sea; and the valleys, changed into estuaries and bays, permitted the limestone to be deposited on their flanks, filling them up entirely, and this continued until the ridges even were deeply buried beneath it.

The origin of any extraneous materials the Carboniferous Limestone contains may also with probability be referred to the disintegration of land in the neighbourhood; but its large area and great thickness indicate the prolonged degradation of some large continental area

---

* Mr. (now Professor) T. McK. Hughes, when referring to these strata in Westmoreland and Cumberland.—*Memoirs of the Geological Survey—Kirkby-Lonsdale*, p. 15. Mr. J. Goodchild, of H.M. Geological Survey, also says that in the valley of the Eden this basement series "seems to be mainly composed of locally derived materials."—*Quart. Journ. Geol. Soc.*, vol. xxx, p. 396. Mr. Tiddeman has remarked that the Mountain Limestone is 3,000 or 4,000 feet thick in the Lake district, and in the Pennine chain, at a distance of 15 miles, only 600 feet.— *Quart. Journ. Geol. Soc.*, vol. xxx, p. 400.

during the period of deposition.* The *débris* must have been carried by its river as sediments into the sea at some locality unknown to us; whilst the lime, held in solution by its waters, was at the same time conveyed and distributed by currents, being utilised where found by corals, mollusks, and other organisms, or was otherwise deposited.

The effects produced were immense, though the physical changes which induced them may have been small, by which the great submarine plateau of Carboniferous Limestone became the basis on which were distributed materials as different from it as are those which constitute the Millstone Grit (including also, under that term, the Yoredale series of rocks), and those which were subsequently deposited—the delta-formed strata of the English Coal-fields. The abundance of mica and of quartz in these deposits, refers their origin to the disintegration of granitic or gneissic rocks, probably of an extensive mountain range; whilst the Coal-measures must be compared to the delta of some large river, on whose alluvial plains grew the abundant vegetation now represented by the various beds of coal; the clays, shales, and sandstones being mud and sand which overspread these plains when the river overflowed or broke through its banks.

The circumstance of the general and persistent depression of the bed of the sea as the accumulation of limestone progressed, and the fact that, in the neighbourhood to which especial attention is being directed, there was an isthmus sixteen miles wide, forming a division between two seas,† may afford a clue to determine the

---

* "In the open sea, at a distance from any land, lime is said to be rarely, if ever, discoverable by analysis."—Jukes' "Student's Manual of Geology," 1862, p. 125.

† It was reduced to twelve miles during the deposition of the Millstone Grit,

circumstances under which these changes have taken place. The abundance of the lime must have required the existence of a large river flowing through a limestone district, emptying itself into the sea, probably within at the utmost a few hundred miles of the place where the limestone has been deposited. This proximity is not an absolute necessity, for the lime in the *globigerina* ooze of the mid-Atlantic has its source in the great rivers of America. A large river was needed to convey the sand, mica, and mud of the Coal-measures from the gneissic and granitic mountains from whose disintegration they have been chiefly derived, and which, as the river overflowed or broke through its banks, and as subsidence of the land progressed, overwhelmed the alluvial plain with waters holding in suspension all but the coarser sediments. A large river would also be required as a means by which the materials derived from the same—at all events, a similar origin—forming the Millstone Grit, might have been brought within the influence of the action of the sea. Many of its particles are much coarser than any found in the Coal-measures; its sands and grits are to a great extent more or less angular, and must have been carried along by the rapidity of the stream without much friction; whilst the larger fragments of quartz are invariably rounded, probably as a result of exposure to constant friction by being pushed along the river-bed. They were subsequently distributed by tidal and other currents over the bed of the sea; filling up the space between the upper surface of the Carboniferous Limestone almost to the surface level of the sea, and, though there was a considerable amount of subsidence continually taking place whilst this accumulation was progressing, they sometimes, as in Yorkshire, formed low-lying land, which remained above the sea-level sufficiently long to admit of the growth of vegetation to produce beds of coal. The beds of coal interstratified with the Yoredale shales and Millstone Grit of Penygent may be cited as examples. This *débris* would also have been carried into bays, like that at Coalbrook Dale, where they would have been distributed in a similar manner to the sands in Morecambe Bay, derived chiefly from the degradation of the Triassic rocks of Lancashire and Cheshire, forming a plain at a level between high and low water mark.

A difficulty arises in determining the causes by which the barrier was removed between the Carboniferous sea of the north-west of England and the great river, whose existence I think is certain, but its course unknown. An isthmus, as has been shown, divided this great northern bay from another situated further south, the elevation of the ridge between them being so small that, had subsidence progressed there during the period of the marine deposits of the Carboniferous formation, to an extent moderate compared with what occurred in other places, a junction or strait must have been formed between the two seas. Let us suppose a circumstance somewhat similar, and not unlikely to have happened. That the marine area, in which the Carboniferous Limestone was being deposited, was separated by a ridge or range of hills from the valley through which the supposed large river flowed; the limestone area we know was persistently subsiding; and, if there was much sediment brought down by the river, judging from what is observed in so many great rivers, subsidence would take place and a delta be formed at its embouchure.* This depres-

---

* The St. Lawrence, in consequence of the detritus being detained in numerous extensive lakes, *may* be an exception.

sion would continue as the accumulation progressed, so
that the valley would be entirely filled with the deposit
forming the delta and alluvial plain ; and the bed of the
river might also become somewhat higher than some
lower portion of the ridge. The tendency would then be
for a channel to be formed communicating with the bay,
which, uniting with the main stream, would, according
to its size, divert into it a large portion of materials
such as had previously passed into an adjoining sea.

Though there is no known deposit during the
Carboniferous period which can be referred to delta-
accumulations, such as have been supposed, the suggestion may be made whether the Calciferous Sandstone
series in the neighbourhood of Edinburgh may not
represent sediments which have filled up the valley
formed by a large tributary of such a river. These
strata amount altogether to a thickness of 3,500 feet;
and they, as well as the Carboniferous Limestone and
Millstone Grit, have been formed under conditions differing in a most marked manner from those deposits in
England which have been under consideration and are
referred to the same periods.

The diversion of a continental river into such an area
as that occupied by the Carboniferous Limestone, however it may have originated, would have brought into it
the *débris* derived from the degradation of the land, which
would have been distributed over the bed of the sea by
tidal and other currents. As deposition went on, depression of its bed would have progressed, not always continuously in any single locality; for sometimes, as in the
Yoredale series and Millstone Grit of Yorkshire, it
became filled up to the surface level of the sea, and land
surfaces were formed, on which vegetation flourished, so
as to form beds of coal; such surfaces subsequently

became depressed and covered with other beds of micaceous shales, sandstones, and grits; and this process was repeated many times in succession. In some districts the total thickness of these sediments amounts to 5,000 feet; whereas at the extreme limit of the bay at Coalbrook Dale, where they overlie the Limestone, but were in the immediate neighbourhood of land, they are represented by 80 or 100 feet only; thinning out entirely at Barrow Farm. This slight subsidence may be due to the accession of pressure from accumulation occurring from one direction only, whereas at so short a distance as thirty miles, at Llanymynech, where a greater thickness of Limestone indicates the existence of a more expansive sea, the accumulation amounts to 560 feet.

The *débris* brought down into this sea overspread and filled up the whole area until, subsidence ceasing to progress in equal ratio with the deposition, no more was distributed from seaward, and the stream passed along a channel in this marine plain. In the subsequent deposits, forming the Coal-measures, there are sandstones and shales, with abundance of quartz and mica entering into their composition, similar in character to those in the Millstone Grit; they may therefore be referred to the same origin, but the grittier and coarser particles are wanting, and there is an entire absence of the rounded quartz pebbles. These pebbles must, with other materials, have still been propelled seaward; but portions, which consisted of such fine materials as were capable of being suspended in the current, were deposited upon the inundated plain when the river broke through or overflowed its banks.

By comparing the delta-deposits of the Coal-measures with those of large rivers, such as the Mississippi, it will be perceived that, though the bursting of the banks would have overwhelmed the plain, covering it with sand and silt, it could not exceed the height of the banks, amounting in the Mississippi to a mean depth of fifteen feet.*   There must, therefore, in order to permit the accumulation of the great thickness of strata which exists between the different beds of coal in the more northern districts, have been a successive depression of the land as accumulation progressed.   Near the course of the river through the delta the greatest amount of accumulation would occur, becoming lessened and the sediment being finer, as the distance increased, whilst at its extreme limits there would remain only the finest particles of mud. This has been the case in the Coalbrook Dale district, situated in the depressed and filled up site of the commencement of one of the minor tributaries of a large valley or system of valleys, situated on the northern slope of the division of the watershed which separated it from a similar area to the south.

Whether or not this is the correct explanation of the formation of the Carboniferous rocks of the northwest of England, the fact is evident that subsidence of the land progressed simultaneously with the accumulation.   Every seam of coal represents the surface of a plain or delta, situated but little above the sea-level, each representing the product of vegetable growth which had flourished for a prolonged period of time; every considerable accumulation between each bed indicates subsidence of the land. This depression is shown to have been in accordance with the amount of accumulation, occurring in some places to an enormous extent in each of the several divisions of the Carboniferous system; whilst in others, as in that of Coalbrook Dale, in each of them it has been small.   Nor is the simultaneous occurrence of

---

* Sir Charles Lyell.

accumulation and subsidence by any means peculiar to the Carboniferous rocks, but can be proved to be coincident during all geological time—from the Laurentian rocks of Canada to the deltas now forming at the mouths of large rivers. Its occurrence is proved wherever in lower beds there are data to determine at the period of their deposition the near proximity to the horizon of the then sea-level or of shallow water, and the subsequent deposition of strata upon them.

Such a simultaneous occurrence of these phenomena during every age and through all time, can only be regarded as the result of cause and effect: that the one is dependent upon the other. Depression may *permit*, but cannot *cause* accumulation. In the instances which have been under consideration the materials have been derived, not from the neighbourhood, but from distant sources, whilst the accumulated weight of the sediments deposited in seas, bays, and deltas is, by the pressure exerted on the crust of the earth, an adequate cause for the occurrence of the depression; the amount of subsidence being greater or less, in accordance with that of the accumulation.

JANUARY 11TH, 1876.

THE PRESIDENT, T. MELLARD READE, C.E., F.G.S.,
in the Chair.

The following communications were read:—

A FEW NOTES ON THE PHYSICAL GEOLOGY OF THE SHILLONG PLATEAU, NORTH-EASTERN BENGAL.

BY ALFRED MORGAN.

ON THE ROCKS OF NEW YORK ISLAND AND THEIR RELATION TO THE GEOLOGY OF THE MIDDLE STATES.

BY D. S. MARTIN, A.M.

Prof. of Geology and Nat. Hist. Rutger's Female College, U.S.

(READ BY THE HONORARY SECRETARY.)

ABSTRACT.

"THE rock of which the Island of New York is composed is almost exclusively of what may be termed a gneissoid schist. It is rarely a true gneiss, its general character being that of a coarse-grained mica-schist, traversed here and there by heavy veins of felspar or quartz. The dip is extremely various, the beds being thrown into many folds and arches, often within short distances. The strike, however, is remarkably uniform, having a general course from N.N.E. to S.S.W. It is this uniform strike that determines the whole form of the island, as a long narrow tongue, cut through at its upper end, and so separated from the main land, merely by the Harlem River and Spuyten Dugvel Creek.

"At this point it may be proper to observe the important fact that this ridge, upon which the city of New York stands, is part of a range of crystalline rocks which runs rudely parallel to the Atlantic coast-line for seven hundred miles; and which, though not conspicuous geographically, has yet a great geological interest that has not been duly recognised. This ridge presents, throughout much if not all of its length, a great uniformity of mineralogical and lithological characters, and an equal distinctness from those of the Blue Ridge, with which it has sometimes been confounded.

"North and east of New York this crystalline belt merges into the wide and complicated metamorphic regions of New England; and its distinctness is therefore obscured. By some of its mineralogical features, however, it can be traced with more or less definiteness, through western New England and even north of Vermont, beyond the Canada line. South of New York its course is perfectly clear. Immediately below the city the ridge sinks ·beneath the general level of the country, and is covered by Mesozoic rocks, until it rises to the surface at Trenton, New Jersey, sixty miles away. The exposure here covers only a few square miles; and the ridge again becomes covered up, until it rises once more at Philadelphia. This time it forms important hills, beginning with the heights of West Philadelphia and Fairmont, and stretching thence in a broad metamorphic belt over all the south-eastern corner of Pennsylvania, and across the state of Maryland into Virginia."

Professor Martin referred to the importance of the ridge, in a geographical point of view, as having determined the site of nearly all the important towns and cities on the coast of that region, and stated that, "Throughout the Atlantic Middle States it divides the earlier from the later Mesozoic beds—the Triassic from the Cretaceous. The former rest upon its western flank and dip westward; the latter, together with the Tertiaries that overlie them, rest upon its eastern or seaward flank and dip eastward. So definite is this arrangement that it may safely be said that a proper understanding of the relations of this ridge is the key to the Mesozoic geology of the whole region referred to."

The author minutely described the petrological and lithological characters of this great metamorphic belt, which distinguish it from the Blue Ridge more to the westward; and remarked that – "The indication afforded by the facts above stated, when regarded in their general bearings, is to the effect that the whole range of the Atlantic (or Montalban) gneiss has undergone, at some period, what may be termed a secondary metamorphism." "The period of this alteration could scarcely be any other than at or shortly before the close of the Triassic— when the beds of that age, which rest upon and against this range, received a dip which can only be explained with any clearness by supposing an elevation of the gneissic ridge."

Prof. Martin concluded by stating that Prof. Hitchcock agreed with him with regard to both the mineralogical and lithological views advanced in his paper.

THE FORMBY AND LEASOWE MARINE BEDS, AS SHOWN IN A SECTION NEAR FRESHFIELD.

By T. Mellard Reade, C.E., F.G.S.

At a point in North Moss Lane, 5 furlongs S. by E. of Formby Hall, and 1 mile 5 furlongs in a direct line E.

of Freshfield Station, excavations are being carried out by the Patent Fuel Company. These excavations have disclosed the following section:—

		Ft. In.
1.	Blown Sand	3·0
2.	Peat, containing stools of trees *in situ* at various horizons, beginning at the Clay below, also, skull of horse, and many other bones......	8·0
3.	Fine Blue Clay	3·0
4.	Thin bed of Peat	0·2
5.	Blue Clay, sandier than No. 3, containing at the base	6·0
6.	Shell Bed, containing *Cardium edule, Scrobicularia piperata, Tellina tenuis, Natica Monilifera.*	
7.	Bore hole in Blue Clay, not bottomed	10·0
	Total about.........	30·2

The following statement occurs in my "Post-Glacial Geology of Lancashire and Cheshire," p. 23:—"In a well at Martin's Farm, Hightown (section 18, plate 4), at 20 feet deep, a bed of marine shells occurred, and *I have no doubt more would be found in other places, did the excavations extend deeper than they usually do.*" The section just described is a remarkable confirmation of this prediction; and situated as the locality is, nearly half way between the excavations at Hightown and those at Birkdale—where marine shells were also found by me in the "Scotch" under the peat—as well as being over 2 miles inland of high-water mark, must, I think, finally settle the question of the Marine origin of these important deposits, showing also that a microscopic determination of these beds, where no mollusca had been discovered at that time, was a reliable one.

For any one who wishes to study, to my mind, the most interesting of local deposits—viz., those from the Glacial era up to the present time—there is now every opportunity, as I have presented to the Liverpool Museum a complete series of specimens, and have arranged them in a way to be readily understood by the aid of my original paper on the subject. I trust shortly that the accompanying maps and sections will also be hung up near the cases to further elucidate the subject. Since that communication was made to the Society, the bones of a *Bos longifrons* and a very pretty skull and horns of a goat have been taken out of Mr. Sawyer's clay pit at Formby (No. 4 on map), and these also are deposited in the Museum. In a gulley in the Canada Docks Extension, two fine skulls of the horse were found and presented to the Museum, by the Engineer, Mr. Lyster. A very fine pair of horns of the red deer were also found in the excavations for the north wall at the Rimrose. It is difficult to determine the ages of these remains: they most likely are later than the Formby Beds, and correspond with the overlying silts. It is interesting, however, to find these records of a former elevation of the land, in the gulleys near low-water mark, so general around our coasts.

FEBRUARY 8TH, 1876.

THE PRESIDENT, T. MELLARD READE, C.E., F.G.S.,
in the Chair.

The following communications were read:—

DESCRIPTION OF VALLEY SECTIONS AT LLANDUDNO.

By HUGH F. HALL, F.G.S.

RECORDS OF GLACIAL STRIÆ IN DENBIGH-SHIRE, FLINTSHIRE, AND ANGLESEA.

By GEORGE H. MORTON, F.G.S.

DURING the last few years I have observed the following localities presenting Glacial Striæ in Denbighshire, Flint-shire, and Anglesea. Some of them may have been noticed before, especially in Anglesea; but they all seem to deserve a permanent record, particularly those in the neighbourhood of Llangollen.

LLANYMYNECH.

In October, 1873, I discovered a striated area on the south of Llanymynech Hill, near the top, and close to the face of the quarry. Several yards were exposed, the Car-boniferous Limestone presenting an uneven surface, but entirely covered with striæ in the direction E.N.E. and W.S.W. The elevation above the sea is somewhere about 600 feet. Last year, 1875, I found another exposed surface of striated limestone, also near the hill-top, a few hundred yards to the N.E., perhaps 30 square yards. The surface drift, a few feet in thickness, had been removed along the edge of the quarry and the limestone presented the most interesting area I have seen, so clear and distinct were the striæ running N.E. and S.W. Being a larger area and on a flatter part of the hill, the direction indicated is probably more likely to represent the general course of the ice than the former one, which is just under the highest eminence.

LLANGOLLEN.

At Llangollen I found, at the upper edge of the most eastern quarry under Pen-y-Caer, the Carboniferous Limestone to be striated over between two and three square yards. The direction is E. and W., or a few degrees N. of W.

I also found ice marks on the Silurian rock in the valley in front of the entrance to Trevor Hall. Possibly the rock may not be in situ, but a large Boulder partly covered up. However, the direction of the striæ is E. and W., coincident with the valley, which tends to show that it is a rock exposure and not a detached block.

Since this paper was read I have discovered very distinct Glacial striæ, near the highest part of the ridge Pen-y-Caer, just two miles nearly due west from Llangollen. The ridge consists of "Cefn-y-Fedw Sandstone"— Millstone Grit—the highest elevation, close to Whalley's Tower, being 1,280 feet above the sea-level. The striæ occur close to the edge of the precipitous cliff at several spots, and from 40 to 90 feet from the highest part of the ridge as it gradually descends to the south-east towards Trevor Hall. The direction of the striæ is exactly E. and W., just the same as in the valley below, and the elevation fully 1,200 feet above the sea.

HOLYWELL.

Mr. George W. Shrubsole, F.G.S., of Chester, has recently informed me of a Glacial area or striated surface near to Pen-y-ball, Halkin Mountain. It was discovered on baring the surface of the rock for quarrying. The direction of the striæ is N.E. and S.W., and the altitude 900 feet above the sea.

ANGLESEA.

In the Carboniferous Limestone to the north of Pentraeth, in Anglesea, there is a thick bed of coarse grit cropping out from about the middle of the formation. It is shown in the quarries which are now worked to be at the least 15 feet thick. The stone is obtained in large blocks and roughly formed into millstones, which are exported to Iceland. At the edge of the quarries at Penrallt, about three miles N.W. from Pentraeth, I observed the surface to be perfectly level and strongly marked with distinct striæ N.E. and S.W., the rock being very hard, resembling typical Millstone Grit, and the striæ very sharp and not likely to be defaced for a long time.

Nearly 2 miles to the N., at a place called Tyddyn-bach, where the road diverges, I discovered another similar area of the same rock, presenting distinct striæ on a worn down surface in the same direction N.E. and S.W. Part of the area occurs in a field at the side of a cottage, but it extends across the road which runs over the bare rock; and it is very remarkable that the passage of cart wheels and the traffic along the road have not effaced the striæ, so hard is the gritty rock.

Three-quarters of a mile to the N.W. near Penrhos-lligwy, on the south side, but close to the River Lligwy, there is another striated area. The rock there is a coarse hard grit which is quarried. It crops out below the lowest beds of Carboniferous Limestone, and is coloured as "Yellow Sandstone" on the survey map. There is a fine surface exposed, striated in a direction N.E. and S.W., as in the former localities.

On the south side of Lligwy Bay there occurs one of the most interesting sections of the Lower Carboniferous strata in N. Wales. But in addition to the stratigraphical interest of the section, the evidence of ice action on the surface is very remarkable. The low cliffs are contorted in such a manner as to indicate a crumpling by the lateral pressure of ice, as shown in the diagram. Below the contorted strata there are three beds of limestone, perfectly horizontal, and uninfluenced by the force which exerted the pressure on the higher beds. Below these horizontal beds, on the sea shore in front of the outcrop, the surface of a lower stratum of limestone extends for several yards, and its surface is striated in the usual direction N.E. and S.W. The waves of every high tide cover the striated surface, and must have done so for years, and still the striæ seem just as fresh as on the road, where carts pass daily over it, or as in the other localities which have been exposed to the weather for years in succession.

All these ice-marked areas seem to be very permanent, and the flat surfaces offer so little resistance to aqueous action, that they retain the sharp striæ and grooves for a long time before they are obliterated.

MARCH 14TH, 1876.

THE PRESIDENT, T. MELLARD READE, C.E., F.G.S.,
in the Chair.

The following communications were read:—

LIST OF WORKS ON THE GEOLOGY, MINERALOGY, AND PALÆONTOLOGY OF CHESHIRE.

BY WILLIAM WHITAKER, B.A., F.G.S.,

*Of the Geological Survey of England, Editor of the
" Geological Record."*

In this List, as in those already published, a chronological arrangement has been adopted, ending with the year 1873, after which date the "Geological Record" supplies fuller information.

INDEX OF AUTHORS, WITH THE NUMBERS AFFIXED TO THEIR PAPERS.

LIST OF WORKS.

1680.

1. LEIGH, C. Natural History of Lancashire, Cheshire, and the Peak in Derbyshire, &c. *Fol. Oxon.* ? another Edition in 1700.

1669.

2. JACKSON, DR. W. Some Inquiries concerning the Salt-Springs and the Way of Salt-making at Nantwich in Cheshire. Answered. *Phil. Trans.*, vol. iv, No. 53, p. 1,060.

1670.

8. MARTINDALE, A. Extracts of two letters from Rotherton in Cheshire, concerning the Discovery of a Rock of Natural Salt in that Country. *Phil. Trans.*, vol. v, No. 66, p. 2,015.

1684.

4. LISTER, DR. M. Certain Observations of the Midland Salt-Springs of Worcester-shire, Stafford-shire and Cheshire. *Phil. Trans.*, vol. xiv, No. 156, p. 489.

1691.

5. RAY, J. Collection of English Words not generally used, with Account of the Making of Salt at Nantwych in Cheshire, &c. *Ed.* 2, 12*mo.*

1740.

6. SHORT, DR. T. An Essay Towards A Natural, Experimental, and Medicinal History of the Principle Mineral Waters of . . . . . . Cheshire, &c. *4to. Sheffield.*

1781.

7. JARS, M. G. Voyages Metallurgiques, *tome* 3. (Cheshire, p. 332). *4to. Paris.*

1795.

8. AIKIN, J. Description of the Country from thirty to forty miles round Manchester. *4to.*

1809.

9. FAREY, J. Observations on a late Paper by Dr. W. Richardson, respecting the basaltic District in the North of Ireland, and on the Geological Facts thence deducible; in conjunction with others observable in Derbyshire and other English Counties . . . . &c. *Phil. Mag.,* vol. xxxiii, p. 257.

1810.

10. FAREY, J. A List of about Five Hundred Collieries in and near to Derbyshire. *Phil. Mag.,* vol. xxxv, p. 431.

1811.

11. BAKEWELL, R. [Description of Alderley Edge, in Cheshire.] *Monthly Mag.,* vol. xxxi, No. 209, p. 7.

12. FAREY, J. A List of about 280 Mines of Lead,—some with Zinc, Manganese, Copper, Iron, Fluor, Barytes, &c., in and near to Derbyshire. *Phil. Mag.,* vol. xxxvii, p. 106.

13. HOLLAND, A. A Sketch of the natural History of the Cheshire Rock-Salt District. *Trans. Geol. Soc.*, vol. i, p. 38.

1817.

14. AIKIN, A. Notice on a Green waxy Substance found in the alluvial soil near Stockport, in Cheshire. *Trans. Geol. Soc.*, vol. iv, p. 445.

15. TRAIL, DR. Notice of some magnetic iron sand, Cheshire. *Ibid.*, p. 447.

1824.

16. ANON. Fossil Elephant's Tooth found in Cheshire. *Edin. Phil. Journ.*, vol. xi, p. 417.

1825.

17. SEDGWICK, REV. PROF. A. On the Origin of Alluvial and Diluvial Formations. (Cheshire, p. 23). *Ann. of Phil.*, Ser. 2, vol. x, p. 18.

1826.

18. HIBBERT, DR. S. On some Remarkable Concretions which are found in the Sandstone of Kerridge in Cheshire. *Edin. Journ. of Sci.*, vol. iv, p. 138.

1828.

19. STEVENSON, R. Remarks upon the Wasting Effects of the Sea on the shore of Cheshire, between the rivers Mersey and Dee. *Edin. New Phil. Journ.*, vol. iv, p. 386.

1829.

20. BRAYLEY, E. W. On the Existence of Salts of Potash in Brine-Springs and in Rock-Salt. *Phil. Mag.*, Ser. 2, vol. v, p. 411.

21. NICOL, W. On the cavities containing Fluids in Rock-Salt. *Edin. New Phil. Journ.*, vol. vii, p. 111.

1830.

22. DAUBENY, DR. C. Memoir on the occurrence of Iodine and Bromine in certain Mineral Waters of South Britain. (Cheshire, pp. 229, 230). *Phil. Trans.*, vol. cxx, p. 223.

23. OEYNHAUSEN, C. VON, and H. VON DECHEN. [On Rock Salt in England.] *Karsten's Archiv.* 1, i, p. 56.

1832.

24. HALL, E. A Mineralogical and Geological Map of the Coal Field of Lancashire, with parts of . . . Cheshire . . . (an inch to a mile). 2 other Editions.

1833.

25. TRIMMER, J. Discovery of marine shells of existing species on the left bank of the river Mersey, and above the level of high-water mark. *Proc. Geol. Soc.,* vol. i, p. 419.

1835.

26. EGERTON, SIR P. G. On a Bed of Gravel containing Marine Shells of recent species, at "The Willington," in Cheshire. *Proc. Geol. Soc.,* vol. ii, p. 189.

27. MURCHISON [SIR] R. I. On an outlying basin of Lias on the borders of Salop and Cheshire, &c. *Ibid.,* p. 114.

28. ———— The Gravel and Alluvia of S. Wales and Siluria as distinguished from a northern drift covering Lancashire, Cheshire, &c. . . . *Ibid.,* p. 230.

1836.

29. EGERTON, SIR P. DE M. G. A notice on the occurrence of marine shells in a bed of gravel at Narley Bank, Cheshire. *Proc. Geol. Soc.,* vol, ii, p. 415.

1837.

30. ANON. Cheshire. "Geological Character." *Penny Cyclopædia,* vol. vii, p. 43. (*Fol. Lond.*)

31. TOOKE, A. W. The Mineral Topography of Great Britain. (Cheshire, p. 40). *Mining Review,* No. 9, p. 39.

1838.

32. ANON. (Liverpool Natural History Society). An account of Footsteps of the Chirotherium, and other unknown animals lately discovered in the quarries of Storeton Hill, in the peninsula of Wirrall, between the Mersey and the Dee. . . . illustrated with drawings by J. CUNNINGHAM. *Proc. Geol. Soc.*, vol. iii, p. 12.

33. DENHAM, CAPT. On the Tidal Capacity of the Mersey Estuary—the Proportion of Silt held in solution . . . the Excess of Deposit upon each Reflux, and the consequent Effect . . . *Rep. Brit. Assoc. for* 1837, *Trans. of Sections*, p. 85.

34. EGERTON, SIR P. DE M. G. On two Casts in Sandstone of the impressions of the Hind Foot of a gigantic Chirotherium, from the New Red Sandstone of Cheshire. *Proc. Geol. Soc.*, vol. iii, p. 14.

35. TRIMMER, J. On the Diluvial or Northern Drift of the Eastern and Western Sides of the Cambrian Chain, and on its Connexion with a similar Deposit on the Eastern Side of Ireland. . . . *Journ. Geol. Soc., Dublin*, vol. i, part 4, pp. 286, 335.

1839.

36. CUNNINGHAM, J. An Account of Impressions and Casts of Drops of Rain, discovered in the Quarries at Storeton Hill, Cheshire. *Proc. Geol. Soc.*, vol. iii, p. 99.

37. EGERTON, SIR P. DE M. G., and J. TAYLOR. Letters on a slab of sandstone, exhibiting footmarks, and supposed to be from the Kelsall quarry. *Ibid.*, p. 100.

38. GRANT, PROF. [R. E.] Footmarks of Chirotherium at Stourton Hill. *Mag. Nat. Hist.*, Ser. 2, vol. iii, p. 43.

1840.

39. BUCKLAND, REV. PROF. W. (On fossil impressions of rain, and ripple marks . . . and fossil
footsteps of Cheirotherium and other unknown animals
recently discovered on strata of the new red sandstone
formation in the counties of Cheshire, Salop, and
Warwick). *Proc. Ashmolean Soc., Oxon.*, No. xvi, p. 5.

40. HODGKINSON, E. On the Temperature of the Earth
in the deep Mines of Lancashire and Cheshire. *Rep.
Brit. Assoc. for* 1839, *Trans. of Sections*, p. 19.

41. YATES, J. B. On the rapid changes which take
place at the Entrance of the river Mersey, and the
means adopted for establishing an easy acccess to Vessels
resorting thereto. *Ibid.*, p. 77.

1841.

42. BINNEY, E. W. Sketch of the Geology of Manchester and its Vicinity. *Trans. Manchester Geol. Soc.*,
vol. i, p. 35.

43. ———— Observations on the Lancashire and
Cheshire Coal Field. *Ibid.*, p. 67.

44. BULLFINCH, —. Report on the Casts of Fossil
Footsteps from Cheshire, England. *Proc. Boston Nat.
Hist. Soc.*, p. 45.

45. HODGKINSON, E. On the Temperature of the
Earth in the deep Mines in the neighbourhood of Manchester. *Rep. Brit. Assoc. for* 1840, *Trans. of Sections*,
p. 17.

1842.

46. HEYWOOD, J. Remarks on the Coal District of
South Lancashire. (Refers to Cheshire). *Mem. Lit.
Phil. Soc., Manchester*, Ser. 2, vol. vi, p. 426.

47. ORMEROD, —. On the Salt of Cheshire. *Geologist*, p. 150, and *Trans. Manchester Geol. Soc.*, vol. viii,
p. 25. (1869).

1843.

48. BINNEY, E. W. Notes on the Lancashire and Cheshire Drift. *Geologist*, p. 112, and *Trans. Manchester Geol. Soc.*, vol. viii, p. 30. (1869).

49. ———— On the Great Lancashire and Cheshire Coal Fields. [Brit. Assoc.] Reprinted from *Annals of Philosophical Discovery and Monthly Reporter of the Progress of Practical Science.* 10 pp. 8vo. *Manchester.*

50. BUCKLAND, REV. DR. W. On Recent and Fossil Semi-circular Cavities caused by air-bubbles on the surface of soft clay, and resembling impressions of raindrops. *Rep. Brit. Assoc. for* 1842, *Trans. of Sections*, p. 57.

51. HAWKSHAW, ——. Notice of the Fossil Footsteps in the New Red Sandstone Quarry at Lymm, in Cheshire. *Ibid.*, p. 56.

52. ORMEROD, G. W. On the Geology of Central Cheshire. *Geologist*, p. 1, ? and *Trans. Manchester Geol. Soc.*, vol. viii, p. 25. (1869).

1845.

53. HUME, REV. DR. A. An Account of a recent Visit by several Members of the Society, to the Submarine Forest at Leasowe. *Proc. Lit. Phil. Soc., Liverpool*, vol. i, p. 97.

1846.

54. BINNEY, E. W. On the Relation of the New Red Sandstone to the Carboniferous Strata in Lancashire and Cheshire. *Quart. Journ. Geol. Soc.*, vol. ii, p. 12.

55. BLACK, DR. J. Observations on a Slab of New Red Sandstone from the Quarries at Weston, near Runcorn, Cheshire, containing the Impressions of Footsteps and other markings. *Ibid.*, p. 65.

56. HUME, DR. [A.] Notes of an Oral Lecture, delivered on Geological Subjects during a recent Excursion to Stourton. *Proc. Lit. Phil. Soc., Liverpool, No. ii, p. 52.*

1847.

57. CUNNINGHAM [J.] On the Geological Conformation of the Neighbourhood of Liverpool, as respects the Supply of Water. *Proc. Lit. Phil. Soc., Liverpool,* No. iii, p. 58.

58. ORMEROD, G. W. On the Extent of the Northwich Salt-field. *Rep. Brit. Assoc. for* 1846, *Trans. of Sections,* p. 62.

1848.

59. BINNEY, E. W. On the Origin of Coal. *Mem. Lit. Phil. Soc., Manchester,* Ser. 2, vol. ix, p. 148.

60. ———— Sketch of the Drift Deposits of Manchester and its Neighbourhood. *Ibid.,* p. 195.

61. CHAMBERS, R. Ancient Sea-Margins, as Memorials of Changes in the Relative Level of Sea and Land. (Cheshire, pp. 223–228). *8vo. Edin. and Lond.*

62. CUNNINGHAM, J. Description of Plates (Impressions on Sandstone, &c., Stourton). *Proc. Lit. Phil. Soc., Liverpool,* No. iv, p. 127.

63. ORMEROD, G. W. Outline of the principal Geological features of the Salt-field of Cheshire and the adjoining districts. *Quart. Journ. Geol. Soc.,* vol. iv, p. 262.

1850.

64. HARKNESS [PROF.] R. Notice of a Tridactylous Footmark from the Bunter Sandstone of Weston Point, Cheshire. *Ann. Nat. Hist.,* Ser. 2, vol. vi, p. 440.

65. HULL [PROF.] E. Sheet 79, S.E. of the Geological Survey Map (N.E. corner). Additions in 1855.

66. ———— Sheet 79, N.E. of the Geological Survey Map (greater part: Birkenhead, Neston). New Edition in 1855.

67. ———— Sheet 44 of the Horizontal Sections of the Geological Survey. No. 1 (part). Section . . . . across . . . the New Red Sandstone of Holt and the Peckforton Hills.

1851.

68. DICKINSON, J. On the Physical Geography of Liverpool and Wirral. *Appendix* (The Flora of Liverpool) to *Proc. Lit. Phil. Soc., Liverpool,* No. vi.

69. TRIMMER, J. On the Erratic Tertiaries bordering the Penine Chain, between Congleton and Macclesfield; and on the Scratched Detritus of the Till. *Quart. Journ. Geol. Soc.,* vol. vii, p. 201.

1852.

70. BINNEY, E. W. Notes on the Drift Deposits found near Blackpool. *Mem. Lit. Phil. Soc., Manchester,* Ser. 2, vol. x, p. 121.

1853.

71. RAWLINSON, R. On Foot-tracks found in the New Red Sandstone at Lymm, Cheshire. *Quart. Journ. Geol. Soc.,* vol. ix, p. 37.

72. TRIMMER, J. On the Erratic Tertiaries bordering the Penine Chain. Part 2. *Ibid.,* p. 352.

1855.

73. BINNEY, E. W. On the Permian Beds of the North-West of England. *Mem. Lit. Phil. Soc., Manchester,* Ser. 2, vol. xii, p. 209.

74, 75. HULL [PROF.] E. Sheets 80, S.W. (Chester, Delamere Forest), and 73, S.W. (small piece on N.) of the Geological Survey Map.

76. SELWYN, A. R. and [PROF.] E. HULL. Sheet 73, N.W. of the Geological Survey Map (N.E. part: Malpas).

1856.

77. BINNEY, E. W. On some Footmarks in the Millstone Grit of Tintwistle, Cheshire. *Quart. Journ. Geol. Soc.,* vol. xii, p. 350.

78. MORTON, G. H. On the Sub-divisions of the New Red Sandstone between the River Dee and the Up-throw of the Coal Measures east of Liverpool. *Proc. Lit. Phil. Soc., Liverpool*, No. x, p. 68.

* 1857.

79. NORTHCOTE, A. B. On the Brine-springs of Cheshire. *Phil. Mag.*, Ser. 4, vol. xiv, p. 457.

80. RENNIE, G., J. BOULT, and A. HENDERSON. Report from the Committee . . . . to investigate and report upon the effects produced upon the Channels of the Mersey by the alterations which within the last fifty years have been made in its Banks. *Rep. Brit. Assoc. for* 1856, p. 1.

81. SMYTH, W. W., A. R. SELWYN, and [PROF.] E. HULL. Sheet 73, N.E. of the Geological Survey Map (N.W. half: Crewe, Nantwich).

1858.

82. HIGGS, S. Notice of the Copper Mines of Alderley Edge, Cheshire. *Trans. Roy. Geol. Soc., Cornwall*, vol. vii, p. 325.

83. HULL [PROF.] E. Sheet 43 of the Horizontal Sections of the Geological Survey (part). Section across . . . . the New Red Sandstone of Chester and Delamere Forest.

84. ———— Sheet 80, S.E. of the Geological Survey Map (Northwich, Middlewich).

1859.

85. ATKINSON, J. (On a curiously-shaped fossil found in the Upper New Red Sandstone near Runcorn). *Proc. Lit. Phil. Soc., Manchester*, vol. i, p. 164.

86. HULL [PROF.] E. Sheet 80, N.W. of the Geological Survey Map. (S. part: Frodsham, Runcorn).

1860.

87. ATKINSON, J. On the Drift Deposits in the Neighbourhood of Thelwall, Cheshire. *Trans. Manchester Geol. Soc.*, vol. ii, Part 6, p. 63.

88. BINNEY, E. W. Observations on the Fossil Shells of the Lower Coal Measures. *Ibid.*, Part 7, p. 72.

89. HENDERSON, W. Economic Treatment of Poor Copper and other Ores [refers to the Alderley Edge deposits, *Mining Journal*, vol. xxx, pp. 686, 690.

90. HULL, E. On the New Subdivisions of the Triassic Rocks of the Central Counties. *Trans. Manchester Geol. Soc.*, vol. ii, Part 3, p. 22.

91. ———— The Geology of the Country around Prescot, Lancashire [refers partly to Cheshire.] *Geological Survey Memoir*, 8vo. *Lond.* Ed. 2 in 1865.]

92. MORTON, G. H. [printed "Hillotson."] Slickensides. *Geologist*, vol. iii, p. 87.

93. ———— Evidences of Ancient Ice-action near Liverpool, and on Pleistocene Deposits near Liverpool. *Ibid.*, pp. 197, 349. See also p. 277.

1861.

94. HULL, E. Sheet 80, N.E. of the Geological Survey Map (all but N. edge: Altrincham, Knutsford).

95. ———— The Geology of the Country around Altrincham, Cheshire. *Geological Survey Memoir*, pp. 8, 8vo., Lond.

96. MITCHENER, J. H. On a New Red Sandstone Quarry at Stourton in Cheshire. *Proc. Geol. Assoc.*, vol. i, p. 75.

97. MORTON, G. H. On the Basement Bed of the Keuper Formation in Wirral and the Southwest of Lancashire. *Proc. Liverpool Geol. Soc.*, Sessions 1 and 2, p. 4.

98. ———— On the Pleistocene Deposits of the District around Liverpool. *Ibid*, p. 12. [Brit. Assoc.]

1862.

99. BINNEY, E. W. (On the Crystal of Selenite found in the till in North Cheshire). *Trans. Manchester Geol. Soc.*, vol. iii, p. 8.

100. ———— On 'Jelly Peat'—found at Churchtown near Southport. *Ibid*, p. 19.

101. HULL, E. The Lancashire and Cheshire Coal Fields. *Mining and Smelting Mag.*, vol. i, p. 85.

102. JONES, PROF. T. R. A Monograph of the Fossil Estheriæ. (Cheshire, pp. 64, &c.) *Palæontograph Soc.*

103. TAYLOR, J. On Pleistocene Deposits on the Stockport and Woodley Railway. *Trans. Manchester Geol. Soc.*, vol. iii, p. 147.

1863.

104. BINNEY, E. W. Section of the Drift near Rainford. *Geol. Mag.*, vol. vi, p. 307. See also p. 308.

105. HULL, [PROF] E. Sheet 88, S.W. of the Geological Survey Map. (E. Part, Staleybridge).

106. MORTON, G. H. On the Surface Markings near Liverpool, supposed to have been caused by Ice. *Proc. Liverpool Geol. Soc.*, Session 3, p. 9.

107. ———— On the Thickness of the Bunter and Keuper Formations around Liverpool. *Ibid*, p. 15.

108. ———— Report of the Society's Field Meetings at Storeton and Leasowe. *Ibid*, Session 4, p. 5.

109. ———— Description of the Footprints of Cheirotherium and Equisetum, found at Storeton, Cheshire. *Ibid*, p. 17.

110. ———— The Geology of the Country around Liverpool. *8vo. Liverpool.*

111. PLATT, —. [Records of Borings at Middlesborough, Bradford, and Wirrall.] *Proc. Lit. and Phil. Soc., Manchester*, vol. iii, No. 3, Session 1863-4, p. 188.

112. TATE, A. N. On the Composition of Black Sandstone occurring in the Trias around Liverpool. *Proc Liverpool Geol. Soc.*, Session 4, p. 16.

1864.

113. BARR, W. R. On the Quaternary Deposits of the Valley of the Mersey, near Stockport. *Trans. Manchester Geol. Soc.*, vol. iv, (No. 15), p. 835.

114. BINNEY, E. W. A few remarks on the Lancashire and Cheshire Drift. *Proc. Lit. Phil. Soc., Manchester*, vol. iii, No. 10, (Session 1863-4) p. 214, (and *Geologist*, vol. vii, p. 140).

115. DARBISHIRE, R. D. Notes on Marine Shells found in Stratified Drift at Macclesfield. *Ibid*, vol. iv, No. 5, (Session 1864-5), p. 41.

116. ESKRIGGE, R. A. On the Lias of Cheshire and Shropshire. *Trans. Manchester Geol. Soc.*, vol. iv, (No. 14), p. 818.

117. GRANTHAM, R. B. A Description of the Works for Reclaiming and Marling parts of the late Forest of Delamere, in the County of Cheshire. *Journ. Roy. Agric. Soc.*, vol. xxv, p. 869.

118. GREEN, [PROF.] A. H. Sheet 81, S.W. of the Geological Survey Map, (Macclesfield, Congleton).

119. GREENWELL, G. C. On the Copper Sandstone of Alderley, Cheshire, *Trans. S. Wales Inst. Eng.*, vol. iv, p. 44.

120. HULL [PROF.] E. On the Occurrence of Glacial Striations on the Surface of Bidston Hill, near Birkenhead. *Trans. Manchester Geol. Soc.*, vol. iv, p. 288.

121. ———— On the New Red Sandstone and Permian Formations, as Sources of Water-supply for Towns. *Mem. Lit. Phil. Soc., Manchester*, Ser. 3, vol. ii, p 256.

122. ———- On the Copper-bearing Rocks of Alderley Edge, Cheshire, *Geol. Mag.*, vol. i, p. 65.

123. HULL, —. Sheet 64 of the Horizontal Sections of the Geological Survey. Section from Northwich on the South-West to Marsden Yorkshire, on the North-East, &c.

124. ——— Sheet 81, N.W. of the Geological Survey Map. (Greater part: Stockport).

125. ——— The Geology of the Country around Oldham, including Manchester and its Suburbs. *Geological Survey Memoir.* 8vo. Lond.

126. HULL, E. and A. H. GREEN. On the Millstone Grit of North Staffordshire and the adjoining parts of Derbyshire, Cheshire, and Lancashire. *Quart. Journ. Geol. Soc.*, vol. xx, p. 242.

127. SAINTER, J. D. Sandstone Hammer in a Diluvial Deposit at Macclesfield. *Geologist*, vol. vii, p. 56.

128. TAYLOR, J. On the Drift Deposits in the Neighbourhood of Crewe, Cheshire. *Trans. Manchester Geol. Soc.*, vol. iv, p. 308.

1865.

129. BINNEY, E. W. A few Remarks on Mr. Hull's Additional Observations on the Drift deposits in the Neighbourhood of Manchester. *Mem. Lit. Phil. Soc. Manchester*, Ser. 3, vol. ii, p. 462.

130. BOULT, J. On the Alleged Submarine Forests on the Shores of Liverpool Bay and the River Mersey. *Journ. Polytech. Soc., Liverpool.*

131. BRODIE, REV. P. B. Remarks on three outliers of Lias in North Shropshire and South Cheshire, Staffordshire, and Cumberland, and their correlation with the main range. *Proc. Warwick Field Club*, p. 6.

132. HULL, E.   Additional Observations on the Drift deposits, and more recent Gravels in the Neighbourhood of Manchester. *Mem. Lit. Phil. Soc. Manchester*, Ser. 3, vol. ii, p. 449.

133. HULL —.   Sheet 67 of the Horizontal Sections of the Geological Survey.   No. 2 (Part).   From Arley Hall, Cheshire, on the South-East, to Windle Moss Lancashire, on the North-West, &c.

134. HULL, E. and A. H. GREEN.   Sheet 65 of the Horizontal Sections of the Geological Survey.   No. 1 (part).   From Manchester on the West, to the River Etherow in Lougdendale, on the East, &c.   No. 2 (part). From Bowdon, Cheshire, on the West, to Westend Moor, Derbyshire, on the East, &c.

135. MORTON, G. H.   Section of the Strata from Hilbre to Huyton.   Scale 2 inches to a mile.

136. ————— On the Recent Shell-bed at Wallasey. *Proc. Liverpool Geol. Soc.*, Session 6, p. 26.

137. SMITH, H. E.   A Record of Archæological Products of the Sea Shore of Cheshire in 1864.   *Quart. Archæol. Journ. and Rev.*

1866.

138. BOULT, J.   Further Observations on the Alleged Submarine Forests on the Shores of Liverpool Bay and the River Mersey: in reply to Dr. Hulme's Communication of July 10, 1865.   *Trans. Hist. Soc. Lancash. and Chesh.*, vol. vi.

139. GREEN, A. H.   Sheet 18 of the Horizontal Sections of the Geological Survey (part).   Section from the Red Marl plain of Cheshire, across the Lower Carboniferous Rocks of North Staffordshire, &c.   Ed. 2. (Ed. 1 does not refer to Cheshire).

140. HARDWICK, C.   A few Thoughts on Geology in its Relation to Archæology.   *Trans. Manchester Geol. Soc., vol. v, p. 201.*

141. HULL, E., and A. H. GREEN. The Geology of the Country round Stockport, Macclesfield, Congleton and Leek. *Geological Survey Memoir, 8vo Lond.*

142. HUME, REV. DR. On the Changes in the Sea coast of Lancashire and Cheshire. *Trans. Hist. Soc. Lancash. and Chesh.*, vol. vi.

143. MORTON, G. H. On the Geology of the Country bordering the Mersey and the Dee. *Proc. Liverpool Geol. Soc.*, Session 7, p. 37, *and Liverpool Naturalists Journ.*, No. 1, p. 15.

144. RICKETTS, DR. C. On a Wooden Implement found in Bidston Moss. *Proc. Liverpool Geol. Soc.*, Session 7, p. 3.

145. SAINTER, [J. D.] Macclesfield Drift Shells, &c. *Trans. Manchester Geol. Soc.*, vol. v, p. 114.

1867.

146. BINNEY, E. W. The Drift of the Western and Eastern Counties. *Geol. Mag.*, vol. iv, p. 231.

147. HULL, E. Sheet 70 of the Horizontal Sections of the Geological Survey (part). From Swan Bank, near Alderley Edge, across the New Red Sandstone Plain of Cheshire; the Coal Measures, Millstone Grit, and Carboniferous Limestone of Kerridge, Saltersford Valley, &c.

148. MORTON, G. H. On the Presence of Glacial Ice in the Valley of the Mersey during the Post Pliocene Period. *Proc. Liverpool Geol. Soc.*, Session 8, p. 4.

149. THOMAS, J. E. Prize Essay upon the Encroachment of the Sea between the River Mersey and the Bristol Channel. *8vo. Lond.*

150. WILLIAMSON, PROF. W. C. On a Cheirotherian Footprint from the Base of the Keuper Sandstone of Daresbury, Cheshire. *Quart. Journ. Geol. Soc.*, vol. xxiii, p. 56.

1868.

151. MAW, G. On the Disposition of Iron in variegated Strata. (Cheshire pp. 370, 395). *Quart. Journ. Geol. Soc.*, vol. xxiv, p. 351.

1869.

152. BOSTOCK, R. The New Red Sandstone as a Source of Water Supply. *Proc. Liverpool Geol. Soc.*, Session 10, p. 58.

153. HULL, E. On the Evidences of a Ridge of Lower Carboniferous Rocks crossing the Plain of Cheshire beneath the Trias, and forming the boundary between the Permian Rocks of the Lancashire Type on the North, and those of the Salopian Type on the South. *Quart. Journ. Geol. Soc.*, vol. xxv, p. 171.

154. ———— The Triassic and Permian Rocks of the Midland Counties of England. *Geological Survey Memoir*, pp. x, 127, *8vo. Lond.*

155. POTTER, C. Observations on the Cheshire Coast. *Proc. Liverpool Geol. Soc.*, Session 10, p. 37.

156. SAINTER, DR. J. D. The Geology and Archæology of some of the Macclesfield Drift Beds. *Geol. and Nat. Hist. Repertory*, vol. ii, p. 269.

1870.

157. BOSTOCK, R. The Mersey and the Dee—Their former Channels and Change of Level. *Proc. Liverpool Geol. Soc.*, Session 11, p. 41.

158. DE RANCE, C. E. Notes on the Geology of the Country around Liverpool. *Nature*, vol. ii, No. 46, p. 391.

159. EYTON, Miss C. On the Age and Geological Position of the Blue Clay of the Western Counties. *Geol. Mag.*, vol. vii, p. 545.

160. MAW, G.   On the Occurrence of the Rhætic Beds in North Shropshire and Cheshire.   *Ibid., p.* 203.

161. TAYLOR, J. E.   Note on the Middle Drift-beds in Cheshire.   *Ibid,* p. 162.

162. WOOD, S. V., Jun.   Observations on the Sequence of the Glacial Beds.   [2nd part.]   *Ibid.,* p. 61.

1871.

163. Report of the Commissioners appointed to inquire into the several matters relating to Coal in the United Kingdom.   Vol. i General Report, &c.   J. DICKINSON.   Lancashire, Cheshire, &c., p. 16.   Prof. A. C. RAMSAY (and others).   Report of Committee D, appointed to inquire into the probability of Finding Coal under the Permian, New Red Sandstone, &c., p. 118. ——— Vol. ii.   General Minutes and Proceedings of Committees.   J. KNOWLES.   Temperature of Air and Strata, p. 192.   On the Probability of Finding Coal under the Permian, &c., p. 413.   *Fol. Lond.*

164. AITKEN, J.   The President's Address.   (Note on a Section at Stockport).   *Trans. Manchester Geol. Soc.,* vol. x, No. 1, p. 26.

165. ——— On Faults in Drift at Stockport Cheshire.   *Ibid,* p. 46, and *Geol. Mag.,* vol. viii, p. 117.

166. BINNEY, E. W.   Notes on some of the High Level Drifts in the Counties of Chester, Derby and Lancaster.   *Proc. Lit. Phil. Soc., Manchester,* vol. x, p. 66.

167. DE RANCE, C. E.   On the Glacial Phenomena of Western Lancashire and Cheshire.   *Quart. Journ. Geol. Soc.,* vol. xxvi, p. 641.

168. ——— On the Postglacial Deposits of Western Lancashire and Cheshire.   *Ibid.,* p. 655.   [Both these papers published with the first No. of vol. xxvii, and therefore in the year after the greater part of vol. xxvi.]

169. ———— On the Pre-Glacial Geography of Northern Cheshire. *Geol. Mag.*, vol. viii, p. 158.

170. Morton, G. H. On the Glaciated Condition of the Triassic Rocks around Liverpool. *Rep. Brit. Assoc. for* 1870, *Trans. of Sections*, p. 81.

171. ———— Anniversary Address. *Proc. Liverpool Geol. Soc.*, Session 12, p. 3.

1872.

172. Anon. (M.S.) Land-slip near Northwich, Cheshire. *Science Gossip*, No. 89, p. 107.

173. Mackintosh, D. On a Sea-coast Section of Boulder-clay in Cheshire. *Quart. Journ. Geol. Soc.*, vol. xxviii, p. 388.

174. Morton, G. H. Minerals that occur in the Neighbourhood of Liverpool, with the Localities, &c. *Proc. Liverpool Geol. Soc.*, Session 13, p. 91.

175. ———— Shells found in the Glacial Deposits around Liverpool, with the Localities, &c. *Ibid.*, p. 92.

176. Morton, Dr. [T.] On Geological Systems and Endemic Disease. *Rep. Brit. Assoc. for* 1871, *Trans. of Sections*, p. 107.

177. Reade, T. M. The Geology and Physics of the Post-Glacial Period, as shewn in the Deposits and Organic Remains in Lancashire and Cheshire. *Proc. Liverpool Geol. Soc.*, Session 13, p. 36.

178. ———— The Post-Glacial Geology and Physiography of West Lancashire and the Mersey Estuary. *Geol. Mag.*, vol. ix, p. 111.

179. ———— (Letter on boring for Coal.) *Liverpool Daily Post*, Sep. 16. (Noticed in *Nature*, No. 151, p. 421.)

180. Ricketts, Dr. C. Valleys, Deltas, Bays, and Estuaries. (President's Address.) *Proc. Liverpool Geol. Soc.*, Session 1871-2.

181. Ward, T. The Landslips at Northwich. *Nature*, vol. v, No. 119, p. 289.

1873.

182. Anon. (P. S.) Ancient Cheshire Forest [W. of Warrington]. *Science Gossip*, No. 99, pp. 67, 68.

183. Boult, J. The Mersey as known to the Romans. *Proc. Lit. Phil. Soc. Liverpool*, No. xxvii, p. 249.

184. De Rance, C. E. The Cyclas clay of West Lancashire. *Geol. Mag.*, vol. x, p. 187.

185. ———— The Lower Scrobicularia and Lower Cyclas Clays of the Mersey and the Ribble. *Ibid.*, p. 287.

186. Mackintosh, D. Observations on the more remarkable Boulders of the North-west of England and the Welsh Borders. *Quart. Journ. Geol. Soc.*, vol. xxix, p. 351.

187. Morton, G. H. The Strata below the Trias in the Country around Liverpool; and the Probability of Coal occurring at a Moderate Depth. *Proc. Lit. Phil. Soc. Liverpool*, No. xxvii, p. 157.

188. Reade, T. M. Formby and Leasowe Marine Beds, or the so-called "Cyclas Clay." *Geol. Mag.*, vol. x, p. 238.

189. ———— The Buried Valley of the Mersey. *Proc. Liverpool Geol. Soc.*, Session 14, p. 42.

190. Ward, T. The Cheshire Salt District. *Proc. Lit. Phil. Soc. Liverpool*, No. xxvii, p. 39.

OBSERVATIONS ON THE SUB-WEALDEN BORING.

By Charles Potter.

APRIL 11th, 1876.

The President, T. MELLARD READE, C.E., F.G.S.,

in the Chair.

The following communications were read:—

REMARKS ON THE COPPER LODE AT DYFFRYN
ALED.

By William Semmons, F.G.S.

A NOTE ON ITACOLUMYTE, OR FLEXIBLE
SANDSTONE.

By Alfred Morgan.

The somewhat fanciful name of Itacolumyte has been
given to the Brazilian variety of Flexible Sandstone, which
is said in some treatises on gems to be diamondiferous
in its nature, though I have not met with any authen-
ticated instance of its being so. Indeed, the only reliable
information we possess tends to a decided negative of the
assertion. My interest in this remarkable rock was
awakened during an investigation of the mineralogy of
the precious crystals, those "flowers of the mineral kingdom;" and I found in the "Records of the Geological
Survey of India,"* a paper by Mr. H. B. Medlicott, A.M.,
F.G.S., containing fuller information on the subject than
I had hitherto met with. According to Dana, "the Ita-

* Vol. vii., p. 31, Calcutta, 1874.

columyte of Brazil, which is associated with Gold and Topaz," is a micaceous, granular quartz rock, which breaks into slabs like gneiss or mica slate. A similar Flexible Sandstone is found in South Carolina and in the neighbourhood of Delhi. The Indian variety is a modified condition of a massive Quartzite or Metamorphic Sandstone. It contains but few and isolated plates of mica, and is devoid of any schistose (foliated) structure.

The only known habitat in India of the Elastic Sandstone is Kaliana, five miles west from Dadri, a town in the Jheend State, sixty miles nearly due west from Delhi. The hill, which is one of the Trigonometrical Survey Stations, is 1477 feet above the sea, and about 740 feet above the plain. It is one of the many ridges which in this region of the Punjab stretch far into the plains, the alluvial areas between being confluent with the Indo-Gangetic Deposits. These ridges are prolongations of the great Aravali system. The highest part of the ridge overhangs the village of Kaliana. " It is here double crested, the projecting ribs being formed by two strong beds of Ironstone, a quartzite strongly impregnated by massive Specular Iron (black hæmatite) and some Magnetic Iron, strings of pure ore occuring locally in the mass. These bands of ferruginous quartzite are regularly inter-stratified with the mica and hornblende schists; and the earthy, cellular quartzite so largely quarried for millstones is distinctly an intercalated member of the same series, all being nearly vertical. The Elastic Sandstone is only found in patches in this band of millstone quartzite. There is no regular seam of it; the stone-cutters, of whom there is quite a colony at Kaliana, come upon it suddenly when cutting out slabs of the ordinary stone. Often the rock in immediate contact with a nest of the Elastic Sandstone is highly indurated and quartzose. The stone-cutters declare they sometimes find it in the line of bedding and sometimes in the joints. Their idea of the matter is that it is a mere local peculiarity of the Sandstone rock caused by the percolation of rain water and *miti* (earth) from the surface."

It is probable, as Mr. Medlicott observes, that if the *miti* had been omitted the natives' explanation is the correct one. Superficially examined, the only difference observable is the greater porosity and friability of the flexible stone, as compared with the quartzite. And the peculiar property of flexibility is probably due to the mechanical removal of some thinly permeating cement to which the strong rigidity of the quartzite is due. The stone bends very readily up to a certain point and then comes to an abrupt stop. Mr. F. R. Mallet* found that a slab of the Kaliana stone 24·5″ × 6·7″ × 1·8″, resting on supports 24″ apart, gave a deflection of 0·7″; and that after saturation with the deflection was reduced to 0·65.

The only tenable account of this property of elasticity is that given by Professor Haughton.†

" A most remarkable circumstance sometimes occurs in the formation of these Sandstones, which are not composed of pure particles of quartz, but a clay mixed with them, namely, that the particles of quartz mixed in this clay or paste are permitted a certain amount of motion. If you take an ordinary sandstone, it is like any other rock ; and with a lens you can see the separate particles, and that each separate particle is touched on every side by a number of other rounded particles that hold it in its place, and it in turn contributes to hold them in their places, so as to form of the whole a rigid rock like any other. But, occasionally in some rare cases—which, as far as I have any knowledge of them, are confined to

---

* Op. Cit. † Manual of Geology—Haughton Lecture ii., p. 51.

Brazil, South Carolina, and Delhi—you have a rock composed of particles of sandstones, which are not in contact with each other, but lie in a paste of felspathic clay, which clay permits a certain amount of motion between the particles of the mass."

The flexibility is certainly not attributable to the presence of talc or mica, the rock not having any schistose appearance and the few small plates of mica being very widely separated. It would seem that doubly metamorphosing conditions were concerned in its production—a solidifying process to give tenuity to the earthy paste, and a partial dissolution to remove the rigidity of its first solidification.

I am indebted to the Committee of the Liverpool Free Public Museum for permission to bring before the Society the beautiful specimen of the Indian variety that was presented to the Museum by Mr. Robert Gladstone. The Museum also contains a specimen of the Brazilian stone which differs considerably in appearance from the Indian specimen, in possessing a finer grain and a greyish, mottled, colouring. The question—what is the true matrix of the Diamond? yet remains unanswered, but all that we know of Itacolumyte dispels the idea that they are in any wise associated.

THE CARBONIFEROUS LIMESTONE

AND

MILLSTONE GRIT OF NORTH WALES,

BY GEORGE H. MORTON, F.G.S.

LIST OF WORKS RELATING TO THE SUBJECT.

The author does not pretend to have made a complete List, and will therefore be glad to hear of any Papers that are unnoticed.

1778.

PENNANT, T.—"Travels in North Wales."

1816.

CLARK, E. D., LL.D., F.G.S.—"Analysis of One Hundred Parts of Dark Bituminous Limestone, from the Parish of Whiteford, in Flintshire, North Wales."—*Trans. Geol. Soc.*, Ser. 1, Vol. iv., p. 430.

1819.

GREENOUGH, G. B., F.G.S.—Geological Map of England and Wales.

1822.

CONYBEARE, Rev. W. D., F.G.S., and PHILLIPS, WILLIAM, F.L.S.—"Outlines of the Geology of England and Wales."

1829.

YATES, Rev. JAMES, M.A., F.G.S.—"Observations on the Structure of the Border Country of Salop and North Wales, and of some Detached Groups of Transition Rocks in the Midland Counties." (*Read* 1825.)—*Trans. Geol. Soc.*, Ser. 2, Vol. ii., p. 237.

1839.

MURCHISON, Sir R. I., F.R.S., F.G.S.—"The Silurian System."

1841.

BOWMAN, J. E., F.L.S.—"Notes on a Small Patch of Silurian Rocks to the West of Abergele, on the Northern Coast of Denbighshire." (*Read* 1838.)—*Trans. Geol. Soc.*, Ser. 2, Vol. vi., p. 195. An Abstract in *Proc. Geol. Soc.*, Vol. ii., p. 666.

1845-57.

GEOLOGICAL SURVEY of the United Kingdom; Maps and Sections of North Wales. Quar. Sheets, 74 N.E. and S.E. Horizontal Sections, 39 and 44. Vertical Section, 24.

1846.

SEDGWICK, Rev. Prof. A., F.G.S.—"Outline of Geological Structure of North Wales." (*Read* 1843.)—*Proc. Geol. Soc.*, Vol. iv., p. 212.

————— "On the Older Palæozoic (*Protozoic*) Rocks of North Wales." (*Read* 1843.)—*Proc. Geol. Soc.*, Vol. iv., p. 251, and *Jour. Geol. Soc.*, Vol. i., p. 5.

SHARP, D., F.G.S.—"Contributions to the Geology of North Wales." (*Read* 1844.)—*Jour. Geol. Soc.*, Vol. ii., p. 283.

1853.

HAUGHTON, Rev. Prof. S., A.M., F.G.S.—"On the Newer Palæozoic Rocks which border the Menai Straits in Carnarvonshire." (*Read* 1853.) *Jour. Geol. Soc. of Dublin*, Vol. vi., p. 1.

1857.

MOISSENIT, M. L., Ingenieur des Mines.—"Mémoir sur le Gisement du Minerai de Plomb, dans le Calcaire Carbonifére du Flintshire."

1862.

DUCKWORTH, H., F.G.S.—"Report of the Excursion made by the Society to Holywell, July, 1861."—*Proc. L'pool Geol. Soc.*, Vol. i., Sess. 3.

1863.

DAVIDSON, T., F.G.S.—"Carboniferous Brachiopoda." —*British Fossil Brachiopoda*, Vol. iii.

1864.

DAVIES, D. C.—"Geology and Botany of the District" in *Roberts' Llangollen Guide*, p. 53.

1865.

DAVIES, D. C.—"On the Discovery of Fossils in the Millstone Grit near Oswestry." (*Read* 1860).—*Rep. Oswestry and Welshpool Nat. Field Club*, p. 41.

———— "The Mountain Limestone of North Wales." (*Read* 1861).—*Rep. Oswestry and Welshpool Nat. Field Club*, p. 50.

PROSSER, W., F.G.S.—"The Fossiliferous Character of the Millstone Grit at Sweeney, near Oswestry, Shropshire."—*Geol. Mag.*, Vol. ii., p. 107.

JUKES, J. B., Prof., F.G.S.—"Former Extension of the Coal Measures."—*Geol. Mag.*, Vol. ii., p. 135.

MAW, G., F.G.S.—"On some Deposits of Chert, White Sand, and White Clay in the Neighbourhood of Llandudno, North Wales."—*Geol. Mag.*, Vol. ii., p. 200.

DAVIES, D.C.—"The Outlier of Carboniferous Limestone near Corwen, North Wales."—*Geol. Mag.*, Vol. ii., p. 283.

JUKES, J.B., Prof., F.G.S.—"The Outlier of Carboniferous Limestone near Corwen."—*Geol. Mag.*, Vol. ii., p. 326.

MAW, G., F.G.S.—"Permian Strata of the Vale of Clwyd."—*Geol. Mag.*, Vol. ii., pp. 380, 523.

———— "Letter on a White Sand Deposit at Talargoch Mine, near Prestatyn, Flintshire, North Wales."— *Geol. Mag.*, Vol. ii., p. 428.

DAVIES, D. C.—"Denudation, Unconformability, and the Vale of Clwyd."—*Geol. Mag.*, Vol. ii., p. 476.

RICKETTS, C., M.D., F.G.S.—"On the Outlier of Carboniferous Limestone near Corwen, North Wales." *Proc. L'pool Geol. Soc.*, Vol. i., Sess. 8.

1866.

RAMSAY, A. C., Prof., LL.D., F.G.S.—"The Geology of North Wales."—*Mem. of Geol. Surv. of Gt. Brit.*, Vol. iii.

1867.

GREEN, A. H., M.A., F.G.S.—"On the Lower Carboniferous Rocks of North Wales."—*Geol. Mag.*, Vol. iv., p. 11.

DAVIES, D. C.—"The Lower Carboniferous Rocks of North Wales."—*Geol. Mag.*, Vol. iv., p. 92.

BOSTOCK, R.—"The probable source of Holywell Spring."—*Proc. L'pool Geol. Soc.*, Vol. i., Sess. 9.

1869.

MORTON, G. H., F.G.S.—"Palæontological Observations on the Carboniferous Limestone in Flintshire."— *Proc. L'pool Geol. Soc.*, Vol. i., Sess. 10.

1870.

DAVIES, D. C.—"On the Millstone Grit of the North Wales Border."—*Geol. Mag.*, Vol. vii., pp. 68 and 122.

AITKEN, J., F.G.S.—"The Grit-rocks of the Eastern Border of North Wales."—*Geol. Mag.*, Vol. vii., p. 263.

MORTON, G. H., F.G.S.—"The Mountain Limestone of Flintshire and part of Denbighshire."—*Rep. Brit. Assoc.* for 1870, p. 82.

1873.

DAVIES, D. C., F.G.S.—"On the overlapping of several Geological Formations on the North Wales Border."—*Proc. Geol. Assoc.*, Vol. ii., p. 299.

——— "On Coal Seams in the **Permian at Ifton,** Shropshire."—*Proc. Gecl. Assoc.*, Vol. iii., p. 138.

MORTON, G. H., F.G.S.—"The Strata below the Trias in the Country around Liverpool, and the probability of Coal occurring at a moderate depth."—*Proc. Lit. & Phil. Soc., L'pool,* Vol. xxvii., p. 157.

1876.

DAVIES, D. C., F.G.S.— "On some causes which have helped to shape the land on the North Wales Border."—*Proc. Geol. Assoc.*, Vol. iv., p. 340.

LLANGOLLEN.

REVIEW OF WORKS RELATING TO THE CARBONIFEROUS
LIMESTONE AND MILLSTONE GRIT OF LLANGOLLEN.

STRATA of the Carboniferous Period in North Wales **are** most fully developed in the country between **Minera** and Llanymynech, and the grandest section of the Carboniferous Limestone in the Principality may be seen from the summit of Castell Dinas Bran, close to the town of Llangollen. A section of such interest naturally attracted the attention of geologists many years ago; and so early as 1778 Thomas Pennant, in his "Travels in North Wales," after accurately describing the succession of the Carboniferous Series in the neighbourhood of Mold, mentions the "Glisseg rocks" and "Craig Arthur" as part of the great ridge of limestone he describes.

In the "Outlines of the Geology of England **and** Wales," 1822, by Conybeare and Phillips, under **the** heads of "Carboniferous Limestone of North Wales," and "Flintshire," there is a notice of the Eglwyseg rocks and the district to the south of Llangollen. A few years later, in the *Transactions of the Geological Society*, 2nd Ser., vol. ii., for 1829, the following paper occurs:— "Observations on the Structure of the Border Country of Salop and North Wales; and of some detached Groups of Transition Rocks in the Midland Counties." By the Rev. J. Yates, M.A., F.G.S. This paper contains a graphic description of the Eglwyseg rocks. The author states:—

"At the distance of about two miles to the N.E. (of Llangollen) is presented the perpendicular face of the rocks of Edlw-y-seg. These are part of the edge of the great basin of limestone, containing the coal formation of North Wales. Their direction is generally from east to west, but in a waving course, and through a tract of many miles in length. A steep talus of *débris* covers about two-thirds of their height; and above this their face rises almost perpendicularly, presenting a remarkable specimen of regular stratification, and a striking contrast to the forms of the slate mountains in their vicinity. The divisions of the strata of limestone are rendered conspicuous at a distance by beds of black bituminous shale, which lie between them. This shale is for the most part perfectly soft and friable; it is, however, frequently indurated by the addition of calcareous matter, and thus passes into fœtid limestone. It is also sometimes mixed with a large proportion of sand, and then resembles very much the mud deposited in the estuaries of the Dee and Mersey.

"These cliffs contain various shells and corals, usually considered as belonging to the Mountain Limestone of England. In the case of shells occurring in the limestone beds, the matter of the shells is generally removed, only casts remaining, or newer depositions of calcareous spar in place of the original substance. But in the beds of shale the testaceous matter seems to be preserved, with very little alteration in its texture or composition. In a formation of so great antiquity in the geological history of the globe, this circumstance appears not a little curious and interesting. The softness of the shale in which they are imbedded, also contributes to render these specimens of fossil shells remarkably perfect, the muscular impressions and interior structure of the larger *Terebratulæ* being exhibited with great distinctness." The author also refers to "the lively red colour of the ploughed fields, and the rounded masses of red conglomerate scattered among the *débris* of the limestone" in front of the Eglwyseg range.

The Millstone Grit, as it occurs to the west of Oswestry, particularly in the neighbourhood of the Race Course and Mynydd Myfyr, is minutely described. The lowest beds immediately above the Carboniferous Limestone are shown to be conglomeratic, succeeded by red sandstones resembling the New Red Sandstone of Lancashire, Cheshire and Shropshire; and these are overlaid by other sandstones, containing *entrochi*, and finally by hornstone strata passing into flint. The author evidently examined the district thoroughly, and he has given one of the best descriptions that we have of the strata of the Lower Carboniferous Series in the neighbourhood of Oswestry.

In 1839, Sir R. I. Murchison, F.R.S., in the "Silurian System," described the same strata a little to the southeast, at Treflach Hall, in the vicinity of Sweeney, where Mr. D. C. Davies has since obtained a large collection of fossils from sandstone strata, about which several recent communications have appeared.

The next work in the order of date which contains any description of the Lower Carboniferous rocks in the country around Llangollen, is a paper entitled "Outline of Geological Structure of North Wales," by the Rev. A. Sedgwick, F.G.S. *Proc. Geol. Soc.*, vol. iv., 1846. The paper principally refers to the Silurian; but the Carboniferous Group of Denbighshire is noticed. The author refers to the red sandstones and conglomerates at the base of the Mountain Limestone in the county; the outliers of limestone at Corwen and Caergwrle, and other subjects connected with the Geology of North Wales. There is another paper by the same author, "On the Older Palæozoic (*Protozoic*) Rocks of North Wales," *Proc. Geol. Soc.*, vol. iv, 1846, in which he gives a description of those stratified rocks in the northern counties of the Principality, which are of anterior age to the Carboniferous Limestone. At page 268, there is a section showing the Eglwyseg rocks resting unconformably on the folded Upper Silurian flagstones of the Dee. There is a map of North Wales appended, which shows the Carboniferous Limestone of Denbighshire and Flintshire, including its extension south to Llanymynech, the patches in the Vale of Clwyd, and the outlier at Hafod, near Corwen.

"Contributions to the Geology of North Wales," by D. Sharp, F.G.S., *Jour. Geol. Soc.*, vol. ii., 1846, is another paper wherein mention is made of the Eglwyseg rocks, and the author states that "the Ludlow rocks of Llangollen dip at a low angle, and pass conformably below the Mountain Limestone of the Eglwyseg Crags." It has been since determined that these Silurian Strata are of Wenlock age, and Prof. Sedgwick had previously shown that the Carboniferous Limestone rests unconformably upon them.

The country around Llangollen was surveyed by the officers of the Geological Survey about 1845, and the "Quar. Sheets," 74, N.E. and S.E., containing it, were published soon afterwards. The "Horizontal Sections," Nos. 39 and 44 and the "Vertical Section" No. 24 appeared about the same time. The geologists engaged on that survey were Professors Ramsay, Jukes, Forbes, Geikie, and Messrs. Aveline, and Williams.* This valuable map and the sections show the area and position of the Carboniferous Limestone and Millstone Grit in relation to the formations with which they are associated. However, on minutely examining the map, it appears that the boundary line between the Carboniferous Limestone and Millstone Grit does not continue on the same Geological horizon; there having evidently been a difficulty in dividing the two formations. The discrepancy between the two horizontal sections is still more remarkable, considering that they both traverse the Eglwyseg rocks within half-a-mile from each other.

The Millstone Grit of North Wales does not of necessity represent exactly the same formation in Derbyshire and Yorkshire. It probably includes both the Millstone Grit and the Yoredale, or Upper Carboniferous Shale of those counties; and there is no reason for supposing that the deposition of the Carboniferous Limestone terminated at precisely the same time in districts nearly one hundred miles apart.

In 1864, Mr. D. C. Davies' "Geology and Botany of the District" of Llangollen, appeared in *Roberts' Llangollen Guide;* and in 1865 a paper by the same author (read 1861), was published by the Oswestry and Welshpool Naturalists' Field Club, entitled "The

---

* Geikie's "Life of Forbes," page 444,

Mountain Limestone of North Wales." It is the first communication entirely devoted to the subject, and is a description of the Carboniferous Limestone of Denbighshire and Flintshire. There are very few details given respecting any of the numerous localities referred to by the author, who rather gives the general results of his observations over the whole area described.

Mr. Davies describes three main divisions of the Mountain Limestone of North Wales, as follows:— "In ascending order, there is, first, a series of beds of pale-coloured stone, extensively quarried along the belt for fluxing purposes, interleaved with five principal layers of red marl. Above there is a succession of beds, varying from a bituminous texture through a sandy limestone impregnated with copper, to a hard compact grey limestone; and, lastly, an alternation of thin layers of limestone, with dark blue and black deposits of fossiliferous shale, and the whole series attaining a maximum thickness of about 400 feet." Although this is a general description of the formation as represented in North Wales, it seems to apply particularly to the south-east of the Eglwyseg ridge, and to the country between Llanymynech and Oswestry.

With regard to Llangollen, Mr. Davies states that *Productus hemisphericus (comoides)* occurs in the lower limestone, and above is *P. cora*, which is abundant in the Trevor Quarries, near Llangollen. These he considers characteristic of the lower beds, and next to them *P. semireticulatus*. The *Terebratulæ*, he says, are well represented in the lower beds, and *Sanguinolites clava* attains to a great size in the middle beds near Llangollen. Many other fossils are mentioned, though it is not clear that he refers to Llangollen as their locality, though it seems to be so; indeed, he says that the beautiful corals *Lonsdaleia, Sarcinula Phillipsi.* and two species of *Stylaxis* attain to luxuriant growth on the Eglwyseg ridge. At the conclusion of the paper the author promises a list of the fossils collected from the Mountain Limestone, but unfortunately no such list has appeared. Both the communications are written in a popular form, without the exactness which a purely scientific description would have rendered necessary.

A paper by Mr. D. C. Davies appeared in 1865, "On the Discovery of Fossils in the Millstone Grit near Oswestry," in the *Rep. Oswestry and Welshpool Nat. Field Club,* five years after the communication had been read. Another paper appeared in the *Geological Magazine* for 1865, vol. ii, on "The Fossiliferous character of the Millstone Grit at Sweeney, near Oswestry, Shropshire," by W. Prosser, F.G.S. The author gives a section from Murchison's "Silurian System" of the Carboniferous strata, near Oswestry, which includes the Millstone Grit, and gives Mr. D. C. Davies the credit of having been one of the first to describe the fossiliferous character of the formation. He also describes the strata around Sweeney, the typical locality, and concludes with a list of sixteen fossils that he had found in the neighbourhood.

In 1866, the 3rd vol. of the *Memoirs of the Geological Survey of Great Britain* was published, and devoted to "The Geology of North Wales," by Prof. Ramsay. It contains (at page 226) a paragraph on Llangollen, as follows:—"South-east of the Vale of Clwyd, between the Bala beds of Cyrn-y-brain and the Berwyns, the Wenlock Shale fills a space about six miles broad, consisting of steep-sided round-topped hills, intersected from east to west by the river Dee. Numerous subsidary valleys branch north and south from the river into the heart of the hills. On the east, between Craig Arthur and Ty-uchaf,* the Old Red Sandstone rests unconformably upon it. From thence to Tan-y-Castell,† a fault passes from Y-fron-fawr to the south-east, and throws first the Old Red Sandstone, and then the Carboniferous Limestone and Millstone Grit, against the Wenlock Shale above the river Dee, to a point four miles east of Llangollen." No sections exhibiting any of the subdivisions of the Carboniferous Limestone have been published. Those of the Geological Survey (Nos. 39 and 44,) merely show the Carboniferous Limestone and its thickness in relation to the formations with which it is associated; though with a separation of 175 feet of the lower beds, described as the "Yellow Sandstone and Dark Shale," corresponding in position to the Lower Brown Limestone, but no yellow sandstone occurs there.

During 1867 a paper appeared "On the Lower Carboniferous Rocks of North Wales," by Mr. A. H. Green, M.A., F.G.S., in the *Geol. Mag.*, vol. iv., where the author gives the result of a survey of the country to the north-east of Tan-y-Castell. He gives two sections, and, from the lithological characters of the Millstone Grit, considers that the greater part of the formation belongs to the Yoredale series; a conclusion favoured by the presence of a band of earthy limestone and Mountain Limestone fossils associated with a bed of shale 15 feet thick, near Tyfyn-uchaf. The conglomerate above the shale-bed he thinks may represent the Rough Rock, or First Grit of the Millstone Grit Series, and that the lower strata may be Yoredale beds, as they agree very well with the middle division of that formation in North Staffordshire.

* About two miles N. of Llangollen.
† One mile N. of Llangollen.

In 1870 another paper appeared "On the Millstone Grit of the North Wales Border," by Mr. D. C. Davies. *Geol. Mag.*, vol. vii. The author supports the assumption that the Grit rocks of North Wales are Millstone Grit, and adds to the number of species contained in Mr. Prosser's list. The same year Mr. J. Aitken, F.G.S., contributed the following paper on the same subject, to the *Geol. Mag.*, on "The Grit-rocks of the Eastern Border of North Wales." The author supports the Yoredale affinities of the strata, on similar grounds to those arrived at by Mr. Green; and it is important, because both of these writers have been long familiar with the Lower Carboniferous Series of Yorkshire and Lancashire. Mr. Aitken, however, does not appear to have seen the sandstone, shale, and conglomerate at Tyfyn-uchaf, described by Mr. Green.

In 1870 I read a paper before the British Association, and gave a general description of the Carboniferous Limestone of North Wales; but particularly of the formation as developed near Llangollen.

During 1873, Mr. D. C. Davies, F.G.S., read a paper "On the Over-lapping of several Geological formations on the North Wales Border." *Proc. Geol. Assoc.*, vol. ii. There is a Geological map of the district appended to it, showing the formations which occur in that part of North Wales. On this map, Mr. Davies adopts Mr. Green's Yoredale rocks and Millstone Grit. The same year, Mr. Davies read another paper, *Proc. Geol. Assoc.*, vol. iii, "On Coal Seams, in the Permian at Ifton, Shropshire," from which it appears that the strata around Moreton, north-east of Llanymynech, may be Coal Measures or Permian, and not Millstone Grit.

From the numerous contributions that have appeared relating to the Millstone Grit of North Wales, it is evident that it possesses considerable interest. It is difficult to correlate it with the same formation in Staffordshire, Derbyshire, and Yorkshire; for it has somewhat peculiar lithological characters, and an unusual number of fossil shells and corals indicating the marine conditions under which the strata were deposited. Several sections of the Millstone Grit country have appeared in illustration of the numerous papers referred to; but there is no indication of drawing to an exact scale, with a correct contour of the ground, and the line of country represented is only roughly given.

No list of the fossils of the Carboniferous Limestone of North Wales, or of any restricted area in the Principality, has appeared. The lists of the Millstone Grit fossils, by Messrs. Davies and Prosser, may be considered complete for the Oswestry district; but little or nothing has been done elsewhere.

CARBONIFEROUS LIMESTONE AND MILLSTONE GRIT.

LLANGOLLEN.

CREIGIAU EGLWYSEGLE AND THE TREVOR ROCKS.

ONE of the grandest and most accessible exposures of the Lower Carboniferous Series in Great Britain occurs near the town of Llangollen. The precipitous and lofty ridge known as Creigiau Eglwysegle, or more commonly as the Eglwyseg rocks, presents the whole of the Carboniferous Limestone in an unbroken series of strata, from the Old Red Sandstone at its base to the Millstone Grit of the Geological Survey at the summit. Almost every bed of limestone is exposed so that the lithological character of the rocks and the fossils they contain can be easily examined. The interstratified beds of concretionary shale, which occur at frequent intervals, are usually obscured by the limestone strata breaking down over their disintegrated edges. This description of the strata refers particularly to the magnificent natural section exposed in the Ty-nant ravine (Frontispiece, Plate 2), between Craig-yr-ogof on the north, and Y-Craig-bensyth on the south side of it; two massive terraced hills, whose summits are about 1350 feet above the level of the sea, and 600 feet above the narrow road at the base. A similar section is presented in Tan-y-Castell ravine (Pl. 1), which is steeper, not being so deeply cut into the rocky ridge, just half-a-mile northwest of the farm house bearing the

This grand exposure of the Carboniferous Limestone is rendered still more interesting by the regular succession of a great thickness of sandstone with interstratified shale, which rises with a bold outline, and forms the mountain mass of Cefn-y-Fedw, above all the terraced sections of the underlying limestone, and probably represents the Yoredale and Millstone Grit formations. The surface of this high ground presents a rounded series of eminences which gradually descend to the east, where the Millstone Grit or Cefn-y-Fedw Sandstone is succeeded in regular sequence by the Coal Measures.

The whole of the strata described is exposed in such a clear series of sections from Cefn-y-Fedw to Fron Deg, south of Minera, that the country under review must be considered as the typical area of the Lower Carboniferous Series in North Wales.

Mr. W. H. Wilson has interested himself in the Geology of the district, and taken large photographs of the typical sections of the Carboniferous Limestone. The Frontispiece, Plate 2, has been reproduced in its original form; but Plates 1 and 3 have been reduced. They afford the means of explaining the contour of the surface, and the subdivisions into which the Carboniferous Limestone is divided, just as if actually on the ground in front of the rocky ridge.

TAN-Y-CASTELL RAVINE.

Plate 1, presents a view of the south-west escarpment of the Eglwyseg ridge and the Tan-y-Castell ravine, taken from the summit of the isolated hill in front—Dinas Bran —777 feet above the River Dee. From this elevation the whole of the Carboniferous Limestone is displayed in one grand natural section along the line of the outcrop of the strata. The highest beds have been denuded from same name. This ravine is indicated by a wall built along its ascending slope, and which is conspicuous from the summit of Castell Dinas Bran, 1052* feet above the sea. The Ty-nant ravine is just a mile due north of Dinas Bran, and the Tan-y-Castell ravine about half that distance.

Fine sections of the strata are also exposed at the south-east end of the Eglwyseg ridge, at the Trevor rocks, where extensive limestone quarries are worked and the ridge ends, or is rather cut back by the little brook, the R. Erwen of the 1-inch Ordnance Map. At the other side of this brook the worked face of Bron-heulog quarry (Pl. 3), exposes about 162 feet of limestone at a lower level, and above it there is a scar of the Upper Grey Limestone, with the Millstone Grit of Garreg Pen-gruch at a considerable elevation above it. The latter sections are much reduced in thickness by the attenuation of the Carboniferous Limestone to the south-east, and are traversed by two faults, parallel with the boundary fault which throws up the Wenlock Shale; and, consequently do not exhibit the whole of the limestone formation in an unbroken series as in the typical ravines referred to, where no faults occur.

Under these conditions in addition to the terraced escarpment there are two fine natural sections, affording the clearest possible view of all the Carboniferous Lime-stone strata 1200 and 1025 feet in thickness. Then there are two other sections, where the strata are attenuated, faulted, and so extensively quarried that they can be examined more minutely than in the sections where the rocks have been exposed to atmospheric influences for untold ages.

---

* This altitude was courteously communicated by the Ordnance Survey.

This grand exposure of the Carboniferous Limestone is rendered still more interesting by the regular succession of a great thickness of sandstone with interstratified shale, which rises with a bold outline, and forms the mountain mass of Cefn-y-Fedw, above all the terraced sections of the underlying limestone, and probably represents the Yoredale and Millstone Grit formations. The surface of this high ground presents a rounded series of eminences which gradually descend to the east, where the Millstone Grit or Cefn-y-Fedw Sandstone is succeeded in regular sequence by the Coal Measures.

The whole of the strata described is exposed in such a clear series of sections from Cefn-y-Fedw to Fron Deg, south of Minera, that the country under review must be considered as the typical area of the Lower Carboniferous Series in North Wales.

Mr. W. H. Wilson has interested himself in the Geology of the district, and taken large photographs of the typical sections of the Carboniferous Limestone. The Frontispiece, Plate 2, has been reproduced in its original form; but Plates 1 and 3 have been reduced. They afford the means of explaining the contour of the surface, and the subdivisions into which the Carboniferous Limestone is divided, just as if actually on the ground in front of the rocky ridge.

TAN-Y-CASTELL RAVINE.

Plate 1, presents a view of the south-west escarpment of the Eglwyseg ridge and the Tan-y-Castell ravine, taken from the summit of the isolated hill in front—Dinas Bran —777 feet above the River Dee. From this elevation the whole of the Carboniferous Limestone is displayed in one grand natural section along the line of the outcrop of the strata. The highest beds have been denuded from

out in the extreme back ground, where several small quarries expose the strata, and have yielded many species of corals and brachiopoda. Still higher ground succeeds as the Sandy Limestone crops out, but the surface is covered with peaty soil, and scattered blocks of white sandstone lie about until the highest portion of Cefn-y-Fedw is attained, when the Lower Sandstone and Conglomerate occurs, and blocks of the rock project above the peaty soil. The highest bed of Carboniferous Limestone at Tan-y-Castell ravine is about 600 feet above its base, which is assumed to be parallel with the road skirting the ridge. The dip of the strata is 15° N.E. or E.N.E.; and the entire thickness of the limestone about 1025 feet.

TY-NANT RAVINE.

Plate 2—Frontispiece—presents a view taken from near the top of Y-Craig-bensyth, looking north towards Craig-yr-ogof and down into the Ty-nant ravine, presenting the most rugged section of the Carboniferous Limestone in its natural grandeur. The subdivisions into which it is divided present such distinctive characters that they can be recognised at a considerable distance by the great differences of their stratification, and by the manner in which the rocks break up along their respective outcrops. The fields at the bottom of the ravine cover the upper beds of the Old Red Sandstone, and the talus which skirts the lower part of the hill obscures the Lower Brown Limestone, which is quarried in several elevated positions. The massive beds of the Lower White Limestone project boldly forward near the top of the precipice, and the *thick-bed* is the stratum just over the top of the talus. The wide terrace above the Lower White Limestone, previously described, is well defined, and it is partly covered by débris from the ends of the Upper White Limestone above it. The peculiar manner in which the strata of the latter subdivision break up is well shown along the outcrop in the centre of the foreground. Higher up to the right the Upper Grey Limestone succeeds, with its usual talus of *small* stones, presenting a great contrast to the Upper White Limestone. The highest beds of the Upper Grey Limestone, which are remarkably fossiliferous, are well marked by the light-coloured line in the middle distance; and further on the Sandy Limestone and the Lower Sandstone and Conglomerate succeed on the highest portion of Cefn-y-Fedw. The contrast between the country composed of the Carboniferous Limestone, and that of the Cefn-y-Fedw Sandstone is very remarkable. Over the limestone a short grass covers the surface like a carpet, and patches of ferns occupy the sheltered hollows and recesses; but over the sandstone the ground is soft, dusty, and uneven in summer, and often like peaty mud in winter. The highest part of this heathy waste is encumbered with loose stones, so white from the numerous quartz pebbles they contain, that when seen from a distance, even in summer, the ground seems to be covered with a sprinkling of snow; it is a desert waste where very few travellers care to venture. From this elevated position the surface of the country slopes towards the east, and the strata dip in the same direction. Immediately above the Lower Sandstone and Conglomerate, there are some hard, cream-coloured shales, and these are succeeded by other sandstones and black shales, and finally by the Aqueduct Grit—which resembles typical Millstone Grit. The latter is succeeded by a thick bed of black shale, and the Aqueduct Coal, forming the base of the Coal Measures. The highest bed of the Carboniferous

Limestone at the Ty-nant ravine is about 650 feet from its base, which is assumed to be forty yards east of the main road below. The dip of the strata is 12° E. or E.S.E., and the entire thickness about 1200 feet.

BRON-HEULOG QUARRY.

Plate 3, is a photograph of the large Bron-heulog Quarry, below Pen-y-gloppa,* and much nearer the River Dee than the Trevor quarries, at the south-east end of the Eglwyseg ridge. The Erwen brook runs down the hollow in the centre; and the tramway in the foreground down an incline of 275 feet, then along the front of the quarry, and after passing through a cutting descends another incline of 300 feet to the wharf on the canal bank. The strata which crop out on the left hand belong to the Upper Grey Limestone, and the ridge higher up above the road is the Sandy Limestone, which is well exposed where the road winds round the hill. There is a fault to the left of the large quarry, nearly parallel with the foot-path, and it runs through the slight hollow at the top of the natural scar. This fault throws up the strata on the right (south-east). The scar represents the lower portion of the Upper Grey Limestone, the upper beds of the subdivision having been denuded, and the strata exposed in the quarry belong to the Upper and Lower White Limestone. The boundary fault which throws up the Wenlock Shale is under the field, on the right hand side below the quarry; but there is another parallel fault which runs along the floor of the quarry, and is visible at the south-east end. This latter fault continues along the tramway, and throws up the strata here and in the Trevor quarries in a similar manner. The

---

* Pen-y-gloppa is the scar of limestone just above Bron-heulog quarry, " 392 " on the 25-in. Ordnance Map; but the name is not inserted.

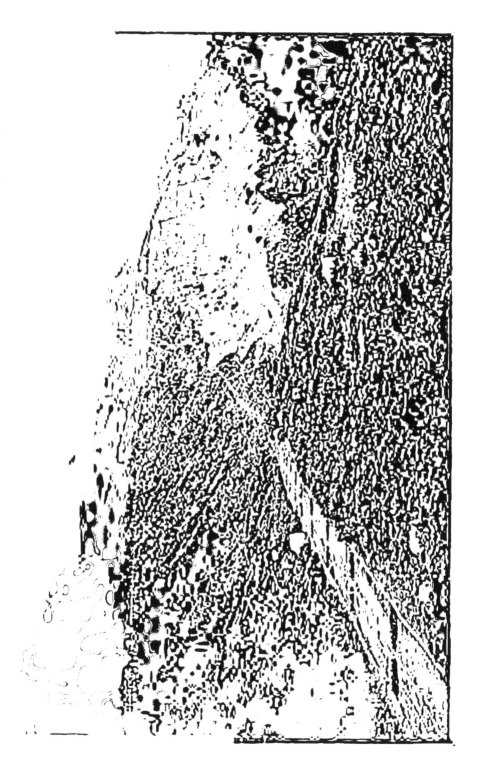

top of the limestone scar is nearly 300 feet from the floor of the quarry below; and the strata dip at an angle of 5° N.E. The thickness of the successive beds has been measured; the total amount being 269 feet, and as the section is almost perpendicular, a slight addition necessary for the dip is sufficient to account for the difference. Plate 4 is a ground plan of the faults showing the nature of the dislocation to which the Carboniferous Limestone has been subjected.

In describing the preceding sections as exhibited in Plates 1, 2 and 3, frequent reference was made to the subdivisions into which it is proposed to divide the Carboniferous Limestone and Cefn-y-Fedw Sandstone in the country around Llangollen. The latter formation probably represents both the Yoredale and Millstone Grit, though it does not lithologically resemble either. All the subdivisions succeed each other in regular sequence, and the Coal-measures repose conformably on the Aqueduct Grit, which is the uppermost member of the Cefn-y-Fedw Sandstone.

The following is a Tabular View of the whole of these subdivisions, with the thickness of each, as exhibited along the line of section from the base of the Ty-nant ravine due east to Tyfyn-uchaf, the distance being rather less than three miles.

TABULAR VIEW OF THE CARBONIFEROUS LIMESTONE AND CEFN-Y-FEDW SANDSTONE IN THE COUNTRY AROUND LLANGOLLEN.

		FEET.	
Cefn-y-Fedw Sandstone	Aqueduct Grit, or Upper Sandstone and Conglomerate	70	Upper Cefn-y-Fedw, Dee Bridge, or Millstone Grit Series.
	Upper Shale	80	
	Dee Bridge Sandstone	80	
	Lower Shale, with Fire-Clay and Bands of Limestone	18	Middle and Lower Cefn-y-Fedw or Yoredale Series.
	Middle Sandstone	200	
	Cherty Shale	50	
	Lower Sandstone and Conglomerate	250	
	Sandy Limestone	75	
Carboniferous Limestone.	Upper Grey Limestone ...	300	Upper Carboniferous Limestone.
	„ White „ ...	300	
	Lower „ „ ...	120	Lower do.
	„ Brown „ ...	480	
		1923	

Upper Old Red Sandstone 300

All these subdivisions are founded on lithological differences, and they can each be traced over a considerable area. Both the Carboniferous Limestone and the Cefn-y-Fedw Sandstone contain numerous beds of shale; but the first is essentially a limestone and the second a sand-*stone formation.*

OLD RED SANDSTONE.

The upper strata of this formation occur on the west of the Eglwyseg ridge. They crop out from under the Carboniferous Limestone near Craig Arthur, and extend along the bottom of the Ty-nant ravine round to the south-east as far as Tan-y-Castell; though the breadth of the outcrop scarcely exceeds a quarter of a mile, even where the strata are most fully developed. The extent of the area is for the most part indicated by the red colour of the ground; though there are exposures near Dinbren-uchaf and along the base of Craig-yr-ogof. When the Rev. James Yates examined the country, in 1825, the latter section was probably more fully exposed; for the débris from the limestone quarries at a higher level is now gradually covering it up, and it is the only exposure worthy of notice. The strata consist of dark red sandstone with some brecciated conglomerate interstratified with it, and the included fragments seem to have been derived from the Silurian rocks. With the exception of some annelid tracks, no trace of any organism has been detected. The fragments of red sandstone and sand of the same colour which occur along the outcrop indicate the probable thickness to be about fifty feet, though the downward extension of the beds is evident over the surface of the adjoining fields. The juncture of the strata with the overlying Carboniferous Limestone is not exposed; but it is certain that the Old Red Sandstone rests unconformably on the Wenlock Shale. According to the sections of the Geological Survey, the thickness of the formation approaches 500 feet; but it is impossible to estimate it with any degree of accuracy.

The Old Red Sandstone is more fully exposed in several places along the west of the Vale of Clwyd, but particularly at Berllan-bach, near Denbigh, where it is interstratified with the lowest beds of the Carboniferous Limestone; and in Anglesea, where it is more fully developed than anywhere else in North Wales.

CARBONIFEROUS LIMESTONE.

LOWER BROWN LIMESTONE.

This is the lowest subdivision of the Carboniferous Limestone, and it rests conformably on the Upper Old Red Sandstone. Though much obscured by the talus along the base of the Eglwyseg ridge, it is quarried in several places. It is well exposed on both sides of the Ty-nant ravine, at Tan-y-Castell, and in some old excavations on the road below the Trevor quarries. The lithological character of the Lower Brown Limestone is very similar along the whole of its outcrop, and consists of thin bedded dark brown limestone interstratified with partings of shale of the same colour. The limestone strata are usually 9 to 15 inches thick, though sometimes the beds are much thicker, especially towards the upper portion of the subdivision along the western escarpment of the Eglwyseg ridge. At the Trevor quarries the line of separation is very distinct; but in Bron-heulog quarry the juncture is not exposed. The thickness of the Lower Brown Limestone is 480 feet at the Ty-nant ravine, 360 feet at Tan-y-Castell ravine, and probably not above 100 feet at the Trevor quarries, where it has been worked at a lower level. It is not much exposed about Bron-heulog quarry, and has probably almost thinned out there; for at Fron, on the other side of the vale of Llangollen, the Upper Grey Limestone rests on the Wenlock Shale, the underlying limestone not having been formed, in consequence of the rapid *rise of* the sea bottom in which the Carboniferous

Limestone was deposited. This attenuation of the limestone towards the south-east diminishes the importance of the fault described by Prof. Ramsay, in "The Geology of North Wales" (*Mem. Geol. Survey*, vol. iii, p. 226), and which is the only fault shown on the Map of the Survey. The 12-feet bed at the base of the Lower White Limestone is the lowest that can be seen at the bottom of Bron-heulog quarry. The 20-feet bed of shale represents the top of the Lower Brown Limestone, and it is faulted against the *thick-bed* of the Lower White Limestone. It is well exposed close to the tramway—which crosses it—at the south-east end of the quarry. The same bed of shale is again seen in a similar position above Plas-Ifan, where it is entirely composed of small rounded fragments of slaty rock, evidently derived from the Silurian rocks in the vicinity, proving the deposit to have been formed along the old coast-line. At Bron-heulog quarry a bed of limestone, of which about six feet can be seen, underlies the shale; but there is no other indication of the Lower Brown Limestone cropping out there. The boundary fault runs along in front of the quarry; but the ground is so deeply covered with débris that its exact position cannot be determined. Some limestone is reported to have been obtained below the level of the quarry, and the Silurian rock is known to come in close to where the fault is supposed to be; though it is uncertain as to how far the Lower Brown Limestone has thinned out, because the strata may be thrown down by the fault.

The Lower Brown Limestone was formerly burnt for lime, and also used in glass-making; but it is not in request now for either purpose. The strata occur in a very inaccessible position, away from the canal and any good road, which is probably the cause of the limestone not being worked at the present time.

The shale associated with the limestone contains many minute crustaceans *Leperditia suborbiculata* and obscure impressions of plants. The most characteristic fossil is *Productus comoides*, which is very abundant in both limestone and shale. The following species are also common:—*Nautilus globatus*; *Euomphalus Dionysii*; *Murchisoniæ Verneuliana*; *Spirifera lineata*; *Productus cora*; *P. punctata*; *Alveolites septosa*; and *Syringopora geniculata*.

LOWER WHITE LIMESTONE.

The next subdivision in ascending order is composed of three thick and some inferior thin beds of white limestone, interstratified with several beds of reddish shale of a concretionary character, all of which are exposed in the Trevor quarries. The following is a section of the strata of the Lower White Limestone and some of the upper beds of the Lower Brown Limestone beneath, as they occur in those quarries:—

		FEET.	IN.
Lower beds of Upper White Limestone.	Limestone		
	Concretionary Shale	7	0
	Shale	3	0
		10	0

		FEET.	IN.	
Lower White Limestone.	Limestone	24	0	
	Shale	2	0	
	Limestone *thick-bed*	46	0	
	Shale	1	6	
	Limestone	5	0	
	Shale	1	6	These beds vary considerably.
	Limestone	6	0	
	Shale	11	0	
	Limestone	20	0	Basement-bed.
		117	0	

		FEET.	IN.	
Upper beds of the Lower Brown Limestone.	Rubbly Limestone.	6	0	These beds vary considerably.
	Limestone	6	0	
	Rubbly Limestone.	6	0	
	Shale	8	0	
	Limestone	12	0	
		88	0	

The Lower White Limestone is exhibited in the following woodcut of the farthest Trevor quarry, opposite Castell Dinas Bran, at a right angle to the tramway (under the letter *a*) with the fault, No. 2 plate **4**, to which frequent reference is made:—

FIG. 1. FAULT NO. 2 IN THE TREVOR QUARRIES.

i. Drift—2 ft.
h. White Limestone—24 ft.
g. Shale—2 ft.
f. *Thick bed*—46 ft.
e. Shale—1 ft. 6 in.
d. Limestone—5 ft.
c. Shale—1 ft. 6 in.
b. Limestone—6 ft.
a. Shale—11 ft.

The *Basement-bed* is below the Shale, *a.*

The *thick-bed* of limestone forms the precipitous scar along the front of the Eglwyseg ridge, to which frequent attention has been directed. It is this bed and the one over it that are principally worked; but the lower beds of interstratified limestone and shale with the *basement-bed* are exposed along the tramway and floors of the quarries. The continuous and rapid changes in the character of the shales are very remarkable. A few yards often produces a difference in the section, and there is usually a complete alteration in a hundred yards. The thicker overlying beds, however, preserve their uniform appearance, with the shale parting between them over a considerable area.

At Bron-heulog quarry farther to the south-east the Lower White Limestone is again exposed at a much lower level and the *thick-bed* is near the bottom, with three compact beds of limestone below it; but with much less shale associated with them than in the corresponding section at the Trevor quarries. The following is a section of the whole of the strata from the top of Pen-y-gloppa, the scar of Upper Grey Limestone, down to the lowest beds exposed in the quarry, including those of all the four subdivisions into which the limestone is divided.

		FEET.	IN.
Lower beds	Denuded surface.		
of the	Limestone, light grey..	12	0
Upper Grey	,, grey and thin-bedded...........	54	0
Limestone.		66	0

		FEET.	IN.	
	Limestone and Shale..	40	0	Obscured by base of talus.
	Limestone	7	0	
	Shale	4	0	
	Limestone...............	15	0	
Upper	Shale	6	0	
White	Limestone...............	12	0	
Limestone.	Shale	5	0	
	Limestone...............	9	0	
	Shale	1	0	Correlates with the 5-feet of shale above the 24-feet bed at Trevor quarries,
		99	0	

		FEET.	IN.	
	Limestone	30	0	
	Shale	2	8	
	Limestone, *thick-bed*	45	0	
Lower White Limestone.	Shale	1	8	
	Limestone	5	6	
	Shale	1	0	
	Limestone	5	0	
	Shale	2	0	Correlates with the 11-feet bed of shale at Trevor quarries.
	Limestone	12	0	Basement-bed. Lowest bed in quarry, and correlates with the 20-feet in the Trevor quarries.
		104	0	

		FEET.	IN.	
Upper beds of the Lower Brown Limestone.	Shale with bands of limestone at the top	20	0	Outside the quarry.
	Limestone	6	0	,,
		26	0	
		295	0	Total.

The passage-beds from the Lower Brown into the Lower White Limestone are better seen at the Trevor quarries than anywhere else.

At Tan-y-Castell ravine the Lower White Limestone is too much obscured by the débris on its successive terraces to admit of the measurement of the separate beds; but the thickness of the whole seems to be about 115 feet. At Dinbren-uchaf, about half-a-mile to the north, the strata are of a massive character, with less shale, as the following section shows:—

		FEET.	
	Limestone	25	
	Shale	5	
Lower	Limestone, *thick-bed*	45	
White	Shale	1	
Limestone.	Limestone.................	10	
	Limestone with shale partings	10	
	Limestone.................	25	Basement-bed.

121

The following is a section of the Lower White Limestone as presented in the Ty-nant ravine; but they cannot be so accurately measured as in a quarry, and the terraces at the base of the *thick-bed* and other strata are so obscured by débris that the thickness of the beds of shale is doubtful:—

		FEET.	
	Limestone	25	
	Shale	5	
Lower	Limestone, *thick-bed*	45	
White	Shale	1	
Limestone.	Limestone—three beds........	15	
	Shale	1	
	Limestone	25	Basement-bed.

117

These measurements present a near approximation to the actual thickness in each section, and they so closely agree that it is evident that the subdivision has an average thickness of about 120 feet.

Towards the north the beds of interstratified shale become still thinner, so that Craig Arthur presents a very lofty precipice, for the beds both under and over the *thick-bed* are almost united in consequence of the absence of shale—except thin partings of it. A mile farther on Craig Aderyn and Craig-y-Forwyn present similar rocky escarpments, beyond which the Eglwyseg ridge subsides into a comparatively flat country.

The Lower White Limestone is used for fluxing purposes, and it can be profitably worked on account of its great thickness and elevated position. The *thick-bed* is, however, in request for its excellent quality.

Fossils are not abundant in the Lower White Limestone, or in the shale interstratified with it. Although the large quantity of limestone that is broken up in the quarries affords facilities for collecting, the number of species is small. The following are the most characteristic, that is, the species which are usually to be found:—
Euomphalus tabulatus; Myacites sulcata; Spirifera bisulcata; Productus cora; P. semireticulatus; Alveolites septosa; Syringopora geniculata; S. ramulosa; Cyathophyllum Stutchburyi; and *Clisiophyllum turbinatum.*

UPPER WHITE LIMESTONE.

This subdivision consists of a series of beds of light coloured limestone, inclining from grey to buff, divided, at intervals, by shale of a concretionary character, which often graduates into limestone. The beds of shale are less able to resist the influence of the atmosphere than the solid limestone, which has a very compact structure, with very few fossils. The section of Upper White Limestone, at Bron-heulog quarry, (page 180) exhibits the general arrangement of the beds of limestone and interstratified thick shales at irregular intervals; but only 59 feet are actually exposed, and there is no other quarry where the strata have been worked. In the natural sections at the Ty-nant ravine and along the

Eglwyseg ridge, it is evident that the same alternation of the strata prevails, though it is impracticable to draw a correct section, as the beds of shale are nearly always hidden by débris, or the subsidence of the overlying limestone.

The Upper White Limestone, in some of the beds, especially at the Ty-nant ravine, is as compact as lithographic marble; though it varies, and even the same beds are liable to changes. It breaks up along the line of outcrop into large tabular masses very different to the beds of any other subdivision. It never forms a talus of small stones; but breaks off in pieces of a flat tabular form, many being four or six feet across, and where there are smaller fragments they are usually thinnest along the line of stratification. This peculiar arrangement of the broken outcrop of the strata, is caused by the frequent occurrence of beds of shale, which gradually yield to the pressure of the overlying limestone as it breaks off along the outcrop. The flat masses of limestone are very remarkable on the ground, and distinctly indicate the space on every hill-side where the Upper White Limestone crops out. On the Frontispiece, Plate 2, this is remarkably distinct, and the strata may be traced along the successive outcrops in five or six lines of stratification. Lower down in front of the ravine the confused heap of ruinous masses of rock presents a scene of fallen grandeur seldom to be surpassed. Although the Upper White Limestone is more broken down in the Ty-nant ravine in consequence of its steepness, the same rugged outcrop is common to the strata all along the Eglwyseg ridge; though less conspicuous about the Trevor rocks, on account of the subdivision being thinner and somewhat obscured by the fault that runs through the quarries. In Bron-heulog quarry the same tendency of the Upper White Limestone to break down in tabular masses is again remarkable, and there is an enormous heap of fallen rock in the middle, which has much increased since the year 1873 when the photograph was taken.

The thickness of the Upper White Limestone is 300 feet at the Ty-nant ravine; 250 feet at Tan-y-Castell; 140 feet at Trevor rocks, and 99 feet at Bron-heulog quarry. It has been used for fluxing purposes, but it is not worked at present.

There are very few fossils in the strata of this subdivision. The compact limestone or marble, seldom contains a trace of any, and in no instance are these beds very fossiliferous. In the coarser limestone, however, a careful search will generally result in the following species being found:—*Spirifera bisulcata; Productus giganteus; P. cora; Syringopora geniculata.*

UPPER GREY LIMESTONE.

This is the highest subdivision of the Carboniferous Limestone, and it is well developed along the top of the Eglwyseg ridge, where some of the middle beds form the prominent scar which is so conspicuous, above all the others, with a deep talus fringing its base as shown in Plate 1. The limestone is usually of a dark grey, or slaty colour; but there are some beds of a light grey. The quarry-men call the dark limestone blue, and the lighter strata white, to distinguish the one from the other. The dark grey limestone is usually thin bedded and interstratified with partings of black shale; but the light grey beds are more massive and are principally in the middle of the series, where they are liable to changes in colour within short distances.

It is with great pleasure that I take this opportunity of acknowledging, that I am much indebted to Mr. Isaac Williams of Bron-heulog, for the uniform kindness with which he has assisted me during the survey of the district. He has taken great interest in the subject, and has always been ready to aid me; and I entertain a very high opinion of his practical knowledge, guided as it is by long and shrewd observation in connection with his occupation.

The following is a section of the strata composing the Upper Grey Limestone as measured by Mr. Williams, in the vicinity of the Trevor quarries :—

Sandy flagstones.

		FEET.
	Light Grey Limestone with quartz pebbles at the top......................	5
	Dark Grey thin-bedded Limestone...	13
	Light ,, Limestone..................	6
	Dark ,, thin-bedded Limestone...	45
	Light and Dark Grey thin-bedded Limestone.............................	33
Upper Grey Limestone.	Light Grey Limestone..................	19
	Dark ,, thin-bedded Limestone...	24
	Black Shale	2
	Light and Dark Grey thin-bedded Limestone	9
	Light Grey Limestone..................	12
	Dark Grey thin-bedded Limestone...	54
		222

Upper White Limestones.

Mr. Williams measured the beds in succession, but considering the difficulty of doing so accurately, I have adopted my own calculated result, which gives a thickness of 250 feet for the whole of the subdivision.

Although these divisional bands of strata are not of any general importance on account of their limited range, they can be identified in the scars and quarries where they occur, and afford the means of ascertaining the amount of denudation when the upper beds of the subdivision have been denuded. The limestone that is worked at the top of the Trevor rocks and in several quarries to the south-east of Bron-heulog, belongs to the 19-feet and 24-feet bands in the section, and in these there are some thinner beds of black shale above the 2-feet bed, in addition to the partings between the beds of limestone. The 12-feet bed of light grey limestone near the bottom of the section forms the scar along the top of the Eglwyseg ridge and that of Pen-y-gloppa above Bron-heulog quarry, as shown in Plates 1 and 3. The thin beds of black shale in the Upper Grey Limestone, present a great contrast to the much thicker beds of the same strata which occur in the subdivision at Minera, Chirk and other places both to the north and south of Llangollen.

The thickness of the strata belonging to the Upper Grey Limestone is 300 feet at the Ty-nant ravine; 300 feet at the Tan-y-Castell ravine; and 250 feet at the Trevor rocks; but further south-east the upper beds are either denuded or thrown down by the fault No. 2, Plate 4, so that only about 66 feet are visible, as at Pen-y-gloppa. The limestone is extensively burnt for lime, but it is only the lower portion that is worked.

Fossils occur in all the strata of the Upper Grey Limestone, though the highest beds are the most fossili-ferous, and are well exposed in several small quarries at the top of the Tan-y-Castell ravine, where the upper 24-feet in the section crop out from under the Sandy Limestone. The same strata are also repre-sented by a long narrow heap of loose stones, which marks the outcrop to the east of the Ty-nant ravine. In the Frontispiece, Plate 2, this fossiliferous zone can be seen extending in the form of a grey line in front of the distant high ground, and it extends along the top of the Eglwyseg ridge for several miles. The strata comprising the 19-feet and 24-feet in the section, however, yield many species, and as most of the quarries are worked in this part of the subdivision, many of the fossils in the list are from those beds. The most abundant species are :—*Bellerophon cornu-arietes; Euomphalus Dionysii; Natica sp.; Spirifera bisulcata; S. crassa; Productus giganteus*, and the young *latissimus; P. punctatus; Cyathophyllum regium; Clisiophyllum turbinatum; Lithostrotion Portlocki; L. junceum*, and *L. irregalare*; and *Lonsdaleia rugosa*.

In these lists the most common fossils have been selected, rather than what seem to be peculiar species, which are usually of rare occurrence. In the list of fossils at the end of the Paper, the horizon of species which have only been found in particular strata is given.

The thickness of the subdivisions and of the whole of the Carboniferous Limestone, at the four localities to which frequent reference has been made, is shown in the following Table; and the thickness at Fron on the south side of the River Dee, a locality to be described hereafter, is appended :—

	Ty-nant.	Tan-y-Castell.	Trevor rocks.	Bron-henlog.	Fron.
Upper Grey Limestone...	300	300	250	66*	80*
„ White „ ...	300	250	140	99	27†
Lower „ „ ...	120	115	117	104	—
„ Brown „ ...	480	360	100‡	26‡	—
	1200	1025	607	295	107

* Upper portion has been denuded.
† Reposes on the Wenlock Shale.
‡ Lowest beds cannot be ascertained with certainty.

At the Trevor quarries and Bron-heulog the lowest beds of the Lower Brown Limestone cannot be seen, being probably thrown down by the boundary fault, so that the absolute thickness cannot be ascertained. However, at the Fron quarries the upper beds of the Upper White Limestone repose on the Wenlock Shale—the Carboniferous Limestone having thinned out about 900 feet in the four miles south-east between the Ty-nant ravine and Fron. At Tan-y-Castell the attenuation is about 200 feet, so that there are strong reasons for supposing the diminution in thickness to continue gradually with the rise of the Wenlock Shale on which the limestone unconformably rests.

According to the two Horizontal Sections of the Geological Survey the thickness of the Carboniferous Limestone at Dinbren-uchaf a little north-west of the Tan-y-Castell ravine is 1,300 feet, and at the Trevor rocks 1,200 feet. If, however, the thickness is corrected, according to the subdivisions here adopted, it is considerably reduced. The contour of the Eglwyseg ridge allows of this test being accurately applied, and it shows that I have not over-estimated the thickness. In the Survey Sections the base of the Carboniferous Limestone is higher than on the map, and also higher than the one I have assumed in the measurements that have been given, There is an uncertainty about the base line, and if it should occur higher than I have supposed, the thickness of the Lower Brown Limestone would be diminished and the difference added to that of the Upper Old Red Sandstone. Another important difference arises from the Sandy Limestone and part of the Lower Sandstone and Conglomerate to the extent of 200 feet in the Dinbren-uchaf section (No. 39), and 400 feet in the Trevor section (No. 44), being included in the Carboniferous Limestone. Taking all these corrections and differences of the Survey Sections into consideration, the result is 1,100 feet for the thickness at Dinbren-uchaf— half way between the Ty-nant and the Tan-y-Castell ravines—a result remarkably near that I have arrived at; and 1,000 feet about Tan-y-Castell and the Trevor rocks, which is more than I have concluded the thickness to be.

CEFN-Y-FEDW SANDSTONE.

SANDY LIMESTONE.

This forms the lowest subdivision of the Cefn-y-Fedw Sandstone. It is well exposed in a roadside quarry at the turn of the road above Pen-y-gloppa, and in the cliff which runs from it in a north-westerly direction. It is a limestone containing a large proportion of sand, or a sandstone with carbonate of lime as a cementing medium; but it is a very variable bed, some portions being a limestone and others a regular sandstone. The quarry-men call the rock the "flaggy sandstone," and were surprised to hear that it contained lime. The quarry and cliff just referred to are distinctly traceable at the top of the hill on the left-hand of Plate 3. The Sandy Limestone can be traced along the top of the Eglwyseg ridge; but it is generally covered with a peaty soil and consequently cannot be seen except where a few narrow roads have worn down the surface. About the Ty-nant ravine it occupies a considerable area of boggy land, and the strata beneath it can only be seen in a few holes, where water has opened a passage and exposed narrow fissures in the rock, which seems to be an alternation of sandstone and limestone. Two miles further to the north the Sandy Limestone is a soft sandstone where crossed by a narrow road half a mile north-east of Craig-y-Forwyn. East of the Ty-nant ravine the Sandy Limestone is included in the Carboniferous Limestone on the Geological Survey Map, but in other places it is doubtful on account of the small scale of the 1-inch sheet; on the Survey Sections it is certainly so included. Associated with the Sandy Limestone, east of the latter ravine, there is a bed of dark grey limestone, 11 feet thick, which is evidently near the upper part of the subdivision. It contains numerous Encrinite stems with *Productus giganteus; P. semireticulatus;* and *P. cora,* and is succeeded by yellow flaggy sandstone containing annelid tracks. The limestone can only be traced for about 100 yards along the strike, and does not seem to occur elsewhere on the Eglwyseg ridge. The thickness of the subdivision is about 75 feet, as shown in the Tabular View of the Cefn-y-Fedw Sandstone, Plate 5.

The Sandy Limestone contains fossils, even where the beds are of sandstone, and there is a small opening between Trevor Hall and Trevor-uchaf, where *Modiola sp.; Productus semireticulatus,* and corals too obscure for indentification occur.

LOWER SANDSTONE AND CONGLOMERATE.

This subdivision is directly above the Sandy Limestone, and it always presents an abrupt ascent of the ground, for it is a very hard rock and its base has little or no carbonate of lime in its composition. It invariably forms the highest part of Cefn-y-Fedw and sometimes crops out through the peaty soil, though more generally the line of strike is indicated by thousands of stones projecting from the surface. The sandstone is very hard and white, and most of the beds, especially near the base, are conglomeratic from the number of white quartz pebbles, less than an inch in diameter, which occur in bands, without any actual separation of the massive sandstone. The rock itself is not much exposed, though it is evidently of a very solid thick-bedded character, and the lower portion of the subdivision forms a rounded eminence, with a semicircular outline, which extends for about seven miles along the highest part of the Eglwyseg ridge, from Garreg Pengruch* to Minera. In Plates 1 and 2 the Lower Sandstone and Conglomerate is the highest visible portion of the hill in the background. The hard white conglomeratic beds seem to be succeeded by sandstone strata of a softer character; but there is no good exposure of them nearer than Minera, where they are exposed in a fine cliff section across the strike of the stratification and are mostly impure limestones; which are coloured Carboniferous Limestone on the Geol. Sur. Map. In that locality the limestone contains numerous fossils; but the conglomerate is very similar to that described. I have not found any fossils in the Lower Sandstone and Conglomerate at the Eglwyseg ridge. Reference has already been made to the contrast between the surface over the Carboniferous Limestone on the one hand, and that of the Cefn-y-Fedw Sandstone on the other; and where the country has not been reclaimed, the geological boundary between the two formations

---

* Garreg Pengruch is the precipitous hill between Pen-y-gaer and the Monumental Tower, "356" on the 25-in. Ordnance Map; but the name is not inserted.

might be safely drawn, by observing the dry and bright green aspect of the former, and the brown and dreary appearance of the latter.

CHERTY SHALE.

Immediately over the Lower Sandstone and Conglomerate some beds of hard cherty shale crop out, with a general strike from north to south along the middle of Cefn-y-Fedw. This shale occurs in the course of a brook about half-way between the top of the Tŷ-nant ravine and Tyfyn-uchaf, in a very inaccessible place. About 50 feet of the shale are actually exposed; but it may be double that thickness. It crops out in thin beds of a whitish colour, though somewhat stained to yellow where weathered. It is very hard, and the fine grained varieties closely resemble porcelain; but some of it contains visible grains of crystalline quartz. There is reason to suppose that the cherty shale crops out on the side of Garreg Pengruch, for there is a trail of cherty fragments with fossils on the talus about half-way up. At my suggestion Mr. I. Williams very kindly set a man to try and penetrate to it, but he found the thickness of débris on the hill side so deep that it was dangerous to continue the attempt.

In the Vertical Section, No. 24, of the Geological Survey, which is represented on a reduced scale on Plate 5, a bed of Coal is shown on the horizon of the Cherty Shale, but I have not been able to find any such Coal-seam. Mr. Joseph Davies, of Rhos, informed me that a boring is reported to have been made, about 70 years ago, in the Cherty Shale on Cefn-y-Fedw, and that a bed of coal 3 ft. 6 in. had been discovered, but that he had not been able to obtain further particulars about it. That the boring may have been made is probable enough, but finding a bed of coal seems very improbable.

The number of fossils in the Cherty Shale is remarkable and includes *Spirifera bisulcata ; Rhynchonella pleurodon; Productus semireticulatus; P. punctatus;* and other species too imperfect for determination. *P. semireticulatus* is the most common, and stems of Encrinites are abundant.

MIDDLE SANDSTONE.

This subdivision succeeds the Cherty Shale, and consists for the most part of beds of very hard white sandstone, sometimes like quartzite and often containing scattered quartz pebbles. There are strata of a softer character and yellow in colour associated with the harder beds ; though they are not so well exposed and can only be seen on several narrow roads, which cross Cefn-y-Fedw from east to west. The Middle Sandstone crops out at Tyfyn-uchaf and at Garreg Pengruch, at both of which places the hard massive character of the rock is well exposed. That the Cefn-y-Fedw Sandstone is of considerable thickness is proved by its outcrop at Garreg Pengruch, which is the south-east continuation of Cefn-y-Fedw. The hill is 360 feet high, with the base of the Lower Sandstone and Conglomerate on the road below, from which the height was determined, and it is succeeded by the Middle Sandstone with the Cherty Shale between them. The strata dip at an angle of 20°, and as the horizontal distance between the road and the top of the hill is 396 feet, the addition to be made to the height of 360 feet is 136=496 feet. The Middle Sandstone does not, however, terminate at the top of Garreg Pengruch, for there is a bed of flinty shale, 20 feet thick, followed by about 30 feet of sandstone which are included in the subdivision, giving a total of about 556 feet as the thickness of the Lower and Middle Cefn-y-Fedw Sandstone alone, but in order to guard against an error in the measurement, I have assumed the actual thickness to be 500 feet. The flinty shale is exposed in a field at Pen-y-gaer,* and the overlying sandstone is the bed on which Mr. Whalley's Monumental Tower is built. The following diagram (Fig. 2) exhibits the Cefn-y-Fedw Sandstone at Garreg Pengruch, and the subdivisions into which it is divided :—

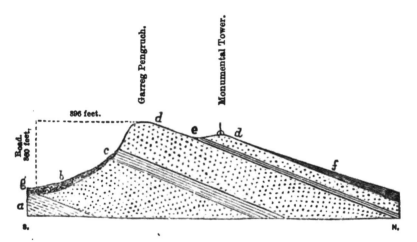

FIG. 2.   GARREG PENGRUCH SECTION.

g. Talus on hill side.	*c.* Cherty Shale.
f. Lower Shale and Limestone.	*b.* Lower Sandstone.
e. Flinty Shale.	*a.* Sandy Limestone.
d. Middle Sandstone.	

LOWER SHALE.

This subdivision is fully exposed at Tyfyn-uchaf, where it rests on the Middle Sandstone, and is about

---

* Ordnance Map 25-in., "1244."

18 feet in thickness. It is chiefly a black shale; but with some bands of impure limestone a few inches thick interstratified with it. The following fossils have been collected:—*Avicula sp.; Posidonomya sp.; Athyris ambigua; Spirifera bisulcata; Streptorhynchus crinistria; Productus semireticulatus; P. longispinus;* and *Chonetes Hardrensis.*

At Garreg Pengruch the Lower Shale reposes on the Middle Sandstone to the east of the Monumental Tower, and the lowest beds can be seen on the hill-side and the road. The higher strata are not exposed, though they probably occur in the fields east of the old limekiln, and seem to have been proved in a trial pit sunk through the overlying Dee Bridge Sandstone on the rising ground near Bryn-Morfydd. The pit was probably sunk in search of fire-clay, when a thin seam of coal, $3\frac{1}{2}$ inches thick, was found. A miner informed me that the same coal-seam had frequently been reached before in the valley, and that it was 10 and 15 inches thick in some old pits that had been sunk. He also stated that it was discovered about 40 years ago in sinking a well. This is the only evidence I have obtained of any seam of coal in the Cefn-y-Fedw Sandstone.

At the Dee Bridge—Pont-y-Cysyllte—near Trevor Station, the Lower Shale is again exposed. It is much thicker than at Tyfyn-uchaf; and probably the same subdivision at Bryn-Morfydd would be found very similar if it were exposed. The strata crop out in the river, and although most of the beds can be examined, it is difficult to measure them exactly, for some are in the water, and others covered with gravel and stones. However, the following section (Fig. 3) shows the position of the Lower Shale and the succeeding subdivisions.

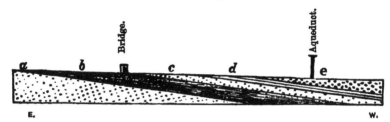

FIG. 3. DEE BRIDGE SECTION.

e. Aqueduct Grit, or Upper Sandstone.

d. Upper Shale.	*b.* Lower Shale and Limestone.
c. Dee Bridge Sandstone.	*a.* Middle Sandstone.

The Lower Shale at Dee Bridge presents the following beds :—

		FEET.	IN.
	Fire clay	3	3
	Hard brown sandstone	2	0
Lower Shale and Limestone.	Shale, obscured in the water	15	0
	Black shale and limestone	15	0
	Brown sandstone	10	0
	Limestone	1	6
	Shale, said by a miner to contain mussels	4	0
		50	9

DEE BRIDGE SANDSTONE.

This sandstone subdivision succeeds the Lower Shale, and is fully exposed at Tyfyn-uchaf. It is a bedded yellow sandstone, jointed, and very different to any of the underlying sandstone. It is 80 feet in thickness, and contains plant remains :—*Stigmaria* and *Calamites* associated with several annelid tracks.

At the Dee Bridge section the position of the sandstone is so well seen above the Lower Shale that I have named it from the bridge, the piers of which rest upon its lowest beds. It is about 80 feet thick, and exactly resembles the same subdivision at Tyfyn-uchaf. It also contains impressions of plants : – *Stigmaria* and *Lepidodendron*.

This sandstone in the trial pit at Bryn-Morfydd presents its usual aspect, and contains annelid tracks as at Tyfyn-uchaf, though no remains of plants were observed.

UPPER SHALE.

This band of shale succeeds the Dee Bridge Sandstone. It is not much exposed at Tyfyn-uchaf, but is visible at the east of the Dee Bridge, cropping up at the sides of the river. It is not a subdivision of much importance, except that it extends over a considerable area beneath the following and overlying deposit. A trial pit recently sunk in the Aqueduct Grit quarry at Mount Pleasant, near Bryn-Morfydd, was abandoned after passing through 10 feet of shale which seems to belong to this subdivision.

AQUEDUCT GRIT.

This subdivision is very important for its distinct lithological character, and for the large area over which it presents a uniform thickness. At Tyfyn-uchaf it is exposed in a large quarry, with a bed of shale, 30 feet thick, and the Aqueduct coal resting on it. At the Aqueduct, east of Dee Bridge, it is also exposed on both sides of the river, with another thick bed of shale, 50 feet thick, above it. At Australia, near Trevor Station, there is a large quarry of the Aqueduct Grit, which is faulted against the thick shale which usually overlies it. This shale is worked as brick-clay at Messrs. Mason and Shelmerdine's brick and tile works, and the following is a section for which I am indebted to them :—

	FEET.	
Coal....................	2	Aqueduct Coal.
Sandstone	6	
Shale................	48	
,, ...	5	
Coal, 1 ft. 6 in. to	2	Chwarele Coal.
	63	
Aqueduct Grit	70	(75 feet in bore hole on account of the dip.)

The Aqueduct Grit closely resembles typical Millstone Grit, and it is the same rock as the Garth Stòne, a well-known building material which has been used in the neighbourhood of Llangollen for more than 500 years. Valle Crusis Abbey, Llangollen Bridge, Carnarvon Castle, and docks at Bristol are built with it. The Aqueduct Grit is supposed to extend over an area of ten miles, and it can usually be recognised in a hand specimen. This grit is the uppermost subdivision of the Cefn-y-Fedw Sandstone.

The following (Fig. 4) is a section from the bottom of the Tynant ravine across Cefn-y-Fedw in an easterly direction to Tyfyn-uchaf, near Trefechan, a distance of three miles. It is the typical section of the Lower Carboniferous Series, and the lower strata are the same as those shown in the Frontispiece, Plate 2. Each subdivision of the Carboniferous Limestone and Cefn-y-Fedw Sandstone is presented in regular succession, and the thickness of the whole is about 1923 feet.

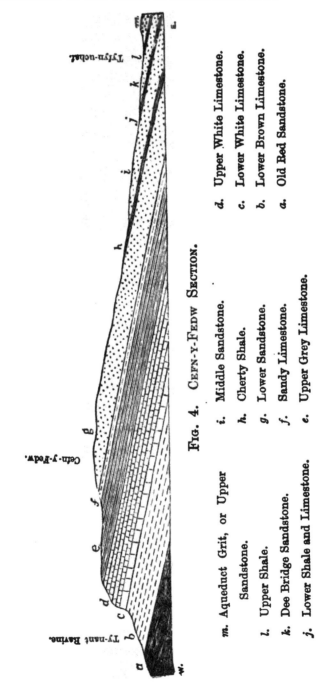

FIG. 4. CEFN-Y-FEDW SECTION.

m. Aqueduct Grit, or Upper Sandstone.
l. Upper Shale.
k. Dee Bridge Sandstone.
j. Lower Shale and Limestone.
i. Middle Sandstone.
h. Cherty Shale.
g. Lower Sandstone.
f. Sandy Limestone.
e. Upper Grey Limestone.
d. Upper White Limestone.
c. Lower White Limestone.
b. Lower Brown Limestone.
a. Old Red Sandstone.

MAP SHEWING FAULTS

BETWEEN THE

TREVOR ROCKS AND TREVOR HALL

The subdivisions of the Cefn-y-Fedw Sandstone seem to be of more uniform thickness than the underlying Carboniferous Limestone; but there are not the same facilities for measuring them. The only section where the Cefn-y-Fedw Sandstone presents a steep escarpment is at Garreg Pengruch, above Pen-y-gaer, where it has already been shown to be 500 feet thick; but the deep talus which covers its steep slope prevents the thickness of the lower strata being so accurately measured as in the underlying limestone. The litho-logical character of each subdivision presents remarkable uniformity; but beyond the prescribed limits, both to the north and south, differences begin to appear, and great changes are presented as the distance from the typical district increases. The correlation of the subdivisions is shown on four vertical sections on Plate 5, viz.:—Tyfyn-uchaf, Garreg Pengruch, Dee Bridge, and at Newbridge and Acrefair—the latter being a reduced copy of the Vertical Section (No. 24) of the Geological Survey. The general resemblance of these sections to each other is remarkable, and as the strata in the three first named localities are well exposed, especially the Upper Sand-stones and Shales, it is evident that the succession has been made out with accuracy. I have not been able to discover the source of the Survey section, but conclude that it was either from borings in search of coal, or an epitome of general observations over Cefn-y-Fedw and in the Dee Bridge section, though Newbridge and Acre-fair are the localities given.

FAULTS.

The faults that have broken up the Carboniferous Limestone in the Eglwyseg ridge are of considerable interest and importance. They were probably all pro-

K

duced at the same time, when the strata were thrown up to the south-west-south during the Permian period. Although there are four faults, they may be collectively considered to be a compound fracture, for they are intimately connected with each other. Plate 4, is a ground plan of these faults, and although it may not be correct in all its details, it is the result of careful observation over a lengthened period.

Fault No. 1, Plate 4, is the boundary fault by which the Wenlock Shale is thrown up, and the Carboniferous Limestone let down; but to what extent it is impossible to ascertain. It is laid down on the Map of the Geological Survey, and appears to throw down the Old Red Sandstone, Carboniferous Limestone, and, finally, the Cefn-y-Fedw Sandstone against the Wenlock Shale; and had I not discovered the attenuation of the limestone in a south-easterly direction, it must have been described as a more considerable fault than it really is. It seems to be an important fault at the east-south-east end, where it brings the Cefn-y-Fedw Sandstone into contact with the Wenlock Shale; but not of much importance between Castell Dinas Bran and the Eglwyseg ridge. This fault is not exposed anywhere about the base of the limestone talus, though its position has been closely determined; for below the Trevor quarries the Wenlock Shale is seen on the road near the spot where the cross-road branches off towards Llangollen; and a little to the south-east along the same road the limestone strata are turned up —30°—probably in consequence of the downthrow on that side of the fault. Although little is actually known of this fault, its course has been traced with tolerable certainty from near Tan-y-Castell, in a curved line to the Park in front of Trevor Hall, and it may have some connection with the springs just beyond that place.

Fault, No. 2, may be a bifurcation of the boundary fault, No. 1, and branch off from it to the east of Trevor Hall. From there it runs west-north-west up a valley, with the Sandy Limestone on one side, and first the Upper White Limestone and then the Upper Grey Limestone on the other—the highest beds of the sub-divisions having been denuded. The course of the fault is then across the scar above Bron-heulog quarry, at the north-west end of which, by the Erwen, it unites with fault, No. 3, when the two form a single dislocation, continuing parallel with the incline and through the Trevor quarries, where it can be seen in several places. It runs along the strike of the Lower White Limestone, and throws the beds down to the north-east-north about 20 feet, so that on crossing the fault the *thick-bed* is that much lower than where worked at the outcrop along the Trevor rocks. The dislocation, however, caused by the fault seems to increase in amount as it runs east-south-east, and it causes the massive beds of the Lower White Limestone to present an imposing scar; though the grand precipitous wall of limestone has been almost destroyed by the quarrying operations. Towards Trevor Hall where the Lower White Limestone is brought up against the Sandy Limestone the dislocation is still further increased.

Fault, No. 3, strikes north-west from near Plas-Ifan, at a slight angle to the boundary fault, No. 1, through some old excavations and Bron-heulog quarry, at the north-west end of which it runs into No. 2, near where the tramway crosses the brook. It can be seen exposed in sections at several places along its course, throwing up the thick shale-bed belonging to the top of the Lower Brown Limestone about 50 feet, against the *thick-bed* of the Lower White Limestone, particularly at the south-east end of Bron-heulog quarry, close to the tramway, where it can be seen on Plate 3. The juncture of this fault with No. 2 cannot be seen for it is beneath the tramway; but the disturbed condition of the strata close to it can be observed in the quarry, about the place where it has encroached on the footpath which winds up the side of it.

Fault, No. 4, is a cross fault from No. 1 to No. 2, and it runs through Wright's most eastern quarry. It is of less importance than the other faults, though the dislocation caused by it is remarkable—175 feet—bringing up the Lower White Limestone on the south-east-south side against the lower beds of the Upper Grey Limestone on the other.

To ensure accuracy, these faults were drawn on the 25-inch Ordnance Maps, and the ground plan, Plate 4, is reduced to the scale of three and a half inches to the mile. That the faults are intimately related to each other is evident from their being downthrows to the north-east-north; and it seems that when the strata were thrown up in the opposite direction, they broke off, and formed a series of fractures, all having a downward tendency in opposition to the upheaving influence of the boundary fault.

MINERAL VEINS.

It is remarkable that no mineral veins of any importance occur in the Eglwyseg ridge; while only five or six miles to the northward there is the rich mining ground of Minera. Reference has been made to the diminution in the thickness of the beds of shale, interstratified with the limestone as they continue northwards. At Minera the Upper and Lower White Limestones form one series of strata, in consequence of the absence of shale and the solid-bedded character of the rock; and it seems very probable that the shale associated with the limestone in the neighbourhood of Llangollen, may have found its way into the open faults and fissures and prevented the deposition of metalliferous deposits.

DENUDATION.

The recession of the upper beds of the Carboniferous Limestone and Cefn-y-Fedw Sandstone along the top of the Eglwyseg ridge is a remarkable illustration of subaerial denudation. This receding contour has been determined by several conditions, but principally by the more exposed position of the highest beds to the disintegrating action of frost, which breaks up the sandstone for it yields sooner to its influence than limestone. The Cefn-y-Fedw Sandstone has been denuded from the front of the ridge, and the hard beds of the Upper Grey Limestone present a precipitous scar, which continues unbroken except where the ravines run deeply into the ridge. Lower down the thicker beds of limestone form cliffs, while the thinner limestone and shale disintegrate, and terraces are formed over the massive beds; in this manner the *thick-bed* of limestone presents the most precipitous scar, and it is succeeded by the widest terrace.

MEMBERS

OF THE

LIVERPOOL GEOLOGICAL SOCIETY.

HONORARY MEMBERS.

A. C. RAMSAY, F.R.S., F.G.S., London.
JOHN MORRIS, F.G.S., London.
S. J. MACKIE, F.G.S., F.S.A., London.
WILLIAM PENGELLY, F.R.S., F.G.S., Torquay.
EDWARD W. BINNEY, F.R.S., F.G.S., Douglas, Isle of Man.
WILLIAM BRYHAM, Wigan.
HENRY HICKS, F.G.S., M.R.C.S.E., London.
W. KING, D. Sc., Queen's College, Galway.

MEMBERS.

ABRAHAM, J., Riverham, Grassendale Park.
      87, Bold Street.
ARCHER, F., B.A., Boundary Cottage, Crosby.
      14, Cook Street.
ARNOTT, T. R., Bramshill, Harlesden Green, London.
      6, Mersey Chambers.
ATKINSON, S., 123, Falkner Street.
*BEASLEY, H., Acre-field House, Woolton.
*BOSTOCK, R., 8, Grange Lane, Birkenhead.
BREWSTER, C., Rev., 115, Huskisson Street.
BROWN, C. H., Low-wood, Alexandra Road, Southport.
BROWN, J. CAMPBELL, D. Sc., F.C.S., 67, Bedford Street.
DAVIES, C., 8, Kinglake Street, Edge Hill.

DAWBARN, W., Elmswood, Aigburth.
    The Temple, Dale Street.
DIXON, T., 27, St. James' Road.
DODD, J., 2, Derby Terrace, Rock Ferry.
ECCLES, J., F.G.S., Springwell House, Blackburn.
† * ESKRIGGE, R. A., F.G.S., Fir Cottage, New Brighton.
    18, Hackins Hey.
FABERT, C., 3, St. James' Walk.
FITZPATRICK, M., 62, Seel Street.
FITZPATRICK, J. J., 62, Seel Street.
FLEMING, E. L., F.C.S., Borax Works, Old Swan.
FOSTER, E., 7, Newstead Road, Smithdown Lane.
FOSTER, R. M., 34, Oxford Road, Waterloo.
GOLDSWORTH, W., Prescot.
GREGSON, S. L., Aigburth Road.
    Slater Court, 5, Castle Street.
GREEN. A., York House, Old Chester Road, Rock Ferry.
    9, Canning Place.
GRIFFITHS, J., 14, Queen Street, Chester.
* HALL, H. F., F.G.S., Green Heys, Grove Road, Wallasey.
    17, Dale Street.
HANCE, E. W., LL.B., Municipal Offices, Dale Street.
HATHAWAY, T., C.E., The Mount, Bangor, North Wales.
* HIGGINS, H. H., Rev., M.A., Rainhill.
JEVONS, G., Jun., 5, Chapel Street.
JONES, T., Top Lane, Wallasey,
    Orange Court, Castle Street.
KEEN, R. J., 85, Edge Lane.
    17, South Castle Street.
KERSHAW, J., Nevill Street, Southport.
KIRBY, C., C.E., Newport, Monmouthshire.
LEA, T., Vale Cottage, Huyton Quarry.
* McCLAY, J. L., Spring Bank, Church Road, Higher Tranmere.
M'KAIG, W. R., 11, Seaton Buildings, Water Street.
* MARRAT, F. P., 21, Kinglake Street.
MAYER, J., F.S.A., Pennant House, Lower Bebington.
* MOORE, T. J., C.M.Z.S.L., 44, Osborne Road, Tue Brook.
    Liverpool Museum.
* MORGAN, ALFRED (Honorary Treasurer), 2, Rathbone Terrace,
  Wellington Road, Wavertree. Office, 126, London Road.
MORTIMER, Captain, Liverpool.
† * MORTON, G. H., F.G.S., F.R.G.S.I. (Honorary Secretary), 10, Sheil
  Road.   122, London Road.

† MOTT, C. G., Sunnyside, Cavendish Road, Birkenhead.

McMILLAN, A., Conway, North Wales.

PARIS, T. J., 68 and 70, Lord Street.
> Rake Lane, Liscard.

PATERSON, J., Palmyra Street, Warrington.

PEARSE W., 15, Harrington Street.
> Green Bank Farm, Wavertree.

† * PICTON, J. A., F.S.A., Sandy Knowe, Wavertree.
> 4 and 5, Queen Buildings, Dale Street.

* POTTER, C., 101, Miles Street.

PEARSON, J. E., Golborne Park, near Newton-le-Willows.

† * READE, T. M., C.E., F.G.S., Park Corner, Blundellsands.
> Canning Chambers, 4, South John Street.

† * RICKETTS, C., M.D., F.G.S., 22, Argyle Street, Birkenhead.

* ROBERTS, I., F.G.S., 26, Rock Park, Rock Ferry.
> 39, Gardener's Row.

RICHARDSON, W. A., Holt Hill, Tranmere.

SHONE, W., F.G.S., 86, Watergate Street, Chester.

* SEMMONS, W., 20, Canning Place.

STRONGITHARM, G., 77, Whetstone Lane, Tranmere.

SPARGO, E., Bangor, North Wales.

SHERLOCK, C., 63, South John Street.

STOWELL, J. T., 36, Exchange Street East.

WASON, J., 26, Hamilton Street, Birkenhead.
> 4, Harrington Street.

WILSON, W. H., St. Michael's Hamlet, Aigburth.
> 31, Wapping.

WESTWORTH, R., 31, King Street.

WHALLEY, E., London and Lancashire Insurance Company, Queen Buildings.

WRIGHT, B. M., F.R. Hist. Soc., 90, Great Russell Street, Bloomsbury, London.

WARD, T., Northwich, Cheshire.

WARD, J. R., 57, Garth Road, Bangor, North Wales.

* Have read Papers before the Society.
† Contribute annually to the Printing Fund.

INDEX.

PROCEEDINGS

OF THE

𝕷iverpool 𝕲eological 𝕾ociety.

SESSION THE EIGHTEENTH.

1876-7.

(The Authors having revised their own papers, are alone responsible for the facts and opinions expressed in them.)

PART III.--VOL. III.

LIVERPOOL:
C. TINLING & CO., PRINTERS, VICTORIA STREET.

1877.

h Rainfall Area and Group of Strata in England and Wales.

r	Total Tons of Water per Annum.	Solids in Solution, Parts per 100,000.	Total Solids in Solution, in Tons.	Total Solids in each Rainfall Area, in Tons.
..	....2,957,568,000....	......4·7	139,000	
				139,000
..	....7,271,968,000....	......5·0	363,590	
.	.... 893,692,800....	......5·5	 49,150	
.	....4,129,452,800....	.... 12·1	499,660	
.				912,400
.	....6,842,480,640....	......5·6	383,170	
.	....5,722,252,800....	......5·7	326,160	
.	....5,297,941,760....	.... 12·9	683,430	
.				1,392,760
.	....2,671,776,000....	......5·0	133,580	
.	.... 787,888,000....	.... 10·0	 78,780	
.	....2,065,040,000....	.... 10·8	223,020	
.	.... 238,318,080....	......4·7	 11,200	
.	....4,035,450,880....	.... 26·0	.. 1,049,210	
.	.... 642,816,000....	.... 14·5	 93,200	
.	....1,446,336,000....	.... 17·7	256,000	
.	....8,251,152,000. ..	.... 12·0	990,130	
.				2,835,120
.	....9,520,748,800....	.... 18·4	....	1,751,810
.	....5,676,054,400....	.... 23·6	....	1,339,540
	68,450,936,960			8,370,630

Solids removed in Solution = 143·5 tons per square mile per annum.

ɔt to the Ton, = 125,559,450 feet, or = ·0077 of a foot per century, or
of one foot of matter soluble in rain water.

PROCEEDINGS

OF THE

Liverpool Geological Society.

SESSION THE EIGHTEENTH.

1876-7.

(The Authors having revised their own papers, are alone responsible for the facts and opinions expressed in them.)

PART III.—VOL. III.

LIVERPOOL

COURIER PRINTING WORKS, VICTORIA STREET.

—

1877

OFFICERS, 1876—7.

President.
HUGH F. HALL, F.G.S.

Vice-President.
WILLIAM SEMMONS.

Honorary Treasurer.
ALFRED MORGAN.

Honorary Librarian.
EDWIN FOSTER.

Honorary Secretary.
GEORGE H. MORTON, F.G.S., F.R.G.S.I.

Council.
CHARLES RICKETTS, M.D., F.G.S.
FREDERICK P. MARRAT.
HENRY BEASLEY.
ROBERT BOSTOCK.

PROCEEDINGS

OF THE

LIVERPOOL GEOLOGICAL SOCIETY.

SESSION EIGHTEENTH.

OCTOBER 10TH, 1876.

THE PRESIDENT, T. MELLARD READE, C.E., F.G.S.,
in the Chair.

JOSEPH T. STOWELL was elected an Ordinary Member.

The President read the Annual Address.

PRESIDENT'S ADDRESS.

SINCE the time when Hutton laid the foundation of our present knowledge of Physical Geology, our acquaintance with the structure of the Earth has advanced with rapid strides. The various formations have been reduced to order and sequence through the combined influence of Palæontology and careful Stratigraphical Surveying. But to make Geology essentially a science, the mathematical method must step in to measure, balance, and accurately estimate.

Though fully recognising that there still remain vast and varied unexplored fields for original research, the direction of advancement will be towards reducing those comprehensive generalisations for which we have to thank the old generation of Geologists—now almost passed away —and their rough though wonderful approximations to truth, to careful and accurate measurement.

Instead of giving you, as is usual on these occasions, a *resumé* of geological progress during the year, I purpose devoting the time to what I trust will prove in my case more valuable, viz., an investigation of the nature and amount of the solvent action of rain-water upon the crust of the earth, and its influence in that direction as an agent of denudation.

There have, as you know, been various estimates made of the amount of mechanical denudation caused by rain, calculated upon the amount of mud held in suspension and carried annually to the ocean by our great rivers; and all of us who prize Lyell's Principles will remember the masterly manner in which he treats the question in the case of the Mississippi and the Ganges, with the Brahmapootra. Other geologists have also calculated from the same data and the area of the river basins, the amount of time it takes to reduce the whole of these river basins one foot in depth; the result being in the case of the Mississippi 6,000 years, and the Ganges 2,800 years.

There have also been estimates of the amount of carbonate of lime carried into the sea annually by the Thames and other rivers draining calcareous districts; but, even if they exist, I am not aware of any attempt having been made to estimate as a whole the soluble constituents removed annually from the varied formations which constitute the crust of the earth. Most of you, no doubt, are aware of the valuable information contained in the Sixth Report of the Rivers Pollution Commission, and the wonderful elaboration and accuracy of all the information relating to the potable waters of Great Britain.

When first I turned over its pages, it at once occurred to me that here is the very thing which a geologist wants for the solution of several interesting problems. I made up my mind that I would use it on the very first opportunity. The present I consider a suitable occasion. In

page 131 of the report is a table of the average composition of unpolluted potable waters, commencing with
rain water, but it is chiefly the upland surface waters
that I purpose dealing with to-night. In the first column
we get the "total solid impurity," which means the total
ingredients held in solution, consisting practically of the
soluble inorganic ingredients, as the proportion of organic
constituents is almost invariably very weak. For an
explanation of the other columns I quote from a letter
Dr. Frankland kindly sent me, and without which I could
have made but a limited use of the stores of information
collected, through the analyses having been made in a
form suited to the immediate object of the Commission.
He says:

. . "'*Ammonia*' is generally present in very small
quantity, and may be left out of consideration. It is
probably always present as Carbonate of Ammonia, and
is therefore an *inorganic* constituent.

'*Nitrogen*' as nitrates and nitrites means almost
invariably nitrogen as nitrates, since the occurrence of
nitrites in any but shallow well water is exceedingly rare.
If you multiply the numbers in this column by six, you
will obtain with close approximation the weight of nitrates
in the water.

'*Chlorine.*'—This exists practically as 'chloride of
sodium,' and if you multiply the numbers in the chlorine
column by 1·65, you will get approximately the proportion
of common salt. 'Temporary hardness' means in most
cases (except water from Dolomite or Coal-measures, in
which there is a good deal of carbonate of magnesia)
carbonate of lime, with a little carbonate of magnesia.

'*Permanent hardness*' means, except as aforesaid,
hardness produced by sulphate of lime; and if you
multiply the numbers in the column by 1·86, you will

get approximately the proportion of *sulphate of lime*, with a little sulphate of magnesia.

Of ingredients of any importance there only remain: Alkaline sulphates—that is, sulphate of soda and sulphate of potash.

Carbonate of Soda.

Silica.

Iron.

Of these, the last two are rarely present in any but very small proportion—about 1 part of silica and 0·1 part of peroxide of iron in 100,000 parts of water."

With this preliminary information I proceed to explain my application of the data for a solution of the problem before us—that is, the estimation of the total solids annually removed by the solvent action of rain from the surface of England and Wales.

To have guaged every river and stream delivering into the sea during a period of say ten years, and to have analysed the water in each case from day to day under the varying circumstances of the dry weather and flood flow, would no doubt have been the most accurate way of determining the question. It is needless to say such a course is fraught with too much labour and expense to be practicable to any individual. There is, however, another method used by engineers, accustomed to design water-works, for estimating, in the absence of gaugings, the flow off the land which gives us what we want with sufficiently close approximation.

By taking the mean rainfall over a given area, and then allowing a certain depth for evaporation and absorption, with judgment, the flow off the land can be arrived at with tolerable accuracy. In the case of several rivers, through elaborate gaugings and observations of the mean *rainfall* of the basin, it is known with certainty what the proportion is. In the Thames basin, for instance, with a mean rainfall estimated at 27 inches, only 8 inches reaches the sea; whereas in the basin of Loch Katrine, in the area of rainfall exceeding 75 inches of Symons' Hyetographical map, 81·7 inches, according to Bateman, and at Rivington Pike, in the area of between 40 and 50 inches of the same map, according to Stephenson, 39·8 inches runs off the ground. The yield of a gathering-ground is in all cases determined by the total rainfall, the nature of the rocks, and the steepness of the land surface.

In a porous area and small rainfall, like the Thames basin, the maximum of loss takes place, measuring in that case 19 inches per annum; while in the mountainous tracts of siliceous rocks in Wales and Cumberland it is doubtful if more than 10 inches is lost.

My method of procedure thus has been to take out the areas of rainfall from Symons' Hyetographical map attached to the report, to allow to the best of my judgment for evaporation, and then, grouping the formations together in each rainfall area, to estimate the number of tons of water yielded by each gathering-ground annually. Instead of, however, taking out each group exactly as given in Dr. Frankland's table referred to, I have roughly divided them where it could readily be done; and in other cases, judging their relative proportions, I have added up the figures opposite the "Total solids in solution" given for surface water off each formation, and then averaged the results before multiplying the total yield of water by the fraction of 100,000 in that way obtained. I consider that this method is more likely to be near the truth than a more minute analysis. A reference to the table prepared will, however, explain the operation better than any description by me. I have exercised very considerable care in the calculations, so I trust they may be relied upon as close approximations.

As there is a certain amount of chloride of sodium in most rain water, due to the spray of the sea being carried inland, I have deducted the average amount from the "Total solid impurity," as not being a product of denudation; but I have not deducted the other solids in solution in the rain, for primarily they must emanate from the land itself. This, however, is but a small fraction of the whole.

Looking at the more remarkable features developed by this analysis, perhaps the one I was least prepared for is the curious way in which the smallest percentages of solids in solution, such as is contained in water from granitic and metamorphic rocks, rise in the aggregate, through the greater rainfall on these formations, to the total solids in solution from such specially soluble rocks as constitute the Thames basin.

With few exceptions, in England the greatest rainfall follows the older formations, whether as cause or effect it is difficult to say; but the older formations constituting the higher grounds they collect more rain, while the denudation being so much greater has no doubt had a tendency to cut down the rocks formerly overlying them so as to expose the old rocks forming the core beneath. Will not this help us to understand those grand examples of denudation in Wales so forcibly shown by Ramsay to have taken place, and which I called your attention to in my last address.

Is it not strikingly apparent from this what a leveller the rain is? Certainly it was never brought to my mind so vividly before.

A reference to the Geological and to the Rainfall maps of England, and a comparison of them, shows that the

mountainous districts, generally composed of rocks from
the Cambrian to the Carboniferous, being situated on the
west coast intercept the greatest rain, which is from the
south and north-west, and that here in Devon, Wales,
and the Lake district of Cumberland and Westmoreland,
the rainfall ranges from 50 to over 75 inches.

The extremes of rainfall in 1874 were at five stations
in the Lake district, from 107·53 at Little Langdale to
148·79 at Seathwaite; while in Wales, at three stations,
it was from 116·56 to 149·00 inches. The smallest, as
might be expected, was on the east coast, ranging from
12·85 at Chatteris, in the Isle of Ely, to 14·97 at Ipswich;
and in Wales from 22·33 at Holywell, to 27·96 at St.
Asaph.

The rainfall, expressed in inches, if distributed evenly
over England and Wales, would have been for 1874, 34·02,
or 1·50 below the average from 1860 to 1865, if we take
the mean of all the stations. Estimated, however, by
areas, as given in Symons' map, the mean rainfall of
England and Wales, is 31.988 or say 32 inches.*

Dividing the country in sections, as shown in the
table, and estimating each separately, gives a total of
68,450,936,960 tons of water run off the area of England
and Wales annually, equal to 18·3 inches in depth, which
leaves 13·7 inches for evaporation.† The total solids in

---

* The difference arises from the fall at some of the mountain
stations being much in excess of the average; and the areas of this
excessive fall being restricted, the mean of all the principal stations
naturally gives the excess we see. Mr. Symons, in a letter to me, says
he has never worked out the mean rainfall, but is "under the impression
it would come out about 35 inches."

† It must not be lost sight of that it is the *evaporation* only that
affects our calculations. Water that *percolates* will find its way eventually
into the river system, or directly by springs into the sea itself. This
water is, of course, more highly charged with mineral matter than surface
water, and may help to balance flood surface water, which often contains
less than the mean quantity of soluble mineral matter. On the whole,
it will be seen that the figures work out fairly in unison with each other.

solution amount to 8,370,630 tons, or 12·23 parts in every 100,000 of water. This total includes, calculating on the method pointed out by Dr. Frankland, and on the averages of the samples 9·50 parts of the carbonates and the sulphates of lime and magnesia, the sulphates predominating in the averages of the water from all the rocks below the New Red and the carbonates in those above the Permian, reaching its maximum in the cretaceous. The average amount of chloride of sodium, deducting ·36 as that contained in the rain, is 1·66 for the upland waters. The nitrates amount to ·08.*

There is now left ·99 for the alkaline sulphates and carbonates of soda, silica, and peroxide of iron.

I have intentionally taken the upland surface water as a Geological basis to work upon, for in consequence of drainage works, artificial manures, and other disturbing causes incidental to a thickly populated country, the primitive denudation of the world is not accurately represented by the constituents held in solution in most of our river waters far down their course. The chloride of sodium in the Thames water, for instance, as supplied by five different companies, averaged in 1873 3·1 parts in 100,000, and most of this is no doubt of artificial origin. In the Mersey at its junction with the Irwell the chloride of sodium is 4·12, and in the Irwell at its junction with the Mersey it reaches the enormous amount of 21·28 per 100,000.

Again, the drainage and culture of calcareous soils adds considerably to the amount of the carbonates and sulphates of lime held in solution, and these disturbing

---

* The averages of all the samples of upland water give 12·66 as the total solids in solution, which is a very close approximation to the 12·23 estimated in the totals as before described, and is calculated to verify the accuracy of the method I have adopted.

causes I have endeavoured to eliminate from my calculations.

If we may estimate the various solids held in solution at 15 feet to the ton, the weight of limestone,* the amount of denudation if distributed equally over the area of England and Wales reckoned at 58,300 square miles would be .0077 of a foot per century, that is it would take 12,978 years to reduce it one foot.

It is certainly a rather remarkable coincidence of figures that Professor Prestwich, I find, in his address to the Geological Society of London, 1872, calculates that the Thames removes from the Chalk, Upper Greensand, Oolitic strata and Marlstone, carbonate of lime alone to the extent of 1 foot over its basin in 13,200 years. This he arrives at by referring 10 grains to the gallon on the total discharge at Kingston to these strata, estimated at 2072 square miles. The total denudation due to solids in solution over the whole area is, as will be seen further on, 149 tons per square mile per annum, as against 140 tons of carbonate of lime alone removed from the restricted area calculated by Professor Prestwich.

Taking the carbonates and sulphates of lime and magnesium at 9·5 and 15 feet to the ton, that would represent the removal of those substances in solution at the rate of 1 foot in 16,707 years.

The Chloride of Sodium estimated at 1·66 would represent the removal of 1 foot in thickness (16 feet to the ton) of Rock Salt in 89,640 years.

The remaining portions consisting of Silica, Alkaline Sulphates, Peroxide of Iron, &c., have not been directly determined by analysis, and are therefore only very

---

* Some very compact limestones only contain 18 feet to the ton.

rough approximations. The analyses of river waters by
Bischof* shew these ingredients to be very variable,
even in the same river at different times. If we estimate
them at 12 feet to the ton, ·99 parts per 100,000, would
give 200,405 years to remove 1 foot in thickness.

After very carefully reviewing my data and calculations, I am of opinion that these figures in the main
represent very nearly what would be the denudation of
England and Wales in their primitive condition, before
the hand of man had interfered much with the surface.

If, however, we desire to know what is now being
removed, I think we must increase this estimate by
one-fifth, as Dr. Frankland's analyses clearly shew that
cultivation of the land, and drainage especially in
calcareous districts, increases the soluble substances in
the water to a very considerable extent.

It would have been impossible to rely upon the data
had not a very great number of samples been analysed,
taken, be it observed, at all seasons of the year, for we
find these averages tend to correct one another, and to
give a very close approximation to the aggregate result.

Stated simply, this then, is the result. If we imagine
the area of England and Wales, consisting of 58,300
square miles, to form one river basin, the delivery of
water by such river would be 68,450,936,960 tons, or
18·3 inches per annum, containing a total of 8,370,630
tons of solids in solution, representing a general lowering
of the surface from that cause alone of ·0077 of a foot
per century, or one foot in 12,978 years.

Thus far we have got with our geological modulus of
time; but before attempting to apply it to the solution of
the larger problems of Geology, let us see if we can

* Chemical and Physical Geology, Vol. 1, p. 76.

institute a comparison between England and the other parts of the world best known and Geologically surveyed.

A reference to the Geological Map of the world, constructed by Jules Marcou, shews that in the continent of Europe the principal difference from the Geology of England is the much greater development of what in his classification are Crystalline Rocks, consisting of gneiss, metamorphic rocks, granite, porphyries and trappean rocks, principally situated in Norway and Sweden, and the Tertiaries in mid-Europe, between the Baltic and the Black Seas. Roughly speaking it is easy to see that in England and Wales a line may be drawn, dividing them into two nearly equal halves, on the western side of which are the rocks from the New Red downwards, and on the eastern the rocks from the lias upwards, including the Tertiaries. I have, at considerable trouble, calculated the areas of the several formations of Europe from Jules Marcou's Map.

They are approximately as follows:—

	English Square Miles.
Modern Rocks	468,277.
Tertiary do.	613,043.
Cretaceous Rocks	552,282.
Jurassic do.	246,983.
New Red Sandstone	466,292.
Carboniferous Rocks	181,940.
Paleozoic or Grauwacke	463,661.
Crystalline Rocks	714,960.
Volcanoes and Basalt	13,062.
Total	3,720,500.

It will thus be seen that the formations from the base of the Jurassic up to the Modern Rocks constitute almost exactly half of the continent, and those from the New

Red downwards, inclusive of the Volcanoes and Basalt, the other half; consequently the dividing line is nearly the same in the Continent as in England and Wales. The Geological structure of England is almost an epitome of that of Europe, excepting that in the Continent the Carboniferous rocks are in less force, and the Tertiary and Metamorphic in greater.

The average solubility of the rocks, I suspect, is not very different on the Continent from that of England, but the rainfall is less, averaging, according to Sir John Herschell,* 23 inches for the *non*mountainous districts, and 42 inches for the mountainous ones.

We may, therefore, assume that the total solids in solution removed annually are proportionately not so great as in England, excepting in the Swiss mountains, where, no doubt the denudation is more rapid than in any area in England or Wales.

As bearing upon this comparison, I have collected all the available information I could as to the discharge of several of the principal rivers of Europe; and, though the data is imperfect in many particulars, the facts bear out the views I have just stated.

The Rhine, the Rhone, and the Danube all rise in the Alpine district, and flow to the west, the south, and the east, through formations of which the basin of the Thames and the Severn would form, perhaps, the nearest English equivalents. The basin of the Rhine is rather more than the area of England and Wales; so we may readily institute a comparison between the country drained by the Rhine and England. Above Lauterbourg, its area is 63,000 square miles, and the annual discharge of the river is 34,216,560,000 tons, equal to a depth of 8·53

---

* Physical Geography, 4th Edition, p. 241.

inches.* The rainfall is from 16·4 inches at Frankfort-on-the-Main to 26·3 at Bonn; but, of course, it is also fed by the Alpine snows through the Lake of Constance. The mean of the analyses of solids in solution, as given by Bischof, is 17·1, say 17 in 100,000, this gives 5,816,805 tons per annum, or 92·3 tons per square mile.

The Rhone at Avignon has an area of 35,745 square miles, and an annual discharge of 53,144,040,600 tons, equal to 22·86 inches in depth. The mean of four analyses given by Bischof is 15·6, which will give 8,290,464 tons of solids removed per annum in solution, or 232 tons per square mile.

The Danube has an area of 310,000 square miles, and the mean discharge into the Black Sea, from ten years' observation is, according to Sir C. A. Hartley, M.I.C.E.,† 207,000 cubic feet per second, equal to 181,332,000,000 tons per annum.

The discharge appears, however, to be very variable, the maximum being 383,000 cubic feet per second in 1871, and the minimum 125,000 cubic feet per second in the years 1863 and 1866.

The rainfall at Sulina also varies from 10·03 inches to 34·28; but whether it is as variable over the whole basin I cannot say.

This discharge equals a depth of 6·8 inches run off the ground, or one-third of the mean rainfall at Sulina. The amount of solids in solution was 12·42 at Vienna. Bischof, however, only gives the one analysis. If this is an average quantity, the total solids in solution would amount to 22,521,434 tons per annum, or 72·7 tons per square mile, or as nearly as possible one-third of the

* Beardmore's "Manual of Hydrology."

† "Minutes of Proceedings of the Institution of Civil Engineers," vol. xxxvi, p. 224.

average amount of matter held in suspension, which is given as 67,760,000 tons, estimated from surface samples.

The total drainage area of these three great rivers is, therefore, 408,745 square English miles, their annual discharge 268,692,600,600 tons, and the total solids in solution 36,628,703 tons.

Comparing this with the calculated denudation of England, it amounts in England to 143·5 tons per square mile and 90 tons per square mile in the three European river basins.

The data for these latter calculations are, indeed, insufficient, more especially as regards the Danube, from the absence of analyses at more points than Vienna. I think it extremely probable that the estimate should be increased, as the direct determination of the solids in solution amounts to 14·14.

The result is, however, in accordance with what we should *a priori* expect; the greater rainfall on the western coast produces its effect upon the land, not only in removing detritus mechanically, but in its solvent action upon the rocks. It works more quickly.

The Garronne removes 142 tons per square mile.

The Seine contains, according to two analyses by Bischof, 21·72 parts per 100,000. The drainage area is at Paris 17,111 square miles, and the discharge equals 6·98 inches per annum; it therefore removes about 97 tons of solids in solution per square mile.

The Thames, estimating the discharge at eight inches per annum and the total solids in solution at 29·26, as given by Prestwich, removes 149 tons per square mile per annum.

It is thus seen that there is much less variation than one would have expected between the soluble constituents removed by one river and another; for if we compare the maximum of our examples, which is the Rhone at 232 tons per square mile per annum, with the minimum, the Danube at 72·7 tons, we find there is only about the same difference between them as there is between the maximum and minimum annual discharge of water of the Danube itself! If, on the other hand, we compare the quantity of solids in solution removed to the solids in suspension, we find that the former is a much more constant quantity. The detritus carried down to the Black Sea by the Danube was, in 1866, 12,500,000 tons, and in 1871 it rose to 154,000,000.

It is also evident that the character of the solids in solution is determined by the nature of the rocks the water flows over. On the western half of England the sulphates of lime in the upland waters predominate over the carbonates in the proportion of 7·15 to 2·9; while in the Thames area the carbonate of lime is in excess of the sulphate in the proportion of about two to one. It is extremely probable, therefore, that over the whole area of England and Wales the carbonates and sulphates of lime are about equal.

On taking the mean of eighteen analyses of water from European rivers, given by Bischof, I find the carbonates in excess of the sulphates of lime in the proportion of 9·32 to 1·79. Bischof, himself, says, "Among the mineral substances in these rivers, carbonate of lime is always in the largest quantity." The basins of these rivers are, however, composed nearly wholly of the strata above the New Red Sandstone, excepting as regards the Crystalline rocks. The Volga is a river flowing through the New Red; of this water I have no analysis, but, as might be expected, the sulphates of lime predominate over the carbonates in the Caspian

Sea, which receives its waters. The mean of two analyses, one by Göbel, the other by H. Rose, gives 89·6 parts per 100,000 of sulphate of lime to 18·9 of bicarbonate of lime.

It is evident, therefore, that, estimated over the whole Continent of Europe, and taking into consideration the proportions of the various rocks, the carbonates of lime will still be in excess of the sulphates.

The extensive development of Carboniferous strata in England, together with the New Red, to a large extent accounts for this diversity between England and the Continent; but the proportional excess of sulphates of lime in the Thames water over the Continental European river waters may perhaps be partly traced to the more artificial state of the Thames basin. If the information we require is limited with respect to Europe, it is still more restricted in relation to the rest of the world. Of the geology of Asia our knowledge is very partial and very indefinite, as a glance at Jules Marcou's map will show. To calculate the proportion of the various formations would be impossible, with the accuracy required for our purpose. Dr. Frankland has, however, kindly supplied me with several unpublished analyses of water in various parts of the world, and among them is one of Tienshan Lake, in China, in which the total solids in solution are 13·10 per 100,000. Of these 5·31 are due to carbonate of lime and 1·91 to sulphate of lime. The River Wangpoo, above the influence of ordinary tides, has 10·46 per 100,000 of solids in solution, of which 4·14 are carbonates and 1·57 sulphates of lime.

Above the bridge at Wangdoo the water holds 21·54 of solids in solution, of which 9·31 are carbonates and 1·65 sulphates of lime; at Tyking 30·52 of total solids in solution, of which 11·30 are carbonates and 3·88 sul·

phates of lime.* The chloride of sodium in Tienshan Lake amounted to 1·71, and in the Wangpoo to 1·48. The Tisai (Tienshan) Lake, according to another analysis, holds 10·90 solids in solution, of which 5·31 are carbonate and 2·32 sulphate of lime, while the chloride of sodium is 1·73.

There are other analyses by Dr. Frankland, but I cannot make any deductions from them, as the samples were apparently taken within the influence of the tides.

In South America an analysis of the Parana in front of Carabelos gives 10·08 of total solids in solution, of which ·28 was carbonate of lime and 3·03 sulphate, and 2·97 chloride of sodium, the nitrates amounting to ·42·

It is rather a pity this analysis did not determine the separate amount of each constituent, as there is a large balance to be accounted for, viz., 3·38 to be divided between the alkaline sulphates, carbonate of soda, silica, and iron.

I have now pretty nearly exhausted all the information I can bring to bear on what, for brevity, I shall call "*Soluble Denudation.*"

The rainfall is so variable in different parts of the world, that it is difficult to make an estimate of the average "Soluble Denudation" of the globe; but we find that Nature, on the whole, averages the results; and, though there is as much as 300 inches of annual rainfall in some places in the Tropics, and 600 inches, or 50 feet, on the Khāsi Hills at Cherra Poonjee, on the other hand we have great rainless districts in the interior of Africa and Asia. The River Nile, with a basin of 600,000 miles, above Cairo, according to Girard, runs off only 3·78 inches per annum; but this, if the data of my calcula-

---

* Probably affected by the tide,

tions are reliable, must be in excess of the actual depth.*

The Ganges at Sikreegulee, with a basin of 330,000 English square miles, runs off 20·51 inches per annum; while if we take the Ganges and Brahmapootra together as having a joint basin of 432,000 geographical miles,† equal to 570,240 English square miles, and the joint discharge at 12,736,154,880 cubic feet per annum, according to Lyell's statement, based on Mr. Everest's calculation,‡ the amount run off the ground per annum will be 50·8 inches.

This tremendous depth is due to the rainfall on the Himalayas, and is greater than the Rhone at Geneva, which is 48·20. The Mississippi and Missouri have a basin of 1,300,000 English square miles; and according to Messrs. Humphreys and Abbott, as quoted by Lyell, 132·36 cubic miles of water are discharged annually, equal to 8.19 inches in depth over the whole area.§

Keeping the above facts in view, and seeing how constant a quantity the solids in solution are, for when the rainfall is small the river water as a rule holds a larger proportionate quantity of dissolved matter; and taking into consideration what we know of the geology of the world, I think we have sufficient grounds for a provisional assumption that about 100 tons of rocky matter is dissolved by rain per English square mile per annum.

---

* The mean annual delivery of the Nile is calculated by M. Talabot at 101,000 cubic feet per second, and its supposed drainage area, according to Herschell, 520,000 square geographical, or 686,400 statute miles. This would give only 2·01 inches run off the ground. (See Herschell's "Physical Geography," p. 210, 4th Edition.)

† Herschell's "Physical Geography."

‡ "Principles of Geology," 10th Ed., pp. 481–3.

§ This is arrived at by dividing the cubic quantity of sediment by the fraction representing the proportion it bears to the water, that is $\frac{1}{1531}$ Beardmore calculates the depth run off the ground at 8·40 inches.— "*Manual of* Hydrology."

Of this total, if we allot 50 tons to carbonate of lime, 20 tons to sulphate of lime, 7 to silica, 4 to carbonate of magnesia, 4 to sulphate of magnesia, 1 to peroxide of iron, 8 to chloride of sodium, and 6 to the alkaline carbonates and sulphates, we shall probably be as near the truth as present data will allow us to come.

Before leaving the subject, let us now see what light, if any, these figures throw upon geological time.

How can we approach the question? If, as is generally supposed, the sea contains only what is washed into it from the land,* and we can estimate its mineral contents in tons, we at once get a minimum measure of the age of the Earth; whether it will be possible to arrive at a maximum we shall see further on. According to Herschell, the ocean contains 2,494,500 billions of tons of water; and the mean of Dr. Frankland's analyses of sea water gives 48·9 tons of carbonate of lime and magnesia, and 1017 tons of sulphate of lime and magnesia in 100,000 tons. Taking the area of all the land in the world at 51 millions of English square miles, there is in the ocean, in round numbers, 1,222 billions of tons of carbonate of lime and magnesia, or sufficient to cover the whole of it at 15 feet to the ton 12·9 feet thick; and of sulphate of lime and magnesia 25,369 billions of tons, or sufficient to cover it 267·6 feet thick. If, then, we reckon the whole of the sulphates removed from the land at 20 tons per square mile per annum, it would take in round numbers 25

---

* Herschell says. "Physical Geography," p. 21. As the sea continually receives the drainage of all the land, besides having in the course of countless ages, washed over and over again the disintegrated materials of successive continents, it must of course hold in solution all the saline ingredients capable of being separated and taken up by such lixiviation in cold water; in fact, in greater or less quantity, every soluble substance in nature—such, at least, whose existence in extremely dilute solution are not incompatible.

millions of years to accumulate the quantity of sulphate of lime and magnesia contained in sea water, but only 480,000 years to renew the carbonate of lime and magnesia, at the rate of 50 tons per square mile of land surface per annum. We know, however, that the carbonate of lime is constantly being removed by testaceous animals, corals and foraminifera.

There is also good reason to suppose that the sulphates of lime are also decomposed by decaying organic matter, and we know from numberless analyses that there is always present in sea water a large quantity of free carbonic acid,* which the result of the "Challenger" expedition proves is sufficient to entirely dissolve the calcareous portions of the dead foraminifera before they in sinking reach the bottom of the greater ocean depths.

The quantity of sulphuric acid in sea water also varies considerably. It is probable, also, that marine organisms can in some way directly utilise the sulphate of lime. Bischof shows very beautifully and clearly that the amount of carbonic acid in sea water is subject to very little variation, and that it is present in sufficient quantity to dissolve five times as much of the earthy carbonates as are actually dissolved, and "that the sea water is so far below its point of saturation as regards carbonate of lime, can only depend upon the constant separation of this carbonate by testaceous animals. By this separation, however, the carbonic acid which had dissolved this carbonate always returns again into the sea water. In the sea, therefore, the solution of carbonates and their separation by organic agency go on constantly, no addition of carbonic acid from without being required." He also shows that the carbonic acid which has been

* Bischof, "Chemical Geology," vol. i, p. 103.

removed in the vapour of water returns to the sea by the rivers.

If we turn to the chlorides consisting principally of chloride of sodium, we find the mean of Dr. Frankland's analyses to be 3,259 parts in every 100,000, which gives 81,295 billions of tons; or, at 16 feet to the ton, sufficient to cover the whole of the land 914·9 feet deep! * This is certainly a startling result. Reckoning all the chlorides brought into the sea by the rivers annually at 8 tons to the square mile, it would take, in even numbers, 200 millions of years to renew the chlorides of the sea. I have now, I hope, enabled you to form a quantitative idea of the soluble constituents of the globe, so far as we can measure them in water.

The greater portion of the land of the globe is composed of sedimentary rocks, themselves laid down in the sea, lakes, inland seas, or estuaries.

The constituents of the crust of the earth have been again and again dissolved, carried into the sea, separated therefrom by organisms, or by evaporation from portions that have from time to time been cut off from the general ocean, or in that minute chloride dust Dr. Frankland so beautifully shews is constantly being carried into the air through the spray of every wave. What a lengthened vista does not this disclose?

We cannot see the beginning, all that is plain to us is the sequence, the circulation.

The matter of the world is continually changing place —its solvent is the rain, its carrier the river, its receiver and distributor the ocean. How many times

---

* As shewing the necessity to the Geologist of a quantatitive knowledge of the constituents of the Earth, even so great a reasoner as Lyell imagines it possible that all the salt in the sea could, during a subsidence of the land, be evaporated in the Runn of Cutch.—See "Principles."

the matter of this solid land on which we stand has been in solution, suspension, or moving to and fro on the shore or the sea bottom, it is impossible to say. In the present state of science it defies calculation to reach a maximum beyond which we can say the age of the earth does not extend, for the calculations based upon the form of the earth and tidal retardation * are fallacious, through leaving out agencies that we know are at work, and which the calculations I have to-night submitted to you bring out in greater force.

I have said nothing as yet of the comparative potency of mechanical erosion as compared with chemical in reducing the crust of the earth. Strictly speaking, one, however, is the complement of the other. The chemical agency decomposes the matrix, and separates the particles, which the mechanical force of the river in flood carries to the sea. The actual degradation of the rocks by mechanical movement of water containing stones, is a very small matter. The effect of tidal action I have before dwelt upon and explained.

The ocean, I consider, acts merely as a mechanical distributer of matter, which has been introduced from the land; and though tidal action has the power in certain cases of excavating very wide, deep, and long gullies in the shallow seas, its effect is limited by the force and direction of the current, so that it cannot work out its hollows beyond a certain depth below the general floor of the sea. The action of subaërial denudation is on the other hand unlimited, except by the sea-level. It can degrade, excavate, and deepen, so long as anything is left above the water.

The amount of matter brought down mechanically into the sea, in the case of the Danube, we see was

---

* Sir William Thompson.

$\frac{1}{3060}$ of the water, or about three times the calculated solids in solution. The maximum amount being $\frac{1}{465}$, and the minimum $\frac{1}{73600}$. The solids in solution come down constantly; the mud is pushed along in times of flood. According to Messrs. Humphreys and Abbott the solids in suspension in the Mississippi are $\frac{1}{1321}$ of the water. If we were to take the solids removed mechanically and in solution at six times those in solution, which is a very high estimate, we should have over the whole of the globe 600 tons of denuded matter annually per square mile. Taking the sedimentary crust of the earth at ten miles thick throughout—a moderate estimate—and allowing for the denudation of the sea and the amount added to sediments by volcanic ejections, matter equal to one-third that which is denuded from the land, we should have annually removed and deposited matter equal to 800 tons per square mile of land surface, or 40,800 million tons annually. The total surface of the globe is 197 millions of English square miles. A cubic mile of rock at $13\frac{1}{2}$ feet to the ton would weigh 10,903,552,000 tons, so that to cover the whole surface of the globe one mile deep with sediment from the land at the rate of 800 tons per square mile of land surface, would take 52,647,052 years, or 526 million years in round numbers for ten miles deep.*

---

*It is not necessary for the accuracy of this calculation that the sedimentary crust of the earth should everywhere now measure 10 miles thick, or even that it should average that thickness, indeed if it were so the estimate of time would have to be enormously increased, because the rocks of one formation are largely derived from the sediments of preceding formations, therefore it is probable that the *maximum* thickness of the whole of the sedimentary deposits is a true guage of the average thickness of rock which has been removed by denudation from the entire surface of the globe. The maximum thickness of the whole of the known sedimentary formations is variously estimated at from 14 to 17 miles.

At 13½ feet to the ton, 800 tons per annum would give one foot of denudation of the land each 2,581 years; so it will be seen that the above is a very moderate estimate of the time which has elapsed since the first of the sedimentary rocks, we are acquainted with, were laid down, on the hypothesis that the denuding agencies had the same average potency as now, and that the area of land surface has been constant.

But it will be said—What proof have we that the denuding agencies were not formerly much greater and more active than now? I reply with Lyell: We have no evidence that such was the case.

It is true that, according to fossil evidence in the earlier periods, the earth appeared to be of a more uniform temperature than now.[*]

This, it seems to me, would act in the contrary direction, and tend to reduce the rainfall, as it is the mixing of air of different temperatures that produces rain. Again, if we assume the land surface to have been proportionately to the sea greater than it is at present, the evaporating surface would have been lessened; in fact, the forces of nature in this, as in other cases, tend to equalise themselves.

In opposition, therefore, to astronomical calculations, I am prepared to maintain the position of Hutton and Lyell. We may speculate on a beginning, but we can find no trace of it by geological methods, for in no respect do these earlier sediments, so far as they have yet been investigated, lead us up to a particular rock from which the first sediments were derived. The beginning may be a logical necessity, and astronomical and mathematical reasoning may eventually throw some

---

[*] See Hooker on Carboniferous plants, Memoirs of the Geological Survey, Vol. II. Also papers by Nordenskiöld and Judd in Geological *Magazine* and Dana's Manual of Geology.

light upon it, but before then a multitude of circumstances will have to be considered by the mathematician,
which he often ignores, through unfamiliarity with
geological reasoning.

· The calculations I have had the pleasure of laying
before you have been laborious, but they have given
proportion and definiteness to my ideas of geological
cause and effect, and their relations to time. Probably
I have dealt too much in figures to make my address
as interesting in its delivery as the subject will be found
on closer study. It is so vast and complicated that I
cannot hope to have given you more than a faint outline
of the whole picture as it presents itself to my mind.
The value of figures is best seen by those who work them
out; but if I have succeeded in demonstrating that the
views of geology taken by our greatest masters come out
with greater force and truth, the more they are put to
the test of calculation—then I have achieved quite as
much as I can expect to do, or could hope that you would
patiently listen to.

In resigning the Chair of the Society, I can only
express to you the satisfaction it has been to me to meet
you all from year to year since I first joined the Society,
and during the term of my Presidentship, and to thank
you for the uniform consideration and courtesy with
which all, I have said, has been treated. In welcoming my successor to the chair, I can only say that
we shall all extend to him the same feeling of good
fellowship, begotten of kindred pursuits, which will
enable him to perform his duties in the satisfactory
manner we know he is capable of, and assist him in
upholding the dignity of the science we all love.

NOVEMBER 14TH, 1876.

THE PRESIDENT, HUGH F. HALL, F.G.S., in the Chair.

JAMES H. JOHNSON, F.G.S., and WILLIAM H. COOKE were elected Ordinary Members.

The following communications were read:—

SOME NOTES OF THE GEOLOGY OF LONDON-DERRY, MADE DURING HOLIDAY RAMBLES IN THAT COUNTY.

BY JAMES L. McCLAY.

IF, on leaving Derry, you ascend any of the hills which command a view of the valley of the Foyle, you will be much struck with the physical features of the country. You will see that it is all dotted over with hills, many of them of considerable height. For instance, here is Slieve Boe, or the " Hill of the Cow," which is about 1,000 feet high. From the hill between the Foyle and Glendermott on to the Knockanduns, or " Hill Forts," in the parish of Tamlaghtfinlagan, hill after hill meets the view. But there is one thing which can be seen from the valleys of the Foyle, the Faughan, or the Roe, and that is what is called Magilligan Rock. At a distance it resembles two steps or terraces, and presents the appearance of a single rock, but when you come to close quarters you find it to be part of the basaltic mountain called Benevenagh. The next thing here which would attract attention is the remarkable regularity of the face of the basalt. The rocks curve and wind about from Downhill to Larganteagh in a manner which forcibly reminds one of a coast line. Up in the higher part, near Duncroon, I searched for marine shell, but found none; but at the base of the mountain, and even as far inland as Bovevagh, marine shells are dug up in great quantities, which plainly enough indicate that this basin was formerly covered by the sea. After having carefully examined the physical geology of this part of the country, I came to the conclusion that the valley of the Foyle was never entirely roofed over with basalt, as some geologists suppose. You will observe that the River Roe forms a sort of rough natural boundary between the Palæozoic and the newer formations. The ancient sea shore must have trended from above Bovevagh, along the left bank of the Roe, to near Limavady, from thence past Eglinton to the "foot" of the Faughan, and from Culmore to Greencastle, as at present. You also see that the basalt is spread over the chalk, and as we know that the chalk was formed under the sea, we may reasonably conclude that all the country from the Roe to near Carrickfergus was submerged at the time of the volcanic eruption in the North of Ireland. After the bulk of the volcanic rocks had been spread over the counties of Derry and Antrim, and before the volcanic disturbances had ceased, the older land which connected Ireland and Scotland must have subsided. The bed of the Foyle was slightly elevated at the time of these eruptions, but, being almost outside of the upheaving force, its basin was not much changed. My reason for stating that the channel between Scotland and Ireland must have subsided at this time is that the basalt, the chalk, and the clay all dip towards the sea at a small angle. I did not quite satisfy myself on this point, but my attention was called to it by reading a passage in "Sampson's Statistical Survey of the County," in which he says, referring to a bed of clay on which the chalk rests: "It dips with the lime under the sea near Downhill; at Benbradagh it rises with the lime nearly to the summit of the mountain." There is no doubt that the same force that caused the upheaval of the basin of the Foyle and the counties of Derry and Antrim also caused the channel to sink. The glens which separate Benevenagh from Kedy, and Kedy from Donald's Hill are the result of subaërial denudation. The country between Coleraine and Swatragh has all been overspread with igneous rocks, but a great body of water must have swept over it from the west, as we find quantities of quartz, schist, and granite pebbles on the surface, and the stone at Ballyclough must have travelled or been carried by ice from the western side of the county. I visited Lough Feagh, which lies between Slieve Gallion and the Fir Mountains. How did the lake come to be here? is about the first question one would ask oneself. It stretches for more than a mile in length, and half-a-mile in breadth, and the peculiar state of the weather made it look much larger. I must say that for the first time I saw the force of Professor Ramsey's theory of the formation of lake basins. Situated as it is so much above sea level, and in such a position, we are naturally puzzled as to its origin. Slieve Gallion, or what may be taken as a continuation of it, slopes down to its north and north-east sides, and on the Tyrone side we have the Fir Mountains hemming it it in. Scattered over these mountains, and all along the Tyrone side, we find enormous blocks of granite. Perhaps I should say syenitic granite, because I noticed, besides quartz, felspar, and mica, an ingredient which I took to be hornblende, in addition to iron pyrites, which is very distinctly seen. These huge blocks are tossed promiscuously over the drift, some of them have sunk a few feet in it, but we see that they were dropped after the *drift* had been deposited. We know that the parent rock from which these boulders were broken off is situated on Slieve Gallion, and that they must have travelled from there over Mobuy, or the "Yellow Plain," and thence across the lough to these mountains. Now, as some of these blocks measure from 500 to 800 cubic feet, or even more, we at once see that no known power except ice could have transported them. Between Draperstown and Feeny we have splendid examples of subaërial denudation. At Lagnapaiste, or the "Hole of the Beast," there is a very pretty waterfall, caused by the outcrop of the schist. At this place we again find our matter-of-fact geology stepping in and spoiling a fine legend. As I have already explained, the pool is called the "Hole of the Beast." From this diagram you will see that another small stream flows into the Owen Reagh, or "Grey River," a little below Lagnapaiste. At the time the Drift was deposited, the meeting of two bodies of water here caused an eddy, and piled up this little gravel hill. At Lagnapaiste, Drumslieve, and Streeve we have nothing but Palæozoic and Post-tertiary rocks, the former dipping south-west, west, and north-west; whereas, if we draw a line from Knockan Bridge to Carric on the one side, and from Carric to Donald's Hill and along the valley of the Roe to a little beyond Dungiven on the other side, we have the Post-tertiary, Cainozoic, Mesozoic, and Palæozoic all represented. At Raliagh, and extending west and north-west, the secondary rocks rest unconformably on the schist, and dip in an opposite direction. If the Coal-measures have not been denuded previous to the deposition of the newer rocks, we might calculate with tolerable certainty on finding coal in this basin. There is also a natural basin near Limavady, where coal might be looked for. I will not ask you to accompany me to the top of Sawel, which might be considered the best proof of the ice age in this county. Dart, or the "Lump," is merely a continuation of Sawel, and presents a bold face to the west. You will hardly meet with anything but schist or limestone until you arrive at Altahoney, where there is a bed of very fine slate, much used for flags and slabs. Up the glen, on to Donemana, limestone occasionally crops out. When we arrive at Donemana we are greatly struck with the gigantic scale on which Nature has sculptured the country. Here, in Altnachree Glen, we see the tremendous force which the surface water exercised. The current from this glen and the current from the glen below Benone met, and so formed Leitrim, or the "Round Hill." Indeed, all the gravel hills in the neighbourhood were formed from the matter brought down from the higher lands at the close of the Glacial Period. In the Bond's Glen we have some rocks which show the force of water in opposition to ice. At the breaking up of the ice, or after that period, an immense body of water must have swept through this glen with irresistible force towards the Faughan. Near Lackagh, or the "Stone Field," we see the rocks standing out in the glen as if the torrent had but swept down yesterday. When we reach Ardground we see an immense block of limestone or hornblende standing in the middle of the glen, and known as the Giant's Grave. It bears a striking resemblance to what the French call *roches moutonnees*. At Ballyarton Bridge the slate or shale is well exposed by a road cutting, and rests unconformably on the schist beneath it. I intended to make a drawing of an alteration in the course of Burn Tollet, in addition to that noticed by Portlock, and also a very considerable alteration in the course of the Faughan, but time did not permit me. The Faughan at one time flowed about fifty yards in the field below the residence of Hugh Lyle, Esq., and, passing over its present bed, it flowed close under the the cliffs which skirt the orchard of James Acheson Lyle, Esq. It continued its course on to what was known as the Puddle Green, in the townland of Crossballycormick, so that formerly nearly all the fine meadows on the right bank were on the Goshedun and Knockbrack side of the river. I meant also to refer to my rambles in Donegal, but time will only permit me to touch on one point which is of some importance—viz., that the whole of the west and north-west of this county appears to be sinking. A few years ago I took an active interest in the Irish fisheries, and in order to inform myself on this subject I visited various stations along this coast, and and it then appeared to me that the coast line was sinking. Last year I had a communication from William Harte, Esq., C.E., in which he states that the coast is *now* sinking, and his word must carry very considerable weight, as there is no one in the North of Ireland better qualified to give an opinion on this subject.

"GLACIAL STRIATIONS AT LITTLE CROSBY."

By T. Mellard Reade, C.E., F.G.S.

At Little Crosby, just north of the village, is a large quarry in the Lower Keuper Sandstone. The Hall at Little Crosby, and the Roman Catholic Church, is built of this stone, and I am told it has been used in some of the Liverpool buildings. Be that as it may, it is but little used now, excepting by the owner, Col. Blundell, for purely estate work. The quarry is nearly overgrown with gorse, which has taken possession of the rubbish heaps; and I think those who wish to know how soil is formed cannot do better than study a disused quarry, where the artificial disintegration of the rocks brings the process before us more rapidly than Nature does, if left to herself. Nor is an old quarry of less interest to the sketcher and lover of the picturesque than to the geologist; but I feel I am digressing as an artist, so must return to the present object of my communication, viz.: the marks of Glacial action which I have discovered.

Strange to say, I have visited the quarry for the last ten years, and generally have looked round to see if any striations were to be discerned, but, until lately, without avail. The top rock is of a very shelly or shaley nature generally, unfitted to retain or even to receive groovings. A short time since I observed on the surface of some quarried blocks, unmistakable signs of glaciation. I could not, however, get the direction of the markings, as none of them were to be found *in situ*. At the first opportunity I met the quarryman on the ground, and he showed me from whence the blocks had come. The rock had been cut back to the boundary wall of the quarry. I at once arranged with him to bare the rock in the farm-yard on the other side of the wall, and, on next visiting the spot, was pleased to find the striations visible. The rock was covered with about two feet of soil, its surface rubbed smooth in the usual way, and the striations pointing 22° W. of N., or nearly magnetic North.

Some time since I communicated to the Society the discovery of Glacial markings opposite the Police Station in Great Crosby. The direction in that case was 40° W. of N., or 18° variation from those at Little Crosby, which are almost exactly parallel with the set of the striations I discovered at Miller's Bridge, which are described in our Proceedings.

No better example of the universality of these markings could be found than those I have just described at Little Crosby; for, as far as we can see, where they occur is the only bit of top rock in the quarry fitted to receive them, and there, as usual, we find them.

If I may be allowed to append a moral, I think my little story shows the necessity for constant watchfulness on the part of the geologist, if he wishes to wrest any fact, however small, from oblivion.

DECEMBER 12TH, 1876.

THE PRESIDENT, HUGH F. HALL, F.G.S.,
in the Chair.

JOHN T. LEWIS, B.A., was elected an Ordinary Member.

The following communication was read:—

SOME NOTES ON SURFACE SCULPTURE,

BY HENRY C. BEASLEY.

THE object of this paper was to draw attention to the phenomena to be observed upon Wansfell, a mountain at the head of Windermere, as illustrating the great variety of causes that have given its present outline to the earth's surface.

Wansfell is a pointed ridge rising to a height of 1,580 feet, and is composed of the members of the Coniston series dipping a little to the east of south at an angle of 30°, and resting upon the Green Slates and Porphyries which compose the summit and the north-eastern slope. The direction of the ridge corresponds with the strike of the beds. The author pointed out how Plutonic agencies originally gave the strata their high inclination, without which no amount of denudation could have formed a mountain of this contour. He then suggested the probability of a comparatively level surface of marine denudation having been formed at a relatively higher level than the present summit (of which, of course, no trace is left) on which rain and running water eroded the main lines of the present valley system of the district. The action of rain and frost, as exhibited upon the peaked summit of the mountain were then described, and the Glacial groovings and rounding of the rocks on the shoulder of the mountain at an elevation of about 1,000 feet.

The hollow on the S.E. side was ascribed to the action of running water originally, its outline having since been rounded by Glacial action, and the valley again seamed with steep ravines by the present streams, whose action in cutting valleys along the strike of the rocks is very clearly exhibited. It was then shown how a considerable delta was being formed of the *débris* from the valley above, where the stream entered the lake close to Lowwood Hotel. Here all the phenomena of a large river might be seen on a small scale.

The tract of country extending eastward from Bideford Bay and drained by the Torridge and its tributaries, was then described. The strata there are also inclined at a high angle, and an ancient plain of marine denudation is still discernible, at a height of about 400 feet above the sea level into which the rivers have cut deep and wide valleys, separated by rounded or flat-topped hills. The absence of pointed ridges here was explained as due to the comparatively short time during which denudation had been going on here, and also to the influence of a climate particularly favourable to the rapid and luxurious growth of vegetation, which protects the hills from the washing effect of rain. It was pointed out that, although the sides of the valleys were very steep, as far as the author had been able to observe there was not a single bare cliff in the district, with the exception of some of the sea cliffs. The effect of vegetation on the contour of the land was particularly insisted on, and attention was drawn to the Ill-bell range of mountains, a few miles to the east of Windermere. This ridge runs in a direction at right angles to the out-crop of the strata, so that the geological structure of both sides is exactly similar. The slope open to the south and west winds and enjoying a larger share of sunshine presents tolerably even grassy slope, whilst the other is bare and precipitous, and rapidly wearing away under the influence of frost and rain.

JANUARY 9TH, 1877.

THE PRESIDENT, HUGH F. HALL, F.G.S., in the Chair.

The following communication was read:—

THE CONDITIONS EXISTING DURING THE GLACIAL PERIOD; WITH AN ACCOUNT OF THE GLACIAL DEPOSITS IN THE VALLEY BETWEEN TRANMERE AND OXTON.

BY CHARLES RICKETTS, M.D., F.G.S.

THE examination only of the beds, or of the materials which constitute the major portion of any geological formation, will rarely enable us satisfactorily to determine the circumstances under which deposits have been laid down, the manner in which they have originated, or from what sources derived. Due consideration must certainly be given to the evidences afforded by those sediments which have a similar character over large areas ; but it is necessary that an equal regard be given to the deposits which in different localities are situated at and form their base; the contour of the underlying rocks must also be taken into consideration before a satisfactory elucidation of the problem can be discovered.

When attention had been so far directed to the Boulder-clay formation that the erratic pebbles, so many of which have all irregularities ground away and their surfaces rendered smooth, often grooved and striated, had been in some instances traced to certain known localities, it was at first considered that not only had these ice-marked boulders been floated on floes or bergs, which on melting dropped them in the localities where they are found, but also that the whole of the clay in which they are embedded had been conveyed in a similar manner. This idea was entirely set aside when, in many places in the valley of the Mersey, on the removal of this clay, the underlying rock-surfaces were, over large areas, discovered to be smoothed and striated, the grooves being so regular in direction that, by no possibility, could the opinion be maintained that these striations were caused by the grounding of icebergs; but, as they correspond entirely with markings on rock-surfaces formed by glaciers now existing, their origin can only be attributed to a similar action; and there is no other known agency by which they could be produced. The inference almost necessarily followed that, as streams issuing from beneath glaciers are always highly surcharged with mud, the clay itself deposited in this glacial sea had resulted from the degradation of rocks in the district, as a consequence of the eroding action of such glaciers in their passage down the valleys, which terminated in what is now the Bay of Liverpool.

Of the possibility that such was the method of the production of this clay, convincing proof has been given by the eminent Arctic observer, Dr. Robert Brown, F.R.G.S. He shewed that in Greenland a clay, so similar that no appreciable difference can be found between it and the brick-clay or fossiliferous Boulder-clay, is formed as a deposit from the waters which issue from beneath the Glaciers as Sub-glacial rivers, thickly loaded with the mud resulting from the grinding of the Glaciers on the infrajacent rocks. These Sub-glacial rivers pour out from beneath the Glacier, whether it lies at the sea or in a valley; their stream flows in a torrent the whole year round, and, reaching the sea, discolours the water for miles, and finally deposits on the bottom a thick coating of impalpable powder.*

Much attention has been directed to the consideration of the causes which induced a climate of such intensity as to cover with a mantle of perennial snow not merely Britain, but also, and at the same time, immense districts now amongst the most fertile in the Northern Hemisphere. Some, without, as I think, any sufficient evidence, imagine that the area surrounding the South Pole is entirely covered with a thick capping of ice; that the whole of this supposed continent, about 2,800 miles in diameter, is covered with one continuous sheet of ice, gradually thickening from its edge to its centre; and it

---

* "Physics of Arctic Ice," by Robert Brown, Ph. D., F.R.G.S.—
Quart. Journ. Geol. Soc., vol. **xxvi**, p. 681.

is presumed that twelve miles would be a moderate amount to ascribe to the thickness of this cap at the Pole. They overlook the effects of intense cold in precipitating moisture contained in the atmosphere. With a winter of such severity as occurs within the Antarctic Circle, the whole of the water would be removed before the winds could pass over a radius of 1,400 miles. Certainly there would be no snow covering the ground within many degrees of the Pole which would not be removed by the heat of the sun during the long day of summer.* The existence of such a monstrous ice-cap at the South Pole having been taken for granted, it has been imagined that, during the Glacial Period, the whole of the waters of the Arctic Ocean formed one mass of ice, with snow thickly piled upon it, and on the larger portion of the land situated in the Northern Hemisphere. Such an accumulation of snow as is here supposed is not only at variance with physical laws at present existing, but, if it possessed the motion which Glaciers have, would have entirely swept away the remains of the Mammoth, Woolly-haired Rhinoceros, and other animals so commonly found in Siberia and the northern parts of America.

Appearances have been observed in Central America which have been *supposed* to indicate the former existence of Glaciers within 13° of the Equator, and it has been considered that these " covered all the higher ranges, and descended in great Glaciers to at least as low as the

* Captain Nares reports that, in the Arctic Expedition, on June 13th and 21st, a thermometer, with a blackened bulb *in vacuo*, exposed to the sun's rays, registered + 128° and + 129° Fahr. respectively; the temperature of the earth's surface at the time being + 27°, and of the air + 34°.

line of country now standing at two thousand feet above the sea, and probably much lower."* Such a condition has been referred to what is known as the Glacial Period. Mr. Belt's examination of the deposits on which he founds this opinion was too cursory, and the inferences are so entirely opposed to the physical conditions now existing there, for them to be readily accepted without further examination. The determination must be left to the investigation of future observers.

Such an hypothesis is incompatible with observations made by the United States Geological Survey of Colorado.† In the district of the Upper Arkansas, about the latitude of 39° N., where "the general elevation of the Sawatch Range for 60 or 80 miles is 13,000 or 14,000 feet above the sea," and that of the bed of the River Arkansas from about 7,500 to 9,800 feet, there is abundant evidence of Glacier erosion, and "the sides of the mountains are worn smoothly and exhibit signs of Glacial action to the height of at least 1,500 feet above the valley," an immense amount of moraine *débris* resulting from it remaining unremoved; whilst about 80 miles to the east, upon the same parallel of latitude, near Colorado City, situated at a height of 6,000 feet in the river-bed, and at about 7,500 feet at the water-divide, so far from there being this evidence of the previous existence of Glaciers, there are most remarkable examples of *sub-aërial* erosion—massive Triassic (?) Sandstones, fifty feet and upwards in height, weathered into the most fantastic shapes, some of which are isolated monoliths; amongst them is a magnificent natural obelisk, 250 feet

---

* "The Naturalist in Nicaragua," by Thomas Belt, F.G.S.; p. 262.

† "Report of the United States Geological and Geographical Survey of Colorado, &c., for 1874."

high, called the "Cathedral Rock," situated in the "Garden of the Gods," Colorado; (Fig. 6.) whilst in rocks of later formation are numerous peculiar columns in "Monument Park." (Fig. 7.) Any of these would have been broken away by the pressure of an accumulation of snow persisting during comparatively a few years.

If, by any possibility, such a climate could have existed in Equatorial regions, there must necessarily at the same time have been a period of most intense cold during winter in higher latitudes; but, with such conditions, the atmosphere could not be supplied with watery vapour, as it is now, more or less directly from Equatorial waters; so that there would be but little contained in it to be precipitated in more northern climes, and therefore Glaciers could not exist there. It would be as impossible for there to have been the system of Glaciers which *are known* to have existed in North America and in Europe, as it would be for a steam engine to be set in motion without a fire underneath the boiler. "The lessening of the sun's heat would infallibly diminish the quantity of aqueous vapour, and thus cut off the Glaciers at their source." *

Respecting the conditions which prevailed in our own country, it has been assumed that "the Irish Sea was filled with an immense Glacier moving southwards, having a thickness of at least 2,000 feet; that it butted against the Welsh mountains, and, dividing, one part pushed *up* the valleys of the Mersey and Dee, and through what has been called the Straits of Malvern." †

---

* "The Forms of Water," by John Tyndall, LL.D., F.R.S., p. 21.

† "The Climate of the Glacial Period," by Thomas Belt, F.G.S. *Quarterly Journal of Science*, Oct., 1874.

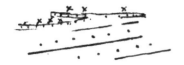

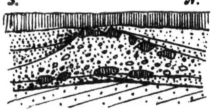

Fig. 3. S.   N.

Fig. 4.

E.   W.

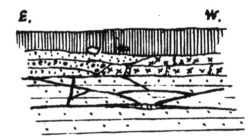

Mt.¹ Colorado.
right 250 feet.

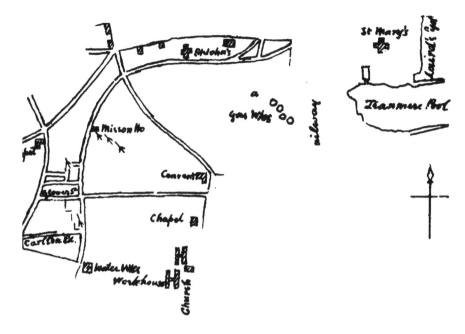

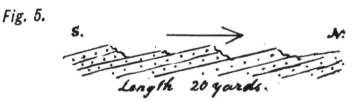

Scale – 3 inches to a Mile.

Fig. 5.

S. ——————→ N.

Length 20 yards.

g. 7.

mument Park, Colorado.

Boulder Clay
Clay blocks
Boulders
Pebbles & Sand
Sand
Moraine Sand
Trias

Sections 1 to 4 = ⅟₁₀ mi

Seemarks →, loc
shown by the

Prof. Ramsay, in a paper read before the Geological Society last year, * without recognising a polar ice-cap, attributes the glaciation of Anglesey to a vast mass of ice moving southwards from Cumberland, reinforced by ice-streams that came from the Mountains of Carrick, in the south of Scotland, and perhaps even from the basin of the Clyde. He considers that this enormous Glacier overspread the region now occupied by the low ground of Anglesey, and went to some unknown distance beyond. There are exposures in Anglesey which afford evidence that the *latest* glaciation of the island did not result from such a system of Glaciers as has been supposed. Thus in the circumscribed area of Serpentine, lying a little south of Valley Station, on the Holyhead Railway, there is exposed a smooth and striated surface covered with a moraine *débris,* so completely derived from the imme- diate locality that it *entirely* consists of angular frag- ments of the Serpentine itself; and at Llanerchymedd, on the Anglesey Central Railway, the striæ on a boss of rock situated close to the station have a direction *towards* S. 10° W., varying, as they curve round it, to S. 20° W. Professor Ramsay remarks that the Glacial striæ of the Island of Anglesey run generally in a direction from 30° to 40° west of south, and that "these striations point directly to the mountains of Cumberland;" but this is also very nearly the same direction as that of the Pre- Carboniferous valley, in which, on its subsidence, the Carboniferous Limestone and Millstone Grit were depo- sited; so that the Glaciers flowed in channels, which had been marked out by the comparative hardness of different rocks that have existed from Palæozoic times.

Observations made in the valley of the Mersey are altogether at variance with the idea of such an enormous

* " How Anglesey Became an Island," by Professor A. C. Ramsay, F.R.S., *Quart. Journ. Geol. Soc.,* vol. xxxii, p. 116.

ice-sheet as has been supposed. There are abundant
evidences that it and its tributaries were filled with
Glaciers, not progressing from an immense accumulation
in the north, but formed by the snowfall in the respective
valleys, being of such an extent only as might reasonably be considered due to the amount of deposition on
their water-slopes. In numerous localities around Liverpool the Triassic rocks, where protected from the action
of the weather by the overlying Boulder clay, and sometimes by beds of sand, on the removal of these accumulations, have displayed smoothed and striated surfaces,
the direction of the striæ varying in different places;
but, so far as I have observed, always taking a direction
similar, or nearly so, to that of the valleys in which
they are situated. Besides these striated surfaces there
are other evidences of the local action of Glaciers. I
have seen beneath the Boulder-clay, in the section
exposed in the making of the Huyton and St. Helens
Railway, and near Whiston, accumulations of unstratified
materials, derived from the adjacent rocks, consisting of
loose sand where there are Triassic rocks; of grey mud,
containing fragments of coal, where there are Coal-
measures. Combining these collections with the striated
rock-surfaces, they can only be considered as moraine
débris.

In Happy Valley, the tributary of the Mersey which
forms the division between Oxton and Tranmere, and
terminates at Tranmere Pool, the removal of the Boulder-
clay has revealed several examples of these glaciated
surfaces, whilst the excavation from time to time of those
deposits which in the bottom of the valley overlie the
sandstone, have afforded sections, limited in area, but
not the less instructive in assisting to determine the
circumstances under which the glaciation of the rocks

and the accumulations of sand and gravel in the bottom of the valley have taken place; whilst the consideration of the whole will assist in forming an opinion respecting the manner in which the Boulder-clay has been deposited, not only here, but likewise in the surrounding districts.

There is now visible, close to the Presbyterian Mission House, grooves deeply cut in the Triassic sandstone, sufficiently large to receive a man's finger; and another striated surface is situated in the adjoining field at a very short distance from a pond, though superficial, these striæ are very distinct. A few years ago an example might be seen at the further end of the field, but, being in a soft sandstone, the grooves have now been entirely erased by weathering. In these instances the striæ have a direction of N. 40 W. There is another, now covered over, higher up the valley, in the unfinished street, nearly opposite a boss of current bedded sandstone, cut through in making the Happy Valley road, from which it is sixty yards distant; the direction of the striæ is due magnetic north. A small surface, about a yard in length and a foot and a half in breadth, is exposed close to the road, about seventy paces from Carlton Road, the striations being placed thickly together, and having a direction of N. 20° W. (See sketch Map.) *

Between Glover Street and Carlton Road the Triassic strata dip up the valley at an angle of 10°. As a consequence, at the basset edges the beds appear as if the rock has been broken off in the opposite direction in a steplike manner, as represented in the diagram Fig. 5; the hollows thus formed are filled with sand and gravel, the whole being covered with Boulder-clay.

---

* Mr. Bostock was the first who observed striated surfaces in Happy Valley.

In one of the sections (Fig. 4) the fracture appears to have progressed to the extent of cracking the upper portion of the bed only, slightly displacing the rock, and forming fissures in various directions, from half an inch to an inch and a half in width, which have been filled with sand and clay, having minute erratic pebbles intermingled.

On the bottom, and extending somewhat up the flanks of the valley, there are, underlying the Boulder-clay, beds of loose materials, sometimes of sand and fragments of sandstone derived from the immediate neighbourhood, not distributed by the action of water nor mixed with materials derived from distant sources. This I will designate *moraine*-formation; also similar sands which have been re-distributed, some of which contain an abundance of pebbles, sometimes fine, in other places larger, similar in kind to the erratics which occur in the Boulder-clay. These beds of drifted materials, as well as the underlying Triassic Sandstone, have at different times been excavated in various places, sometimes as areas for building, at others in order to make use of them for building materials. The most interesting sections are situated between Glover Street and Carlton Road. (A record of each exposure should be made at the time, lest it suffer damage from the weather, or be covered up in subsequent operations by the workmen.) At the corner of Carlton Road the sandstone is covered with an accumulation of yellow sand, so little altered in appearance from the underlying rock that, were it not for the occurrence of thin bands of brown sand and of patches of sand containing erratic pebbles, it might, without special attention, be easily mistaken for the soft Triassic Sandstone *in situ*. In some places a band of this pebbly sand separates this moraine-like accumulation from the sandstone; in others the moraine itself is divided by this washed sand, whilst in this locality a thin layer of it separates the moraine from the Boulder-clay. (Figs. 1 and 2.)

Two or three years ago an excavation was made in irregularly stratified beds of gravel and sand containing small rolled fragments of shells, accumulated in a channel nine or ten feet wide, which had cut through a moraine accumulation and the Triassic Sandstone to a depth of eight or nine feet. The sides of the moraine and also of the sandstone were perpendicular, the latter even over-hanging at one part. (Fig. 1.) There are other places where the sandstone has been hollowed out and worn as if by streams of water, the channels having been subsequently filled with gravel and sand (as in Fig. 2).

" Sub-glacial rivers are familiar in all alpine countries, and in Greenland pour out from beneath the Glacier, whether it lies at the *sea* or in a valley, in summer and winter."* It appears most in accordance with concurrent phenomena, to attribute the formation of these channels to the action of such streams issuing from beneath a Glacier extended some distance into the sea. The striæ left on the Triassic rocks and the moraine sand indicate that a Glacier existed immediately before the excavation; whilst the thin beds of pebbly sand interbedded with the moraine show that, at the time of their occurrence, the latter was beneath the water; so also do the perpendicular walls, especially of the loose sand, which, had it experienced a few days of subaërial exposure, would have been reduced to an acute angle, or washed away entirely.

Not a very long time could have elapsed—not long enough for tidal or other currents to remove the moraine

* Dr. R. Brown, *Quart. Journ. Geol. Soc.*, vol. xxvi, p. 681.

accumulation—before the Sub-Glacier stream ceased to flow through this channel with sufficient force to counter-act the action of the sea. The Glacier must have receded, possibly by its diminution; but, as the period of intense cold continued long afterward, it may quite as probably have been from persistent depression of the land, causing a greater depth of water, by which a Glacier of the same thickness would be floated and broken off higher up the valley. At all events, the force of the current issuing from beneath the ice was so lessened that it no longer kept for itself this passage, but the channel became filled up in the manner described.

On the bottom of the valley, between Carlton Road and Glover Street, and somewhat up its western flank, the Triassic Sandstone and the moraine accumulations, where they exist, are covered with beds, sometimes of sand only, sometimes of sand mixed with small frag-ments of rock foreign to the district, such as are so abundant in the Boulder-clay, but never, so far as I have observed, having any striæ upon them; there are also beds of gravel, chiefly consisting of these erratic pebbles of various sizes, occasionally containing large boulders of Granite, Trappean, and other rocks, as well as frag-ments of Triassic Sandstone, and sometimes blocks of the Boulder-clay itself. (Figs. 2–4.) The beds of sand are also sometimes interstratified with thin bands of this clay. In different beds there are also a considerable number of fragments of marine shells, so broken and rounded by attrition as not to admit of identification. The area in which the individual beds retain the same character is very limited; their materials have been repeatedly heaped together, portions have been again removed, to be afterwards overlaid by others in which the deposit differs somewhat in composition; these pro-cesses have been repeated again and again.

Some years ago there were exposed at the lower part of the valley, near the Gas-works (*a* on Map), beds of sand and small erratic pebbles, containing an abundance of shells, mostly comminuted, but many were perfect, or nearly so; the species of these have been determined by Mr. Morton.* These shells could not have lived at the place where they were found, but must have drifted from a locality situated at a comparatively short distance, and where there must have been conditions suitable for their existence; but as yet I am not aware that any beds refer-able to the Glacial Period have been discovered, with similar shells in the place where they had existed.

There was at first considerable difficulty in making a reasonable explanation of the presence, in the Drift gravel and sand, of the blocks or pebbles of Boulder-clay (Figs. 2, 3); they are angular in form, and therefore had not been exposed to attrition, or rolled, in the same manner as are the balls of clay so commonly found upon our shore. In accounting for them, circumstances which are known to have been then existing must be taken into consideration: that a Glacier extended into the sea within a few score of yards of this place; that the bay was closely packed with innumerable ice-bergs and floes; that the Boulder-clay, with its countless ice-borne erratics, was after a short time deposited above the sand and gravels in which these blocks lie; and that the deposition of this clay must have been in progress at the same time near the mouth of the Mersey. Regard must also be paid to the recorded effects of Glaciers in the Arctic Regions which appear somewhat similar. Dr. Brown remarks that "if a

---

* " Proceedings of the Liverpool Geological Society," Session 1871.72, p. 92.—Excavations have very lately been made near the Gas-works, in thick beds of similar sand; but only fragments of shells were found, all very much comminuted.

berg grounds on a bank or shoal, or in any water not deep enough for its huge bulk to float in, it will often bring up from the bottom boulders, gravel, &c., deposited by former bergs," and "the clayey bottoms of shallow inlets will be grooved and torn up by grounding bergs." * I think it is more than probable that icebergs may have grounded upon some lately deposited bed of Boulder-clay, and again floating off, bore away portions of it, and drifting to this locality, on melting, dropped their load here. If this is the true explanation of the origin of these blocks, the production of the thin and localised bands of clay before alluded to may have arisen from the same cause; some of these blocks after they have fallen down may have become dissolved, and thus spread over a more extended surface.

Lower down the valley, from about the Mission House to the Gas-works, beds of sand which have been exposed beneath the Boulder-clay are remarkably free from erratics, excepting those of a minute size, which are there in abundance. The same may be considered to be the general condition of those cut through near Grange Lane in making the new railway tunnel (b on map), though some larger ones were thrown out amongst the materials removed. So great a difference between these beds and those situated higher up the valley, leads to the inference that each had been formed under somewhat different conditions; there must, in the former instance, have been some impediment to Glaciers, laden with erratics, floating over the immediate locality, otherwise there would not be this absence of large pebbles; the smaller ones are such as might have been brought from a short distance by currents, and thus became mingled with sand derived from the disintegration of the Trias.

* *Quart. Journ. Geol. Soc.*, vol. xxvi, pp. 687 and 690.

Mr. Morton has described these "Lower Drift Sands and Gravels" chiefly as they occur beneath the Boulder-clay in the cliffs forming the boundaries of the Mersey :— "The beds of gravel are of limited extent—mere nests or patches distributed through the sandy strata—frequently containing fragments of shells, and sometimes perfect specimens;" and he considers that "the deposit has probably originated from the disintegration of the Triassic rocks, immediately before the deposition of the Boulder-clay."* The late Mr. John Cunningham C.E., F.G.S., found beds of loose sands and gravels, with fragments of shells, in sinking for water close to Wallasey Pool; these loose strata proved so great an impediment that he was obliged to sink the well in another place. Mr. Bostock found the same in boring in the valley of the Fender on the Upton Road to determine the character of the underlying rocks. He has also supplied other localities, where the same have been met with in borings and well-sinkings, which Mr. T. M. Reade, F.G.S., has recorded in our Proceedings, with many that have occurred to himself and friends.† These gravels and sands appear to occur either on the bottom of valleys which had lately been filled with Glaciers or a little way up their flanks.

My observations lead me to the conclusion that 225 feet, or it may be something less, was the greatest thickness of the Mersey Glacier in mid-channel. In excavating for the foundations of a building connected with the Birkenhead School, at the height of 200 feet above the rocky bed of the Mersey, there was

* "Geology of the Country around Liverpool," by G. H. Morton, F.G.S., p. 42.

† "The Buried Valley of the Mersey."—Proceedings of the Liverpool Geological Society; Session 1872-73, p. 42.

exposed, in an accumulation of moraine breccia, consisting of angular fragments of sandstone and loose sand, a hollow place or channel about a yard and a half wide and a foot and a half thick, filled with a whitish clay, such as is commonly found as balls or pebbles in the Keuper Sandstone or as beds interstratified with the sandstone; both the *débris* and the clay are covered with Boulder-clay. This moraine covers a considerable surface, both below and above the schoolhouse, and has been derived from the sandstone in the immediate vicinity. It does not appear possible that the Glacier which originated it could have formed an integral part of that which filled the valley of the Mersey, and, extending over the present site of Birkenhead, passed through the gorge between Bidston Hill and Wallasey.* Had such been the case, everything must have been swept onward in its passage towards the sea. It is more probable that this *débris* may be ascribed to the effects of an accumulation of snow on the land between it and the water-parting, causing the degradation of the rocks, and by its movement carrying down the disintegrated materials to near the sea-level at that time. The limited deposit of clay would have originated from percolation of water through this moraine, washing out from the disintegrated sandstone of the Keuper the clay it contains in such abundance; and this settled in this hollow or pool, separated in some way from the waters of the ocean. If such was the cause of its formation, or if the Glacier of the Mersey, by floating, was separated from that upon the summit of this ridge, the greatest thickness of the the Glacier could by no possibility be greater than the amount specified, being the height of the locality above

---

* "Glacial Phenomena of Western Lancashire and Cheshire," by C. E. De Rance, F.G.S.—*Quart. Journ. Geol. Soc.*, vol. xxvi., p. 652.

the rocky bed of the Estuary, with the addition of one-eighth for flotation. It is desirable for the confirmation or refutation of this suggestion that advantage be taken of any opportunity afforded by excavations on either side of the Mersey, at heights from 120 to 160 feet above the sea level.

The Boulder-clay containing abundance of ice-marked pebbles derived from distant sources* is so well known that there is no necessity to direct attention to its characteristics further than to notice the occasional occurrence in it of flints. They have been observed but seldom by Mr. C. E. de Rance, F.G.S., of H.M. Geological Survey; more frequently by Mr. D. Mackintosh, F.G.S., and by others. Though not common, these flints may generally be found after a prolonged search, but sometimes several are situated close together. I found five or six thus placed off the Red Noses, New Brighton, and about the same number within an area of a square yard on a bank by the roadside at Neston. Mr. A. Strahan, F.G.S., of H.M. Geological Survey, told me that he also has met with several near together.

I have met with flints in almost every brickfield in the Birkenhead district, but some from Happy Valley are so remarkable as to deserve particular notice. The largest specimen has a portion split off at one end, and appears much weathered; projections on its rounded end are abraded, not smoothed as flints usually are which have been exposed to grinding action on the shore, but as if little fragments had been chipped out by forcible

---

* Since the reading of this paper, I have found a very large number of erratic boulders, some of which, sculptured by the action of the weather, bear no evidences of glaciation or rolling; the others, with a greater or less amount of ice-polishing and scratching, are also distinctly weathered.

pressure against some hard substance. This erosion does not affect even superficial depressions on the surface. A fragment of another has been exposed to the same chipping, and has also several small patches rubbed smooth and polished; one of these places is also striated. This and another of about the same size have been so altered by weathering that they are white throughout their whole substance. Another has a fragment of white limestone attached. This has a granular appearance; but, though thus altered, its hardness is such that it can only be referred to the Chalk or White Limestone of Antrim. I have also obtained a piece of similar limestone granular upon one side, whilst the other is smoothly polished and striated. The flints, weathered but not waterworn, coincide with those so abundant on the eroded surface of the Chalk of the North of Ireland, where they are overlaid by Basalt.*

Marine shells, all of littoral species, are found, but not frequently, in the Boulder-clay. Excepting *Turritella communis* and a solitary specimen of *Litorina litorea*, they are very seldom in a perfect state, being more or less broken, generally into small fragments. Embedded in a soft matrix of clay, their fractured state indicates that they have not existed where found, but have probably been conveyed and deposited in the same manner as the erratic boulders.

The smoothed surfaces of the rock, striated here and elsewhere in the general direction of the valleys, and in a similar manner to what occurs in countries where Glaciers now exist, indicate a period when here also the

---

* Mr. Isaac Roberts, F.G.S., possesses a specimen of flint exactly similar to those which, at Belfast, are situated in the hollows formed on the eroded surface of the Chalk, and lying immediately under, have been altered by exposure to the action of the Basalt.

valleys were filled with Glaciers and perennial snow covered the district. The loose unstratified sand which I have called 'moraine,' containing no materials foreign to the neighbouring rocks, is found in numerous places elsewhere. Combining these accumulations with the existence of Glacier markings on the rock surfaces, they can only be considered as having been derived from the grinding of Glaciers upon the rocks, and were carried forward in their progress until this *débris* has been left behind at the termini. As they have been formed at the foot of the Glacier, it follows that the Glacier must have moved *down* the valleys; and, with the occasional occurrence of interbedded bands of sand containing fragments of marine shells in connection with them, it follows that the termination of the Glacier was in the sea. These conclusions respecting the local origin of the Glacier have been confirmed by other observations; as the tributary Glacier from Tranmere meeting that from Happy Valley at an acute angle; the Triassic beds fractured off where the rock projects at Glover Street (Fig. 5); and the channels, especially the one at Carlton Road (Fig. 1), formed immediately after the recession of the Glacier.

The land during the Glacial Period must have been covered with perennial snow, and many a Glacier, filling the valleys of Cumberland, Wales, and Ireland, extended into the sea, and gave origin to bergs, numbers of which, under the influence of prevailing winds, drifted into the Bay of Liverpool and Estuary of the Mersey, and, melting, dropped their load of ice-marked pebbles; but every phenomenon is in direct antagonism to the hypothesis of a monstrous Glacier filling the Irish sea, or of one extending from the mountains of Cumberland, across the Bay of Liverpool, and over the Island of Anglesey. With such supposed barriers, no sea could have existed between them and the mainland; none of those pebbles with which the Boulder-clay is studded could have passed over and reached the situations where they are embedded in it; least of all could those ancient Irish immigrants, the flints and pieces of Chalk from the Antrim district, have crossed such an obstruction.

That there were no powerful currents is shewn by some of those accumulations in the sea, which I have termed moraine sand, not being re distributed; by the removal of the sandy and gravelly beds being partial only; and their re-deposit, though frequently repeated, being very localised, as is shewn by the different sections, especially in the one represented in Fig. 3. Little more could have been effected by the tide than was due to its rise and fall. The bottom of this valley appears to have been somewhat deep in the water, but there must also have been an obstruction to the water rushing up and down it, constituting the ebb and flow of the tide. The presence of a Glacier within a short distance of these Drift sands and gravels, as proved by other evidence, would act as such a barrier to the ingress of the sea. So that, on that account, and the deep water occupying the Bay and Estuary, the tidal currents must have been exeedingly slight, and probably much of the erosion of these beds, and their re-distribution was due to Sub-glacier streams. The absence of stratification in the Boulder-clay is most remarkable, whether it has been deposited in what must be presumed to have been deep water, as in the bottom of the valleys, or where it has been shallow, as on their flanks and ridges. Had currents existed of even moderate force during the time it was being deposited, some re-arrangement of the sands and pebbles would have taken place, giving to it a bedded appearance. Reasons have been shewn why the rise and fall of the tide should not have affected these deposits; but there would have been some evidence of stratification, at least in what is now higher ground, had there been such wave action as occurs now. The Boulder-clay contains in the arrangement, or, rather, want of arrangement of its innumerable ice-marked pebbles, the clearest evidence that never in these waters did wind-waves then exist. The floating ice and bergs which conveyed these pebbles must have covered the bay so entirely that, protected by an immense accumulation of pack-ice, the winds, however tempestuous, had no such effect in disturbing the water as to distribute the constituents of the Boulder-clay in a stratified manner.

In attributing the great difference of climate prior to, during, and after what is called the "Glacial Period" to astronomical causes, whether due to increase of the obliquity of the ecliptic or of the eccentricity of the earth's orbit, or to other influences, it has usually been considered that the effects produced were dependent upon a general increase in the intensity of cold only; that the more the temperature was diminished the greater would be the amount of snow precipitated, and, in the Northern Hemisphere, the farther south Glaciers extended the greater would be the snow-fall in the north.

Before intense cold could precipitate water contained in the atmosphere in the form of snow, heat at or near the Equator was required to saturate the air with this moisture. In reference to this subject, Professor Tyndall remarks:—"In this process of distillation, *heat* plays quite as necessary a part as *cold*. Before Bishop Heber could speak of 'Greenland's icy mountains,' the Equatorial ocean had to be warmed by the sun."*

---

* "Forms of Water," p. 21.

In passing over land surfaces, even in temperate climes, the atmosphere parts with much of its moisture. In our own island the rainfall on the east coast is only about a third of what it is upon the west, where the winds which have traversed the Atlantic first impinge upon the land.

Though in Siberia the intense cold of winter has for ages so far exceeded the warmth of summer that the ground is frozen to the depth of at least six hundred feet, yet sufficient moisture has not been retained in the air which traverses the continents of Europe or Asia to produce perennial snow; for in passing, during August, 1875, up the River Jenisei from its mouth, Professor Nordenskjold, of Sweden, "saw snow only at one place, a deep valley cleft of some fathoms extent." But the severe cold and long absence of light of the Arctic winter had not prevented the warmth of the summer's sun producing within the Arctic Circle "a vegetation remarkable for a luxuriance, to which he had seldom before seen anything corresponding. In a territory, part of which lies north of the Arctic Circle, are found the most extensive and finest forests of the Globe."[*] He refers to a fact which he considered improbable beforehand, that "the northern limit of many plants in Siberia is situated farther towards the north than in Sweden. It appears that the severe winter of Siberia has by no means any specially injurious influence on the vegetation of the summer."[†]

Compared with Greenland, no great accumulations of snow takes place in the Parry Islands, "no Glaciers of any size exist, westward of the 85th meridian of west longitude in Lancaster Sound, and no true icebergs are met with in the Great Arctic American Archipelago.

[*] *Nature*, vol. xiii., p. 97.   [†] Page 275.

Here and there, in dark and sunless ravines of North Devon and Melville Island, a diminutive Glacier may be found, but it never reaches the sea so as to form icebergs."[*]

Reasoning from Professor Nordenskjold's report, it appears that, if there is the warmth of summer—in other words, if there is no greater amount of snow on the ground than can be readily melted by the sun's rays —no intensity of cold or absence of light in winter has the effect of preventing, even within the Arctic Circle, the growth of luxuriant vegetation. It may have been quite possible that trees and plants, as abundant as those found at Disco, Banks Land, Discovery Bay, Spitzbergen, &c., may have flourished in these latitudes during a Glacial Period affecting more southern localities; for, after passing over land covered with snow and seas filled with bergs and floes, there would remain in the air no more moisture than would supply snow readily melted when summer commenced.

On the discovery of these plant remains in these high northern latitudes, it was generally—I believe universally —considered that it would be quite impossible at the present time that vegetation, such as can be called luxuriant, could exist within the Arctic Circle. Dr. R. Brown, the chief collector of them in Greenland, says, "the very large number of species obtained from a very small space betokens a flora more tropical than temperate, for he is not aware that any similar area in Italy (with the temperature of which Dr. Heer compares the climate of Greenland at the time of their growth) produces a similar number of species. Yet the plants found are not those

---

[*] "McClure's Discovery of the North-west Passage," edited by Captain Sherrard Osborn, C.B., p. 149.

of the tropics, but of temperate regions." * The information respecting the River Jenisei supplied by Professor Nordenksjold may render necessary the re-consideration of the climatic conditions under which these fossil Arctic plants flourished. But if the species are such that they could not have existed with an intense winter followed by a warm summer, such as occurs in Northern Siberia, before attributing this difference in climate to astronomical causes, it will be well to determine whether any physical change has taken place or might reasonably be supposed to have occurred which, altering the relative positions of land and water might change the direction or force of the currents of the ocean, and induce in these regions a climate comparable with that of the temperate zone. The depression of Florida below the sea level (a circumstance which occurred in the Tertiary epoch) would greatly increase the warmth of the North Atlantic Ocean. Not only would the Equatorial waters escape from the Gulf of Mexico three hundred miles further north, but they would do so in much greater volume.

In 1851 Mr. William Hopkins, F.R.S., † then President of the Geological Society, considered the effects which various *possible* changes in the configuration of the land, during recent geological times, would have in causing alterations in temperature. Amongst others he took into consideration the hypothesis of depression of the valley of the Mississippi so as to permit the Equatorial waters to pass in that direction into the Arctic Ocean. He concluded that the Gulf Stream would lose all sensible influence on the coasts of Western Europe, but would

---

* " Geological Notes on the Noursoak Peninsula, Disco Island, &c."
Transactions of the Geological Society of Glasgow, vol. v, part 1.
† *Quarterly Journal of the Geological Society*, vol. viii.

necessarily increase the temperature along its altered course, and especially in the cold regions of North-western America, towards the present shores of the Arctic Sea. Evidence is yet wanting of this supposed communication between the Mexican Gulf and the Arctic Ocean. The results of the examination of the Rocky Mountain district by the United States Survey indicate a period, referred to the Tertiary, when the relative conditions of land and water must have most materially modified the climate of the whole of the North American Continent. The base of the "Great Lignite" group of strata (Lower Tertiary) proves that "extensive tracts of country in the regions of the Rocky Mountains, and east of them in Nebraska and other north-western territories, were occupied by bays, inlets, estuaries, &c., of brackish water. The shores of these ancient estuaries, &c., supported dense forests of large trees, and a growth of other vegetation far exceeding in luxuriance anything now met with in these latitudes. The presence of true fan palms of large size, the remains of crocodiles, as well as the affinities of the mollusca found in these beds to southern forms, all point to the existence of a tropical rather than a temperate climate during their deposition."*

The Equatorial waters, constantly propelled by the influence of the Trade Winds through such an extensive land-locked bay, inducing upon its shores a tropical vegetation, would by the warmth infused into the air so modify the climate farther north that the winter, rainy, cloudy, and foggy, would probably in no part of North America have had a temperature differing much from that of Britain at the present time.

---

* "United States Geological and Geographical Survey of Colorado, &c.," 1874, pp. 22, 23.

The general idea that in high northern latitudes the country must be a desert waste, either covered by ice or snow, or by an exceedingly scanty moss vegetation, being so contrary to the startling fact, as described by Professor Nordenskjold, the re-consideration of the fossil flora of the Polar Regions may become a necessity; whether it may so far agree with that of the forests of Western Siberia that the plants of which it consists may have lived if placed under similar circumstances, and whether the geological position of all or any of these plant-beds would coincide with such a supposition as co-ordinates them with that of the Glacial Period farther south. The accounts of the fossil and sub-fossil plants of the Parry Islands may probably favour the idea of a Siberian climate, whilst those of Disco, &c., may be incompatible.

The subsidence which, allowing the influx of Equatorial waters, produced a tropical climate in the central parts of North America, if it progressed farther south, and caused submergence to any considerable depth of the low ridge of land which forms the Isthmus of Panama, would permit the Equatorial waters to be propelled by the Trade Winds directly into the Pacific Ocean; and thus, in accordance with the extent of the immersion, the climate of the Northern Hemisphere would be entirely altered. Probably the accession of the Equatorial water of the Atlantic to that of the Pacific would so much increase the moisture of the atmosphere that, amongst other changes, the Himalayas would be covered with a greater fall of snow, and its Glaciers extend to a much lower level, especially on their southern aspect. The warm Equatorial waters would cease to circulate in the bay which once stretched into the interior of the North American Continent. The power which causes the Gulf Stream being diverted, this great ocean current would no longer exist; and that immense portion of the Equatorial water for which there is not sufficient area in the Straits of Florida to form part of its volume, and as an overflow mixes with the North Atlantic, would also be diverted in the same way. A diminution of temperature would follow sufficient to change the winter rainfall of Britain and Western Europe into a fall of snow; at the same time sufficient warmth would remain in the ocean to generate the vapour from which the snow would be derived, not in quantities such as many imagine occurred during the Glacial Period, but plenty to fill the valleys entirely with their respective Glaciers. This I have illustrated in the case of a minor valley, tributary to the Mersey, not because I do not think that the principle is of general application, but because I have there had special opportunity of examining the phenomena which have resulted from its action.

The observations on Central America have been too few to determine, from geological evidence, the former existence of such a depression as I have supposed, yet there is good ground for supposing that such has taken place.* All around the Bay of Mexico and on the western coast of Central America there has been a former subsidence of the land to a considerable extent below its

---

* In reference to recent investigations of the fauna of Lake Nicaragua, by Drs. Gill and Bransford, it has been considered that "the element of especial interest is the association of characteristically marine forms, such as a species of Megalops, a shark and a saw-fish, with fresh-water types. The most probable cause of such a combination is the detention and survival of salt-water fishes in inlets of the sea that have become isolated and gradually transformed into fresh-water lakes." *Nature*, Oct. 11th, 1877 ; page 505.

present level. Many Mollusks* and Echinoderms† are found in the two oceans which are either identical or very similar in species. The altered conditions in the Pacific, upon a re-elevation of the land, must have been the destruction of a very large number of species; but the number in which this similarity exists is sufficient to lead the late Mr. P. P. Carpenter, Mr. Alexander Agassiz,‡ and Professor Wyville Thomson to consider that they may be indicative of a former intercommunication between the two seas.

FEBRUARY 13TH, 1877.

THE PRESIDENT, HUGH F. HALL, F.G.S.,
in the Chair.

The following communication was read:—

ON SOME OF THE INFUSORIAL EARTHS, AND THE USES TO WHICH THEY ARE APPLIED.

BY ALFRED MORGAN.

THE student of Lyell's "Elements of Geology" has his interest awakened at an early stage of his enquiries by the narrative there given of the discoveries of Professor Ehrenberg, of Berlin, as to the organic origin of a silicious stone called Tripoli, a substance which has long been well known in the useful arts, being used in a pulverised form for polishing stones and metals.

---

* "The Mollusca of the West Coast of North America," by Philip P. Carpenter.—Report of the British Association, 1856, p. 363.

† "The Depths of the Sea," by Professor C. Wyville Thomson, F.R.S., &c., p. 13.

‡ Quoted in "Depths of the Sea," p. 14.

Ehrenberg found that this deposit is composed of the remains of countless millions of microscopic Infusoria, such as abound in fresh water lakes and ponds, and which naturalists now concur in regarding as vegetable organisms, and describe by the terms Diatomaceæ and Desmidæ.

At Bilin, in Bohemia, there is a single stratum of wide area no less than 14 feet in thickness; and under microscopic examination the entire mass is found to consist of the silicious plates of Diatomaceæ. united together without any visible cement. "It is difficult to convey an idea of their extreme minuteness; but Ehrenberg estimates that in the Bilin Tripoli there are 41,000 millions of individuals of the *Gaillonella distans* in every cubic inch, which weighs about 220 grains, or about 187 millions in a single grain. At every stroke, therefore, that we make with this polishing powder, several millions, perhaps tens of millions, of perfect fossils are crushed to atoms." *

The observations of Ehrenberg led to the discovery of similar deposits in many other localities, and we now know that such beds are in process of formation over extended areas. The indestructible shells of the minute organisms occurring so abundantly in the tripoli are found in immense numbers beneath peat bogs, where they constitute strata often many feet in thickness and of great extent. The cake or "pan" of bog iron ore found in such positions consists of the slender articulated threads or plates, partly silicious and partly ferruginous of *Gaillonella ferruginea*. The source of the iron which imparts the jet black colour to the oak embedded in the peat was not known until Ehrenberg demonstrated its

* Lyell's "Elements," 6th Edition, p. 25.

x

vegetable origin.* Bog iron ore is largely used in gas manufacture in the purifying process, and when super-saturated with the impurities of which it deprives the newly-made gas, it becomes deodorised and pure on exposure to the atmosphere. Other minute organisms, whose skeletons constitute the mass of the deposits which may be grouped under the term infusorial, inhabit the ocean in inconceivable multitudes, and, while living, produce the beautiful phenomenon of luminosity of the waters. In the harbour of Wismar alone, Ehrenberg calculated that an annual deposit of 18,000 cubic feet was laid down. The countless numbers, rapid multi-plication, and wide distribution of these microscopic organisms, place them among the most powerful agents that operate in the production of physical changes. The mind is filled with astonishment in the contemplation of the aggregate results of the life history of such minute forms. Ehrenberg's two great works are his " Mikrogeologie " and " Die Infusionsthierchen als Vollkommene Organismen," in which the geographical distribution and natural history of the group is elaborately worked out.

The "Challenger" explorations of deep sea areas, not to refer to other investigations, have shown that the impalpable mud or ooze of the Atlantic is made up almost entirely of such minute organic bodies as these. Some of the shells or skeletons are calcareous, and appear to be identical with the organisms which abound in the chalk of Europe, while others are silicious. One of the Atlantic deposits has been traced over a distance of 1,300 miles in length by 600 miles in breadth. We have here all the conditions in operation for the produc-

* Lyell's " Principles," 10th Edition, vol. ii, 501.

tion of a vast chalk deposit, and additional evidence in support of uniformitation theories in geology.

In tropical seas the great agents in the extraction of carbonate of lime from the ocean are the corals; but in extra tropical regions this result is accomplished chiefly by the Rhizopoda. Rivers discharge into the ocean carbonate of lime, &c., in solution, and the Testacea perform the same function, but to a less extent, as do the Foraminifera, in separating the lime again in a solid form. The only means by which a limestone rock could, at this period of our earth's history be formed, is, so far as we can tell, by the agency of organic life. Bischof has estimated that the water of the sea contains five times the amount of carbonic acid which would be necessary to hold in solution the total quantity of carbonate of lime that it holds; and, if so, before any could be precipitated, the amount of carbonate of lime would have to be increased five fold. The segreation of the carbonate of lime is now accomplished by corals and Rhizopoda for the most part.

In peat bogs, swamps, &c., there are often found layers of a white silicious paste, composed of the remains of minute organisms which, when dry, present the appearance of a friable chalk, and which, under microscopic examination, proves to be an aggregation of diatomaceæ, many hundreds of which have been described by Ehrenberg and Bailey. Infusorial deposits may, therefore, be either of marine or of fresh water origin.

Bischof mentions a diatomaceous clay amongst the deposits lying under Amsterdam, at a depth of 138 feet from the surface. It is eight feet in thickness, and contains silicious remains to the extent of about one-half of its entire mass.

The Calcaire Grossier of the Paris Basin contains the remains of foraminifera in countless millions; and we may see in the buildings of Paris, where it has been extensively used, a monument of their existence.

The deposit at Bilin is not the only one of large extent that has been investigated. There are beds of scarcely inferior dimensions of a similar nature at Berlin and at Planitz (Saxony). It also occurs at Lüneberg, in a stratum of 28 feet in thickness, and at Kliecken, near Dessau, and in the vicinity of Cassel.

In England a stratum of considerable magnitude has been found in Surrey, at the base of the chalk hills, and elsewhere. In Ireland there is a celebrated stratum on the banks of the River Bann, County Down, and which, from its being much in request for polishing purposes, is locally known as Lord Roden's plate powder.

A similar earth is found in Lapland, in the Isle of France; at San Fiora, in Tuscany; and in Africa, Asia, and New Zealand. In America it has been found in a great number of localities, and occasionally in enormous quantities. Perhaps the most remarkable deposit in the United States is that upon which the city of Richmond, Va., is built; this deposit is in places more than 20 feet in thickness, and has been traced by Professor W. B. Rogers, who was the first to make known its nature, from Herring's Bay, on the Chesapeke, Md., to Petersburg, Va. Professor George H. Cook, State Geologist of New Jersey, in his papers for 1874, reports on an interesting deposit at Drakeville, N.J. He says:—" It has been known as a white earth, or marl, for a long time, and some years since was dug out and spread upon the soil as a manure; it has also been observed to possess remarkable excellence for scouring silver. The establishment of a manufactory for making nitro-glycerine and giant powder at M'Cainsville, in which infusorial earth imported from Germany was used, led to an examination of the deposit, when it was found to be the same material with that they were bringing from Europe."* Professor Cook describes the deposit as occurring in a depression of the surface at the foot of Schooley's Mountain, and covered by a swamp of black earth about a foot thick. A trial pit sunk in the middle of the swale indicated 12 inches of black earth, 8 inches of very light infusorial earth, and 12 inches more of denser infusorial earth. Professor Cook continues :— " There is little doubt that other deposits will be found in this gneissic region, . . . and it can easily be distinguished from any other white earth by its not effervescing with acids, as white marl does; by its not becoming plastic when wet, as white clay does; and by its dissolving almost entirely in a strong solution of boiling water and washing soda."

On the Uses to which Infusorial Earth is Applied.

As an Article of Food.—Strange as it may appear to us, the Laps are said to mix this earth with the bark of trees, as an occasional "famine-fare," when better provisions fail. A deposit occurring at Lillhaggsjon (Sweden) has long been described as "edible," and it is said the Indians dwelling along the banks of the Amazon are accustomed to eat certain white earths found there.

In the Manufacture of Dynamite.—Infusorial earths are of considerable importance in this manufacture. According to Professor Cook, the industry is valued at £600,000 per annum, and some dynamites require as much as 25 per cent. of infusorial earth in their production. Professor Cook gives 47·12 per cent. of soluble

---

* See a paper by Dr. Wall, *Quarterly Journal of Science*, vol. vi, N.S. London, 1877.

silica as the result of his analysis. As an absorbent and carrier of liquids, the infusorial earth has been found to be the substance most adapted for use. It takes up three to five times its weight of water, oil, &c., and is extensively used with disinfectants.

In order to bring nitro-glycerine within the range of articles of transport, Nobel devised the substance known as dynamite, in which the explosive oil is simply carried by the inert, pulverulent silicious earth. After careful preparation, which consists in the thorough removal of all organic matter by heat, &c., the earth is rolled and pressed and sifted when it is ready for use. Fifty pounds of the earth is put into a flat wooden tank and covered with 150lbs. of nytro-glycerine, which is then thoroughly mixed with it. After half an hour has elapsed it is ready for removal to the cartridge moulds, in which parchment paper is used.*

In Agriculture.—As silica enters largely into the composition of the stalks and outer coverings of cereals, the use of infusorial earth as a fertiliser for lands deficient in silica has been suggested; and Professor P. B. Wilson has shown that the very minute skeletons or shells of which infusorial earths are composed are *carried up as such* into the body of the plant during the process of growth. Professor Wilson made many examinations of wheat grown under such conditions, and was led to expect that the undissolved diatomaceous forms that occur in the earth, used as a fertiliser, would be found in the tissues of the plant. With this idea he subjected several growths of wheat to a careful microscopic examination, and thus expresses the result of his investigations: —"My labours have been amply rewarded by one of the

---

* Dr. Wahl: op. cit.

most enchanting views that has ever fallen to my lot to behold through twenty years of varied scientific investigations. When the epidermal siliceous coating was adjusted upon the field of the microscope, some 36 forms of the diatomaceæ were observed." Professor Wilson failed to find a single diatom in wheat straw not so grown. He thus concludes his report:—"I look upon this application of vegetable silica to fertilising purposes as the most important adaptation of matter for the reproduction of vegetation that has ever been discovered." Its *miscellaneous applications* include the employment of the earth as a polishing agent. For this purpose its hardness and wonderfully fine state of division fit it admirably. Under the name of "Electro-Silicon," &c., the Nevada earths are extensively sold in the United States; and, as the Tripoli of commerce, its wide reputation in Europe attests its excellence for the purpose.

Being a very poor conductor of heat, it forms a suitable covering for ice, beer cellars, fire-proof safes, steam boilers, powder magazines, refrigerators, &c. Its superiority over the substances generally used would seem to be placed beyond doubt. "It is extremely light, being nearly five times as light as dry earth, and only about half the weight of dry coal ashes; it is not combustible, remaining unaffected by the hottest fire."

Floating bricks may be made of infusorial earth, clay being added to assist in binding it firmly together. Such bricks were said to have been made by Vitruvius, Pollio, and Pliny. In 1791 they were again produced by Giovanni Fabroni in Tuscany. Fabroni's bricks were equal in strength to those made from ordinary clay, were infusible, and, being very poor conductors of heat, might be held by one end while the other was red hot. Fabroni, as an experiment, constructed the powder magazine of a wooden ship of these bricks ; the vessel being set on fire, sank, without exploding the powder. In 1832, Count De Nantes and Fourriet employed such bricks in the construction of powder magazines, &c., on board ships.

In the preparation of cement and of artificial stone, infusorial earth is largely used. In the "Ransome stone" or apoenite, which is composed of sand and silicate of soda thoroughly mixed and moulded into blocks, which are saturated with a solution of chloride of calcium, the result is the formation of an insoluble silicate of lime, which firmly cements the particles of the stone together, and of chloride of sodium. This latter has to be removed by the free application of water to prevent efflorescence and secure the durability of the stone. This washing process was found to be so tedious and expensive in its thorough application that Mr. Ransome devised, after many experiments, the following process, in which the use of chloride of calcium is avoided.

Suitable quantities of lime (or substances containing lime) and soluble silica (*i.e.*, infusorial earth) are mixed with sand and a solution of silicate of soda or potassa, which, when intimately incorporated, are moulded, and allowed to harden gradually. As rapidly as the soda or potash is set free, it dissolves some of the infusorial silica, and again gives it up to the lime, forming more cement, and thus acting as the carrier of the silica to the lime until eventually all is combined, and, as the result of chemical changes, the whole of the alkali is fixed, leaving nothing to be washed out. The mass gradually becomes thoroughly indurated, and is converted into a compact stone capable of withstanding enormous pressure, and increasing in strength and hardness *with age.*

In pottery, infusorial earth has received several important applications. When fused, for example, with borate of lime, an excellent glazing is produced, which is useful not only for pottery of all kinds, but for enamelling iron and other metals.

The enumeration of all the uses to which this earth is applied would lead us over a very wide field. It has been of service in the manufacture of sealing-wax, soap, paper, ultramarine, &c. And, no doubt, as it becomes more widely known, the extent of its applicability will be comensurably increased.

In addition to the paper by Dr. Wahl, to which reference has been made, I have had before me one by Dr. Birkenhead, on "Micro-geology," which is contained in Vol. XV. of the "Transactions of the Historic Society of Lancashire and Cheshire," and which is of great interest.

MARCH 13TH, 1877.

THE PRESIDENT, HUGH F. HALL, F.G.S.,

in the Chair.

The following communications were read:—

COPPER PITCH-BLENDE AND ITS ASSOCIATIONS.

BY W. SEMMONS.

THIS mineral, formerly of such rare occurence as to be unnoticed in almost every work on Mineralogy, has been lately imported into Liverpool in considerable quantities.

Dana in his edition gives the analyses of some varieties of this ore; but its very existence was almost forgotten, and a writer well known among Mineralogists only twelve months since included it in his list of doubtful minerals.

Its physical characters are :—

Colour—Brown, almost black ; lustre pitch-like.

Streak—Same as colour.

Hardness—6.

No crystal has yet been found.

This high degree of hardness is remarkable, as it far exceeds that of any other ore of copper. It is found associated with Chrysocolla in the great mining district of North-west Mexico. It occurs in nodules of various sizes, also in veins, varying from $\frac{1}{8}$ to $1\frac{1}{2}$ inch in width, and covered on all sides by different varieties of the Chrysocolla. Its composition appears to vary, also its fusibility. In some cases it is quite infusible, at others it melts with ease before the blow-pipe. The most fusible varieties seem to contain a large percentage of manganese.

The following analyses, by Mr. W. M. Hutchings, of Copper Pitch-Blende and the associated Chrysocolla show their marked distinctness and individuality :—

	Chrysocolla.	Copper Pitch-Blende.
Silica	66·25	27·98
Oxide of Copper	25·69	28·59
,, Lead	·12	·41
,, Iron	·26	10·94
,, Zinc	·34	1·54
Lime	·74	·92
Magnesia	1·06	—
Water	6·13	8·30
Alumina	—	·15
Oxide of Manganese	—	17·53
,, Cobalt	—	·35
Oxygen	—	3·60

From the above it seems this ore differs from Chrysocolla in containing much less silica and much more iron;

while manganese, which is absent from the Chrysocolla, is found in considerable quantities in Copper Pitch-Blende.

In order to pass any opinion on the formation of this ore, it is necessary to look at the Chrysocolla and other minerals associated with it. They are:—

Silica, in the form of quartz and of calcedony, as also jasper, is found freely disseminated through the whole, and often incrusting the mammillated Chrysocolla.

Gypsum occurs in veins from a line to three inches thick. Calcite is also found in small quantities.

Pyrolusite in thin botryoidal incrustations occurs on the Copper Pitch-Blende. This is easily separated from the parent mass, and seems to be a seggregation from it.

Looking at the tendency in compounds of manganese to assume dendritic and other forms, and to separate themselves from the minerals by which they are surrounded, I am inclined to consider these nodules— which, occurring so frequently, have amounted to hundreds of tons in the past few months' importations at this port—are secondary products. By this I mean a deposit not existing in its present form in the original mass. The manganese molecules have separated themselves from the parent mass, together with the iron molecules, and have thus set up a new combination, much poorer in silica than the surrounding Chrysocolla.

The Chrysocolla associated with the Copper Pitch-Blende is so remarkable in many respects, that I reserve its description for a future paper.

THE GLACIAL STRIÆ OF THE COUNTRY AROUND LIVERPOOL.

By George H. Morton, F.G.S.

In this communication I propose to give a general description of the Glacial Striæ which are of such frequent occurrence on the surface of the sandstone rocks in the country around Liverpool.

This is the only area in England so far south, and so far away from a hilly or mountainous district, where the rocks have been found to be striated, except, perhaps, the coast of Durham, where similar striæ occur on limestone near the coast. In Leicestershire, at Mount Sorrel, in 1867, I saw the Syenite striated, probably by ice. The occurrence of such indications of moving ice in North Wales, the north of England, and in Scotland is more easily accounted for, on account of the proximity of hills or mountains from which glacial ice may have radiated.

In 1859 * I described for the first time, evidences of the action of ice on the surface of the sandstone in this neighbourhood. Having at that time only found such indications in a single locality, I attributed the striated surface to the grounding of an iceberg in the Glacial sea.

In 1866, † having discovered several additional examples of glaciation on both sides of the Mersey, though at no great distance from it, I began to entertain

---

* "Traces of Icebergs near Liverpool."—Proceedings, Literary and Philosophical Society, 1859-60.

† "On the Presence of Glacial Ice in the Valley of the Mersey during the Post-Pliocene Period."—Proceedings, Liverpool Geological Society, 1866-7.

the opinion that a Glacier, or at least a field of moving ice, had descended the valley of the Mersey during the early part of the Glacial period.

By 1870 [*] I had discovered similar evidences of ice-action at greater elevations, several miles from the river, and was consequently compelled to adopt another theory, viz.: that a great ice-sheet had passed over this part of the country from the S.E. to the N.W. This direction seemed the most probable from the general contour of the ground; and was supported by an examination of the quartz pebbles protruding from the striated surfaces being rubbed or broken on the side from which the ice was supposed to have travelled.

The following are the descriptions of the striated surfaces, in the order in which they were discovered.

PARK HILL ROAD.

The first striated surface discovered was between Park Hill Road [†] and the Dingle. It has since been covered by the erection of cottages over it. The surface of the rock was 120 feet above the Ordnance datum, and the strata belonged to the Pebble-beds of the Bunter formation. The direction of the striæ was N. 42° W., of course allowing $22\frac{1}{2}$° W. for magnetic variation. In this instance, as in all the other areas, the rock had been originally covered with Boulder-clay; otherwise the striæ would have been obliterated. The clay had been removed for brick-making, and when the surface of the rock had been washed by rain the grooves and striæ became visible. A slab of sandstone was taken from the

---

[*] "On the Glaciated condition of the surface of the Triassic Sandstone around Liverpool."—Report, British Association, 1870.

[†] "On Glacial Surface Markings near Liverpool.—*Quarterly Journal Geological Society*, 1862.

surface and deposited in the Liverpool Free Museum. It shows the character of the striæ, which present a remarkably uniform appearance when seen extending over a considerable area. Such sandstone does not take a polish, like the glaciated greenstone and slaty rock of North Wales; but it assumes a flat surface and exhibits numerous striæ and long grooves which frequently extend several yards in perfectly straight lines—parallel with each other. Ice would not striate the rock over which it passes in this manner, unless it enclosed stones and boulders embedded in the bottom of it.

BOUNDARY STREET, KIRKDALE.

The second locality was situated in a brickfield, about 50 yards north of Boundary Street, and 150 yards west of Heriot Street (formerly Gore Street), where an area of about ten square yards of striated rock was exposed for several years, but is now covered with houses.* The surface was about 80 feet above the Ordnance datum, and the sandstone belonged to the Keuper formation. The direction of the striæ was N. 15° W.

STANLEY ROAD, KIRKDALE.

The third locality was also discovered in brickfields on the west side of Stanley Road, opposite the Stanley Hospital, more recently erected, and about 600 yards from the locality last described, with which it may have possibly communicated.* The rock surface was about 80 feet above the Ordnance datum, and the direction of the striæ N. 15° W.

FLAYBRICK HILL, CHESHIRE.

The fourth locality was at Flaybrick, and is a locality of considerable interest, for striæ have been

* Ibid.—Quar. Jour. Geol. Society, 1862.

found both on the sides and base of the hill. The
form of Flaybrick Hill was formerly very remarkable,
and it attracted attention many years ago, for it had a
very steep escarpment facing the east or north-
east,* which is unusual in this neighbourhood, but
it has now been almost entirely removed for building
purposes. It is an outlier of the Bidston range of
hills, and seems to have been worn into its precipitous shape by the passage of ice rather than by the action
of water. The strata belong to the Keuper formation,
which rests on the Bunter Sandstone near the base of the
hill. The striæ were first observed at an elevation of
one hundred and twenty feet above the Ordnance datum,
half a mile S.E. of the Telegraph Station on Bidston
Hill, and again at seventy feet, the direction being
N. 32° W., and N. 30° W.† They were soon after observed
on the western side of the hill one hundred feet above
the same datum-line, where the direction was N. 20° W.
Mr. D. Mackintosh, F.G.S., has recently described striæ
W. 30° S. on Flaybrick Hill, just half-a-mile due south
from St. James's Church. The striæ are nearly effaced,
but the rock seems to have presented a glaciated surface,
which was too thinly covered with drift to have been
preserved.

NORTH HILL STREET, NORTH OF ST. SILAS'S CHURCH.

The next striated surface was found in 1863, in the
fields on both sides of North Hill Street, and it presented
two of the largest areas discovered, each fully five hundred square yards, but they are now almost entirely
covered with rubbish.‡ The surface of the rock is one

---

* Proc. Literary and Philosophical Society, 1844-5, p. 97.
† Ibid.—Quar, Jour. Geol. Society, 1862.
‡ Ibid.—Rept. Brit. Assoc., 1870.

hundred and sixty feet above the Ordnance datum, and the strata belong to the Pebble-beds of the Bunter formation. The direction of the striæ is N. 35' W. On the rock surface on the north of North Hill Street I noticed an oblique grove, crossing the regular striæ at an angle of 35°, that was N. 70° W., and a specimen was obtained showing this exceptional grove and deposited in the Museum of the Royal Institution.

WAVERTREE.

Near the village of Wavertree, in Victoria Park,* I found the rock to be striated, but an excavation for building destroyed the surface, which was 170 feet above the Ordnance datum. The rock belongs to the Pebble-beds of the Bunter formation, and the direction of the striæ was N. 32' W. Specimens were obtained and placed in the Liverpool Free Museum.

THATTO HEATH.

A fine striated surface occurs along the top of the rock on each side of the railway-cutting a little west of Thatto Heath. It is on the south-west slope of the hill, about 290 feet above the Ordnance datum, and the strata belong to the Pebble-beds of the Bunter. This area is of especial interest on account of its distance being nine miles from Liverpool, and was discovered by Dr. Ricketts, F.G.S., in 1870.† The direction of the striæ is W. 40' N.

OXTON, CHESHIRE.

At Oxton, about half-a-mile S.E. of Christ Church, there is a small area of striated sandstone, at an elevation of 100 feet, on the Keuper formation. The direction

* *Ibid.*—Rept. Brit. Assoc., 1870.
† "The Sections of Strata exposed on the Huyton and St. Helens Branch Railway."—Proc. L'pool Geol. Society, 1869-70.

of the striæ is N. 24° W. Mr. Robert Bostock discovered the locality. Close to the spot the surface of the yellow-beds of the Upper Bunter Sandstone present a very remarkable flat surface beneath the Boulder-clay, probably caused by the planing action of ice on strata too soft to be permanently striated. Recently Dr. Ricketts described two additional areas in the locality, one close to the Mission House, on the Happy Valley Road, N. 40 W., and another between Carlton Street and Glover Street, Happy Valley Road, and Woodchurch Road, N. 22½° W. The elevations being respectively 62 feet and 105 feet above Ordnance datum.

PARK ROAD.

In 1870 I found loose blocks of striated sandstone on the broken surface of the Keuper formation east of Park Road—opposite Northumberland Street—indicating a striated area close to the place.

MILLER'S BRIDGE.

Another striated area has recently been discovered to the east side of Regent's Road, near the toll-gate at Miller's Bridge, by Mr. T. Mellard Reade, C.E., F.G.S.,[*] about 90 feet above the Ordnance datum. The strata belong to the Keuper formation, and the direction of the striæ is N. 28° W. On this surface there are several cross grooves at a considerable angle to the regular striæ.

CROSBY.

At the village, in a field south-west of the Police Station, Mr. Reade found another striated surface.[†] It is only 25 feet above the Ordnance datum. The rock is

[*] "Glacial Striæ at Miller's Bridge, near Liverpool."—Proc. L'pool Geol. Society, 1872-3.

[†] Proc. L'pool Geol. Society, 1873-4, p. 72.

the Keuper Sandstone, and the direction of the striæ N. 40° W. In the adjoining quarry there is a fine section showing the perfectly flat glaciated surface, with the super-imposed Boulder-clay. A large decomposed green-stone boulder rests on the sandstone.

LITTLE CROSBY.

Last year, 1876, another striated area was discovered by Mr. Reade,* in a yard attached to a farmhouse close to the large quarry at Little Crosby. The surface of the rock, Keuper Sandstone, is about 35 feet above Ordnance datum, and the direction of the striæ N 22° W.

The parallelism of the striæ in each of these glaciated areas is remarkable. Although particular grooves occasionally run into each other, it may be explained by stones at the bottom of the ice having gradually altered their position.

Several instances have been noticed where oblique grooves intersect the principal striæ at a considerable angle, as at North Hill Street and at Miller's Bridge. I do not regard these exceptional striæ as of any importance, for they appear to have been formed after the surface had been striated in a uniform direction, and seem to have been caused by the final breaking up of the ice.

There are large areas around Liverpool where the rock is exposed with a denuded surface, and consequently where no indication of the passage of ice has been preserved. It is only in situations where the Boulder-clay has been deposited on the rock, that the striated surfaces

* "Glacial Striations at Little Crosby."—Proc. L'pool Geol. Society, 1876-7.

have been found, and only in exceptional places then. In the low-lying land, where the soft sandstones of the Bunter occur, no trace of moving ice has been observed --excepting the flat surfaces already described.

Since the foregoing descriptions of striated areas were written, Mr. A. Strahan, F.G.S., of the Geological Survey, has kindly given me a list of several additional localities where he has observed glaciated surfaces in this neighbourhood; and Mr. C. E. De Rance, F.G.S., has allowed me to see a proof sheet of the "Memoirs of the Superficial Deposits of the South-west of Lancashire." These important additions to the areas previously known have enabled me to compile the following list of glacial surfaces in the country around Liverpool; but I have added a number of localities from a paper "On the Evidences for the Ice-sheet in North Lancashire and adjacent parts of Yorkshire and Westmoreland," by Mr. R. H. Tiddeman, M.A., F.G.S., which continue the connection of this district with the country about Preston and Lancaster. It seems unfortunate that there is no recorded instance of glacial striæ on the south-eastern side of Wirral, or near Chester, for the discovery of such an area would connect this district with North Wales, glacial striæ having been recorded in the neigh-bourhood of Holywell.*

* Discovered by Mr. G. Shrubsole, F.G.S. "Records of Glacial Striæ in Denbighshire, Flintshire, and Anglesea," by G. H. Morton, F.G.S.—Proc. L'pool Geol. Society, 1875-6.

LOCALITIES OF GLACIAL STRIÆ IN SOUTH-WEST LANCASHIRE AND CHESHIRE,
ARRANGED ACCORDING TO DISTANCE FROM LIVERPOOL EXCHANGE.

NO.	LOCALITY.	DIRECTION.	DISCOVERER.	WHERE DESCRIBED.
1	Park Road, Liverpool	Loose Blocks only.	G. H. Morton, F.G.S.	Not previously described.
2	North Hill Street, Liverpool	N. 35° W.	Do.	*Rept. Brit. Assoc.*, 1870.
3	Boundary Street, „	N. 15° W.	Do.	*Quar. Jour. Geol. Soc.*, 1862.
4	Stanley Road, „	N. 15° W.	Do.	Do.
5	Park Hill Road, „	N. 42° W.	Do.	Do.
6	Miller's Bridge, Bootle	N. 28° W.	T. M. Reade, F.G.S.	*Proc. L'pool Geol. Soc.*, 1872-3.
7	Christ's Church, Oxton	N. 24° W.	R. Bostock.	*Rept. Brit. Assoc.*, 1870.
„	„ „ „	N. 22½° W.	Dr. Ricketts, F.G.S.	*Proc. L'pool Geol. Soc.*, 1876-7.
„	„ „ „	N. 40° W.	Do.	Do.
8	Flaybrick Hill, Birkenhead	N. 30° W.	G. H. Morton, F.G.S.	*Quar. Jour. Geol. Soc.*, 1862.
„	„ „	N. 32° W.	Do.	Not previously described.
„	„ „	N. 20° W.	Do.	Do.
„	„ „	N. 10° W. N. 22° W. W. 30° S.	E. Hull, F.G.S.	*Trans. M'chester Geol. Soc.*, 1864.
„	„ „	N. 32° W.	D. Mackintosh, F.G.S.	*Quar. Jour. Geol. Soc.*, 1877.
9	Wavertree	N. 32° W.	G. H. Morton, F.G.S.	*Rept. Brit. Assoc.*, 1870.
10	Crosby	N. 40° W.	T. M. Reade, F.G.S.	*Proc. L'pool Geol. Soc.*, 1873-4.
11	Little Crosby	N. 22° W.	Do.	Do., 1876-7.

NO.	LOCALITY.	DIRECTION.	DISCOVERER.	WHERE DESCRIBED.
12	Thatto Heath	W. 40° N.	Dr. Ricketts, F.G.S.	*Proc. L'pool Geol. Soc.*, 1869-70.
13	Pool Hall Rocks	N. 43° W.	A. Strahan, F.G.S.	Not previously described.
14	Farnworth Church Yard	W. 8° N.	Do.	*Mem. S.W. of Lancashire, Geol. Survey,* [1876.
15	Appleton, near Church	W. 8° N.	Do.	Do.
16	Runcorn—Bed of Mersey	W. 8° W.	Do.	Do.
17	Runcorn—Bridgewater Company's Quarry	?	Do.	Not previously described.
18	Middlehurst's Delf, St. Helens	W. 33° N.	Do.	*Mem. S.W. of Lancashire, Geol. Survey,*
19	Crank, St. Helens	W. 30° N.	Do.	Not previously described.
20	Garswood, St. Helens	W. 30° N.	Do.	*Mem. S.W. of Lancashire, Geol. Survey,*
21	Horwich Colliery	W. 12° N.	E. Hull, F.G.S.	Do.
22	Grey Heights, Chorley	N. 22° W.	B. H. Tiddeman, F.G.S.	*Quar. Jour. Geol. Soc.*, 1872.
23	Euxton, Preston	N. 22° W.	Do.	Do.
24	Ordsall, Manchester	N. 40° W.	J. Plant, F.G.S.	*Trans. Man. Geol. Soc.*, 1868.
25	Mellor Beacon, Blackburn	{ W. 10° S. / W. 13° S.	J. Eccles. / B. H. Tiddeman, F.G.S.	*Quar. Jour. Geol. Soc.*, 1872.
26	Heysham	N. / N. 10° E. / N. 40° E. / N. 10° E.	Do.	Do.

During the last few years several important communications have been brought before the Geological Society of London, descriptive of similar phenomena in districts north of Liverpool, in which attempts have been made to show that during the Glacial period a great ice-sheet from Norway and Scotland advanced over the north of England. Mr. D. Mackintosh, F.G.S., contributed a paper "On the Traces of a Great Ice-sheet in the Southern part of the Lake-district and in North Wales;" this with Mr. Tiddeman's paper, previously referred to, afford evidence that the theory of this great ice-sheet has been very generally accepted. Mr. Tiddeman's subject is intimately connected with this district, for he describes glacial striæ at Chorley, running N.N.W., only 15 miles from Thatto Heath—one of the glaciated areas I have described. He is of opinion that the great ice-sheet he describes advanced over this district, and that the direction was S.S.E., instead of N.N.W., as I supposed it to be in my paper read before the British Association in 1870.

Geologists are beginning to think that the ice-cap theory has been pushed too far; and with regard to this part of England, it seems to be a question whether a great thickness of glacial ice moving over the country would not have produced a more uniform direction of the striæ in the numerous areas recorded. It seems probable that the drifting and frequent grounding of field-ice in a shallow sea would be more likely to produce the striated surfaces that have been described, and at the same time account for the varying direction, which extends over 65° in the immediate neighbourhood of Liverpool, without regarding the area discovered by Mr. Mackintosh, where the surface has been weathered. If that the variation would amount to no less than 112.° The passage of field-ice carried along by tidal currents in the same general direction, and occasionally grounding on the sandstone bottom, would be very likely to cause striæ with the amount of variation I have shown the respective areas to possess; whereas a rigid mass of ice would have probably striated the rocks in a more uniform direction —within a fewer number of degrees than we find to be recorded.

Whichever of these two theories is finally adopted, it seems to me that the striæ were produced before much if any of the Boulder-clay was deposited, and that there is little if any connection between the striated surfaces and the superincumbent clay.

If the ice-cap theory is adopted, it must be admitted that the sandstone surface was partially denuded, after the rock had been striated, otherwise the striæ would have been more generally present; and where the Boulder-clay covers the denuded surface, which it usually does, it is obvious that the denudation must have occurred before the clay was deposited. If, on the other hand, the field-ice theory is supported, it seems unnecessary to suppose any such denudation after the striation of the rock, but that we find the striated surfaces just where ice happened to ground, that the grounding of the ice was exceptional, and that the places where it occurred were at various and irregular distances from each other.

It was my intention to have supplemented this communication with a description of the interesting section of Upper Boulder-clay, Middle Sands and Gravels, and Lower Boulder-clay recently exposed at the north of Liverpool,* but as I have arrived at the conclusion

* A full description of the section will be found in the Rept. Brit. Assoc., p. 110, and *Geol. Mag.* for 1876, p. 526.

that the Glacial Striæ in this neighbourhood are altogether of pre-Boulder-clay origin, it is unnecessary to describe such overlying deposits, although they also belong to the Glacial period. However, I may state that in my opinion the Boulder-clay in the country around Liverpool has been deposited in rather deep water, except during the deposition of the Middle Sands and Gravels, which indicate shallow water conditions and a connection with those great deposits of a similar character which are so conspicuous over North Wales.

I have only to add that the Lower Drift Sand of my former papers is the same formation as that more recently described as the Middle Sands and Gravels, and that the section at the north Docks has presented the only example of what I consider to be a Lower Boulder-clay in the country around Liverpool. The Upper Drift Sand is now described by Messrs. De Rance and Reade as the Shirdley Hill Sand.

ON THE GRAPTOLITES FOUND IN THE LOWER LLANDEILO STRATA NEAR THE CHURCH, SHELVE, SHROPSHIRE.

By G. H. Morton, F.G.S.

In my paper on "The Geology and Mineral Veins of the Country around Shelve" there is a description of the Lower Llandeilo series, a section showing the position of Shelve Church on the upper beds of the series, and a list of fossils containing *Bellerophon perturbatus* and *Dictyonema sociale* from beds close to the church that are well known to contain graptolites.

The position of these Church-beds I very carefully worked out, and considered to be at the top of the Lower Llandeilo or Arenig, and that is the position assigned to them in the section of the Geological Survey (No. 34).

The graptolite *Dictyonema sociale* in the list of fossils represented several species, which I was unable to name when my paper was printed in 1869. I have not been able to visit the place since, but during the years I was working in the district I preserved all the specimens that I found, though it was not until Messrs. Hopkinson and Lapworth's paper appeared in the *Journal of the Geological Society* that I was able to name them.

In 1873 Mr. J. Hopkinson, F.G.S., read a paper before this Society on "The Graptolites of the Arenig Rocks of St. David's, South Wales," when he referred to the Shelve Church graptolites. An abstract of this paper is in the Report of the British Association, 1872. Early in 1874 Mr. Hopkinson read another paper before the society "On some Graptolites from the Upper Arenig Rocks of Ramsay Island, St. David's." In this paper he speaks of the graptolites "having been found in the *lower beds* of the Arenig at Shelve." This paper appeared in abstract in the Report of the British Association, 1873.

In a letter to me, dated 13th January, 1873, Mr. Hopkinson remarks that the Shelve Church-beds are lower than those of the White Grit Mine, and in another, dated 23rd September, 1874, he states that he is "convinced from their graptolites that they are low in the Arenig series—that they are at least nearer the Lower than the Upper Arenig Rocks."

Finally, another paper appeared: "Description of the Graptolites of the Arenig and Llandeilo Rocks of St. David's," by John Hopkinson, Esq., F.L.S., F.G.S., and Charles Lapworth, Esq., F.G.S. (read December 16, 1874); *Quar. Jour. of the Geological Society*, vol. xxxi., for 1875, p. 631. In this paper the authors refer the Shelve Church graptolite beds to the middle of the Arenig series. There is a list of the graptolites found by the authors at Shelve.

I had found the following before 1869:—

1. *Didymograptus patulus.*
2. *Clematograptus implicatus.*
3. *Dendrograptus flexuosus.*
4. *Callograptus Salteri.*
5. *Ptilograptus acutus.*

The latter *Ptilograptus acutus* is not in Messrs. Hopkinson and Lapworth's list of Shelve Church species, but they have the following, which I did not find:—

6. *Dendrograptus difflusus.*
7. *Callograptus elegans.*

So that according to their list the beds belong to the middle of the Arenig, with one species indicating a lower and one an upper horizon; while my species indicate the middle, with, however, one species indicating a higher horizon altogether. The position of the Church-beds geologically is Upper Arenig, and there seems little in the palæntological evidence to throw doubt on that conclusion.

Besides, Mr. Hopkinson wrote to me on the 18th January, 1876, in answer to a letter containing my list of species as follows:—"*I am much obliged to you for the list you give. It certainly looks like a higher position for the Shelve Church-beds than I had thought.*"

It seems to me that too much importance is attached to the occurrence of particular species in distant localities, and that they will ultimately be found to occupy *different* horizons when followed over an extended area.

THE CARBONIFEROUS LIMESTONE

AND

MILLSTONE GRIT OF LLANGOLLEN.

By GEORGE H. MORTON, F.G.S.

(Continued from Page 205.)

THE following List of Fossils contains the names of 76 species, all of which I have collected myself—no others having been admitted. The Upper Grey Limestone is very fossiliferous, 61 species occurring in it, while in the Lower Brown Limestone only 16 species have been found, and of these 4 species are peculiar to it. If the Carboniferous Limestone is simply divided into Upper and Lower Limestone, 37 species are peculiar to the two upper subdivisions, and 14 species peculiar to the two lower subdivisions, 25 being common to both. The species that are peculiar to the upper and lower subdivisions are often quoted from higher and lower horizons in the formation in other districts, so that perhaps all the information to be gleaned from the list is the general absence of particular zones of species in the Carboniferous Limestone. No doubt diligent search would add to the number of species, and modify the results deduced from the list, but the ·general conclusions would remain unchanged.

LIST OF FOSSILS FOUND IN THE CARBONIFEROUS LIMESTONE OF THE EGLWYSEG RIDGE, LLANGOLLEN.

	Lower Brown Limestone.	Lower White Limestone.	Upper White Limestone.	Upper Grey Limestone.
PISCES.				
1 *Cochliodus oblongus*, Ag.	.	.	.	*
2 *Helodus* sp.	.	.	.	*
3 *Petalodus Hastingsiæ*, Owen	.	.	.	*
CEPHALOPODA.				
4　　　　　*Goldfussianum*, Koninck	.	.	.	*
5　　,,　　　sp.	*	.	.	.
6 *Nautilus globatus*, Sow.	*	.	.	*
HETEROPODA.				
7 *Bellerophon cornu-arietes*, Sow.	.	.	.	*
8　　,,　　*tenuifascia*, Sow.	*	*	.	*
GASTEROPODA.				
9 *Euomphalus Dionysii*, Goldf.	*	*	.	.
10　　,,　*pentangulatus*, Sow.	.	*	*	*
11　　,,　*rugosus*, Sow.	.	*	.	.
12 *Murchisonia Verneuiliana*, M'Coy	*	*	.	*
13 *Natica tabulata*, Phil.	.	.	.	*
14 *Natica spirata*, Sow.	.	*	.	.
15　　,,　sp.	*	.	.	.
16 *Pleurotomaria* sp.	.	.	.	*

	Lower Brown Lime-stone.	Lower White Lime-stone.	Upper White Lime-stone.	Upper Grey Lime-stone.
17 *Pleurotomaria* sp., Sow	.	*	.	.
18 *Stroparollus costellatus*, M'Coy	.	*	.	.

DIMYARIA.

19 *Cypricardia*, sp.	.	.	.	*
20 *Myacites sulcatus*, Flem...............	.	*	.	*
21 *Pinna flabelliformis*, Mart...............	.	.	.	*
22 *Sanguinolites arcuatus*, Phil.	.	.	.	*
23 *clava*, M'Coy	.	.	.	*

MONOMYARIA.

24 *Aviculo-pecten micropterus*, M'Coy......	.	.	.	* .
25 ,, ,, *plicatus*, Sow.	.	.	.	*
26 ,, ,, sp.	.	*	.	.

BRACHIOPODA.

27 *Athyris ambigua*, Sow..................	.	.	.	*
28 ,, *expansa*, Phil.	.	*	.	*
29 ,, *Royssii*, Léveillé	.	*	.	.
30 *Chonetes papilionacea*, Koninck.........	.	*	.	*
31 *Orthis Michelini*, Koninck	.	.	.	*
32 ,, *resupinata*, Mart..................	.	.	.	*
33 *Productus aculeatus*, Mart..............	.	.	.	*
34 ,, *comoides (Llangollensis)* Sow...	*	*	.	.

	Lower Brown Limestone.	Lower White Limestone.	Upper White Limestone.	Upper Grey Limestone.
35 *Productus cora*, D'Orb.	*	*	*	*
36 ,, *costatus*, Sow.	.	.	.	*
37 ,, *fimbriatus*, Sow..............	.	.	.	*
38 ,, *giganteus*, Mart...............	.	.	*	*
39 ,, *latissimus*, Sow..............	.	.	.	*
40 ,, *longispinus*, Sow.	.	.	.	*
41 ,, *Margaritaceus*, Phil.	.	.	.	*
42 ,, *Martini*, Sow.	.	.	.	*
43 ,, *punctatus*, Mart.	.	*	.	*
44 ,, *semireticulatus*, Mart.	.	*	.	*
45 ,, *Youngianus*, Dav.	.	.	.	*
46 *Rhynchonella pleurodon*, Phil.	.	.	.	*
47 *Spirifera bisculata*, Sow.	*	*	*	*
48 ,, *crossa*, Koninck	.	.	.	*
49 ,, *glabra*, Mart.	.	.	.	*
50 ,, *lineata*, Mart.	*	*	.	*
51 ,, *striata*, Mart..................	.	.	.	*
52 *Streptorhynchus crinistria*, Phil..........	.	*	.	*
53 *Strophomena analoago*, Phil.	.	.	.	*
54 *Terebratula hastata*, Sow.	.	.	.	*
BRYOZOA.				
55 *Fenestella membranacea*, Phil.	*	.	.	*

	Lower Brown Limestone.	Lower White Limestone.	Upper White Limestone.	Upper Grey Limestone.
ECHINODERMATA.				
56 *Archæocidaris Urii*, Flem.	.	.	.	*
57 *Poteriocrinus crassus*, Koninck	.	*	*	*
CRUSTACEA.				
58 *Griffithides longiceps*, Portl.	.	.	.	*
59 *Leperditia suborbiculata*, Münster	*	.	.	.
ZOOPHYTA.				
60 *Alveolites septosa*, Flem.	*	*	.	.
61 *Chætetes tumidus*, Phil.	*	.	.	.
62 *Clisiophyllum turbinatum*, M'Coy	*	*	*	*
63 *Cyathophyllum Murchisoni*, M. Edw.	.	*	.	*
64 *rngium*, Phil.............	.	,	.	*
65 ,, *Stutchburyi*, M. Edw..	.	*	*	.
66 *Lithostrotion basaltiforme*, Phil.	.	.	.	*
67 *irregulare*, M'Coy.........	.	*	*	* .
68 *junceum*, Flem.	.	*	.	*
69 *Martini*, M. Edw.........	.	*	*	*
70 ,, *Portlocki*, M. Edw.......	.	*	.	*
71 *Lonsdaleia rugosa*, M'Coy	.	*	.	*

	Lower Brown Limestone.	Lower White Limestone.	Upper White Limestone.	Upper Grey Limestone.
72 *Lonsdaleia floriformis*, Flem..............	.	.	.	*
73 *Phillipsastrea radiata*, M. Edw.	.	.	.	*
74 *Syringopora geniculata*, Phil.	*	*	*	*
75 ,, *ramulosa*, Phil.	.	*	.	.
76 *Zaphrentis cylindrica*, Scouler	.	*	*	*
FORAMINIFERA.				
(Of undetermined species)*				

The fossils found in the Carboniferous Limestone of the Eglwysèg ridge are seldom in a good state of preservation. In the Lower Brown Limestone *Productus comoides* is the most abundant, but it is difficult to find a specimen with both valves. The minute crustacean *Leperditia suborbiculata* is also abundant, in brown shales about the middle of the subdivision, north of the Tynant ravine. The most frequent species are given at page 178†, though they are all in a very imperfect condition.

In the Lower White Limestone *Productus cora* is the most common species, and fragments of the large *Euomphalus rugosus* (not *tabulatus*) are of frequent occurrence, so that these two species may be considered the most characteristic. In the Upper White Limestone the fossils are few in both species and individuals, but *Productus cora* is the most frequent. A list of the

---

* *Endothyra ammonides* and *Textularia*, sp. occur in the Upper Grey Limestone.

† *Productus punctatus* was entered in the list by mistake, and printed in some of the copies, but I have not found it in this subdivision.

ordinary species found in each subdivision is given at pages 183 and 185.

In the Upper Grey Limestone the greatest number of species occur, many being exceedingly abundant, while others are very rare, though most of the latter are common in other localities. The Zoophyta and Brachiopoda are the most abundant, and the specimens sufficiently perfect for accurate determination. In the highest beds *Productus latissimus* and *P. giganteus*, with the corals in the list of characteristic species at page 188, occur in profusion. *Orthis Michelini, O. resupinata*, and *Strophomena analogo* are rare, though the first-named *Orthis* is very common at Chirk and other localities to the southward. The Monomyaria, Dimyaria, Gasteropoda, and Cephalopoda are each représented by a few specimens of each species—often by single examples as *Natica tabulata*—but they are usually in such a bad condition that the determination has often been difficult and sometimes uncertain. *Sanguinolites clava* occurs in a fine state of preservation, and is a characteristic species in the subdivision. The Echinodermata is represented by a few ambulacral plates of *Archæocidaris Urii* and numerous stems of *Poteriocrinus crassus;* and the Crustacea by *Griffithides longiceps* which occurs in black shale about 75 feet from the base of the subdivision in Wright's quarry near the limekiln.

This list is the result of frequent visits to Llangollen, extending over a period of seven years. A few other species, including *Productus sub-lævis*, have been referred to the locality, which I have not found myself, and consequently excluded from the list.

HAFOD-Y-CALCH, NEAR CORWEN.

THE outlier of Carboniferous Limestone at Hafod, near Corwen, is about seven miles from the same formation at the Eglwyseg ridge, near Llangollen. The area is coloured on Mr. Greenough's Geological Map of England and Wales published in 1819. It also appears on the map prefixed to Prof. Sedgwick's Memoir "On the Older Palæozoic Rocks of North Wales," *Jour. Geol. Soc.*, vol. i., 1845. Although it does not appear on the Map of North Wales appended to Mr. D. Sharp's paper, "Contributions to the Geology of North Wales," *Jour. Geol. Soc.*, vol. ii., 1846, it is described by him in that communication under the head of "Outlier of Mountain Limestone at Guerelas, West of Corwen." He says it is "about half a mile long and a quarter of a mile wide," and that "it is well exposed in open quarries, and consists of thick beds of light grey limestone, alternating with dark and black argillaceous shale, agreeing in character with shale that, in the neighbouring districts of Mountain Limestone, is found in the lower part of that formation." The author states that he "obtained from these quarries many well-known fossils of the Mountain Limestone," and that the strata "dip to the north-east, from a low angle up to 45°. In Sir R. I. Murchison's Geological Map of England and Wales (Society of Useful Knowledge), 1843, the Hafod outlier is omitted; perhaps it is to be found in the more recent editions, unless it is too small to be represented; and I need scarcely say that it is inserted on the Geological Survey and more recent maps.

Prof. Jukes, in the *Geological Magazine* for 1865, vol. ii., p. 186, states that "the patch of Carboniferous

Limestone near Corwen, together with the Flintshire escarpments, makes it almost certain that the whole Carboniferous formation spread formerly over the greater part of North Wales, with just a few island-peaks of older rocks, perhaps, rising up through it;" and there is a letter in reply from Mr. D. C. Davies, headed "The Outlier of Carboniferous Limestone near Corwen," containing a section of the strata and the following list of fossils :— *

Rhynchonella .... }
Chonetes, &c. .... } in the Black Shale.

Productus giganteus ....
Phillipsastræa radialis ....
Lithostrotion junceum ....
    Do. *fasciatum* .... } in the Limestone.
Diphyphyllum latiseptatum (?) and
    small *Producti* and *Terebratulæ.*

After describing the strata, he says that "the beds quarried at Corwen correspond to those in the *upper portion* of the main band; the dirt and shale-beds, together with the fossils found all serving to confirm the identity." "The beds are perched up at very great angles; the lower beds are not worked, but, by measuring the outcrop of the strata, it is evident that we have the whole series of beds as developed in the main band" —that is at Llangollen.

. Mr. Davies then gives his opinion regarding the deposition of the strata in "a little inland sea," in consequence of which a letter from Prof. Jukes appeared in the same magazine, p. 326, headed "The Outlier of Carboniferous Limestone near Corwen." After disposing of Mr. Davies's theory, he added some remarks and rough

* *Geol. Mag.,* vol. ii., 1865, p. 283.

diagramic sections of interest regarding the Hafod strata.
He states: "The country around Corwen was examined
by Mr. Talbot Aveline and myself, who spent many
pleasant but laborious months in it, so that not only was
no rock-exposure unknown to us, but there was hardly a
boulder with which one or other of us could not claim a
personal acquaintance. If, therefore, our conclusions
are wrong (and I, for one, utterly abjure all pretension
to infallibility), it is not that we spared our labour in
examining the ground, and collecting data for arriving at
them." After some descriptions of his sections (woodcuts),
he says:—"It is, therefore, a by no means improbable
supposition that the preservation of that little patch near
Corwen is due to the joint action of the downthrow of
the (great Yale and Bala) fault, and a local basin-shaped
depression of the beds there. An undulation in the beds
at that particular spot perhaps enabled the fault to bring
down higher beds than it did just north of it." No
opinion is given regarding the position of the Hafod beds
in the Eglwyseg ridge, or nearest Mountain Limestone.

The last paper on the subject seems to be the one by
Dr. Ricketts, F.G.S., read before the Liverpool Geolo-
gical Society, and published in abstract, 1866, vol. i,
"On the Outlier of Carboniferous Limestone, near
Corwen, N. Wales." He refers to the different degrees of
dip first described by Mr. Sharp, F.G.S., and supports
Prof. Jukes' opinion that a synclinal curve occurred prior
to the faulting of the strata, but gives no list of fossils.

The thickness of the Carboniferous Limestone in
North Wales varies in different localities in consequence
of the undulating surface of Silurian upon which it
rests, and the variation in the most extreme cases
exceeds 1,000 feet. There can be no doubt that the
limestone of Hafod was deposited on the same open

Carboniferous sea as that at Llangollen, and that denuding influences have caused the separation. The actual base of the limestone at Hafod is not exposed, neither can its relation to the Silurian strata be seen. At the southwest boundary of the area the lowest visible limestone occurs in an old though disused quarry just behind some cottages, Plas-uchaf, on the Turnpike road. The limestone is of a light colour, contains *Euomphalus* sp. and *Productus cora*, and closely resembles the Lower White Limestone of Llangollen. The strata seem to dip at 70° S.W., but the exposure is too obscure to render the observation satisfactory, and the occurrence of a fault between the limestone and the Silurian seems probable. Just beyond where the limestone abruptly terminates along the south-west margin of the area, behind the cottages referred to, the drift and surface soil become thicker, and no rock is visible, but the numerous embedded fragments of slaty rock indicate the presence of the Silurian strata beneath. The Lower White Limestone can also be seen on the side of the road in front of the cottages, and it is exposed on the grounds in front of Plas-isaf, the residence of Mrs. Lloyd, where it has evidently been worked, but there is nothing known of any limestone under the house, as shown on the Geological Survey Map.

There is no exposure of any limestone south-west of the places referred to, so that the Lower Brown Limestone of Llangollen does not appear to occur, and there certainly is no exposure of it, at Hafod. The surface of the ground slopes from the centre of the limestone area in every direction, except the south-west, where it rises and forms the hill Cefn Mawr, 200 feet above the Alwen. The area is covered with drift, except at the quarries and rock exposures described; everywhere else the horizontal beds of sand and gravel obscure the underlying strata from view—even the ends of the limestone strata on the strike are covered by the drift, although there is a rapid descent of about 100 feet in each direction.

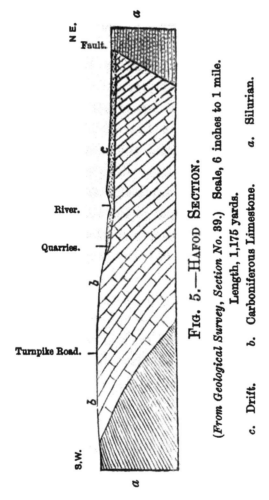

FIG. 5.—HAFOD SECTION.

(*From Geological Survey, Section No. 39.*) Scale, 6 inches to 1 mile. Length, 1,175 yards.

c. Drift. *b.* Carboniferous Limestone. *a.* Silurian.

The Section of the Geological Survey, Fig. 5, is drawn on the scale of six inches to the mile, and shows the outcrop of the Carboniferous Limestone to extend about 1,000 yards; the average dip of the strata being 45° N.E. and the thickness 2,000 feet, with the upper beds terminating against the Yale and Bala fault.

According to the Geological Survey Map, Sheet 74, S.E., the limestone does not extend so far to the north-east,—not beyond the Alwen.

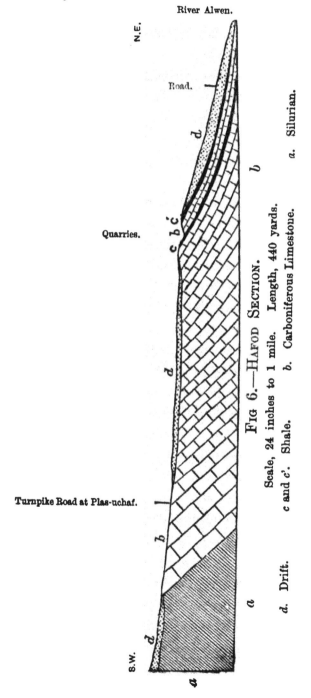

FIG 6.—HAFOD SECTION.

Scale, 24 inches to 1 mile. Length, 440 yards.

a. Silurian. b. Carboniferous Limestone. c and c'. Shale. d. Drift.

The Section Fig. 6, is on the scale of 24 inches to the mile, showing the outcrop of the limestone to extend about 400 yards; the average dip to be 45° N.E., and the thickness 750 feet. The line of this section is directly across the strike, whereas the Survey section deviates to the extent of about 30 degrees.

The section given by Mr. Davies in the *Geological Magazine* seems merely intended to exhibit the limestone strata in and about the quarries, where it is burnt for agricultural purposes.

It is evident from these sections that it is difficult to estimate the entire thickness of the Carboniferous Limestone at Hafod-y-Calch, for there is not only an uncertainty about the position of the lowest beds, but according to the Section of the Geological Survey there is a considerable extension of the limestone upwards under the alluvial deposits on the north-east of the Alwen, although unsupported by the Survey Map. Possibly when the district was surveyed by Messrs. Jukes and Aveline there may have been some other exposures visible, but though I have very frequently been over the ground I have not been able to find any limestone in situ on the north-east of the river, and therefore conclude that the map is more reliable than the section. Close to the bridge, on the south-west side, the strata dip at the angle of 20° or 25°, as shown on the section, Fig. 6, and the numerous blocks of limestone on both sides of the river are evidently derived from these upper beds. However, both the Geological Survey Map and Section seem to extend the Carboniferous Limestone too far to the south-west, and it seems improbable that there is limestone beneath Mrs. Lloyd's residence; indeed, the late Mr. Lloyd informed me that none had been observed below the drift, which is of considerable thickness. Still, it is probable that the geological surveyors had some reason for concluding that the limestone existed beyond where I have been able to find it, though, after a careful examination of the area, I have concluded that the Lower White Limestone is either faulted against the Silurian on the south-west, or that it reposes directly on the Silurian rocks, the Lower Brown Limestone being absent.

The thickness of the Carboniferous Limestone at Hafod-y-Calch, including the Lower and Upper White Limestone and the Upper Grey Limestone, as described in the Eglwyseg ridge at Llangollen, seems to be about 750 feet, but the subdivisions cannot be separately measured. The limestone worked in several large quarries is all on the same horizon and is about 80 feet in thickness, including interstratified shale. The lowest band of rubbly limestone and black shale (c) is about 6 feet thick, and it is from this bed and the thin bedded limestone below that the numerous fossils have been obtained; collecting being much facilitated by the great inclination of the beds and the extent of the surface exposed. Hafod is one of the most prolific localities for fossils in North Wales, being remarkable for the profusion of individuals, the number of species, and the perfect condition in which they occur; and from its frequent mention as a locality must for a long period have yielded the beautiful corals, particularly *Phillipsastrea radiata*, for which it is celebrated. This and most of the fossils in the list are common in the beds just below the dark band c. The fossils indicate that the strata in which they occur belong to the Upper Grey Limestone, and most probably the upper beds in the subdivision. Some, however, viz., *Stroparollus costellatus*, *Orthis Michelini*, and *Alveolites septosa*, have only been observed lower in the series, but taken collectively the fossils are remarkably similar to those found in the highest beds of the Upper Grey Limestone at the Eglwyseg ridge. The highest strata at Hafod are about 50 feet of thick bedded white limestone, succeeded by 10 feet of shale and rubbly limestone (c'), it being very improbable that there are any higher Carboniferous strata on the north-east of the Alwen.

Although the fossils in the following list, from the limestone and shale in the quarries at Hafod, are on the horizon of the top of the Upper Grey Limestone, the lithological characters of the strata do not present much similarity to that subdivision. The band of dark lime-stone and black shale (c) is very similar, but the overlying 50 feet of limestone is much thicker and of a lighter colour than any corresponding beds in the Eglwyseg ridge. The strata seem to have altered with the distance, and no minute co-ordination of the particular beds can be recog-nised. That the 50 feet of white limestone represents the· Sandy Limestone seems to be unlikely, for it is succeeded by shale and thin beds of rubbly limestone. The limestone about Plas-uchaf is very similar to the Lower White Limestone near Llangollen, and is evidently on the same horizon.

LIST OF FOSSILS FOUND AT HAFOD-Y-CALCH.

PISCES.

1 *Pscphodus* sp.

HETEROPODA.

2 *Bellerophon cornu-arietes*, Sow.
3   ,,   *tenuifascia*, Sow.

GASTEROPODA.

4 *Stroparollus costellatus*, M'Coy.
5 *Natica ampliata*, Phil.

DIMYARIA.

6 *Modiola* sp.

BRACHIOPODA.

7 *Orthis Michelini,* Koninck.
8 *Productus cora,* D'Orb.
9   ..   *giganteus,* Mart.
10   *fimbriatus,* Sow.
11   *longispinus,* Sow.
12   *Martini,* Mart.
13   *punctatus,* Mart.
14   ,,   *semireticulatus,* Mart.
15 *Rhynchonella pleurodon,* Phil.
16 *Spirifera bisulcata,* Sow.
17   ,,   *crassa,* Koninck.
18   *glabra,* Mart.
19   ,,   *lineata,* Mart.
20 *Streptorhynchus crinistria,* Phil.
21 *Strophomena anologa,* Phil.
22 *Terebratula hastata,* Sow.

BRYOZOA.

23 *Fenestella fastuosa,* Koninck.
24   ,,   *membranacea,* Phil.

ECHINODERMATA.

25 *Archæocidaris Urii,* Flem.
26 *Poteriocrinus crassus,* Koninck.

ZOOPHYTA.

27 *Alveolites septosa,* Flem.
28 *Chætetes tumidus,* Phil.
29 *Clisiophyllum bipartatum,* M'Coy.
30   ,,   *Keyserlingi,* M'Coy.
31   *turbinatum,* M'Coy.

32 *Cyathophyllum regium*, Phil.

33 *Lithostrotion irregulare*, M'Coy.

34 „ *junceum*, Flem.

35 „ *Portlocki*, M. Edw.

36 *Lonsdaleia rugosa*, M'Coy.

37 *Phillipsastrea radiata*, M. Edw.

38 *Syringopora ramulosa*, Phil.

39 *Zaphrentis cylindrica*, Scouler.

FRON-Y-CYSYLLTE.

At Fron, about three and a half miles to the east of Llangollen on the south side of the Dee, the Carboniferous Limestone occurs in an elevated position, and forms a capping on the hill, with the Wenlock Shale beneath, as shown in the following wood-cut (Fig. 7):—

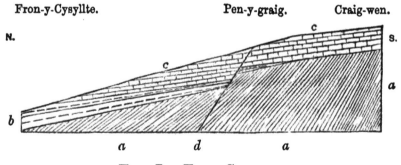

FIG. 7.—FRON SECTION.

d. East and west fault.   *b.* Upper White Limestone.
c. Upper Grey Limestone.   *a.* Silurian.

The limestone has been broken up by several faults running north-north-east and south-south-west, and east and west, but particularly by one in the latter direction (*d*), which causes the limestone to present two areas at different elevations, that of Fron-y-Cysyllte being the lowest, and that of Pen-y-graig or Craig-wen the highest. Both of these areas exhibit the Carboniferous Limestone resting on the underlying Silurian strata in steep escarpments on the north-west of the hill, from which a magnificent view of the Vale of Llangollen is obtained. There are several large quarries, and in one of them, about half way up the hill, the east and west fault referred to is exposed for a considerable length—the limestone having been removed on the north or downthrow side of it. The following is a section exposed in an old quarry close to the Primitive Methodist Chapel at Fron-y-Cysyllte:—

FEET.

Lower beds of the Upper Grey Limestone.	Limestone thin-bedded..	10
	Limestone	8
	Limestone	3
		21

Upper beds of the Upper White Limestone.*	Concretionary Shale ...	8
	Limestone	2
	Shale	2
	Limestone	7
	Rubbly Limestone	2
	Limestone	7
		28

The lower beds in this section belong to the Upper White Limestone which terminates upwards with the 8-feet bed of concretionary shale, and the 3-feet bed of limestone above it forms the base of the overlying Upper Grey Limestone. This section presents the most considerable exposure of the Upper Grey Limestone, which

* In these beds I found *Alveolites septosa*, a coral not found in the overlying subdivision.

gradually thins out higher up the hill. Two almost continuous sections are exposed along the north-west of the hill, the 8-feet bed of shale being conspicuous in the lower one near the base of the limestone. The upper section along Craig-wen does not present any indication of the 8-feet bed of shale, which seems to have thinned out. There is a large circular quarry at the lower end of the upper area, and the Upper Grey Limestone seems to rest directly on the Wenlock Shale. Mr. Isaac Williams, who worked the quarries many years ago, informed me that the Wenlock Shale is just below the floor of these quarries and the limestone has been removed to its base—the Upper White Limestone being absent—so that the rapid attenuation of the limestone with the rise of the Silurian strata at Fron is evident.

The following is a section of the strata exposed in the upper area, Pen-y-graig or Craig-wen quarries:—

FEET.

Lower beds of	Dark Grey thin-bedded Limestone...	25
the Upper Grey	Light ,, Limestone	10
Limestone.	Dark Grey thin-bedded Limestone...	50
		85

These beds are above the horizon of the 8-feet bed of shale in the lower quarries, and consequently nearly the whole of the limestone quarried about Fron is from the Upper Grey Limestone. The upper beds have been denuded, so that the strata exposed in the quarries represent the lower beds of the subdivision at Trevor rocks, the band of light grey limestone being about the same distance from the base in both localities.

The Upper Grey Limestone at Fron contains the usual fossils found in the lower part of the subdivision on the Eglwyseg ridge, and the strata are faulted against the Cefn-y-Fedw Sandstone on the east of the limestone area. The sections exposed at Fron are very important, for they prove that the Carboniferous sea bottom shallowed there, and was much higher than it was three or four miles to the north-west; and that the limestone attained a considerable thickness in that direction before any was deposited over the former area. It seems probable that the country south-west of Fron may have been dry land during the deposition of the lowest limestone on the north-west. This supposition is strongly confirmed by the beds of shale in the Eglwyseg ridge being in some places largely composed of flattish fragments of Wenlock Shale, only slightly rounded, derived from the coast-line of the old Carboniferous sea.

Proceeding towards the south there is an exposure of the Carboniferous Limestone at Bron Freian, where it must be very thin. It is, however, only exposed on the surface of the road through the village, so that little can be seen of it. It is difficult to measure or approximate the thickness, but it appears to be under 100 feet. Whether there is a greater attenuation of the limestone at this place cannot be ascertained with certainty, for neither the base of the limestone nor its juncture with the overlying Cefn-y-Fedw Sandstone is exposed, and it may be faulted. It has been remarked that the diminution in the breadth of the country occupied by the outcrop of the Carboniferous Limestone varies, in conse- quence of an alteration in the inclination of the strata,[*] but an examination of the country dispels any such conclusion. There are very few exposures of the Cefn-y- Fedw Sandstone in this locality.

---

[*] Excursion to the North Wales Border, "Proc. Geol. Ass.," vol. iv., p. 559.

BRON-Y-GARTH, NEAR CHIRK.

The Carboniferous Limestone probably extends south-wards through Chirk Park, though I have not seen any exposure there, but the valley of the River Ceiriog, one and a half miles east of Chirk, presents a fine section through the formation. All the limestone strata belong to the Upper Grey subdivision, and the thickness is about 137 feet. Along the strike of the strata there is another valley, running towards the south-west for about half-a-mile, and the following section is across this valley, with the Bron-y-garth limestone quarries and the overlying Cefn-y-Fedw Sandstone at a higher level on the south-east, as shown in the following wood-cut (Fig. 8):—

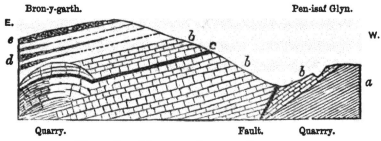

FIG. 8.—BRON-Y-GARTH SECTION.

e. Cefn-y-Fedw Sandstone.   d. Sandy Limestone.
c. Shale-Bed.   b. Upper Grey Limestone.
a. Silurian.

The Lower Cefn-y-Fedw Sandstone is exposed in quarries and other sections. It is a yellowish sandstone, and has been used for building purposes. The lower beds are well seen toward the top of the valley, and present the following section in a hillock west of Castle Springs.

		FEET.
Lower beds of the Cefn-y-Fedw Sandstone and Conglomerate.	Soft Sandstone, light colour, with many quartz pebbles.	12
Upper beds of the Sandy Limestone.	Soft Sandstone	10

These beds represent the base of the Lower Sandstone and Conglomerate and the top of the Sandy Limestone, but all differ from the typical strata above the Eglwyseg ridge in being much softer—almost loose sand in some places. Higher beds are exposed along the road above this section, and contain very few pebbles, though nests of sand are frequent, and the rock weathers with a honeycombed appearance.

The Sandy Limestone crops out in the field just above the quarry at Bron-y-garth, and is an impure limestone which has been but little used. These passage beds between the Carboniferous Limestone and the Cefn-y-Fedw Sandstone are not well exposed, so that the sequence of the strata cannot be given.

In the Bron-y-garth quarry the Upper Grey Limestone consists of a series of beds of limestone and shale, the most remarkable being a 12-feet bed of shale. The lowest bed of limestone, 50 feet thick, is said by the quarrymen to rest on some soft clay, with the slate rock —Silurian—beneath, but there is no exposure to prove the statement. At the other side of the valley by Pen-isaf-Glyn there is a large quarry, the strata in which are same as the 50-feet bed at Bron-y-garth, and the fossils, *Productus giganteus*, *Lithostrotion Portlocki*, and *Syringopora geniculata* are common to both. Between the two quarries there must be a fault as shown on the section, but its exact position is uncertain. Higher up the valley the lower beds of the limestone are faulted against the Lower Cefn-y-Fedw Sandstone, and the continuation of the fault is obvious. In appearance the section across the top of the valley is very different to the one given at the bottom Fig. 8, but the difference is easily explained by the greater denudation of the valley toward the north-east. The locality is very interesting, for it presents several geological conditions rarely found in such close contiguity.

The following is a section of the whole of the strata from the base of the Carboniferous Limestone to the lower part of the Sandy Limestone, as correct as it has been possible to render it. When the measurements are given the description and thickness are strictly correct. The 12-feet bed of shale is remarkable for the fossils it contains, especially *Leptæna Hardrensis* and *Orthis Michelini*, both of which occur in profusion.

		FT.	IN.	
Lower beds of the Sandy Limestone.	Impure Limestone ...	,,	,,	
	Shale	4	0	
	Limestone	4	6	
	Shale	8	0	
	Limestone	10	0	
	Shale	1	0	
Upper Grey Limestone.	Limestone, thin beds.	8	0	Represent the 15-feet of Shale at Craignant.'
	Shale	12	0	
	Limestone	12	0	
	Shale	1	6	
	Limestone	30	0	
	Shale	2	0	
	Limestone	50	0	
	Soft Clay ?	4	0	
		187	0	

The following fossils occur in the 12-feet bed of shale: *Buccinum imbricatum; Myacites sulcatus; Athyris Roissyi; Chonetes Hardrensis; C. papilionacea; Orthis Michelini; Productus longispinus; P. punctatus; P. semireticulatus;*

Rhynchonella pleurodon; Spirifera bisulcata; Fenestella membranacea; Poteriocrinus crassus; Clisiophyllum pro-lapsum; C. turbinatum, and *Lithostrotion irregulare;* and the following occur in the thick bedded limestone at the base of the formation, viz.:—*Productus cora; P. gigan-teus; Lithostrotion Martini; L. Portlocki,* and *Syringopora geniculata.*

Still further to the south-west, about a mile from the river there are several small quarries at the top of the valley, "L'stone Quarries" on the Survey Map, where the lowest beds of the Upper Grey Limestone are exposed and the ordinary fossils occur. The limestone contains numerous nests of sand, but although close to the Wen-lock Shale, there is no section showing the one resting upon the other.

At Grug-fryn, above half a mile to the south, the Carboniferous Limestone is again exposed, with the Cefn-y-Fedw Sandstone on the east and the Wenlock Shale on the west, and along such a narrow space that the limestone seems to be only 50 or 100 feet thick. The few exposures seem to present the lower beds of the Cefn-y-Fedw Sandstone reposing on the Upper Grey Lime-stone, but probably there is a fault between them, the 12-feet bed of shale having been denuded, for it occurs in several localities south of this place, and presents the same appearance and fossils as at Bron-y-garth.

CRAIGNANT.

The next section is at Craignant, where there is a fine exposure of the Carboniferous Limestone. The strata belong to the Upper Grey Limestone, and the following is a section of the whole of the beds exposed:—

		FT.	IN.
Lower beds of the Sandy Limestone.	Impure Limestone...	,,	,,
	Shale	?	
	Limestone	?	
	Shale		
	Limestone	15	0
	Thin beds of Limestone		
Upper Grey Limestone.	Shale, with beds of Limestone at base.	15	0
	Limestone	20	0
	Shale	0	6
	Limestone	3	0
	Shale	0	6
	Limestone	25	0
		74	0

Represents the 15-feet of shale and Limestone at Bron-y-garth.

Base not exposed.

This section closely resembles that near Chirk, and the occurrence of the 15-feet bed of shale with the same species of shells and corals as at Bron-y-Garth is very remarkable.

The following fossils occur in the 15-feet bed of shale, viz.: *Chonetes Hardrensis; C. papilionacea; Orthis Michelini; O. resupinata; Productus longispinus; Spirifera bisulcata; Rhynchonella pleurodon; Poteriocrinus crassus; Chætetes tumidus; Cyathophllum Murchisoni.*

The general order of the strata is so similar that it may be considered conclusive evidence that the upper beds of the Upper Grey Limestone were deposited continuously over the intervening country, though they have been denuded and only the lower portion of the subdivision left exposed. The thickness of the Upper Grey Limestone at Craignant, as shown in the section, is about 74 feet, and it is not likely that the actual thickness is much greater, for it includes the whole of the outcrop. It seems that the Silurian rocks on the west of the country described formed land during the deposition of the lowest Carboniferous Limestone, and that it was only after a lengthened subsidence that some of the upper beds were deposited along the old coast line. There is no reason to suppose that the country further west, about Glen Ceiriog, was ever covered by the limestone, though it seems probable enough that the Cefn-y-Fedw Sandstone and Coal Measures may have extended over it.

The succession of the strata from the Carboniferous Limestone up to the Cefn-y-Fedw Sandstone cannot be seen in detail about Craignant. The limestone at the top of the quarry is covered with drift, but probably some shale comes in, and then the Sandy Limestone, which can be seen on the dip of the strata, at a lower level, about 200 yards along the road to the east. The Sandy Limestone has been worked and evidently burnt for lime, and it must occur just over the upper beds in the section, being immediately below the Lower Cefn-y-Fedw Sandstone and Conglomerate, which rises to the south and forms the bold outline of Sclattyn Hill.

[To be continued.]

MEMBERS

OF THE

LIVERPOOL GEOLOGICAL SOCIETY.

HONORARY MEMBERS.

A. C. RAMSAY, F.R.S., F.G.S., London.
JOHN MORRIS, F.G.S., London.
S. J. MACKIE, F.G.S., F.S.A., London.
WILLIAM PENGELLY, F.R S., F.G.S., Torquay.
EDWARD W. BINNEY, F.R.S., F.G.S., Douglas, Isle of Man.
WILLIAM BRYHAM, Wigan.
HENRY HICKS, F.G.S., M.R.C.S.E., London.
W. KING, D. Sc., Queen's College, Galway.

MEMBERS.

ABRAHAM, J., Riverham, Grassendale Park.
   87, Bold Street.
ARCHER, F., B.A., Boundary Cottage, Crosby.
   14, Cook Street.
*BEASLEY, H., Acre-field House, Woolton.
*BOSTOCK, R., 8, Grange Lane, Birkenhead.
BREWSTER, C., Rev., 115, Huskisson Street.
BROWN, C. H., Low-wood, Alexandra Road, Southport.
BROWN, J. CAMPBELL, D. Sc., F.C.S, 67, Bedford Street.
COOGAN, P. M., C.E., 47, Mersey Road, Rock Ferry.
COOKE, W. H., Aughton Springs, Town Green, Ormskirk.
DAVIES, C., 8, Kinglake Street, Edge Hill.
DAWBARN, W., Elmswood, Aigburth.
   The Temple, Dale Street,

DODD, J., 2, Derby Terrace, Rock Ferry.

†*ESKRIGGE, R. A., F.G.S., Fir Cottage, New Brighton.
18, Hackins Hey.

FABERT, C., 3, St. James' Walk.

FITZPATRICK, M., 62, Seel Street.

FITZPATRICK, J. J., 62, Seel Street.

FOSTER, E., 7, Newstead Road Smithdown Lane.

FOSTER, R. M., 34, Oxford Road, Waterloo.

GOLDSWORTH, W., Prescot.

GREEN, A., York House, Old Chester Road, Rock Ferry.
9, Canning Place.

GRIFFITHS, J., 14, Queen Street, Chester.

*HALL, H. F., F.G.S., Green Heys, Grove Road, Wallasey.
17, Dale Street.

HANCE, E. W., LL.B., Municipal Offices, Dale Street.

HATHAWAY, T., C.E., The Mount, Bangor, North Wales.

*HIGGINS, H. H., Rev., M.A., Rainhill.

HEWITT, W., B. Sc., 67, White Rock Street.

JEVONS, G., Jun., 5, Chapel Street.

JOHNSON, J. H., F.G.S., 64, Albert Road, Southport.

JONES, T., Top Lane, Wallasey.
Orange Court, Castle Street.

KEEN, R. J., 85, Edge Lane.
17, South Castle Street.

KERSHAW, J., Neville Street, Southport.

KIRBY, C., C.E., Newport, Monmothshire.

LEA, T., Vale Cottage, Huyton Quarry.

LEIGH-GREGSON S., Aigburth Road.
Slater Court, 5, Castle Street.

LEWIS, J. T., 131, Park Street.

*McCLAY, J. L., Rose Villa, Victoria Road, Oxton.

*MARRAT, F. P., 21, Kinglake Street.

MAYER, J., F.S.A., Pennant House, Lower Bebington.

*MOORE, T. J., C.M.Z.S.L., 44, Osborne Road, Tue Brook.
Liverpool Museum.

*MORGAN, ALFRED (Honorary Treasurer), 2, Rathbone Terrace,
Wellington Road, Wavertree.   Office, 126, London Road.

MORTIMER, Captain, Liverpool.

†*MORTON, G. H., F.G.S., F.R.G.S.I., (Honorary Secretary), 10, Sheil
Road.   122, London Road.

†MOTT, C. G., Sunnyside, Cavendish Road, Birkenhead.

McMILLAN, A., Conway, North Wales.

PARIS, T. J., 68 and 70, Lord Street.
    Rake Lane Liscard.
PATERSON, J., Palmyra Street, Warrington.
PEARSE, W., 15, Harrington Street.
    Green Bank Farm, Wavertree.
†*PICTON, J. A., F.S.A., Sandy Knowe, Wavertree.
    4 and 5, Queen Buildings, Dale Street.
*POTTER, C., 101, Miles Street.
PEARSON, J. E., Golborne Park, near Newton-le-Willows.
†*READE, T. M., C.E., F.G.S., Park Corner, Blundellsands.
    Canning Chambers, 4, South John Street.
†*RICKETTS, C., M.D., F.G.S., 22, Argyle Street, Birkenhead.
*ROBERTS, I., F.G.S., 26, Rock Park, Rock Ferry.
    39, Gardner's Row.
RICHARDSON, W. A., Holt Hill, Tranmere.
ROBINSON, J. J., 113, Shaw Street.
SHONE, W., F.G.S., 86, Watergate Street, Chester.
*SEMMONS, W., 20, Canning Place.
STRONGITHARM, G., 77, Whetstone Lane, Tranmere.
SPARGO, E., Bangor, North Wales.
SHERLOCK, C., 63, South John Street.
WILSON, W. H., St. Michael's Hamlet, Aigburth.
    31, Wapping.
WESTWORTH, R., 31, King Street.
WRIGHT, B. M., F.R. Hist. Soc., 90, Great Russell Street, Bloomsbury,
 London.
WARD, T., Northwich, Cheshire.
WARD, J. R., 57, Garth Road, Bangor, North Wales.
YOUNG, H., 12, South Castle Street.

   * Have read Papers before the Society.

  † Contribute annually to the Printing Fund.

INDEX.

PROCEEDINGS

OF THE

𝔏iverpool 𝔊eological 𝔖ociet

SESSION THE NINETEENTH

1877-78.

*(The Authors having revised their own papers, are alone respon
for the facts and opinions expressed in them.)*

PART IV.—VOL III.

LIVERPOOL:

C. TINLING & CO., PRINTERS, VICTORIA STREET

PROCEEDINGS

OF THE

Liverpool Geological Society.

SESSION THE NINETEENTH.

1877-8.

*(The Authors having revised their own papers, are alone responsible
for the facts and opinions expressed in them.)*

PART IV.—VOL. III.

LIVERPOOL:
C. TINLING & CO., PRINTERS, VICTORIA STREET.
—
1879.

OFFICERS, 1877-8.

President.
HUGH F. HALL, F.G.S.

Vice-President.
WILLIAM SEMMONS.

Ex-President.
T. MELLARD READE, C.E., F.G.S.

Honorary Treasurer.
ALFRED MORGAN.

Honorary Librarian.
EDWIN FOSTER.

Honorary Secretary.
GEORGE H. MORTON, F.G.S., F.R.G.S.I.

Council.
MICHAEL FITZPATRICK.
J. CAMPBELL BROWN, D.Sc., F.C.S.
CHARLES RICKETTS, M.D., F.G.S.
FREDERICK P. MARRAT.

PROCEEDINGS

OF THE

LIVERPOOL GEOLOGICAL SOCIETY.

SESSION NINETEENTH.

OCTOBER 9TH, 1877.

THE PRESIDENT, HUGH F. HALL, F.G.S., in the Chair.

The President read the Annual Address.

NOVEMBER 13TH, 1877.

THE PRESIDENT, HUGH F. HALL, F.G.S., in the Chair.

WILLIAM HEWITT, B. Sc., JOSEPH J. ROBINSON, and HENRY YOUNG were elected Ordinary Members.

The following communication was then read:—

ON THE GEOLOGICAL SIGNIFICANCE OF THE CHALLENGER DISCOVERIES.

BY T. MELLARD READE, C.E., F.G.S.

No knowledge can be more interesting than that which connects us with the past—which attempts to bring the sequence of events in an unbroken history from the earliest geological period to the present time. As a contribution towards the geological history of the world, the discoveries made during the three years' voyage of the *Challenger* have a special significance.

Although the scientific staff are still engaged in for-
mulating the results of the observations, and naturalists
in this and other countries are studying the forms of life
brought up from the ocean depths, I trust it will not be
considered premature and presumptuous of me to call
attention to some of the physical problems of geology
affected by the remarkable facts which have been now for
the first time brought to light.

Without going minutely into details, which can be
best studied in the Admiralty Reports* and the Reports
to the Royal Society†, it appears to be pretty clearly
established that there is a definite relation between depth
and temperature throughout the ocean, obscured, it may
be in some cases, by local circumstances, but, on the
whole, remarkably general and uniform.

Excepting in depths of between 100 and 200 fathoms
and under the exceptional circumstances produced
by the melting of the Antarctic Ice, the water decreases
in temperature from the surface to the bottom. In the
North Atlantic ranging from above 70° Fah. at the surface to 35˝ at 2,000 fathoms, continuing at 35° for the
greater depths, which reach, in some cases, over 3,000
fathoms. In the South Atlantic the lowest temperature
is 31° in what is called the Western tongue of the Atlantic
basin; the lowness of the temperature, it is supposed,
being due to an indraught of the Antarctic waters. The
temperature sections, to my mind, reflect the greatest
credit on the Admiralty and their officers; they are the
work of careful practical men, who have not allowed
theory to run away with them, and evince a commen-

---

* "H.M.S. *Challenger's* Reports on Ocean Soundings and Temperature," Nos. 1 to 7.

† "Reports from the *Challenger*."—Proc. of Roy. Soc., vol. xxiv.,
p. 463 to p. 636.

dable common-sense and scientific grasp of the subject. So regular, however, do they find the results of their temperature soundings, that if in any special cases the minimum is reached at a certain depth and below that the water is uniform in temperature, they assume that it is cut off from the general oceanic basin by ridges at a depth approximately the same as that at which the same temperature is found in the general ocean. This is the case with the Celebes, China, and Japan seas, which, if raised above the general ocean, would, in fact, become lake basins or inland seas.

Now, this lowering of the bottom temperature over such immense areas is certainly a remarkable and unexpected fact, and shews that the secular cooling of the earth must be extremely slow, as to all appearances contact with the bottom does not in any case appreciably influence the temperature of the bottom water.

The water is heated at the Equator and cooled at the poles, but the rate of interchange is unknown, and probably very slow. No undercurrents at great depths are recorded. Of course all currents from the Equator to the poles must come back in some form or other, but the greater bulk of water is just as likely to return in undercurrents at small depths as by a general movement of the whole depth of ocean water. The materials for making an exact calculation do not exist, but I am inclined to think the indraught of bottom water from the poles is decidely slow. The heaviest water, always the coldest, excepting it be more saline, necessarily keeps to the bottom, and when we find that contact with the bottom does not influence the temperature of water that has travelled many miles from the poles to the Equator, we must pronounce it to be an interesting and unexpected fact.* Not less remarkable is the fact that, after penetrating the surface waters of the Equator, the colder temperatures are reached nearer the surface than in more northern latitudes.

Thus we see the conditions of increase of temperature in the ocean are the reverse of those on the land. All investigations of underground temperature show a gradual increase of heat as the earth is penetrated, so that if we take it at 1° per 60 feet,† at 3,000 fathoms (the depth of part of the Atlantic), the temperature of the earth at that depth, with the surface of land at the sea level would be—allowing 55° as the normal of the surface—355°, or more than half as high again as boiling water at the surface, while at the same zone beneath the Himalayas it would not be less than 600°. The influence of surface heat and cold extends therefore, by convection, to the greatest depths of the ocean, while on land it is limited by conduction to about 80 feet. What influence on climate this great body of ice-cold water can have it would be difficult to say, but it certainly must make itself felt, and in all speculations on changes of climate the effect of former shallow or enclosed seas must not be

---

* Mr. Mallet, in the "Introduction" to his translation of Professor Palmieri's Eruption of Vesuvius in 1872, says, p. 67:—"By application of Fourier's theorem to the observed rate of increment of heat in descending from the Geothermal *couche* of invariable temperature, and the co-efficients of conductivity of the rocks of our earth's crust, as given by the long-continued observations made beneath the Observatories of Paris and Edinburgh, it results that the annual loss of heat into space of our globe at present is equal to that which would liquefy into water, at 32° Far. (0°C), about 777 cubic miles of ice." This would equal a film of ice all over the globe ·25 of an inch thick, or say 1 yard deep of fresh water raised 1° Far.

† I do not consider this by any means established, the increase varies greatly in different localities, and also with the nature of the rock. See my " Age of the World, as viewed by the Geologist and the Mathematician."—*Geo. Mag.*, April, 1878.

lost sight of. It is also quite clear that the tendency of the spreading of the cold water of the poles over so large an area of the globe must be to ameliorate the climate of the poles as its place is taken by water of a higher temperature, and it would thus seem that the great depth of the Atlantic and Pacific Ocean is a means of equalizing the temperature of the globe. In addition to the climatic effect of the geographical distribution of land and sea, the actual form and depth of the ocean bottom is a factor that has not been previously considered.

Not the least interesting of the facts brought to light by the *Challenger's* work is the distinctive character of the deposits in relation to the depth. The extended deposits of Red clay which are found to fill up most of the basins below 2,000 fathoms, * and the accompanying nodules of per-oxide of Manganese are discoveries of great geological importance. They not only show that chemical changes are taking place, previously unsuspected, but the nature of the deposit is pointed to as an indication of the great age of the present oceans. Of course, it is impossible to tell the thickness of this Red clay, but if Mr. Murray's explanation be the correct one, and it is the most reasonable yet advanced, the deposit is the result of the decomposition of volcanic products.

Who, I ask, would have suspected so large an area of the globe to be coated with matter emitted from volcanoes ? The rate of accretion must have been extraordinarily slow, as the area covered by the Red clay, compared with volcanic ejections contributed annually direct to the ocean, supplemented, even as Mr. Murray suggests, by the denudation of ancient volcanic deposits on land, is so very great.

---

* Mr. J. Murray, on Oceanic Deposits.—" Proc. of Roy. Soc.," vol. xxiv. p. 527.

The Globigerinæ ooze, first discovered by the "Porcupine" soundings as an extensive oceanic deposit, gradually shades off into the Red clay, and usually finally disappears at about 2,000 fathoms. * Now, there is no reason to suppose that the pumiceous matter is not deposited in moderate as well as great depths, and the inference therefrom is that it is obscured by the quicker accumulation of Carbonate of Lime from the tests of Foraminifera, in depths of less than 2,000 fathoms, at about which point the two deposits usually blend. As reinforcing the argument of its age, the profusion of sharks' teeth and ear bones of cetaceans found in the Red clay has been justly dwelt upon. If we assume that foraminiferal organisms (with calcareous tests) remove annually from sea water the same amount of Carbonate of Lime as is contributed by rivers from the land, we have a rough mode of arriving at the rate of accumulation of Globigerinæ ooze.

In my address on "Geological Time," which I had the honour to read to this Society, I estimated the average amount of carbonate of lime annually removed from each square mile of land surface over the whole globe at 50 tons.†

---

* In an exceptional case it was found at 2925 fathoms in the Mid-Pacific—the depth at which it is found is variable within certain limits. —Mr. J. Murray—"Proc. of Roy. Soc.," p. 525.

† It is fair to assume that the amount of Carbonate of Lime in the sea remains pretty constant, otherwise it would soon be all used up, as there is only sufficient in the sea to cover it to a depth of 4·5 feet. See Address on "Geological Time." I omit Sulphate of Lime from consideration, because if organisms can decompose it, which is a moot point with naturalists and chemists, it must be in a small degree, otherwise the sulphate would not form, as it does, the bulk of the lime in the ocean, it being contributed by the land only, at the rate of 20 tons per square mile per annum, according to my approximation. Being used up slowly, it accumulates more rapidly.

"Geological Time." — Presidential Address to the Geo. Soc., Session 1876–7; p. 21 in reprint.

At 15 feet to the ton the weight of compact limestone, this would give a uniform deposit over the whole ocean of ·0000094 of a foot per annum, but if considering the deposit as one of loose mud holding much water, we assume it to accumulate at three times that rate, it would give ·0000282 of a foot per annum, or, in round numbers, 35,500 years for a deposit of chalky mud 1 foot in thickness. If, however, we say that calcareous deposits are absent where the Red clay is present, and the whole of the Carbonate of Lime from the land is used upon the remaining area, we may reduce the period to 20,000 years. These calculations are made quite independently of any deposit of coarser materials, because they do not, as a rule, exist, except in the form of volcanic products at the depth affecting my argument. Of course, in shallower water the deposits increase much more rapidly by the admixture of other materials.

We thus find that the maximum average rate of accumulation cannot be more than 1 foot of calcareous ooze in 20,000 years,* but probably it takes much longer for that thickness to be deposited; for we may not unnaturally surmise that coral animals and molluscs remove more lime from sea water, area for area, than the minute Foraminifera. Locally, the deposit may take place more rapidly, but what is deposited in one area is robbed from another area, and I think we may safely assume that not more carbonate of lime is used up

---

* Professor Martin Duncan, F.R.S., says of deep sea deposits, in his "Presidential Address to the Geological Soc. of London," vol. xxxiii., p. 74—"I have satisfied myself from late researches that the rate of deposition is extremely slow. Thus an electric cable was laid down in the *Globigerinæ* ooze regions, and five years after a considerable coral growth had taken place on it. Some of these living calices were close above the cable, and, therefore, the deposit had been infinitesmal in that time."

annually than what is contributed annually by the land; otherwise, the quantity in the sea would finally, before this, have become reduced to nothing.* These forces of nature, in my opinion, tend to balance each other.

Where the Globigerinæ ooze ends the Red clay begins —the one shades into the other. Pumice and the materials of the Red clay are found in the ooze, and more abundantly as the Red clay is approached; hence the scientific men of the *Challenger* were driven to the conclusion that the Red clay is found in the greater depths because in them the tests become destroyed by carbonic acid before reaching the bottom.

If, then, it takes 20,000 years for an average thickness of one foot of chalky mud to accumulate over the area occupied by it, how long a period will be required for one foot of Red clay?—the mind stands aghast at the problem. Probably 10 times as long.† Certainly the volcanic emissions annually directly deposited in the sea, combined with those due to denudation, must be excessively small compared to the amount of carbonate of lime annually contributed by the whole surface of the

---

* Mr. Murray says ("Proc. of Roy. Soc.," vol. xxiv., p. 531): "When there has been no reason to suppose that the trawl has sunk more than one or two inches in the clay, we have had in the Bag over a hundred shark's teeth and between thirty and forty ear-bones of cetaceans; some of them have been imbedded in over an inch of the Manganese arranged in concentric layers, while others have had just a trace of Manganese on them, or none at all. . . . In the *Globigerinæ*, Radiolarian and Diatom oozes we have found during the whole cruise only one or two shark's teeth and perhaps one tympanic bone. In shore deposits they were even more rare. These facts, taken with others that will at once suggest themselves, go to show, as might be expected, that the shore deposits accumulate faster than the organic oozes, and these last faster than the deep sea clay."

† See Geological Time before quoted.

Land. Not only does Geology tell us this, but the arrangement of the deposits in the sea also tells us the same thing.

The nodules of per-oxide of Manganese, and the profusion of sharks' teeth both point to the same conclusion, and it is not to be wondered at if some Geologists are almost ready to believe that our great oceans, from the beginning of geological time, have always been as they are now. It has been said that this Red clay deposit has no equivalent in any of the known rocks, and this is used as another argument. *

While believing that the ocean depths are of enormous age, it is impossible to resist other evidences that they have once been land. The very continuity of animal life on the globe points to it. The molluscous fauna of the Eastern Coast of North America is very similar to that of Europe, and this could not have happened without littoral continuity, and at no very distant period, geologically speaking; yet there are depths of 1,500 fathoms between these continents. Again, the form of the bottom of the North and South Atlantic is so like a continuation of the land; the Dolphin, Challenger, and Connecting Ridges follow so naturally the outlines of the continents they lie between, that it is difficult to believe they have not been formed by sub-aerial denu-

---

* The President of the Royal Soc., Dr. Hooker, stated ("Proc. of Roy. Soc.," vol. xxv., p. 354) that Mr. Sorby informed him that a microscopic examination of the "Red Clays" showed them to be, in composison, like the Gault. This is singular, as the Gault is associated with the chalk, but where are the pumice stones and per-oxide of Manganese? On the other hand, Mr. J. Starkie Gardner believes the Gault to be a shallow water deposit.—*Quar. Journ. of Geo. Soc.*, vol. xxxiii., p. 206.

dation—that they are not, in fact, valleys and mountains.*

The probable causes of these subsidences and up-heavals I am at present engaged in investigating; so I will not touch upon them now, but will simply confine myself to a consideration of the significance of the alleged absence of rocks corresponding to the Red clay deposit of the ocean.

In the first place, we are not by any means prepared to prove a negative. With so much of the area of the Globe unexamined geologically, he would be a bold man to declare that equivalents in the Earth's crust do not exist. Again, if they do exist, it would probably be in sporadic patches, for any one acquainted with sub-aerial denudation will know what havoc the rain and weather would make with a thin coating (like the deposit in question would probably be), unless protected by denser deposits above. Of all the dangers that beset a geologist, that of reasoning from the absence of an expected thing is the worst, as conclusions are so readily based upon it. Again, it is quite within the bounds of possibility it may turn out the true explanation that seas of the depth of over 2,000 fathoms never existed on the sites of our present continents. It is quite consistent with the sup-position that the extreme depths of the ocean may at one time or other have been dry land—that only shallow seas or seas of moderate depth may have at the same time flowed over portions of the present continents. The ocean depths may thus prove to be *relatively* permanent indentations. Certainly the character of the rocks,

---

* Mr. Judd says, speaking of these ridges: "Hence it is not difficult to picture to ourselves the existence in later Tertiary times of a great band of volcanic peaks, comparable in magnitude and parallel in position with the range which now forms the western boundary of the great American continent."—"Contributions to the Study of Volcanos," *Geo. Mag.*, 1876.

generally composed so largely of sediments, would rather tend to confirm this view. If we consider the Globe in its present form as liable to equal subsidences and up-heavals over large areas, it follows that an upheaval bringing the present Atlantic bottom 400 fathoms nearer to the surface, balanced by an equal subsidence in Asia, would lay a great area of land under water without affecting the Atlantic as an ocean to any material extent. As so clearly shown by Darwin 30 years ago in respect to South America,* there are general and tolerably equable upheavals, extending for thousands of miles, occurring independently of the actual fracturing of the Earth's crust, so that it is extremely probable that the deposits over continental areas may be greater, more fluctuating and variable in character than those which take place over the areas now occupied by the oceans.

The time has not yet come for taking a comprehensive view of the bearings of this recently acquired knowledge of the ocean depths : that must be deferred until all the information is published ; and facts are so interlocked and dependant for their thorough comprehension on classification, system and arrangement, that until each specialist has finished his work it were impossible to generalise with complete success. Sufficient is known to enable us to say the work of the *Challenger* will be an important contribution to natural Science, and of the greatest value in assisting to solve some great and enthralling problems of the Earth's history, the interpretation of which has been reserved for the present age.

* " Geological Observations ": We have seen that upraised marine remains occur at intervals, and in some parts almost continuously, from lat. 45° 35.' to 12° S along the shores of the Pacific. This is a distance in a North and South line of 2,075 geographical miles." " Judging from the upraised shells alone, the elevation in Chiloe has been 350 ft., at Conception certainly 625 ft., and by estimation 1,000 ft.; at Valparaiso 1,300 ft," &c.—Sec. Edit., p. 276.

DECEMBER 11th, 1877.

The President, HUGH F. HALL, F.G.S., in the Chair.

Patrick M. Coogan, C.E., was elected an Ordinary Member.

The following communications were read:—

ON EXAMPLES OF SUB-AERIAL EROSION DURING INTERVALS IN THE DEPOSITION OF THE CARBONIFEROUS LIMESTONE.

By Charles Ricketts, M.D., F.G.S.

NOTES OF CHRYSOCOLLA.

By William Semmons.

Situate on the Triassic rocks, with frequent coverings of the Boulder-clay, Liverpool seems completely shut out from any relation with mineral deposits. Its extensive commerce, however, sometimes affords collectors opportunities for acquiring valuable specimens from foreign lands, and the following notes were prompted by observations on some heavy arrivals of Copper Ores from Lower California. These ores were of a very remarkable character. They consisted almost wholly of Chrysocolla, and the carbonates of copper, which generally accompany this mineral, were present only to a very minute extent. When Carbonate was present, it was always as "Azurite," the blue variety. Occasionally a little chloride of copper, "Atacamite," was found, interstratified with gypsum, &c.; both these two compounds being formed in the neighbourhood of volcanoes, might point to igneous action being connected with the deposits. The other associated minerals, Kupferfrechez (see Trans. L'pool Geol. Soc., 1876–7, p. 282), &c., are not within the purpose of the present paper.

The remarkable varieties of Chrysocolla met with, and their peculiar behaviour before the blow-pipe, induced me to compare them with varieties from Chili, Peru, Cornwall, and other localities. The results to which I have been led are stated at the end of this paper, and I will, in the first place, give a brief description of the several varieties I have found.

No. 1, FROM LOWER CALIFORNIA.

This large stone shows strikingly a series of gradations from the light earthy variety of Chrysocolla, with hardness 1, to the vitreous variety, hardness 5. Beautiful dendritic formations of manganese ore are scattered throughout the specimen, and Kupferfrechez is also present. Commencing with the vitre us variety, we find it of a dark, blueish green colour; this passes gradually into a lighter shade, until we reach a variety with the faintest tinge of blue green, almost white. The light-coloured variety is quite adherent and fuses in blow-pipe flame, while the dark-coloured variety (typical Chrysocolla) is quite infusible, and is non-adherent. Thin veins of the vitreous variety permeate the other, and a layer of chalcedony covers them both; this, in its turn, is covered by a layer of calcite crystals.

No. 2 (SAME LOCALITY).

Similar to the light earthy variety described above, but so porous that it floats on water. Colour, light blue green; hardness, 1 to 1½. Remarkably absorbent of

of water, and when saturated becomes of a much
darker colour. Fuses before the blow-pipe. Mr. W. M.
Hutchings, F.I.C., whose assistance in these examinations I would here acknowledge as being of the highest
possible value, has analysed this variety with the following result, which I have placed for comparison with
an analysis made, by the same gentleman, of the hard
and vitreous variety from No. 5.

	VARIETY, Hard and Vitreous.	VARIETY, Soft and Earthy.
$Si\ O_2$	67·07	46·45
$Cu\ O$	24·95	39·15
$Pb\ O$	·26	·41
$Fe_2\ O_3$	·27	·48
$Al_2\ O_3$	·55	3·65
$Zu\ O$	·09	·10
$Ca\ O$	·81	·80
$Mg\ O$	·37	·82
$H_2\ O$	5·82	7·99

These minerals were heated to 95° Cent. for some hours,
and the water determined by heating to redness.

No. 3 (SAME LOCALITY).

Layers of amorphous felspar and chalcedony, sometimes containing crystalline quartz. The felspar,
apparently when unchanged of a dull greyish brown
colour, passes through various shades of blue to a very
dark blue, at the same time becoming richer in silica
and much harder. The silica appears to increase still
more, until the variety is hard enough to scratch glass.
In one instance the hard blue variety graduates into
almost pure chalcedony of a dull grey colour.

No. 4 (SAME LOCALITY).

A series of layers, each about 2 millimetres of gypsum, soft brown Hepatinerz, black Kupferpechez, and Atacamite, with Calcite.

No. 5 (SAME LOCALITY).

Resembles vari-coloured jasper so much in appearance, that were it not for an unmistakable piece of typical Chrysocolla of the usual hardness thereon, it would probably be taken as such. The colours are blue, blueish green, brown, grey of all shades, from black on one side to white on the other. Dendritic manganese ore is disseminated throughout the entire mass. In some cases there is semi-opalescent quartz mixed with the Chrysocolla.

No doubt can be entertained that this stone represents various stages of deposits of copper and silica in solution, sometimes the one, at other times the other in excess. The solution would also at times have more or less iron or manganese present. The analysis of this hard vitreous variety shows no less than 67 per cent. silica and 5·8 water, so that the surmise by Berthier of opal silica being present is probably correct, as both physical and chemical examinations confirm it.

No. 6, FROM UTAH.

Is composed of both brown and blueish green varieties. The fibrous radiations of malachite pervade the stone, and as some of these are completely converted into Chrysocolla, the stone possesses great interest.

No. 7, FROM PERU.

As typical of a parcel of some 300 tons, this is instructive. It consists of a mixture of Chrysocolla, Malachite, and Atacamite, the latter two being generally

B

crystallised. As some characteristic crystals of Ataca-
camite are partially converted into Malachite, and this
passes into Chrysocolla, it would appear that the above
sequence represents the age of these minerals in this
locality. I also find crystals with the characteristic form
of Malachite converted into a Silicate of Copper.

No. 8, FROM PERU.

Represents another large importation of quite a
different characterr It looks as if it had been subjected
to decomposing agencies. Numerous cavities occur in
which the Chrysocolla is almost crystalline. In some
instances layers of small quartz crystals are found, and
on these, very minute crystals of Dioptase of a rich
emerald green occur.

No. 8, FROM CHILI.

In this stone are nodules of a brown-red variety,
encircled by the blue. As the depth of the blue increases
as the kernel (other colour) is neared, there seems to be
a connection between the two. The red probably existed
formerly as Cuprite, or native Copper, and has since
been decomposed. This view of the origin of Chrysocolla
is maintained by Dr. Burghardt. It is interesting to
notice that at one portion of the stone minute Crystals
of Dioptase are met with, while in another, quartz
Crystals, with native Copper interspersed between them,
are found.

No. 9, FROM CORNWALL.

One of the typical specimens from the celebrated
Wheal Gorland Mine contains well defined crystals of
Olivenite on pseudomorphous layers of quartz. At the
base is a mass of Green Chrysocolla passing into Kaolin.
It fuses with ease before the blowpipe.

No. 10, FROM CORNWALL.

A piece of ordinary Cornish Granite, from South Carn Brea Mine. It has a small vein of Cuprite, about 2 metres wide running through it. The Felspar crystals on either side have been partly converted into Chrysocolla, and this alteration is greater as the Cuprite is neared. The small quartz crystals seem to be surrounded with layers of Chrysocolla, while the Mica has been quite changed into thin hexagonal flakes of a bright green colour, resembling Chalcophyllite.

No. 11, FROM CORNWALL.

This stone, from South Caradon Mine, shows very clearly how Chrysocolla may be found in the decomposition of other Copper Ores. One portion consists of almost pure Kaolin, but in another part several nodules of Chrysocolla surround inner kernels of Chalcocite. Examining one of these nodules we find the central portion to be quite compact Chalcocite, with the ordinary streak and sectility of that mineral. Proceeding outwards the streak becomes less metallic, and nearly earthy, of a white colour. The mineral assumes gradually a reddish brown colour, as if some small quantity of iron present had been converted into oxide, and then a layer of Chrysocolla is reached. This is first of a deep blue colour, and then shades gradually away to pure white Kaolin. The depth of its blue colour appeared to coincide inversely with the adherency of the stone, as if with the increased per centage of Copper, the Kaolin lost its ordinary property of adhering to the tongue.

An examination of the literature on this ore shows such a variety in the per centage of Copper and Silica, of what are called pure specimens, that I am tempted to lay down the proposition that no formula can be tabulated for the mineral. In fact, the term "Chrysocolla" should be taken as representing a group of Hydrated Silicates of Copper, varying in chemical composition and behaviour, also in physical character and blowpipe reaction.

Dane ("System of Mineralogy," p. 403) gives the results of 15 analyses of what I presume are pure varieties, as in p. 404 he gives 11 analyses of impure ones. The results of these fifteen show the following per centages :—

	Min.	Max.	
Oxide of Copper	28 to	45	per cent.
Silica	26 ,,	52	,,
Water	16 ,,	31	,,

This seems sufficient to show the absurdity of giving a fixed formula for the mineral, but Mr. Hutching's analyses, showing in one case (No. 3) 67 per cent. Silica and 25 per cent. Oxide of Copper, and in the other (No. 5) 47 per cent. Silica, with 39 per cent. Oxide of Copper, and 3·6 per cent. Alumina, demonstrate the absurdity in even a more striking manner. These varieties, so different in all their characters, are, as I have shown, connected together by others of an intermediate character, so that a complete gradation can be established from a variety hard enough to scratch glass to one soft enough to be scratched by the finger nail; from one infusible before the blowpipe to another fusing easily; from an ore containing 25 per cent. Oxide of Copper to one containing 39 per cent. Again, every gradation can be traced from the typical varieties of Chrysocolla through others containing less and less copper, until we arrive at Chalcedony on the one side and pure Kaolin on another.

Some little light, too, is thrown on the probable formation of Chrysocolla by the examination of so many varieties, and I think we shall have to allow of at least more than one mode. In the specimen, No. 11, where a gradual change can be seen in the condition of the Ore acted on, and also in the condition of the Kaolin surrounding, there seems but little doubt of its resulting from the action of these minerals on one another in the presence of water. In specimen No. 5 the mineral appears to have been formed from a solution, in which Copper and Silica were both present, sometimes the one and sometimes the other in excess. Dioptase crystals would seem to be formed when the proportion of Copper and Silica, such as it is composed of, existed.

JANUARY 8TH, 1878.

The Vice Persident, WILLIAM SEMMONS, Esq., in the Chair.

The following communication was read:—

ON THE BEDS IMMEDIATELY OVERLYING THE UPPER PEAT OR SO CALLED FOREST-BED OF THE CHESHIRE SHORE.

By Charlrs Potter.

FEBRUARY 12TH, 1878.

THE VICE-PRESIDENT, WILLIAM SEMMONS, ESQ.,
in the Chair.

The following communications were read : —

NOTES ON THE MINERALOGICAL STRUCTURE OF SOME CORNISH GRANITES.

BY WILLIAM SEMMONS.

THE Granite districts of Cornwall have by some writers been compared to islands which rise out of a sea of clay slate. The three largest patches, which form, as it were, prominent processes in the backbone of the county, also contain the chief veins of metallic ores for which Cornwall has been celebrated so many centuries.

The scanty vegetation of these Granite districts, with their scattered boulders and Logan rocks seems to make a fit home for the giants and piskies which the interesting legends of the people say resided here. Passing, too, from the fertile meadows on the southern shore to the bleak wild moorlands of the Granite districts, we can easily trace the relation between the Geology and Agriculture of a district.

Of late years the commercial value of Cornish Granite has vastly increased, and now many thousand hands are employed in connection with the various Granite works. Chief among these are the fine quarries of the Messrs. Freeman, whose enterprise and skill have caused the various kinds of Cornish Granite to become known. Not only do they furnish large blocks for dock works, &c., but their polishing department shows some of these

Granites to have a highly ornamented character. This process of polishing, while it renders the stone more pleasing to the eye, also enables its structure to be examined more easily, and as, through the liberality of the Messrs. Freeman, I have been enabled to examine no less than eight distinct and characteristic varieties from their various quarries, I have great pleasure in stating the results thereof. The specimens being of large size, I have been able to investigate sections of crystals of the various minerals at every angle, so that the innermost structure could be ascertained.

Before describing in detail the special characteristics of each variety, it may be well to first speak of these Granites in general terms. They may be considered as typical members of their class, being composed generally of orthoclose quartz and mica. Sometimes oligoclase is present. The micas are represented by both the principal groups, Muscovite and Biotite. The quartz is usually white or dull grey, but sometimes is of other tints as red, brown, &c. Many other minerals are found in it, sometimes forming a large portion of the rock. Amongst these are schorl (tourmaline), fluor spar, &c. The description given by Dr. Haughton ("Trans. Royal Irish Academy," vol. xxiii.) of the great Leinster mass of Granite seems fairly to represent those of Cornwall.

The felspar never forms less than one-third, rarely less than one-half, and generally a still larger proportion of the mass. The whole of the four or five minerals seem embedded in a felspathic paste, which does not assume any definite crystalline form, and seems to be the superfluous mineral which remained unused when the other minerals were formed.

Prof. Ramsay ("Physical Geography and Geology of Great Britain," p. 51) says:—"In Granites there is generally a quantity of free silica, not always crystallised in definite forms like the two other minerals enveloping the crystals of felspar and mica." The Cornish Granites resemble the description of Haughton rather than that of Ramsay.

I now proceed to describe the structure and mineralogical characters of the different varieties.

No. 1.—CARNSEW.

May be considered as a Granite of ordinary appearance, having the cold grey colour of Granite hills, as usually seen.

Composed of felspar, quartz, and mica; the quantity of the former being rather in excess of the other two.

Felspar, in imperfectly formed crystals, sometimes $\frac{3}{4}$ in. by $\frac{1}{4}$ in., and enveloping the quartz and mica.

This seems to be the last mineral which consolidated, if the mica is not derived from it. It forms the paste spoken of by Professor Ramsay. The colour is generally white. H = 6.

Quartz occurs in detached crystals, and in long continuations of these crystals. In some cases the crystals are cut across perfectly, and show the section of the hexagonal prism, and occasionally the layers of growth are to be seen. The quartz is of a light purplish grey colour.

The mica is frequently found embedded in the quartz and around the edges of the felspar. Sometimes very small flakes are found along small lines of fissure or cleavage in the felspar, but this only rarely.

The variety is generally that known as Muscovite. It generally occurs in layers of from $\frac{1}{100}$ in. to $\frac{1}{6}$ in. by $\frac{1}{6}$ in. to $\frac{1}{2}$ in. in length.

No other minerals seem present in the rock, and it presents the character of having undergone but little change since its formation.

No. 2. CARN GREY.—CORNWALL.

In this Granite the felspar is much in excess of the other ingredients.

Felspar is of a white colour, sometimes in imperfect crystals 1 in. in greatest length by $\frac{3}{8}$ in. wide. It also forms the ground mass of the rock, and has evidently been formed after the quartz. Colour, white. H = 6.

Quartz.—This mineral occurs in detached crystals, larger than in No. 1, and not in the long continuous lines. In some cases sections of the hexagonal prism are shown with a diameter of $\frac{1}{4}$ in., but they are more often $\frac{1}{16}$ in. The lines of growth are beautifully seen in some instances, and occasionally what appears to be hollows in the quartz crystals. These are probably the cavities investigated by Sorby. The mica occurs in disseminated patches of $\frac{1}{100}$ in. to $\frac{1}{4}$ in. Probably the latter is the width and the former the thickness of the mica deposits. The variety is again Muscovite, mostly of a dark colour, but with an occasional flake of white variety.

As a rule, it is found around the quartz crystals, but in one instance it looks as if a crystal of felspar were being decomposed into a mica. No other instance of change can be seen in the stone.

No. 3.—LAMORNA. CORNWALL.

A porphyritic variety of a greenish yellow colour, when viewed as a whole.

The appearance is rather pleasing, owing to the large crystals of white felspar being well shown up by the considerable quantity of black mica and vari-coloured felspars surrounding them.

Felspar of two varieties.

1st. White variety, resembling albite, occurring in crystals $1\frac{1}{2}$ in. by 1 in. down to $\frac{1}{4}$ in. by $\frac{1}{16}$, frequently containing flakes of mica embedded. This has a hardness of 6 —

2nd. Green and yellow variety in crystals $\frac{1}{4}$ in. by $\frac{1}{16}$ in., and forming the enveloping compound. The quartz is found in small crystals $\frac{1}{16}$ in. to $\frac{1}{10}$ in. Mica usually in very fine flakes, scattered throughout the ground mass, which, in fact, consists of amorphous felspar, and mica. Few of the large felspar crystals are quite free from flakes of mica in them. In one instance, the mica has assumed the shape of a felspar crystal, and also sets off branches into another crystal, as if it resulted from the decomposition of the latter. This crystal is $1\frac{1}{4}$ in. long by $\frac{3}{8}$ in. at shortest width.

One would say this rock shows a somewhat altered appearance to its original structure.

No. 4.—LUXULYAN. CORNWALL.

In this variety the surface to the extent of about one-eighth is occupied by mica, the remaining portion being about equally divided between felspar and quartz. There is also a saponaceous or greasy feeling mineral (a variety of lithomarge), sometimes occurring in distinct spherical nodules, but more frequently occupying the centre of felspar crystals, and occasionally having the perfect shape of the felspar crystals.

The felspar appears in large crystals $1\frac{1}{2}$ in. long, sometimes down to $\frac{1}{2}$ in., but does not appear to form an enveloping paste, as in some other instances. Colour, white. H = 6, and frequently contains small flakes of mica.

The quartz occurs in long continuous sinuous lines, showing an appearance similar to the columnar structure noticed in Basalts. In one crystal a pear-shaped cavity is seen about $\frac{3}{10}$ in. long, and in some others, irregular shaped cavities, from $\frac{1}{100}$ in. wide are seen.

The mica is black, in groups of flakes about $\frac{1}{8}$ in. by $\frac{1}{8}$ in., generally surrounding the felspar crystals, occasionally embedded in them. This is probably a rock in which some change has been caused, as when the felspar crystals show signs of change they are softer, and the change to the saponaceous mineral is gradual.

No. 5.—TROWLESWORTHY. DEVON.

In this the quartz occurs in irregular patches of various shapes, sometimes 1 in. by $\frac{1}{4}$ in., at others $\frac{3}{8}$ in. by $\frac{3}{8}$ in. The felspar forms the ground mass, and certainly more than half the bulk.

The quartz preserves the ordinary appearance, and shows some of the cavities noted by Sorby.

There are two varieties of felspar—one of a white colour, which occurs in crystals of varying size, from $\frac{1}{4}$ in. by $\frac{1}{16}$ in. to $\frac{1}{2}$ in. by $\frac{1}{4}$ in.—the other of a red colour, forming the ground mass, and encircling the white variety, also frequently the patches of quartz.

The micas are of the dark variety, also the silvery— probably two varieties of Muscovite.

The quartz crystals are much more perfect than the felspar, and are occasionally seen *protruding through the latter.*

The rock seems to have consolidated under conditions which allowed but little play to the crystalline forces, and to have had a large quantity of iron in it.

No. 6.—WHITE ROCKS. CORNWALL.

A remarkably fine grained Granite, looking as if the mass were made up of minute crystals of orthoclase, quartz, and mica.

The quartz in crystals seldom more than $\frac{1}{10}$ in. diameter. Some of these show cavities, which are generally round.

Felspar appears in an amorphous paste, and also small crystals, of a grey colour ; some larger ones are also found confusedly scattered throughout. These vary from $\frac{1}{8}$ in. by $\frac{1}{4}$ in. to $\frac{1}{4}$ in. by $\frac{3}{8}$ in., and are generally white, sometimes tinged with yellow.

Mica is generally scattered throughout the stone in minute specks. Sometimes clusters are found $\frac{3}{16}$ in. by $\frac{1}{4}$ in.; black colour. No other mineral seen.

The consolidation of this Granite seems to have taken place under conditions which allowed less play to the crystallising forces. In one instance the largest felspar crystal on the stone has one end imperfect, owing to the quartz *crystal occupying the space*. The quartz is perfectly formed.

No. 7.—GRANITE FROM NEWLYN.

A highly schorlaceous variety, in which by far the greatest portion is made up of very minute crystals of felspar quartz and chorls, giving rise to an almost black ground mass, whilst scattered through it are crystals of yellowish white felspar, evidently undergoing decomposition.

On examination with a low power the rock is seen to be covered with small hollows, showing decomposition has been at work.

Almost all trace of the original Granite structure is lost, and were it not that it can be traced by degrees into Granite of normal appearance, its origin would be a matter of speculation.

No. 8.—LUXULLIANITE.

This is evidently an altered rock. Essentially large crystals of felspar, with two kinds of tourmaline, and crystals of quartz.

The felspar crystals vary in size from 2 in. by $1\frac{1}{2}$ in. down to $\frac{1}{16}$ in. by $\frac{1}{20}$ in.

The edges of the felspar crystals are jagged, and show it has undergone change. This is confirmed by the general appearance of the specimen, which presents a marked contrast to the firm and compact nature of Granite.

It is considered—and, to me, it seems with very good reason—to be an altered Granitic rock.

This remarkable rock occurs in Boulders only, as the parent rock is unknown. The sarcophagus of the late Duke of Wellington is made from it. It is described very fully by Prof. Bonney in *Mineralogical Magazine*. In this most valuable essay the relation between tourmaline and mica is shown in an altogether new light.

Closely related to the Granites are the Elvans of Cornwall. These two consist largely of felspar: in some cases to the extent of three-fourths of the mass. They also contain, often perfectly formed, crystals of quartz, and occasionally a variety of other minerals. The relations of these dykes to the Granitic masses and overlying clay-slate would constitute material for another paper.

Summarising the facts observed, we find an examina- of the eight varieties before described shows :—

1st. The felspars are usually in excess of the other constituents, and present the following features:

 a. They form by far the larger portion of the ground mass.

b. The crystals are sometimes imperfect, from their edges being cut off by those of quartz.

c. The crystals are frequently penetrated by quartz crystals, which latter have their form perfect and not distorted.

d. The crystals and ground mass sometimes show traces of pseudomorphism into tourmaline (schorl) and mica.

2nd. The quartz is usually in well-defined prisms, with, in some cases, perfect pyramidal terminations. A consideration of the foregoing facts leads to the following conclusions or deductions:

A. We find, from a consideration of "b" and "c," that the quartz was evidently the first mineral to crystallize.

B. Metamorphic action has been at work even in these rocks which appear to retain their original hard structure.

C. This metamorphism seems to be related to the appearance in the rock of schorl (which contains boracic acid and fluorine).

This latter deduction confirms the results spoken of by Bonney, Foster, and Collins. Probably the immense masses of decomposed Granite and Elvan in Cornwall and elsewhere may hereafter be found to have resulted from emanation of gases or percolation of water charged with such gases from below, rather than, as formerly taught, through the influence of waters which have been acidulated at or above the surface of the Earth.

ON THE MICROSCOPIC STRUCTURE OF THE CARBONIFEROUS LIMESTONE WITH REFERENCE TO ITS MODE OF DEPOSITION.

By Henry C. Beasley.

Having lately examined, microscopically, a number of specimens of Carboniferous Limestone, principally from North Wales and Somersetshire, the author brought a few notes of his observations before the Society.

A piece of Limestone free from any large fragments of shells or other fossils, when examined under a 1-inch objective, is usually found to consist of more or less opaque amorphous particles, and fragmentary or perfect fossil Microzoa scattered through a transparent crystalline matrix; but the various proportions of each vary greatly. The Microzoa often are entirely absent. In some cases the opaque particles are so numerous that there is scarcely any of the matrix visible; in others they are very scarce, whilst the fragments of fossils stand out clear and distinct from each other in the transparent matrix.

The most common Microzoa are Foraminifera of the Genera, Trochammina, Endothyra, and Textularia, fragments of the skeletons of Polyzoa, spines of Echini. Occasionally the calcareous bodies found in the skin of many Echinoderms, Sponge spicules, and in some Limestones are bodies supposed to be the tests of radiolarians.

Certain dark coloured Limestones contain fragmentary forms of apparently vegetable origin, and this supposition is confirmed by the fact that a Limestone of this character at the base of rocks forming the Great Ormeshead has been found to contain 3 per cent. of carbon.

Besides the appearance above described, there are many beds in the Carboniferous formation exhibiting öolitic structure. This is not so common in North Wales as in the South of England. Mr. Morton has kindly given me a specimen from Llanymynech which exhibits this structure, and which is remarkable for the large size of the öolites, which lie in a granular matrix, the whole held together by a transparent cement. Mr. G. W. Shrubsole, of Chester, also mentions a bed in the Vale of Clwyd. This structure is, however, very commonly met with in the Carboniferous Limestone in the neighbourhood of Bristol and the Cheddar cliffs in the Mendips.

The öolites are spheroidal bodies more or less opaque, and shew, in section, a number of concentric rings, the latter often crossed by numerous radiating lines. The nucleus consists generally of a fragment of a Foraminifer or a minute crystal, or occasionally a perfect fossil. The space between the öolites is usually filled with a transparent crystalline matrix, but occasionally, as in the specimen from Llanymynech, with minute granules. It is not at all unusual to find a Foraminifer between the oolites, and having no trace of any deposit or aggregation of particles upon it.

The conclusions arrived at with reference to its deposition was that the bulk of the Carboniferous Limestone was the result of the disintegration of coral reefs, by the action of the waves. Sea water is rarely found to contain more than one-fifth of the amount of Carbonate of Lime it is capable of holding in solution; it, however, acts so slowly on organically formed Carbonate of Lime, of which, of course, coral reefs are composed, that the detritus is carried away in much larger quantities than the sea water can dissolve before it is deposited in deeper water as a calcareous mud, entombing the remains of the organisms inhabiting the superjacent sea. Comparing a section of Limestone with one of Chalk, the difference in the microzoa is at once apparent. Foraminifera are abundant in each, but the genera differ greatly, the Chalk showing oceanic forms, such as are found in the recent Globigerina ooze, whilst the genera found in the Limestone point to shallower water. Again, the chalk is almost entirely made up of organic remains, whereas the amorphous particles before mentioned form by far the greater part of the Limestone. The deposits now forming in the enclosed seas between Torres Straits and the Straits of Malacca are apparently the modern representatives of the Carboniferous Limestone.

Some beds are undoubtedly the remains of coral reefs *in situ*, as may be seen from the abundance of reef forming corals they contain. Other beds, and probably all containing vegetable remains, have been formed nearer shore, as well as those Limestones which are mainly composed of the shells of Mollusca ; but, as far as the microscope throws a light on the subject, the finer and more massive beds appear to have been formed in moderately deep water of, say 400 to 1,000 fathoms, in the manner mentioned above.

With regard to the oolitic beds, their modern representatives are certain beach sands and sandy patches, or coral reefs, now consolidating with a distinct oolitic structure, as described by Dana, Jukes, and others ; but it is hardly probable that all the limestone shewing this structure should have been formed in a similar manner; and the author suggested the possibility of a tendency in very finely comminuted detritus to form spheroidal concretions, so as to form an öolitic rock in deep water.

MARCH 12TH, 1878·

CHARLES RICKETTS, M.D., F.G,S., in the Chair.

HENRY BRAMMALL was elected an Ordinary Member.

The following communications were read—

SOME FURTHER NOTES ON THE SUB-MARINE FOREST AT THE ALT MOUTH.

By T. MELLARD READE, C.E., F.G.S., F.R.I.B.A.

My attention having of late been more particularly directed to the remains of the submarine forest at the Alt mouth, in consequence of finding a great many mammalian bones—which I purpose describing at some future time—and also by the rapid changes which are taking place, I invited several of our Society to the uprooting of one of the stumps. This I have described in a short paper sent to the London Geological Society.*

I have since inspected the forest, to ascertain in what manner the trees grew and were preserved. The bases of the trees are represented in some cases by stools a couple of feet high, in others only by the ramifications of the roots; while where the peat has actually been skinned off we see nothing but tap roots in groups on the surface of the blue clay. The roots are invariably in a very spongy and decayed condition. In one or two cases the star-like ramification of the roots from the basal stump along the surface of the peat is very prominent, and these again throw out tap roots penetrating the blue clay or sand beneath. I took the positions and distances apart of the trees in a group which I here represent. They varied from 8 yards to 2 yards apart. In another case there was an oak stool with two appa-

---

* "The Submarine Forest at the Alt Mouth."—Quar. Journal of Geol. Soc., vol. xxxiv., pp. 147–8.

rently smaller trees, represented only by basal roots, 1½ yards from it, measuring from centre to centre. The whole of the group were oaks.

The roots of another stump measured, so far as they extended and were exposed on the surface of the peat, 4 yards across. Our excavation showed that the roots struck diagonally into the blue clay in the two examples we tested, and I have little doubt but that all are pretty much the same as those we tried.

I have also closely examined the constitution of the peat, and I find that the bulk of it is composed of decayed woody fibre and bark, with some grasses and water plants. The silvery bark of the birch is very prominent, and I find it in some cases resting upon the sandy soil of the upper part of the shore which the blue clay graduates into. The lower part of the peat is especially prolific in branches and bark.

From the abundance of forestal remains it is quite clear to me there has been a long succession of growth. The proximity of some of the stumps in various groups also shows that the trees cannot all have grown at the same moment. The fact that the stumps are actually rooted into the ground is positive evidence the trees grew in situ. The difficulty that some of the members of this Society feel in conceiving how the first growth of trees could have rotted before the next set grew is therefore only a difficulty, if it be one, to be explained.

The stumps of the trees are in various stages of decay, as we should expect from a successive, not a simultaneous growth. I think it probable that the situation was at the first a moist one, favourable to the growth of the alder, of which there exist remains. It is quite clear it was never a swamp or bog until the whole forest became finally destroyed. It is also evident that there existed some antiseptic conditions which allowed the remains to accumulate and be preserved. In many cases the bark of the branches is pressed close together, the internal woody fibre having decayed.

The tree we dug up, portions of which are in my garden, grew after the first layer of vegetable matter had accumulated, for the basal portion of the trunk has a layer of peat about 4 or 5 inches thick, largely composed of bark and branches, adhering to it now, and there is peat under the roots where they commence to branch off from the stool.

When a layer such as this had accumulated, it is easy to see that the deposit would have strong preservative qualities.

The roots of the trees must in all cases have been preserved; had they not been, we should find casts of them in the blue clay. To my mind, the whole question of the growth and decay of these forests never presented any serious difficulties. Now the evidence is certain, complete, and full.

One positive fact is worth a mass of negative evidence, and I cannot help regretting the prevalence of a style of reasoning on facts of Geology which appears to me more like the arguments used by a few singular people who maintain that the world is flat, than the scientific induction we expect from those who investigate Nature with a view of eliciting truth, by methods which any observer, if he takes the trouble, can test for himself. *February 4th, 1878.*

Since writing the preceding notes I have several times visited the site of the forest. The denudation from day to day reveals more clearly the nature of the deposit. Where there formerly only appeared to be peat, the sea, skimming off a layer of it, reveals the roots of trees branching out on the surface in all their various ramifications; and at other places we see when we come to the broken edge of the peat, the roots striking into the clay below. I have over and over again traced in this way the roots to the parent stem. From day to day I have collected the bones washed out of the deposits, and lately have been fortunate enough to find a number of them in situ. Just south of Thornbeck Pool there is a patch of much denuded peat, revealing the blue silt below in places. In this patchy piece I have found several bones embedded in the surface of the silt or peat. In one case particularly I noticed a small, dark, shining substance peering above the surface; on digging down I found it was the right ramus of a horse, embedded vertically, the hollow of the bone being filled with a sandy matrix. Its position was close to some roots striking through the clay, which I cut through in extracting it.

A microscopic examination of the silty sand inside the bone showed it to be principally composed of grains of quartz, partially rounded, but many angular and broken—in fact, what is known as "sharp sand." I found one or two very minute fragments of shell among it.

Excepting on this patch, I have not found any bones in situ. It appears to me they are mostly derived from the surface layer of silt under the peat, or from the peat itself.

One peculiarity of the bones is the glossy surface they usually present, appearing as if polished.

In one or two cases the bones were covered with a sandy scale, which the microscope showed were grains of quartz, cemented together with iron pyrites. It would appear that the bones in some cases antedate the forest; and, as they are scattered about in a fragmentary manner, have probably been washed into their positions by streams trickling over the sand. From the levels of the land, it is not improbable that some of the inland water has been ponded up by the tides. The deposits have all an estuarine character.

At the request of the Historic Society of Lancashire and Cheshire, I gave that Society a brief account of the digging up of the oak tree previously alluded to. Judge of my astonishment, when two gentlemen well known in connection with the subject, without in any way calling the accuracy of my description in question, passed over the facts stated as a matter of no moment, and attempted to argue that the trees had not grown in situ because *such was an impossibility*. It has been stated over and over again by the same gentlemen—unless my memory very much betrays me—that the principal evidence against the trees ever having formed part of a forest which existed on the same spot was, that the roots never penetrated the ground below. Having demonstrated to eight gentlemen of various professions and occupations, and possessing considerable scientific attainments, that the trees are rooted in the ground, I certainly thought the matter settled. Mr. Potter and Mr. Boult think otherwise; and, although I consider their objections of no weight against the positive evidence of the rooted trees, it may not be altogether lost time to examine the nature of their difficulties.

1st. "The trees could not be preserved unless embedded in water." 2nd. "Water is absolutely necessary to fossilisation." 3rd. "If there was water the trees could not grow." I have shown the place was a moist one, and that the remains of the birch, alder, and willow underlie the whole of the peat beds. Mr. John Blenkarn, Agricultural Engineer and Surveyor, says in "British Timber Trees":—"The alder is an aquatic and grows best in boggy ground and a black wet sandy soil, and may be seen sometimes flourishing amid standing water; but it will also grow on a moderately dry soil. The roots appear to have the power of attracting all the moisture and nourishing juices from the earth, rendering it totally barren round the tree." Of the birch he says: "There is hardly a soil so dry, so poor, so wet, so exposed, that this tree will not thrive in: the Earl of Haddington calls it 'an amphibious plant,' and the manner in which it endures removal from one extreme to another appears to justify this remark." The willow, he says, delights in wet and moist situations and the banks of rivers and running water, but may be found occasionally flourishing in higher ground.

Of the Oak:—" There is scarcely any land, however barren, if in some degree elevated, upon which this tree will not grow; stiff clay, hard gravelly soil and black gravelly earth are alike suitable, and fine trees are often seen growing in low and damp situations. The finest quality of oak timber will often be found growing in elevated clay districts."

Of the Pine:—" The various kinds of fir trees will grow well in almost every kind of soil, preferring generally that which is dry and elevated, whether sand, chalk, rock, or gravel."

In a paper on the "Alluvial Strata of the Lower Ouse Valley" (Pro. of the Geo. and Poly. Soc. of the West Riding of Yorkshire), Mr. Franklin Parsons, M.D., F.G.S., says: "There are large woods of Scotch fir in the East Riding growing on the wet heathy surface of the same bed of sand (sand under the peat), and I am of opinion that, therefore, they may be lineal descendants of those which anciently inhabited the district." *

* The accepted opinion is—see Lardner's "Aboretum et Fructicum Britannicum"—that the Scotch pine had died out at the time of the Roman occupation of England.

The Alder, Birch, and Willow are all found in these forest beds, and probably formed the first growth, and this being the case, the conditions for the preservation of succeeding trees would be found. The earliest trees have mostly decayed, and only the roots are found when the peat is skinned off. Of Willows there are portions to be seen, distinguished by the crookedness and branching character of the trunks, but they are very much riven, split up, and decayed, though some sound wood is to be obtained. This applies also to the Alder, of which there is little left, except branches, bark, and roots.

The Oak is the most easily recognised tree in the forest remains. It is remarkable for the soundness of its timber and the straightness of the trunks, appearing as if the trees had grown thickly together—(It is probably *Quercus Sessileflora*)—and the remains of its timber is by far the most abundant. Of the Pine there are examples, and towards the most northern part of the forest the remains of the branches and needle-shaped leaves are most abundant, showing like plumes of feathers spread out on the surface of the peat.

It seems to me rather absurd having to explain to you that it is possible for a thing to have occurred which we know by the best of geological evidence *has* occurred. I will venture to affirm that any other hypothesis than that the trees have grown in the places they now occupy is entirely out of court. If they did not grow on the spot, the alternative is they were washed there by water, or else, what is more absurd, carried there by human agency.

That they could be carried by water and carefully planted so regularly in the ground is a physical impossibility, or, at least, is too great a draught on our credulity to believe. Nor could the vegetable remains have been separated from the alluvial by any known process of water carrying. If water had transferred them to their present site, we should have had interlaminations of silt and a confused mass of vegetation.

With an apology for this expression of my views, I take leave of the subject.

APPENDIX.

"In the time of the Romans the Danish Isles were covered, as now, with magnificent beech forests. Nowhere in the world does this tree flourish more luxuriantly than in Denmark, and eighteen centuries seem to have done little or nothing towards modifying the character of the forest vegetation. Yet in the antecedent bronze period there were no beech trees, or at most but a few stragglers, the country being then covered with oak. In the age of stone again, the Scotch fir prevailed see p. 9), and already there were human inhabitants in these old pine forest."—Lyell's "Antiquity of Man," page 17.

"According to Rennie, many of these mosses of the north of Europe occupy the place of forests of pine and oak, which have, many of them, disappeared within the historical era." * * * *

"Thus, in Mar Forest, in Aberdeenshire, large trunks of Scotch fir, which had fallen from age and decay, are said to have been soon immured in peat, formed partly out of their perishing leaves and branches, and in part from the growth of other plants. We are also told that the overthrow of a forest by a storm, about the middle of the seventeeth century, gave rise to a peat moss near Lockbroom, in Ross-shire, and that, in less than half a century after the fall of the trees, the inhabitants dug peat there."

"At Tierra del Fuego almost all plants contribute by their decay to the production of peat, even the grasses; but it is a singular fact, says Mr. Darwin, as contrasted with what occurs in Europe, that no kind of moss enters into the composition of the South American peat, which is formed by many plants, but chiefly by that called by Brown, *Astelia Pumila*."—Lyell's "Principles of Geology."

"Abernethy Pine Forest: Some of the trees have attained the age of 200 years; many of them had been thrown down by a great flood of 1829, the stumps of which still remain in soil or sandy moss from 4 in. to 8 in. deep."—Lardner's "Arboretum et Fructicum Britannicum."

"The trees and shrubs known to our Saxon ancestors were the Birch, Alder, Oak, Wild or Scotch Pine, Maiden Ash or Rowan Tree, Juniper, Elder, Sweet Gale, Dog Rose, Heath, St. John's Wort, and the Mistletoe."—*Ibid.*

"Native Birch and Alder are frequently met with in Pine forests, but never are large or valuable."—*Ibid.*

"The Highland Pine in early life grows, although crowded together, to a greater girt; it is found to attain a greater size in very wet ground."—*Ibid.*

"All Oaks when young are remarkable for throwing out long and vigorous tap roots." " The roots of the Oak not being so liable to rot in the ground as those of the Elm, Beech, and other trees, full grown Oaks are not so likely to be blown down by the wind."

The wood of the Alder is homogeneous, tender, and without much tenacity. The bark at the rising of the sap separates from the wood with great facility. It has great durability in water, and Vitruvius recommends it for piles. The wood when worked has the colour of mahogany, but in peat bogs it is black as ebony. The bark of both the Willow and Alder contains a great deal of tannin.

SECTION OF DRIFT-BEDS OBSERVED IN SINKING FOR WATER AT AUGHTON, NEAR ORMSKIRK.

By George H. Morton, F.G.S.

The Author gave the following section of the drift deposits, observed in sinking the shaft at the Springfield Pumping Station, Aughton, near Ormskirk:—

	FT.	IN.		FT.	IN.
Surface Soil	1	0	Sandy Boulder Clay	15	6
Sand	3	0	Gravel	2	0
Sandy Boulder Clay	5	0	Stony Boulder Clay .	5	0
Gravel and Sand ...	15	0	Gravel and Sand...	15	0
Boulder Clay	16	0			
Gravel	1	6		79	0

When Mr. Morton saw the shaft the walls were timbered, but his attention was called to the hard stony character of the "Stony Boulder Clay 5 feet" near the bottom of the section. He was informed that it was very different to any of the higher beds, and on examining a quantity of it that had been brought up, found it remarkably like the "Lower Boulder Clay" described by him in the "Report British Association" for 1876, p. 112.

THE CARBONIFEROUS LIMESTONE

AND

MILLSTONE GRIT OF LLANGOLLEN.

By GEORGE H. MORTON, F.G.S.

(Continued from Page 325.)

CRAIGNANT.

The next section is at Craignant, where there is a fine exposure of the Carboniferous Limestone. The strata belong to the Upper Grey Limestone, and the following is a section of the whole of the beds exposed:—

		FT.	IN.	
Upper Grey Limestone.	Limestone	3	0	
	Shale			
	Limestone	15	0	
	Limestone, thin beds			
	Shale, with beds of Limestone at base..	15	0	Represents the 15-feet of Shale and Limestone at Bron-y-garth.
	Limestone...............	20	0	
	Shale...................	0	6	
	Limestone...............	3	0	
	Shale...................	0	6	
	Limestone...............	30	0	Base not exposed.
		87	0	

This section closely resembles that near Chirk, and the occurrence of the 15-feet bed of shale with the same species of shells and corals as at Bron-y-Garth is very remarkable.

The following fossils occur in the 15-feet bed of shale, viz.: *Chonetes Hardrensis; Orthis Michelini; O. resupinata; Productus longispinus; Rhynchonella pleurodon; Spirifera bisulcata; Streptorhynchus crinistria; Poteriocrinus crassus; Chœtetes tumidus; Cyathophyllum Murchisoni.*

The general succession of the strata is so similar that it may be considered conclusive evidence that the upper beds of the Upper Grey Limestone were deposited continuously over the intervening country, though they have been denuded and only the lower portion of the subdivision left exposed. The thickness of the Upper Grey Limestone at Craignant, as shown in the section, is about 87 feet, and it is not likely that the actual thickness can be greater, for it includes the whole of the outcrop. It seems that the Silurian rocks on the west of the country described formed land during the deposition of the lowest Carboniferous Limestone, and that it was only after a lengthened subsidence that some of the upper beds were deposited along the old coast line. There is no reason to suppose that the country further west, about Glen Ceiriog, was ever covered by the limestone, though it seems probable enough that the Cefn-y-Fedw Sandstone and Coal Measures may have extended over it.

The succession of the strata from the Carboniferous Limestone up to the Cefn-y-Fedw Sandstone cannot be seen in detail about Craignant. The limestone at the top of the quarry is covered with drift, but probably some shale comes in, and then the Sandy Limestone, succeeded by the Lower Cefn-y-Fedw Sandstone and Conglomerate, which rises to the south and forms the bold outline of Selattyn Hill.

LLAWNT, NEAR OSWESTRY.

To the south of Craignant the Upper Grey Limestone continues along a band of country usually about one-third of a mile in width. Between the Tumulus and Gorsedd-wen there is a quarry where it has been worked for a long period, and there are several other places where small limekilns indicate spots where limestone has been obtained for agricultural purposes by farmers in the neighbourhood. The limestone is also to be seen along the course of a brook, the Morda, near the same place. About a mile further south the Upper Grey Limestone occurs in a large quarry at Maes-y-graig, and dips 24° to the east. A series of limestone quarries extends along the crest of the ridge trending south, with a steep escarpment to the west; the lower part being formed of Bala-beds on which the limestone unconformably rests. Still further south the Upper Grey Limestone is well exposed resting on similar Silurian strata north of Llawnt, where it is about 108 feet in thickness and presents the following section in the quarries and the ground above them:

		FT.	IN.
Lower beds of the Sandy Limestone.	Calcareous Sandstone?		
	Soft Sandstone, three beds...	3	0
	Dark Red Shale	0	6
	Limestone	10	0
		13	6

		FT.	IN.	
	Shale, with bands of Limestone	10	0	Represents the Bron-y-garth and Craignant Shale-beds.
	Concretionary Shale	10	0	
	Limestone	7	0	
Upper Grey Limestone.	Shale	2	0	
	Limestone	20	0	
	Shale	1	0	
	Limestone	10	0	
	Shale	3	0	
	Limestone	45	0	
		108	0	

The position, colour, fossils, and general appearance of the limestone and shale in this section and others in the neighbourhood, conclusively prove that the strata belong to the Upper Grey Limestone, which reposes directly on the underlying Silurian strata, and that the average thickness is about 100 feet.

Assuming that the 10-feet bed of shale is on the same horizon as at Bron-y-garth and Craignant, it is the most persistent and remarkable bed in the district. At Llawnt the shale-bed is not so fossiliferous as at the other localities, having a concretionary character, but *Athyris ambigua, Rhynchonella pleurodon*, and *Lithostrotion irregulare* occur in it.

The lowest beds of the Sandy Limestone occur in a small quarry a quarter of a mile to the east of Maes-y-graig, at Careg-y-big, as shown in the following section:—

		FT.	IN.
Lower beds of the Sandy Limestone.	Thin beds of sandy lime-stone, concretionary at the base, with fucoids, or annelid tracks...............	9	0
	Light Grey Shale, with beds of concretionary limestone	3	0
	Limestone, thin beds	3	0
	Limestone with quartz peb-bles	6	0
		21	0

Mr. D. C. Davies, F.G.S., of Oswestry, who for many years investigated the so-called Millstone Grit (Cefn-y-Fedw Sandstone) of the district, first described this section and another at Craig Forda, further south, which shows the succession more completely. However, on the hills on both the north and south of the Llawnt-road the line of juncture between the Upper Grey Limestone and the overlying Sandy Limestone may be easily traced.

The Lower Cefn-y-Fedw Sandstone and Conglomerate forms the commanding eminence, Selattyn Hill, the summit being about 1,000 feet above the Ordnance datum, and 250 feet above the village of the same name. There are no quarries on the hill, but the surface about the summit, where not reclaimed, is scattered over with blocks of white sandstone, containing numerous quartz pebbles, and presents exactly the same appearance as at Cefn-y-Fedw, the general aspect of the hill-top being very similar to the typical area of the formation on the north-west of Llangollen. There is a monument on the top of the hill in.

commemoration of a battle between the English and
Welsh, while the Tumulus close by, and Offa's Dyke,
which runs along the strike of the Upper Grey Limestone, all mark the locality as a long-contested battlefield. Rather more than half-a-mile to the north-west
of the village, on the hill beyond the brook, there is a
quarry in the Cherty Shale, which dips about 20° to the
south-east and is fifty feet thick—that thickness being
actually exposed. The rock has much the same appearance as on Cefn-y-Fedw, but no fossils were observed.
There is another exposure a little to the north-west,
where beds of weathered sandstone appear, evidently
below the Cherty Shale.

About two miles further south the Cefn-y-Fedw
Sandstone is represented about Oswestry race-course, in
the picturesque defile or valley of the River Morda, and
is also exposed in several quarries in close proximity.
The exposures of the Sandy Limestone at Careg-y-big
and on the hill above the limestone quarries at Llawnt,
have been shown in the sections at pages 373–5, and
above those sections the Lower Sandstone and Conglomerate presents a rocky ridge, or is indicated by numerous large fragments of the sandstone containing pebbles
of white quartz. The thickness of the Sandy Limestone
in this locality is probably about 75 feet, and is
certainly represented by the calcareous sandstone and
limestone which occur between the ~~top of the~~ Lower
Sandstone and Conglomerate and the Upper Grey
Limestone at Craig Forda. The latter can be seen
exposed at the Forest quarry on the ridge between
Offa's Dyke and the race-course, half-a-mile north
of the Llawnt and Oswestry-road. The strata present the usual characters: hard white sandstone
with white pebbles, 12 feet thick, succeeded by the

same thickness of similar sandstone without pebbles. The beds dip 22° E.S.E. At Cwm-sych, close to the south end of the race-course there are two quarries, in higher strata, where the following section is visible, particularly in the one near Offa's Dyke, where the thickness was measured:—

		FT.	IN.
Lower beds of the Cherty Shales.	White cherty sand-stone	12	0
Upper beds of the Lower Cefn-y-Fedw Sandstone.	White sandstone, with the upper beds wea-thered to a brownish colour	20	0

Below the strata exposed in this quarry much lower beds of the Lower Sandstone and Conglomerate crop out in the defile of the Morda, below Craig Forda, along the eastern side of which they present a ridge extending nearly its entire length of two miles. The depth of the defile is above 300 feet, the rocky ridge being 250 feet above the river, and the strata dip 20° E.S.E. The strata, both above and below the ridge, are hidden by a talus of débris, and a thick covering of soil supporting a plantation, so that the lower beds and the underlying limestone cannot be seen. The beds above those crop-ping out are evidently composed of hard white sandstone, with occasional quartz pebbles, as fragments of it are numerous on the surface, and the walls of the fields above are built of stone taken from a series of holes along Offa's Dyke, which presents a conspicuous embank-ment of earth and stones along the top of the defile. The sandstone cropping out in the ridge is usually very

D

hard, and probably was originally white, but long exposure and weathering at the sides of the ravine have produced a mottled red shade, and in one spot it has been reduced to sand, which contains quartz pebbles. There is a small quarry in the ridge about 50 feet below Offa's Dyke, and exactly opposite Bron-y-Gell, where the thickness of sandstone exposed is about 20 feet, and the dip east-south-east.

The thickness of the Lower Sandstone and Conglomerate seems to be about 220 feet, including the 20 feet exposed in the quarry at Cwm-sych, of which a section has been given, and in Allinson's quarry, about 200 yards to the north. In the latter fossils are abundant in the upper beds, and also occur in the overlying Cherty Shale, which are there composed of regular beds of Chert and very fine grained white sandstone.

Along the greater portion of the Morda defile the direction is coincident with the strike of the strata, but south of Candy it gradually winds round towards the east—crossing the strike and exposing a fine section of the Sandy Limestone, as follows:—

		FT.	IN.
	Calcareous Sandstone	20	0
	Soft Brown Sandstone	4	0
	Limestone, with shales at the base	7	0
Sandy Limestone.	Sandstone, with weathered cavities	1	9
	Dark Red Shale	0	6
	Dark Grey Limestone	18	0
		51	3

The 20-feet of calcareous sandstone crops out *below* the inferior beds in the section, half-way up the side of the ravine, having been dropped by a fault or recent landslip, and that explanation is confirmed by the limestone strata cropping out again below the sandstone just above the Morda.

The strata at the base of the Lower Sandstone and Conglomerate, which must come in over this section, cannot be seen, though there can be little doubt that they are composed of soft red sandstone, for there are indications of such a rock in the débris overlying the outcrop. The upper beds of the Carboniferous Limestone crop out a few yards below the calcareous sandstone in the section, but there must be some beds at both the top and bottom of the section, which would probably increase the thickness of the Sandy Limestone to about 75 feet.

The Cefn-y-Fedw Sandstone is again exposed on the east of the race-course on the north side of the road to Oswestry, in a quarry near Underhill, where the rock has much the same appearance as at Cwm-sych, and the cherty rock is worked for road-stone, the large quantity of broken-up material affording great facilities for examination. It is a very fine grained cherty sandstone, but does not seem to contain any fossils—at least, I was not able to find even a trace of any. Only about 6 feet of the Cherty Shale and 4 feet of the underlying Lower Sandstone are visible, and dip at an angle of 10° S.E.S. Half-a-mile to the east there is another quarry, near a farm house, where there is a hard white sandstone with yellow spots, and a bed of soft shale over it. The beds dip 20° S.E.S., and probably underlie the Cherty Shale at Underhill, but the surface is so covered with drift that no regular succession can be seen. Although the Sandy Limestone and the Lower Cefn-y-Fedw Sandstone and Conglomerate are clearly represented in the country west of Oswestry, no exposure of the Upper Cefn-y-Fedw Sandstone has been noticed, for the country as it descends to the east is all under cultivation. Probably the underlying sandstone is of a soft character and has been so denuded and covered with drift, that it seldom appears at the surface, and the succession clearly exposed to the northeast of Llangollen is not to be seen.

Besides the fossils that occur in the quarries that have been described, stones of various sizes are thrown off the fields about Cyrn-y-Bwch which contain numerous species, and judging from the lithological character of the rock, have been derived from strata about the top of the Lower Sandstone. Mr. D. C. Davies, F.G.S., was the first to describe the fossils at Cyrn-y-Bwch, and it would seem to be the most northerly locality, except Selattyn Hill, where he has discovered them in the Oswestry district. The most frequent species that occur at Cyrn-y-Bwch are : *Athyris ambigua; Productus longispinus; P. semireticulatus; Rhynchonella pleurodon; Spirifera bisulcata;* and *Streptorhynchus crinistria,* all species that occur in Allinson's quarry.

The Cefn-y-Fedw Sandstone is continued to the south of Craig Forda, when it again rises and forms the commanding elevation of Mynydd Myfyr. All the upper portion of the hill is the Lower Sandstone and Conglomerate, and there are many exposures where it can be seen presenting its usual characters. The Cherty Shale and higher strata in the formation cannot be seen, the country on the east of Mynydd Myfyr being all under cultivation; but there is a bed of coal, to which no name has been given, represented as in the Cefn-y-Fedw Sandstone according to the Geol. Survey map, though it probably represents the Aqueduct Coal at the base of the Coal-measures. This coal was worked about forty years ago, and the line of outcrop is indicated by the débris that was thrown out of the shallow pits. The thickness of the seam is reported to be about 18 inches, but little is actually known respecting it. The upper beds of the Cefn-y-Fedw Sandstone do not occur at Mynydd Myfyr, and it is probable that the seam is the Aqueduct Coal faulted against the Lower Cefn-y-Fedw Sandstone, all the country to the east being Coal-measures. On the Geol. Survey Map the outcrop is continued to the east of Craig Forda and the race-course, though thrown off its continuity a quarter of a mile by a fault which crosses it, and represented as terminating a little north of Underhill, near the quarry in the Cherty Shale already described. However, I have not succeeded in obtaining any confirmation of its occurrence north of Mynyd Myfyr, even from persons who have long resided in the neighbourhood.

TREFONEN.

The Cefn-y-Fedw Sandstone and the underlying Carboniferous Limestone are broken up by a succession of east and west faults, which, excepting the one just north of Mynydd Myfyr, are upthrows on the south side; and in consequence of the easterly dip of the strata, cause both formations to crop out further to the east with each succeeding dislocation. These faults are shown on the Geol. Survey Map, and explain how the Cefn-y-Fedw Sandstone has been continued so far to the east between Oswestry and Llanymynech.

About Craig Forda and Mynydd Myfyr the Lower
Cefn-y-Fedw Sandstone and Conglomerate presents a
remarkable change in aspect and colour, and becomes for
the most part a soft red sandstone with a conspicuous
outcrop, overlaid by a hard white sandstone which
retains its original characters. The lower red beds are
well exposed 200 yards east of the Upper Grey Limestone quarries at Treflach wood, about half-a-mile south-
east of the village of Trefonen, at the spot marked + 10°
on the Geol. Survey Map; along the road south-west
from Treflach Hall and Bellam Farm—though coloured
Carboniferous Limestone on the map; and near the
south end of the old tramway constructed some years
ago in connection with coal-pits near Trefonen, where
the lowest beds form a conglomerate. In all these
places the Hard White Sandstone may be seen over-lying
the Soft Red Sandstone, though the change in colour
seems gradual, and there are some soft yellow beds about
the horizon where they blend into each other. The
section exposed along the tramway presents nearly the
whole of the Cefn-y-Fedw Sandstone, and affords the
means of comparing the subdivisions of the formation
with those of the typical area. Although the lower beds
are obscured by a thick covering of drift they can be
seen close to the section, which is of great interest, and
was first described by Mr. D. C. Davies, F.G.S., in the
" Geological Magazine" for 1870, where there is a wood-
cut and description of it. Plate 6 is representative of
the strata exposed in the tramway, drawn to scale,
showing the top of the Carboniferous Limestone, the
embankment and drift which cover some of the lower
beds, and the subdivisions into which the Cefn-y-Fedw
Sandstone is divided, as follows :—

PLATE 6.

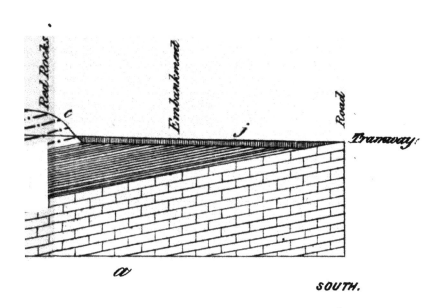

SOUTH.

HALL.

SUBDIVISIONS OF THE CEFN-Y-FEDW SANDSTONE AT SWEENEY MOUNTAIN.

		FEET.
Middle Cefn-y-Fedw Sandstone.	Sweeney Mountain Sandstone	100
Cherty Shale.	Pink Sandstone and Shale...........	25
	Summer-house Sandstone	60
	Red Sandstone and Shale	25
Lower Cefn-y-Fedw Sandstone and Conglomerate	Hard White Sandstone	70
	Soft Red Sandstone....................	150
Sandy Limestone.	Sandy Limestone not exposed	75?
		505

The section, Plate 6, runs nearly north and south, and is 1,000 yards in length, the north end being 65 feet higher than the south. The actual dip at the south end is 10° N.N.E., increasing to 16° N.E. about the middle, and finally decreasing to 10° N.E. The thickness of the subdivisions and of the whole has been determined from the above data, combined with observations on the other exposures close by.

The Pink Sandstone and Shale, *g*, is only partially exposed along the tramway, but a parallel fault on the east brings it down in the quarry 100 yards off, where the fossils in the list were obtained. The rounded hillock at the north end of the section is composed of the Sweeney Mountain Sandstone, *h*, a very white and soft rock; but the hill on the east, upon which the summer-house of Stanley Leighton, Esq., M.P. stands, is formed of the Summer-house Sandstone, *f*, resting on the Red

Sandstone and Shale, *e*, the Pink Sandstone and Shale, *g*, having been denuded. The Hard White Sandstone, *d*, is exposed in the section, but little is seen of the underlying Soft Red Sandstone, *c*, though it is conspicuously prominent over a large area on the south of Treflach Hall. The base of the Soft Red Sandstone is not visible, neither can any of the strata between it and the Carboniferous Limestone be seen where the upper beds of the latter dip into the hollow underneath the embankment.

Although there is a considerable lithological difference between the Cefn-y-Fedw Sandstone near Llangollen and the same formation at Treflach Hall and Sweeney Mountain, there are several points of resemblance which assist in correlating the strata of the two areas. There are no strata about Sweeney Mountain resembling the Aqueduct Grit, and there are no black shales and yellow sandstones likely to be on the same horizon as the Upper Cefn-y-Fedw Sandstone. The Sweeney Mountain Sandstone is very similar, but much softer than the Middle Sandstone of the typical area, and though it is succeeded at Gron-wen and Nant by a few feet of yellow sandstone and white shales, it does not seem that the highest beds occur in the district, having probably been thrown down by a fault bringing in the Coal Measures in the direction of Oswestry. There are no beds resembling the Cherty Shale, which occur as far south as Craig Forda, but they are probably represented by the shale interstratified with the Pink, Summer-house, and Red Sandstones of the old tramway section, all of which contain similar fossils. The Lower Cefn-y-Fedw Sandstone around Treflach presents, as already described, a peculiar lithological aspect in its lower beds, which so much resemble the soft sandstones of the Trias as to have attracted the attention of geologists many years ago,* though the upper beds of hard white sandstone with occasional quartz pebbles continue to characterise the subdivision. In the tramway section there is a space between the Carboniferous Limestone and the red beds of the Lower Cefn-y-Fedw Sandstone where the strata cannot be seen under the embankment. The Sandy Limestone is supposed to occur there, but it is merely conjectural, the nearest sections where such transitional beds occur being at Careg-y-big, Craig Forda, and north-east of Little Nuttree Bank.

The following list of fossils has been compiled from the papers by Mr. D. C. Davies, F.G.S., and Mr. F. C. Prosser, F.G.S., already referred to, only one additional species, *Productus longispinus*, having been added. In several localities described by them I have not succeeded in finding any, as in the Soft Red Sandstone in the tramway section, but Mr. Davies explained to me how the lower beds have been gradually covered by débris during the last seven years. Generally, however, I have found sufficient to confirm the fossiliferous localities, while the Pink Sandstone quarry close to the tramway, Allinson's quarry, and other places about Oswestry race-course, have afforded fully half the species in the list. The localities have enabled me to tabulate the species found in the subdivisions here adopted. They are all ordinary Carboniferous species; nearly all found in the underlying Upper Grey Limestone, just as might be expected considering that further north, at Minera, the Lower Cefn-y-Fedw Sandstone becomes a regular limestone with the conglomerate beds cropping out beneath, apparently forming the upper portion of the Carboniferous Limestone, and is so coloured in the Geol. Survey Map:—

* "The Silurian System." (By Sir R. I. Murchison, F.R.S.)

LIST OF THE FOSSILS FOUND IN THE CEFN-Y-FEDW SANDSTONE, NEAR OSWESTRY.

	SPECIES.	SUB-DIVISION.	LOCALITY.
	CEPHALOPODA.		
1	Orthoceras giganteum,* Sow.	Summer-house Sandstone	About 220 yards east of the Treflach Tramway, Field No. 2,574 in Parish Map, S.W. corner.
	HETEROPODA.		
2	Bellerophon, sp.	Hard White Sandstone	Oswestry Race-course.
	GASTEROPODA.		
3	Metapoma, sp.	Soft Red Sandstone	Treflach Hall and Tramway.
4	Pleurotoma decipiens ?	Do.‡	Sweeney.†
5	Edmondia sulcata, Phil.	Do.‡	Do.
6	Pecten, sp.	Do.‡	Do.
7	Sanguinolites variabilis, M'Coy	Do.	Treflach Hall and Tramway.
8	Schizodus, sp.	Red Sandstone and Shale	Treflach Tramway.
	BRACHIOPODA.		
9	Athyris ambigua, Sow.	Hard White Sandstone	Oswestry Race-course & Selattyn Tower.

	SPECIES	SUB-DIVISION.	LOCALITY.
10	Chonetes, sp.	Soft Red Sandstone	Treflach Tramway.
11	Lingula mytiloides, Sow.	Do.‡	Sweeney.
12	Orthis resupinata, Mart.	Hard White Sandstone	Llanforda-isaf.
13	Productus concinus, Sow.	Soft Red Sandstone ‡	Treflach Tramway.
14	,, cora, D'Orb.	Do.	Do.
15	,, costatus, Sow.	Cherty Shale	Allinson's Quarry.
16	,, longispinus, Sow.	Hard White Sandstone	Do.
17	,, semireticulatus, Mart.	{ Pink Sandstone Summer-house Sandstone Hard White Sandstone Soft Red Sandstone	Treflach Tramway, Allinson's Quarry, &c.
18	,, punctatus, Mart.	Cherty Shale	Do.
19	,, Youngianus, Dav.	Do.	Do.
20	Spirifera bisulcata, Sow.	Hard White Sandstone	Do.
21	,, striata, Mart.	Do.	Oswestry Race-course.
22	Streptorhynchus crinistria, Phil.	Do.	Do.

23	*Rhynchonella pleurodon*, Phil.....	Soft Red Sandstone.....	Sweeney.
	CRUSTACEA.		
24	*Phillipsia*, sp..........	Hard White Limestone....	Sweeney & Oswestry Race-course.
	ECHINODERMATA.		
25	Encrinital stems undetermined....	{Red Sandstone.............. / Hard White Sandstone.........}	Sweeney & Oswestry Race-course.
	ZOOPHYTA.		
26	*Cyathophyllum Murchisoni*, M. Edw.........	Hard White Sandstone.....	Sweeney & Oswestry Race-course.
27	*Clisiophyllum*	Do.	Oswestry Race-course.
28	*Petraia* ?	Do.	Llanforda-isaf.
	PLANTÆ.		
29	*Calamites*.............	Pink Sandstone........	Treflach Tramway.
30	*Sigillaria*...........	Do.	Sweeney.

* The only specimen found is now in the Liverpool Derby Museum, and it is fully described in the "Proceedings of the Literary and Philosophical Society of Liverpool" for 1875—6; the following paragraph being an extract:—

"This specimen is now three feet eleven inches long, the width at the summit three and a half inches, and at the base fourteen inches; the apical angle being about twelve degrees. It measures only twelve inches in diameter perpendicular to the line of the original being, probably from which seems to have been the cavity which domed a portion of the animal, and this cavity is eighteen inches in length. Originally there must have been, at the base, and the entire length of the shell was probably nearly six feet, so that it is an exceptionally large specimen."

† Sweeney as a locality probably includes the Treflach Tramway and other places around Sweeney Mountain.

‡ Some of these species may be found in the Hard White Sandstone.

The Cefn-y-Fedw Sandstone is represented on the Geol. Survey Map as occurring over an area of two square miles about Llync-lys, Moreton, and Crickheath Hall. The surface is entirely covered with a thick deposit of drift, consisting of a coarse gravel of pebbles and sandy clay. There is no opening showing the rock, and the wells at the various farms are not supposed to reach it, so that it is difficult to surmise the data upon which the formation below the drift was determined. Mr. D. C. Davies refers to the strata of this area, and seems to consider them to be Permian, and states that they rest upon the Carboniferous Limestone, but without giving any description or any section where they may be seen.* Not having seen any exposure of the strata, no opinion can be here given respecting them. There are some red beds exposed on the west of the road between Lync-lys and Sweeney Old Hall, which might be mistaken for Permian; but they are the Soft Red Sandstone of the Lower Cefn-y-Fedw Sandstone. They are coloured as Carboniferous Limestone on the Survey Map, and may have no relation to the strata below the drift on the east, around Moreton.

UPPER GREY LIMESTONE.

Proceeding southwards from Llawnt, the Upper Grey Limestone forms the gradually ascending ridge of Craig-y-rhiw, where the rock has been quarried in several places, and presents a precipitous scar, with the underlying Bala-beds of the Silurian exposed at intervals beneath. The limestone exposed along the ridge belongs to the lower portion of the subdivision, and is on the same horizon as the lower beds at Llawnt. The scar is

* * "On the Coal Seams in the Permian at Ifton, Shropshire."—Proc. Geol. Assoc., Vol. iii., p. 188.

most precipitous at the highest part of the ridge, where the limestone is about 70 feet thick, having broken down in large masses, and a scene of ruinous grandeur produced. The limestone rests unconformably on the Bala-beds, and there is a fine exposure of the latter on the hill side close to the broken masses of rock. A walk along the road from Llawnt to Llansilin affords a good view of the ridge of Upper Grey Limestone; the underlying Bala-beds; the great heaps of limestone that have fallen down the side of the hill, and a deep cutting in the drift, exposed by the flow of the stream in the valley below. At Craig-y-rhiw some of the lower beds of the limestone become very compact, like marble, a condition still more remarkable further south.

At Coed-y-Gaer the Bala-beds rise to the west and to the height of the Upper Grey Limestone, but the lower beds of the latter are exposed by an old limekiln close to Llynrhyddwyn, and are of a reddish colour. Further south, near Pant-hir, there is a quarry where about 27 feet of the same subdivision are exposed. The beds are very near the base of the limestone, the lower half being of a compact structure. Near Pentre-cefn, on the road side, there is another quarry in the same subdivision where the strata are very similar to those at Pant-hir, the following beds being exposed :—

		FEET.
Lower beds of the	Light Grey Limestone	5
Upper	Shale	1
Grey Limestone.	Compact Light Grey Limestone	10
		16

These beds are about the lowest in the subdivision, and are on the same horizon as those at Pant-hir and

Llynrhyddwyn. Higher strata occur at New Inn, a quarter of a mile along the road, in a large quarry, where the following section is exposed :—

		FEET.
Middle beds of the	Light Grey Limestone, in thin beds..	30
Upper	Black Shale and Rubble	3
Grey Limestone.	Dark Grey Limestone, in thin beds...	40
		73

The limestone in this section is all of a grey colour, and evidently on the same horizon as the beds below the thick-shale at Llawnt. There is no exposure of any higher beds of the subdivision in the locality, though they must occur further east.

About a mile due south of Pentre-cefn there is a conspicuous hillock, Craig Sychdin, where the Upper Grey Limestone is worked in a quarry near Wern-ddu, and the following section occurs:—

		FEET.
	Grey Limestone, with rubble at base.	21
	Shale	1
Middle and Lower	Limestone, thin beds—some compact	30
beds of the	Grey compact Limestone...............	4
Upper	,, ,, ,, ...	4
Grey Limestone.	Black Limestone, thin beds............	8
	Limestone—reddish colour	10
	Limestone, thin reddish beds	8
		76

The strata shown in this section belong to the middle and lowest portion of the subdivision and are of the usual grey colour, but with a reddish shade towards the base. Although the underlying Bala-beds are not actually seen, as in some of the sections previously described, they probably occur just outside, to the west of the quarry. It is seldom that the very lowest beds of limestone can be seen in a quarry, for they are usually sandy or useless from other causes, and consequently left untouched. The highest beds of the Upper Grey Limestone are not exposed in the locality, and a considerable fault running east-north-east from Craig Sychdin brings up the Bala-beds, throwing the limestone considerably to the east. At Craig Sychdin a lower subdivision of the Carboniferous Limestone—the Upper White Limestone—first presents its appearance, and crops out from under the Upper Grey Limestone, proving that an earlier series of strata was deposited at the southern extremity of the Carboniferous area, as I have previously shown to have been deposited in the country to the north of Llangollen. This lower subdivision rises into three conspicuous hills, is extensively quarried in many places, and is the most important economically considered.

There are several large quarries about Treflach Wood, which is about a mile to the south of Trefonen, where the Upper Grey Limestone again occurs, cropping out from under the soft red beds of the Lower Cefn-y-Fedw Sandstone, the Sandy Limestone not being exposed. The following is a section of the strata forming the subdivision as exposed near the middle of the area in quarries on the east side of the road, which runs north and south, where the beds dip 15° east.

		FEET.
	Shale, base only seen.....................	1
	Light Grey Limestone, two beds......	3
	Shale	4
Upper beds of the Upper Grey Limestone.	Light Grey Limestone	4
	Shale	1
	Light Grey Limestone	10
	Shale and rubble, which graduate into the beds below, many fossils.	7
	Dark Grey Limestone, thin beds, with thicker below..................	18

48

The thickness of the shale at the top of the section is uncertain, as it is partly denuded and covered by drift. The 7-feet bed of shale and rubble graduates into the beds of limestone below, but is on the same horizon as the persistent and similar bed referred to so frequently before, and it is remarkable about Treflach Wood for the abundant corals and other fossils it contains. About half-a-mile further south there are other quarries in the Upper Grey Limestone, where the beds dip 16° N.W., and present a ridge bounded on the south side of the fault shown on the Geol. Survey Map. This fault is the same as the one which will be described as occurring on the south of the Nant Mawr quarries and running east and west, and is supposed to be continued towards Sweeney Old Hall, where there is some complicated ground caused by faults. Close to the stream and fault shewn on the Geol. Survey Map, the Soft Red Sandstone at the base of the Lower Cefn-y-Fedw Sandstone crops up from under the Sandy Limestone, both being well exposed along the stream. The fault is susposed to have cut off both subdivisions across the strike of the strata.

The following is a list of the fossils collected in the quarries in Treflach Wood, but principally in those at the southern part of the area, one-third of a mile north of the word Camp.

LIST OF FOSSILS FOUND IN THE UPPER GREY LIMESTONE
AT TREFLACH WOOD.

1 *Orthoceras giganteum*, Sow.*
2 *Euomphalus*, sp.
3 *Loxonema*, sp.
4 *Athyris Royssii*, Léveillé.
5 *Orthis resupinata*, Mart.
6 *Productus cora*, D'Orb.
7   ,,   *costatus*, Sow.
8   ,,   *giganteus*, Mart.
9   ,,   *longispinus*, Sow.
10 *Spirifera bisulcata*, Sow.
11   ,,   *glabra*, Mart.
12 *Alveolites septosa*, Flem.
13 *Clisiophyllum coniseptum*, M'Coy.
14   ,,   *turbinatum*, M'Coy.
15 *Cyathophyllum Murchisoni*, M. Edw.
16 *Lithostrotion irregulare*. M'Coy.
17   ,,   *junceum*, Flem.
18   ,,   *Martini*, M. Edw.
19   ,,   *M'Coyanum*, M. Edw.
20   ,,   *Portlocki*, M. Edw.
21 *Lonsdaleia floriformis*, Flem.
22 *Syringopora geniculata*, Phil.
23 *Zaphrentis cylindrica*, Scouler.

The highest beds of the Upper Grey Limestone, dipping 16° N., can be seen at the south end of the old tramway near Treflach Hall; and at Dolgoch, east of

* In the Powys Land Museum, Welshpool.

Nuttree Bank, on the north of the road leading to Llync-lys station, there is a large quarry where the strata dip slightly to the north, and the upper half of the subdivision is exposed as shown in the following section :—

		FT.	IN.
Upper beds of the Upper Grey Limestone.	Light Grey Limestone	4	6
	Dark Grey Limestone, six equal beds	7	0
	Black Shale, with many fossils ...	2	0
	Light Grey Limestone...............	5	0
	Black Shale	2	0
	Light Grey Limestone...............	4	6
	Shale	2	0
	Light Grey Limestone...............	9	0
	Black Rubble and Shale...........	3	6
	Dark Grey Limestone, seven equal beds	10	0
		49	6

This section differs considerably from those already described, as it presents more limestone and less shale. However, the 3-feet 6-in. bed of rubble and shale seems to be on the horizon of the persistent shale-bed, and it contains corals, particularly great branching masses of *Lithostrotion*. The regular bedded limestone at the bottom of the section is used for similar purposes there and at Treflach Wood quarries, where it occurs beneath the shale-bed; and the thick bed of limestone above the shale is very much alike at both places.

The following is a list of the fossils collected in Dolgoch quarry, principally in the 2-feet bed of shale towards the top of the section, which may represent the thick shale, though the 3-feet 6-in. bed near the bottom more closely resembles it, both lithologically and in position.

LIST OF FOSSILS FOUND IN THE UPPER GREY LIMESTONE
AT DOLGOCH.

1 *Euomphalus Dionysii*, Goldf.
2 *Athyris Royssii*, Léveillé.
3 *Chonetes Hardrensis*, Phil.
4 *Orthis Michelina*, Koninck.
5 *Productus giganteus*, Mart.
6 ,, *latissimus*, Sow.
7 ,, *longispinus*, Sow.
8 *Rhynchonella pleurodon*, Phil.
9 *Spirifera cristata*, Schloth.
10 ,, *bisulcata*, Sow.
11 ., *lineata*, Mart.
12 *Alveolites septosa*, Flem.
13 *Syringopora geniculata*, Phil.
14 *Streptorhynchus crinistria*, Phil.
15 *Lithostrotion irregulare*, M'Coy.
16 ,, *junceum*, Flem.
17 *Lonsdaleia floriformis*, Flem.
18 *Zaphrentis cylindrica*, Scouler.

Between Craig Sychdin and Dolgoch little is known respecting the lowest beds of the Upper Grey Limestone, but south of the latter quarry and the Llync-lys road, there is a deep quarry on the opposite hill-side, known as Jones' Quarry, where the lower beds are well exposed as follows;—

FEET.

		FEET.
	Rubble and Shale	4
	Light Grey Limestone	10
	Rubble	9
Middle and Lower	Light Grey Limestone, two equal beds	2
beds of the	Shale	7
Upper	Rubble	7
Grey Limestone.	Light Grey Limestone	8
	Dark Grey Limestone, thin beds......	10
	„ „ Limestone, three beds ...	10
	Rubble and Shale........................	4
		71

The colour of the limestone in the section is of the usual grey shade, and the beds of shale are black or a dark grey. The strata dip rapidly 30° N., and appear to run under the beds at Nuttree Bank and Dolgoch quarry, without any fault between. The upper beds in the section may be observed on descending the hill as they dip towards the road, and the rapid changes that take place within the distance of one hundred yards is remarkable. There are some of the usual fossils to be found, but they are not numerous.

There is an important fault, running north and south, exposed in the middle of Jones' quarry, which throws up some of the highest strata of the Upper White Limestone to the surface on the west side of the quarry—beds that lie beneath the Upper Grey Limestone on the east side. This fault is more fully described and a woodcut given of it, Fig. 10, page 403, under the head of Porth-y-waen. There is no trace of the Upper Grey Limestone further south, and though it must have extended over the Upper White Limestone some miles in that direction, all trace of it has been removed by denudation.

Reference has already been made to the Upper White Limestone which underlies the Upper Grey Limestone, and crops out in thick beds at Nant Mawr and other places to the southwards. In general appearance it differs considerably from the Upper White Limestone at Eglwyseg ridge, for the interstratified thick shales are limited to its upper beds, and it does not appear in such conspicuous natural sections as in the typical district. Lithologically the limestone is very similar, being of a compact structure, and often like marble, especially the beds about the middle of the subdivision. The shale that alternates with the upper beds is usually of a reddish shade, so that the water that trickles down the sides of the quarries gives a red appearance to the limestone, which, when it is broken, is found to be generally of a light grey, though sometimes it assumes a drab, yellow, or brown colour. Being on the horizon of the Upper White Limestone near Llangollen, under the Upper Grey Limestone, it is assumed to represent the former subdivision—its thickness at Nant Mawr and Porth-y-waen not being sufficient to include the Lower White Limestone, which is only represented along the base of the Llanymynech Hill by a series of beds of red shale and limestone, resembling the 5-feet of shale above the *thick-bed* at Llangollen. The fossils in the subdivisions do not much aid in identifying them, for although there are some peculiar species found in the 30-feet bed at the top of Llanymynech Hill, others are common to both the Upper Grey and the Upper White Limestone. The distinctive characters that serve to identify and to separate the two subdivisions are purely lithological, the Upper Grey Limestone being composed of grey and black limestone, and shale exactly similar to the same beds in the Eglwyseg ridge; while

the Upper White Limestone is usually of a light grey
or cream colour, the beds being interstratified with
red and purple shales, so that it is usually easy at a
glance to determine the subdivision to which the strata
belong, especially where the rock is quarried and well
exposed. The difference between the two subdivisions
was shown to be remarkable in the Eglwyseg ridge, and
it is equally clear and distinct over the Llanymynech
area.

NANT MAWR.

At Nant Mawr the uppermost strata of the Upper
White Limestone consist of beds of rubble and interstratified red shale, and occur on the top of Moelydd and
Nant Mawr. They make their first appearance under
the Upper Grey Limestone at Craig Sychdin, increase in
thickness towards the south-west, and can always be
distinguished by the red shale and reddle associated with
them. The whole of the Upper White Limestone presents
a remarkable similarity to the same subdivision at Porth-
y-waen and Llanymynech Hill, for at each of these
places the strata are much alike, and extensive quarries
are worked on the precipitous flanks of steep hills, the
limestone being exposed in vertical sections from 150 to
175 feet in height. The following is a section of the beds
exposed in the large quarry facing the south, along the
bottom of which a fault runs nearly east and west and
brings in the Bala-beds :—

		FT.	IN.
	White Limestone, with red streaks	25	0
	Reddish Shale..........................	0	9
Middle and Lower	White Limestone	2	0
beds of the	Reddish Shale.......................	1	6
Upper	White Limestone, in thick beds,		
White Limestone.	with thin partings of purple shale	125	0
	White Limestone and thin shale		
	with Pyrites......................	5	0
		159	3

The strata dip about 10° E.N.E. and appear to be reddish rock, but when broken of a light cream colour. The highest bed in the section is a very variable stratum, and at a distance often appears to be a single bed, though it is usually more or less divided by a few thin partings of shale. It is persistent over the Nant Mawr and Llanymynech district, and may be designated the 30-feet bed. At the east end the dip brings this bed down near the floor of the quarry, and another fault throws the strata up to the east, where the 30-feet bed has been denuded, though it comes in again over the hill in a plantation. It may be traced half-a-mile further north, where it occurs about a hundred yards west of, and parallel with the road through Treflach Wood in the form of a low ridge, sufficiently distinct to be shaded on the Survey Map, and a quarry has recently been opened in it for road-stone. There must be a fault a little to the west of this outcrop of the 30-feet bed, for there is a small exposure of the Upper Grey Limestone about a quarter of a mile west of the road. This fault is probably the continuation of the north and south fault which throws the strata up on the east of the large quarry at Nant Mawr already referred *to,* but it is not shown on the Geol. Survey Map.

The underlying Bala-beds are exposed not only in a road section at the entrance of the large quarry, but are faulted against the Upper White Limestone by the east and west fault in a smaller quarry about a hundred yards to the east. Fig. 9 is a representation of the fault as

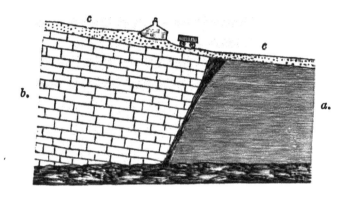

FIG. 9.—FAULT AT NANT MAWR.

c. Drift. *b.* Upper White Limestone. *a.* Bala-beds.

it appeared three years ago, but the excavating continually alters the appearance of the section from year to year.

PORTH-Y-WAEN.

The numerous quarries worked at this place afford great facility for the examination of the Upper White Limestone, which is the only subdivision that occurs in the hill. A fine view of the quarries may be obtained from the opposite hill by Offa's Dyke. From that elevation the massive 30-feet bed is conspicuous along the top of the highest quarries, but the strata gradually incline down the hill towards smaller quarries and the road below, where it has been denuded or quarried away with some of the inferior beds. The general inclination of the strata is about 16° S.E., and the following is the section shown in the quarries:—

		FEET.
Middle and Lower	White Limestone, often sandy & earthy	30
beds of the ·	Reddish Shale ....:.......	3
Upper	White Limestone in thick beds, with	
White Limestone.	thin partings of purple shale ...	130
		163

Above the strata shown in this section, there are higher beds of limestone, rubble and red shale, perhaps 50 feet thick, which belong to the same subdivision and can easily be identified, though no exact succession of the beds can be made out. They occur on the highest ground above the quarries.

The lowest beds of limestone are not actually seen, but they evidently repose directly on the Bala-beds, which are exposed between the quarries and the road below. There is a quarry called the Farmer's Quarry, close to and north-east of the others, where a bed of shale 6 feet thick occurs. This shale is the same as the 3-feet bed in the section, the overlying 30-feet bed of limestone having been removed by the quarrymen. An east and west fault runs nearly parallel with the tramway above the road, and throws the strata up on the south side. It is visible in the quarry, nearly opposite the Methodist Chapel on the road below, but is sometimes *obscured* by débris at the entrance.

LLANYMYNECH HILL.

On the north-western extremity of Crickheath Hill the fault which runs through Jones' quarry nearly north and south, already referred to, has an upthrow of about 70 feet on the west side. It is not shown on the Geol. Survey Map, but it is probably much more clearly exposed now than it was twenty years ago when the district was surveyed. It exposes the Upper Grey Limestone faulted against the Upper White Limestone, as represented in following wood-cut, Fig. 10. This

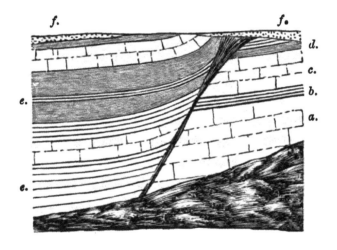

FIG. 10.—FAULT AT JONES' QUARRY.

f. Drift.   e. Lower beds of the Upper Grey Limestone.
d. Rubble and Reddle.   c. Limestone with Copper Ores.
b. Rubble and Reddle.   a. Top of 30-feet bed.

fault is of importance, for the beds of the Upper White Limestone on the west or upthrow side of it are some of the highest in the subdivision, and are distinguished by very remarkable beds of reddle and small deposits of Malachite and Chalcopyrite, as shown in the following section:—

		FEET.
	e. White Limestone or broken rubble	3
Upper beds	*d.* Reddle	3
of the	*c.* White Limestone, containing	
Upper White	Malachite, Chalcopyrite, &c. ...	15
Limestone.	*b.* Rubble and Reddle	4
	a. White Limestone, top of 30-ft. bed	6
		31

These upper beds of the Upper White Limestone crop out on the ascending ground above Jones' quarry, and the 30-feet bed then forms the highest parts of the hill and is continued, though denuded in places, to the precipitous escarpment overlooking Llanymynech. But towards Pant the strata as they descend the hill with a gradually increasing dip—finally 30°—to the east, have been less denuded, so that the higher beds of the Upper White Limestone again occur above the 30-feet bed, and are exposed close to the railway in a quarry opened a few years ago, and known as Eaton's quarry. There are other quarries and cuttings along the railway showing the upper beds of the subdivision, but the following section is from Eaton's quarry, which is worked at the present time:—

		FT.	IN.
	e. White Limestone	4	0
	e. Rubble and Shale	4	0
Upper beds	*d.* Reddle and Purple Shale	2	6
of the	*c.* White Limestone	14	0
Upper	*b.* Shale, with Malachite, &c.......	4	0
White Limestone.	*a.* White Limestone, top of 30-feet		
	bed	20	0
		48	6

Still further east of the railway and close to the canal, these upper beds of the Upper White Limestone are more completely developed, as follows:—

		FT.	IN.
	k. Rubble and Red Shale	4	0
	j. White Limestone	10	0
	i. Reddle	8	0
Upper beds	*h.* Rubble and Red Shale	4	0
of the	*g.* White Limestone	1	6
Upper	*f.* Rubble and Red Shale	20	0
White Limestone.	*e.* ,, and Purple Shale	7	6
	d. Purple Shale	2	6
	c. White Limestone, base not seen	10	0
		62	6

North of Pant there are several quarries on the west of the road, where the 30-feet bed and the strata immediately above it are exposed in as many different sections. The following section occurs in a quarry, not now worked, by an old limekiln, and the strata are on the same horizon as the two previous sections:—

		FT.	IN.
	e. White Limestone, thin bedded	10	0
Upper beds	*d.* Reddle	0	6
of the	*c.* White Limestone	17	0
Upper	*b.* Rubble and Shale	4	0
White Limestone.	*a.* White Limestone, top of 30-feet bed	17	0
		48	6

The strata shown in this and the previous sections of the uppermost beds of the Upper White Limestone, show their correlation at several places about Llanymynech Hill; and although the succession of the beds is not so clear on the hills to the north-west, the thickness and lithological appearance seem to be very similar. At Pant they are the highest visible beds of limestone, but it seems to be a question whether they are faulted against some higher subdivision of the Carboniferous series, or whether they may not present an escarpment covered by more recent deposits.

A fine section of the Upper White Limestone is exposed on the south and south-east of Llanymynech Hill, and it is almost a continuous outcrop along the railway to the sections at Pant already described. The strata are so clearly exposed, with a regular dip of 12°, N.E.N., that the succession and thickness of limestone can be easily determined. Llanymynech Hill was originally a precipitious escarpment, but quarrying operations during the last fifty years have produced a grand rocky wall about half-a-mile in length, and the strata exposed form one of the finest mural sections in North Wales. The height is usually about 170 feet, and the beds can be seen as they lie one above another like courses of masonry. The highest cliff at the side of the round quarry, at the southern end of the hill, is 175 feet above the base, and being vertical it represents the thickness of the limestone, with the exception of a few feet below the bottom of the quarry. The following is a section of the strata exposed :—

				FEET.
	White Limestone, often sandy.........			20
Middle and Lower	White Limestone, oolitic and shelly			7
beds of the	,,	,,	flaggy beds	2
Upper	..	,,	thick-bedded, with	
White Limestone.			purple shales...	150
		,,	sometimes sandy..	5

184

The upper portion of the 30-feet bed is somewhat denuded, the highest remaining part being of a sandy character, and occurs only at the edge of the round quarry at the southern termination of the hill, having been denuded further north; but the oolitic and shelly limestone extends along the top of the other quarries. The upper part of the 30-feet bed is taken off by the quarrymen and the stone thrown on the top of the cliff as useless, except as road-stone; while the oolitic and shelly portion is also left on the top in large heaps, for if thrown down to the floor of the quarry, 170 feet below, it is so shattered and broken up as to be of little value.

The Llanymynech limestone is chiefly used for fluxing purposes, and is sent away by railway to the iron smelting districts, though a large quantity is sent by canal for burning elsewhere. At Nant Mawr and Porth-y-waen a larger proportion is burnt for lime at the quarries. The general similarity of the limestone at these places has already been referred to, but the 30-feet bed at Llanymynech is not so distinctly visible as at Nant Mawr and Porth-y-waen, for there is no prominent bed of shale separating it from the inferior beds, and it is usually considerably reduced in thickness by denudation. It can, however, be easily identified above the round quarry, and its oolitic and shelly base traced along the top of the continuous line of quarries which extends to the north-east. It may also be traced through the quarries about Pant, and in those on the railway until the limestone becomes covered with drift deposits. The fossils that occur in the 30-feet bed at Llanymynech are of considerable interest, for some of them have not been found anywhere else in the district, and others not even in North Wales. They occur in the oolitic **and** shelly portion, which has not been observed at the base of the 30-feet bed at Nant Mawr, or Porth-y-waen. The fossils in the lower beds seem to be of the same species in the three localities, so that the list refers to those found in all those places, though principally collected at Llanymynech. The oolitic structure referred to is not so perfect as that of the Carboniferous Limestone at Clifton, on the banks of the Avon, for the little concretions are mixed up with shelly fragments of various organisms and Foraminifera.

LIST OF THE FOSSILS FOUND IN THE UPPER WHITE LIMESTONE
AT LLANYMYNECH.

1 *Cochliodus oblongus.* Ag.
2 *Patalodus Hastingia,* Owen.
3 *Bellerophon cornu-arietes,* Sow.
4   ,,   *tenifasia,* Sow.
5 *Eulima Phillipsiana,* Koninck.
6 *Euomphalus,* sp.
7 *Macrochilus imbricatus,* M'Coy. *
8 *Murchisonia striatula,* Koninck.*
9   ,,   *verneuliana,* M'Coy.
10 *Solarium planorbe,* Koninck.*
11 *Cypricardia striato-lamellosa,* Koninck.*
12 *Productus cora,* D'Orb.
13   ,,   *comoides,* Sow.
14   ,,   *fimbriatus,* Sow.
15   ,,   *giganteus,* Mart.
16   ,,   *longispinus,* Sow.
17   ,,   *punctatus,* Mart.
18   ,,   *semireticulatus,* Mart.
19 *Spirifera bisulcata,* Sow.

* Found in the 30-feet bed at Llanymynech only.

20 *Spirifera cristata,* Schloth.*

21 ,, *glabra,* Mart.

22 ,, *striata,* Mart.

23 *Streptorhynchus crinistria,* Phil.

24 *Terebratula hastata,* Sow.

25 *Rhychonella pleurodon,* Phil.

26 *Fenestella membranacea,* Phil.

27 *Griffithides longiceps,* Portl.

28 *Alveolites septosa,* Flem.

29 *Clisiophyllum,* sp.

30 *Lithostrotion Martini,* M. Edw.

31 *Syringopora reticulata,* Phil.

32 *Zaphrentis cylindrica,* Scouler.

LOWER SHALE,
OR
LOWER WHITE LIMESTONE OF LLANGOLLEN.

It has been shown that the Upper White Limestone rests directly on the Silurian strata at Nant Mawr and Porth-y-waen, and probably it does so at Crickheath Hill. However, at the east of Llanymynech Hill, in the quarry at the end of the tramway close to the "Cross Guns," some inferior strata crop out from under the limestone and represent the Lower Shale, as in the following section :—

		FT.	IN.
Lower Shales, or Lower White Limestone of Llangollen.	Dark Grey Shale	2	0
	White Limestone	4	0
	Grey and Red Shale, with bands of sandy limestone, the base not exposed	10	0
		16	0

* Found in the 30-feet bed at Llanymynech only.

Another section of the Lower Shale was discovered by Messrs. Savin & Co., 13 years ago, in sinking a shaft about 50 yards north-east of the field "63" on the 25-in. Ordnance Map, for the particulars of which I am indebted to Mr. J. Lester, of Pant, the strata in the following section being immediately under the limestone, the base of which can be seen at the place.

		FT.	IN.
Lower Shale or Lower White Limestone of Llangollen.	Soft Red Shale	13	6
	Sandy Limestone	1	6
	Soft Red Shale	6	0
	Sandy Limestone	1	6
	Hard Red Shale...................	40	0
		62	6

The débris around the shaft still remains with a depression in the centre, and consists of weathered red shale containing many rounded fragments of Silurian rock, exactly similar to those common in the shale-bed below the *thick-bed* of limestone at Llangollen. From Mr. Lester's description of the strata, it appears that the Bala-beds were not reached, but that the lower beds of shale were much tougher and harder than those near the surface. Lower down on the side of the hill the soil is of a red colour, and probably the Lower Shale crops out along the west and south end of Llanymynech Hill, though obscured by the limestone débris from the cliffs above, and the quarries and numerous shafts on the hill side.

The final results derived from the foregoing sections prove the thickness of the Carboniferous Limestone at the several places described, and the maximum at its southern *termination* at Llanymynech Hill. It has been proved that the Upper Grey Limestone rests on the Silurian rocks from Fron-y-Cysyllte to Craig Sychdin, a distance of seven miles; and that from the latter place southwards, the Upper White Limestone underlies and continues below it, resting on the Bala-beds as far as Crickheath Hill. Further south at Llanymynech Hill a still lower series, the Lower Shale, comes in below the Upper White Limestone, and forms the lowest subdivision. The thickness of the whole of the Carboniferous Limestone about Crickheath and Llanymynech Hill is as follows:—

SUBDIVISONS OF THE CARBONIFEROUS LIMESTONE
AT LLANYMYNECH HILL.

	FEET.
Upper Grey Limestone	125
Upper White Limestone	250
Lower Shale, or Lower White Lime-stone	75
	450

If the Sandy Limestone, 75 feet, were added to the Carboniferous Limestone, instead of being included in the Cefn-y-Fedw Sandstone, the thickness would be increased to 525 feet; and it is a question as to which formation should include it, for it is subject to constant lithological changes, and is rarely exposed. The thickness of the Lower Shale certainly exceeds the 62 feet 6 inches shown in the section, and has been provisonally made 75 feet.

Reviewing the subdivisions in the order of deposition, and describing them from the south toward the north, it appears that the earliest Carboniferous deposit at Llanymynech was a series of shales, which gradually became interstratified with thin bands of limestone and formed the Lower Shale. This subdivision became gradually overlapped by the Upper White Limestone, which seems to have filled all the minor inequalities of the underlying rocks, and finally the deeper part of the sea bottom; when the deposition of the Upper Grey Limestone succeeded, and not only covered the whole of the Upper White Limestone, but a much wider area of shallow sea with a very uniform series of strata.

FAULTS AND MINERAL VEINS.

All the faults shown on the maps of the Geological Survey representing the country between Llangollen and Llanymynech, run in an east and west direction, or a little to the north of east. They are important faults, whose influence on the strata and the contour of the ground is obvious, although they can seldom be actually seen. With a single exception, all these faults are up-throws on the south, and in consequence of the easterly dip of the strata, the Carboniferous Limestone and overlying Cefn-y-Fedw Sandstone are both carried gradually further to the east, on the up-throw or south side of the fault, than they would otherwise have been. The fault with an up-throw to the north is at that end of Mynydd Myfyr—a Cefn-y-Fedw Sandstone hill—which is bounded by the Upper Grey Limestone, except on its eastern side.

The only mineral veins indicated on the Geol. Survey Map are two at Moelydd, north-west of Nant Mawr, the direction of both being east-south-east and west-north-west; and another at the south end of Llanymynech Hill north-east-north and south-west-south, from which it might be inferred that the area was not a mining district. It does not appear that any mineral veins have been discovered in the northern portion of the area, but at Moelydd, Crickheath, Pant, and on Llanymynech Hill,

it is evident that mining operations for copper and lead
have been in progress from remote ages, and probably
during distant periods. It is difficult to ascertain what
amount of success, if any, attended mining in the district during former periods; but the indications of
mineral wealth are so remarkable as to present strong
temptations to search for the copper ore which is of
such frequent occurrence in the upper beds of the Upper
White Limestone. In and about the bed, c, in Jones'
quarry (Fig. 10), Eaton's quarry, and in some of the old
quarries on the west of the road at Pant, the quantity of this
ore, in the form of blue and green Carbonate of Copper,
is very remarkable. It is not unusual to see a heap,
enough to fill a wheel-barrow, in these quarries, so that
the indications of ore are favourable enough to promise
success by regular mining operations. In Jones' quarry
the ore is in open joints in the bed, c, in Eaton's it
occurs in the shale bed, d, and in a fissure or lode
through the bed c, and in other quarries it occurs on the
same horizon. It is only in these beds that the ore is
so abundant, and they are of very limited extent, having
been denuded from the high ground as already described. In lower beds of the Upper White Limestone
in quarries near the "Cross Guns" copper-ore occurs in
limited nests of shale which fill hollows between the
beds of limestone. Galena and other ores of lead, as
well as Blende, have been obtained in many places, but
do not appear so frequently in the rocks near the
surface.

Recently Mr. Joseph Henderson, Mining Engineer,
has been engaged in surveying and developing the
mineral resources of Crickheath and Llanymynech Hill,
under the direction of Messrs. R. and C. Gill. He has
very kindly given me access to an elaborate mineral map

of the district, a verbal account of its mining history, and the general result of his explorations, all of which I take this opportunity of acknowledging.

Mr. Henderson has carefully surveyed the district and laid down the lodes that have been worked at different periods, with others that he has discovered himself during the progress of his mining operations, from which it appears that the numerous lodes vary considerably in importance, some being mere open joints and others considerable faults. The fault or lode through Jones' quarry, Fig. 10, is shown on the map running N. 14° W., some old shafts being upon it, and lead is supposed to have been obtained. The principal lode at the south of Llanymynech Hill runs N. 38° and then 32° E., and terminates at the marshy ground in the hollow, west of the Entrenchments, "2," on the 25-inch Ordnance Map. There are several old shafts along the line of the lode, from which lead is said to have been obtained. A little to the west of the termination of this lode there are evidences of old surface workings to be seen, and Mr. Henderson considers them to be of Roman origin, for two ingots of copper were obtained there, with the name of the Emperor Hadrian cast on them. Just beyond, to the north, along the edge of the cliff known as Blodwel Rocks, there are many evidences of surface work to be seen, and the direction of the lodes can be ascertained. About Crickheath Hill on the north-east there are several shafts, and the mines have evidently been worked at a more recent date—perhaps forty or fifty years ago. It is improbable that any of them are deep, or that they exceed 200 feet, at which depth the base of the Limestone would usually be reached from the top of Crickheath or Llanymynech Hill.

There is nothing very remarkable in the direction or relative age of the lodes. There are many that run about north-east and south-west which are crossed and thrown off their courses by others running about north-west and south-east, and consequently of later origin—except on the west of the hill, where the reverse is the order of dislocation, so that there is no general order of formation observable. There are, however, three important and nearly parallel lodes, known as the North Lode, running W. 24° S. hading N.; the Main Lode, W. 24° S. hading S.; and the South, or Llanymynech Lode, W. 15° S. hading S., which appear to cut and throw out all the veins they intersect, and consequently are the most recent in the district.

None of the lodes are important faults, except that shown in Fig. 10; and the amount of dislocation is of trifling extent, the one referred to being the only fault which brings down the Upper Grey Limestone against the Upper White Limestone, and there are many that are mere fissures with no throw whatever.

Mr. Henderson is driving two levels, one under Crickheath and another on Llanymynech Hill which will intersect several lodes if continued a sufficient distance, and by that means he will ascertain whether the deposits of copper and lead ores supposed to have existed near the surface are continued at a greater depth. No doubt this information will be soon obtained, and it is to be hoped that success will be the result of the skill and capital employed.

The following minerals occur:—Blende, Calamine, Calcite, Cerussite, Chalcopyrite, Chessylite, Galena, Hæmatite, Malachite, Pyrolusite, Pyromorphite, and Quartz.

MINERA.

The Carboniferous Limestone and Cefyn-y-Fedw Sandstone between the Eglwyseg ridge and Minera have now to be described, and the formations retain their interest as they approach the northern limit of the country under description. The precipitous scars of Craig Arthur, Craig Aderyn, and Craig-y-Forwyn are all within two miles from the Ty-nant ravine, and are well worth a visit on account of the majestic grandeur of their outlines. They all present similar sections to Craig-yr-ogof, the Lower Brown Limestone forming the base, with the higher subdivisions in regular ascending order and overlying them towards the east. There is a deep ravine between Craig Aderyn and Craig-y-Forwyn, and an east and west lode was recently worked in it for lead. In front of the ravine the Bala-beds crop up from under the Wenlock Shale and rapidly rising form the mountain Cyrn-y-Brain, the Carboniferous Limestone resting on its eastern slope. The Bala-beds ascend so rapidly towards the north that the Lower Brown Limestone suddenly ends, and both it and the Lower White Limestone are over-lapped by the Upper White Limestone, within half a mile north of the ravine. The latter subdivision con-tinues exposed for about a mile, presenting a succession of low terraced ridges along the heathy and fern-clad surface, the rock having the usual compact structure. Further on, there is a long valley between the Bala-beds of Cyrn-y-Brain and the Carboniferous Limestone; the highest ground on the east being the Lower Cefn-y-Fedw Sandstone and Conglomerate. This valley is very deeply covered with drift, so that the underlying strata cannot be seen, and it continues so until near Minera, where a deep transverse valley exposes a grand section through the Carboniferous Limestone and Cefn-y-Fedw

Sandstone—the base of the former being exposed as it rests on the underlying Silurian in the bed of the stream which flows down the valley towards the east. The precise direction of the valley from the west is east-north-east for half a mile, when it runs east-south-east for about a mile. The source of the stream, or River Clywedog, is on the eastern flank of Cyrn-y-Brain and it flows by Minera, south of Wrexham into the Dee. The Upper White Limestone comes in over the Bala-beds along the course of the Clywedog, where it flows north. Near Ty-hir, about a hundred yards east of the spot where the stream receives a tributary and turns round to the east, the lowest beds of the limestone are exposed, overlying the vertical Bala-beds, and again about a quarter of a mile lower down the latter rise and form a ridge for about fifty yards across the bed of the stream. A little further on in the quarry they were found below the tramway, when they finally disappeared. At the Hush Mine, a quarter of a mile to the north, the Silurian rock occurs at the bottom of the shaft 135 feet below the surface, that thickness of the Upper White Limestone reposing on it. All the limestone along the upper course of the Clywedog belongs to the Upper White Limestone, and at its greatest thickness is about 160 feet. It is succeeded by the Upper Grey Limestone on both sides and lower down the stream towards Minera. The lowest beds of the Upper White Limestone are composed of beds of compact white limestone containing numerous pebbles of various sizes, from that of a pea to some two inches in diameter, composed of quartzite and other hard rocks probably derived from the underlying Silurian strata.

The Upper White Limestone is of a very uniform character, though it does not present such a compact structure as in some of the southern localities. It is a thick-bedded limestone, separated by mere lines of shale, though between the lowest and highest beds they approach a foot in thickness. There are extensive quarries worked on both sides of the river, and those on the south belong to the Minera Lime Co. The Secretary, Mr. J. A. Broadbent, and the Manager, Mr. J. Jones, gave me all the information and rendered all the assistance they could when surveying the district. During the progress of excavating, old shafts and levels driven along the lodes are continually brought to light, for several faults cross the quarries, and one of them, the Ragman vein, running north-west and south-east, with a down-throw of about 60 feet on the south-west, brings the Upper Grey Limestone against the Upper White Limestone at the end of the large quarry above the office of the Company. In the same quarry a fine mural section exposes about 70 feet of the Upper Grey Limestone resting conformable on 80 feet of the Upper White Limestone, so that the gradual change from typical beds of the one to those of the other can be examined, and there is not a more interesting section between Minera and Llanymynech. The highest bed of the Upper White Limestone is a compact light-coloured rock, 17 feet thick, with a bed of rubble about a foot thick over it, which separates it from a coarse-grained light grey bed overlying it, succeeded by a thin bed of black shale and then by a dark grey limestone—typical of the Upper Grey Limestone.

Minera Hill is the northern termination of Fron Deg, which is the continuation of Cefn-y-Fedw, and rises to an elevation of about 500 feet above the Clywedog. The range ends with a steep escarpment at Minera, where the strata have been abruptly cut off and thrown down by the Minera fault several hundred feet. The strata present a very uniform dip of about 8° towards the south-east. There are several quarries, mine heaps from shafts, and levels driven into the hill, so that the succession of the beds is particularly well exposed. Along the top of the hill, opposite the village of Minera, there is a bold and precipitous ridge, which forms a conspicuous object even at Wrexham, four miles off. The ridge is divided by an indentation where the rocks have broken down about the middle, and the two lines of cliff are known as Craig Fechan on the east and Craig Mawr on the west, the latter exposing the strata in a section where every bed of the Sandy Limestone and the highest beds of the Upper Grey Limestone may be examined. The quarries worked at the extreme west of Minera Hill are in the Upper White Limestone, and there are others higher up on several horizons in the Upper Grey Limestone, the rocky ridge of Sandy Limestone just described being above them, while the Lower Cefn-y-Fedw Sandstone and Conglomerate forms the still higher background of the hill. The latter is seldom actually exposed, but is represented by thousands of large angular stones, which crowd the hill far below the actual base of the subdivision, and usually cover the outcrop of the Sandy Limestone, which from its softer character has been more rapidly denuded. The following is a general section of the whole of the strata exposed at the end of the hill.

SECTION OF CARBONIFEROUS STRATA EXPOSED IN

MINERA HILL.

FEET.

| Lower Cefn-y-Fedw Sandstone and Conglomerate. | *k.* White Sandstone, with quartz pebbles .... | 100? |

Sandy Limestone ...	*j.* White Sandstone, with concretions of limestone	30
	i. Grey Limestone, solid bed......	11
	h. Yellow Sandstone, graduating into limestone at the top and bottom	12
	g. Shale, with beds of limestone, 8 or 9 in. thick	18
		71

Upper Grey Limestone.	*f.* Grey Limestone, massive bed..	35
	e. Grey Shale, with bands of limestone	20
	d. Grey Limestone, thin bedded..	25
	c. Black Shale.......................	25
	b. Grey Limestone, thick bedded, with black bands..............	100
		205

Upper White Limestone.	*a.* White Limestone, thick beds...	160
	Total	536

The subdivisions into which the strata are divided
may be easily identified and examined, and especially
the Sandy Limestone at the top of Craig Mawr and
Craig Fechan, just above the office and other works of
the Minera Mining Co. The strata forming the 30-feet
bed, *j*, of the Sandy Limestone at the top of Craig
Mawr and Craig Fechan, with the beds below, altogether
about 71 feet in thickness, may be considered a typical
example of the subdivision—the white sandstone with
numerous concretions of limestone of a lenticular shape,

resembling the chert nodules in the Upper Grey Limestone at Mold and other places. The concretions contain fossils, and there are casts of them in the sandstone itself, which will often effervesce in acid. *Chonetes Hardrensis* and *Productus longispinus* were found in the concretionary limestone nodules. The massive 35-feet bed, *f*, at the top of the Upper Grey Limestone is well exposed along Craig Mawr, but the 20-feet of shale with bands of limestone, *e*, is only visible in a water-course, which runs down the hill, and must be always dry, except in very wet weather, for it descends the steep slope of the hill. It can be examined in the bed of the water-course below the limestone at the entrance to an arched level driven into the hill, the limestone there exposed being the base of the 35-feet bed, a fault or land-slip having brought it down to a lower level. The lower 25-feet bed of shale, *c*, above the 100-feet of grey limestone, *b*, is conspicuous in two quarries nearer the Minera quarries, with the thin bedded limestone, *d*, resting on it.

The ridges and terraces along the slope of Minera Hill, near the Upper White Limestone quarries, well deserve attention, for they indicate the outcrop of the successive strata with remarkable exactitude, whether seen from the opposite Berwig Mountain, or on the ground itself. The two beds of shale, *e*, and *c*, are each represented by terraces, with the thin bedded limestone, *d*, forming a ridge between. The thickness of the grey limestone, *b*, was measured from the ridge at the top of it down to its base where exposed in the quarry below.

LIST OF FOSSILS FOUND IN THE UPPER GREY LIMESTONE AT MINERA.

1 *Aviculo-pecten micropterus,* M'Coy.
2 *Athyris ambigua,* Sow.
3   ,,   *Royssii,* Léveille.
4 *Orthis Michelini,* Koninck.
5 *Productus cora,* D'Orb. *
6   ,,   *giganteus,* Mart.
7   ,,   *latissimus,* Sow.
8   ,,   *longispinus,* Sow.
9   ,,   *semireticulatus,* Mart.
10 *Spirifera crassa,* Koninck.
11   ,,   *bisulcata,* Sow.
12 *Poteriocrinus crassus,* Koninck.
13 *Alveolites septosa,* Flem.
14 *Cyathophyllum Murchisoni,* M. Edw.
15   ,,   *regium,* Phil.
16 *Clisiophyllum turbinatum,* M'Coy.
17 *Lithostrotion ensifer,* M. Edw. †
18   ,,   *irregulare,* M'Coy.
19   ,,   *junceum,* Flem.
20   ,,   *Portlocki,* M. Edw.
21 *Lonsdaleia rugosa,* M'Coy.
22 *Syringopora geniculata,* Phil.
23 *Zaphrentes cylindrica,* Scouler.

---

* Occurs also in the Upper White Limestone, but it is the only species I was able to determine, fossils being remarkably scarce in the subdivision at Minera.

† A single specimen, the only one I have so far found in North Wales.

Foraminifera seem always present in the Carboniferous Limestone, except, perhaps, in the Lower Brown Limestone. Mr. G. W. Shrubsole, F.G.S., found beautifully weathered specimens of *Saccammina Carteri* in a black bed about the middle of the lowest 100-feet of the Upper Grey Limestone at Minera, with the following additional species:—*Trochammina incerta,* D'Orb; *Endothyra Bowmani,* Phil; *Endothyra ammonoides,* Brady; *Valonlina palæotrochus,* Ehren.; *Valonlina decurrens,* Brady; *Archædiscus Karrari,* Brady.

FAULTS AND LODES.

The faults exposed in the quarries in the limestone in the country about Minera are all regarded as lodes, or mineral veins, and the numerous shafts sunk over and the levels driven along them prove that they are identical. The principal lodes laid down on the Geol. Survey Map are also the principal faults, and the most general direction is about north-west and south-east. The Minera vein, the great fault or lode which throws the Carboniferous Limestone up on its south-west side, is evidently the most important dislocation, and is supposed to extend nearly five miles.

Capt. J. Ball, of Minera, informed me that the Silurian rock occurs at the depth of 870 feet from the surface in the Minera Mine, which is in the valley, the overlying Carboniferous Limestone and Cefn-y-Fedw Sandstone being nearly that thickness, for the general dip of the strata is only 8°, but it is so long since any shaft was sunk that he could not give the thickness of the sandstone which overlies the limestone. Capt. S. Mitchell has, however, given me the following section of the strata passed through in sinking No. 3 Shaft at the Park mine, on the top of Minera hill. The position of the shaft is close to the letter "P" in the word "Pen-y-Craig," apparently in the Lower Cefn-y-Fedw Sandstone, and ending downwards at the Minera upper day-level, 235 yards below the surface.

		FEET.
Cefn-y-Fedw Sandstone and Sandy Limestone.	? Coal-measures	90
	k. Millstone Grit, including thin beds of sand, clay, & shale...	279
	h, i & j. Dark Limestone	82
	g. Chert	21

	f. Dark Limestone	82
	e. Limestone with thin shale beds	80
Upper Grey Limestone.	*d.* Dark Limestone	51
	c. Black Shale	21
	b. Dark Limestone, to adit level...	99

Total depth of Shaft......... 705

The strata agree closely with those given in the section of strata exposed on the escarpment of the hill, especially considering that the sections are about half a mile apart, so that a change in the beds would be likely to occur. The letters in *italics* show the correlation of the strata in the two sections; the Minera upper day-level being near the base of the Upper Grey Limestone. The supposed Coal-measures at the top of the section require investigation, but as the shaft was sunk many years ago, and the strata are not visible on the surface, it is difficult to give an opinion about them; probably they belong to the Middle or Upper Cefn-y-Fedw Sandstone and contain two thin seams of coal as reported, perhaps correlating with the coal seams on the east of Cefn-y-Fedw and Mynydd Myfyr already described. If ever the strata are proved to be Coal-measures it will be time enough to endeavour to explain their occurrence in such an unexpected position, and whether introduced by faults, or proving some unconformity between them and the underlying Lower Cefn-y-Fedw Sandstone.

The Minera fault running north-west and south-east along the valley brings in the Cefn-y-Fedw Sandstone, and forms the hill known as Berwig mountain. The longest direction of the hill is about north-west and north-east, which nearly coincides with the strike of the strata exposed in several quarries. The highest strata closely resemble the Aqueduct Grit of the typical locality, especially at the Minera quarry near the church, worked by Mr. R. A. Rylands, where the coarse grit is a good building stone. This, and another quarry in similar rock, are assumed to be about six or seven hundred yards from the Coal-measures, but the intervening space is all cultivated, so that little or nothing is known about it. The lower beds are of a yellow colour, very much false-bedded, and crop out at Cae-fadog, but there is no black shale associated with them, which might have been expected if on the horizon of the Dee Bridge Sandstone near Llangollen, and below that of the Aqueduct Grit. Probably a fault occurs on the north-west of Berwig mountain, being a continuation of three mineral veins which meet at a point south-west-south of the Bwlch-gwyn mining ground, so that the middle beds of the Cefn-y-Fedw Sandstone, including the Cherty Shale, are not exposed at the surface. The Horizontal Section, Sheet 44, of the Geol. Survey, passes through Bwlch-gwyn. There is no such fault represented, but the thickness of the Millstone Grit (Cefn-y-Fedw Sandstone) is shown to be nearly 1,000 feet; and the Carboniferous Limestone 1,200 feet, whereas in the foregoing sections the latter is proved to be only 436 feet including the Sandy Limestone, which was probably included by the Surveyors.

The Lower Cefn-y-Fedw Sandstone and Conglomerate crops out at Bwlch-gwyn and other localities on the north-east, along the course of the Bala fault. The rock is a well-known local stone, as it is extensively used for repairing the roads, for which purpose it is very suitable. Originally it seems to have been a fine grained sandstone, but with occasional beds of conglomerate interstratified with it. Mostly it has been converted into quartzite, and some of the finer beds into chert, which often contains chalcedony. Small crystals of quartz occur along the joints with earthy Sulphate of Lead; which is so common that a large proportion of the road-stone is coated with this yellow mineral, and the stems of encrinites occur in the form of *screw-stones*.

CONCLUSION.

The great Bala fault, which runs from the south-west to the north-east, forms the northern boundary of the Carboniferous rocks in the country between Llanymynech and Minera, and the uniform character of the subdivisions is remarkable over the whole area that has been described. The identification of the subdivisions of Carboniferous Limestone and the Cefn-y-Fedw Sandstone has resulted in proving the varying thickness of the former along the country described, while the latter formation presents remarkable uniformity. The lowest subdivisions of the Carboniferous Limestone, the Old Red Sandstone, and the Lower Brown Limestone only occur in the deepest hollows, and represent the most ancient Carboniferous deposits. The Upper Grey Limestone, however, extends over the whole area, and no doubt once extended far and wide over the Silurian rocks beyond its present boundary. The Cefn-y-Fedw Sandstone seems invariably to have succeeded the deposition of the Upper Grey Limestone, but it is impossible to define its extent before the great denuding influence set in, which produced the extended escarpment along its western termination.

The Bala fault throws down the Cefn-y-Fedw Sandstone on the north-west, and presents a series of geological phenomena between Llandegla and Ffrith which are of considerable interest, though they can be only described in a very brief manner. Between Llandegla and Minera the fault seems to be a double-fault, with the Upper Grey

Limestone between the two lines of dislocation. At Hafod-
dafalog the road passes over the latter subdivision, which is
quarried for roadstone, the strata inclining at various
angles, as might be expected when faulted between the
Bala-beds on the one side and the Cefn-y-Fedw Sandstone on the other. Nearer Minera the narrow ridge of
limestone is conspicuous along a portion of the old
Llandegla road as shown on the Geol. Survey Map. As
the fault runs below Bwlch-gwyn the Sandy Limestone
occurs, and can be seen on both sides cropping out from
under the Lower Cefn-y-Fedw Sandstone. Still further
north-east the Sandy Limestone is again presented under
similar conditions, but with its continuity along the
main fault broken by small cross-faults. Gwern To
is a grand old hill of Cefn-y-Fedw Sandstone on
the north-west of the fault, with the Sandy Limestone
at its base, faulted as described, and presenting a precipitous cliff above the stream in the valley; for the
fault, the valley, and the stream follow the same course.
On the south-east of the fault there are several mineral
veins where mining operations have been in progress.
The direction of the veins is at a considerable angle to
those at Minera, the principal running into the Bala
fault. The veins have been worked in the Lower Cefn-
y-Fedw Sandstone or Bwlch-gwyn rock, which, according
to several miners, is about 180 feet thick. Between
Bwlch-gwyn and Llandegla there are frequent trial-pits,
though they seem to have been abandoned after short
trials. The country to the north-west of the Bala fault
rises rapidly and is of a mountainous character, being
Cefn-y-Fedw Sandstone with the Carboniferous Limestone cropping out and presenting its usual subdivisions,
including the Lower Brown Limestone, towards Llandegla and Llanarmon, but all at a lower level.

The number of fossils found in the Carboniferous Limestone between Llanymynech and Minera, and given in the foregoing lists, amounts to 106 species. The greatest number of these occurs in the Upper Grey Limestone, and there is a remarkable similarity between those found in the various localities. A few species are represented by single specimens, while some, common in one or two places, are altogether absent in others. Comparatively few of the species occur in the lower subdivisions, probably because the conditions were unfavourable for their preservation, and it is improbable that they did not exist in the area during the deposition of the whole of the limestone. A tabulated list showing the range of the species over the entire area might have been interesting, but it would have been of such a provisional character as not to have been of permanent value. However, the general result of such a list would have been similar to the tabulated list of the typical locality at Llangollen where the most thorough search for fossils was made (page 299), except that a greater number of peculiar species would appear in the Upper White Limestone, as shown by the rare forms found in that subdivision at Llanymynech. Further search will no doubt add to the foregoing lists, but the Upper Grey Limestone will always present the greatest number, though additional species may be found in the lower subdivisions.

The fossils of the Cefn-y-Fedw Sandstone, with the exception of the plants, seem to be of the same species as those in the Carboniferous Limestone; some of the most common being found at Tyfyn-uchaf, in the Lower Shale, near the highest beds in the formation.

MEMBERS

OF THE

LIVERPOOL GEOLOGICAL SOCIETY.

HONORARY MEMBERS.

A. C. RAMSAY, F.R.S., F.G.S., London.
JOHN MORRIS, F.G.S., London.
S. J. MACKIE, F.G.S., F.S.A., London.
WILLIAM PENGELLY, F.R.S., F.G.S., Torquay.
EDWARD W. BINNEY, F.R.S., F.G.S., Douglas, Isle of Man.
WILLIAM BRYHAM, Wigan.
HENRY HICKS, F.G.S., M.R.C.S.E., London.
W. KING, D. Sc., Queen's College, Galway.

MEMBERS.

ABRAHAM, J., Riverham, Grassendale Park.
          87, Bold Street.
ADDISON, W. H., Deaf and Dumb Institute, Oxford Street.
ARCHER, F., B.A., Boundary Cottage, Crosby.
          14, Cook Street.
*BEASLEY, H., Acre-field House, Woolton.
*BOSTOCK, R., 8, Grange Lane, Birkenhead.
BRAMALL, H., 3, Balmoral Road.
BREWSTER, C., Rev., 14, Selborne Street, Prince's Road.
BROWN, C. H., Low-wood, Alexandra-road, Southport.
*BROWN, J. CAMPBELL, D. Sc., F.C.S., 27, Abercromby Square.
COOGAN, P. M., C.E., 28, Green Lawn, Rock Ferry.
COOKE, W. H., Aughton Springs, Town Green, Ormskirk.
DAVIES, C., 8, Kinglake Street, Edge Hill.
DAWBARN, W., Elmswood, Aigburth.
          The Temple, Dale Street,

DODD, J., 2, Derby Terrace, Rock Ferry.

*†ESKRIGGE, R. A., F.G.S., The Woodlands, New Brighton.
18, Hackin's Hey.

FABERT, C., 3, St. James' Walk.

FITZPATRICK, M., 62, Seel Street.

FITZPATRICK, J. J., 62, Seel Street.

FOSTER, E., 7, Newstead Road, Smithdown Lane.

FOSTER, R. M., 34, Oxford Road, Waterloo.

GREEN, A., York House, Old Chester Road, Rock Ferry.
9, Canning Place.

GRIFFITHS, J., 14, Queen Street, Chester.

*HALL, H. F., F.G.S., Green Heys, Grove Road, Wallasey.
17, Dale Street.

HANCE, E. W., LL.B., Municipal Offices, Dale Street.

HATHAWAY, T., C.E., The Mount, Bangor, North Wales.

*HIGGINS, H. H., Rev., M.A., Rainhill.

HEWITT, W.. B. Sc., 67, White Rock Street.

JACKSON, G. O., 15, Trafalgar Road, Birkdale, Southport,

JEVONS, G., Jun., 5, Chapel Street.

JOHNSON, J. H., F.G.S., 64, Albert Road, Southport.

JONES, T., Top Lane, Wallasey.
Orange Court, Castle Street.

KERSHAW, J., Neville Street, Southport.

LEA, T., Vale Cottage, Huyton Quarry.

LEIGH-GREGSON, S., Aigburth Road.
Slater Court, 5, Castle Street.

LEWIS, J. T., 131, Park Street.

MACKINTOSH, D., F.G.S., 32, Whitford Road, Higher Tranmere.

*McCLAY, J. L., Rose Villa, Victoria Road, Oxton.

*MARRAT, F. P., 21, Kinglake Street.

MAYER, J., F.S.A., Pennant House, Lower Bebington.

*MOORE, T. J., C.M.Z.S,L., 44, Osborne Road, Tue Brook.
Liverpool Museum.

*MORGAN, ALFRED (Honorary Treasurer), 2, Rathbone Terrace,
Wellington Road, Wavertree.   Office, 126, London Road,

MORTIMER, Captain, Liverpool.

*†MORTON, G.H., F.G.S., F.R.G.S.I. (Honorary Secretary), 10, Sheil
Road.   122, London Road.

†MOTT, C. G., Sunnyside, Cavendish Road, Birkenhead.

McMILLAN, A., Conway, North Wales.

PATERSON, J., Palmyra Street, Warrington.

PEARSE, W., Wellington Buildings, Chapel Walks.
Green Bank Farm, Wavertree.

*†PICTON, J. A., F.S.A., Sandy Knowe, Wavertree.

       4 and 5, Queen Buildings, Dale Street.

*POTTER, C., 101, Miles Street.

PEARSON, J. E., Golborne Park, near Newton-le-Willows.

QUILLIAM, W. H., Fern Bank, Fairfield Crescent.

*†READE, T. M , C.E., F.G.S., Park Corner, Blundellsands.

       Canning Chambers, 4, South John Street.

*†RICKETTS, C., M.D., F.G.S., 22, Argyle Street, Birkenhead.

*ROBERTS, I., F.G.S., Kennessee, Maghull, Lancashire.

       39, Gardner's Row.

RICHARDSON, W. A., Holt Hill, Tranmere.

ROBINSON, J. J., Blundellsands Road, Great Crosby.

SHONE, W., F.G.S., Upton Park, Chester.

*SEMMONS, W., 20, Canning Place.

STONE, T., Jun., Newton Park, Newton-le-Willows.

STRONGITHARM, G., 77, Whetstone Lane, Tranmere.

SPARGO, E., Bangor, North Wales.

SHERLOCK, C., 63, South John Street.

WILSON, W. H., St. Michael's Hamlet, Aigburth.

       31, Wapping.

WRIGHT, B. M., F.R. Hist. Soc., 90, Great Russell Street, Bloomsbury, London.

WARD, T., Northwich, Cheshire.

WARD, J. R., 57, Garth Road, Bangor, North Wales.

WOOD, J. J., Olive Mount, Wavertree.

       20, Lord Street.

YOUNG, H., 12, South Castle Street.

       * Have read Papers before the Society.

       † Contribute annually to the Printing Fund.

Lightning Source UK Ltd.
Milton Keynes UK
UKHW021930180219

337529UK00011B/888/P

9 780282 994310